Frontispiece

It is a definition of a sociologist that he/she is someone who analyses his/her own society. There are no sociologists who do not also live through the complexities and incoherencies of a concrete historical situation and who do not try at the same time to bring out and define general processes of functioning or transformation. I claim for all sociologists not only the right but the duty to be both committed and uncommitted, partisan and independent, realistic and prophetic. How could we set apart the unity of our thought from the history of our personal lives and the experience of profound historical transformations? We not only work on our societies; we work on ourselves.

Alain Touraine
'A sociology of the subject' in J. Clark and M. Diani (eds)
Alain Touraine. (1996, p.326).

Abbreviations

AIM	Action, Information, Motivation
AP	Associated Press
CAP	Common Agricultural Policy
CCTV	Closed Circuit Television
CEO	Chief Executive Officer
CORI	Conference of Religious Ireland
CSO	Central Statistics Office
CWC	Community Workers' Co-operative
DDDA	Dublin Docklands Development Authority
DTEDG	Dublin Travellers' Education and Development Group
ENFO	Environment Information Service
EPA	Environmental Protection Agency
ERI	Economic Research Institute
ESR	*Economic and Social Review*
ESRI	Economic and Social Research Institute
EU	European Union
FDI	Foreign Direct Investment
FGM	Female genital mutilation
GAA	Gaelic Athletic Association
GDP	Gross Domestic Product
GDI	Gross Domestic Income
GNP	Gross national product
GRS	*Gerry Ryan Show*
HEA	Higher Education Authority
IBTS	Irish Blood Transfusion Service
ICA	Irish Countrywomen's Association
ICT	Information and Communications Technology
IDA	Industrial Development Authority
IHA	Irish Housewive's Association
IJS	*Irish Journal of Sociology*
INM	Independent News and Media
IPA	Institute of Public Administration

IT	Information technologies
JNLR	Joint National Listenership Research
MNC	Multinational Corporation
MRBI	Market Research Bureau of Ireland
NAPS	National Anti-Poverty Strategy
NDP	National Development Programme
NESC	National Economic and Social Council
NIC	Newly industrialising country
NIRSA	National Institute for Regional and Spatial Analysis
NSM	New social movement
NUIG	National University of Ireland, Galway
OECD	Organisation for Economic Co-operation and Development
PLAC	Pro-Life Amendment Campaign
REPS	Rural Environment Protection Scheme
RMT	Resource mobilisation theory
RSE	Relationships and Sexuality Education
RTC	Regional Technical College
RTÉ	Radio Telefís Éireann
SAI	Sociological Association of Ireland
SPUC	Society for the Protection of the Unborn Child
SSIS	Statistical and Social Inquiry Society
TCD	Trinity College, Dublin
TD	Teachta Dála (Member of Parliament)
TNC	Transnational corporation
TWG	Technical Working Group
UCD	University College, Dublin
UN	United Nations
UTV	Ulster Television
VAT	Value-added tax
VEC	Vocational Education Committees
WTO	World Trade Organisation

Contents

Part I

Sociology in Ireland

Introduction

This is a book about Irish society from a sociological perspective.

What exactly do we mean by this?

First, we offer an interpretation of aspects of Irish society that we hope will illuminate and resonate with the experiences of those living in, or connected with, or curious about, contemporary Ireland. You may already be expert in the analysis and practice of living in Irish society, but we may perhaps add some unexpected, neglected or half-forgotten insights to that expertise. Second, we provide an introduction to the discipline of sociology itself, as a system of thought and a form of imagination that aims to make sense of our everyday life experiences and to place them in the context of their social surroundings. The sociological perspective (in contrast to historical, aesthetic, psychological or even philosophical approaches to reality) is often ignored and under-utilised in Irish social, cultural and intellectual life. We aim to show something of its strength and fascination while also recognising its limitations.

With these two elements together, then, this book is intended as an introduction to Irish sociology: it tries to convey a sense of how Irish sociologists and sociologists in Ireland have thought about, researched and interpreted their society. The idea that Irish sociology could be a valid topic for investigation may seem surprising. After all, sociology generally presents itself as the 'scientific study of society'; it claims to study social life in general: social groups, relationships and social activities wherever they occur. But in practice there is a close connection between the discipline of sociology and the idea of the bounded and unique nation state. Each emerged and was consolidated within the same milieu — the overlapping intellectual networks of nineteenth-century Europe. Sociological accounts of 'society', as a result, are usually those of the social institutions and practices found within the boundaries of specific national societies (especially the United States, Germany, France and Britain), though they are presented as if universal.

Teachers and students of sociology in smaller countries such as the Irish Republic, New Zealand or Finland may read about 'society' only to find that the texts are in reality accounts of British or North American society. Readers may find that the occupational structure of their own country, its political or educational systems or how it organises relations between the genders are not those described. But because such structures and systems are presented as those of 'society' in the abstract, readers may learn little of the specificities of their own society and be unable to ask significant questions about it. They may even come to see their own society, with its different institutional forms and practices, as inferior or uninteresting, since it does not correspond to the 'norm' for a modern society.

In effect, all sociologies are 'national' sociologies. While they share common frameworks of analysis and guiding ideas, they are marked by specific historical and social circumstances. We must read them not as innocent descriptions of 'reality', but as being deeply influenced by where and how they have developed. Irish sociology has been shaped by our incorporation into an English-speaking intellectual world dominated comprehensively by British and American participants. As a product of recent history and 'modern' ways of thinking, the sociological perspective is associated with a secularised self-consciousness characteristic of 'modern' actors. If we fail to recognise its national origins, it can become a vehicle for cultural dependency, promoting cultural change that imagines a particular and limited form of modernity, that ignores the specificities of space, time and power.

We thus address the sociology of Ireland in a deliberately *reflexive* way. Neither the discipline itself nor its application to Irish society is transparent or unproblematic. In Part I of the book we briefly sketch the historical background from which the discipline of sociology emerged and which shaped its subsequent development. We take Irish society as a case study to demonstrate and to reflect upon the questions that sociologists ask about society and the interpretations and explanations they offer.

The chapters of Part I are linked by the idea of 'modernity'. In Chapter 1 we argue that for the past 150 years sociology has developed specifically as the study of modern — effectively industrial — society. This does not mean that sociologists have no interest in the study of other sorts of societies, but that much sociology assumes modern industrial society to be the typical or normal case that the discipline should seek to analyse and explain. However, Irish students may find that many claims in typical sociology textbooks about 'modern industrial society' do not adequately reflect Irish experience. For example, Irish society has industrialised only recently; 40 per cent of the Irish population lives outside large cities and towns; and religion remains a strong, if currently contested, force in Irish social life. In a number of ways Irish society seems to be distinctive or exceptional, even though it shares many features with other contemporary societies. Irish society today is certainly modern, but it may also reveal that the conception of modernity that underpins much sociology is rather narrow and limiting. We need to query these conceptions and expose the assumptions that influence how we understand our own historical experiences and how we anticipate our future development.

In Part I, and indeed throughout this book, we argue that there is more than one way to be modern. The more sociology identifies 'society' with the social arrangements found in specific, usually advanced and powerful, states, the more this impoverishes the discipline, as it prevents us from recognising the open-endedness of all social development. In Chapters 3 and 4 we discuss the Irish experience of development and modernisation in the light of an analysis of the normative assumptions of core sociology. We suggest in Chapter 3 that to understand Irish economic and social development it is crucial to address the transformations in agriculture as well as in industry. The significance of agriculture and food production is not an indication that we are somehow 'less than modern', but emphasises the importance of recognising the variant pathways into modernity.

In Chapter 4 we pay particular attention to the state as an agent of modernisation in Ireland. We suggest that how the Irish state has managed the process of economic development has been fundamental in the production of modern Ireland, particularly in terms of its power and class structures. Other agencies, internal and external, including transnational corporations (TNCs) and the European Union (EU), have also been very important; the contemporary world is one where societies are interdependent and no society develops alone. The significant contribution of the state to the shaping of contemporary Ireland distinguishes our experience of modernity from that of many societies referred to as 'typically modern'.

Chapter 5 examines some dimensions of collective social life in Ireland. In particular we address the part played by local community memberships and the idea of community as a guiding social ideal. A discussion of community and community-related research in Ireland is framed within the concept of 'civil society'. This is often thought of as a realm of solidarity, citizenship and democratic participation, outside of the state and its controls, that enables people to live a genuinely autonomous and self-sustaining social life. Civil society has been seen by sociologists as a key element of 'modern society', but also as under continuous pressure from modernisation processes. We suggest that while there are clear tendencies for 'community' to be appropriated and used by the Irish state for its own ends, the persistence of local solidarities and their creative and reflexive mobilisation by community members remains a distinctive feature of Irish civil modernity.

Our analysis of the dynamics of Irish development is preceded by a discussion of the development of sociology in Ireland. Chapter 2 is central to our attempt at an element of reflexivity in this book. We argue that, while sociology sets out to provide interpretations of reality that are in some sense objective, it remains relative to the cultural and social/institutional context in which it is produced. To 'do sociology' in Ireland is not necessarily the same as in other countries: Irish sociology may emerge from a unique constellation of values and aims and may address different audiences and publics. This of course is true of this book as of any other sociological work; we encourage the reader to treat it as a small part of an unfolding 'national tradition' of Irish sociology that, we hope, will itself become an object of sociological analysis and reflection.

1
Sociology and modernity

This chapter is a brief and selective introduction to sociology in general and contains little specifically Irish material, except for some illustrative examples. We sketch the historical context in which the study of social matters was first formalised into the discipline of sociology and outline some of the key ideas that emerged during that formative period. These ideas remain central to sociological thought today. We aim to connect with 'the high tradition' in sociology that can be traced back to the revolutionary discoveries about society by thinkers such as Karl Marx, Max Weber and Émile Durkheim in the period from 1850 to 1920.

The nature of Irish modernity is a key theme of this book and in this chapter we focus in particular on how sociology has interpreted this concept. The classic sociological debates about modernity offer a degree of intellectual vigour, emotional depth and engagement rarely found in Irish discussions of the topic. Sociology has also contributed to a specific conception of 'modern society' that can marginalise or confuse the experience of modernity in societies like Ireland. Our brief discussion of the classic sociological theorists, and how their ideas related to particular issues of social change, form the basis of this opening chapter.

THE ORIGINS OF SOCIOLOGY

Sociology, as a distinct form of enquiry, is a product of the nineteenth century. The term itself was coined around 1838 by the French writer Auguste Comte. A long tradition of thought about the nature of society and social change can be traced back to the Ancient Greeks and to Islamic culture, but most of this earlier thinking was philosophical (depending on reasoning from basic assumptions); theological (drawing from divine revelation); or psychological (in the sense that it started with some first principles about human nature and argued from these to an account of society). Writers like Comte sought a new approach with its own distinctive label that took society rather than human nature as its starting point and that used systematic methods to collect empirical evidence. Harriet Martineau is also increasingly being recognised as a major founder of the discipline of sociology (Giddens, 2006, p.20). As well as translating the work of Comte into English, and thus introducing his work to the English-speaking world, she was a significant theorist and social analyst in her own right. Her book, *How to observe morals and manners* (1838), was an early primer in social research, and she also carried out extensive study tours, including a number of visits to Ireland (Hill, 2005).

Two features of the time help us to understand the emergence of sociology, its subsequent development and the central issues that remain of concern to sociologists. The nineteenth century was the age of industrial and political revolution. It was also the age of science. Together, we could say these made it the age of control: of people and of nature. The application of science, particularly through industrial technology, enormously increased the scope of human control over the natural environment and its resources. In politics, radical thinkers similarly tried to bring the institutions of the state under the control of human reason. Inevitably the desire to control through the accumulation and application of knowledge would be extended into the field of society.

The British sociologist Bryan Turner (1996, p.3) suggests that it was then that the idea of 'the social' as a human creation separate from 'nature' became widely accepted:

> Modern industrial society was not a natural community . . . it dealt with needs and the satisfaction of wants in a wholly revolutionary and unique fashion. Natural communities were bound by tradition and by the traditional or conventional satisfaction of wants and needs.

The discipline of sociology, he suggests, developed in order to analyse this new concept of a 'separate and autonomous world of the social'; indeed the ideas of society, modernity and sociology emerged together. For some, sociology was a science that could be used to control both human behaviour and the development of societies. For others it appeared to offer a form of reasoning that could emancipate humans from external control and, by helping them to understand their own social situation and circumstances, increase their autonomy. These dual — and often competing — views of sociology persist. They often meet in debates over whether sociology is a science and, if so, what sort of science it should be.

The growth of sociology was part of the formation of modernity. By the early nineteenth century the conviction was widespread in Europe and North America that the most profound changes yet experienced by humanity were under way. The Industrial Revolution, first in Britain and later in France, Germany and the United States, precipitated new economic processes that seemed likely to alter for ever the organisation of societies and social relationships. The 'democratic revolutions' in the United States (1776) and France (1789) provoked intense debates about human nature, legitimate authority and the proper relationship between the individual and society. The speed of social change seemed to have accelerated tremendously and social thinkers became preoccupied with trying to identify modernity and to chart its likely future path. Contemporary sociology has inherited a view of itself not just as the study of society, but of *modern* society. By contrast the cognate discipline of anthropology is often defined as the study of pre-modern, or traditional, social forms, though many contemporary anthropologists would challenge this distinction.

Nineteenth-century social thinkers disagreed over how to characterise and evaluate modern society. They differed in their emotional and moral responses to social change. Some feared that the modern world posed a threat to social order; their aim was to discover how social stability could be restored and secured. This preoccupation has developed within contemporary sociology as *the problem of social order*: the attempt to explain how the organisation of society is maintained and reproduced over time. Other thinkers were far more excited by the potential of modernity to expand human control over social arrangements and to overcome existing constraints on human freedom. Their response shaped contemporary sociology's second core preoccupation: *the problem of social inequality*.

Most sociologists today see both these concerns as central to sociological inquiry. We may understand better what is common to all in a society (such as beliefs, values, shared identity and social consensus) when we recognise what divides individuals and social groups (unequal access to power and social respect, conflict over beliefs and values). We cannot explain social order in any society unless we can show how social inequality is managed within it; equally, the type and experience of social inequality is deeply influenced by how the society is ordered and organised.

We have considered above the emotional and moral responses to modernity of the social thinkers of the nineteenth century and their intellectual or analytic responses. However, we shall now see how the ideas and interpretations of modernity of some major sociological theorists of the period have influenced the way all of us today, whether sociologists or not, think about and interpret the world in which we live.

SOCIOLOGY AS THE STUDY OF MODERN SOCIETY

The nineteenth-century writers who tried to interpret the changing world around them agreed on one thing — it was new and unique in historical experience — but they differed as to how to describe and characterise it. As a result their writings offer at least four distinct themes for characterising modern society. Three derive from attempts to identify the most important effects of the economic transformation introduced by the Industrial Revolution; the fourth is more concerned with tracing the social effects of cultural change. We might summarise them as follows:

- modern society as *industrial* society
- modern society as *capitalist* society
- modern society as *urban* society
- modern society as *rational* society.

Modern society as industrial society

The Industrial Revolution is normally understood to be the transformation of an economy dominated by agriculture to one based on manufacturing. It was a process that spread from eighteenth-century Britain to the rest of the Western world. The technological changes involved, such as the invention of new machines and new ways of harnessing power for the production and transport of goods, had far-reaching effects on people's livelihoods and on the social organisation of work. In the early nineteenth-century British cotton industry, for example, the introduction of power looms brought weavers out of their cottages and small workshops and into factories where they experienced new work routines (the 'tyranny of the clock') and new work relationships of authority and control (Thompson, 1982).

The French thinker Émile Durkheim interpreted the social changes that accompanied industrialisation as an increase in the *division of labour* in society. This refers to how work tasks are divided and shared among the working population. Durkheim argued that in pre-industrial societies, one worker or workgroup (such as a family) did a range of different work tasks necessary to meet survival needs and work was organised sequentially so that each stage in the production process was completed before the next was begun. This allowed a single worker to see the whole process through from beginning to end and to have a wide range of skills with limited specialisation.

By contrast, in industrial society, each worker now specialises in a single activity that has to be complemented by those of other specialised workers. With the shift from handicraft to machine production and from the workshop to the factory, all the processes necessary to produce a given item can be carried out simultaneously. The industrialisation of agriculture and food provides a good example of Durkheim's thesis. In Ireland, in the earlier part of the twentieth century, butter was produced manually by farm families who also tended, fed and milked the cows. Today the labour of producing butter is divided between the farmer who produces the raw milk; the factory that processes it into butter; the factory that produces feed for the cows; the factory that produces the computer programmes to regulate the timing and content of the cows' meals; and so on. We can see the same process in other areas of society. The job of 'teacher' has become divided into first-, second- or third-level teacher; and into educator, career guidance advisor, counsellor or youth worker. The role of 'enterprise boss' is now divided into financial controller, production manager, sales manager, human resources manager and so on. The outcome is a much more complex and detailed system of occupational divisions and identities in modern industrial society.

A question that preoccupied Durkheim was how a society with an advanced division of labour could retain the social bonds between individuals that he thought necessary for social order. Such societies tend to be very individualistic, with a danger that those within them may lose a sense of social connectedness or obligation to others. Pre-industrial societies were unified on the basis of similarities — most people shared the same sorts of skills, responsibilities, values and life experiences. This unity is destroyed by industrialisation. For Durkheim, an answer could be found in the fact that as people become more specialised occupationally, they become more dependent on their fellow citizens. As each of us provides only a specialised service to others, we rely on them to provide us with their services and skills. In a modern, industrialised society, collective social order depends more on the acceptance of difference and on co-operation between individuals and groups than on feelings of sameness and collective identity.

Durkheim sometimes went so far as to suggest that industrial society is synonymous with 'civilisation' because of the new order of *moral individualism* that a highly developed division of labour can create. This moral code reverses earlier understandings of the proper relationship between the individual and society. It shifts the emphasis from the duties the individual owes to society to the duties society owes to the individual. Moral individualism treats the individual as the source of all ethical value and encourages the organisation of society to ensure maximisation of individual rights.

Durkheim realised that individualism could sometimes be amoral rather than moral. He argued that modern society constituted an abnormal form of the division of labour and a breeding ground for amoral individualism. The industrial society that emerged at the end of nineteenth-century Europe did not extend equal rights to all of its citizens. It was full of arbitrary inequalities and severely restricted the opportunity for an acceptable lifestyle for some social groups. Instead of generating feelings of solidarity and mutual respect between specialised and differentiated individuals, it tended to encourage either unbridled egoism (selfishness) or what Durkheim termed *anomie*.

This concept is one of Durkheim's most significant contributions to sociology. He used it to identify a condition of society that arises when the rules by which social life is organised are incoherent, incomplete or widely disregarded. Examples might include a society that publicly prides itself on its impartial exercise of justice but where everyone knows that in practice there is one law for the rich and another for the poor; or a society that legitimises divisions between rich and poor on the grounds that anyone can succeed if they work hard enough, yet system- atically discriminates against some groups so they can never succeed no matter how hard they try. The result of living in an anomic society is that people may suffer a deep sense of isolation and meaninglessness in their lives and work. In certain social conditions anomie can, as Durkheim famously argued, lead to suicide, the ultimate statement of the collapse of the bond between the individual and society.

Modern society as capitalist society

The society that has emerged over the past two centuries is often described as industrial capitalist society. Though the terms 'industrial' and 'capitalist' are often used in tandem in this way, they are not synonymous. Instances of capitalism can be found prior to the development of modern industry. Some forms of agricultural production in eighteenth-century Britain were capitalist, as were many business enterprises in fifteenth-century Italian city states. Similarly, the twentieth century has seen the development of industrial societies that were not capitalist, such as the former Soviet Union. Sociologists generally use the term 'capitalist' to describe a particular way that economic production is organised: it is oriented to exchange on markets; we produce things in order to sell them; the wealth or resources used in production are held in private ownership; and these resources are invested and reinvested to produce the greatest possible profit. Capitalist societies are those where this type of economic organisation predominates.

The major interpreter of modern society as capitalist society was Karl Marx. Marx understood capitalism very specifically as an economic system in which profit is made by those who own the means of production (land, money or credit, machinery, buildings) through exploiting the labour of those who do not. Owners, or 'capitalists', realise a profit when they can sell products on the market for more than they cost to produce. This is possible mainly through paying those who labour to create the product less than the true value of their contribution to its final market price. But how could they achieve that? It is only possible in a society where private ownership of wealth is concentrated in the hands of a minority and the rest of the population, reduced to owning nothing but their own capacity to work (their labour power), have to sell this to the capitalists in order to survive. Capitalism as an economic system, Marx argued, both produces and depends upon a particular type of social structure peculiar to capitalist societies — division into two major and opposed classes, the capitalist class or *bourgeoisie*, and the working class or *proletariat*.

While the concept of industrial society led Durkheim to ask questions about social order and stability, the concept of capitalist society enabled Marx to focus on questions of inequality and conflict. In his view, it is the relationship between the two major classes — a relationship of conflict — that determines the form and development of modern society. Capitalist economies are very dynamic and characterised by continual technological innovation as capitalists strive to reduce production costs, increase profits and diminish their dependence on human labour. But capitalist society is also a society that alienates human beings from each other and its structures reduce human freedom.

The Marxist concept of *alienation* is as significant to sociologists as Durkheim's notion of anomie. Marx used the term to attack what he saw as the profoundly dehumanising effects of capitalism. Under capitalist conditions, workers become alienated — separated — from the products of their work. What they produce does not belong to them but to the capitalist, the owner of the means of production who has bought their labour. Instead of being a recognisable outcome of their own human creativity, what they produce appears foreign to them, disconnected from their identity and lives. But alienation does not stop here, on the production line. The result of a capitalist division of labour is that people become alienated from work itself as it is subdivided into fragmented tasks, mechanised and managed from above, thus denying workers the use of their own skills and knowledge or control over the timing and sequence of their work. In these conditions work becomes a meaningless activity undertaken for purely instrumental reasons — to make money to survive. Inevitably, workers also become alienated from each other. They no longer see themselves as engaged in a joint productive task but merely as atomised individuals. Ultimately, since Marx believed that it is creative interaction with the environment through meaningful work that makes us human, this means that capitalism alienates people from their own essential humanity. Finding no meaning in their working lives, they become obsessed with material possessions and work harder and harder in order to acquire more and more, whether or not the possessions have any intrinsic value. They learn to see themselves as no more than consumers. It is inevitable that capitalist societies are dominated by an ideology that glorifies material possessions unless the working class can find the means to mobilise against it and regain humanity for modern human beings.

Marx's analysis of social change is often described as *materialist*. He understood the development of modern capitalism to be the result primarily of changes in economic organisation. While not denying the key role of the economy, Max Weber stressed that ideas and values also influence social change. Weber thought it important to ask how people could come to accept the new economic relations and behaviour that capitalism demands. In particular, he asked how they could accept that the search for profit should be the central, overriding goal of life, when in previous 'traditional' societies work was more often simply a means to achieve an acceptable standard of living, only to be abandoned once that was reached. How do we explain this change in people's values?

Weber argued (1970[1920]) that a key influence here was religion. He focused in particular on the religious changes that took place in the seventeenth and eighteenth centuries in Western Europe, especially the emergence of a puritan type of Protestantism (most clearly seen in Calvinism) whose followers came to believe that an austere, self-denying life of unremitting work was the best way to glorify God and to calm anxieties over whether they were one of the 'saved' who would find a place in heaven. Weber's sociology is laced with irony. The materialism of modern capitalist society can be traced back to the 'work ethic' of an ascetic religious world view.

Weber, like Marx, saw modern capitalist society as characterised by inequality. But whereas Marx's focus was on the material bases of inequality, Weber was more interested in the ideas that are used in modern society to explain and to justify inequality. Weber's view of sociology as the study of human action and of the meanings that actors give to their world has been of great influence on sociologists since.

Modern society as urban society

As we have seen, industrialisation is widely associated with a switch from an agricultural to a manufacturing economy. It is also associated with urbanisation — the growth of towns and cities and the depopulation and decline of rural areas. Of course, cities existed in pre-industrial societies (for example, Alexandria or Lima), but industrialisation boosted and accelerated their development as well as transforming their character in important ways. The concentration of factories in urban areas attracted immigrants pushed out of the countryside by the commercialisation of agriculture, and the numbers of working-class inhabitants in cities swelled enormously. Rapidly expanding, badly built and overcrowded working-class housing areas were prone to epidemics and seen by many upper- and middle-class urban people as symbolic of the threat to social order posed by a chaotic and uncontrolled poor.

Urbanisation was perhaps the most visible of the massive changes that modernity brought to society. It attracted the attention of many social commentators, including some sociologists who saw it as evidence of regress rather than progress. They mourned what was being lost with the passing of 'traditional' rural society. The influential German sociologist Ferdinand Tönnies, for example, wrote (2001[1887]) that urban industrial society was characterised by a loss of community. He argued that industrialisation increases the scale and thus the impersonality of society and that, with urbanisation, the close personal relationships of small-scale, pre-industrial local societies are replaced by impersonal, calculative relationships where others may be seen as no more than a way to achieve one's own aims. Though Tönnies did not explicitly identify 'community' *Gemeinschaft* with rural areas or a rural way of life, nor 'impersonal association' *Gesellschaft* with urban areas, many writers subsequently did, with the result that 'rural society' is often confused with 'traditional' or 'pre-industrial' society, while the urban is inevitably linked to modernity.

Another important German social theorist, Georg Simmel, wrote about the city as the key location of the everyday experience of modernity. For him modern individuals are formed within and by an urban or metropolitan world. In cities people are constantly involved in interactions with strangers that engage only fragments of the individual personality, leaving most of it unknown. On the city streets people are bombarded by a constant stream of impressions and are brought into contact continuously with anonymous others. City dwellers typically respond to this by developing stratagems of defence such as inward retreat, social distance and an attitude of blasé indifference towards everything they encounter (Simmel 1971, p.326):

> The metropolitan type of man . . . develops an organ protecting him against the threatening currents and discrepancies of his external environment which would uproot him. He reacts with his head instead of his heart . . . Metropolitan life, thus, underlies a heightened awareness and a predominance of intelligence in metropolitan man.

But if city living is associated with intelligence and heightened self-consciousness in a way that rural living is not, Simmel (1971, p.326) also emphasised that the city is the seat and the visual representation of the modern money economy:

> The metropolis has always been the seat of the money economy . . . money economy and the dominance of the intellect are intrinsically connected. They share a matter-of-fact attitude in dealing with men and with things; and in this attitude, a formal justice is often coupled with an inconsiderate hardness. . . . Money . . . reduces all quality and individuality to the question: 'How much?'

While Simmel's fascination with the metropolis was tempered with ambivalence, subsequent sociological characterisations of the urban way of life were far more positive. The American sociologist Louis Wirth, writing in 1938, claims the city to be the source of innovation in the modern world and the dominant, controlling centre of modern society. For him modern culture is virtually identical with urban culture. At the same time, the supposed absence from urban life of community was and is used to explain the high rates of crime and other social problems that seem to be a feature of modern society.

There is in fact little evidence to support the idea that settlement patterns, whether concentrated and large-scale as in urban settings, or dispersed and small-scale as in rural ones, determine either social relationships or psychological characteristics. The belief that there is a characteristically 'urban way of life' to be contrasted with the 'rural way of life' has come to hinder sociologists when investigating the very different ways that different social groups experience life. Nevertheless the modern city distinguishes our world from that of earlier periods in history and the experience of modernity in the urban setting remains a focus of research for contemporary sociologists.

Modern society as rational society

Political revolutionaries in late eighteenth-century Europe tried to replace tradition with reason and law as the basis for societal organisation. They claimed, for example, that rulers should no longer govern by inheritance or divine right, but should be selected in accordance with clear, formal and universally acceptable procedures. Behind this lay the belief that human beings are naturally sociable, co-operative and reasonable; if they often appeared to be the opposite, this was due to the distorting effects of oppressive and unreasonable forms of social organisation. With the removal of these distortions, people would be free to create the type of society in which these natural qualities would gain full expression. The spread of democracy, universal education and beliefs in individual rights seemed to indicate the benign progress of reason in society, as did the development of law, science and, as suggested earlier, sociology itself. Nevertheless not all sociologists were convinced that the increasing rationalisation of social life equated to undiluted progress, nor that it necessarily advanced human happiness.

Simmel, as we have already noted, connected the hard-headed rationality of the inhabitants of large cities with the colonisation of all areas of urban life and experience by the money economy and monetary values. Weber argued that one important form of rationalisation in modern society was the development of bureaucracy as a way to administer and control large organisations. Modern bureaucracies are organisations whose official functions are set out in writing (for example, in 'rules and procedures') and are divided into sets of distinct tasks allocated to specific officials. These officials are given the necessary authority and resources to carry out these tasks, but no more; they do not 'own' their positions within the organisation but are selected for them on the basis of explicitly specified qualifications. Positions within the bureaucracy are organised in a hierarchical way, with each position being under the control and supervision of a higher one; administrative actions, decisions and rules are recorded in writing and organisational records provide the basis for continual review and improvement of the organisation's performance. This type of administrative apparatus is quite different from any found in earlier societies and is above all a rational way to organise administration. Though today we often use the term 'bureaucratic' to mean 'inefficient', Weber at the time believed this type of rational administrative system to be extremely efficient.

For Weber, rationality refers primarily to a way of acting. *Rational action* is taken on the basis of a calculation of the relationship between means and ends: 'I choose to do x because I want to achieve y, and doing x is the most effective way to achieve y.' This contrasts with *customary action*: 'I'll do x because this is what people in my group have always done.' Modern society, according to Weber, is one where rational action, involving the application of knowledge, calculation and rules, increasingly replaces customary action. This spread of instrumental rationality undermines religious belief and fundamental values. A rationalised world thus threatens to become secularised, 'disenchanted' and, ultimately, meaningless.

Weber associated the growth of rational systems of administration with the development of large-scale capitalist enterprises, but linked it in particular to the state. Modern capitalist society characteristically involves an expanded bureaucratic state which, in Weber's view, means that modern states possess the power to supervise, assemble information on, monitor and organise citizens to a degree unprecedented in the pre-capitalist world. Bureaucracy and democracy are in conflict, since the former centralises power and concentrates it in the hands of those who control the bureaucratic organisation. Ironically, therefore, the very advance of reason may lead to a reduction in human freedom and happiness.

Sociological theorising did not, of course, end in the 1920s. Later in this book you will encounter further references to Weber, Durkheim, Marx and Simmel and also modern theorists such as Habermas, Bourdieu, Giddens and Parsons and many Irish authors whose work is cited and discussed. They continue to carry forward the task of understanding the world in which they live, if not always by building on, at least in dialogue with, the ideas of the classic social theorists.

SOCIOLOGY AS A SCIENCE OF SOCIETY

Restivo (1991, p.4) describes sociology as 'a field of inquiry simultaneously concerned with understanding, explaining, criticising and improving the human condition'. We have already devoted some attention to the 'understanding', 'criticising' and 'improving' aspects of sociological work, but not much to 'explaining'. Sociological inquiries are not only about exploring theories and ideas. Theories and ideas must be tested against reality if they are to be any use as explanations. Sociology is an empirical discipline that makes discoveries about social reality through the application of theoretical ideas and methods of research. Here we discuss briefly the practices and status of sociology as a research-based discipline or what many would call a (social) science.

There are many ways to research social life, such as large-scale questionnaire surveys; structured or unstructured interviews; ethnographic observation; or the collection and analysis of documents. For most sociologists, research is not just a matter of choosing a technique — it involves reflection on the fundamental issues of how we 'gain our knowledge of the social world, the relationships that are held to exist between theory and research, and the place of values and ethics in research practice' (May, 1997, p.1). The attention paid to these issues makes sociology somewhat unique as a research discipline.

The technicist assumption that doing sociological research is just a matter of selecting appropriate tools implies an unproblematic relationship between researcher and social reality. Early sociologists such as Comte or Durkheim may have held such a view, but it is not easily accepted by contemporary sociology, with decades of reflection on the difficulty of trying to do good social research. Durkheim, who in 1895 authored one of the first textbooks of sociological research (*The rules of sociological method*), said that the social researcher should study social phenomena 'in the same state of mind as the physicist, chemist or physiologist when he probes into a still unexplored region of the scientific domain' (1964, p.xiv). Here he was following Comte, who believed that sociology could and should be modelled closely on the methods and procedures of the natural sciences to produce similar systematic knowledge of and control over the social world. Comte thought the social world could be explained as could the natural world — by deriving objective laws or generalisations about the behaviour of phenomena (in the case of sociology, people and groups) that would allow us to predict their future behaviour patterns. Prediction was important to him because the capacity to predict enhances the potential for control. In reality since then, sociologists have rarely been interested in prediction (now more a concern of economists) and have tended to concentrate on close description and interpretation of what has already occurred.

There are major difficulties with any attempt to treat the social and natural worlds identically or to argue that sociology can only be scientific if it models itself on the natural sciences. Indeed it has become increasingly clear (see Woolgar, 1988) that there is no single model of natural scientific inquiry that all scientists agree on and follow. As suggested above, it is also important for social researchers to be reflexive, that is, *critical of their own methods of generating knowledge*. As a result, sociology has had to devise its own distinctive methods and procedures for research.

A number of key considerations govern the practice of sociological research. First, people within the social world already understand to some degree how their world operates. As a consequence they cannot be treated as would the elements that make up the natural world. Objects in the natural world such as atoms, molecules or ecological systems 'behave' — they are governed by the laws of cause and effect. Humans 'act' — they have reason and purpose, they make choices and they confer meaning on their world. They have their own theories about why their world is as it is and these are also empirical facts for the sociologist to study. Second, sociologists are members of the world they research. Indeed without access to the social world as participants as well as researchers, it would be extremely difficult, if not impossible, for sociologists to understand anything about it. Social reality is a product of people's ideas and interpretations and is not automatically accessible to the senses or to measuring tools in the way that natural phenomena are. To grasp someone's interpretation of reality we need to participate, even in a minimal way, in their culture.

Sociologists differ in their responses to these difficulties. We can distinguish three main positions. *Positivism* refers to those who, in the tradition of Comte, hold the view that for the purposes of research people can be seen to react to their environment as molecules react to heat — without conscious knowledge of what they are doing. Positivism implies that we do not need to ask people *why* they do what they do but we can learn this from our own observation of them. Thus, for example, we need not ask heroin users why they take the drug since we can see that they are 'addicted' to it. More broadly, positivism assumes that there are 'facts' about the social world that are independent of how people define them. It may deduce, for example, that Irish society is class-divided, though most people in

Ireland would claim that class is irrelevant and that people rise or fall largely on their own merits. It is argued that social facts can be revealed to us by research and it is possible to generate an 'objective' knowledge of social reality. This does not depend on the researcher's feelings about or interpretations of that reality, but is produced by detached and impartial observation and measurement.

Subjectivism insists that 'the only thing we can know with certainty is how people interpret the world around them' (May, 1997, p.13). It rejects the positivist claim that research can provide privileged access to 'facts' of which people in the social world are not themselves aware. Extreme versions of subjectivism abandon the idea that there are such facts, indeed that there is *any* external reality beyond people's ideas and definitions of it. Less extreme versions redefine the goal of sociological research as description — it should reveal how interpretations are constructed and how people reach mutual agreements on working definitions of reality. A subjectivist approach to environmental problems, for example, might focus on how the idea that we are threatened by global catastrophe in the form of global warming has come to dominate contemporary environmental politics, rather than on how the 'fact' of global warming is a result of collective human behaviour.

Subjectivist positions have been boosted by feminist critiques of conventional or positivist research (Byrne and Lentin, 2000). Feminists have revealed, in particular, how much supposedly objective and impartial knowledge generated by sociological research has been gender-blind or gender-biased. It has produced accounts of the social world that are only 'real' from a male point of view. Feminist sociologists have forcefully challenged the positivist claim that the good researcher is disengaged from the subject they study. They argue that research is in fact a two-way process where the findings are as influenced by the social identity, status and biographical experiences of the researcher as those of the 'researched'. Research knowledge is always the product of collaboration between researcher and researched and is thus relative to the conditions under which it was generated. There is no detached vantage point from which the absolute truth can be discerned.

A third position, *critical realism* or, as it is often called, *critical theory*, is mainly associated with Marxist sociologists, though it also shares elements with Freudian approaches to researching human behaviour. Both take as a starting point the idea that there are underlying mechanisms in society or in people's subconscious that operate outside consciousness and generate surface phenomena (losing your job; a 'Freudian slip') that we cannot fully explain just by looking at the surface. Critical theorists share with positivists the idea that research should do more than just describe how people act towards each other and how they develop shared ideas about reality. Research should go beyond description to explanation and try to identify the conditions that allow such interaction and interpretation to happen. This does not mean we should ignore the sense that people make of their world, but we should recognise that it is often distorted or incomplete. Critical theorists part company both with positivists and subjectivists over the issue of detachment and disengagement in research. For them, the purpose of research is to reveal what needs to be criticised in contemporary society; for example, oppression and inequality. Their standpoint is engaged and passionate, not detached. They ultimately accept, with caution, the notion that ordinary people can sometimes be wrong about how they understand and evaluate their own social world. The insights of critical research can help to illuminate more adequately the 'true' nature of the world.

Apart from the issues raised above, others that sociological researchers face include the place of ethics and values in research and the relation between theory and research. It was held as orthodoxy for many years that 'objective' research, in the social as in the natural sphere, does not allow an attachment to values to bias the gathering and interpretation of data. We have seen that there is now far less consensus among social researchers that this is possible or even desirable. The emphasis has shifted from trying to keep values out of research to developing codes of *research ethics*.

Ethical research is honest and avoids manipulating or exploiting subjects, readers, sponsors or funders unless there are, in rare cases, compelling reasons for deception. Reflection on ethics encourages researchers to examine the research process as a whole, in particular the values and interests, often unanticipated or unconscious, that shape it. Also of importance are the circumstances under which the research is being carried out: who has funded it; to what end; who has defined the core 'research problem'; and what is to happen to research findings. The fact that a government department, for example, has funded a piece of research and has an interest in how it is done and what it discovers does not necessarily make the research invalid, but it is important for researchers to keep in mind that they are operating in a world where there is unequal power, both in the definition of 'a problem suitable for researching' and in avoiding the intrusions of the researcher. The rich and powerful are far less often the subject of social research than the poor and marginalised. Social scientists are encouraged, with promises of funding, media attention and participation in policy-making spheres, to do research that is 'relevant'. For the sociologist, the construction of a relevant research topic is itself a social phenomenon that can be researched.

The sociologist of education Kathleen Lynch (1999a; 1999b) has argued strongly that even critical models of sociological research typically exclude the 'researched', who usually have no control over the research project and may never see the final product. Successful instances of genuinely participatory research are rare and if those researched have some control over the research methodology, this seldom extends to participation in the development of theory or analysis. The lack of any real engagement with those who experience inequality means, for Lynch, that sociologists are debarred from moving beyond a critique of existing systems towards any truly transformative or emancipatory practice.

Much social research is done without reference to theory — C. Wright Mills (1961) described this as 'abstracted empiricism' and Restivo (1991, p.1) calls it the 'low tradition' in sociology. The career world of the modern sociologist is organised so as to widen the gap between research and theorising. There are strong pressures to specialise in one or the other and those whose areas of competence are the most specialised tend to receive the highest rewards. Publication outlets, such as journals and books, are divided according to the specialised markets they serve. A widening gap between research and theorising leaves sociology vulnerable to a process whereby its research problems are determined by others. A sense of development or cumulation of knowledge about social reality becomes difficult to achieve. The discipline tends to fragment into a series of disconnected sub-fields of research that lack interconnection or possibilities for dialogue; for example, the sociology of childhood, urban life, economic development, food, religion, management, health and illness and so on. But research *can* draw on theory and contribute to the rebuilding and refinement of theoretical frameworks in many different ways. There is no single right way of relating the two, yet some mutual engagement appears to be essential to a dynamic and coherent sociology.

SOCIOLOGY, MODERNITY AND POST-MODERNITY

Our brief review of the early sociological responses to the massive social changes of the eighteenth and nineteenth centuries showed how the experience of these changes led to interpretations of modern society that are still potent and continue to largely define what sociology is about. Sociologists are now aware that the development of modernity is not only a series of historical changes or processes in the material world, but that it also involves intellectual assumptions that legitimate and sanction these changes. They are captured particularly in the taken-for-granted identification of modernity and progress.

It is part of the modern attitude to assume that human history has a meaning and a destiny and that it consists of a sequence of movements towards a higher, more civilised, more orderly, more humanly satisfying way of organising social and individual life. It is characteristic of modernity to assume that people have developed ways to research reality that allow them to arrive at truth, and that the uncovering of truth aids and expands the realisation of human freedom. It is part of modernity to take for granted that revolutionary changes in society — political (the French Revolution) and technical (the Industrial Revolution) — are incremental advances in the unfettering of human reason so that it can be put to use to improve the world. It is, finally, a quintessentially modern belief that the development of science and its application in the empirical world through industrial technology enhances human control over and capacity to manage the natural environment for the greater benefit of all.

Such assumptions are so ingrained in modern thinking about the world, including sociological thinking, that we have come to accept them as largely unquestioned. Sociologists have begun to draw attention to the novelty of such ideas, in historical terms, and what we might call their fragility. Kumar (1995) points out that to seventeenth-century Europeans the very idea of historical change would have been strange as most believed that human life was fundamentally unchanging. For them the object of studying history was primarily to discover, as the Scottish philosopher David Hume put it, 'the constant and universal principles of human nature' under varying sets of circumstances. The idea of progress — that human history could be thought of as, in effect, a movement towards the realisation of Heaven on Earth — would have struck them as downright blasphemous. Similarly the idea that underlay the advance of science, that nature is made up of inert matter that can be partitioned, manipulated, combined and recombined to realise human ends, contrasts markedly with earlier understandings of nature as an unpredictable and explosive living system to be placated through ritual or co-operated with through long experience and observation (Merchant, 1980).

Ironically, perhaps, the excavation of intellectual history in the period before modernity has helped the emergence of what is today widely referred to as *post-modernity*. Post-modern thinking contextualises and relativises modernity. Instead of believing, with the modernisers, that the intellectual assumptions of modernity are objectively true and absolute in all historical eras, it emphasises how they are historically quite novel, unique and contingent. The concept of post-modernity is notoriously difficult (Rose, 1991) and we do not propose to go into it in great depth here. We will simply try to disentangle some of the different ways that it has been understood, in order to indicate some of its impacts on contemporary sociology.

It is most common to understand post-modernity as a historical period that comes *after* modernity. Thus, if we are now post-modern, it is because we have moved into an era characterised by new social, economic, political and intellectual conditions. Thus, while existing sociological analyses may not be entirely out of date in post-modern society, they may fail in some crucial ways to capture its core experiences. Ulrich Beck (1992), for example, argues that societies today are increasingly organised around struggles to escape from 'bads' (such as threatened environmental disasters) instead of struggles for access to 'goods' (social equality, well-paid work, education, housing). In the 'risk society' that is now replacing industrial society, your position in relation to environmental risks is more significant than your position in relation to the class structure. Class analysis, central to modern sociology, no longer tells the full story of how people's 'life-chances' are shaped. A number of sociologists have suggested that contemporary society has shifted from a society organised centrally around work to a society organised around consumption. In modern society work provided people with their core identities and the important relationships that tied them to the larger society. In post-modern society, we locate our identities and social ties in our patterns of consumption — what we acquire and how we display it. While much classical sociological theorising about modernity emphasises shifts in the world of work as basic to social change, we need to move beyond this to develop new theories for post-modern society. Sociologists do not necessarily agree on these points, in particular on whether contemporary society is so fundamentally different that it needs a radical revision of existing theories.

According to a second interpretation, post-modernity is about the abandonment of the intellectual assumptions of modernity, especially the notions that human history has a discoverable meaning and that science can uncover absolute truth. While modernity took it for granted that we can establish 'overarching narratives' of history and progress, post-modernity involves turning our backs on any such attempt since all truth is relative and thus no interpretation of the course of history can ever claim absolute correctness. While the idea that truth is relative is perhaps hard for some scientists to accept, it may be easier for sociologists, especially those who work in the Weberian tradition. They are interested in the meanings that people use to guide their actions rather than in establishing whether those meanings are correct or incorrect. But the call to abandon *all* overarching narratives is rather more difficult. The impetus to practise sociology reflects a desire to interpret the world in ways that make it meaningful, even if these are only fragmentary and partial interpretations. Sociology involves the construction of narratives and depends upon a belief that these narratives are more than just 'stories', that they have some scientific basis. Many sociologists, faced with this way of understanding the concept of post-modernity, deny that it makes any sense or has any relevance for their discipline.

A third approach to post-modernity sees it not as a historical successor to modernity nor as a rejection of its intellectual assumptions, but as an occasion to reflect on the experience of modernity (Kumar 1995, p.67) or, in Bauman's words, 'as modernity conscious of its true nature — *modernity for itself*' (1992, p.187). Bauman argues that, while modernity struggled to order and organise the world, much of the time this struggle gave rise to chaos, to 'variety, contingency and ambivalence'. Instead of trying to repress these outcomes as evidence of the failure of modernity, we should embrace and reflect on them in order to develop new sociological understandings of the contemporary human condition. From this point of view, post-modernity is best understood as a *stance* adopted by the sociologist. It involves an acceptance of social and cultural difference, a readiness to revise interpretations and an openness to competing perspectives. Above all it implies a willingness to stand back and rethink the bases on which judgments and interpretations are made and the fundamental ideas that the discipline has developed. This approach is often called *reflexive sociology*. It is one that, as far as we can, we try to maintain throughout this book.

2
Irish sociology

The dominant view of sociology in Ireland is that it is an applied social science. Governments, funders of research, media commentators and publishers expect sociology, like other social sciences such as demography, economics and political science, to provide empirical data by which public policy can be guided. Its task is to analyse patterns and predict trends and to help the powerful to manage society, solve social problems and bring about desired forms of social change. Of all the social sciences, however, sociology is probably regarded as the least satisfactory and reliable public servant. It is often seen to be less serious than other more 'scientific' disciplines, particularly economics. Kane suggests that, for both the public and the policy-makers, 'social scientists are seen to be, at best, jaywalkers, losing fact to science and meaning to literature' (1996, p.133).

For many sociologists, this understanding of the discipline is one-sided, 'slighting both the nature and potential of public life and the importance of other, more critical and theoretically informed versions of sociology' (Calhoun, 1996, p.429). For Calhoun sociology can do a lot more than provide the data needed to carry out the 'technical activities' of ruling elites. It can also generate and inform public debate on the important issues of the day and subject 'the concepts, received understandings and cultural categories constitutive of everyday life and public discourse to critical theoretical reconsideration' (1996, p.429).

In her analysis of the role of social scientists in Irish public life, Kane (1996, p.136) distinguishes between 'intellectuals' and 'the intelligentsia'. The former provide independent critical commentary on the state of the world, while the latter produce knowledge that tends to be 'market-driven [and] readily identifiable, particularly to other "intelligentsias" in management and public administration'. Such knowledge is used to produce, evaluate and extend existing modes of knowing in specific, well-defined areas of inquiry. As it works within established ways of conceptualising the world, it tends to be 'less threatening than the free-floating interpretation of intellectuals'. Lynch (1999b, p.53) is sceptical even about this role, arguing that the 'free-floating intellectual' is a myth. As she points out, 'even radical intellectuals are culturally and relatively financially privileged' and are part of the structures of power within Irish society.

Such analyses suggest there can be a variety of reasons for 'doing sociology'. These include a *managerial* objective to make government more effective and rational; a *democratic* objective to inform and develop individuals so they can participate more fully in society and its government; and an *intellectual* objective to critically examine the social world and better understand it. In Figure 2.1 we can see the connection between these objectives and the four 'founding theorists' of sociology whose ideas about modernity and its development we outlined briefly in Chapter 1.

Figure 2.1 Sociological approaches of the 'founding theorists'

Playful/intellectual	*Managerial*	*Critical/democratic*
Simmel	Weber, Durkheim	Weber, Marx

Durkheim's writings reflect an instrumental and positivistic approach to sociology: it can provide the state with diagnoses of social trends that help it to manage society in a more rational and progressive and less conflictual manner. Marx offers a very different model: the sociologist as politically engaged critic who seeks to awaken and shape the consciousness of the public, in particular that part of it — the working class — that can bring about revolutionary social change. Simmel offers a third model. He was the first theorist to suggest that sociology should examine and analyse society at play as well as at work. It is possible to see his sociological work as a form of 'play' — a disengaged intellectual activity that recognises no external rules and sees playing the game as its own reward. The hardest person to locate in this simplified scheme is Weber. Less optimistic than Durkheim about the benefits of rationality and rational social management, Weber is closer to Marx in his attempts to develop sociology as a critical reflection on the long-term processes of social 'modernisation', but Weber, unlike Marx, had no alternative vision to capitalist modernity. His work often seems, like Simmel's, to provide only its own reward in the intellectual pleasures of understanding and creative interpretation.

From its earliest days, then, sociology has been characterised by disagreement over its nature, purpose and social role. When we look at the history of the discipline in Ireland, we may expect to find similarly competing views as to what it is or should be about. This chapter is an attempt to sketch that history. It argues that sociology in Ireland has tended most often to reflect the Durkheimian managerial model. Its desired contribution has been to help improve, reform and rationalise how Irish society is governed, but there have been occasional flights from this position towards the critical/democratic stance, particularly in the late 1970s, and towards the playful/intellectual approach, particularly since the 1990s. We will try to explain, sociologically, why this has been the case.

EARLY FORMS OF SOCIAL INQUIRY IN IRELAND

In recent years there has been an emerging literature that has sought to trace the history and development of sociology in Ireland. Though a full-length study has yet to emerge, a number of important writers, documents and institutions have been identified. Writers such as Hill (2005), Garvin and Hess (2006) and Conway (2006) have begun to explore the nineteenth-century roots of sociological analysis of Irish society. The study of seminal writers such as Harriet Martineau and Gustav de Beaumont, as well as a recognition of Marx's and Engels' work on Irish society (Hazelkorn, 1980), has helped to locate Irish sociology within a broader sweep of European and American social and political analysis.

Conway (2006, p.8) asserts that (as in other countries) 'Irish sociology was likely born sometime during the nineteenth century' and that this was 'outside the university setting' (p.12). The foundations can be found, on the one hand, in the writings on Ireland of a number of seminal international figures and, on the other, in the foundation of institutions that were dedicated to the understanding of social conditions in Ireland.

The work in and on Ireland of some major international thinkers has only recently begun to attract attention. In particular Garvin and Hess (2006) and Conway (2006) have sought to bring to light the work of the nineteenth-century writers Martineau, Beaumont and Tocqueville. None of these writers was Irish — Harriet Martineau was English, while the latter two were French. They visited Ireland in the first half of the nineteenth century (between 1831 and 1852) and reported on their experiences to an international audience. Conway (2006, p.10) suggests that 'all three applied a sociological lens to Ireland's then impoverished situation'. The full implications of their contribution to Irish sociology have yet to be developed.

As we outlined in Chapter 1, Harriet Martineau is increasingly being recognised as a major founder of the discipline of sociology. Her writings spanned many topics and fields, but Ireland was a significant one. Her work can mainly be found in *Ireland: A tale* (1832), which, like much of her other work, made use of the novel form to express her observations, and in *Letters from Ireland* (1852), which was based on a series of letters she dispatched from post-Famine Ireland to the London newspaper, the *Daily News* (Conway, 2006, p.9).

In 1835 the French writer Gustav de Beaumont travelled to Ireland with his friend and fellow-writer Alexis de Tocqueville, the celebrated author of *Democracy in America*. He returned in 1837 and two years later his observations and analysis of pre-Famine Ireland were published in two volumes as *L'Irlande sociale, politique et religieuse*. This book was republished in 2006 with an introduction by Tom Garvin and Andreas Hess (2006), who describe it (p.vi) as 'one of the first sociological bestsellers in France'. Beaumont was highly critical of the role of landowners in Ireland and noted the poverty and inequality brought about by an inequitable society.

He argued that 'Ireland was to the United Kingdom what slavery was to the United States' (Garvin and Hess, 2006, p.xi). He prophesied 'the emergence of an Ireland of small owner-occupier farmers'. His book is 'a classic account of the painful birth pangs of Irish democracy, Ireland providing in miniature a model of the struggle for democracy against feudalism in Europe' (Garvin and Hess, 2006, p.xiii).

Beaumont's analysis is reminiscent of anthropologist Clifford Geertz's notion of 'thick description', i.e. 'a wide range of readings and possible interpretations, usually derived from a broad variety of sources. Detailed note-taking, interviews with experts and other knowledgeable sources, direct observation, the collection and careful study of secondary sources such as journals, government reports, books and studies, as well as detailed notes from travel books and diaries, all contributed to the final draft' (Garvin and Hess, 2006, p.xiv).

In 1934 the American anthropologist Conrad Arensberg reported that he 'could not source any material on Irish sociology, indicating the absence of sociology (or anthropology) as a professional discipline at that time in Ireland' (Byrne et al., 2001, p. XXXVn). Despite this valid claim, social inquiry of certain types has a long history in Ireland. The first population census (a 'private census of Mr Dobbs') was attempted in 1732 (Kennedy, 2001, p.10) and was followed by another in 1821. The year 1824 saw a detailed educational census and in 1847 the first agricultural census was carried out. In 1854 there was an exhaustive census of landholding (Griffith's Valuation) throughout the country. The first association in Ireland devoted to empirical social inquiry, the Dublin Statistical Society, was formed in 1847. Fifteen years later it was renamed the Statistical and Social Inquiry Society (SSIS). It celebrated its 150th anniversary in 1997 and continues its work to the present day (Daly, 1997; 1998).

Sociologists of science, in particular those who study the social construction of knowledge (for example, Woolgar, 1988), point out that science, like all knowledge systems, arises from social activity. With regard to the social sciences, Wagner (1994, pp.xiv–xv) argues that we should not take at face value the categorisation of modes of inquiry such as 'social science', 'political science', 'natural science' and so on, but should investigate the historical circumstances under which the discourses now known as the 'social sciences' were constructed. He suggests that they have tended to be closely interwoven with the practices they have claimed to observe, particularly the activities of the state and the market. This means that we must treat the writings of social inquirers 'in a double way' — not just as a source of information about society, but also as an indicator of the 'ways of seeing society' available to people at the time. So what were the historical circumstances relating to the establishment of the Statistical and Social Inquiry Society? Who were its members and how did they see Irish society?

Two circumstances, one external and one internal to Ireland, are worth noting. First, an interest in statistics, and the formation of 'statistical societies', was not unique to Ireland. It was a feature of nineteenth-century European society generally and was linked to the emergence and development of the modern nation state (see Chapter 4). The word 'statistics' originally related to the study of how a state should be organised, and embraced the legal, educational, public health, welfare, criminal and economic aspects of society. It gradually came to mean, more narrowly, quantitative information or 'figures' as states began to collect more and more numerical data as a way of monitoring and regulating populations.

The development of 'modern statistics' was founded on an assumption that, through the collection of objective information about social conditions and behaviour, states could find solutions to the major social problems confronting them. As Daly notes (1997, pp.19–28) it was no coincidence that the Dublin Statistical Society was founded at the height of the Great Famine in Ireland. The discourse of social inquiry in Ireland was shaped early on by the assumption that better information about the major problems and trends in society would produce better government by the state. This implies a belief that the state acts in response to appeals to rationality rather than, as a Marxist view might emphasise, in the interest of powerful groups in society.

This 'rationalist' view of the state, and of what social inquiry is about, would have been widely shared across nineteenth-century Europe. But for Ireland there was an additional factor. At this time Ireland was a colony of Britain and was, moreover, disruptive and difficult to control. As with military technology, the technology of social inquiry found colonial Ireland a good terrain on which to experiment. The early formation of the discourse of social inquiry in Ireland occurred in circumstances where it was deemed important not only to increase the rationality of the state, but also to increase its control over society. This may help to explain the underdevelopment of a 'democratic' objective for sociology in Ireland until quite recent times.

The early membership of the Dublin Statistical Society was, as we might expect, drawn from the city's affluent male professional and intellectual elite — lawyers, Trinity College academics, some businessmen, senior Dublin Castle officials and leading members of the Church of Ireland (Daly, 1998, p.2). Few members of the Society were interested in statistical techniques as such. Rather, they believed that some sort of systematic and objective, or 'scientific', information would help to answer the great social questions of the day and suggest a direction for reformative action on the part of the state. Daly describes them as people who were generally optimistic about how Ireland was progressing economically in the wake of the Famine and who tended to share the 'assimilationist' view that 'the best recipe for further prosperity was to bring Irish laws and administrative practices into line with those in England and Wales'. For Boylan and Foley (1992) the social scientific inquiry that the Society helped to popularise was not a 'value-free universalistic science', but a key part of the 'civilising' project launched by a colonial elite that aimed to transform Ireland into, as Archbishop Whateley put it, 'a "really valuable portion of the British Empire" rather than a sort of "morbid excrescence"' (quoted in de Guistino, 1995, pp.228–9).

During the first twenty-five years of its existence the SSIS had a considerable impact on the United Kingdom's Irish legislation, and on other matters such as the management of poverty and of children in need. From the 1870s, however, its influence was undermined by the rise of nationalist politics. None of those actively involved in the new social movements such as Sinn Féin or Labour, or even in the Irish Parliamentary Party, was a member of the Society. Yet, remarkably, within a few years of the establishment of the Irish Free State, the SSIS had become a highly significant political arena once again. It was able to establish close links with the new civil service — perhaps even closer than those it had enjoyed with Dublin Castle — and a large number of senior public officials became active members (Daly, 1998, p.4). The new Irish state continued to measure, count and analyse its population as part of its system of government. It found in the Society an appropriate forum for the generation of data and advice on the direction of policy. In turn, members of the Society appeared to have no difficulty in redefining the object of their research — 'Irish society' — to reflect the territorial boundaries of the new state, illustrating how, as Wagner notes, discourses of inquiry and the social practices of the state tend to be interwoven.

By the 1950s the SSIS had become a prominent advocate of 'economic planning', particularly through the papers read to it and published in its *Journal* by T.K. Whitaker. By the 1960s, it was entering into 'a golden age . . . Many views first aired at its meetings had now been accepted as official policy. Economics and statistics appeared to offer a blueprint for a modern and prosperous Ireland, precisely as the Society's founders had hoped in 1847' (Daly, 1998, p.7). In the process, however, 'social inquiry' had become very largely redefined as economic and statistical inquiry. A large proportion of the papers presented to the SSIS came from economists and statisticians, especially those employed by government departments and semi-state bodies; also, the Central Bank and the Central Statistics Office (Daly, 1997, p.165). The marginalisation of sociology within the SSIS foreshadowed the marginal position it would occupy within the larger society, but it was also set free to begin to develop different understandings of its role and purpose over time.

THE SHAPING OF IRISH SOCIOLOGY

The SSIS's understanding of the purpose and conduct of social inquiry strongly influenced the shaping of Irish sociology, in particular through its links to the Economic and Social Research Institute (ESRI), the major source of sociological research in Ireland and chief employer of professional sociologists. In 1959 the SSIS was instrumental, with funding assistance from the American Ford Foundation, in the establishment of the Economic Research Institute (ERI).

Relations continued to be close between the SSIS and the Institute, with broadly overlapping memberships and similar intellectual concerns. The foundation of the ERI was directly linked to the economic and social development in Ireland that was taking place under the 1960s Programmes for Economic Expansion. The ERI's early concerns — European integration, productivity and tariff protection — mirrored the concerns of the government of the day (Daly, 1997, p.161). Despite this congruence, the ERI was explicitly 'non-political'. Following a review by the Danish social scientist Henning Friis (Jackson, 2004, p.25) it had 'social' added to its remit, and became the ESRI in 1966. Over the following three decades, it was to become a key location for sociological research in the country.

The ESRI has specialised in conducting large-scale social research that is numerical or quantitative in form. Research is addressed to issues seen as significant social or policy problems by the state or other elite groups (business or employers' associations, for example) and is undertaken with a view to making public policy and action more rational and effective. ESRI research has contributed in particular to our knowledge of class structure and mobility patterns in Ireland and of, in particular gender-related, inequalities in access to education. The influence of the ESRI in defining what constitutes useful sociological knowledge has been felt in other research institutions such as the Agricultural Institute/Teagasc, the Health Research Board, the Educational Research Centre, the Linguistics Institute of Ireland and the National Economic and Social Council (NESC). Sociology has over time acquired a footing in all these sites but what constitutes the discipline is fairly tightly defined.

In the current decade the ESRI has continued to conduct policy-driven research: some of it in established fields where it has an international reputation, such as social mobility, poverty and disadvantage, education and labour market studies. It has also been active in areas that reflect the concerns of Ireland of the 2000s: immigration, social capital and sexuality, for example. It continues to have a strong influence on social research in Ireland.

In addition to the state-centred sociology practised by the ESRI and other official research bodies, Irish sociology has been shaped by two other key influences with rather different impacts. The first is Catholic social teaching and the involvement of the Catholic Church generally in the early promotion of sociology in Ireland. The second is research by 'foreign', predominantly American, sociologists and anthropologists. The combination of these three powerful influences has produced a sociology in Ireland that is distinctive and not easily assimilated into just a regional variant of, for example, British or American sociologies.

In an analysis of the emergence of sociology in the West, Langer suggests that Catholicism has been less than helpful to the development of sociology, drawing attention to the comparative lack of development of the discipline in countries such as Austria and Spain. He argues (1992, p.5) that:

> Catholicism always generated its own 'social theories' which are usually less individualistic and less complex than the dominating theories of sociology. On the other hand they have more normative implications . . . when sociology developed in a Catholic milieu it was either occupied with the question of 'social order' (especially how to stabilise the state) or strongly empirically oriented (usually in a later stage). Sociology as the secularised self-consciousness of modern society did not flourish on Catholic foundations.

The development of a Catholic-influenced sociology in Ireland reflected aspects of the experience elsewhere. Sociology made sporadic appearances in academic circles in Ireland from as early as 1910, when it was taught in University College, Dublin, under the name of 'social philosophy'. Its adoption in the National University of Ireland reflected the interest in social ethics stimulated by the Papal Encyclical *Rerum Novarum* (1891) and later by the Encyclical *Quadragesimo Anno* (1931) 'with its concern for a counter to the trades unions and what was perceived as a drift on the part of the working class towards socialism and communism' (Jackson, 1998, p.1).

In 1944 the Catholic Truth Society published Father Peter McKevitt's book *The plan of society* (McKevitt, 1944). This textbook was intended to underpin the course in 'Catholic sociology' at the Maynooth seminary. The book, however, had very little to say about Irish society *per se*. It was based on an interpretation of aspects of European society in the context of Papal Encyclicals, and on the works of prominent European Catholic writers, with references to a very small number of American and British sociologists. It also reflected the fact that apart from some state-derived statistical information, there was a dearth of indigenous sociological research within Ireland. By the 1950s, the Catholic Church's interest in pastoral and community issues and its strong involvement in voluntary associations and voluntary service provision (see Chapter 14) had led a number of its members to take an interest in the discipline of sociology. The Christus Rex Society organised the teaching of sociology to selected groups of religious in the late 1950s. It also published a journal, *Christus Rex* (renamed *Social Studies* in 1973) that became an important outlet for Irish sociological writing during the 1970s and 1980s. In addition, Catholic sociology continued to exert considerable influence through its role in journals, institutions and even the locations where sociologists met (Conway, 2006, pp.13–15).

As in Spain (Langer, 1992, p.12), clerics and former clerics were prominent as early sociologists in Ireland. In 1937 the formerly mentioned Father Peter McKevitt was appointed to a Chair of Sociology and Catholic Action founded at the Maynooth seminary, a position he occupied until 1953 (Kennedy, 2001, p.154). The first Chairs in university sociology departments were also held by Catholic priests, at University College Dublin, where James Kavanagh, later Archbishop of Dublin, was appointed in 1966, and at National University of

Ireland, Galway. Clerics with a strong interest in sociology, including Professor Edward Coyne and Father Bill McKenna, were also instrumental in the establishment and development of the College of Industrial Relations, now the National College of Ireland (Kennedy, 2001, pp.181, 205). The first lay professor of sociology in the Republic of Ireland, Professor Damien Hannan, was appointed to University College Cork in 1971 and the second, Professor John A. Jackson, came to Trinity College Dublin, in 1974.

In the universities, then — in contrast to the research institutions — Irish sociology was, from the outset, heavily influenced by Catholic social teaching and philosophy, particularly by the 'Catholic corporatism' that had developed in other European societies such as Belgium, Italy and the Netherlands. Whereas the positivist tradition in sociology inherited from the SSIS and similar organisations emphasised a social research that served the state, the Catholic corporatist tradition focused on what is often called 'civil society'. This referred to core institutions 'outside the state', for example, the family, the community and the parish, that, through a supposed better grasp of the dynamics of social processes, could be assisted and encouraged to take control of and manage their own affairs.

The relationship between the 'Catholic' and the 'official' elements in Irish sociology is interesting. Both discourses tended to be positivistic and rather uninterested in theoretical issues and debates. Each took for granted that they could easily identify the proper objects of sociological research in the 'real world' (social problems) and tended to encourage empirical research rather than theoretical or conceptual development. Lynch (1987, p.117), talking about the sociology of education, though her remarks can be applied to the discipline as a whole, suggests that 'the Catholic view of the good — in terms of social order — has been transformed from being a religious ideal into a conceptual model of the world that purports to represent empirical reality.' O'Dowd (1988, p.9) has suggested that the empiricist emphasis of 1950s Catholic social philosophy explains why sociological research developed earlier in the Republic of Ireland than it did in the North. Yet the perceived consumers of 'official' and 'Catholic' research were quite different in each case: for the former, the state and its agents; for the latter 'the people', variously defined.

The extent to which early Irish sociology approached any form of social critique, or defined social problems independently of a statist perspective, was due to the influence of the Catholic tradition. It is a tradition carried forward today in the work of the Conference of Religious of Ireland (CORI) and Trócaire, for example, and is a discernible influence on the research of bodies like the Combat Poverty Agency and Focus Ireland. Catholic social teaching, on the other hand, had provided considerable opposition to the enthusiasm among members of the SSIS during the 1940s for the introduction into Ireland of a British-style welfare state (Daly, 1998, p.6; Kennedy, 2001, p.192). There is also no doubt that some Catholic clergy sought to appropriate Irish sociology so as to prevent it from becoming a vehicle for the importation of socialist or Marxist ideas into Irish society.

A third important influence on the early formation of Irish sociology has been that of 'foreign' sociologists and anthropologists, particularly the latter. Anthropology normally deals with 'other' societies perceived to be very different to our own. Thus, we are familiar with the idea of anthropologists leaving the Western world to go and inquire into the 'primitive' peoples of Africa or the South Pacific but, for anthropologists in Britain, Europe, the United States and Australia, Ireland itself often provided a suitably exotic, or even 'primitive' location for research, made even more attractive by the fact that the society was English-speaking. This generated a steady stream of anthropological researchers, from Browne and Haddon in the 1890s (Curtin and Wilson, 1989, p.ix) to Eipper, Wilson, Peace and others in the 1980s and 1990s, seeking to understand our mysterious ways (Wilson and Donnan, 2006).

The most influential piece of anthropological research carried out in Ireland remains that by two American social anthropologists, Conrad Arensberg and Solon Kimball, in a farming locality in north Co. Clare in the early 1930s (for a more detailed discussion of this study, see Chapter 5). The most striking feature of Arensberg and Kimball's work, compared to other social research carried out in Ireland at that time or in the following forty years, was that it addressed a problem set not by the state, the church or any other 'external' body, but from within the discipline of anthropology itself (Byrne et al., 2001). Arensberg and Kimball, following the research practices developed in America by Lloyd Warner (in his 'Yankee City' studies) and Robert and Helen Lynd (Middletown, 1929), wanted to discover how communities work — how do people who live in communities behave towards each other? And how does this behaviour add up to a set of patterns or a 'social system' that can reproduce itself over long periods of time, even when the individuals involved have gone and have been replaced by new ones? Warner and others had developed the idea that communities (or micro-societies) can be analysed as integrated systems made up of interrelated parts that are 'functionally interdependent'. They had tested this theory through research into American, largely urban, communities. Arensberg and Kimball wanted to see if the theory held true in a remote and isolated rural community. Their interest was not initially in Irish society at all but in testing and developing a theoretical idea about how societies should be understood.

We could locate Arensberg and Kimball towards the 'playful/intellectual' end of the spectrum outlined in Figure 2.1, but it was their detailed observations about rural Ireland that made the greatest impact on Irish social researchers. Almost inevitably, given how social inquiry has been understood in Ireland, they were seen to be writing about a 'social problem': small or marginal farming in the underdeveloped western periphery. Arensberg and Kimball's work set the agenda for sociological research into urban (Humphreys, 1966) as well as rural Ireland and the context for analyses of the 'modernisation' of Irish social and cultural development for much of the next 40 years. It was only in the 1970s that critical assessment and discussion of their approach began to take place, marking a watershed in the development of sociology as a discipline in Ireland (Tovey, 1992a).

By the 1970s sociology was finally becoming consolidated in Ireland as a distinct discipline. Sociology departments were established in all of the universities of the Republic that did not already have them and new professors were appointed in two of these. Many of the staff that still work in university sociology departments today were appointed during this decade. By 1975 there were four or five sociologists in each of the departments in University College, Dublin, University College, Cork and Trinity College, Dublin (TCD), and two in the Department of Political Science and Sociology at National University of Ireland, Galway (NUIG) (Jackson, 1998). Similarly, lecturers in sociology began to be appointed within the teacher training colleges and the Regional Technical Colleges (RTCs). Publication outlets for sociological work were increasing. The *Economic and Social Review* (*ESR*), a journal produced under the auspices of the ESRI, was first published in 1970. Though it published more papers from economists than from any other discipline (O'Dowd, 1988, p.20), it did publish an increasing number of sociological papers over time. In 1973 *Social Studies* rose out of the ashes of the previous *Christus Rex* journal (Conway, 2006, p.15).

Moreover, new perspectives and influences were coming in to Irish sociology as more appointments were made within universities and research institutions. The ESRI employed a significant number of researchers, both Irish and foreign, who had received their sociological training abroad, especially in the United States. Within the university sector, while many staff had taken a first degree in Ireland, virtually all had received postgraduate sociology training abroad. Staff employed in the National University colleges had generally trained in America — strong links existed with certain American universities such as Southern Illinois and St. Louis. In TCD the links were predominantly with Britain. All university sociology departments contained at least one staff member who was not Irish; in TCD, from the mid-1970s until 1991, four of the five sociology staff were recruits from Britain. The RTCs were more likely to employ Irish-born lecturers.

Both foreign and foreign-trained sociologists were instrumental in carrying out a form of 'technology transfer' in the importation to Ireland of British and American models of sociological theorising and research. A more critical analysis might depict the development of sociology in Ireland as dependent, in a similar way that the sociology of most smaller Western countries was, for example, in Australia, Scandinavia and Canada. The sociology of the core countries, in particular the United States, the UK, Germany and France, has long dominated the development of the discipline in smaller peripheral countries. In the latter the resources devoted to sociology are comparatively small and these countries rely heavily on their 'big brothers'. This is especially the case when, as with Ireland and

Britain, the similarities between the countries appear at least on the surface to be substantial. This may explain why Irish sociologists have long drawn on the work of those in the core economies, rather than in countries that may have more in common economically, politically and perhaps socially, such as Finland, Austria or New Zealand.

American-trained sociologists working in Ireland largely adhered to structural functionalist theoretical models (see Chapter 3), while staff from Britain were largely followers of one or other variant of Marxism, which enjoyed a revival in Britain and Europe in the late 1960s and 1970s. During the following decade the study and debate of a wide range of other, imported, theoretical perspectives also began within Ireland. The social constructivist perspectives of symbolic inter-actionism, phenomenology and ethnomethodology, for example, confronted both Marxist and functionalist realist world views, while a growing interest in researching language and meaning, using qualitative rather than quantitative methods, challenged the dominance of positivist orientations in research. The growth of theoretical and methodological pluralism in Irish sociology during this time stimulated the opening up of new topics for research and new issues for debate. O'Dowd notes (1988, p.4) that some sociologists feared that such pluralism 'hindered the development of the discipline' and, in particular, 'undermined its potential contribution to policy-making'. It seemed likely to alienate prospective funders who were unable to take seriously a discipline riven with internal contro-versies and arguments about its own theoretical assumptions and research practices.

One of the most significant events in the development of sociology in this period was the establishment in 1973 of the Sociological Association of Ireland (SAI). The Association was organised on a 32-county basis and welcomed as members both practising and non-practising sociologists and graduates of some cognate disciplines. Since 1975 it has hosted an unbroken series of annual conferences, has organised a variety of other events, and has published a newsletter (and more recently a website) for members and others with an interest in Irish sociology. The impact of the SAI as a forum for debate and self-recognition has been invaluable. During its first decade, its conferences were the site of lively arguments that pitted Marxism against functionalism; modernisation theory against dependency theory; revisited Arensberg and Kimball and the conception of Irish 'peasant' society; or disagreed over how to interpret the place of 'community' in Irish life. Irish sociology was beginning to understand itself and to recognise its distinctive approach to reality with its own particular issues and concerns. The process was, however, a rather halting and insecure one and continued to be dominated by the idea that the prestige of the discipline depended on its 'relevance' to society, defined in quite narrow statist/social-problems terms.

As the 1970s came to an end, it looked as though sociology might be able to secure for itself a place within Irish cultural and literary life that could offer an alternative model. Sociologists at TCD were invited to create a sociological exhibition on contemporary Ireland to form part of the Irish government-sponsored festival 'A Sense of Ireland' at the Institute of Contemporary Arts in London in 1980, which also included living art performances, poetry readings and concerts. The sociology section of the exhibition, 'No Country for Old Men', used text, photographs, graphs and cartoons to represent and celebrate the demographic, economic, social and cultural transformations of Ireland in the 1970s (McHugh, 1980). However, the invitation was not repeated at later international festivals on Ireland, and the idea that sociology could be presented in a cultural rather than 'scientific' milieu was largely forgotten for another one and a half decades.

CONTEMPORARY IRISH SOCIOLOGY

The 1980s were a time both of stagnation and consolidation for Irish sociology. During this decade sociology increased steadily in popularity as a university subject in Ireland, in contrast to the experience of decline in other countries such as Britain, but the possibilities for a graduate of gaining employment in Ireland as a sociologist declined substantially. There was very little recruitment to permanent posts in sociology in the universities, where most of those recruited in the 1970s were still in place and no expansion in positions had occurred (O'Dowd, 1988). The situation in the research institutions and RTCs was only slightly better. Increasing numbers of sociology graduates who left Ireland to get postgraduate qualifications found themselves unable to return to employment, while many of those who completed PhDs in Ireland subsequently had to go abroad to work. A study of sociology graduates of TCD between 1974 and 1996 (Jackson, 1998) located around 16 per cent who were pursuing a professional career in sociology; half were doing so outside Ireland. Irish sociology was successfully integrated into an international labour market but, consequentially, with the of loss of new voices and of critical mass at home.

The SAI continued to perform a key role in providing a place to discuss and reflect on how Irish sociology was developing, but it also became a force for the professionalisation of sociologists. It began to address such issues as the establishment of a set of principles of employment for people working in research, who were often temporary or contract appointees with few rights over how they conducted research or what happened to their findings; and the development of a code of ethics to guide research practice. At one point the Association appeared to be moving towards becoming a professional body that would seek to defend practitioners and monitor and regulate the right to practise. Understandable as a largely defensive response to the employment constraints of the 1980s, this trend created difficulties over the Association's generous rules on eligibility for membership and provoked some stormy debates about the purpose of the SAI and, more broadly, of sociology itself.

A very positive contribution by the SAI during the 1980s was its role in sponsoring the publication of sociology texts, including a series of readers, 'Studies in Irish Society'. The first, *Power, conflict and inequality*, was published in 1982, followed by *Culture and ideology in Ireland* (1984), *Gender in Irish society* (1986) and *Whose law and order? Aspects of crime and social control in Ireland* (1988). The SAI also commissioned chapters for a text on Irish society: *Ireland — a sociological profile* (1986; a second edition, with entirely new chapters, appeared as *Irish society: Sociological perspectives* in 1995). This was not the first attempt at a comprehensive integrated text on Irish society — Michel Peillon's *Contemporary Irish society* (see Chapter 4) was published in 1982 — but it was the first to target the growing interest in sociology among Irish third-level students.

The ESRI also contributed significantly to Irish sociological output, publishing throughout the 1980s reports based on its research into educational access and performance; education and gender; distribution of income; employment; social class and social mobility; and social change in rural Ireland. At the end of the decade it published *Understanding contemporary Ireland* (Breen *et al.*, 1990), an analysis of social change since the 1950s that focused almost exclusively on social structural trends, integrated through the concept of social class.

The 1990s seemed to open up a range of new development possibilities. The Irish government's decision in 1991 to make funds available for a programme of university expansion in response to demographic and social pressures on third-level places brought a number of new staff into existing sociology departments. The teaching of sociology increased in the two new universities, in Dublin and in Limerick, and in the RTCs. Postgraduate teaching also expanded, as a range of taught Masters and diploma courses supplemented the traditional postgraduate degrees by research. In the 1990s sociology departments across the Republic contributed to Masters courses in communications and cultural studies; European social policy analysis; peace studies; women's studies; the sociology of development; equality studies; community development; rural development; social research methodology; and racial and ethnic studies.

New sources of funds for research became available, particularly from the EU. This expanded the resources available to the ESRI and for the first time made large-scale research a real possibility for some academic sociologists. Government departments such as the Department of Health and Children became more interested in funding research either through the employment of researchers or commissioning research from the universities and research institutes. Small, independent research consultancies were set up by sociology graduates and flourished in the new research climate. The Royal Irish Academy's National Committee for Economic and Social Sciences lobbied for funding for social science research and, in 1995, was able to set up a Social Science Research Council with a small fund, disbursed annually on a competitive basis, to support research projects and postgraduate training and to reward high achievement by postgraduate students (Jackson, 2004, pp.35–38). In 1998 the Higher Educational Authority (HEA) made scholarships available to social science postgraduates and, in 1999, state funding for third-level research, via the HEA, included for the first time the Humanities and Social Sciences.

As a result of this funding a number of major new interdisciplinary research centres in the social sciences, some embracing sociology, were established, including the National Institute for Regional and Spatial Analysis (NIRSA), centred on the university at Maynooth; the Institute for the Study of Social Change at UCD; and the Institute for International Integration Studies at TCD. The former narrowness of the funding base meant that research had tended to be closely tied to specific policy issues (Lynch, 1999b, pp.44–46). This led to a lack of research in some fields and a tendency to adopt a highly positivist approach towards the production of 'useful results'. It can be argued that the more generous funding environment has led to the emergence of a broader approach to sociological research within the country.

In 1993 the SAI celebrated its twentieth anniversary with an Annual Conference on 'Irish Sociology — Themes and Tensions'. It then had a membership of some 180, of whom 10 per cent were based outside Ireland, about 14 per cent in Northern Ireland and about 7 per cent in non-university research institutions in the Republic of Ireland. The other two-thirds were predominantly third-level teachers and postgraduate students from the Republic. By 1996, membership had risen to 226, though this was to be a high watermark (Conway, 2006, p.21). Two key developments in Irish sociology took place around 1990. The first was the introduction by the SAI of the annual *Irish Journal of Sociology (IJS)*, to replace the now defunct *Social Studies*. The *IJS* showed itself to be distinct from both *Social Studies* and the *ESR* right from the first issue which included papers on cultural studies and post-modernism, ideas scarcely mentioned in public in sociological writings before this point. It also reviewed eighteen books, mainly about aspects of Irish society, reflecting the growth of publishing in the field. The journal's commitment to providing a forum for lively and rigorous critique of developments in both Irish sociological writing and sociology in general, established in this first issue, has remained a significant feature of all issues since. The interest in topics ignored in more statist versions of sociology has also persisted. Over the last decade, the journal has published papers on a broad range of topics, ranging from the sociology of landscape; to studies of the sociology of various sports; to the sociology of art and of animals. In recent years special issues have been compiled on issues such as sexuality; mass media; the Irish diaspora; masculinities; and 'the war on terror'. These have reflected a conscious decision to 'internationalise' the journal, with contributions from internationally renowned writers such as Raymond Boudon (France), Nathan Glazer (USA) and Bob Connell (Australia).

The second important development is the growth of feminist sociology. This took place in close liaison with the rise of the Irish women's movement (Mahon,

1995). Writing in 1988, O'Dowd could still comment on the need for Irish sociology to address 'the perspective of gender'. He noted 'the extent to which all social science has been shaped by male perspectives' and, in particular, that 'Irish intellectual life, especially higher education, has been male-dominated. It is only very recently that social and historical research has sought to take full account of Irish women' (1988, p.16). Yet one might argue that sociology has been the *least* male-dominated among Irish social sciences. The SAI was chaired by women within the first decade of its establishment. Sociologists pioneered research on gender issues both in institutional and academic circles, for example, the ESRI study, *Schooling and sex roles* (1983) and *Gender and Irish society* (1986), respectively. In 1992, the first issue of the NUIG *Women's Studies Review* appeared, edited by, among others, a NUIG sociologist. In 1993/4 the *IJS* carried a debate between Ronit Lentin and Evelyn Mahon over the possibility of a feminist research methodology (see Chapter 8). Interest in and debates about feminist sociology continued during the second half of the 1990s with the establishment of the Cork-based *Irish Feminist Studies Review*; major studies of the gender aspects of areas such as health, education and rural life; and the publication of *Women and Irish society: A sociological reader* (Byrne and Leonard, 1997) and *Emerging voices: Women in contemporary Irish society* (O'Connor, 1998). Women were appointed professors of sociology in the Universities of Ulster and Limerick, but the proportion of women at senior academic level does not yet reflect the dominance of women in sociology undergraduate and postgraduate courses, nor their increasing equality among the teaching staff of sociology departments. It is sometimes suggested that the feminisation of Irish sociology is related to its marginalisation within Irish public life, but whether sociology, of all the social sciences, has been most open to women's voices and concerns because it has been more marginalised, or the other way round, is open to speculation.

Since the early 1990s the number of sociology books published in and about Ireland has significantly increased, reflecting the dynamic nature of contemporary Irish society. Subjects have included 'established' topics such as education; religion; inequality; housing; the family; and community, but have also explored topics of popular interest such as globalisation and the mass media; Travellers and Irish society; immigration, multiculturalism and racism; and sexuality. These issues continue to reflect matters that are of immediate concern to politicians, public servants and opinion formers: they might be interpreted as sociologists' attempts to address public issues that have arisen in contemporary Ireland. But there have also been attempts to analyse the perhaps more everyday and mundane indicators of change in Irish society and culture, such as food and drink, traffic, popular music, public art, shopping and celebrity culture. The series published by the Institute of Public Administration, *Sociological chronicles*, has, in particular, provided a platform for this type of analysis. It remains to be seen whether Irish sociologists go on to produce a significant number of book-length studies in these fields, though there are encouraging indications that this may be starting to occur (e.g. Wickham, 2006, on Dublin traffic).

Despite this expansion of output, it is perhaps surprising that sociology has not really managed to establish itself within Irish life as a significant or stimulating guide to how that life is changing. This has been a concern of Irish sociologists for as long as they have been organised as a discipline (Conway, 2006). While Langer (1992, p.1) suggests that in Western society as a whole 'sociology has become the most popular way for society to interpret itself . . . firmly integrated into . . . everyday communication', in Ireland such influence seems to rest more clearly with historians, literary critics and, increasingly, psychologists. Sociologists rarely appear in the mass media as interpreters of everyday life. Compared to economists, sociologists are seldom called upon to discuss or determine policy matters in the public sphere. How then, with its history to date, should we evaluate the contribution that Irish sociology, has made to Irish society? Does Irish society need Irish sociology at all?

Reviewing *Irish society: Sociological perspectives* in the *IJS* in 1996, Kieran Bonner clearly regards this as open to question. He contends (1996, p.219) that the 'domain assumptions' of much of the sociology displayed in the text and elsewhere:

> are very much intertwined with the modernist project. The reflexive turn which emerged in sociology as a consequence of the influence of phenomenology provides the tools for a self-conscious reflection about the philosophical and political implications and meanings of these domain assumptions. Yet . . . one gets the sense from this book that Anglo-American empiricism (which is embedded in the modern project) rather than European continental theorising (which seeks to move some distance from the project) dominates Irish sociology.

Bonner suggests that Irish sociology has been good at producing a great deal of factual knowledge about Irish society but it has left questions of sociological theory largely unexplored. In this respect, it reflects the underdevelopment, as identified by historian J.J. Lee (1989, pp.562–643), of an intellectual tradition of philosophy or theorising in contemporary Irish life compared to our much stronger aesthetic and literary traditions. History and psychology are thus very popular ways to interpret reality, given their emphasis on the narrative and on the individual.

Anthropologist Eileen Kane (1996, pp.139–145) provides a similar, perhaps harsher, critique. She distinguishes three paradigms, or dominant approaches, that have shaped Irish social science. These are similar to those we have identified in this chapter and Chapter 1 — a dominant positivism/post-positivism; an emergent body of critical theory; and an essentially absent phenomenology or interpretative sociology. As social scientists in Ireland have drawn almost entirely from a post-positivist paradigm, they have been led into the production of 'facts, albeit second-class ones, rather than interpretation and . . . an emphasis on refinements of methodology, usually quantitative'. Positivistic thinking has been endemic within Irish society. It has 'shaped not only the social sciences, but official and public expectations about the nature of reality and what constitutes credible evidence as a basis for action'. The result is a 'stultifying empiricism'; a sociology oriented towards 'social engineering' that sees its primary audience as the state and the Catholic Church. As a result, Kane argues, Irish sociology has emphasised pathology, crime and deviance; poverty and unemployment; violence, drugs and alcohol; the conditions of some minorities; and the problems of rural areas. These are all fields that 'have symbolic and political resonance for both church and state'. A further consequence for Kane is that Irish sociology (like most others) studies 'down, in class and power terms, rather than up', with very little if any research being done on the powerful social groups in society. That is left to (a few) investigative journalists and, in recent years, various public tribunals of inquiry.

Kane contrasts this type of sociology with critical theory, which sees research as part of an attempt 'to facilitate transformation towards a desired end' (1996, p.140). For critical theorists, knowledge is always embedded in its socio-historical context. They ask 'knowledge for whom?'; 'knowledge for what?' Inquiry is thus 'a political act'. Kane remarks that critical theory can also produce a top-down or paternalistic perspective on the subjects studied. It sees others as in need of truth and empowerment, not the theorists themselves. It 'seeks to transform the world view of others, while failing to seek the insights of those whose thinking we are liberating to liberate our own' (1996, p.141). Thus, it can become a form of Western cultural imperialism. It is interesting that, while Kane mentions feminism, Marxism and neo-Marxism, liberation theology and participatory research as versions of critical theory, she does not name any Irish sociologists as examples of critical theorists nor does she discuss their work. We might question how well her comments apply to, for example, Drudy and Lynch's *Schools and society in Ireland* (1993) or Lynch and McLaughlin's 'Caring labour and love labour' (1995). Indeed Kathleen Lynch has been a major critic of contemporary Irish sociology from within the discipline and has (1999b) urged sociologists to adopt an approach to research that empowers those researched and overtly addresses issues of power within the research process.

For Kane, as for Bonner, it is ultimately the absence of a strong phenomenological or interpretative strand in Irish sociology that is most problematic and puzzling. It is easy enough to find explanations, Kane suggests, for the growing appeal of critical theory in Ireland's 'post-colonial marginal position, historical missionary association with the Third World, notional subscription to socialism, and exposure by some to liberation theory', but it is harder to understand why a discipline that could have had 'an interpretative brief' has been 'so bogged down in emphases on positivistic, "quantitative" methodologies' (1996, pp.142–3). Kane calls for more interpretative work in Irish sociology: research that recognises multiple realities and the multiplicity of alternative theories that can explain a given body of material. As facts are value- and theory-laden, research becomes a process of interpretation, and its product a narrative rather than a report. She argues that an interpretative approach is particularly germane to rapidly changing Irish society, with its significant levels of inequality and division and increasing uncertainty about its identity — where 'some speak of one nation, of two traditions, of the "fifth province", of a unique perspective,' we have to ask 'how many voices does Ireland have and how many perspectives?' Within such a context the essential task of an interpretative sociology is 'to discover the diversity and commonality of Irish meanings and experiences, and what the lived life is like' (1996, p.151).

In the decade since Kane and Bonner made their critiques of Irish sociology, there has been substantial growth in publishing in the discipline. The terrain of Irish sociological research and writing has expanded to embrace a more diverse and eclectic range of approaches, ranging from state-sponsored, large-scale quantitative research, to more speculative, qualitative and interpretive work. Much of this work is outlined and discussed in the remainder of this book, though it is not possible to span the whole field and we have not had the space to consider some important work.

In order to examine the trends in sociological writing, we briefly consider three relatively recent texts. These reflect the three sociological approaches that we outlined earlier in this chapter and can tell us something about the concerns of Irish sociologists in the early twenty-first century. The three texts are: *Conflict and consensus* (Fahey *et al.*, 2005), an all-Ireland study of values and attitudes; *The end of Irish history?* (Coulter and Coleman, 2003), a critical analysis of post-Celtic Tiger Ireland; and *Collision culture* (Keohane and Kuhling, 2004a), a set of essays on the nature of contemporary Irish culture.

The first of these books, *Conflict and consensus*, is published by the Institute of Public Administration (IPA), an organisation that, as its name suggests, is closely linked to the interests of public administration and government in Ireland. Though it has also made an important contribution in publishing the more interpretive and 'playful' *Irish sociological chronicles* series of books, the bulk of its output comprises material that is of direct utility and relevance to the governance of the country. The IPA is a major educator of civil servants and policy-makers and its publications support this role. It has also published some of the more important sociological texts of recent years, including O'Connor's (1999) analysis of women in Irish society and Kennedy's (2001) description of family change.

Conflict and consensus is a quantitative study of values and attitudes in Ireland — north and south. In this it is unusual, as cross-border or all-Ireland research is still rare, as O'Dowd, amongst others, has repeatedly pointed out (Goldthorpe *et al.*, 2002, p.102). The research is based on an analysis of data from a multinational sample survey — the European Values Survey — carried out across thirty-two European societies in 1999–2000. This data is supplemented by another cross-cultural survey, the European Social Survey, conducted in Ireland in 2002–3. Such multinational attitudinal surveys are becoming more important as a basis of sociological knowledge, but inevitably are expensive to conduct and complex to administer. They provide a large corpus of quantitative data that can then be made available to researchers across Europe (in Ireland through bodies such as the Social Science Data Archive based at UCD) for analysis and commentary.

This book focuses in particular on cleavages — in particular the perennial questions of politics, nationalism and religion — in Irish society: attempting to compare and contrast sets of attitudes amongst the populations of both sides of the border. These attitudes are then correlated with basic characteristics of the populations in question: such as their religious identification, ethnic identity, age, gender and education. In some cases (such as ethnic identification) there are (perhaps unsurprisingly) deep divisions between (say) northern Protestants and southern Catholics. But the authors remark on the striking similarities between the attitudes and values of people in the two parts of the island; for example, each is far more religious than nearly all other societies in Europe. This then makes them 'more similar to each other on certain key moral issues [such as divorce and abortion] than they are to any other national population' (Fahey et al., 2005, p.232). Interestingly, the authors identify a similar division that is opening up in both the north and the south: the emergence of a significant division between secular/liberal people on the one hand and religious/conservative people on the other. It is this emergent cleavage that might, they suggest, lead to a decline in the importance of sectarian religious divisions.

This research thus has the potential to cast Irish society in a new light. Fahey et al., in drawing on extensive survey data, provide a solid empirical basis for their findings, which goes beyond anecdotal or speculative writing. It shares some of the limitations of survey research of this type: the scale and complexity of these international surveys means that there is considerable lag between survey and publication — up to six years in this case. Furthermore, the findings are shaped by the questions asked, and these are inevitably limited to the particular interests of those commissioning the survey. On the other hand, the authors do go to considerable effort to make use of series of surveys over time: this allows them to provide a historical dimension to their data often lacking in sociological research. Survey research of this type provides a broad overview of societal attitudinal patterns, but of course can capture little or nothing of how such attitudes are expressed in everyday interaction. For policy-makers it can provide a broad picture of how legislative changes and social policy interventions might be perceived and received by populations. For other sociologists it provides a broad picture of how a population may be 'thinking' at a particular point in time.

The writing in The end of Irish history? serves a very different set of purposes. While Fahey et al. (2005, pp.140–150) conclude that the left/right or socialist/conservative divide is of little salience amongst Irish people, the contributors to

Coulter and Coleman's book would continue to place themselves on the political left. Theirs is a critical form of sociology that seeks to analyse the shortcomings of 'Celtic Tiger' Ireland from a number of angles. Specifically, it draws on the key sociological concepts of class, inequality, gender, racism and globalisation to attempt to puncture the apparent positive consensus about the Irish economic boom and its associated cultural and social repercussions. In challenging the 'orthodox reading' (2003, p.12) of the Celtic Tiger phenomenon, the contributors to this set of essays seek to provide alternative explanations to those offered by mainstream economics, history and psychology. Thus, they argue that the origins of Ireland's economic turnaround lie not in the actions of particular politicians or business people or trade union leaders, but in the operations of global capitalism: in particular in the activities of transnational corporations who transfer large sums of money in and out of the state in order to minimise exposure to taxation. Furthermore, they point out the extent to which the increase in wealth in Ireland is not equitably distributed amongst the population, but that much of the contemporary period of prosperity is supported by poorly paid workers, many of them women (Kennedy, in Coulter and Coleman, 2003).

The empirical basis of the essays in this volume is varied: some, such as the contribution by Kieran Allen, draw extensively on published government-produced statistics, combined with reference to critical material in academic journals and broadsheet newspapers such as *The Irish Times* and the UK *Financial Times*. Others (the contributions by Keohane and Kuhling, and by Slattery) are based as much in literary techniques of criticism and creative writing as in more conventional sources of social data. These aim to provide new perspectives on contemporary realities. None of the contributors draw, to any extent, on the type of survey data that provides the basis for the previously discussed text; nor is there any detailed analysis of social interaction at the micro-level. Rather the approach is framed within a critique of the broader national or global structures that are seen to contribute to specific social realities within the Irish context. Where Fahey *et al.* focused very much on the 'Republic of Ireland' and 'Northern Ireland' as their units of analysis, many of the authors (e.g. Fagan, Allen) in this book are concerned with broader global trends and interactions — stressing the place of Ireland in a broader analysis of global capitalism. Conversely, others (Slattery, Coleman) focus on the local (Dublin city, the Gaeltacht) but as these are shaped by broader global understandings. While the work by Fahey *et al.* implicitly works within existing political and economic structures (which are in a sense taken as given) the essays in this work actively seek to challenge the status quo and as such fall clearly within the critical/democratic tradition of sociology.

The third work considered here, *Collision culture* (Keohane and Kuhling, 2004a), shares with the previous work a critical approach to the social phenomenon of 'Celtic Tiger Ireland'. But it speaks in a different language (though the authors also have an essay in Coulter and Coleman's book). The approach is to make use of a wide range of the theoretical language developed mainly by European sociological thinkers (such as Bauman, Virilio, Habermas, Giddens, Beck) to interpret aspects of contemporary Irish society. The topics are not the standard sociological categories of class, inequality or social problems. Rather the authors have selected a number of incidences or aspects of everyday Irish life — often taken from media coverage — that can be used to extrapolate broader discussions about the nature of change in Irish society. Such aspects include car crashes, judicial cases, celebrity culture, New-Age Travellers, Christmas shopping. Such phenomena are rarely, if ever, considered by policy-driven social research or, if they are, they are generally considered in terms of the implications for social or economic policy.

Keohane and Kuhling are interested, following Kane and Bonner, in the micro-processes of everyday Irish life. They use the term 'collision culture' in two senses: in one sense it refers literally to the incidence of traffic accidents, which are at the centre of three of their essays, but more broadly it operates as a metaphor or symbol for contemporary Irish society, where rapid social change leads to clashes between different ways of living (Keohane and Kuhling, 2004a, p.11):

> The traffic accident is a spectacular and literal representation of more general 'collisions' occurring in Irish society today: between vestigial traditionalism and accelerated modernisation, between the local and the global, between the values and organising principles of action of community and society.

Collisions take place because people are moving at different speeds and in different ways, but trying to occupy the same space. For the authors, Ireland is not moving in some neat linear direction towards modernity, but is experiencing multiple social realities at the same time, which rub up against each other (sometimes literally) in all sorts of interesting and illustrative ways. These may take the form of the elderly man tragically killed while cycling on a new motorway; the judge forced to resign when his 'traditional' approach falls foul of the new 'modern' rules of accountability; the New-Age Travellers who confront Ireland's rampant consumerism. Each of these conflicts is described in some detail by the authors, drawing on a mixture of types of data, including primary research materials such as interviews, government statistics and media reports. But while the detail of the cases is interesting, their main purpose is not to serve as 'information' about Irish society (we would not turn to this book for a comprehensive analysis of road accidents or suicides), but to provide a set of symbols through which the authors can interpret contemporary Ireland, drawing on a rich array of theoretical sources, some of which we mentioned earlier. The result is a stimulating effort to make us think in different ways about Irish life; to go beyond the obvious and the taken-for-granted. It is an approach that falls clearly within the playful/intellectual tradition of sociological writing.

What, then, can these three examples tell us about the direction of Irish sociological research? Initially, their existence reflects the relatively healthy state of the sociological endeavour in Ireland. The combined authors and contributors span a broad range of academic institutions, north and south, and include younger and more established figures, and a balanced number of women and men. The writing styles and audiences are diverse, yet each book is produced and distributed by a mainstream publisher, one of which (in the case of *The end of Irish history?*) is located outside Ireland. Some of the research has been funded by the Irish state through various mechanisms. Compared with just two decades ago, the volumes reflect the greatly increased range of sociological writing about Ireland that is now available.

Second, there is some evidence of a degree of convergence across the research practices. Though founded in quantitative attitude research, Fahey *et al.* (2005) make reference to broader cultural and social patterns in order to locate their findings; the contributors to the Coulter and Coleman volume, while critical of many aspects of the Irish state, make generous use of statistics generated by that state; while *Collision culture* combines a style of literary analysis with more 'traditional' sociological material such as interview data. These may reflect the theoretical and methodological eclecticism that has come to typify contemporary sociology, where the 'sociology of the research centres' and the 'sociology of the departments' (Goldthorpe *et al.*, 2002, p.97) are perhaps less separated than heretofore. Each remains bound to a large extent by its institutional setting, its aims and its funding mechanisms, but there are signs that a common language and an interpenetration of methods and approaches may be possible. Such combinations are beginning to make themselves apparent in some types of 'official' sociological research, such as in the work of the Crisis Pregnancy Agency (Hyde and Howlett, 2004) and the National Advisory Committee on Drugs (Loughran and McCann, 2006). If this reflects a new direction in Irish sociology, it bodes well for the future relevance of the discipline.

3
The dynamics of Irish development

In Chapter 1 we introduced sociology as *the study of modernity*. We suggested that to sociologists a 'modern' society is one that is rational, industrial, urban and, usually, capitalist. But is Irish society modern? An industrial society, for example, is often defined as one where most people live in urban areas and very few — perhaps one in fifty — work in agriculture. In the Republic of Ireland just a generation or two ago, as late as 1971, nearly a third of employed men worked in agriculture, either as farmers, as relatives assisting on the farm or as agricultural labourers, while over a third of the population lived in the countryside or in rural settlements of fewer than 200 people. Of those who lived in urban areas, over half lived in just one city, Dublin.

Clearly Irish society has become more urbanised and more industrialised in the past thirty-five years. But in comparison to other European states like Britain, Germany or France, it is doing so considerably later. As a consequence, Ireland is often described as a 'late moderniser', a latecomer to modernity. Much debate about Irish society and how it is changing still uses this notion. It assumes that there is a condition called 'being modern' or 'modernity' and that change in Irish society represents a shift towards this condition. But when we consider this further, some interesting questions are raised. If we say Ireland is becoming modern, what are we comparing it to? Are we implying it has become more like those societies that industrialised early? Or is there a different, specific way of 'being modern' that characterises late modernisers like Ireland? And if we say that Ireland is modern now, what are we implying about the past and about the processes of change that have occurred?

We begin this chapter, therefore, with a brief overview of sociological accounts of how societies 'become modern'. These are usually referred to as theories of social change or theories of development. Two general points can be made about these before we go on to look at specific examples. First, the question of how to explain change or development has been central to the growth of sociology as a discipline. It has produced much disagreement between sociologists, not just about details of the theory but about the theories themselves as broad perspectives or paradigms for understanding social life. They are also more than just academic disagreements. As we see in Chapter 4, states and other powerful actors in society have, for at least the last century, been preoccupied with achieving social change, particularly progressive change or *development*. In the contest between sociological theories of change we find resonances of the clash of ideas between elites in Irish society about how to understand our past history and how to locate Ireland as part of the contemporary world. Sociological theories both influence and are influenced by the ideas held by important social groups in society. Nowhere is this more obvious than in relation to social change since interpretations of the past are often used to explain and justify movements towards a particular sort of future.

The second point relates to the concept of development itself. Until recently much sociology identified 'development' with 'becoming modern' but this is increasingly seen as simplistic. As sociologists become more reflexive in thinking about society, they correspondingly become less certain that modernity is the most 'developed' condition to which societies can or should aspire. The values that underpin the ideal of modernity, discussed in Chapter 1, no longer command automatic allegiance as the problems generated by the continuous pursuit of 'progress' threaten to outweigh its benefits.

The sociological debate over development is itself, in a sense, characteristic of modernity and may lose its rationale as ideas about history as progress are abandoned or eroded. The debate has not become irrelevant, but we should approach it in a more questioning and critical way than before. In particular, we should recognise that there is more than one way for a society to be modern. This is especially helpful to a society such as ours, that has for so long felt the pressure to see itself as 'unmodern', or backward, compared to the rest of the world, and as a society that has only recently begun to 'catch up'. The idea that there are *varieties of modernity* liberates the potential for making choices about how we want to develop in future. It also lets us rediscover the value of our past instead of downgrading it as 'less than modern'. Sociological theorising helps us to examine not only how the world is but also how we think about the world.

THEORIES OF DEVELOPMENT

In this section we outline the three dominant ways of thinking about social change and development: the theories of *modernisation, dependency* and *globalisation*. We will not discuss them in great detail, as we are mainly interested in providing a context within which to examine recent change in Irish society.

Sociological studies of development long assumed the best way to understand social change was to take a single society, analyse it in detail and then compare it with others to see what resemblances could be found on selected dimensions. This seemed a natural way to proceed as theorists took for granted that the societies of the world could be ranked on a *continuum* of development, from the most developed or 'modern' (say, Southern California) to the least (say, Chad). It was suggested that if we knew the main structural or cultural features of the most modern societies, we could interpret change in other societies as evolution towards these. This approach underpins modernisation theory. It has shaped the ideas of elite social groups, academics such as sociologists and historians, policy-makers and ordinary people, in Ireland and in many other countries, during much of the period since the Second World War.

In the 1980s and 1990s a very different perspective on development emerged in sociology. It argued that to understand the changes taking place in particular societies, we must start with an examination of the relationships that connect countries and regions into an international 'system'. This implies that no society exists in isolation. All are influenced in very significant ways by international trends and relationships. This approach underpins both dependency and globalisation theory. Below we note some contrasts in how these theories explain social change in general, before going on to look specifically at Irish society.

Modernisation theory

Modernisation theory is used in sociology to mean a complex set of interconnected ideas, but two of its key features are:

- an evolutionary account of social change
- the belief that all societies in the world are converging at different speeds and from different starting points, towards the same point — modern industrial society.

Many nineteenth-century social thinkers (including Comte, Tönnies and Durkheim, see Chapter 1) were much influenced by Charles Darwin's ideas about evolutionary change in nature. They sought to apply these ideas to an understanding of social change, suggesting that we could treat societies as analogous to natural species that developed through the process of 'survival of the fittest'. More complex forms of social organisation are better adapted to survival within their environment and thus replace simpler forms. Therefore nation states replace tribal societies; factory production replaces the individual craft-worker; the supermarket replaces the local grocery.

Evolutionary interpretations of social change encouraged the assumption that change is unidirectional — that there is but one pattern of change, from primitive (simple, 'traditional') to modern (highly complex, highly adapted to survival) — and that all societies must eventually follow this pattern. They also encouraged the belief that development is 'an imitative process, in which the less developed countries gradually assumed the qualities of the industrialised nations' (Hettne, 1990, p.60). Ultimately they reflected a belief that change is the same as progress, thereby establishing the most 'modern' societies as the model that developing societies should try to emulate. Since the social theorists involved were all from the West and took for granted that that was where the most 'advanced' countries were found, this approach also encouraged an ethnocentric vision of development that saw 'modernisation' as identical to 'Westernisation'. Thus, modernisation theory defined a clear task for development analysts (including sociologists, economists and political theorists) — to identify the qualities of modern societies that are to be imitated and to suggest ways to facilitate their imitation.

Rostow (1960) argued that as societies converge towards modernity, they pass through a sequence of distinct stages of development ('traditional', 'pre-modern', 'modernisation take-off' and so on). We can take a society and, by looking at specific features within it (does it have a mass education system? how developed is its banking system? how urbanised is it?), can say what stage of modernisation it has reached. We can then use this finding to explain other features such as its type of family structure or the extent of secularisation. This indicates further changes needed to move the society to the next development stage. We can see that modernisation theory is often used not just as an explanation for social changes, but also as a set of prescriptions for putting directed social changes into practice. Its influence on leaders of both modern and modernising societies has made it something of a self-fulfilling prophecy.

If societies change by evolving through particular development stages into the 'modern' form, what starts the process off? Some modernisation theorists see *technological innovation*, perhaps imported into the society by a modernising elite, as the starting point. Technological change in agriculture, such as the introduction of mechanical harvesters or tractors, may set off a process in which large numbers of agricultural workers become redundant, move to urban centres and contribute to the development of urban industry. Modernisation theorists argue that social change follows a 'logic of industrialisation' — once the technology is present, industrialisation and its accompanying social changes inevitably follow. In turn, the division of labour becomes more complex as large-scale industrial production requires a wide range of specialised and technical skills. The society becomes more 'open' or meritocratic as jobs need to be assigned to people on the basis of their skills and talents, rather than any inherited social position. There is increased equality of opportunity and social mobility and reduced social conflict as different class, ethnic or regional groups come to share the same goals of further development and higher standards of living. Other cultural changes follow, for example, secularisation (see Chapter 14). In short, once the technological changes occur that allow industry to 'take off', social changes follow the same logic in all industrialising societies — they become more and more alike.

For other modernisation theorists social change is driven by cultural change, especially changes in *social values*, and it is the values and attitudes of the developed West, rather than its technology, that must be implanted into more traditional societies before industrial development can begin. There is a parallel here with Weber's theories (see Chapter 1) about the relationship between particular sets of ideas and capitalist development. Cultural modernisationists brought the term 'traditional' into widespread use to describe societies that not only lacked the science and technology of the advanced world but were still trapped within traditional values or culture. For example, they valued people more for their 'ascribed' than their 'achieved' characteristics; they preferred face-to face, personalised relationships to impersonal, detached ones; and social interaction was influenced more by kinship or familiarity than by universal rules. Modernisation theory implies that such values are an obstacle to cultural and, ultimately, economic development.

In summary, modernisation theory suggests that the social organisation and cultural features of a society can largely be explained by identifying the 'stage of development' it has reached on the path towards modernity. It seems to offer a very powerful analysis of change, because it treats societies as integrated systems where change in one part (for example, the organisation of work) leads to changes in almost every other part. While its roots go far back into the thinking of the 'classical' social theorists, particularly Durkheim and Weber, in the hands of later theorists discussions of modernity have often narrowed into checklists of technical and cultural criteria.

A major concern of the classical theorists had been to understand specific historical patterns of change in the countries of early Europe, but theorists subsequently universalised these analyses into an account of global evolution. Modernisation theorists gave up the strong sense of ambivalence towards modernity that had characterised the classical theorists' discussions, such as Weber's concerns about the effect of increasing bureaucratisation and rational-isation on the human spirit, Durkheim's analysis of anomie or Marx's scathing analysis of the roots of alienation. Hettne (1990, p.72) concludes that:

> On the winding road towards a theory of social change there are many mistakes, both magnificent and more trivial. Modernisation theory certainly belongs to the first category. . . . It had a long tradition in Western social thought. . . . It had a great appeal to a wider public due to the paternalistic attitude towards other non-European cultures . . . [and] it is probably correct to say that the general outlook of modernisation theory still constitutes the popular image of developing countries.

The most damaging legacy of modernisation theory may be the simplistic conception of change as a transition from 'traditional' to 'modern'. The term 'traditional' took on pejorative overtones. It no longer simply referred to societies whose culture and ways of organising political, social or economic life were different from those of the most powerful European societies, but suggests they were inferior — they lacked or had failed to develop modern forms. This position of innate superiority became a particular target in the critique of modernisation theory launched by dependency theorists.

Dependency theory

Modernisation theory treats traditional societies as unchanging and isolated from contact with the outside world and, once technological or cultural change is introduced, the process of differentiation and evolution towards higher stages of development unfolds according to its own logic, independent of relationships with other societies. On both counts the theory has been heavily criticised, particularly by dependency theorists.

The first to outline dependency theory was a German-born economist working in South America, André Gunder Frank. It is significant that he came from Latin America, a part of the world that has had long experience of colonial domination. To Frank it was inconceivable that the pattern of social change in any single society could be explained without reference to its past and present relationships with others. Moreover, by the late 1960s when he put forward his theory, Latin American countries were no longer colonies. Most had been politically independent since the nineteenth century and had been trying to develop and modernise themselves, yet most remained economically underdeveloped. To Frank it was clear that there was no universal, linear pattern of change by which less developed countries 'converged' with more developed ones. He argued (1967) that all countries are part of an international system that affects societies in different ways. Some, mainly early-industrialising Western countries that had been colonisers, have been able to establish relationships with others, particularly those that had been colonised. These are essentially relationships of exploitation. Through these relationships the dominant or core countries systematically funnel out the wealth created in the underdeveloped countries. The wealth accumulates in the developed countries, both as capital and as 'human capital'. Frank argued, therefore, that it was wrong to see underdeveloped societies as being behind or outside the development process; rather, both developed and underdeveloped societies are part of a single international system. Underdeveloped societies have been underdeveloped and are maintained in a state of underdevelopment by the core countries that have developed at their expense. Lack of development is therefore not the result of the value systems or technologies of the underdeveloped countries, but lies with the core countries and the resultant relationships.

Frank refused to label less developed societies 'traditional'. For him this was a term that 'denies all history' to the society concerned. Developed societies do not have a monopoly on history. Underdeveloped ones also have a history, usually one of colonisation where the economy and social institutions were restructured to suit the colonisers. Their agriculture was reorganised, for example, to produce cash crops such as coffee, soybeans or rubber for export as industrial raw materials rather than food for home consumption. Thus, Brazil became a major exporter of coffee; the Middle East of oil; Malaysia of rubber. Irish agriculture under colonial rule specialised in the production of live beef cattle for export and processing in

Britain. The history of colonised countries was therefore one of restructuring resulting in dependency. For the sale of their agricultural exports and the import of industrial products they became increasingly dependent on the core countries that profited from their underdevelopment. For Frank this was 'the development of underdevelopment'. He argued that even when such countries gained political independence they remained locked into international relationships that promoted the process of underdevelopment.

Modernisation theory saw world development as a process where modern societies helped traditional societies to develop through the transfer of new technology, values or capital. Dependency theory challenged that account. It argued that the transfers were primarily in the opposite direction, from the poor countries to the rich. This generated much debate on whether it was ever possible for underdeveloped countries to break free from underdevelopment. But in the 1970s and 1980s it became apparent that many previously underdeveloped countries *were* experiencing social change in the form of industrialisation. By the late 1970s, for example, there were nearly a million workers employed in industrial production, including car-making, in Brazil, many earning well above the minimum wage. The term 'newly industrialising countries' (NICs) was coined to mark this new phenomenon that seemed to contradict the claim that development was impossible in dependent societies. But what sort of development was it?

Dependency theorists point out that transnational corporations (TNCs) — companies that operate across national boundaries rather than within several or many nations — have played a significant part in the new industrialisation process. TNCs do not just replicate their firms in different countries. Their operations are underpinned by a structured division of labour: the production process is broken down into more and less skilled parts; or into stages further from and nearer to the finished product. These component parts of the process are located in different parts of the world depending on what a region has to offer. There may be a large unemployed or underemployed workforce, cheap to employ or docile to manage, or raw materials or resources and access to markets may be readily available. TNCs engender a new *international* division of labour that operates on a global level and shapes the possibilities for development of both the industrialised and the newly industrialising societies (Klein, 2000).

TNCs operate on a huge scale, with annual turnover often equal to or greater than the total gross national product (GNP) of the country in which they locate branch plants. They can influence government policies on trade unionism or prevent the introduction of controls on environmental degradation if these are likely to push up production costs. Many sociologists therefore refer to the industrial development occurring in NICs as *dependent development*. They argue that the social structure of NICs is not converging with that of early industrialising societies. Their place in the new international division of labour means that the social structure of NICs *remains* different to that of the core countries.

In summary, dependency theorists put forward a number of theses that contrast sharply with the modernisation paradigm. The most important obstacles to development are *not* internal characteristics such as lack of technology, capital or an entrepreneurial culture, but are external to the underdeveloped society and relate to its position in the international division of labour. In the international system, value is transferred mainly from the peripheral and underdeveloped societies to the core or developed societies. Thus peripheral societies are deprived of a surplus that they *could* invest in development and at the same time are providing a surplus to the already developed societies. In this way, development in the core *produces* underdevelopment in the periphery. Development and underdevelopment, taking place in different regions or spaces of the world, are parts of the same single process. Relations with core countries severely constrain the capacity of peripheral countries to develop. Their best prospects would seem to lie in detaching themselves from core–periphery relations or from the world market through some form of protectionism and by working towards national self-sufficiency.

From dependency to globalisation

During the 1970s and 1980s dependency theory was exposed to intensive discussion and debate. Critics asked whether it was really possible to distinguish between dependent and independent economies and to allocate existing societies unequivocally to one category or the other. The problems experienced by peripheral economies, explained by Frank as the outcome of a process of underdevelopment, were said to be the product of a particular — and temporary — stage in global capitalist development and did not represent a permanent relationship of exploitation. Furthermore it was argued that the focus on external relationships encouraged dependency theorists to ignore social or cultural features *internal* to dependent societies that could be very relevant to understanding their situation. In particular, dependency theory was criticised for its lack of analysis of the class and power structures within dependent societies that could explain why they remained underdeveloped.

So intensive was the criticism of dependency theory that by the 1990s it was seen by many to be no longer relevant. However, if few theorists of change currently support it at least in its original version, it has had major impacts on social theorising. Chief among these must be the decline of the modernisation paradigm itself and the growing resistance to all theories of development that simplistically equate modernisation with Westernisation, or that equate 'traditional' societies with societies that are non-Western in practices and culture. Dependency theory opened up the possibility of 'indigenising' development and allowed people in the peripheral countries to think about the process of social change needed in their own countries based on their own cultural traditions and sense of history. The clash between modernisationists and supporters of dependency theory was experienced by sociologists and other intellectuals in many countries, not least in Ireland, as a sort of intellectual revolution or declaration of independence.

As a thesis about social change, the dependency approach has now evolved into theories of globalisation that shift the focus of analysis from dependence to interdependence. They recognise that no countries can exercise wholly autonomous control over their economies and societies and that development cannot be said to result purely from internal factors. To understand change in any society or region we must start from an overview of the world system at a given point in time and work back to locate the networks of cross-national relations in which a particular country is enmeshed.

In a reformulation of dependency theory, some versions of globalisation theory suggest that while all countries are interdependent, the type and extent of dependency varies from case to case. This argument recognises that the global system has a more complicated structure than a simple dichotomy between 'core' and 'periphery' can account for (we at least need a further distinction between peripheries and semi-peripheries).

O'Hearn (1998, p.14) argues that the concept of *interlinking commodity chains* is useful, where 'a global division of labour spans distinct core, semi-peripheral and peripheral regions'. World regions are thus organised into a hierarchy in terms of what they can offer to the commodity chain of a TNC; for example, different forms of 'human capital'. In this context, 'economic development' relates to how able a country or region is to improve its level of participation towards higher-value, more sophisticated and skilled and more profitable activities. Globalisation theory also recognises tensions and competition *within* the core (for example, between the United States and Europe or between different regions within each of these) and that processes of global change continuously give rise to the peripheralisation of some core areas and the development of some peripheries (for example, on one hand the deindustrialisation of Britain and, on the other, the industrialisation of regions of Asia such as South Korea).

Analyses of Irish dependent development within a global system tend to be rather one-dimensional. They tend to focus on the economic level only and have little to say about political or cultural impacts of globalisation. But such aspects cannot simply be read off from economic processes; they must be discussed and analysed in their own right. The extent and manner of Ireland's incorporation into a wider international or global system needs to be treated as something that changes over time. It is widely suggested that in recent decades the world has become globalised in ways that are both quantitatively and qualitatively new. Thus earlier approaches, influenced by dependency theory, may need to be replaced by new theories of globalisation.

The term 'globalisation' is increasingly used in sociology to refer not just to new processes and relationships that are making the economies — and perhaps also the political and legal systems — of different societies more integrated, but also to a subjective change, broadly experienced. This is a change in mindset, or, in the sense of collective identity, a change that is variously expressed when people start to think of themselves as world citizens, global consumers or participants in a world culture. We can think, for example, of the recent rise of 'world music' as a label for a range of ethnically varied indigenous music — including traditional Irish music — that constitutes an organised totality from which the music fan in contemporary Ireland can select. Twenty years ago, traditional Irish music was thought of as belonging to and understandable only as part of national Irish culture. Now it is a globalised entity: almost as likely to emerge from Tokyo, Boston or Sydney as from Dublin or Doolin.

Robertson (1987) suggests that we think of globalisation as referring to the process or processes whereby the world becomes 'a single place'. This means that globalisation perspectives are not just about an increase in the intensity and impact of relationships between societies or nation states, which we might call internationalisation; they are also about how such relationships are helping to contribute to a new sort of world characterised by transnational institutions and relationships. How have sociologists come to recognise that a single world is emerging at this time? We can identify two different positions. One is that recognition of 'the global' is a natural outcome of an analysis of modernity. Globalisation is then simply part of the process of becoming modern, or of the transition to late modernity. In the second case, globalisation is associated with post-modernity. A global world is then seen as more than just the worldwide expansion of modern institutions, characteristics and relationships across the boundaries of the developed world. It is something qualitatively new that may radically transform our experience and understanding of society and social life.

Industrialisation theorists argue that modern industrialism has a 'universalising imperative' (McGrew, 1992, p.82). This is often expressed through the idea of technological determinism: once the technology associated with industrial methods of production is introduced into a society, it inevitably leads to profound rearrangements on the social, cultural and even political level in that society. In a more contemporary version of this argument, the transformative capacity of technology is now so great that it has moved us from industrial into post-industrial society. The latter is based on the use and production of knowledge rather than material resources. In contrast, analyses of modern society as capitalist society produce a rather different evaluation of globalisation. One of the best-known protagonists of this perspective is Wallerstein (1983), who argues that we live in a single world system — the capitalist world system. The driving force that underpins this system is the relentless search for profit and, though it contains a varied range of cultures and political forms, it is characterised by a single international division of labour. The capitalist world system is structured around unequal relationships between core, semi-peripheral and peripheral areas, each of which provides distinctive functions for the system as a whole.

A key way that these accounts of globalisation differ from those of indus-trialisation theorists is their emphasis on the unevenness of capitalist expansion across the world, whereas industrial or technological determinist theories tend to emphasise the homogenising experience of globalisation. Wallerstein emphasises unevenness when he focuses on the international division of labour between core and peripheral areas and regions, as does Sklair when he writes (1995, p.7) that:

> The global system is marked by very great asymmetry. The most important economic, political and cultural-ideological goods that circulate around the globe tend to be owned and/or controlled by small groups in a relatively small number of countries. Until recently it was both convenient and accurate to use the term 'Western' to describe this asymmetry.

The many problems associated with globalisation have been documented by the Nobel prize-winning economist Joseph Stiglitz (2003; 2006), among others: the unfair global trade regime that impedes development; the unstable global financial system that results in recurrent crises that particularly impact on poor countries; and a global intellectual property regime that denies access to affordable life-saving drugs, even at a times when AIDS is stalking the developing world. Stiglitz is not anti-globalisation, preferring to see the enormous potential of globalisation to be a force for change. Thus he suggests (2006) that investments in education and research, together with a strong social safety net, can lead to more productive and competitive economies, with more security and higher living standards for all. What is lacking is that while, economically, countries have become more interdependent, the institutional frameworks for acting together effectively and democratically are absent. Stiglitz argues that it is possible to make globalisation work, but only if political regimes seek to actively manage the process.

DEVELOPMENT IN IRELAND

The major economic and social changes that occurred in Ireland in the 1990s and into this century have given rise to many attempts to analyse and understand what was happening: from journalists (Hourihane, 2000; McWilliams, 2005), social psychologists (O'Connell, 2001) and environmentalists (Clinch et al., 2002), as well as the economists and sociologists discussed in this chapter. Though these works have often reflected the complexity and contradictoriness of the processes of change, an underlying modernisation theme can be detected. It is widely assumed, indeed it has been argued, that the lifestyles, values, occupational structures and political concerns and challenges of the Irish people increasingly resemble those of 'modern' societies of Europe and North America. This process is universally linked to economic change: as our economy increasingly resembles that of the more 'advanced' societies, so does our way of life mirror theirs.

Ireland is often described as a 'late industrialising society'. This version of modernisation theory assumes that industrialisation is the universal end-point of social change, but that some societies reach it more quickly than others. The term 'newly industrialising country' or NIC is another variant of the same idea — it allows that societies can industrialise in different ways but assumes that industrialisation is the prime indicator of advancing modernity.

O'Hearn (1998, p.34) notes that the connection between industrialisation and modernity has a long history in Ireland; Marx remarked that 'every time Ireland was about to develop industrially, she was crushed and reconverted into a purely agricultural land.' This pattern became a powerful element in Irish nationalist mythology: if Ireland was ever to compete as a nation on equal terms with Britain, industrialisation was essential. For Sinn Féin leader Arthur Griffiths, speaking in 1918, 'a nation [could not] promote and further its civilisation, its prosperity and its social progress equally as well by exchanging agricultural products for manufactured goods as by establishing a manufacturing power of its own' (cited in O'Hearn, 1998, p.36).

The struggle of the independent Irish state to develop an industrial economy may have been as much an expression of modernity as a response to material conditions. It is thus quite ironic to find O'Hearn reproducing such ideas in his discussion of the 'Celtic Tiger'. Agriculture is never included in O'Hearn's narrative about Irish economic development and the fact that the main industries left in the Republic of Ireland after partition were all agriculture-based (brewing, distilling and food processing) is offered as evidence of industrial *weakness*. By the 1990s, neither the food and drink industries nor rural-based tourism appeared to play any significant role in Ireland's 'economic miracle'. In O'Hearn's account, rural Ireland features only in the context of a discussion of poverty and inequality in modern Irish society.

In contrast, we could think of Irish society not as 'late industrialising' but as 'early agriculturalising' and it can then be characterised in terms of its achievements rather than its failings. This may not be the form of modernity enjoyed by all 'advanced' European countries but it is still an important variant, especially in countries of Europe's 'Green Ring' such as Finland, Scotland, Southern Italy and Poland (Granberg *et al.*, 2001). To be agricultural is not the same as to be traditional in the sense of 'backward' and so, as we discuss the Irish experience of development, we start, not as is conventional with an account of industrial development, but with one of agriculture and agricultural change.

Agricultural development

The agrarianisation of Ireland

The society that gained political independence in 1922 was highly specialised in agriculture. Some 58 per cent of the male labour force at the time worked in agriculture. Agricultural commodities made up the bulk of Irish exports and, as an earner of foreign currency and a source of livelihood for many Irish families (outside as well as inside farming), agriculture was a key sector both economically and politically. In this respect, Ireland was not unique in Europe. Denmark and Finland had similar economic profiles. Moreover, despite the reliance on agriculture, Ireland was by world standards at this time a comparatively wealthy country.

Ireland was not 'naturally' agricultural, but became so as a result of historical processes, in particular its long relationship with Britain. In the eighteenth century, British rule contributed to the spread of the Industrial Revolution throughout Ireland, with the development of rural industries such as linen and milling and of the urban-based woollen and food-processing industries (Cullen, 1987). By 1821 there were reported to be more people engaged in 'manufacture, trade and handicrafts' than in agriculture in one-third of Irish counties (Haughton, 1995), but this blossoming of 'proto-industrialisation' rapidly reversed outside the north-east of the country during the nineteenth century. A key factor was the incorporation of Ireland as a region of the British economy following the Act of Union. As a result, for a century prior to political independence Ireland, along with Scotland and Wales, was part of a 'common market' centred on England. In this context Irish society underwent specific processes of deindustrialisation and agrarianisation.

Ireland's agricultural economy was not a traditional economy if, by that, we mean one that was uncommercialised and isolated from markets. From the seventeenth-century Irish farmers were integrated into global food markets through their incorporation into British colonial and imperial trade relations. Irish farm and fishery products were exported to countries on the European Continent, particularly France, Spain and Portugal (Cullen, 1987) and to colonial markets in the West Indies where they helped to sustain the slave-based plantation economy (Rolston and Shannon, 2002, pp.7–19). By the end of the seventeenth century almost half of Irish agricultural exports went to Continental Europe, especially to France (Haughton, 1995). Over the next 200 years exports became more focused on Britain as Ireland became an important source, especially of labour and food, for British industrial expansion.

Irish agriculture therefore has a long history of commercialisation and of integration into international markets. Much of what happened in Irish social and economic history can be explained only in terms of this external integration. Sociology in Ireland has generally been slow to recognise this and its implications for theories of development. This is partly because of the frequent dismissal of agrarian or rural Ireland as 'traditional' as a result of over-enthusiastic use of modernisation theory and partly because the form of farming that was inherited by the Irish state and that persisted largely unchanged for decades afterwards was family-based. Family-based forms of production tend wrongly to be linked with 'subsistence' agriculture, regarded as non-capitalist and remote from the modern, urban, capitalist and rationalised economy.

Irish farming in the early twentieth century

This does not mean, of course, that Irish agriculture at the point of political independence was entirely commercialised or that all Irish farmers were equally involved in market relationships. On the contrary, what the new state inherited was a *dualistic* agrarian economy, characterised by wide gaps in wealth, income and political power between large and small farmers and between different farming regions. Smaller, poorer farm households were concentrated in the north and north-west of the country and the midlands; larger, richer farmers were found predominantly in the east and south.

While this dualism has persisted and strengthened up to the present (Commins, 1996), in the early part of the twentieth century it was less obviously a problem. Though there were extremes of size at each end of the scale, overall Irish farms tended to be small, at least compared to those in Britain. Thus, in 1926, 57 per cent of farmers had less than 30 acres and less than a tenth owned 100 acres or more (Breen *et al.*, 1990, p. 191). They were also less specialised than today in terms of output. Despite the massive dominance of cattle production, most farms operated a mixed production regime with some tillage, some dairying, pigs and poultry, either for consumption by the farm family and farm animals, or for sale, or both. They mostly had the same tenure conditions and organisation of farm production. It was therefore possible to view farmers as forming a fairly homogenous class. By the 1920s, as a result of land reforms commenced by the United Kingdom government, the great majority of farmers were owners of their land, rather than tenants. Most worked their farms with family labour or, on the larger farms mainly to be found in the east and south of the country, with the addition of a small number of hired labourers.

Arensberg and Kimball (2001[1940]) show how familial relations, on family farms, were shaped by the fact that they were also relations within a farm business. The father of the family was also boss of an enterprise in which the main workers were his wife and sons. This led to complex and often tense relationships between family members. For example, the marriage of a son had major implications for the continuity of the farm enterprise and so involved business considerations as much as personal choices in terms of timing, choice of partner and the nature of the contract between the new couple. Similarly, family needs influenced the form of farming. In particular, it encouraged the type of mixed farming outlined above. Arensberg and Kimball's account is based on relatively small farms in the west of Ireland. We have little comparable information about family relationships in large-farm, commercialised areas but it seems likely that they did not differ greatly (McNabb, 1964). If anything, the greater value of the property to be managed and passed on to the next generation tended to intensify the patriarchal nature of family relationships on such farms. Gender inequalities on large farms were greater and farm wives and daughters were more actively excluded from a say in the business.

Though commonalities across Irish farming helped to obscure its dualistic structure, class differentiation between farmers was already marked by 1900 and became more pronounced over the course of the century. But it would be wrong to assume that the smaller, more westerly farmers existed independently and in isolation from larger farmers and the national and international markets in which they participated. Much Irish rural sociology implies this and suggests that the small-farm areas of the west were traditional in the sense that they remained outside the modernising capitalist farm economy. In fact, such dualism is more typical of *contemporary* Irish farming, as we see below, than it was in the early 1900s.

Agriculture in Ireland: the 'development problem'

The process whereby the Irish economy became agrarianised prior to independence suggests a further challenge to the 'traditionality' of Irish agriculture. This relates to the role of the British (and subsequently the Irish) state in the development of rural areas and agriculture. Food security has always been an issue of concern to rulers as has the problem of how to pacify and control the inhabitants of open countryside outside easy reach of armies, tax inspectors, census takers and other agents of the state. State intervention in agriculture therefore has a very long history and generally tends to remain an issue even when governments are committed to non-interventionist, *laissez-faire* orientations to the economy. The British government, for example, made a range of interventions into Irish agriculture in the decades after the Famine, including the passing of the Land Acts and the establishment of the Congested Districts Board in 1891. Of key importance was the setting up of a Department of Agriculture and Technical Instruction which subsequently became the first government department of the newly independent state.

The role of the state is highly relevant for two reasons. First, the definition of the Irish 'development problem' — how the state could intervene in and change agricultural and rural Ireland — has gone through a number of shifts (see Figure 3.1). These have profoundly affected the living standards and life chances of different groups of Irish farmers. They also remind us that our definitions of 'development' and 'modernisation' are shaped by the economic opportunities made available by a dynamic global economic system and the political and ideological orientations of those in power.

Second, the state is important in how it has actively facilitated the global diffusion of ideas and assumptions, derived mainly from North America, about 'modern farming'. In modern farming, for example:

- There is the maximum possible distance between farm and family so economic decision-making is not clouded by irrational or emotional attachments.
- Farm women are encouraged to withdraw from farm work into domesticity and to leave the business to their husbands and sons.
- Farmers should respond actively to market trends and changes and should be guided by agricultural scientists and professional farm advisors rather than kinsmen, neighbours and other holders of 'local knowledge'.

Figure 3.1 Policy aims of the Irish state in relation to agricultural and rural development

	Policy aim(s)	Response(s)
1920s	Maximise agriculture's capacity to earn foreign exchange.	Remove rates from agricultural land.
	Reduce costs of production, such as land and capital.	Provide low-interest loans via the state-owned Agricultural Credit Corporation.
1930s 1940s	Restructure agricultural production and employment to make economy and society more self-sufficient.	Encourage farmers to switch from extensive, export-oriented cattle production to tillage — more labour-intensive and oriented to domestic markets.
1950s 1960s	'Modernise' Irish farm production and responsiveness to markets. Maintain and modernise smaller as well as larger farmers to reduce rural depopulation.	Provide technical assistance and grants for modernisation of facilities.
1970s	Remove smaller and 'less efficient' producers.	Target agricultural development resources towards larger farmers. Provide alternative livelihood for small farmers through rural industrialisation.
1980s	Transform Irish farming to meet the needs of growing food-processing industry.	Provide technical assistance and grants. ——➤

Figure 3.1 *(continued)*

	Policy aim(s)	Response(s)
1990s	Further develop commercial agriculture and food processing.	Provide technical assistance and grants.
	Respond to increasingly urbanised society and service-oriented economy.	Manage demands for rural space for tourism, recreation, heritage conservation, environmental protection, access to 'nature'.
2000s	Continue development of commercial agriculture and food processing. Increase interest in niche products (for example, organic produce, specialty foods).	Develop environmental initiatives (such as REPS) for less 'commercial' farms. Increase focus on food rather than agriculture.

The 'modern farming' approach to agriculture coincided with the interests of the food industry and agribusiness which, since the 1960s, have become increasingly powerful actors in world agriculture. For example, the Kellogg food company has been an important agent in the global diffusion of these concepts, through the funding of research centres. But these are powerful ideas in their own right, forming part of a complex of beliefs about modern, rational economic behaviour whose adoption was fostered by the close relationships that grew up between American and Irish agricultural professionals in the post-war period. Indeed a number of Irish agricultural scientists received postgraduate training in American universities during the 1960s (Tovey, 1992a). Subsequently, as part of the Irish state's interventions into agriculture, they helped to introduce the new sets of beliefs and practices associated with 'modern farming'.

These processes fed into a policy orientation, now termed 'productionism', that concerned itself in an increasingly narrow way with the productive function of agriculture — its capacity to produce food or raw materials for a food-processing industry — and disregarded other important functions such as the provision of employment, the underpinning of a vibrant rural community, or the care and management of the environment. Productionism reflects a particular conception of modernity. It has not been peculiar to Irish agricultural policy, but has dominated agricultural thinking in most parts of the 'developed' world since the late 1950s. It underpinned the EU's Common Agricultural Policy (CAP) for some two decades, from around the time of Ireland's accession to the EEC in the early 1970s to the so-called McSharry reforms of the late 1980s and early 1990s. Irish membership of the EU strengthened and consolidated existing productionist tendencies in Irish agricultural policy and it is only in recent years that its dominance as a discourse shaping Irish agriculture has waned.

Changes in social structure

In this section we focus on two processes: the decline in the proportion of rural people who are farmers and consequently in the political power and dominance of agriculture in local country areas; and the transformation of 'family farming'.

Employment in agriculture in Ireland has declined sharply. The proportion of the labour force engaged in agriculture fell from around half in the 1920s to less than an eighth in the mid-1990s (Commins, 1995). By 2003 the numbers employed in agriculture accounted for under 7 per cent of the numbers at work (CSO, 2004). Up to the late 1980s the number leaving agriculture in each intercensal period roughly equalled that of new jobs created (Commins and Keane, 1994), but many of the new jobs were created in urban areas and in the east of the country while most of those lost from agriculture were in the midlands and the west. As a result of the decline in agricultural employment many rural areas are no longer primarily made up of farm households, but of those dependent on other forms of work. This has had important effects on rural politics and on state policy.

Until the early 1980s the fall in agricultural employment was primarily among farm labourers and 'relatives assisting' (family members who lived and worked, often unpaid, on the farm) rather than among farmers themselves, but since then there has also been a marked decline in the number of farmers. This raises critical questions about the long-term future of farming, at least in certain parts of the country. However, it is not simple to identify who is a farmer and who is not: does it depend on owning farm land, or on working that land, or both? Irish Farm Survey figures show that a reduction in the number of farmers does not necessarily mean fewer farms. In fact, the number of farms has not markedly decreased. Many people apparently continue to hold land but have ceased to identify themselves as farmers, possibly due to rental of land to a farming neighbour; it does appear that renting of land is on the increase in Ireland again after nearly a century of pressure to convert tenants into owners. Owners of smaller farms appear most likely to rent out land rather than work it themselves. This may reflect the availability of off-farm income from employment or state benefits or a decline in the perceived status of farming as an occupation. In addition, widespread ownership of land among non-farming people in Ireland distinguishes the Irish class structure from many other 'modern' societies and appears to have quite distinctive effects on the patterns of social mobility and class politics in contemporary Ireland (Hannan and Commins, 1992). It is perhaps one way that Irish society is more usefully compared with French or Finnish rather than British society (Fahey, 2002a).

The demographic patterns noted above have changed the nature of family farming in some interesting ways. Formally, there appears to be continuity in the type of farming that predominates in Ireland — there has been very little movement, for example, towards large capitalist companies taking over farming and using entirely hired labour to work the land, in a similar way to industrial production. But even if Irish farming remains in some sense 'family farming', it is a different situation when the farm is operated individually by the male 'head of household' rather than with the labour and commitment of a number of family members. But we must take care not to overemphasise what may be unreliable data. The claim that 'relatives assisting' have virtually disappeared from Irish farming is based on what farm people report as their occupation, rather than on the contribution they may make, in terms of time or specific tasks, to farm work. The figures may, in particular, underestimate the work of farm wives, who are more likely to report themselves, or be reported in official surveys, as 'engaged in home duties' rather than as farm workers. The solitariness of contemporary farming may therefore be exaggerated. It may also be that the extent and nature of farm women's contribution — managerial and secretarial, for example, as opposed to manual — varies between large and small farms and in different parts of the country. Gender relations in farming is an area that Irish sociologists have only begun to study in any depth (see Ní Laoire, 2001; P. O'Hara, 1998; Shortall, 1997).

The withdrawal of farm sons and daughters from farm work is better documented. The main reason for declining numbers of farmers is not that farmers are moving into other jobs, but that those who retire are not being replaced by a member of the next generation. Increasingly, farm sons (this was always true of daughters — see Chapter 8) aim to secure educational certification and a place in a broader labour market rather than leave school early, go through an agricultural apprenticeship under their father, and in time succeed to the farm. Farm heirs who are already in work outside farming when their father retires or dies are increasingly likely to continue their existing job and work the holding part-time, if at all. This depends on the size and value of the farm and the region in which it is located.

Changes in farming practices

A few key changes will be discussed here. First, and most striking, is how far Irish agriculture has moved away from a mainly mixed type of farming to one that is typified by *specialisation*. When Ireland joined the EEC in 1973, dairying was still carried out on almost two-thirds of farms. Today this has fallen to just over one-third. The average size of dairy herds increased over the same period from around 10 to around 27 cows per farm, suggesting that specialisation is accompanied by increasing scale and intensity of production. The number of dairy farms has fallen further from 40,000 in 1996 to 28,000 in 2006. Average herd size is now almost 40 cows per farm (Teagasc, 2007). The most striking example is probably in pig production. Once widely dispersed on Irish farms, and small in scale, by the 1990s pig-keeping had become an enterprise concentrated on a small number of holdings

— 2,900 in 1991 — and the average herd size — 29 in 1973 — was more than 450 animals (Commins and Keane, 1994, p.44). By 2007 the number of holdings specialising in pigs had consolidated further to just 600 (Teagasc, 2007).

Specialists in the more profitable types of farming, such as cattle fattening, dairying and cereals, tend to be large farms in the east and south-east while specialisation on the small farms of the north-west and west is in virtual monocrop production of 'drystock' (young beef cattle raised for selling on). The latter form of specialisation provides one of the lowest incomes in Irish farming: the outcome of a continuous, decades-long process of exclusion and marginalisation from more profitable types of farming (Tovey, 1982).

A second important change is the *commoditisation* of farming — how farmers become increasingly involved in and dependent on markets, not just to sell what they produce, but also to obtain the resources or inputs they need to complete each round of production. This is generally regarded as the most critical form of change because it means that farmers lose skills and substantial amounts of control over the farm production process through dependency on the manufacturers whose resources or commodities they now buy rather than self-produce on the farm. An example is the switch in Irish farming in the 1960s and 1970s from the production of fertiliser on the farm itself from the previous year's round of animal production to buying in bags of industrially produced chemical fertiliser. Other examples include no longer keeping seeds from previous crops but buying them in from seed companies and suppliers; using the 'government bull' (artificial insemination) to inseminate one's cows instead of keeping one's own bull; and buying in young dairy calves or lambs instead of raising replacements on the farm itself.

Irish agriculture, we argued earlier, has been commoditised for centuries through the sale of its output on domestic and international markets. But input commoditisation has developed into the norm only in the period since the 1960s. It is linked to processes of increasing specialisation on farms and to the trend away from mixed farming. It appears to have been very deliberately encouraged by the state through the agricultural advisory service (Leeuwis, 1989). Agricultural economists and other specialists argued that a core problem in Irish farming was the fact that it generated quite low incomes compared, for example, to industrial wages in the 1970s. They believed that the best way to solve this problem was to increase the level of farm output (an example of 'productionism') and that this could be best done by moving farmers towards a 'high-input/high-output' regime that required extensive use of bought-in inputs. Farmers who resisted this approach were labelled and stigmatised, according to Leeuwis, as irrational, traditional or even stupid — ironic perhaps in the light of contemporary concerns about the environmental impacts of 'modern' farming.

Commoditisation of agriculture, especially of inputs, exposes farmers to external influence and control. The most crucial influences are agribusiness and science.

Commoditisation is accompanied by a third key process: *scientisation*. This refers to a process of technological intensification where tasks once carried out by farm family members, perhaps using farm animals, such as ploughing, are taken off-farm, mechanised, made amenable to industrial production and sold back to the farmer in the form of new tools such as tractors. Such technological intensification has been a marked feature of Irish farming since the 1950s, particularly on larger farms. Scientisation also refers to how the knowledge needed to carry out farm tasks is removed from farmers and farming communities and brought under the control of scientific 'experts', from where it is returned to farmers in the form of state regulations or industrially produced 'technological packages'. A particular example of the hegemonic tendencies of these scientific discourses is provided by Jorgensen (2006). She observes that organic farmers are not just producers of food but also of knowledge, which they extract, debate and develop on an ongoing basis. Whereas organic farmers are aware of and do draw on scientific advancements as well as locally derived knowledge, how information is passed on within the organic movement differs greatly from the knowledge diffusion methods employed in the conventional food system. Increasingly, many farmers and consumers are turning to organics as an alternative to the conventional industrialised production systems in agriculture. Jorgensen argues that when the state takes over the responsibility of passing on knowledge about organic production to interested individuals, it has the potential to reach a greater number of people than the organic movement. But its very involvement in that knowledge diffusion process reverses the traditional system of knowledge transfer, thereby disempowering organic farmers rather than empowering them. Although encouraging organic conversions, state agents still seem to be caught up in the system of knowledge transfer in which their role is that of authoritative expert, giving instructions and providing templates for action. The danger, as Jorgensen sees it, is that local knowledge, with its potential for sustainability, is silenced in this process.

What are the implications of these changes? An obvious one is that dualism and inequality have intensified. Farmers are increasingly polarised between those who can survive and make a good living under these new conditions of production and those who cannot. In Irish farming such polarisation does not manifest itself in the concentration of land into fewer hands but in the concentration of capital and production. About one-third of all farms (fewer than 50,000 holdings) now account for about two-thirds of all farm output; they receive about 70 per cent of all the income generated in Irish farming, and between them hold about two-thirds of all tillage acreage in the country, about 70 per cent of all dairy cows and about half of all grazing livestock (Power and Roche, 1993; Matthews, 2000, p.59). Increasingly, farmers outside this elite are categorised as 'part-time farmers' even if they do not receive any earnings from off-farm work nor have any other occupation to put time into. They are, essentially, those who lack capital or access to educational and informational opportunities needed to adopt scientised, commoditised, specialised forms of farming. They are increasingly seen as surplus to the requirements of an efficient food industry and thus as available to be diverted into other, non-competing farm activities such as farm tourism or non-intensive, environmentally friendly types of agriculture like organic farming.

From co-ops to capitalism: the rise of the Irish food industry

The dominance of the trends outlined above means that agriculture can no longer be thought of as a set of independent, separate farming units but instead as part of an extensive, even globalised, food system. Links, direct and indirect, are growing between farmers and the food industry as well as between farmers and manufacturers of farm inputs. This process of *integration* is encouraged by state policy where increasingly food industry interests, particularly those of the large food processors, transport companies and retailers, take precedence over those of farmers. The food industry also targets and seeks to bring particular sorts of farmers under its control. An important strategy is *contract farming* where farmers are engaged on contract to supply a specified quantity of farm produce, of a specified quality, at a specified time and price, to a processing company. In Ireland contract farming is less common than in the United States or the UK, but is found in some areas of agriculture, such as sugar beet, barley for brewing and peas for freezing or canning (Hoggart *et al.*, 1995, p.148).

In Ireland the farmers' co-operatives (co-ops) have historically played an important role as food processors or as intermediaries between farmers and food-processing companies. Since co-ops are legally made up of their farmer members, it is inappropriate for them to engage in contracts with farmers, but they have been able to use other strategies to achieve integration and control over selected producers, such as giving them privileged access to professional farm development advice or to the purchase of inputs for the farm on credit from the co-op, as well as paying bonuses to farmers who meet particular requirements of quality or timing of supply. Use of such practices is a sign of transformation within the co-ops from social organisations to increasingly capitalistically oriented enterprises. A small number of co-ops (such as Glanbia and Kerry Foods) are now substantial food corporations in their own right, operating at a global level.

Development of this increasingly integrated food system also reflects consumers' changing food preferences or, perhaps more accurately, changes in the sorts of food made available to them by retailers (see Chapter 13 for a further discussion of food issues). Chief among these is the change from relatively unprocessed to highly processed foods. Although this is not as advanced in Ireland as in, for example, North America (particularly in relation to meat where Irish consumers still buy much of their meat butchered and otherwise relatively unprocessed), it is still quite developed in some food lines, such as dairy-based foodstuffs like yoghurts, dairy spreads and milk-based drinks. Growth in the extent of food processing means that the share of the price of food that goes to the farmer steadily declines: it has been estimated that 60 per cent (Europe) and up to 90 per cent (North America) of the price paid by consumers for food now goes to the companies that process, package, transport, advertise and market the food, rather than to farmers. In an integrated food system that links agribusiness, agriculture and the food industry, farmers appear to occupy an increasingly powerless, dependent position.

This position is exacerbated by the fact that the global food industry is exceptional compared to most other industrial chains in the extent to which it is dominated by a very small number of very large TNCs — Cargill, Grand Metropolitan, Nestlé and Unilever are probably some of the better known. It is a very highly concentrated branch of the global economy in which a small number of companies that have multiple interests in different foods or food-related activities command enormous power. These TNCs try to develop controlling positions within each of the different stages of a given food line, through what is known as 'vertical integration'. For example, some American corporations started as grain exporters and shippers, then expanded into supplying feed for chicken farms, then bought up and operated day-old-chick enterprises, established relations of contract with chicken farmers to whom they sold the chicks and the feed and from which they bought the finished birds, and finally bought into or set up outlets for the processed chicken in supermarkets or in fast-food chains. But food TNCs also invest in other areas of production that may not be closely related to food at all. Some move into food while retaining their original base in a quite different area — tobacco companies, for example, have been prominent investors in salmon farming in Ireland and vineyards in Australia. This diversity of interests enables TNCs to manipulate food prices and markets, sometimes making food available at below cost in the interests of removing competitors and to achieve long-term control over the sector.

To some extent Irish farmers have, until recently, been protected from direct manipulation by such powerful companies by the strength of the co-ops. As long as, legally, only co-ops could do the initial stage of milk processing in Ireland, foreign companies could not easily penetrate the dairy food system, although the beef system was more open to them. But the co-ops have, since the early 1970s, become increasingly concentrated. The emergence of a small number of large co-ops coincides with the concentration of dairy farming in Ireland (fewer farms, larger herd sizes) noted earlier. A new stage in this concentration process was reached with the 1997 merger of Waterford and Avonmore Foods to form GlanBia, claimed to be the fourth largest dairy food company in the world. Over the same period the co-ops have been increasingly transforming themselves into conventional companies quoted on the Stock Exchange, thereby opening themselves up to influence from a growing number of non-farmer shareholders. Though still nominally farmer-controlled, the extent to which they can or wish to act on behalf of local farmers is doubtful. These co-ops have been the basis for the development of an indigenous group of Irish TNCs.

Whether the international division of labour in food production that they promote is good for either Irish farmers or Irish food-industry workers is open to question. In a sense, both farmers and industrial workers have become 'employees' of food-industry companies, though there are interesting social reasons why both groups find it hard to recognise any shared status.

From agricultural to rural: a post-productionist regime?

We frequently hear the claim that, since the early 1990s, agriculture in Ireland and Europe has moved into a 'post-productionist' phase. European policy, it is said, is no longer narrowly concerned with agriculture simply as a means to produce food, but now recognises its other important dimensions as well, particularly environmental considerations in how we use the countryside and the importance of finding a way to maintain a rural, as well as an urban, society within an increasingly urbanised Europe. Some try to capture this change by suggesting that European, and by inference Irish, policy has switched from a policy for agriculture to a *policy for rural development*.

In the 1980s growing European enthusiasm for a post-productionist rural policy coincided closely with a realisation that the CAP was leading to problems of overproduction that could financially cripple the EU. It was given a new boost in the late 1990s by pressures on the EU to enlarge and incorporate Eastern and Central European countries that have large numbers of farmers. It has become important to find ways of supporting farmers that do not necessarily translate into the production of more food or, at least, not food already in oversupply. But other factors have influenced policy changes:

- the creation, as outlined above, of a category of 'surplus' farmers that followed from the development of a streamlined food industry
- the urbanisation of European life, leading to new demands on rural areas such as for leisure and housing
- growing concerns about the nature of food produced under the intensive, scientised methods promoted by the CAP in terms of the environment, animal welfare and food quality and safety.

While these concerns have shifted thinking about rural and agricultural areas towards post-productionism, they have not succeeded in moving policy decisively away from the ideal of 'the modern farm'. Rather, they have tended to reinforce support for polarisation and dualism, for it is only as long as we have — somewhere — highly efficient, intensive, technologically advanced farms that produce as much food as we need, as cheaply as possible, that we can enjoy the luxury of allowing large tracts of the countryside to be given over to non-productionist concerns, such as National Parks. The outcome is an increase in regional differences within Europe, and within Ireland, of which the social and environmental impacts have yet to be meaningfully evaluated (Hoggart *et al.*, 1995, pp.21–75).

INDUSTRIAL DEVELOPMENT

It is easier to write more briefly about Irish industrial development, given the body of comprehensive analysis that already exists (Allen, 1997, 2000; Jacobson, 1989; Kirby, 1997, 2002; O'Hearn, 1992, 1998; Ó Riain, 2004; Wickham, 1986, 1997), and we offer only a summary account here. Breen *et al.* (1990, p.5) suggest 1960 as an initial vantage point from which to survey earlier and more recent developments. This was a time when Ireland:

> could be characterised economically as one of the peripheral regions of the United Kingdom. British capital was the major source of foreign investment. Two-thirds of all exports went to the British market. Entry into the labour market for each new generation often meant emigration to Britain.

At a time when most of the developed industrial economies in Europe were experiencing economic growth, the Irish economy was stagnant and emigration rates were very high (see Chapter 6).

During the 1930s the Fianna Fáil government had tried to reduce economic dependency by protecting Irish industry against foreign competition and by encouraging domestic production in both agriculture and industry to replace imported goods. This period of protectionism and import substitution could be interpreted as an early attempt by the Irish state (anticipating dependency theory by some thirty years) to achieve 'independent development' by disengaging the Irish economy from the international exchange relations in which colonialism had entangled it. Allen describes Fianna Fáil's strategy as 'building native capitalism' and compares it to the later *populist development strategies* of countries such as Mexico, Argentina and Brazil (1997, pp.33–4):

> All these movements were concerned with national development and opposed the dominant agro-export model whereby their countries were reduced to supplying primary produce for metropolitan countries. Populist movements became the political instruments by which a shift was made from agricultural interests to the promotion of manufacturing interests.

Similar protectionist barriers were erected by Australia and New Zealand as they sought to develop indigenous manufacturing industries while maintaining an export-oriented agriculture.

Protectionism sought to construct a 'tariff wall' inside which Irish indigenous industries could be nurtured. In an attempt to reduce the influence of foreign capital, the Control of Manufacturers Acts of 1932 and 1934 prohibited such investors from holding more than a 50 per cent stake in Irish companies. It also stipulated that a majority of a company's directors had to be Irish. Special tax and credit arrangements were made available to Irish firms, particularly in commodity lines that did not require much start-up capital such as hosiery or boot and shoe manufacturing. In terms of its own objectives the strategy was quite successful: between 1932 and 1935 nearly 900 new companies were registered; employment in a range of industries doubled or trebled; and output rose by large amounts (Allen, 1997, pp.40–41). But government intervention in the economy did not go far enough to be entirely successful: it 'never induced new producers to step in and produce things that were needed by existing companies' nor did it 'induce domestic capitalists to reinvest after they exploited the profitability of a few "easy" sectors' (O'Hearn, 1998, pp.36–37). In the 1940s growth slowed considerably and the level of imports, particularly from the United States, soared.

In 1958 protectionism was abandoned and a decision was made to 'open up' the economy to foreign investment and promote export-oriented industrialisation. Barriers to foreign firms selling goods on the Irish market were also dismantled, especially with membership of the EEC in 1973. The impact of the new strategy was quickly visible: manufacturing output grew by 5 to 6 per cent per annum in the twenty years from the end of the 1950s, and employment in industry increased from 179,000 people in 1961 to 237,000 in 1981. Manufactured goods as a proportion of exports rose dramatically, from less than one-fifth in 1958 to nearly two-thirds in the early 1980s, while exports of live animals and other foodstuffs fell equally dramatically. By 1984 one-third of exports were going to EC countries other than Britain, with only 28 per cent going to Britain (Wickham, 1986).

The main contributors to this industrialisation process were foreign-owned companies and TNCs. Who were the main beneficiaries? Allen (1997, p.108) argues that the '1958 turn' to an 'open economy' was undertaken by Fianna Fáil governments who still pursued the goal of 'building native capital'. Grant aid and subsidies for foreign firms went to those that were export-oriented and did not compete with native capitalists in the home market. TNCs were perceived as bringing a new dynamism into the economy that could 'revive the Irish business class'. O'Hearn disagrees: he suggests that Irish companies selling in the home market lost out to foreign competitors and were unable to compensate through expansion into exporting (though some, such as food processors, did develop into major exporters). By the mid-1980s employment in Irish-owned manufacturing companies was at its lowest since the 1940s. By 1987, foreign firms accounted for 43 per cent of manufacturing employment, 52 per cent of manufacturing output and 74 per cent of manufactured exports (O'Malley, 1992, p.111). The Irish industrial economy had become heavily dependent on foreign investment for development. The main beneficiary, according to O'Hearn, has been global capital.

Ireland was more successful than any other peripheral area of Europe during this time in attracting foreign investment. This was partly due to the generous packages of tax waivers and grants offered by the Irish government. But there were also social and political reasons for success. Competing peripheral regions, such as Northern Ireland, Scotland and Wales or underdeveloped regions in England, did not possess their own state institutions that could pursue this type of development (see Chapter 4). Moreover, Ireland was attractive to outside investors because there was no internal social or economic group — not even radical left-wing political groups like the Workers' Party — that would oppose the TNC indus-trialisation strategy. Indigenous Irish entrepreneurs were too few in number and politically too weak to challenge the policy even if they had wished to. Farmers, led by the Irish Farmers' Association, did resist briefly but were mollified by government promises that the new policy of industry support would not divert resources from agriculture.

The Irish trade unions were still a significant political force in the 1970s and early 1980s and might have been expected to protest strongly about the anti-union or single-union-only policies of the incoming TNCs. But their objections were muted by the usually substantially higher wages that TNCs offered to their workers compared to native Irish employers and by the 'sweetheart deals' that some individual unions secured with some incoming firms. Many foreign companies set up their branch plants in rural areas that had no living memory of industrial employment and it is often claimed that they were therefore dealing with a workforce that had no interest in or commitment to trade-union ideals, though Allen notes that the Italian experience indicates that 'rural workers who have no trade union traditions can also be less hidebound by some of the more conservative habits that grow up with more bureaucratised structures' (1997, p.126).

Impacts of TNC-led industrialisation

The spatial and social impacts of the industrialisation strategy of the 1970s and 1980s have been the subject of debate. On the spatial side, the regional distribution of growth has attracted considerable attention. During the pro-tectionist period, industrial growth took place mainly in larger urban centres and its distribution was largely unplanned or uncontrolled, despite de Valera's 'ideology of ruralism' (Breathnach, 1985). For a brief period in the 1950s (following the Undeveloped Areas Act 1952) regional development was encouraged through dispersal of industry to the least industrially developed areas of the country, but it was not until the early 1970s that regional planning became an overt part of development policy.

The pattern of regional growth then began to change markedly. In the early 1970s the eastern 'core' regions of the country had been the most attractive to new manufacturing firms, both foreign and indigenous. But the Regional Industrial

Plans of the Industrial Development Authority (IDA) spurred on manufacturing employment in the other regions, particularly the west and mid-west, in rapidly expanding industries such as electronics and chemicals. Thus, by 1990, the highest proportion of hi-tech firms was in the mid-west region, followed by the Dublin area and the western region (Boylan, 1996, p.186). Foreign companies contributed most to the change. By the late 1980s they accounted for almost half of total employment in the 'western periphery of Ireland', that is, in all regions outside the three 'core' eastern ones, compared with about one-third in 1973 (Drudy, 1991, p.166). In the period 1973 to 1989, these regions had a net gain of almost 30,000 jobs (98 per cent of the national net gain in foreign jobs).

Regions that had consistently lost population since the 1950s (or indeed 1850s) began to experience population growth, particularly through immigration or return migration. But, while the more peripheral areas of the country clearly needed the additional employment, the regional policy left the core areas, particularly Dublin, 'in serious difficulty in relation to manufacturing employment' (Drudy, 1991, p.167). Even within the peripheral regions the success of the policy is debated. According to Boylan, for example, rather than promoting rural development, industrialisation policy exacerbated growth disparities between rural and urban settlements, with manufacturing employment concentrated in the larger towns while smaller settlements and rural hinterlands were drained of population, jobs and services. This has particularly affected the rural poor who are excluded from participation in urban-centred regional growth by their limited access to transport (private or public) and a low level of technological skills.

The social impact of industrialisation on the Irish countryside has been much discussed. International research on the effects of 'industrialisation by invitation' has stressed its gendered nature and addressed in particular the significant part played by women in the process. O'Donovan and Curtin (1991) note that in Ireland during the 1960s and 1970s the IDA publicly stressed that jobs in the new factories were for adult males, suggesting that they would be high-quality, full-time, well-paid and highly skilled. In practice, many of the workers recruited were women, particularly rural women. Breathnach (1993) notes that in the 25 years after 1961 women's employment in manufacturing outside of Dublin, Cork, Limerick and Waterford increased by 139 per cent (it decreased by 35 per cent in these urban centres) and concludes that 'access to female labour from a rural/small town background has been a locational determinant of considerable significance to foreign firms investing in Ireland' (1993, p.23). Others (Harris, 1989; Jackson and Barry, 1989; Owens, 1992) have been less interested in the availability of cheap labour for incoming industry than in how the new work opportunities affected the lives of rural women. This research has revealed much about the position of women in Irish rural communities and 'the inequality in gender terms that rural women have encountered in the local development process' (Boylan, 1996, p.189). Breathnach argues that TNCs employ women as part of their broader strategy: to locate the lower-skilled assembly stages of the production process in Ireland. The result has been to produce in Ireland 'a truncated and inferior form of development and therefore a dependent and subordinate position within the New International Division of Labour that emerged in the 1960s and 1970s' (1993, p.27).

TNCs are relatively mobile and can respond quickly to global economic change. Many firms that came to Ireland in the early 1960s were involved in labour-intensive industries such as textiles, footwear and light engineering: by the end of the decade they had moved on to poorer countries with lower wages, such as Morocco and Malaysia. In addition, increasing unemployment throughout Europe in recent years has intensified competition for TNC investment and some firms have moved out of Ireland in response. An American recession in the 1980s meant that fewer new TNC plants were located here and already established ones trimmed their workforces. Kirby (1997, p.131) notes critically that although over 390,000 new industrial jobs were created in Ireland in the two decades to 1994, over 400,000 were lost, leaving the country with a net reduction in industrial employment — despite massive expenditure of taxpayers' money on job creation. But it could also be argued that this investment had improved the 'quality' of the jobs and that shoe-manufacturers and biscuit-bakers had been replaced by 'modern' personnel engaged in computing and the manufacture of health-care devices.

Wickham (1986) examined the Irish activities of US-based TNCs in the 'high technology' sector (computers, pharmaceuticals and electronics) during the 1970s and 1980s. These firms located in Ireland largely to access the EU market. Their activities were mainly in the 'finishing' area: they assembled and/or distributed goods developed or manufactured in the core economies. The research and development [R&D] activities of these science-based industries were rarely carried out in Ireland. As a result, in the 1980s, over half of those working in the Irish electronics industry were semi-skilled assemblers and operatives, while such workers made up just one-third of the workers in the US electronics industry. Managers and professionals constituted 28 per cent of the American workforce but only 12 per cent of those working in the electronics industry here. Wickham concluded that the development of the Irish workforce was diverging from rather than converging with advanced industrial countries.

Dependency theorists generally believe that industrialisation in Ireland has contributed more to the growth of skilled and semi-skilled manual jobs than to managerial and R&D positions. They also argue that expansion of foreign-owned industries has not led to a corresponding growth in indigenous Irish industry or in industry-related services. For them foreign industries remain an enclave within the Irish economy, importing most of what they need for production and exporting most of the products (Kirby, 1997; O'Hearn, 1998). Within the new international division of labour, TNCs organise production across borders: most of the highly-skilled work and the profits remain in the core countries while the less-skilled tasks are distributed to the periphery. Since the early 1980s, industrial policy has largely been oriented towards 'encouraging investment, both foreign-owned and indigenous, in high-technology manufacturing sectors such as electronics, pharmaceuticals and biotechnology, as well as in internationally traded services including financial services, software, shared services and e-commerce' (McCafferty, 2007, p.69).

Ireland's more recent industrial experience has generated new arguments. During the 1990s, the economy experienced a remarkable boom, described by many as an 'economic miracle'. For several years Irish growth rates were the highest in the 15 EU or 29 OECD member states. Between 1993 and 1997 national income rose by around 44 per cent and there was a 16 per cent rise in employment. Many of the new jobs were in services, but manufacturing employment also grew, against international trends: industrial production grew by 15 per cent in 1997 alone. In the mid-1990s Ireland attracted 30 per cent of new TNC investments in the EU, compared to 19 per cent going to Britain. Company profits soared, tax revenues increased and the national debt was dramatically reduced (Sweeney, 1998, p.3). The question that has concerned many analysts — and the Irish people in general — is whether this experience represented a new departure in Irish history, reflecting the fact that we have finally 'got the economy right', or whether the change was a transient and largely unmanaged effect of the convergence of a number of coincidences.

Sweeney argues strongly for the former position. He concludes (1998, p.15) that 'the Irish economic miracle appears to have a solid modern foundation on which a lasting edifice can be built . . . good infrastructure, investment in that important capital — human beings — and a healthy demographic structure'. For him, the key factors that led to the boom have largely been 'internal'. They include good planning and state management; a tighter fiscal regime; investment in education; IDA success in 'picking industrial sector winners'; and acceptance of 'flexible' work practices by Irish workers and trade unions. He places particular emphasis on the social partnership established in 1987 between the state, employers and trade unions which, he argues, has helped to maintain Irish competitiveness. He does recognise some 'external' factors to be important: the effects of EU structural funds; the attractiveness of Ireland to TNCs looking for a location within the EU; and the revolution in telecommunications.

In contrast, Allen (2000) argues that Ireland's economic success arises from conditions in the global economy and has little to do with 'planned modernisation'. He notes that growth rates have fallen in all major industrial economies since the mid-1970s, reflecting falling rates of profit. This has led to increased competition between both firms and states. It has been particularly felt in the US, where business has responded in two ways: first, it has attacked the employment conditions of US workers; second, it has expanded investment abroad in search of better profit opportunities. As a consequence, investment abroad by American-based TNCs quadrupled between 1982 and 1997 (Allen, 2000, p.22). Ireland benefited as it was an attractive location for US investment into Europe. Particularly attractive was the 'spectacularly low' rate of corporate taxation in Ireland (10 per cent as against 34 per cent in the US); a young, English-speaking workforce that 'could be hired at rates of pay which stood at the bottom of the European league'; and the dominance of a stable pro-business government (Allen, 2000, p.25). For Allen, then, the birth of the 'Celtic Tiger' had little to do with Irish initiatives. Correspondingly, he does not believe the boom will be sustained into the future.

Sweeney (1998, p.128) speaks of a second wave of TNC investment in Ireland, which he believes took place between 1987 and 1996, that was qualitatively different to that of the 1960s. In the earlier phase foreign investment came, he suggests, mainly for access to cheaper labour and to grants and tax breaks. In the second phase skilled labour and access to the European market became more important. He further suggests that economic links between TNCs and indigenous industry improved substantially and that there has been a diffusion of skills from foreign to local industry.

Moving away from his earlier dependency perspective, Wickham (1997) also notes that by the end of the 1980s the occupational profile of electronics manufacturing had changed. The proportion of qualified employees in the electronics workforce had increased, as firms automated their production processes and took on ancillary activities (such as customer support) that required more skilled labour than did production itself. Also, new companies entering the sector tended to have a higher skill profile than existing ones. At the start of the 1980s electronics companies were looking for technicians — by the end of the decade they sought graduates in electronic engineering and in computer science.

Wickham also discusses the substantial software industry that has emerged in Ireland. He notes that it contains a much higher proportion of indigenous companies than the hardware industry. O'Hearn (1998, pp.74–78) is more sceptical in this regard, but Wickham's claim has received support from Ó Riain (2000), who describes the growth of 'a significant sector of indigenous Irish-owned companies, often working in knowledge-intensive, high technology products and services' as perhaps the most surprising outcome of the Celtic Tiger economy.

These changes in the structure of Irish industry have also had implications for the nature of the workplace. Hazelkorn (1997) has noted the transformation of the media and cultural sector from one dominated by the public broadcaster (RTÉ) and informed by universal, creative and service values, to a multi-faceted industry defined and influenced by processes of production and exchange. Information/knowledge and cultural production has increasingly been identified in Ireland, as in all advanced economies, as playing the key role in the generation of capital and the invigoration of the national economy. Many of the companies in this sector are small scale, characterised by extreme flexibility and insecurity of tenure. The software industry in Ireland is also dominated by small firms with relatively few layers of management, rapid turnover of staff and little expectation of 'loyalty' or lifetime employment on the part of either employer or employee (Ó Riain, 2000; 2004a). Ó Riain (2004a) has argued that changes in how class relations, between professionals and employers are regulated has not undermined the service relation, but has transformed it for certain employees. 'Service' is still exchanged for the long-term prospect of 'compensation'. But where the service relation of the 'Golden Age' rested firmly on long-term employee and employer expectations, these temporal horizons have been much shortened and even obscured. The reconciliation of the various class positions in which professionals find themselves (worker, self-employed, petit bourgeois, owner of share capital) is less and less effectively carried out through the temporal structure of the career and is telescoped within the structure of work, increasingly organised around project teams. This creates significant instability in class relations among professionals and the co-ordination of professional class relations is increasingly carried out through spatial rather than temporal 'fixes' — at least partly explaining the increasing importance of regional economies relative to corporate hierarchies. The high-tech region becomes not only a 'milieu of innovation' but also a crucible of class relations and the renegotiation of the terms of 'professional service'.

Ó Riain points in particular to the Irish-owned computer software sector which, along with Israel and India (interestingly both societies with a high number of English speakers and with a global diaspora) is one of the world's largest. Out of fragmentary beginnings in the 1970s, a dynamic industry was forged by the 1990s, largely due, Ó Riain argues, to developmental interventions of the Irish state which created not only the economic but also the social conditions for the industry's success. Key figures in state agencies, such as the National Board for Science and Technology, Eolas, Forbairt and the National Software Directorate, created and maintained networks among the new social actors that helped foster this new industry: educators, policy-makers, new employers and employees.

Although the state played an important role in attracting TNCs like Microsoft and Lotus into Ireland in the 1980s, this in itself did not lead to the development of an Irish-owned software industry. The most critical contribution was the active role taken by the state in 'building up a web of associations and social ties that supported information-sharing and co-operation' across and between the new firms and the centres of innovation and advanced technology programmes, located mainly in the universities (Ó Riain, 2000, p.243). Ó Riain argues that the state should apply similar developmental efforts to other groups in Irish society in order to combat the rising income inequality that has accompanied recent economic success.

A related problem is that of the regional disparities that have emerged in terms of inward investment and state support. According to Haynes (2004), national government has tended to restrict its funding primarily to publicly run national networks. She sees this as hindering the capacity of the regions to develop to their full potential and argues that support for regional associationalism would help to unlock the potential of social capital to spur economic growth in the regions. In Haynes's view, an industrial development policy that fails to invest in fomenting social networks among local economic actors can only have limited impact: 'just as public investment in transportation and communication links can be a mechanism for public policy implementation with regard to regional development, so can public investment in social capital. Government can harness local social capital for its public policy purposes.' Her study of information and communications technology (ICT) companies in Galway city reveals two important insights about regional level development: (a) the potential of social capital for mutually beneficial exchange and co-operation; and (b) the need for co-ordinating structures in order to harness its full potential. She identified an informal network within this regional ICT sector that served five main purposes: recruiting employees; acquiring contracts; assigning contracts; sourcing information and resources; and forming formal collaborative ventures.

Similarly, McCafferty (2007) has argued that the imbalance in the spatial structure of the urban system in Ireland poses major challenges for regional development. Most of the new investment has been in the larger urban areas, particularly the cities. As a result, there have been greater levels of job creation in and around urban areas and an attenuation of regional disparities. Crucially, McCafferty concludes (2007, p.70) that 'the spatial distribution of the new growth runs counter to the National Development Plan's goal of balanced regional development'. Urban dominance remains an ongoing challenge in Irish society. Policy-makers have so far failed to identify a mechanism for reducing spatial inequalities.

The contribution that TNCs have made to indigenous economic development has often been seen as disappointing. They import a high proportion of their inputs and withdraw (or 'transfer') substantial profits from the country. Relative to total output, they spend less locally on goods and services for production and on wages and taxes than Irish-owned companies do. Nevertheless Wickham (1997) argues that foreign-owned industry has had a beneficial impact on Irish industry, particularly as it has increased opportunities for Irish managers and developed management thinking in Irish society. He notes that, with the exception of Japanese-owned firms, TNC branch plants tend to be staffed with Irish managers soon after establishment. The indigenous management skills thus created became rooted in the local economy over time.

Allen does not entirely disagree with this portrait. Ireland today, he notes, has the highest level of direct US investment per manufacturing worker of any country in Europe — seven times the EU average — and it is more dependent on US investment than either Costa Rica or the Honduras, often described as American backyards (2000, p.27). But this has not driven out native Irish capital, rather it has created new opportunities for it to expand. The Irish state does not prioritise the interests of foreign over domestic capital; in fact 'their interests converge on almost every issue' (2000, p.20). Allen agrees that the Irish economy is a 'capitalist success story'. But by other, more important, criteria, such as equality and social justice, he judges it an abysmal failure.

Between 1987 and 1997 the share of the expanded national economy claimed by wages, pensions and social security declined by 10%, while the share going to unearned incomes in the form of profits, interest, dividends and rent rose by the same proportion (Allen, 2000, p.59). Between 1990 and 1997 industrial profits increased by 144 per cent, bank profits rose astronomically (the after-tax profits of the Bank of Ireland grew by 570 per cent since 1990) while wages increased by only 59 per cent (Allen, 2000, p.64). Working hours have also increased: Irish workers now work an average of 1,800 hours per year, compared to 1,400 in the Netherlands (Sweeney, 1998, p.13). The rise in profits has not led to a surge of investment in the economy, rather much of the wealth has been exported, legally or illegally, and much has gone into stock market or property speculation. At the same time, 23 per cent of the workforce are categorised as 'low-paid'. Inequality has increased and 'the Celtic Tiger has quite simply one of the worst records on earnings dispersion in the developed industrial world' (Allen, 2000, p.76). Much of the responsibility for this systematic transfer of wealth to the wealthy, in Allen's view, lies with the same social partnership agreements praised by Sweeney. Allen sees such deals as having severed the link between profits and wages, distanced the trade union leadership from rank and file members and incorporated union leaders into state and business ideologies of promoting economic 'competitiveness' and 'flexibility' in employment, rather than advancing the interests of the majority in the society, the workers and employees.

IRELAND — WHERE IN THE WORLD?

It is clear that industrial development strategies have significantly changed Irish society. The economy has become less dependent on a single external 'core' market — Britain — and, in agricultural commodities, on a single type of export, though food-based exports remain highly significant. The occupational structure has become much more diversified: white-collar work in industry, services and the professions has expanded, as has skilled or semi-skilled manual work, while agricultural employment has contracted. The class structure has also changed: in the 1950s about half of each new generation of young people who remained in the country and found work, found it in family-owned businesses, particularly farming. Today people's jobs are related more to their educational qualifications than to their family connections. In many respects, then, we could argue that the Irish occupational structure, and society more broadly, has been 'modernised' by the process of state-led industrial development.

Today Ireland is characterised by the ESRI as a small, open, trade-dependent economy that has one of the fastest growing economies in the developed world. Its openness is reflected in high levels of inward migration and high levels of foreign direct investment (FDI). The Irish economy has been transformed from one based on agriculture and traditional forms of manufacturing to one increasingly based on the hi-tech and internationally traded services sector. In 2005 the services sector accounted for 66 per cent of employment, industry for 28 per cent and agriculture just 6 per cent. Ireland's remarkable growth performance throughout the late 1990s and into the new millennium has led to rapid convergence of output per capita with the

EU average, driven by exceptional rates of growth in employment. The unemployment level has dropped to a historically low level (ESRI, 2007).

But the extent to which this 'modernisation' should be seen as progress can be questioned, as we have seen above. Two further aspects of current occupational and sectoral structures may be mentioned here. First is the position that service employment now holds in Ireland. The record growth in employment since the mid-1990s, as has been pointed out, is primarily in service rather than manufacturing jobs. Indeed, one in three new jobs created in Ireland since 1988 has been in tourism (Flanagan and Conlon, 1999) and around half of these jobs are seasonal and/or part-time (Breathnach, 1994, p.58). While some service work, particularly in the professions, is very well paid, much new service employment is low-paid and casualised. Second, the sectoral organisation of the economy has changed greatly since the early attempts at industrialisation under protectionism. Economic growth and exports have become increasingly concentrated in a small number of economic sectors dominated by TNCs: the so-called '3Cs' of computers (electronics and engineering), chemicals and cola concentrates. These account for around one-third of *all* value-added in Irish manufacturing (O'Hearn, 1998, p.73).

Excessive dependence on tourism is a cause of concern to Breathnach and others, who see it as a highly seasonal and unstable economic sector, easily upset by factors outside Irish control. It may also have cultural and social impacts, such as the transformation of history into 'heritage' for tourist consumption, that may be damaging to the host society. Dominance of a narrow range of economic sectors that are not deeply 'embedded' in the host society is of concern to both O'Hearn and Kirby. Kirby favours an industrialisation process that involves increasingly sophisticated value-adding to indigenous raw materials. His ideal is Denmark, where agricultural-processing contributed to the development of a high-quality food-processing industry, and associated engineering, mechanical and high-tech manufacturing. Such a process 'is far more embedded in that country's social structure than an industrialisation process largely dependent on multinational companies setting up plants' (1997, p.142). One of the consequences of Ireland's high dependence on TNCs is that much of the wealth generated in the country is expatriated. As a result, Ireland scores very well on measures of Gross Domestic Product (GDP) but less well on measures of Gross Domestic Income (GDI). GDP is a relatively straightforward measure of output and, according to the OECD, gives a measure of how well off a country is compared with competitors and past performance. Ireland's position has moved up the GDP rankings since 1999 and it is now in the top five countries in the OECD (OECD *Observer*, March 2005). In 1995, Ireland's GDP per capital was 12 per cent below the OECD average, whereas in 2003 it was 22 per cent above the average. But the question is: does GDP measure the country's actual wealth, since inward investment and immigrant labour generate profits and other revenues, at least some of which flow back to the country of origin? The GDI measure accounts for these inward and outward flows, and on this ranking

Ireland drops to seventeenth place. The gap between GDP and GDI in Ireland is significant and reflects the reality that a significant proportion of the income generated in the country does not stay there.

Globalisation theorists argue that we cannot understand the pattern of change in Irish society unless we use a 'global approach'. We must discuss Ireland not as a locally bounded society, but as an increasingly integrated element of a global capitalist system. Global processes lead to the incorporation, peripheralisation and re-incorporation of different zones within the global economy. By placing Irish experience in relation to these trends we can better understand our own recent history. O'Hearn (1992; 1998) and Allen (2000) argue that the global system is dominated by the United States; Irish history has been shaped, far more than we realise, by changes in the US society and economy and in America's understanding of how the global system should be managed.

According to O'Hearn (1992, pp.22–28), the US began to consolidate its position as a world power in the 1950s, as the British empire declined. American interests required the expansion of a world order based on interdependence through trade, backed by American military might. The global system was to be maintained through a triangular system of trade, wherein the US would sell industrial products to Europe and modernising parts of Asia; the Europeans would sell their own industrial output to their former colonies; who in turn would supply raw materials to the US. This centred the whole system on America and was actively pursued through the Marshall Aid plan for European restructuring. The Irish state, far from choosing to participate in free trade within the system, was unable to remain outside even if it so wished.

Over the following thirty years this regime proved remarkably tenacious, despite its failure to resolve unemployment, stagnation and poverty in Ireland and other incorporated countries. There is evidence that, more recently, changes are occurring, though they are 'hard to characterise because we are still living through the process' (O'Hearn, 1992, p.28).

From the Irish point of view, O'Hearn suggests, the most important change is in European integration strategies. These have shifted from 'a primarily US-inspired plan to reintegrate Europe' into global trade, to a project by the European core itself to increase its economic and military power. The EU has expanded steadily in recent years and has 'sought to strategically reformulate the roles of its territories so that they could collectively contribute to the creation of a more globally competitive Union' (Kitchin and Bartley, 2007, p.11).

Ireland has benefited greatly from its association with the EU since 1973. Kitchin and Bartley (2007, p.9) contend that the unprecedented growth experienced in Ireland in recent years owes much to Ireland's membership of 'the evolving European mega-region'. In the early years of EU membership, Ireland benefited substantially from transfers from Brussels and was later to avail of structural funds. These funds have played a significant role in underpinning the multi-annual National Development Plan (NDP) spending programmes. Ireland was also able to tap into

European markets, thereby significantly reducing trade dependence on Britain. The virtual elimination of trade barriers after the passage of the Single European Act in 1992 impacted positively on the Irish economy. In particular, Ireland provided not just a reliable way for US companies to enter the larger European market, but was also English-speaking.

Furthermore, the new institutional environment that has emerged in Ireland in recent years owes much to the kinds of institutional arrangements pioneered within the EU. Partnership has become the preferred mode of regulation adapted by contemporary European states, seen as a palatable alternative to hierarchies and markets (Benington, 2001, p.203). Partnership has assumed centre stage because of a fundamental shift in the way the economy and society are conceptualised by policy-makers. Finally, Ireland's labour market has relied very heavily in recent years on labour migrants from the former Eastern and Central European countries that became members of the expanded EU25 in May 2004 (and later the EU27 in January 2007) though in the latter case free movement has been restricted. All of these developments indicate that the European periphery, including Ireland, is being reoriented towards the European core and away from the US.

We can argue with details of this portrayal of the recent period in Ireland; and we might question the one-dimensional view of change it offers, where the impact of globalisation on Ireland is confined to the economic level, with politics and culture essentially ignored. But while O'Hearn's 'globalised dependency perspective' can be perceived as narrow, it does point to some of the inherent weaknesses in the Irish economic model that remain to be addressed.

The debate between versions of modernisation theory and versions of dependency theory, as contrasting ways to understand societal change, is clearly not settled (see Kirby, 2002). We have argued that modernisation theory provides only a partial, and in some respects distorted, understanding of social change in Ireland as it overlooks the external relationships that have so strongly influenced how we have developed. At the same time, it is not helpful to assume that Irish social change has been totally externally imposed either: powerful groups within Irish society, and particularly the Irish state, have also shaped our development experience. It is to these 'internal' processes that we turn in Chapter 4.

4

The modernising state

In Chapter 3 we examined some features of Ireland's agricultural and industrial development over the last century and explored theoretical explanations of change and development. Now we ask not what happened or why, but who — who oversaw and managed development, took the decisions and influenced the policies adopted and implemented? The usual response to such questions is 'the state'. After all, for many the rationale for an independent Ireland is that we ourselves can, through our own government, control and manage Irish affairs. Thus, we open this chapter with a discussion of the state:

- as a concept
- as a focus for sociological theorising
- as an actor in Irish affairs.

We conclude with the suggestion that the state is not the only power-holder and, in considering who the others may be, we raise questions about the meaning and nature of power itself.

THE STATE: AGENT OF CHANGE OR REACTIVE FORCE?

In a survey of Irish state research, O'Dowd (1991, p.98) cautions against taking for granted that the state is, or can be, the author of development. Instead we should ask whether the state is an agent of social transformation in society or is best seen in a reactive and intervening capacity — as a response to other agents that initiate social change. The theories of development considered in Chapter 3 generate different answers to this question. For modernisation theorists the state has a major role to play in transforming 'traditional' societies into 'modern' ones, but only in late modernising societies. In those that modernised early, the transition to modernity was stimulated by the bourgeoisie following their own class interests and aspirations. In late modernising societies, this class is not fully developed and its work falls to the state. A key role is then played by intellectuals and professionals, often educated or trained in an 'advanced' society, who express ideas about becoming 'modern' that support and amplify state efforts. In peripheral or post-colonial societies, modernity can be 'a deliberately embraced project, a consciously pursued goal' (Bauman, 1995, p.228) and the intelligentsia takes on a transformative mission, often as part of the project of nationalism. Ironically, the result may be to *imitate* the colonial state, as much as to withdraw from it.

If the modernising state is the main actor in modernisation theory, the picture presented by dependency theory stands in sharp contrast. It argues that in a dependent society *under*development results from incorporation into trade and other relationships with a powerful core society or the broader world capitalist system. The drivers of change are external to the society and the role of the state in a dependent society is to act on behalf of the external power, to facilitate the restructuring of the economy in the desired direction and to persuade or even coerce the indigenous population to accept the changes involved.

Some dependency theorists have argued that at least some 'dependent states' are more autonomous than this account allows; they have been able to develop economically and raise living standards for *some* in society, if not all. This recognition has led to a reconsideration within dependency theory of the role of the state. It has been argued that possession of an autonomous state *can* confer benefits on a dependent society. For Wickham (1997) this is reflected in the advantage that Ireland has enjoyed as a peripheral region of Europe when compared to Scotland and Wales in competition for TNC investment. The Irish state has been able to take its own initiatives to make Ireland an attractive location for investment. Such a pattern of development remains rather different to that of powerful, core societies and is termed 'dependent development'. For most *dependent development theorists*, therefore, the state is not merely a passive recipient of external commands but does have the capacity to secure national interests, albeit within the context of unequal economic and political relationships.

Evans (1995) has developed the notion of the flexible developmental state as a way to explain the relatively autonomous actions taken by a state in order to enhance its production and consumption capacities. Ó Riain (2000) has argued that much of Ireland's economic success is attributable to the 'flexible developmental strategy' adopted by the Irish state. The Irish state's transformative role has facilitated not only the creation of new productive capacities, but also the means through which new consumption capacities can be deployed. For example, at national level, direct fiscal subsidies and indirect infrastructural investment acted as catalysts for an out-of-town shopping mall development on the perimeter of Dublin in the 1990s (see Chapter 16). At local level, networks were fostered between state officials, politicians and commercial developers. The nature, extent and propriety of some of these were the subject of investigation in the Flood/Mahon Tribunal. It is clear that Irish policy-makers have followed what Evans describes as a 'developmental model' in relation to the production of consumption. State agencies have been 'embedded in a concrete set of social ties that binds the state to society and provides institutionalised channels for the continual negotiation and renegotiation of goals and policies' (1995: 12). Such a strategy allows the state sufficient autonomy to transcend the individual interests of its private counterparts in order to resolve collective problems.

What of globalisation theory — how does it understand the state? This is an ongoing debate. Briefly, globalisation theorists share a view of the state with dependent development theorists, but have broadened the analysis in a number of useful ways. They talk of the contemporary world as a globalised economy shaped primarily by the activities of transnational capital, but recognise that the capitalist world system is *also* a system of separate states. Considerable tension results within this system between 'footloose' capital, organising new international divisions of labour as it seeks out economic opportunities across the world, and 'immobile' states, trying to attract capital investment to their territories while dealing with the impact on their own populations of international economic developments.

A key issue for globalisation theorists is whether the rise of transnational capital means the end of the nation state as the basis of world political organisation. With highly mobile capital that sees trillions of US dollars circulating daily in the world money markets, the power of any single state — even a superpower like the United States — to control and direct economic affairs has seriously diminished. But economic globalisation has also helped in some ways to enhance the importance of nation states. State institutions such as Ireland's IDA and its global competitors struggle to offer transnational corporations the most attractive infrastructure and taxation regimes, even as they try to manage the fallout or 'the local consequences of global restructuring'. People increasingly look to the state to organise the conditions that will create and sustain jobs. The state becomes involved in providing education and training for the workforce, advanced telecommunication facilities and joint enterprises in natural resource exploitation. People also now demand protection against the harm caused by international movements of capital, through unemployment benefits, retraining programmes and programmes to stimulate alternative industries.

Some functions normally associated with the state have been diffused downward to the city or urban regions. Indeed, the role of the urban regime has been dramatically reshaped in the post-Fordist era. Since the 1980s, a major spatial shift has occurred that has resulted in cities or metropolitan economies emerging as the key foci of economic development strategies. As Jessop (1997, p.28) points out, 'there have been major shifts in cities' roles as subjects, sites and stakes in economic restructuring and securing structural competitiveness.' These shifts are reflected in the new focus on the 'entrepreneurial' or 'creative' city at regional and local level. Indeed the idea of the entrepreneurial city has been embedded in public narratives about the city and has emerged as the dominant response to urban problems (Jessop, 1997, p.31). The entrepreneurial city promotes economic development to counteract the deleterious effects of deindustrialisation on the one hand and to create new forms of employment and new sites for consumption on the other. The city, in other words, makes a virtue of devising strategies aimed at improving its economic competitiveness. Urban entrepreneurialism is pursued in a variety of ways but, most notably, in European and North American cities, through the creation of 'fantasy' projects, flagship *grands projets culturels* and business/ cultural incubation quarters (Hannigan, 2004; Mikunda, 2004).

Just as states seek to maximise their interests, cities increasingly have developed urban locational policies and compete with each other on the international stage for inward investment. Mayer (1995, p.232) argues that these developments are a response to changes in capital mobility and shifts in the technological and social organisation of production that make it increasingly impossible for the state to retain an organisation and co-ordination role. The economic imperative has come to dominate in the urban regime and so the sphere of local political action has expanded to include not just the local authority, but a range of private and semi-public actors.

We can find examples of all of these views of the state in Irish sociology. The dominant view corresponds closely to that of modernisation theory — hardly surprising, given the influence of this theory on Irish intellectual life over many decades. Such analyses assume that the Irish state has been, and remains, the pre-eminent agent in the transformation and modernisation of Irish society. Studies in this vein sometimes raise questions about how far other groups have challenged or eroded the independence of the state — the Roman Catholic Church, for example, or employers' organisations or trade unions. But they do so in the context of assuming that the state should be the primary initiator of development, even if in practice it is not in sole control.

A sharp contrast can be found in the work of O'Hearn, a globalisation/ dependency theorist, whom we discussed in Chapter 3. He is highly critical of those who suggest that the Irish economic take-off in the late 1950s was a result of the deliberate actions of the Irish state or of specific individuals such as Taoiseach Seán Lemass or modernising professionals and civil servants. O'Hearn (1992, p.23) asserts that when we place Ireland in the context of the global economy, many shibboleths of Irish history dissolve, in particular:

> the great myth that an officer from the Department of Finance named Whitaker wrote a monograph, started a planning bureaucracy, and transformed the nation. The Irish economic regime was transformed by the global economy long before Whitaker wrote *Economic Development* in 1958.

For O'Hearn, changes in the Irish economy since the late 1950s reflect shifts in the world economy, and in particular the strategies adopted by the United States in the post-war period in order to consolidate its position within the global core. The Irish state may have welcomed, even facilitated, the resulting incursion of TNC capital into Ireland, but cannot be considered the initiator of this change. Murray (2004) also takes issue with the historiography that accords a primary role in the transformation of Ireland to Seán Lemass and T.K. Whitaker. Rather he suggests that this interpretation understates the agency of non-state actors in the overall refashioning of Irish industrial policy. According to Murray, capital and labour in Ireland, far from adopting a protectionist stance, championed positive engagement with the task of enhancing and developing Ireland's productivity (2004, p.27).

Between the modernisation theorists and the work of O'Hearn we can locate the analyses of writers like Breen *et al.* (1990) who see Ireland as a semi-peripheral country within a global system. The country's possibilities for development are deeply shaped and limited by that position and in particular by the fact that, along with Spain, Portugal and Greece, Ireland has, until recently, been on the EU periphery. This global position constrains but does not determine the policies adopted by the Irish state. In turn, its policies have major impact on internal social structure, especially in producing certain patterns of class difference and class inequality that are thought to be typical of the EU periphery. The choices open to the state may be limited by external factors, but it would be impossible to understand contemporary Irish society without examining the part played by the Irish state in shaping social change. This is largely the position we adopt in this book. It is, indeed, part of the reason why we have confined ourselves to writing only of society in the Republic of Ireland, excluding the North. To the extent that different states shape and produce different societies, it is not possible to take 'Ireland' as meaning both Northern Ireland and the Republic of Ireland, nor to treat both of them coherently within the confines of this text. (For a sociological analysis of contemporary Northern Irish society, see Coulter, 1999.) In the aftermath of the peace process, the two states have come together to create a range of cross-border agencies and initiatives including integrated planning for the Belfast–Dublin corridor.

DEFINING 'THE STATE'

Before we take our discussion further, we need to clarify how we understand 'the state'. Discussions of the topic can confuse, as sociologists tend to use the term 'state' in two senses. First, as a way to refer to *countries* in the world system — territorially bounded social systems that possess their own institutions of government. In this sense, 'Ireland', 'Irish society' and 'the Irish state' are often used interchangeably (as we have done in many cases ourselves). Second, 'state' refers to a *set of institutions* within a society that have some distinctive characteristics. These include:

- the political institutions of government
- administrative institutions such as the civil service and local government agencies

- discursive institutions such as the mass media and health promotion agencies
- institutions of control such as the courts and prisons
- institutions of coercion, including the army and the police.

Indeed what is *not* part of the state (that is, what sociologists call 'civil society') is not easy to determine. In each of its two senses 'the state' is a difficult concept to define and as a result it is the focus of much debate and disagreement.

But are all societies 'states' and all states 'nation states'? When sociologists talk of particular societies, rather than of society in general, they often equate 'society' and 'country' (thus Ireland = Irish society). They treat the boundaries of the society as congruent with the territorial borders of the state. But such relationships may be hard to establish in practice, as the case of Scotland illustrates. Many people would agree that Scotland is the name of a country — different to Wales, England or Northern Ireland. But Scotland remains part of the United Kingdom; it does not fully possess its own state, despite its distinctive legal and education systems and some devolution of government within the UK. If the boundaries of Scottish society are not provided by a Scottish state, they must then be provided by a Scottish *nation*; but if it is state territorial borders that define a society, then Scotland must be part of UK society (McCrone, 1992).

Sociologists often write as if the contemporary state means 'nation state' and Giddens asserts that 'all modern states are nation states' (2001, p.421). This view assumes that nation boundaries and state borders are the same, reflecting the influence on sociology of nineteenth-century nationalist ideas (see Chapter 12) that said the boundaries of the nation and the borders of the state *should* coincide. Every nation should have its own state — so every legitimate state today belongs to a particular nation. But if the case of Scotland questions the assumption that 'state', 'nation' and 'nation state' are identical, the Irish case makes it even harder to sustain. The *country* of Ireland is divided between two states, neither of which is coterminous with 'the Irish nation'. Indeed the *nation* may include, not just the population of the Republic of Ireland and at least some groups in Northern Ireland, but also the almost one million Irish-born people living in Britain, first-generation emigrants in America, and perhaps even second- and third-generation Irish-Americans and Irish-Britons (not to mention those members of the 'Irish diaspora' in Australia, Germany, and so on). From another perspective, sometimes 'the Irish nation' does not embrace the whole population of the Republic of Ireland. Particular social groups, though subjects of the Irish *state*, may on occasion be defined, or define themselves, as outside the Irish *nation* (Protestants, non-Irish speakers, gays and lesbians and Travellers provide historical and contemporary examples — see Fanning, 2002).

The passing of a controversial referendum and the subsequent legislative change — in the shape of the Irish Nationality and Citizenship Act (2004) — meant that on 1 January 2005 the parameters of Irish citizenship were significantly narrowed. Until then, all children born in Ireland, irrespective of their parents' nationalities, were Irish citizens as of right. This right originated in 1922 when Irish citizenship was defined by state law (and codified in the Constitution in 1999) in terms of territory as well as descent. In the twenty-seventh referendum, the electorate voted to restrict the constitutional provisions on citizenship. Subsequently enacted legislation provided that citizenship would now only be automatically granted to children who had at least one parent as an Irish citizen at the time of the child's birth. As a result of this constitutional change, automatic entitlement to Irish citizenship was redefined exclusively in terms of descent. Analysis by Breen *et al.* (2006) demonstrates how the framing of the citizenship issue was primarily in terms of the risk it posed to Irish nationality. The authors argue that the mass media debate perpetuated a set of negative frames in which immigration was to be viewed. Furthermore the media failed to make any significant interventions in challenging public xenophobia. Indeed the uncritical reproduction and tacit acceptance of politicians' often xenophobic comments surrounding citizenship reinforced the idea that the right to citizenship ought to be contingent.

O'Dowd notes that the lack of coincidence between state and nation is not at all peculiar to Ireland but is 'the empirical reality in much of Europe and the Third World' (1991, p.97). The Irish diaspora is mirrored by others, such as the Chinese, Jewish, Armenian, Indian, to list but a few. In fact, though it is part of the ideology of modernity that each state represents and manages its own nation, countries where this is the case would seem to be the exception rather than the rule. For purposes of clarity, then, it is best to describe the modern international political order as made up of 'states' rather than 'nation states', and to treat the relationship between 'state', 'nation' and 'society' as a matter for empirical investigation in each individual case.

The second use of the term 'state' in sociology has to do with the presence of particular types of institution within a given society. But how to identify state institutions and distinguish them from others? Weber defined the state as that agency within society that has a monopoly on legitimate violence. He suggested that in orderly societies private violence is not acceptable as a way to settle disputes. Rather, violence may be used legitimately only by the central political authority and by those to whom it delegates that right: these authorities and agencies constitute the state. Contemporary sociologists have broadened Weber's approach to include another element — territoriality. Thus the state as an institution or set of institutions has three distinctive characteristics (and no other institutions within society possess these):

- It claims sovereignty over a specific *territory*.
- It holds the sole right to organised use of *violence* within that territory.
- It possesses *legitimacy* — the consent of the citizens to be governed by it.

There is continuing disagreement over whether legitimacy, or the control of the use of force, is the more basic source of state power. States that lose their legitimacy, as happened in the communist states of Eastern Europe, lose much of their power. In stable societies most people obey the state because they accept its authority rather than from fear of its violence. Nevertheless the state's capacity to coerce has been seen by many sociologists as its ultimate 'power resource'.

In practice, of course, we can find examples of states that lack these distinctive characteristics. One state's claim to sovereignty over a territory may be disputed by another state (Taiwan is a good example); organised violence may occur outside state control (as in Colombia); two sets of institutions may contest each other's right to be the sovereign authority within the same territory (as has occurred in many post-colonial African states); or citizens may withdraw their consent to be ruled (again, as in the communist states). Irish history also provides examples of all of these situations. In practice too, the institutional form of 'the state' may vary considerably between societies or in a single society over time. States may be more or less interventionist. In some circumstances the state may undertake tasks that are otherwise left to society, such as industrial production as in 'semi-state companies', or the socialisation of young people through state education systems or youth organisations. The range of institutions that make up 'the state' is potentially very broad and it is therefore difficult to draw an absolute boundary between 'the state' and civil society.

These criteria do not always help us decide whether the institutions we are dealing with constitute a state or not. Is the EU a state? According to our three criteria there seems to be good reason for saying it is not. First, the EU does not clearly possess its own territory; although the Maastricht agreement defines the territorial borders of free movement of people, goods and capital, the territories involved are ruled directly by the member states and only indirectly by the EU. Second, the sovereignty claimed by the EU is problematic; while it can override specific laws of its member states, it has few means to enforce its decisions. Third, no EU agency yet has a monopoly on the organised use of violence across member states. Fourth, the legitimacy of its decision-making processes is frequently called into question given the low level of power accorded to the European Parliament and the 'democratic deficit' apparent in its political institutions. However, while we may agree that the EU is not a conventional nation state, it arguably has institutions (the European Commission, in particular) that operate in 'state-like' ways. Conversely, the EU may also be evidence for the decline of nation states, and the rise of supra-states, as the key players in the global political system.

There is a third, perhaps easier, way to define the modern state: to examine what it does, rather than try to list the institutions and agencies of which it consists. Breen et al. (1990, p.13) suggest, rather cynically, that the modern state is at base an administrative and military organisation that takes resources from a society and uses them to 'maintain order at home and to compete against other states abroad'. This view reveals something about the two key problems that confront the modern state: maintaining order and managing the economy. On one hand, it must ensure that the conditions for capitalist economic development continue. This may involve a defence of private property rights; the introduction of taxation measures to stimulate business expansion; or the provision of a healthy, well-trained and willing labour force. Such challenges relate to the problem of *accumulation*: the need to secure the profitability of capitalist businesses and thus the financial basis of the state itself. Simultaneously the state has to maintain the consent of those it governs and ensure that they support its economic development strategy, even when they derive little benefit from it. This is the problem of *legitimation*.

As the state seeks to resolve one of these problems it may exacerbate the other. For example, a move to control wages to improve business profits can lead to protests from workers; or provision of unemployment benefits for the victims of economic restructuring may mean higher taxes that deter investment in the economy. A particularly difficult problem for the modern capitalist state is the management of social inequality. As it strives to improve the possibilities for capitalist accumulation, it tends to increase inequality and divisions in society and obvious social inequality may put severe strains on the state's legitimacy.

THE STATE IN IRISH SOCIETY

As it has sought to manage the economy and maintain social order, the state has contributed significantly to the formation of contemporary Irish society. To develop this point we focus on inequality to see if the ideas of accumulation and legitimation help us to understand how the state has responded to this issue. We discuss here the historical construction of inequality only; Part II addresses its more contemporary dimensions in some detail.

How has the Irish state responded to social inequality in Irish society? First, it can affect the life chances of individuals and families in two main ways. As an employer and facilitator of job creation and economic activity generally, it influences the occupational positions available and the incomes earned by different occupational groups. Second, the state influences incomes indirectly through its taxation policies and its policies for redistributing state resources across different groups in society.

The consequences of decisions taken by the state can reverberate for many decades, as has been pointed out by Frank McDonald in his various accounts of planning, and the lack thereof, in Dublin (McDonald, 1985; 2000; McDonald and Nix, 2007). Decisions taken by the state in the 1970s to rezone lands around the city of Dublin for development without any linked investment in transport and social infrastructure have had major lifestyle consequences for tens of thousands of people. Corruption in local authority planning is not a victimless crime. People who spend hours every day stuck in traffic jams as they attempt to navigate their way from the suburbs to the city are suffering as a result of the failures of the local state.

The development strategy adopted since 1958 has used incentives to attract foreign capital and to develop an export-oriented industrial base in Ireland. Tax reliefs on export profits, accelerated depreciation and other tax allowances were made available to those who located in particular areas of the country. In agriculture, grants and subsidies for farm development were increased to encourage farmers to raise their output and agricultural exports were directed away from the 'cheap-food' British market to higher-priced European markets.

We can see these measures as an attempt by the Irish state to tackle its accumulation problem. They particularly benefited the owners of foreign capital, larger farmers, and those, for example in the food industry, who set up export-oriented enterprises. The state itself became a major employer between 1960 and 1980. Most of the new public-sector jobs were in white-collar, secure employment, located in Dublin, though much of the state-generated industrial employment was located outside the capital. One group strongly disadvantaged by the state strategy was the existing working class of Dublin and other east-coast centres such as Drogheda and Waterford. Many indigenous companies, in areas such as textiles, engineering and food processing, closed during this period and those made redundant were unable to compete for the new public-sector jobs against better-educated immigrants to the city. Rural areas also experienced increasing inequality (see Chapter 3). While larger farmers expanded their businesses, smaller farmers, unable to take advantage of state development aids, were pushed into less lucrative types of farming such as rearing young cattle.

The new development strategy was primarily directed towards increasing wealth. It was argued that more wealth would translate over time into extra jobs and rising living standards for everyone — *the trickle down effect*. Initially this seemed to be the case as industrial employment increased and emigration declined but, by the late 1980s, unemployment rose to 18 per cent of the workforce and the annual average migratory outflow rose to nearly 34,000 between 1986 and 1990 (see Chapter 6). How the state raised resources through taxation and the way it redistributed these across different social groups contributed to this growing inequality. Between 1965 and 1984 state revenue from taxes on property, inheritance and corporate income fell while indirect taxation (VAT), personal income tax and social insurance contributions increased. Personal taxation increased at a higher rate than increases in earnings, so people on low incomes experienced a *decline* in their real income. In 1980 large proprietors with an average income of £197 a week had the same average tax rate (16 per cent) as unskilled manual workers whose average weekly income was just £63 (Breen *et al.*, 1990, p.92). The tax system benefited owners of capital. The additional existence of secret overseas bank holdings, bogus non-resident accounts and further mechanisms for avoiding and evading tax was revealed in the many tribunals of inquiry that have been a feature of recent public life.

Industrialisation was accompanied by the adoption of a version of the 'welfare state', the rationale here being that it would reduce inequality of access to basic services such as education and medical care and to basic needs for food, clothing, and housing (Kennedy, 2001). If we examine the effect on Irish households of state transfers, through taxation, unemployment benefits, free medical services and education, we find that middle- and upper-middle-class groups in 1980 ended up with 'final incomes' that were slightly less than their direct incomes, while most working-class households ended with slightly more. But large proprietors and professionals still had around twice the final income of unskilled manual worker households. Despite expanded state services and increased expenditure on income-maintenance programmes over the period, the Irish welfare state failed to 'significantly reduce income inequality and certainly failed to abate the importance of class in determining life chances' (Breen et al., 1990, p.97).

Taxation and state services have helped to ensure the survival of two vulnerable groups in the class structure: farmers with very small holdings and/or poor quality land; and low-skilled, urban, working-class people. Breen et al. suggest that in the absence of state intervention these groups would probably not exist today in Irish society but, they note, there is also a group at the top of the class structure — large proprietors — whose existence has depended equally on massive state subsidies. State intervention has provided a 'safety net' that ensured their continued profitability and made it possible for them to continue to hold this class position and to pass it on to their children (1990, p.98). Middle-class families benefit disproportionately from free education and tax relief on mortgages; to that extent they too depend on the state to maintain their position in the class hierarchy. Irish class structure is thus a product, to a large extent, of the interventionist state and the development strategy it has pursued since 1958.

An analysis of trends in income inequality during Ireland's boom period since the mid-1990s reveals that rapid growth has not greatly affected the Irish ranking in terms of income inequality: Ireland has a high degree of economic inequality in comparative terms after the boom, just as it did beforehand. For example, an analysis of estimated income, based on income tax paid, indicates a substantial increase in the share of the top 10 per cent (decile) over the 1990s, from 33 per cent to 38 per cent. The top 1 per cent saw its share rise sharply in the second half of the decade and all the growth in share for the top decile was actually concentrated in the top 1 per cent. According to Nolan and Maitre (2007), this means that by the end of the 1990s the share of the top 1 per cent was more than twice the level prevailing through the 1970s and 1980s. A low redistributive 'effort' is a long-standing characteristic of Ireland's welfare state, and the country continues to compare unfavourably with other rich countries in terms of levels of and recent trends in inequality (Nolan and Maitre, 2007). This is of particular concern as there is now a well-established literature that demonstrates the extent to which the overall health and well-being of a population is related to levels of inequality (see Chapter 10). People fare better in more egalitarian societies and worse in those societies, such as the United States, where there is greater class polarisation and inequality between the better off and the poorer off (Wilkinson, 2005).

This suggests that whatever its response to its accumulation problem, the Irish state has not dealt adequately with its legitimation problem. Or has it? Despite occasional protests (the tax marches of the early 1980s, for example) persistent social inequality has not yet produced widespread and sustained protest or withdrawal of consent to be governed, even among the most disadvantaged groups. Why this is so is a very complex issue to address. It involves, among other things, examining the nature and use of power in Irish society.

STATE, STATE POWER AND SOCIETY

As a small open economy on the European semi-periphery, Irish possibilities for development are constrained by international economic conditions and processes. But the course on which the Irish state embarked in 1958 was not predetermined. Industrialising countries in the European fringe, from Scandinavia to the Mediterranean, have exhibited a variety of ways to manage their development; the strategy adopted in Ireland was not the only one open to us. Earlier we suggested that state development policy has helped to perpetuate social inequality in Irish society. This was presumably an unintended, though perhaps not entirely unforeseen, consequence of policy. But it suggests we need to ask why states adopt the policies they do. On whose behalf do they act?

To take this question further, we must revise and problematise our understanding of the state. So far we have discussed it as something apart from and acting upon society, outside of and relatively untouched by the course of social change. But if the state acts on and influences society, society must act on and influence the state (Peillon, 1995). There are at least two ways that society can influence the state. First, as a set of social institutions the state reflects and is shaped by the power hierarchies and social divisions that exist in society. Over a period of time we find that some social groups have been better able to access state positions and to mould the understanding of, for example, 'the national interest'. Irish society contains different (and competing) social classes, genders, regions, religious and cultural groups, and we could expect the Irish state to recognise and represent the values and interests of some of these more than others. This view of the state still sees the state as being able to take independent action on society, but suggests that how the state defines and selects its favoured projects is strongly influenced by its own history and by the various groups that played a part in its construction. A second, alternative viewpoint queries whether the state is a significant actor at all. It suggests that far from being an autonomous agent for change, the state is controlled by more powerful and less obvious interest groups within society. Variations on these views produce four main types of argument in sociology about the nature of state rule and about who the 'real power-holders' in society are.

The first can be called the *ruling class thesis*. This derives directly from Marx's analysis (see Chapter 1) that portrays capitalist society as sharply polarised between two opposed social classes: capitalist/bourgeoisie and working class. Ruling class theorists contend that capitalist society is ultimately ruled by the capitalist class — the owners of capital and of large productive property. Though the state may appear to be independent, in practice it always acts in the interests of capital, being, as Marx put it, the capitalists' 'executive committee'. Despite occasional apparent conflict, the state has no goals of its own separate from those of the capitalist class. It may pursue goals that appear to militate against ruling class interests, such as certain taxation measures, but these are ultimately in the long-term interest of capital, for example, in development of the labour force.

This approach is resisted by many state theorists. Peillon (1995, p.363) remarks that while the state may emphasise 'the project of the bourgeoisie' this does not automatically make it 'an instrument of this particular class. The conflicts of interest that erupt from time to time between state and bourgeoisie simply rule out such a possibility'. While Peillon agrees that the state does generally privilege the interests of the capitalist class, in his view this is because the capitalist class controls a scarce resource required for economic growth, not because the state is merely its agent or mouthpiece.

A second argument is the *power elite thesis*. This maintains that society is ruled not by a ruling class but by a coalition of elites that includes owners of capital or their representatives. This group, termed the 'power elite' after a 1956 book of the same title by American sociologist C. Wright Mills, may include top financial advisors, employer association lobbyists, military leaders and major formers of public opinion such as politicians, journalists and even academics. The precise make-up of this group varies from society to society: Mills's original analysis was based on America during the Cold War when, he believed, business and military leaders dominated state policy, with government and state executives as junior partners. In contemporary Ireland, we might see military leaders as relatively unimportant but business leaders as a key element of the power elite. In a recent analysis of Ireland from the mid-1930s to 1960, Garvin (2004) has argued that economic, social and cultural stagnation was exacerbated by the lack of imagination on the part of policy-makers, as well as the power exercised by the Catholic Church, the strength of the small farm community and what he describes as the 'gerontocratic' tendencies in the political elites and in society as a whole.

The power elite differs from the ruling class: a class consists of people who share the same economic position and economic interests but who may have few social contacts with each other; an elite is a social group whose members share similar backgrounds, educational experiences and lifestyles. They move in the same social circles, often intermarry and share a common sense of group identity and a belief in their right to lead society. Not surprisingly, it is very hard to prove the existence of such a ruling elite (or 'golden circle') through research, even when one strongly suspects that it exists and exercises considerable power. One of the by-products of the tribunals of inquiry into payments to politicians has been the illumination of the kind of golden circles that formed an intrinsic part of the Irish political establishment, particularly in Fianna Fáil under the leadership of Charles J. Haughey.

Both ruling class and power elite theorists see power as being sharply divided in society: the rulers have all or most of the power while the rest of society has little or none. A third approach rejects this view of power and argues that modern societies contain a plurality of relatively equal interest groups who compete with each other to influence the state. If ruling class theories have their roots in a Marxist analysis of capitalist society, *pluralist theories* owe much to Durkheim's argument that the transition to modernity involves a process of increased differentiation and specialisation of social and occupational roles. According to this view modern society is highly complex and diverse, made up of many pressure groups and associations that represent the outlooks and interests of people in different positions within the division of labour. Pluralist theorists regard the state as outside and above this interplay of interests. The state is a neutral referee that oversees the competition and decides which demands to favour at any given time. The state is portrayed as a rational actor responding primarily to the reason-ableness of the case made by an interest group rather than to traditional loyalties or to threats. The rational state thus reflects the general *rationalisation* of society that accompanies modernisation.

The fourth analysis of power in modern society is often called the *corporatist approach*. This suggests that society is ruled by the state acting in conjunction with a small number of specific interest groups that it has taken into a privileged form of 'partnership'. Employer groups, farmers' associations and trade unions are allowed to participate with the state in the process of policy formation and implementation while this is denied to other interest groups such as the unemployed, consumers or the voluntary sector. In return, the privileged organisations guarantee to secure the support of their own members for state policies and this benefits the state by reducing the level of social conflict.

WHO RULES IRELAND?

Do any of these theories help us to answer the question 'who rules Ireland?' Do they assist in our understanding of the persistent direction taken by Irish state policy in relation, for example, to social inequality? The taxation policies followed in recent decades might suggest to us that power in Irish society is held by a ruling class. Research on the redistributive effect of taxation in Ireland in the 1970s and early 1980s (Rottman *et al.*, 1982; Peillon, 1995) shows that redistribution occurred primarily among people who lived from income: professionals on high incomes, for example, lost substantial amounts of their income in tax that was redistributed, in the form of state services and welfare payments, to those on very low incomes. But virtually no redistribution at all occurred from those who owned property (large business owners, large farmers) to those without property.

This seems to be evidence of a bias in state policy towards owners of capital but it does not necessarily show that Irish capitalists constitute a ruling class. Furthermore, indigenous industrialists and some large farmers feared that the development strategy adopted by the state in the late 1950s would adversely affect them but were unable to prevent its adoption. Much of the capital subsequently invested in Ireland has been foreign-owned. Does this fact then force us to conclude that the class that rules Ireland is located *outside* the country and that capitalists within Ireland are not a ruling class but merely the local representatives of an international capitalist class? Dependency theorists argue that this is a feature of semi-peripheral societies in general and term the local capitalists a *Lumpenbourgeoisie* to indicate their dependent and controlled position. Others argue that this does not sufficiently recognise the power that local capitalists possess, even in dependent or dependently developing societies. The pluralist thesis offers a less conspiratorial account of who rules Ireland but does not fully explain why some interest groups, even when organised into formal associations, obtain little effective recognition in state policy-making. These tend to be the groups already most disadvantaged — the unemployed, small or part-time fishermen and farmers or tenants of under-resourced public housing complexes.

A corporatist analysis may better explain the mechanisms at work. Corporatism in one version or another has a long history in Ireland. It was experienced first in the form of Catholic corporatism: a programme that sought to minimise state intervention in civil society so that people could express their Christianity through the voluntary organisation of their own economic and social lives. It was popular across much of Europe at the beginning of the twentieth century and reached its zenith in the 1930s to 1950s (Kennedy, 2001). Catholic corporatism encouraged people to form local or sectoral organisations to take over the management of their daily lives and saw these also as natural units through which people could participate in the political process. The impact of this teaching in Ireland is evident in the Constitution of Ireland drawn up under de Valera's leadership in 1937 and has left a residue in the contemporary make-up of the Irish senate. However, it failed to make any other significant impact on the Irish social or political system, a fact that Whyte (1979, pp.74–6) attributes to the influence of entrenched political and civil-service structures. Corporatism was revitalised, in a secular mode, in the late 1950s as a way to organise development planning and to provide a system of consultation and conciliation between the state and major interest groups. It has been extensively used since then as a means to secure industrial peace (through national partnership programmes, for example) and to ensure that state development goals are widely disseminated and promoted among significant social groups.

The effect of corporatism in Ireland is that a small group of peak organisations have come to exert particular influence. According to Peillon (1992, p.22) they have 'been co-opted as privileged partners in the dialogue between state and society. Trade unions, employers' associations, [some] farmers' organisations and some professional bodies have come to enjoy privileged access to the state'. This tells us little about the relative power of the groups that are admitted to partnership with the state. Are trade unions, for example, given the same privileged access as business or employers' representatives? If not, this may suggest that behind the corporatist state there *is* a ruling class of capitalists that holds the real power.

Corporatist accounts of the state help to explain how it can maintain social order in an unequal society — in other words, how the state solves the legitimation problem. To involve the main, and often opposed, interest groups in society in the process of policy formation ensures that both will ultimately accept state policy. On the other hand, the more interventionist a state becomes, the more it gets entangled in social conflict. Before the late 1950s the Irish state intervened in civil society in a quite limited way. In many spheres of life (education, the family, health care) it restricted its role to that of support for non-state institutions, in particular the churches, that claimed the main responsibility for organising affairs relevant to themselves. Indeed, Irish society in the 1930s and 1940s was marked by a strong resistance to state interference that emanated largely from the social teachings of the Catholic Church (Whyte, 1980). In recent decades the Irish state has, like most other Western states, become progressively more interventionist. It now seeks to undertake the leading role in modernising not only the economy, but other institutions, such as education and welfare, that can influence economic performance. Thus, it has become an increasing target for its citizens' demands and aspirations; it is expected not only to organise economic growth but also, for example, to prevent environmental pollution that results from industrial production. This widens the arena of conflict and makes corporatist strategies more difficult to maintain.

So far we have said nothing about Irish politics. Where do they fit into theories of state power? If we take the view that Irish society is ruled by a ruling class or power elite, party politics and electoral processes effectively become irrelevant. The only function of the political process is to provide an appearance of democratic control that masks where the real power resides. Even corporatist theories may support that conclusion. But in Irish politics there are some features that may help to explain how the society has developed in recent decades and why there has been little opposition to the form of that development. Political scientists have suggested that the structure of political parties in Ireland during this period has been unusual when seen from the perspective of core societies.

Parties have divided, not along a left/right axis like those in most European or Australasian countries, but around a nationalist cleavage inherited from the early years of the state's foundation (Garvin, 1998). Furthermore Irish parliamentary processes are thought to be particularly influenced by clientelist relationships between politicians and citizens where electoral support is traded for the real or apparent granting of favours or assistance by politicians (see Sacks (1976) for a classic analysis; Komito (1984) for an alternative view). Whether either of these features is peculiar to Irish politics, or is common to semi-peripheral societies, is open to debate, but both processes arguably help to prevent people from recognising or organising themselves in opposition to social inequality.

What remains is the power elite analysis, but this has been little researched in Ireland. On the basis of extant research, it is often claimed that the theory has little application. Peillon argues that there are few links between Irish social elites and thus it is not possible to see them as forming a single ruling group. He argues (1992, p.20) that:

> In the sense that the boundaries of each particular elite are clearly drawn . . . we observe little overlap in their membership and rather limited exchange between them. Higher civil servants rarely retire to high positions in the corporate private sector, and very few politicians transfer to the economic elite. In a similar way, owners or managers of large firms do not belong in a significant way to the political class.

One criterion for the existence of a power elite — overlapping career paths — seems to be absent. But Peillon does go on to warn that there may be other ways elites are interconnected. Members can 'develop close relations and even produce a high level of integration on a totally different basis: a similar background, school networks . . . close social interaction [and] a significant cultural closeness'. Without more research it is difficult to judge how much Irish elites share these characteristics: recent tribunal findings suggest, at least, close connections between elements of the political and business elites. For example, the Moriarty Tribunal, established in order to investigate payments made to politicians, found that payments received by the former Taoiseach Charles J. Haughey from wealthy benefactors during his political career devalued the quality of a modern democracy. The tribunal found that through the period 1979–1996, Mr Haughey lived a life and incurred expenses vastly beyond the scale of public-service entitlements. His income during this time was supplemented by clandestine donations, including funds intended for the medical expenses of his colleague in government, Brian Lenihan.

The power elite thesis is rich in the possibilities it brings to a discussion of power in Irish society. It focuses less on structures than on processes. The power elite is understood as a collective agent and what is of interest are the processes through which this agent assembles, manages and exercises power in particular situations. An implication of the ruling elite thesis is that we must look at the intelligentsia in Ireland as a powerful group. For Mills this sector played primarily a legitimating role within the power elite. Their job was to show that rule by the elite over the masses is right and natural. Is this how the Irish intelligentsia has acted?

Before we consider this question, we need to discuss one final perspective on the state. Much of our discussion has drawn upon the work of Michel Peillon and we should look more directly at how he approaches the question of state–society relations. This was first spelt out in his book *Contemporary Irish society: An introduction* (1982) and was revisited briefly in a more recent (1995) paper on interest groups and the state. Peillon regards the state as a social force, a collective actor, and one of a number that exert a significant influence on Irish society. Others include the business class, the Irish Farmers' Association, the Roman Catholic Church and to a lesser extent the Gaelic League. Social forces, Peillon says, have *projects* — collective understandings about the future state of affairs that they would like to see realised in society; and the state is no exception. Peillon argues that the state must be seen as an initiator of action in its own right, not merely a mouthpiece for another social force (as ruling class theory suggests), nor as a neutral arbiter between the projects of a number of other social forces (as in pluralist theory). While the state project reflects the power structure of Irish society and seeks to promote private enterprise development, it remains an autonomous project that is never identical with that of any other social force. Rather, it seeks to manage the others by integrating or discarding elements of them from time to time and by playing them off against one another when it suits (Peillon, 1995, p.362).

Peillon's approach is in many respects similar to a power elite theory. He too tries to construct a view of the state that emphasises process over structure; for him, the state is a type of actor, with its own goals, principles of action and orientations to the future. However, compared to power elite theory, Peillon's analysis remains abstract. We remain ignorant of who constructs the state's project and who are its main intellectual architects and maintenance workers. As we noted above, power elite theory sees this as an important task of the intelligentsia. These are the people who translate the sectional interests of other members of the elite coalition — the military or big business — into a project for society that appeals to and appears to embrace the interests of all the people. The role of the intelligentsia is to legitimate the elite's hold over power by providing it with ideas and concepts to help mobilise the support of the people it rules. We briefly consider some sociological work on the intelligentsia to conclude our current discussion.

THE INTELLIGENTSIA IN IRISH SOCIETY

Like most of the terms we have encountered in this chapter, the term 'intelligentsia' covers a complex reality. At its broadest it includes the increasing number of workers who create and communicate knowledge rather than material goods and resources and is often referred to as the 'knowledge class'. Here, however, we are using the term much more narrowly, to refer to those often called *intellectuals* (this distinction was first discussed in Chapter 2). Intellectuals are arguably a particularly important group in peripheral and dependently developing societies. Earlier we quoted Bauman's suggestion that in such societies modernity is taken on self-consciously by the state as a deliberate project. Intellectuals participate significantly in this process and contribute to the process of state-building that post-colonial countries like Ireland go through in the early decades of independence, as they try to transfer the allegiance of their populations to the new state institutions that replace those of the ousted colonial rulers.

O'Dowd (1996, p.19) summarises the work of intellectuals in such countries as including the:

- protection of national or religious identity
- modernisation of institutions and building of a 'welfare state'
- introduction of cosmopolitan thinking or the avant-garde into the national stasis.

We could see these three tasks not so much as things that all peripheral-society intellectuals do, but as three different roles or self-images adopted by groups of intellectuals in various periods. In that sense, they correspond rather well to some features of Irish intellectual life.

At the time of political independence the main intellectuals influencing Irish life came from the nationalist movement and the Roman Catholic Church (there was also a significant tradition of Anglo-Irish or Church of Ireland intellectuals, but their influence on society was limited and oppositional). In the following three decades or so, up to the 1950s, the values and goals of this group dominated Irish life: a vision of a social order organised around small to medium property (farms and manufacturing concerns), distinctively Irish in language and values, with a dominant voice for the church in education, health and welfare and a limited role for the state (O'Dowd, 1992).

From the late 1940s, however, a new intelligentsia was developing — senior civil servants, professional economists and other government advisors, journalists — who gradually replaced the established intellectual elite of nationalists and clerics. This 'modernising elite', as it saw itself, believed that the state could play a much greater role in achieving development and it gave significant support to the state when it adopted the strategy of industrialisation through foreign investment in the late 1950s. In turn, these intellectuals benefited from the expansion of state and semi-state activities that accompanied modernisation in the subsequent decades. A considerable proportion of the almost exclusively male (O'Connor, 1998, p.83) intellectual elite was to be found in some form of state employment: as university teachers, members of the judiciary or as managers and scientists in semi-state organisations like Bord na Móna and the Office of Public Works. With the advent of RTÉ in 1961 and the general expansion of media and cultural activities in the 1960s and beyond, the composition and orientation of the intellectual elite changed again. Encouraged by Ireland's membership of 'Europe', the focus of younger intellectuals and media personalities increasingly came to match the third task outlined above: to 'open up' the local society to cosmopolitan values and ideas. After the nation-building intellectuals and the modernising intellectuals came the globalising intellectuals.

Much of the power exercised by intellectuals and the respect they command derives from their claim that the knowledge they produce is 'free-floating', that is, unbiased by any particular social memberships (class, gender, local community, age group or generation) that the intellectual may have. Intellectuals, when speaking as such, claim to be able to transcend social positions, political affiliations and socialisation and produce ideas that are universal and timeless. Intellectuals present themselves as non-partisan and therefore take for granted that their efforts to shape state policy are made in the public interest and not in their own.

Much of the sociology of intellectuals has involved a critical investigation of this self-image. This has taken two main forms. The first argues that intellectuals come from a specific class position that shapes the ideas and knowledge they promulgate. International research suggests, for example, that intellectuals tend to be drawn overwhelmingly from middle- or upper middle-class families of the sort where education is highly valued and where there are plenty of resources available to obtain it. In Ireland, the picture appears a little different since both the strength of the Catholic and nationalist intelligentsia in the early years of the state and the expansion of technical and professionalised intelligentsia in more recent decades has meant that many Irish intellectuals came from a lower middle-class background. But the argument that their class background makes their world views less than 'universal' and non-partisan still stands.

A second sociological position argues that class of origin is less important in terms of explaining the particular values and orientations that intellectuals articulate than class of orientation — that is, the class they move into as adults or the class they would like to be part of and identify with in terms of culture and economic interests. The French sociologist Bourdieu (1984, p.176), on the basis of research into intellectual and academic life in France, argues that intellectuals should be seen as part of the bourgeoisie, the dominant class in capitalist society, albeit a rather 'dominated' part of that class. They may own little material capital but do possess 'cultural capital' and this encourages them to see their interests and those of the bourgeoisie as intertwined. This class position, in Bourdieu's view, profoundly shapes intellectuals' judgments about what is to be regarded as genuine intellectual activity; what political ideas, artistic products, and so on, should be given serious critical consideration and which should be simply ignored, ridiculed or marginalised.

Some sociologists suggest we need to distinguish between two sorts of intellectual:

- the thinker who finds him or herself at odds with society and who responds intellectually as social critic or alienated outsider
- the thinker who is firmly tied into the existing social order, credentialised by the formal education system, employed in an institution controlled or funded by the state, and certified and approved by a professional organisation to practice their skills.

The first is the more popular image of the intellectual and associates intellectual work with great writing or art; the second is more often simply called 'a professional'. In modern society the latter seems to predominate: the typical 'intellectual' now is a professionalised expert, trained to work with a specific and narrowly delimited body of knowledge but who claims to be able when required to rise above this narrow specialism and address issues to do with the well-being of society as a whole. Many Irish historians, psychologists and economists recognised as intellectuals or 'opinion-formers' would fit this second category. In Irish society we tend to accommodate both types of intellectuals, although the second category is probably in the ascendant. Commentators like John Waters in *The Irish Times* or Kevin Myers in the *Irish Independent* frequently adopt an oppositional or contrarian position on the key issues of the day. Waters, for example, has regularly taken issue with the feminist movement, which he holds responsible for the emasculation and marginalisation of men in Irish society. Myers has clashed frequently with those who take a nationalist or republican position on the North. On the other hand, there are now a number of 'professional' intellectuals who make a living from dispensing opinion through various media channels. Eddie Hobbs draws on his financial expertise to develop a critique of personal spending habits and David McWilliams has used a variety of platforms, including a regular newspaper column, a book and a TV series, to promulgate his views on the transformation of Irish society. His book, *The pope's children* (2005), offers a pseudo-sociological dissection of the new class system in Irish society. McWilliams celebrates what he sees as the new-found confident, sassy, go-getting middle class, whose identity is expressed primarily through what and how they consume. Of greater intellectual weight, psychologist Dr Maureen Gaffney, chair of the National Economic and Social Forum and involved in numerous public bodies, provides frequent media comment on lifestyle, gender and health issues, often from a social psychological perspective.

There is some basis for the claim by power elite theorists that intellectuals' main contribution to society is to legitimate the activities of those in power. A number of studies (for example, O'Dowd, 1996; Lynch, 1999b) suggest that Irish intellectual life has been characterised by a lack of significant criticism of or dissent from existing social arrangements. We can explain this by reference to the class background of Irish intellectuals or to their links with the modernising state, or both. But this is not a criticism that Irish sociologists can make of other Irish intellectuals without being willing to turn it on themselves. In Chapter 2 we suggested that Irish sociology has avoided an investigation of its biases, including its avoidance of the more critical traditions in the discipline, and has committed itself to a rhetoric of 'objective knowledge' and 'research expertise'. Sociology in Ireland is remarkable for the slight influence it has had on mainstream intellectual life in comparison with that of other academic disciplines or of artists and writers. But whatever influence it *has* achieved has failed to significantly expand the role of intellectual as alienated outsider or as protagonist of human emancipation.

SOME COMMENTS ON POWER

Finally we need to critique the idea of 'power' itself. Power has always been a central concept in sociology and many sociologists would say that theories of society stand or fall, ultimately, on the basis of how well or how interestingly they are able to deal with this phenomenon. An early but still influential discussion of power was that of Max Weber and we draw briefly again on his ideas to end this chapter.

In our discussion we have associated power with the capacity to initiate action. We suggested that the state can be considered the real power-holder only if it has the capacity to take autonomous action to modernise or develop Irish society. If the state cannot act autonomously in this way, then power may lie elsewhere, perhaps in a ruling class. But, for Weber, power is best defined by the *outcomes* of action rather than its initiation. The powerful person or group is the one who ultimately manages to get what he/she/they want, particularly in the face of opposition from others. This suggests that, in the end, to identify who really holds power we must discover who consistently and over a period of time achieves the outcomes they want and that benefit them most.

Once we have an idea of how to begin researching power, we can go on to ask other questions about it. A central question for Weber was: if an actor or group of actors tries to achieve their goals against resistance from others, what are the main 'resources of power' available to them? One is the capacity to exercise coercion: to force other people — by physical force if necessary — to do what you want. Weber saw that this capacity was such an important power resource that states always try to monopolise it. But coercion is not restricted to physical force; it is possible to speak of economic coercion, for example. If one group in society controls the means of livelihood and others are dependent on them for the necessities of life, then they possess an economic power resource. A key feature of a class-divided society, according to Weber, is that power is unequally distributed within it, largely for this reason.

Threats of violence and of economic damage are very effective ways to ensure compliance with one's wishes, but Weber suggested that ultimately they are rather unstable and easily open to challenge. A more effective method is to persuade people that they should obey you and that you have a right to command them and ensure your wishes take precedence; this, as we have seen, was Weber's problem of legitimation. We have devoted considerable space to discussing this and in particular how the state can enlist the services of the intelligentsia to represent its development projects as the legitimate way forward for the whole of Irish society.

Weber's discussion of power led him into a rich historical analysis of the different types of legitimation. We have no space to develop this here, but end this chapter simply by suggesting that the tension between coercion and legitimation to which Weber draws our attention is a core feature of all kinds of power, and a core management problem for all power-holders, whether agents of the state or groups in civil society. A significant feature of state power is that most of the time, in most societies, the state can take its legitimacy for granted; other groups and organisations have to achieve legitimacy to secure their power. Holding *legitimate* power is part of what it means to be a state. Legitimacy is such an important resource for the state because it must face deep and pervasive inequality in society. In Part II we look in more detail at the extent and types of inequality found in Irish society. However, first we examine issues of power and change within Irish society and how they operate outside the structures of the state, as we turn in the next chapter to a consideration of civil society and community.

5

Civil society: community and citizenship

We have examined the broad scale of Ireland's economic growth and the state's role in development and in maintaining social order. In recent years this type of *macrosocial* analysis has lost some of its appeal. Alexander (1998, p.6) notes a greater sociological interest in 'informal ties, intimate relationships, trust, cultural and symbolic processes, and institutions of public life'. This turn towards intimacy and the *microsocial* has stimulated an interest in the sociology of popular culture and everyday life, from Putnam's (2000) discussions of card-playing and ten-pin bowling, to emerging analyses of food, eating and drinking, clothes and fashion (see Chapter 13). The diffusion of the Internet, with its potential to bring new forms of expression and communication within everyone's reach, is also proving fertile ground for sociological researchers. Allied to this is a revival of interest in the idea of *civil society*.

Informal associations, trust and the institutions of public life are the stuff of civil society. For Alexander this is a sphere in society 'marked by civility, equality, criticism and respect'. In this chapter we discuss the concept of civil society and seek to connect it with Irish sociology's longstanding focus on *community*. Community researchers and civil society analysts share an interest in associational life in society, from informal relations of everyday civility to more formal movements and organisations outside the state. By locating research on community in Ireland within the context of civil society theory, we hope to find something more along the well-trodden community path.

Peripheral or late-developing societies are thought to be typified by a weak civil society: society is seen to be structured around the state, unable to organise itself independently (Peillon, 2001, p.171). In Chapter 4 we suggested that the state has indeed played an important role in shaping social change in Ireland, but this should not be taken to mean that associational life has been weak. The continuing strength of 'community' as a basis for mobilisation and voluntary action in Irish social life indicates the vitality of associational life. Here we ask whether community can be seen as the Irish way to achieve civil society, or whether it is in some respects a barrier to this process. Arguably, too strong a tradition of studying community has deterred Irish sociology from entering into broader debates about the nature of *citizenship* and how people may engage with political and public life.

CIVIL SOCIETY

Civil society is a concept with a long history in Western thought (Keane 1988, 1998; Seligman, 1992; Alexander, 1998). In the eighteenth century it referred to social institutions that fell 'between' the family (the sphere of private life or intimate relationships) and the state (formal public action). In particular it included voluntary associations and forms of collective co-operation, marked off from both state and family by virtue of their voluntary form of participative social engagement. Writers such as Locke, Rousseau and Hegel were interested in these associations as they provided a model of social order that was 'inner-determined and autonomous' (Seligman, 1992, p.16): it showed society acting for and by itself.

In the following century the idea came under powerful attack, particularly from Marx who argued that civil society, far from being an arena of co-operative, associative and democratic action, was simply another terrain within capitalist society on which the capitalist class could enact its dominance, under a veneer of civilised and philanthropic concerns. The Marxist critique had 'fateful effects' (Alexander, 1998): the concept of civil society came to be seen as a historical curiosity with little relevance to actual societies. It came to be superseded in the twentieth century by an interest in 'citizenship', understood as a set of rights held by individual citizens rather than an active engagement in civic life.

What is it about civil society that interests sociologists? What does the concept direct our attention to? It is not easy to grasp civil society: definitions abound, and boundaries are drawn in widely differing ways. Some include, while others exclude, the *economy* from civil life; most see a very clear division between civil society and the *state*, while others suggest the growth of state involvement in civil society makes such a division meaningless. Alexander (1998) suggests we use the term today to refer to a differentiated society that contains a rich variety of institutions and associations that belong neither to the state nor to the economy. Civil society theorists do tend to privilege citizen interaction over other spheres of social life, arguing that it is civil society that provides the fundamental guarantees of freedom in the modern world (Fine, 2000).

Those interested in civil society stress we must be careful not to idealise it. Where earlier philosophers used the concept normatively, to set forth their ideas on how a civilised and democratic society *should* be organised, the task of social science is to describe what public social life is actually like. Alexander (1998) and others (Tonkiss and Passey, 2000; Fine, 2000) seek to break away from 'utopianism' to examine how 'real civil societies' operate in different social, historical and cultural settings.

A major issue is that of violence in social life. Theorists such as Keane define civil society as the absence of violence or, more positively, see it as the sphere that allows people to engage in civilised conversation with those whose opinions and identities vary. Civil society is the realm where we respect difference and use rational argument to solve problems. Recourse to violence as a way of settling disputes signals the end of civil society and the emergence of 'uncivil' social relationships. Keane sees nationalism as one such uncivil force in society: excluding those outside the nation from participation in public life and ultimately treating them as less than civilised or less than human.

Others argue that in reality civil societies are always vulnerable to repression and violence from outside (by the state or the economy) or within (through social inequalities or the conflicting interests of individuals and groups). Alexander argues that contemporary societies provide civic spaces for solidarity among citizens, even while these very spaces can themselves be exclusionary: society is much more complex and conflictual than the idealised versions of civil society recognise. At the dawn of the twenty-first century, there is a widespread view that though the public sphere as a democratic domain may be more necessary than ever, it is increasingly difficult to locate. An essay in *The Economist* contends that the modern equivalent of the coffee house, wherein the seeds of civil society were sown in the seventeenth and eighteenth centuries, may be the Internet. The network is no longer solely the province of the military intelligence and computer boffins, but has grown to become 'a nexus of commercial, journalistic and political interchange' ('The Internet in a Cup', *The Economist*, 20 December 2003). Nevertheless it must also be acknowledged that the Internet is not a universally accessible medium, and that many of the uses to which it is put do not fall within the rather high-minded aspirations of those who would see it as a new digital public sphere. The task of the sociologist is to analyse the social conditions that enable or disable civil society in the control of tendencies towards violence, abuse and repression.

Sociability and democracy

Civil society theorists have been particularly concerned with the negative effects of power and hierarchy, seeing power as the opposite of individual autonomy and self-realisation. They have also focused on the trend towards social atomisation and the tendency in late modernity to deny collective identity and solidarity. Recent writings on civil society thus contain two key themes. One is an interest in the forms of relatively informal and intimate *sociability*. Sociability is seen as a valuable dimension of social life that protects against the anomie of excessive individualism. Analyses of sociability look for conditions that may help to prevent social atomisation; where everyday feelings of solidarity with others are fostered and a sense of belonging to a larger collectivity is created and sustained. Here, civil society is described as that realm of social experience where we learn to reconcile the conflicting demands of individual interest and the collective social good, where 'a certain kind of universalising community comes gradually to be defined, and to some degree enforced' (Alexander, 1998, p.7). This approach follows Durkheim (see Chapter 1) in its concern for the social formation of the individual; relations between the individual and society; how societies manage (or fail to manage) individual and collective difference; and the possibility of a social order organised around social solidarity rather than instrumental relations of power or money.

From within this approach to civil society has emerged an interest in the now widely-used concept of *social capital*. The best-known proponent of this term is Putnam in his influential work *Bowling alone* (2000). Putnam uses the term to try to capture the idea that social contacts and connections (such as recreational 10-pin bowling) 'add value' to society in many spheres, from economic productivity to better health (see Chapter 10). Social capital is indicated by networking in a society, where dense networks of reciprocal social relations mean high social capital, and by social norms of reciprocity and trust. A network can either be 'bonding' (oriented internally towards creating a tightly knit and exclusive social group) or 'bridging' (oriented outward to creating contacts and relationships with other networks). Each is an important source of social capital, despite the danger that the bonding form can have negative social effects.

Putnam is particularly interested in the links between social capital and social connectedness or what he often calls 'civic engagement'. People can be *machers* (formal association joiners and workers) or *schmoozers* (who like to spend a lot of time informally with friends and acquaintances). Both forms of social connectedness, Putnam argues, are important sources of social capital, and his argument is that contemporary American society is steadily losing both. Not only are political, religious, workplace and philanthropic forms of civic engagement declining, but people now increasingly go 'bowling alone' instead of in informal friendship teams.

We can see in Putnam's work an account of the collapse of American civil society, understood specifically as sociability or social connectedness. But while his analysis is often powerful, it is questionable whether the term 'social capital', with its instrumental and economic connotations, is a valid replacement for 'civil society'. For most civil society theorists sociability and solidarity are goods in their own right as expressions of civilisation. The renewed interest in civil society expresses a desire to avoid treating people as 'functions' in or resources for the benefit of a larger social system, but rather to see individuals as having autonomous value (Hess, 2000).

A second theme links civil society to *democracy*. Civil society is seen here as a diverse set of non-governmental organisations and institutions that can act to counterbalance the state and prevent it from dominating the rest of society. Here the most important characteristic of civil society is its public nature: it is in civil society that citizens engage in public debate and argument about issues of concern to them and where genuine 'public opinion' can be formed (Habermas, 1971). For Keane (1998, p.8) an essential ingredient is 'public suspicion of power' — a concern to hold those who wield power accountable to the citizenry and so ensure its responsible exercise. Keane argues that a strong, participatory civil society is essential to ensure the state continues to abide by democratic principles.

Theorists of civil society understand democracy in a rather specific way. A democratic society is not simply one where governments are subject to periodic elections, with competition between political parties and majority rule. Rather it is one that enables and facilitates public engagement of citizens in shaping their own society. Its defining characteristic is that it contains one or many 'public spheres' (Habermas, 1989) — occasions for citizens to come together as equals to exchange and debate opinions in an atmosphere oriented to reaching agreement and compromise. 'Public spheres' are created by the associational life of citizens and can be found in voluntary and professional organisations, in trade union meetings, in the mass media (for example, radio phone-ins, newspaper letters pages, blogs) and in social movements. Though created from the sociable life of citizens acting outside the state, they depend for their vitality and continuance on state support and guarantee. A state may, through its public order legislation, restrict the use of open spaces (parks, streets, public halls) by assemblies of citizens; it can enact legislation to recognise the rights of citizens to join together in trade unions; or can ensure the vitality of public broadcasting and media diversity.

In theory, at least, the two key themes about civil society are interconnected. Some level of sociability and solidarity among citizens, and a sense of a shared identity, seem to be an essential basis for the public, collective engagement that secures a democratic society. But in reality the connections are often less straightforward: solidarity among citizens may be highest where democracy is denied (as in many opposition movements). Indeed some argue that in Western societies the political trappings of democracy, and the institutionalisation of individual citizenship rights, have contributed to the decline of social solidarity and collective identity (the rise in public 'apathy' noted by many commentators).

Despite its difficulties, the concept of civil society allows sociologists to raise interesting questions about contemporary social life. These include questions about voluntary organisations, their persistence, and their impact on social solidarity; about social exclusion or inclusion; about citizenship and the meanings attached to this in different social settings; and about the practices and institutions that help us to enact citizenship as a public role. Current debate on the development of new media technologies overlaps strongly with questions being asked about the nature of community (Stevenson, 1999). The mass media is diversifying (for example into mobile phones, the Internet, 3G technology) just at the point when old communal relations are increasingly open to question. The question that is raised by Stevenson and others is whether new media technologies are responsible for undermining a sense of community by robbing people of participatory public spaces or whether they are the sites where more diversified relations of solidarity can be formed. It is difficult to answer this question. One set of theorists sees new electronic media as destroying communal forms of identification, promoting the progressive privatisation of everyday life and the commodification of public life. People are thus encouraged to be passive rather than active within civil society. On the other hand, it is argued that new technology opens possibilities for bringing in voices from the margins; that it helps to create new forms of social networks; that individuals are now empowered to choose their communities rather than to be passively assigned to them; and that the new means of communication can presage an era of new radicalism. According to Stevenson (1999), a genuinely sociologically informed account of the opportunities and dangers heralded by the development of new media technologies should seek to develop some of the more ambivalently conceived aspects of the relationship between media and society and move beyond this kind of binary thinking.

In this chapter, we raise some of these questions in the Irish context. How does 'real civil society' operate in Ireland? This question is difficult to answer as there has been little discussion of democracy, or even of citizenship, amongst Irish sociologists. There is, however, a great deal of work on sociability and association. Irish sociology has a long history of studying *community*. It is perhaps within the tradition of community studies that Irish sociology has best been able to raise questions about the relationship between the individual and society. How does a national concern about community and communality shape democratic action in Ireland? Does it contribute to, or does it discourage, the vigorous participation in public spheres and suspicion of unaccountable power? Has it shaped how 'citizenship' has been defined and actualised in Ireland? We look now at the Irish sociology of community in the light of such questions.

SOCIOLOGY AND COMMUNITY

While philosophers debated civil society, an interest in community was central to early sociology. As sociological thought developed, two sociological problems emerged, each carrying ideas about community. One was Durkheim's concern to foster 'moral individualism': a relationship between the individual and society that encourages individual autonomy but does not collapse into egocentrism as societies differentiate and become more complex. For Durkheim, the advancing division of labour had the potential to leave individuals without a sense of moral obligation to any social group or collectivity. Contemporary civil society theorists reflect this concern by regarding community as a collectivity that can provide a sense of shared identity and mutual dependence and a basis to act for the common good.

The second sociological problem was seen in Tönnies' concern that industrial-isation encouraged new types of social relationships that could suppress or even destroy human communality. In the pre-industrial world, Tönnies argued (2001[1887]) most of the relationships that engaged people were communal (*Gemeinschaftlich*): intimate, face-to-face, enduring and based on detailed knowledge of others, their biography and their place in local society. But the rise of industrial capitalism replaced these by associational (*Gesellschaftlich*) relationships: impersonal, contractual, calculative or instrumentally rational, based on limited or no knowledge of the personal circumstances of others but on formalised rules for associating with those with whom we may have only distant, partial or transient contact. We learn to know about others only what we need to know, so as to achieve our ends. This led Tönnies to ask if the development of industrial capitalist modernity should be thought of as 'progress' at all. Lee and Newby (1983, p.31) see Tönnies as a major contributor to 'an important tradition in sociology . . . founded in a critique of the dehumanising effects of industrial capitalism'.

Both Tönnies and Durkheim were responding to the profound social and cultural changes that result from industrialisation. But where Tönnies' ideas have underpinned a modernisation thesis that assumes the decline of community to be a key 'fact' about the modern world, Durkheim reminds us of the human *need* for community and its continual recreation in social life.

For Tönnies the concepts of *Gemeinschaft* and *Gesellschaft* did not identify particular social groups, but articulated how industrial society had altered social relationships and rendered them less personal and emotional — less human. But sociologists later took up his critique in ways that substantially changed it. First, they assimilated it into the armoury of modernisation theory to help detail the process — seen as positive — whereby 'traditional' societies give way to 'modern' ones. Second, they turned Tönnies' analysis of changing relationships across *time* into an analysis of contrasting relationships across *space*. *Gemeinschaft* or community became associated with rural space, while *Gesellschaft* (following Simmel, see Chapter 1) was linked with urbanity. Captured by an ideology that equated the city with the modern and progressive and relegated rural society to the backward and traditional, they took for granted that community was linked to 'the rural way of life' while urban living meant a loss of community.

Community became a popular but increasingly confused sociological concept. In the mid-1950s an American sociologist (Hillery, 1955) set out to examine how his colleagues had defined and used the concept. He counted over ninety definitions and concluded, tongue-in-cheek, that the only common element was that they were all 'about people'. The term causes confusion as it is commonly used to refer both to *place* (as in 'the local community') and to *a type of relationship* (some prefer to call this 'communality', or even 'communion'). Often we use community to refer to a particular geographical location, as in 'the Tallaght community' or 'the Gaeltacht community west of Galway'. It would make little difference if we were to substitute 'population' or 'people' for 'community' in such phrases: 'community' here refers to those who live within a territory whose boundaries have been established according to the administrative systems of the state (for example a townland or a Gaeltacht area) or the church (a parish).

But community implies that social as well as spatial features hold people together, that those in a community know each other and share a sense of being part of a defined social group. (Of course, this may not be true.) Here 'community as place' shades into 'community as relationship': we assume that what moulds an aggregate of individuals into a community is a special sense of identity, a 'communality' of spirit that derives from shared interests and position in society. Indeed this consensus may be so significant that we can talk of 'the community' itself as an entity over and above its members, with its own opinions, history and needs.

It is also possible to talk of a community in a social sense without tying it to any location. People may have feelings of shared identity as members of a community that has no common geographical base, such as professional and occupational groupings (the academic community, the business community), religious denominations (the Muslim community) or groups who share a common lifestyle interest (the arts community; Internet communities). This helps to make community a complex and confusing concept, in both sociological theory and everyday usage.

Community refers to relationships between people that are both informal and multidimensional. Such relationships depend on people having considerable knowledge about others' lives. Conversely relationships 'outside the community' are seen as impersonal, formal, specific in their goals and lacking in emotional content — in Parsons' terms 'instrumental' rather than 'affective'. State institutions may be the most extreme example of 'formal organisation' or 'association': they operate not on shared meanings and values but on clear and explicit rules and principles, codified into laws and regulations. Thus the social relationships that produce feelings of shared identity and group belonging are said to be found at the level of community, but not in relationships with more formal, rationalised institutions. In Ireland, where historically 'the nation' or national community was created before and eventually found expression in 'the state', such a distinction may be exaggerated. Irish society is still shaped by the lingering effects of the collective nationalist project to achieve the common good.

The eclipse of community and the rise of 'individualisation'

Many sociological accounts of community are tinged with nostalgia, a sense that the world of communities is past. The critiques of modern urbanism and industrialisation by writers such as Tönnies and Simmel gave rise to an enduring tradition of sociological thought that superimposed a series of binary oppositions on social development. Thus modernity was opposed to tradition; large-scale to small-scale; impersonal to intimate; and city anonymity to rural community. Within this conceptual framework, the development of modernity inevitably meant the loss or 'eclipse' of community.

The 'eclipse of community thesis' (Stein, 1964) combines a number of ideas that need to be examined separately. The *eclipse of locality* argument suggests that attachment to local place, and its significance for one's social identity, declines in modern society. Modern social identities are now constructed from universal categories such as gender, occupation, profession or social class. But this assumption has been strongly challenged within sociology. For dependency and globalisation theories economic development *heightens* differences across societies and increasingly differentiates regions and localities, depending on how they are incorporated into the international division of labour. Spatial change in Ireland seems to support this argument: rather than an even 'urbanisation' of the country, there has been increasing polarisation between east and west (Commins, 1996) and between areas specialising in large-scale commercial farming and those where agriculture has declined and been replaced by industrial and service-sector employment. Territorial boundaries may be redrawn in the process of development, but do not necessarily disappear (Tovey, 1985); people continue to see their own locality as a basis for collective identification, even collective action. 'Glocalisation' is a term commonly used to emphasise how globalisation processes give new importance to the local.

Sometimes when people talk of the eclipse of locality they mean that in the contemporary world local societies can no longer be regarded as self-contained or isolated. We may think of the past as a time when most of people's interactions were with their kin and neighbours, in a circumscribed space. Lives were conducted within the overlapping social boundaries of the local parish, the catchment area for the local school and shops and the local labour market (see, for example, Leyden, 2002). This may not be universally true: while in some previous historical periods people did live in fairly immobile societies, there have been many societies long characterised by large-scale movement of populations, whether as individual migrants or as displaced groups. But it is true that our daily lives are now conducted across a greatly enlarged space, made possible by continual developments in the technology of transport and communications, from the telephone to cheap air travel.

But this differs by class position and income level. In rural, urban and suburban settings, the lives of people from working-class or low income backgrounds still tend to be conducted within quite constrained spatial boundaries, while it is primarily the middle class and affluent who are able to escape from the constraints of locality when they wish (Bartley, 1999, pp.242–3). Bauman (2001, p.58) remarks that 'the successful . . . do not need community'. In some senses, then, 'community' may be experienced by some social groups in Ireland more than others and the eclipse of locality thesis may not apply equally to different social groups. Recent research, for example, has found that a sense of attachment to locality is significant in shaping people's sense of belonging and sense of community in four suburban localities in the Dublin hinterland (Corcoran *et al.*, 2007). Despite the speed-up and changes that have taken place in everyday life in Ireland, people still seek an attachment to the local and, to varying degrees, find solace in such an attachment. But while ideas about place based on a pastoral ideology provide some inducement to prospective suburbanites, they also take much more pragmatic considerations into account. The literature suggests that a combination of aesthetic and functional factors inform the suburban imaginary. Hummon (1992) identifies three sets of imagery volunteered by suburbanites that are salient to a suburban ideology:

- suburbs are 'clean, quiet, natural' places with an easy-going ambience; while they may not be country, they provide readier access to nature than the city
- suburbs are places of domesticity where the focus is on home, family life and children; they offer the best of both worlds for children in terms of freedom and security
- suburbs differ from cities in that they are safe; this safety enables other values such as sociability and family makes good child-rearing practices possible.

Corcoran *et al.* (2007) found that this ideology is extremely pertinent to how many Irish suburbanites think about and interpret suburban living. But it is tempered by very pragmatic considerations to do with flexibility and convenience. Furthermore, the balance between the pull of the pastoral and the promise of convenience manifests itself differently in the four different suburbs.

A second aspect of the eclipse of community thesis relates to the *eclipse of local autonomy*. Stein (1964) coined the phrase 'eclipse of community' to express concern with the spatial distribution of *power*. He argued that throughout the previous century local autonomy enjoyed by small American communities had steadily declined, resulting in a concentration of power in the state and the federal 'centre'. Such centralisation was a result of urbanisation, industrialisation and bureaucratisation, which had combined to reduce the capacity of local decision-making institutions such as local government, local education committees and health boards and local parish organisations, to determine their own affairs.

A third dimension of the eclipse of community thesis could be called *eclipse of communality*. It is argued that modern individuals find it hard to establish authentic relationships with others, or to develop a secure sense of identity, to a degree not found in pre-modern societies. Those aspects of personal identity that used to be pre-ordained by membership of social groups and institutions are now increasingly open to individual choice. We may now choose our religion, nationality, family membership, even (still with some difficulty) our gender. As such identities can increasingly be selected, constructed and manipulated, it seems less easy to accept them as being authentic. Turkle (1999), for example, has argued that the Internet allows for a more flexible self to engage in identity play by cycling through cyberspace. Wellman and Hampton (1999) propose the idea of a networked society, where online interactions provide people with a means of living simultaneously online and offline, allowing them to move between virtual and face-to-face communities.

For Beck and Beck-Gernsheim (2002) the key experience of individuals in late modernity is *individualisation*. Whether we like it or not, contemporary institutions impose on people the obligation to live as individuals and to construct their own 'do-it-yourself' biography: 'we live in an age in which the social order of the national state, class, ethnicity and the traditional family is in decline. The ethic of individual self-fulfilment and achievement is the most powerful current in modern society' (2002, p.22). Categories of collective identity, including community, have become 'zombie categories, which have died yet live on' (2002, p.27). Those charged with managing society continue to talk *as if* people can be assigned to collective groups and identities, but the experience of people themselves is that their identity is not assigned but self-created. This raises very difficult questions about the possibility of continuing social integration, even of 'society' itself as a meaningful term.

The 'eclipse of community' thesis, in its different forms, has shown remarkable staying power in sociology — Putnam's work is a modern version of it. But in much contemporary sociology it is being replaced by concern about and a search for shared, communal identity in modern society: what we might call the *quest for community*. To a large extent this has been due to the political and philosophical movement known as *communitarianism* (Crow and Allen, 1994). This movement has significantly rekindled interest in community among social scientists and political theorists. It favours attempts to build communities as a solution to the problems of modern life, whether at the local level, across national borders (for example, through the EU), or as expressed in the UN's 'Local Agenda 21'. Communitarianism argues that the good society is one that 'nourishes both social virtues and individual rights'; that achieves 'a carefully crafted equilibrium' between social order and individual autonomy (Etzioni, 1997, pp.4–5).

Communitarians call for the rebuilding of collective solidarities, or 'inclusive communities' (Tam, 1998), centred on the citizen and organised so as to enable universal participation. They emphasise that they are not trying to go back towards some idealised pre-industrial community, but to develop new ways to organise social, economic and political life. They see similarities between their movement and the nineteenth-century co-operative movement (which in Ireland led to the establishment of co-operative creameries and other food-processing organisations and to the Credit Unions). They believe that 'co-operative communities' which respect and care for all their members are necessary for social well-being and that social and political progress depends on finding 'a third way' between right and left, or between individualism and authoritarianism.

Communitarians are particularly concerned by the growth of individualism, as outlined above. They fear that 'the individual is the citizen's worst enemy and . . . individualisation spells trouble for citizenship and citizenship-based politics' (Bauman, 2002, p.xviii). Rebuilding communities is a way to 'provide the social bonds that sustain the moral voice, but at the same time avoid tight networks that suppress pluralism and dissent' (Etzioni, 1995, p.122), thus reconciling individual freedom and collective solidarity. But civil society theorists tend to be unconvinced. Communitarianism, in their view, remains normative and prescriptive, rather than attempting to analyse 'real' civil societies. It is seen as a 'radical' movement that is in reality conservative, emphasising the obligations of the individual to the community at the expense of the rights of the individual against community controls.

Communitarians are also criticised for complacency about communal social relations, failing to recognise their capacity for intolerance or repression. Sennett (1977, p.310) argues that attempts to establish 'real communities' are 'a tyranny of intimacy' that converts 'claustrophobia into an ethical principle'. For feminist theorist Iris Marion Young (1990, p.300) communitarianism favours 'unity over difference, immediacy over mediation, sympathy over recognition of the limits of one's understanding of others from their point of view'. It ignores how communities can make illegitimate moral claims on their members. Many find the 'paradigm communities' that communitarians invoke — family, neighbourhood, nation — troubling in this respect. Such communities can never be genuinely inclusive: their identity always *depends* on the exclusion of some people, since 'any definition of what members have in common necessarily implies some form of closure against "outsiders"' (Day, 1998, p.235). Young advocates 'a politics of difference' not a politics of community; one that recognises the extent of heterogeneity and particularity of individuals that can never be exhausted by collective categorisation.

As Curtin (1996, pp.249–50) reminds us, community is a perennially ambiguous concept:

> in the left-populist perspective, community is best understood as expanding participatory democracy, providing for more direct forms of government, decentralised decision-making and even political and economic equality . . . [but] community . . . is also much in favour with the conservative political tradition. Here, however, the emphasis is on the notion of community as common good, on public-spirited individuals with respect for the rights of others, on authority and order and on reducing civil society's dependence on the state. . . . Community is a symbolic construct capable of invoking for all its supporters the positive notion of communality and sharing, but also presenting the possibility of being subjected, in each case, to particular meanings.

Given this ambiguity, it is not surprising that civil society theorists also experience difficulties with the concept. For them, the problem with community is not that it is a 'zombie category', but rather that it may be too much alive. Civil society, they argue, rests on communal solidarities, but these can also lead to exclusionary attitudes to those outside the community. When communal solidarity is strong, it may suppress individual autonomy and democratic dissent. Communal solidarity needs to be counter-balanced in civil society by a well-established public sphere, where people can recognise themselves as *citizens*, not just as members of a particular community. We return to this important issue after a brief discussion of community and its analysis in Ireland.

COMMUNITY IN IRISH SOCIOLOGY

Community is a popular word in Ireland. We like to think our society is made up of communities and permeated by a spirit of community. Public discussions assume that communities are good and desirable forms of social organisation. Those without a community are said to lead impoverished lives or are believed to be unstable and unreliable members of society. Leaders of church and state favour community responses to social problems like poverty, unemployment and crime. Local residents combine to defend the interests of their community against outsiders, whether property developers, road engineers or Travellers. Health professionals, media personalities and educators claim to serve the community. Young people all over Ireland engage in intense virtual interactions via Bebo communities, while (considerably fewer) older people immerse themselves in virtual worlds such as Second Life. Our communality is part of our image of Irishness, reflected in literature, media and politics. So we would expect community to be a core concept in Irish sociology.

If Irish society is often represented as a society of communities, British society has long understood itself as a *class* society. This does not mean, of course, that either representation is necessarily true: class divisions are as significant in Irish society as they are across Europe (see Chapter 7). But community studies have played an important part in Irish sociology as well as in the collective self-representation of Irish society.

Community studies in Ireland

There is a long tradition of ethnographic research on communities in Ireland (Bell, 1982). Such studies include Arensberg and Kimball (2001 [1940]); Humphreys (1966); Cresswell (1969); Messenger (1969); Symes (1972); Leyton (1975); Fox (1978); Sacks (1976); Scheper-Hughes (1979); Harris (1984); Brody (1986); Curtin and Varley (1986); Eipper (1986); Peace (1986, 2001); Tucker

(1987); Curtin (1988); Ruane (1989); Silverman (1993) and Shutes (1991). In this chapter we focus on only a small number of these. Much of this research has focused on rural areas, 'perhaps unduly concentrated on peripheral and island communities in the West of Ireland' (Curtin, 1996, p.252). Some newer studies have redressed this imbalance somewhat. See for example, Humphreys' (2007) work on urban and small-town neighbourhoods in Munster and Corcoran *et al.*'s (2007) work on suburban localities in and around Dublin.

The best-known, indeed the archetypal, account of 'the Irish community', was by American anthropologists Arensberg and Kimball who, over a period of two years in the early 1930s, lived in (though not at the same time) and studied a rural area in Co. Clare. Their work gave rise to a number of publications, amongst them the celebrated *Family and community in Ireland*, originally published in 1940. A third edition, with an informative introduction by editors Byrne *et al.* of NUI Galway, was published in 2001.

The study area was quite remote — a good distance, in those car-less days, from the market town of Ennistymon — and was inhabited predominantly by small farmers. Arensberg and Kimball's description of small farming in the locality emphasised its familial nature. They showed how the fortunes of the farm enterprise were entwined with the survival of the family on the land and how the relationships of family members were also those of boss and workers within an enterprise. They emphasised how this type of farming gave rise to, and relied upon, particular sorts of local relationships outside the immediate family. Individual farm households, which independently met their own needs by working their privately-owned land, were drawn into relationships at the local level through two community institutions: *kinship* (many households in the area were related by marriage) and the practice known as *cooring* (the exchange of labour between households, either routinely or at particular points of the year such as haymaking when labour needs were high).

According to Arensberg and Kimball these institutions reflected the strong value that the local culture placed on the obligations of neighbourliness. They also helped to ensure a level of equality between the farm households in the local area and prevented any from falling into severe poverty or debt, or indeed from becoming particularly wealthy. For Arensberg and Kimball Irish rural life in 1930s was strongly shaped by the local community and the feelings of mutual identification, mutual dependence and collective solidarity to which it gave rise.

The gaze of the young American researchers on the community they studied was quite austere, yet they were able to find not only collective solidarity but also some spontaneous sociability. Soon after arrival they remarked (2001 [1940], p.173) how 'night after night, the day's work done, [our] new acquaintances, at least the males among them, walked out upon the roads to this house and that in search of recreation and companionship'. At first unable to interpret this behaviour, they later came to see that these visitings were structured by gender and age. Women were largely confined to the area around the home and had little opportunity for everyday sociability with others outside the family. Men found their friends mainly among their kin, and even here the dominant impression is of relationships that were work-oriented and serious. The old men's 'cuaird', which gathered to smoke, drink tea, tell stories and debate the issues of the day, saw itself as responsible for the well-being and order of the community. But among the young men, free of responsibility for farm and family, high spirits and playfulness could find expression. As one older man said: 'it wouldn't suit [for the young men to come to the old men's gathering]. They gather in at Jack Roche's and they laugh and joke and play cards. They talk about the next gamble and the next dance, and that is all they know. It is a lot of codology' (pp.173–4). Arensberg and Kimball decided that recreational patterns reflected and consolidated a man's status within the community: the old men of property and experience; the young waiting to attain this position at some future point; and 'Oscair's clique' — those who fitted in neither of the other groups and who held no clearly defined status within the community.

Arensberg and Kimball's methodology and conclusions have, over the years, been heavily critiqued (see Gibbon, 1973). They have been condemned for failing to anticipate how quickly Irish rural life would change as the twentieth century wore on. But the editors of the 2001 edition suggest rather that the work points to 'the developing crisis of modernity' (Byrne et al. 2001, p.lxxxi). In the society they studied, individuals were still:

> bound into their family and local settings. Personal preference [was] a secondary question in comparison with the well-being of the people among whom one lives. But . . . by the end of the century in which they wrote, Irish people had come to have a much stronger sense of their individual rights to make decisions affecting their own lives — but within a socio-economic setting often experienced as immune to control.

Arensberg and Kimball bequeathed a potent image of the 'typical rural Irish community' to later Irish sociologists. Three features had particular force. First, they refer often to the isolation, remoteness and self-containment of the local area, reinforcing the idea that its people constituted a naturally distinct and boundaried local society. Local households are shown as economically isolated from the rest of Ireland as, even though they were part of a country-wide system of cattle production, much of their farming was to meet their own consumption needs. The people are also depicted as culturally distinctive from those living in the more anglicised eastern counties.

Second, the account tends to emphasise the similarities between households and local residents much more than the differences between them. For example, there are few non-farming households in the locality; and there is no big variation in the size of local farms. Though there were both big and small farmers in Ireland at the time, Arensberg and Kimball suggest that each tended to be found in different localities, and thus in different communities.

Third, in a local economy of this sort there are obviously many occasions for conflict, such as between father/farm boss and sons/farm labourers, between family members around inheritance, or between households over ownership of land, but the strongest impression in the study is of agreement and harmony. This image of the rural community, self-contained and separate from 'society in general', homogeneous, bound together by local institutions and characterised by co-operation and consensus, still dominates contemporary community discourse in Ireland. It permeates public belief about what Irish society was like in the past and what, ideally, it should be like today.

Curtin (1988, p.77) has argued that Arensberg and Kimball did not entirely ignore conflict but for 'theoretical and methodological reasons' were more interested in exploring social harmony, stability and integration. The problem was in how their research was taken up by others: 'for long, the generally uncritical acceptance of their account . . . discouraged the discovery and analysis of conflicts of interests as normal social structural features of rural communities'. Subsequent sociological and anthropological study of Irish communities has tended to ignore conflict and the management of difference between community members. Explanations for the maintenance of social order have, in their appeal to qualities of 'nativism' and 'primitivism', tended to produce a rather misleading image of social harmony. Similarly much attention has been focused on the role of the Catholic Church. This has led researchers to exaggerate the Catholic moral virtues embodied in the Irish family and community. Where local disputes have been studied (Leyton, 1966; Messenger, 1969) they have generally been treated 'as events almost separate from the general pattern of social relationships' or 'dysfunctional elements of a taken-for-granted social order' (Curtin, 1988, p.78).

A potential source of dissimilarity, difference and conflict within communities is that of *gender*. Arensberg and Kimball largely sidestep this phenomenon: while recognising the very different lives led by women and men in rural Ireland, they treat gender roles as complementary and mutually reinforcing. Brody, in a study of a western small-farm area carried out in the late 1960s, depicted men and women as living in virtually separate communities, so different were their life experiences, identities and aspirations. According to Brody, the local institutions at the core of rural social life in the late 1960s were the shop and the pub. Those whose social life revolved around the shop were the most marginal to the 'traditional' community: young single women expecting to emigrate, and older married women who, despite active involvement in farm work, were not regarded as having any particular farming skills or knowledge. The pub was frequented by men identified with the agricultural life of the area: older farm owners and some younger expectant heirs. Thus: 'the one place outside the home which people regularly visit thus identifies their relationship to the community' (Brody, 1986, p.164).

Indeed, for young men to visit the shop rather than the pub was an indication that they were seeking an identity outside the local farming community and were highly likely to emigrate in the near future. While the shop was a centre for sociability, the pub, as Brody describes it, was silent and repressed, particularly during the winter months.

For Brody rural Ireland had undergone a process of urbanisation since Arensberg and Kimball's visit. Younger rural people had adopted an urban view that saw little to value or conserve in rural life. Those left behind in rural areas had become profoundly demoralised. Brody, like many earlier sociologists, linked urbanisation to a weakening in the bonds of community. He noted the decline of co-operation or *cooring* in farmwork; the growing isolation of local households from each other; individualism among the young; emergence of social inequality symbolised by the 'gombeen' household; and an increasing emphasis on self and self-realisation against the claims of community membership. For Brody modern life or 'urban capitalism' tolled the death-knell of community. This image resonates in Curtin's (1988, pp.82–3) vivid description of an atomised rural life pervaded by an absence of community:

> households in the villages are intensely private and neighbours seldom visit. On a journey through the area on a winter's night, one sees each house distinguished by the flashing television screen. On entering a house, one finds individuals or families alone. Indeed people are unsure how to handle the unexpected visitor. 'Pure' social calls have little meaning and one is expected to state one's business at the door. People do not like to be caught unaware by a caller and indeed callers seldom catch occupiers unaware. In many houses, the front door is rarely used, which means that one has to go round the house. Barking dogs give advance warning and delay the visitor. On reaching the back door, the impression is of an intensely private order being invaded.

Peace's (2001) community study *A world of fine difference* offers a very different picture of contemporary rural life. Set in 'Inveresk', a mixed fishing, farming and small business locality in the south-west, its interest is in how 'a small Irish community maintains its sense of social distinction, notwithstanding the comprehensive process of modernisation to which it has been subject in the late twentieth century' (2001, p.1). Despite being economically and socially transformed over the previous thirty years, Inveresk retains 'a strong, indeed pervasive, sense of its own distinct identity, of being a special place in the world'. It is actually a diverse place of different occupational groups and spatial domains. Local inhabitants are keenly aware of this diversity: they respect and wish to maintain it and fear pressure from outside to homogenise their local society.

Peace is interested in how Inveresk people can both express local diversity and celebrate a distinctive common identity. He identifies a 'politics of identity' that is performed on different local occasions, sometimes emphasising difference, sometimes collective identity. He describes (2001, pp.104–5) the hilarious annual local concert as 'a collective representation of the community by the community for its own appreciation . . . one of the few occasions each year in which, through the efficient mobilisation of its own resources, the community consciously and conspicuously rises above the differences and the divisions which run through it'. It is a night when 'the sense of collective distinction is shared and savoured by those to whom it is supremely important'.

Peace does not wish to generalise from his local study, as he sees Ireland 'as a richly diverse and heterogeneous economic and political landscape, a multiplicity of spaces and places in which the proliferation of cultural difference is the order of the day' (2001, p.7). But his reworking of 'community' adds considerably to our understanding of its meaning and its expression. Community, he argues, is not a given; rather it is performed by the locals involved, on particular occasions and through particular relationships. This performance is not simply an acting-out of cultural roles: the actors concerned are self-conscious, self-critical, attending to what they are doing and its effects on their audiences. Much of the performance of community in Inveresk occurs through conversation, slagging and *craic*. This picture of how 'community' is reproduced differs greatly from that suggested by Brody or Arensberg and Kimball.

Why should Inveresk people wish to perform or constitute their community? Peace suggests this may be an exercise of local control, a response to feelings of powerlessness and alienation from wider Irish political structures. Those in Inveresk are aware that regional politicians accord them little importance, even while trying to build up clientelist relations (see Chapter 4). For them power is concentrated in Dublin and exercised on behalf of the wealthy and powerful. Inveresk people create a local communal world where they themselves can be powerful as a response to the centralisation of power in the wider society. Here centralisation of power does not inevitably lead to Stein's 'decline of community'. Peace's account of Irish rural modernity is not one of a 'crisis' of (impotent) individualism, as in Byrne *et al.*'s reading of Arensberg and Kimball, but rather one of collective, if circumscribed, empowerment.

Similarly, Corcoran *et al.*'s (2007) investigation of four suburban localities presents a picture that is much less bleak than that of the popular imagination. Generally speaking, respondents 'electively belonged' to their communities: they felt attached to the place where they lived. People still saw the suburbs as good places to raise children. They derived sustenance from close relations with others, particularly those who were at similar stages of family formation. The research also suggests relatively modest but not negligible levels of social and civic participation. In all these respects, local residents are socially embedded in their respective localities. Such a conclusion goes against the dominant perception of suburbs.

While the findings from the four suburban locations did not register a fundamentally deficient social fabric, nonetheless the very intensity of suburban development creates its own difficulties. The built and natural environment, which acts as an important signifier of place, may be obliterated by development that proceeds unabated and attachment to place may be undermined. The family-friendliness of suburbs appears to be linked to a pattern of demographic homogeneity that marginalises those at different family stages, while reinforcing traditional gender roles. Furthermore, such suburbs face immediate and pressing problems that have a negative effect on the quality of life. Local residents clearly identified the main problems they faced in the locality: these related mainly to the unregulated nature of development; the lack of a range of basic amenities; the school situation; and heavy traffic on inadequate roads. Although many residents stated that they had done something to address these problems, they were also aware of the ineffectiveness of their action. Local residents in the suburbs found it difficult to deal collectively with the many problems they faced. The lack of institutions of local government at neighbourhood level meant that they were struggling in their efforts to manage their own local affairs. Local residents encountered an institutional void, which they found difficult to overcome despite their best efforts (Peillon et al., 2006). So while there are many ties that bind in suburbia, those ties are in danger of being eroded by the intensification of development and its attendant problems on the one hand, and the absence of locally embedded institutional structures for responding to community needs on the other.

Community and Irish civil society

Irish community studies suggest that local solidarity and shared collective identity based on locality have a long and dynamic history. As Peace in particular describes it, community is constructed by local people as a framework within which a vibrant, autonomous, self-empowering social life can be played out. Clearly in this respect, community is and remains an important dimension of civil society in Ireland.

But civil society theorists occupy a complex, even contradictory, position in regard to community. They look to the collective solidarity offered by community as a basic guarantee for democracy in late modern societies; but they find it difficult to reconcile sociability and solidarity on the one hand with individual autonomy on the other. They fear that (in Putman's term) 'bonding' forms of community cannot recognise and address the value of individual difference, whether within the bonded community or outside it. One way they try to reconcile community, democracy and individual autonomy is to make a distinction between the 'modern' or civil form of community and the 'traditional'. The former contains 'a community of actors whose patterns of association are voluntary', hence they can 'reinterpret and . . . transform the social and political structures with which they interact'. In the 'traditional' type of community 'belonging is involuntary, government is instinctive, and laws tend to be unchangeable' (Keane, 1998, p.31). Irish evidence suggests this distinction is greatly exaggerated. It challenges the assumption that we can easily differentiate between 'voluntary' and 'involuntary' forms of association, particularly at the local level. It does not show that only 'voluntary' forms of association can be reflexive or transformative.

Alexander deals with the issue rather differently. He suggests that communities are 'uncivil' when they encourage *particularistic* attachments to social group, neighbourhood or place: for him 'civil' community is based on trust in *universalising* values, without exclusionary boundaries. It expresses solidarity with all other humans, even if they are strangers — or in some cases, perhaps, with all sentient species. Some writers argue that civil society is today becoming detached from particular localities or states and that a 'global' civil society may be slowly, if spasmodically, emerging, for example in the development of a global environmental movement (Wapner, 1996).

We might question whether the idea of a universal collective identity is plausible. Community studies suggest that collective solidarity depends on particularisms and on the perceived distinctiveness of a specific social group or way of life as compared with others. Particularistic communities have a place in civil society, but must be able to co-exist with other forms of civil life, in voluntary associations, friendship networks, trade unions, social movements and so on . We return to this issue below, but first we discuss contemporary uses of 'community' by the Irish state and its agencies: do they see community as just a 'zombie category'?

Community as rhetoric and as ideology

For Peace the vocabulary of community is owned and shared by the everyday local actors of Inveresk. Other sociologists have been less sanguine: they argue that the discourse of community in Ireland has been produced, used and appealed to by specific social actors, usually those with social and economic power. Community has indeed been 'eclipsed' but, they suggest, a *rhetoric of community* is alive and well and is persistently and frequently reproduced in public debates and discussions. It persists because it is useful to powerful groups in Irish society, including the state and its agents. Evocations of community, and of what 'the community' wants and needs, are an effective way to legitimise the actions of those in power and to minimise challenges from those who may be disadvantaged.

Harris's (1984) anthropological study of industrial development in North Mayo reflects this approach. The development was a product of globalisation and the new international division of labour: with IDA support two TNC branch plants located in the area and soon came to dominate the local economy in terms of jobs. This brought about some important changes in the local society, not least a large growth in the number of women working outside the home, as the factories mainly sought female workers. In addition the development benefited some locals more than others: it brought most benefits to those who were property-owners or entrepreneurs who could sell land or other commodities to the new factories or could profit from the increased spending power in the area.

Harris argues that the coming of transnational capital to Ireland severely challenges a view of Irish nationhood that sees a self-contained economy as an essential element of the nation. Economic globalisation fractures the unity of the national economy: local areas may become more oriented to the global horizon of the TNC than to other localities within Ireland. As the reality of 'the nation' becomes ephemeral, and change becomes ubiquitous, it becomes necessary to find an alternative source of collective identity. 'Community' provides such an alternative.

It is within this context that Harris explains the uses of community in North Mayo. The management of the new firms, the state (via the IDA) and members of the local bourgeoisie represented the industrialisation process to local people as a way to help the whole local community. Harris argues that this strategy to create a local consensus around economic development does not equally favour everyone in the community; indeed when overt conflict arose, local leaders responded by redefining the boundaries of the community. When fitters in one of the factories took unofficial strike action in pursuit of union recognition, the firm threatened to withdraw its operations from Ireland. This led the local Community Council to intervene and demand that the men should go back to work or leave the area. According to Harris (1984, p.163):

> 'troublemakers working against the interests of the community' were not welcome. The fitters, who might well be seen as part of the local 'community' by virtue of their residence in the town, were thus defined out of the community until such time as they submitted to the local consensus.

O'Carroll (1985, p.147) suggests that organisations such as Community Councils, who claim to 'represent the community' are, in effect, a local extension of the state. When people claim to be community leaders, this encourages others to think that behind them there is 'a solidly united community with whom they have close ties, share a common value system and over whom they can exercise authority'. For O'Carroll, that type of community no longer exists. In reality most community or voluntary organisations are set up with the encouragement of, or at the instigation of, the state; those who emerge as 'community leaders' at the head of such organisations are as likely to owe their position to the operations of the state as to any sort of community franchise.

Irish state and other agencies most commonly use the term community in connection with aspects of service-delivery: for example in the areas of welfare, health, education, or development. Community services are generally not *organised by* the local community on the basis of a diagnosis of its own needs; but are nearly always services delivered to residents in a locality. Community policing is a case in point; it refers not to policing by the community of itself, but to policing by the state, delivered to those living in a particular area with the co-operation of local organisations such as residents' associations. Indeed if a community does attempt to police itself, this is defined as 'vigilantism' and is condemned.

The use of 'community', for O'Carroll, is no more than a rhetorical flourish: it obscures the fact that the state does no more than deliver services to the Irish population on a *territorial* basis — by locality, rather than by gender, class or age. Its primary purpose is to confer legitimacy on state activities. In North Mayo, as discussed by Harris, it maintains an appearance of agreement around a develop-ment process that might otherwise be seen as a source of increasing social inequality. In the case of community policing, it maintains support for localised state intervention to keep social order.

O'Carroll (1998) uses a similar framework to look at the work of the Irish Blood Transfusion Service (IBTS). In Ireland, he notes, blood donation is surrounded by a 'community ethos': it is organised on the principle that it should be a free gift between fellow members of the national community, not a market exchange as in the US. But the transfusion service has not always worked to benefit the community in Ireland. When the system broke down in the case of the Hepatitis C scandal, the IBTS drew on the community ethos in order to 'prevent change and ignore uncertainty while failing to minimise the risk of infection' (1998, p.113). The IBTS, O'Carroll concludes, prioritised the maintenance of 'public confidence' over securing the safety of the public.

Studies such as these bring a useful scepticism to bear on the rhetoric of community. But insofar as they assume that community is *only* a rhetoric, and has no 'on the ground' reality for Irish people, they seem to suggest that Irish society is entirely penetrated by state power, unmediated by civil society institutions and associations. The history and practice of 'community development' in Ireland suggests that the situation is more complex.

Community development

If the state can enhance its legitimacy through a rhetoric of community, we might also expect this to apply to ordinary residents in a locality. Much contemporary collective action in Ireland appeals to the collective identities and solidarities generated by local community rather than to, say, class or gender solidarities. As earlier suggested, in a globalised society spatial inequality is likely to be as much a part of people's everyday experience as are other inequalities. The 'urge towards community' has a long history in Ireland. It goes back at least to the self-help strategies of Muintir na Tíre in the 1930s (Devereux, 1988) and to the influence of Catholic corporatism in the early decades of the last century (see Chapter 4).

As Curtin (1996, p.268) reminds us, the idea that community-based groups could help to tackle problems of rural poverty and disadvantage is neither novel nor peculiar to Ireland. As a response to the problems of rural areas it has been sponsored both by the US government and by development agencies associated with the UN, in Asia, Africa and Latin America. 'Community development' as an idea may have emerged from grass-roots movements, but is today increasingly being adopted by states as a key dimension of development policy — nowhere more so than in Ireland.

Curtin and Varley (1995) argue that in Ireland community action has taken two forms: one that attempts to work *with* the state for local development, which they term *integrationist*; and one that mobilises against the state, in particular against its taking of power from the local level, which they term *oppositional*. An example of *integrationism* can be found in the Muintir na Tíre movement and its structure of Community Councils. Curtin and Varley (1995, p.379) see this movement as remarkable for its 'all-together' ideology. It has an ability to project itself as concerned only with the common good and to transcend divisions of class, party or gender — even of religion. It claims to speak for the locality as a whole and that all locals stand to benefit from its activities. The strategy of the Community Councils is to build partnership ties with the state and to work through established political networks using traditional methods such as lobbying.

A good example of the *oppositional* tendency is the community-based 'Shell to Sea' campaign in North Mayo. As Garavan (2006) points out in relation to the oral hearing into the building of an on-shore gas pipeline, attempts are constantly being made by figures in authority to write risk and unpredictability out of social space. But risk, uncertainty and contingency continue to assert themselves and can be articulated through local knowledge in order to challenge the arguments derived from rational science. According to Garavan, the Corrib Gas oral hearing gave rise to an intriguing effort by local residents to contest the monopoly usually enjoyed by scientific reasoning and to attempt to engage Shell in a real deliberation about the issues that were at the heart of their opposition. As Garavan demonstrates, the burden of the argument advanced by community activists at the oral hearing lay in contesting the validity, or appropriateness, of relying *only* on scientific forms of knowing in arriving at an understanding of place. Community speakers did not attempt to contest the scientific reasoning on its own ground; rather they attempted to show that it simply was not a sufficient basis by which one could come 'to see' their local place accurately or comprehensively. They asserted the value of local discourses, local knowledge and forms of reasoning grounded on 'common and local senses'.

The two approaches to community action are distinguished by their attitude towards the state: part of the solution, or part of the problem? But the Irish state's orientation to community development groups has varied over time. Until the 1980s, it saw such groups as having no more than a marginal contribution to make to local social service provision and as largely irrelevant to economic development. But since then the community sector has come to be constituted as a significant actor in its own right: in policy discourse if not in the political process itself. The change is visible in, for example, the development of the FÁS community enterprise and social economy programmes; the Third EC Programme to Combat Poverty, and a series of EU-inspired 'area-based development programmes' since the late 1980s. These have included the Forum programme in Connemara; the PAUL Partnership in Limerick; the Pilot Programme for Integrated Rural Development, the LEADER I and II programmes, and the establishment of numerous locally-based partnership companies and other 'partnership' organisations (Geddes, 1998, pp.56–60). These institutional mechanisms have helped to place terms like 'partnership' and 'participation' at the centre of contemporary development discourse in Ireland and internationally (Sabel, 1996). They reflect an attempt by national and EU institutions to 'institute a formal structure of co-operation between the state and local actors' (Curtin and Varley, 1995, p.383).

If co-operation is the flavour of the day, is the oppositional tendency in community activism completely dead? There have been instances since the late 1970s where local communities have vigorously resisted the introduction of certain sorts of industrial production. Examples include the opposition by residents of Killeagh, Co. Cork to the siting in their locality of a Merrill Dow chemicals plant (Peace, 1993; Tovey, 1993) and the campaign (mentioned above) mounted by the people of Rossport against the construction by Shell of a gas pipeline (Garavan, 2006). At stake in such struggles is the principle that how local resources should be used (and what 'development' should mean) should be determined by local people, not by the central state or its agencies. Examples of opposition today are more often found in single-issue campaigns, for example against hospital closures or the erection of mobile phone masts. The focus of such campaigns tends to be on resisting the impact of national planning strategies on a specific locality, rather than attacking the strategies themselves. Yet the distinction is not clear-cut. Curtin and Varley point to examples of how local women's groups may understand themselves to be community-based and to that extent 'integrationist', even while using local relationships as an opportunity to forward feminist principles and forms of social analysis. Similarly Murray's (2007) study of opposition to an incinerator in Ringsend demonstrates the important interplay between local, national and global levels in the evolution of the community's campaign. In the course of organising community awareness of the government's proposal for the incinerator, activists made use of both transnational discourses on incineration that emanated principally from transnational NGOs, as well as the NGOs themselves. In other words, there was little evidence of reticence on the part of members of the community in reaching out to 'outsider' help, if this would be useful in resisting the incinerator. But residents do 'critically filter' the impact that transnational factors have on their resistance to the incinerator and the primary determinant in this is attachment to the local or community. Essentially, global or transnational flows are negotiated in this context, with residents not willing to 'buy in' to the global agendas of the NGO, preferring to focus on the specific issue of salience to their own locality. Integrationist and oppositional tendencies can be linked together in particular campaigns in complex ways.

The rise of 'local partnerships'

In recent years it has been state interest, as much as bottom-up pressure, that has elevated 'community' to a prominent policy position (CWC, 1996). For Walsh *et al.* (1998) this is evidence of a 'radical new localism' in Irish public policy. To the grass-roots tradition of community development, they argue, the Irish state has added its own interest in 'social partnership' as a way to achieve consensus on economic and social objectives. Social partnership has enjoyed strong cross-party political support, and a fourth pillar, of non-government or voluntary sector organisations, has been added to the original tripartite representation of employers, trade unions and farmers: 'social partnership has in effect been elevated to a shared political ideology which infuses all aspects of public policy-making and with minimal dissent' (Walsh *et al.*, 1998, p.16). Larragy (2006) suggests that part of the extension of social partnership in its early days into social policy, and the concomitant incorporation of the community and voluntary sector, was due to a legitimation crisis. The economic crises of the 1980s and the resultant problems of social marginalisation required a multi-sectoral response. Larragy found that the community and voluntary sector was able significantly to moderate neo-liberal tendencies in policy and place issues such as unemployment on the partnership agenda. It was perhaps inevitable that partnership would also be applied to overcome spatial inequality. The state has come to see involvement of the local community in development as the best way to tackle the concentrated pockets of unemployment and poverty that have persisted despite overall economic growth. It has argued that state and local community have 'co-responsibility' for economic growth. EU input has contributed significantly to the new policy direction, for example through the Local Development Programme — part of a joint EU-Irish government support framework for the allocation of EU structural funds. But Walsh *et al.* (1998) argue that the main stimulus for the new localism in policy has been indigenous.

They note that in 1996 there were nearly 150 local partnerships, of five main types, in existence in Ireland, working with more than 200 community development organisations (Figure 5.1). They point out that local partnership is characterised by a concern about social exclusion at the local level. All partnerships, with the exception of the Community Development Organisations, are required by the state to formulate an explicit equal opportunities policy for specified groups such as women, Travellers, or the disabled if these are present in their local area.

Figure 5.1 Local partnerships in Ireland

Local Development Partnerships (e.g. EU LEADER programmes)
These draw their membership from a wide range of interests. By way of a voluntary board of directors, they draw up a local plan for integrated social and economic development that must be approved by central government in order to receive funding.

Local Enterprise and Employment Partnerships (e.g. the Western Development Commission)
Membership is determined by central government, but includes local authority representatives, public enterprise agencies and voluntary and community sector representatives. They are chaired by the manager of the relevant local authority and again must have their local development plan approved by central government.

Local Partnerships (e.g. the Ballymun Task Force)
Co-ordinating structures for the delivery of specific social services such as training and employment, drug-use reduction or childcare to a variety of local users. They are often constituted as a subcommittee of a Local Development Partnership.

Community Development Organisations
Receive funding for specific — generally neighbourhood-based — projects, from diverse sources including local supporters, lottery money and private trusts. Usually managed by a voluntary management committee.

Urban Regeneration Partnerships (e.g. Integrated Area Planning in Dublin)
Relatively new bodies that have a distinctive focus on physical regeneration as well as social and economic improvement in disadvantaged urban areas.

Walsh *et al.* (1998) discuss eight local partnerships to illustrate these different types, and outline case-studies of three: the PAUL Partnership (Limerick), the Tallaght Partnership and the South Kerry Development Partnership. Their aim is to evaluate how effectively local partnerships promote social inclusion or increased equality at the local level. We may also be interested in what they might tell us about local partnerships as a form of civil society in Ireland. A number of interesting points emerge, in both respects.

For Walsh *et al.* local partnerships indicate a 'radical new localism': reversing to an extent the centralisation of state power. But they also note a major contradiction at the heart of the approach: 'local partnerships are primarily a project of central government, which defines the parameters of these initiatives and their location and controls their main supply of funding' (p.105). So, rather than indicating a revival of *localism*, it may be more useful to see partnerships as instruments of *national* policy, motivated in the main by questions of 'enhanced national competitiveness' (p.17). National government retains huge influence over how local partnerships operate, directly through its control of budgets and plans and indirectly through its dominance in the framing of policies that impinge on local areas in the domains of housing, industrial and agricultural development, infrastructural development and public services. The state has not devolved substantial power or resources to local administration and local partnerships remain highly dependent on the state. It is significant that the growth of local partnerships has coincided with a period of atrophy and starvation of funds for local government in Ireland; we might say that local partnerships, despite representing 'an innovative form of local governance' (p.106) are in certain respects less than democratic.

Local partnerships are required to promote social inclusion. While involving representatives of disadvantaged local groups in partnerships does give them some input into decision-making, Walsh *et al*. note that such groups remain very marginal to mainstream development policies. There are still discernible barriers to the participation of women in the decision-making procedures of local partnerships, let alone of members of other minority groups. Local partnerships have brought a 'new positive dynamic' to many localities: they have attracted new resources; delivered services more effectively and efficiently; created new assets with a commercial as well as a social value; and encouraged dialogue and consensus-building at the local level. But local participation in their decision-making may be narrow and the rules for deciding their membership are inflexible. Attempts to ensure national uniformity between partnerships through applying a standard membership formula 'undermines the principle of "bottom-up" development' (p.109); people may be selected for membership because of their seniority in their own agency, rather than for their commitment to the partnership ideal.

Walsh *et al*.'s reservations are echoed in other discussions of community development. Curtin (1996, p.268) suggests that 'playing according to the rules of this new game may mean that empowerment of the poor is now to be achieved not through protest and conflict with power-holders, but through consensus-based partnerships'. Local groups that are not included in the local coalition of community and state agencies may find themselves excluded from local development strategies. But even for groups that are included, the experience may be unsatisfactory. The activity open to the partnerships may reflect the availability of funding, rather than a commitment to ideals of community development (CWC, 1996).

The responsibilities shouldered by voluntary groups involved in partnership may be very burdensome and tend to force them towards some form of professionalisation. The development strategies that evolve from local partnerships generally fail to be integrated effectively into regional or national planning.

Finally, despite a growing rhetoric of 'participation' in development policy discourse in Ireland, many elite groups remain hostile to the idea of participatory democracy. Hostility appears particularly entrenched within sectors of the civil service, which has been pervaded (Commins, 1985) by a 'technocratic or managerialist ethos' that conflicts with the democratic and participative ideals of community groups.

Community development and civil society

Given the concerns noted above, we might describe local partnerships not as a 'zombie category' but as 'proto-civil associations'. Keane (1998, p.40) uses this term to characterise groups that function at the local level as the arms of state power, taking over some control of tasks such as trade and commerce, poor relief, water or landscape conservation, or the maintenance of order. They are not 'civil' associations because they are tightly tied to the state, but they do, Keane argues, provide a medium in which social interests can crystallise and the public sphere be extended. As Ó Riain (2006, p.315) points out, 'the constant dialogue and struggle between the horizontal and vertical dimensions of partnership is central to the outcomes of partnership negotiations and processes.' Local partnerships use a rhetoric of community but the local actors involved in partnerships are often not communities but rather spatial coalitions, whose territorial boundaries have been marked out by the state. This can help to overcome particularistic attachments to a locally boundaried social group, and offers a possibility of 'civil repair' to a society characterised by competing and rival local solidarities.

The term 'civil repair' comes from Alexander (1998, p.7) and relates to a particular type of relationship between civil society and other spheres in society (the state, the economy, the family). An example of 'civil repair' is where economically underprivileged members of the capitalist economy make claims for respect and power on the basis that they are also members of civil society and make use of institutions like the law, the mass media, trade unions or the vote to force the state to intervene on their behalf against overweening economic interests. This may mean to prohibit dangerous or inhumane working conditions, prevent labour-market discrimination or redistribute wealth according to non-economic criteria. When this happens, Alexander suggests, we can see that 'important elements of the utopian promises of civil society have in fact been incorporated into actually existing social systems'. To the extent that local partnerships make a claim for the spatially and socially excluded in Irish society to be recognised as equal members of civil society, they have at least the potential to become vehicles for 'civil repair'.

Peillon is less optimistic about the contribution to civil society that local partnerships can make. He says that the partnership discourse that has emerged amongst local groups and community development professionals draws from a model of civil society that envisages 'a communal association of people that is largely self-governing and does not allow the state to exercise too much power' (2001, p.134). But the actual practice of partnerships operates according to a different logic of civil society, an 'administered' rather than a democratic civil society, shaped by the state and for its purposes. 'The state,' suggests Peillon, 'is keen on the idea of partnership because it offers a mechanism through which civil society is shaped, at least to some extent' (p.135). 'Real' civil society here confronts a form of communitarianism.

Powell (2000, p.90) also warns that civil society, like community, is a term that has been embraced not only by academics but also by politicians 'as a prescriptive model of the future organisation of society'. Calls to reinvigorate both these concepts have coincided with a withdrawal from the welfare state and a loss of belief in its capacity to solve social problems. This 'new' kind of politics may be little more than 'neo-conservatism': a view that expects the disadvantaged in society to prevail through their own resources, without any structural change in society.

COMMUNITY, CIVIL SOCIETY AND CITIZENSHIP

As noted earlier, theorists of civil society are concerned not only about sociability and collective solidarity among citizens but also about their capacity to act democratically to reform society. But a society organised around individual communities may hinder the emergence of broad movements for change. A society structured around separate local communities encourages competitive relations between localities (as in the notorious competition between Waterford and Kilkenny, or Portlaoise and Tullamore) and invites clientelistic responses from the state. This leads Tucker (1987, p.298) to conclude that 'community development on its own cannot bring about structural change — that can be brought about only by broadly based national or regional movements with a political agenda'.

Civil society then, is not identical with community. It is both a realm of collective solidarity and an institutional realm that includes, as Alexander (1998, p.97) points out, the law and the courts; the mass media; 'dignitaries' and 'public servants' who exercise power and identity through their work within voluntary organisations; and 'movement intellectuals' who articulate new ideas through their involvement in social movements. We have focused on community because the strength of the community studies tradition in Irish sociology provides a way to explore the issues of sociability and association. To end we look briefly at two other central elements of a developed civil society: the 'voluntary' or 'third sector' and citizenship rights, institutionalised in law.

According to Bauman (2001, p.139) 'a republic is inconceivable without the well-entrenched rights of the individual citizen'. He goes on to suggest that individual citizens need protection from both communal and anti-communal pressures. Marshall (1950) famously distinguished between three forms of citizenship or citizen rights: civil, political and social. Elements of *civil* rights (of individual freedom, including freedom of the person against state violence; freedom of faith, thought and speech; the right to own property or make contracts, the right to justice before the law) existed before *political* rights (the universal franchise; the right to organise collectively as a political party, trade union or interest group). The latest of the three, and still the most contested, is *social* citizenship rights, which provide a basis for social inclusion of all members of society through, for example, rights to health care, to employment, a pension or environmental protection. Most of these rights have been institutionalised in Irish law.

Some have argued that citizenship rights, while indispensable, have not rendered society fully 'civil'. According to Seligman (1992, p.130) the contemporary idea of a society based on equality of citizenship 'has somehow denuded citizenship of that universal solidarity of mutual affections and natural sympathy . . . at the core of the idea of civil society'. There is a particular threat from rationalisation. Every step towards universalising equality has been based on reason, in opposition to particularist forms of solidarity, but this very exercise has undermined citizenship's 'foundations in the shared realm of sociability' (p.146). It is the autonomous individual, not the shared realm of sociability, that has come to represent the ethical foundations of society. For Seligman this has led to a situation where ethical and moral issues are now seen as the concern of the private individual: as private individuals, people 'happen to believe' in this or that ethical agenda, but their private beliefs have little purchase in a world founded on belief in autonomous citizenship. The contradiction between the rationalised civil society of individual citizenship rights and a moral world of social solidarity is one that Seligman fears theories of civil society cannot resolve.

Powell (2000, pp.96–8) distinguishes between two forms of citizenship: 'entitled citizenship' and 'active citizenship'. Social citizenship leads to a view of the citizen as an individual *entitled* to a range of social and economic welfare rights: the assumption is that these entitlements free the citizen to live an active, informed and associational life in society. But in practice it has led to increased individualism, often of a hedonistic and self-oriented form. The institutionalisation of citizenship rights does not necessarily produce the 'active citizen' who 'pursues moral commitment through involvement in the community', supports democracy and indeed is 'the cornerstone of civil society'.

'Active citizenship' can be manifested through the presence of strong voluntary associations and social movements in a society. Indeed the first report of the Task Force on Active Citizenship (Department of An Taoiseach, 2006) maintains that voluntary and community organisations are the backbone of active citizenship, with an ability to achieve trust and cohesion in a way that governments cannot. Furthermore, the report identified cynicism and a lack of confidence in democratic and some other consultative structures, particularly at local level. Civil society theorists emphasise the importance of the voluntary sector in society in ensuring social pluralism. While the state tends to homogenise society and culture, voluntary organisations and movements sustain a diversity of ideas, opinions, institutions and interests. Some, as we have seen above, seek close partnership relations with the state, in return for statutory funding, others 'challenge the state through vigorous social movements that may be seen as constituting "a people's opposition"' (Powell 2000, p.103) (CORI would be a good example in the Irish context).

Social movements can play a key role in the formation and expansion of public spheres, challenging the boundaries of what is conventionally understood to be the concern of politics, and creating new knowledges and new conceptions of the public good (Tovey, 1999b). It is important not to reduce 'civil society', as is sometimes done, to charitable and philanthropic NGOs and voluntary associations, which are increasingly likely to be implicated in state strategies for 'shifting various welfare services from the state' (Hems and Tonkiss, 2000, p.9). It is through social movements in particular that civil society marks out the boundaries between itself and the state. We discuss some significant Irish social movements in Chapter 17. Nationalist, cultural, Catholic, sporting, feminist and environmental movements have all played a part in shaping contemporary Irish society.

Information on participation in voluntary sector organisations in Ireland is limited, though it has recently been prioritised as a research field by the Royal Irish Academy. Though the proportion of those volunteering has dropped (from 39 per cent in 1992 to 33 per cent in 1998), levels of volunteering in Ireland compare well with those in countries such as Germany, Denmark or Canada (NCV, 2002). A survey conducted by Volunteering Ireland in 2006 reported more than 1.5 million volunteers, about 9 per cent of whom were non-Ireland based. From the 2006 census of population figures, this suggests that 37 per cent of the population volunteer, up 4 per cent on the most recent figure (Volunteering Ireland, 2007). Males outnumber female volunteers by a ratio of more than three to one in Ireland, a trend identified in Healy's earlier work (2004) on social capital. Overall, between 17 and 33 per cent of the adult population volunteer on a regular basis. In the European context, Ireland's volunteering rate is average and its citizens' membership of community and voluntary associations is above average. Both rates are on the increase. Irish society does not then appear to be experiencing the sort of 'civic disengagement' that Putnam found in the US, although there are clear changes in recent years in the types of volunteers and the patterns of their commitment, some of which, including an apparent decline in volunteering in the 40–50 age group (NCV, 2002, p.16), reflect US trends. Changes in the rate of volunteering have often been explained by changing trends in participation in work, particularly the increased numbers of women working formally outside the home. The areas where volunteering is increasing is amongst part-time workers and amongst students — both expanding sectors of the population (NVC, 2002, pp.17–19). Another feature of volunteering is that it increases in line with income and education: the lowest levels are found amongst those with minimal education, the unemployed and the unskilled. The National Committee on Volunteering notes that co-ordination and support of volunteering in Ireland is poor: the state has done little to support the health of civil society actively in this regard.

Civil society and the problem of trust

The concept of trust is increasingly being used as a way to think about relations in civil society. If civil society represents the sphere of social relations that are entered into voluntarily — not compelled by state, economy or family — then they are relations of trust. Putnam has identified trust and reciprocity as key elements of 'social capital'. Trusting others makes it easier for us to co-operate with them and to engage in collective endeavours, even with those who are recognisably very different from ourselves. Putnam believes that trust created between individuals can be translated into a more general collective trust in society, but others argue that as relations shift from the level of voluntary individual exchanges to relations with institutions and collectivities, maintaining trust becomes much more problematic.

Some civil society theorists, such as Keane (1998), argue that what civil society needs is not trust but *distrust*: in particular distrust of unaccountable power. Generalised social trust would subvert Habermas's ideal of the public sphere as an arena of open debate where all citizens can participate as reasoning beings and all authorities can be called on to justify, through reasonable debate, their pronouncements and actions. Loss of trust in authority is widely seen as a feature of late modern societies, but it is clear that civil society theorists evaluate that change in different ways.

Sociologists who have studied trust agree it is declining within Irish society. O'Carroll, commenting on the activities of the Irish Blood Transfusion Service in relation to blood contamination, remarks that 'until the disclosures of the blood tribunal, the level of trust in blood in Ireland remained quite high . . . post-tribunal Ireland will be a fundamentally different Ireland precisely because it will be characterised by a shift from trust in experts and public institutions to the calculation of risk involved in participation in them' (1998, p.114). Peillon argues that crises of trust, in the church, in medical institutions and in food, are rapidly propelling Ireland towards the state that Giddens has termed *high modernity*. He suggests (1998, p.118) that Irish society proves Giddens's thesis that a change in trust is central to the transformation of modern societies:

in traditional societies, trust follows the network of face-to-face relations, of community, kinship or friendship. One trusts what is familiar and this trust is sustained by traditional rules and personal loyalty. The development of the industrial society has brought about what [Giddens] calls *simple modernity*, in which trust has become more impersonal. Every day one trusts the technical competence of other people, the expertise of those who possess the relevant specialised knowledge. Today, whole populations are learning that experts disagree with each other and have no monopoly of truth. The unreliability of the expert-systems has created the real possibility of a generalised collapse of trust, and has ushered in another stage of modernity: that of *high modernity* in which we still depend on abstract and expert systems but we are now responsible for the expertise we choose to trust.

Both O'Carroll and Peillon suggest that loss of trust in Irish society contributes to increased individualisation. Our response to the collapse of expertise and expert institutions is an increased interest in calculating the risk to ourselves as we choose from amongst competing claims of expertise. But this process may in itself lead to counter trends that may encourage collective solidarity. Many of the traditional functions associated with the state, such as the minimisation of risks and making provision for the future, are gradually being deregulated. The responsibility to act in the interests of the citizen's welfare and well-being is increasingly shifted back to the individual. This divestment of responsibility from government to the individual places a burden on the latter, but also provides an opportunity. Individuals and groups, required to face up to risks and to manage contingent events, must make their own value judgments and develop their own normative positions. In a sense, the very uncertainty with which people must contend provides a basis for advancing new agendas, and new ways to respond to adversity. For example, the blood crisis of the mid-1990s led to the emergence of organisations to support and represent the victims of contaminated blood. Those concerned about the safety of food have joined organic box schemes or food co-operatives; victims of clerical sexual abuse have set up their own support groups. The numerous crises in Irish institutions, from the banks to the church, have led to increased pressures for accountability by the institutions involved. A concept of civil society points us towards trying to grasp the multidimensional nature of social change: solidarity and individualisation, private suffering and public concern, personal loss of trust and democratic action for accountability.

Part II

Irish society

Introduction

In Part I we have tried to show something of the development of sociology as a discipline: internationally and in its Irish manifestations. We have emphasised the connection between the birth and subsequent growth of sociology and the development of modernity itself. Thus, we have paid considerable attention first to the concept of *development* and second to the question of the *state* and where it sits in relation to civil society.

This discussion provides us with a good launching pad for an examination of Irish society. In the next section of the book we deal with some of the key aspects of Irish social life. Inevitably, for practical reasons, we have had to be selective and our choice of topics — population, class and inequality, education, gender, health, crime and deviance — is driven largely by our own fascinations, experience, and judgments as to what others may see as crucial objects of analysis.

We cannot claim that these topics are necessarily the most important. They may not even reflect how people spend their time. There is evidence that people spend a large proportion of their lives in routinised activities such as watching TV, eating, sleeping, socialising with friends, relatives and neighbours, commuting and working inside and outside the home. Except for perhaps the last of these to some extent, all these aspects of life have been virtually ignored by sociologists across the world. It is only very recently, for example, that a sociology of food and eating has developed or that researchers have begun to pay any attention to how people watch television. As in literature and film, the mundane aspects of everyday reality tend to get short shrift in sociology.

We may speculate as to why this is so. Much of the reason may lie in the powerful influence that a concern with 'social problems' has had over sociology. Sociologists have tended to reflect those areas of life that have generated public discourses of concern; for example, health, the family, poverty and class conflict. As we have seen, this has been cemented by sociology's strong links with the concerns of the state. The modern state is pre-eminently concerned with the management of the economy, and of key aspects of society — often those that take an *institutional* form; the state is intimately involved in the running of prisons, schools, hospitals, sometimes churches. It is inclined to intervene in matters of population, of social conflict, of sexual morality and of gender relationships. Thus, the ubiquity and pervasiveness of the state has helped to generate many of the key areas of interest for sociologists. State intervention also helps to produce voluminous documentation in the form of statistics, reports, enquiries and procedures which in itself makes these aspects of society highly visible to the sociologist. It also provides research funding and supports publication in these fields, again helping to stimulate interest.

It would be too cynical to suggest that it is only the supportive role of the state and its institutions that has contributed to a sociological interest in the matters we address in Part II. The labour movement and the women's movement have been two of the most powerful generators of social change in the modern world. The struggles of workers and of women against the status quo have contributed to the emergence of distinctive sociologies of class and gender. Each area embraces a vast range of human activity, has ramifications into all aspects of human behaviour and has generated a rich body of research and theory. No sociology could ignore these aspects of life.

Similarly sociologists have long been involved in, and frequently passionate about, education. In particular, they are concerned with the relationships between education and inequality, emphasised by Durkheim and especially Weber and still of major interest to sociologists, not least in Ireland. Interest in health reflects similar concerns. Some of the earliest empirical research in the social sciences was focused on the issues of public health and the connections between health, power and inequality remain of key interest to sociologists. In addition, the human interactions that take place in the arena of health — for example, between doctors and patients, or doctors and nurses — are of considerable fascination to sociologists, revealing as they do taboos, vulnerabilities, sometimes huge inequalities of status and abnormal social situations. It is of no surprise that the medical drama has long been a staple of popular TV programming and similarly of no surprise that it has attracted social researchers.

Finally, crime and deviance have fascinated sociologists from the earliest days of the discipline. Here the sociologist has the capacity to focus on an area of social life that is often hidden and rarely treated dispassionately in popular culture or everyday discourse. The sociologist has a number of possible roles here: to carefully sift the evidence and provide a more 'objective' picture of the incidence and effects of crime; to question the whole notion of crime itself, at times asking the awkward question as to why the petty thief receives a three-month jail sentence while the corporate criminal or corrupt politician escapes without a conviction; and perhaps, though not very commonly, to penetrate the hidden world of crime and to reveal to us 'outsiders' how it operates, how it is socially structured and how it has meanings for those involved.

We trace here a line through these topics and, though we leave much unexplored and unsaid in the hope of stimulating the reader to extend their own investigations, we maintain our primary concerns with the nature of modernity as it is experienced in Ireland and with how Irish sociologists have struggled to respond to Irish experience within a largely imported theoretical framework. We focus on issues of inequality, questioning the current practices and perceptions that help to maintain Ireland as an unequal society, one that continues to deprive many of its people of full citizenship. And we draw attention to how people make their own accommodations and live their own lives within the dominant structures, for it is important that sociologists, while stressing the determining influence of social institutions and structures, never lose sight of the agency that people bring to social processes.

6

Population and migration

Apart from geographical location and cultural background, we all live very similar lives: get up, go to work, try not to feel different, try to be normal, similarities between Poland and Ireland are strong, we have very similar views on life, to have a laugh and get on with life.

Magdalene, a Polish immigrant, from *Changing Ireland* (www.nccri.ie)

Population is one of today's most pressing concerns. The relationship between the number of people living on the planet and the resources to support their continued existence and welfare is a complex and dynamic one. We are all familiar with media images of global starvation and famine, of teeming cities and shanty towns, of fleeing refugees and conflicts over resources and territory. Similarly, there is much debate over issues such as the 'greying' of society, family structure, abortion and divorce, all of which are related to population. In Ireland, no less than elsewhere, population has been a perennial social, personal and political concern.

Population is ultimately about birth and death and movement; aspects of every individual's life story that combine together to produce the story of a society. At times the patterns of natality and mortality can be almost static; at others they change with amazing rapidity. Even over the last fifty years the behaviour of Irish people in relation to birth, marriage and family formation has changed quite dramatically. Conversely, trends in mortality appear to have stabilised. Nowadays Ireland seems to present a picture that is in many ways less notable for its exceptionality and more in line with that of our European neighbours, but previous experience shows us that this may change again in the future.

Of particular concern to Irish society historically has been emigration and the demographic and economic effects that the long-term haemorrhage of people from the country has created. Over half a century ago, Geary pointed out that 'of no country in the world is it more true to say that the political and economic boundaries do not coincide' (1951, p.400). It is true that for much of its history, a large proportion of Irish-born people have chosen or have been forced to live outside the geographical confines of the island. But, since the 1990s, Ireland's population profile has changed dramatically. First, a pattern of return migration was established by the mid-1990s, with many Irish emigrants choosing to return home to a buoyant economy. Second, since the turn of the twenty-first century there has been a rise in immigration, accelerating after the accession of new countries to the EU on 1 May 2004. Between May 2004 and May 2006, 230,000 workers from Poland, Latvia and Lithuania arrived in the state and sought personal PPS numbers in order to be able to take up employment here (*The Irish Times*, 25 November 2006). Not all of these have stayed, but it is estimated that immigrant workers now make up one-tenth of the Irish labour force. Ireland's new profile as a country of immigration has generated debates about refugee and labour rights, racism, integration and interculturalism. We must now address the reality of a multicultural Ireland; what that might mean for our social and personal identities, and for social policy and practice. In this time of globalisation, population issues have taken on a new importance. We will return to these issues at the end of this chapter.

POPULATION AND SOCIOLOGY

Population is a social phenomenon. Changes in population not only reflect individual decisions about family size, place of living and lifestyle, but are structured by broader societal patterns. In particular, population may be related to historical development, economic activity, value and belief structures and environmental constraints, and in turn it has a structuring effect on these aspects of social life. In other words population patterns and changes have consequences for society. They can create increased demand for resources and changes in the political, social or economic organisation of society and can shape opportunities for mobility and relationships.

Population phenomena, as they relate to the totality of people's experiences, are necessarily complex. Though they can be reduced to series of discrete figures about births, marriages and deaths, and mathematical formulae for fertility and mortality that can be applied over space and time, the reality behind people's decisions about, literally, life and death matters is inevitably complicated and open to many interpretations and explanations. As a result, in studies of demography and population matters, there is a constant tension between 'objective' analyses that tend to focus on the macro-level and often appear to be highly determinist; and 'subjective', micro-level accounts that try to 'get behind' the figures to probe the personal motivations and experiences of people as they give birth, emigrate or make decisions about familial matters and relationships.

Analysts of Irish population frequently remind us how difficult it can be to understand what is happening. For sociologist Ryan, 'Irish twentieth-century emigration is an extremely complex phenomenon' (1990, p.49) while Hazelkorn suggests (1991, p.135) that the experience of emigration can only be understood as 'a complex process, structured by class and gender inequality'. Immigration is a similarly complex process. The push factors that send people from Central and Eastern Europe and the developing world to Ireland include poverty and unemployment. The prevalence of political, religious and ethnic conflicts throughout the world impacts on refugee movements. But these factors alone cannot explain the mobilisation and the internationalisation of migration flows in recent decades. Structural conditions and technical infrastructure favour more than ever the mass movement of people across continents. Today it is possible to transmit information on earnings prospects, or conditions of asylum or entry requirements, via the mass media and the Internet to even the most remote regions. Thus the 'better way of life', which hitherto may have been a relative concept, is known by and within the reach of those living in poverty and suffering oppression. Pull factors that attract immigrants, both regular and undocumented, include the large-scale economic restructuring that has led to the simultaneous emergence of high-earning professional enclaves in metropolitan centres (that require a range of support services) and the emergence of economic enclaves such as construction or tourism that rely on cheap, compliant labour (Sassen, 1988). In summary, migration is an outcome of multiple and intertwining social factors.

Sociologists have long had an interest in population matters, an interest shared with economists, historians, and the specialists in the population field: demographers. In Ireland the SSIS (see Chapter 2) had a 'perennial interest' in the area (Daly, 1997, p.141) as have more recently founded research and statistical bodies such as the ESRI, NESC and the Central Statistics Office (CSO). However, there has been little active interest in demography within modern Irish sociology, with the work being left to a small number of individuals such as Courtney (1995; 1997; 2000) and to official bodies such as the CSO. Commentary on emigration has largely been left to historians, geographers and cultural practitioners and critics.

The key concerns of demographers are the identification and measurement of those factors that help determine the size and structure of the population, namely, fertility, mortality and migration. Demographic data on Ireland has been poor (Coleman, 1992, p.53), with problems in relation both to the adequacy of census data and the registration of births, marriages and deaths. It was not until the twentieth century that the data began to improve and this makes historical analysis, so crucial to understanding long-run trends such as population change, difficult to carry out. The data sources that demographers use tend to be those produced by official bodies. Of particular importance in Ireland are the national censuses, registries of vital statistics (births, marriages and deaths) and sample surveys such as the Labour Force Survey (now the Quarterly National Household Survey) (Courtney, 1995, pp.43–7). Increasingly such surveys are being co-ordinated across the EU, thus allowing for more effective generation of comparative data. Ireland does not provide for local registration of population (unlike say Japan or the Scandinavian countries) and therefore it can be difficult to obtain accurate data at the local level on an ongoing basis. Even the level of migration is difficult to determine as it is not easy to interpret the nature of movement into and out of the country.

THEORIES OF POPULATION

Conventional approaches

The theoretical basis of demography has been shaped around responses to the eighteenth-century writer Thomas Malthus. Malthus was most renowned for his prediction that, unless checked (for example, by war, famine, birth control or delayed marriage), population would increase more rapidly than food production. He argued that the obstacles presented by the natural environment would thwart attempts to improve the position of humanity (Furedi, 1997, p.14). Ireland's Great Famine was interpreted by many, including the British administration and parts of the Irish middle class, as empirical proof of Malthus's predictions. Despite the many subsequent criticisms of Malthus's theories, from religious, political, scientific and other quarters, he can be said to have made a significant contribution to the development of demography. In particular, he drew attention to the *social* nature of population, showing that it was linked to economic, environmental, social and political factors. Demography as practised in Western societies has subsequently come to be strongly shaped by functionalist sociology and modernisation theory. Courtney (1995, p.40) suggests that as a result there has been an overemphasis on empirical analysis, with far less attention paid to theoretical development.

Demographic transition theory emerged in the 1920s as a response to the apparent stabilisation of population patterns in twentieth-century Europe. The situation where many European governments were expressing concern about low birth rates and slowing population growth was in marked contrast to the rapid expansion in population seen by most European countries during the preceding century. The theory of demographic transition suggests that societies move through five demographic phases as they develop towards modernity. In other words, following Malthus, demographic change is seen to be closely related to economic and technological development (Courtney, 1995, p.41). The stages have been identified as follows:

1 *Static phase* — poor standards of living and lack of education, medical knowledge and facilities result in high mortality and fertility rates (as in some developing countries today).
2 *Early expanding phase* — better living conditions, especially improved diet and sanitation, mean the mortality rate declines while the fertility rate remains high (for example, Ireland in the years preceding the Famine).
3 *Late expanding phase* — increased knowledge of contraceptive practices, improved status of women and higher living standards cause the fertility rate to start to decline (Ireland in the 1970s).
4 *Low static phase* — mortality and fertility rates are both at a relatively low level (the UK after the Second World War).
5 *Diminishing phase* — fertility dips below mortality: the population ages and diminishes as there are not enough people being born to replace those that die (for example, Italy and Germany today).

The theory of demographic transition is firmly linked to that of *modernisation* and similar criticisms have been made of it: it is teleological and unidirectional; it does not allow for the influence of cultural and social diversity. More recently, demographers have spoken of the 'second demographic transition' (Courtney, 1995, p.42) which we discuss later in this chapter.

Critical approaches

As mentioned above, demography has tended to strongly reflect a functionalist approach to sociology. More critical approaches to population issues have derived from Weberian and Marxist positions. From a Weberian perspective, sociologists have focused on how population has increasingly become an object of control for states and elite groups such as the medical profession. Such control has been exercised, for example, in the twentieth-century rationalisation of childbirth and in the eugenics movement. Movements that have attempted to control the growth and nature of the population have operated both within countries and at the global level, for example, the International Planned Parenthood Federation. The Weberian concern with rationalisation has been developed by sociologists who, drawing on the insights of the French writer Foucault, have brought to our attention how populations are increasingly monitored in time and space. For Foucauldians the surveillance and monitoring of the populations of modern states and societies has acquired central importance and it is here that sociological concerns with population overlap with health concerns (see Chapter 10).

Marxist sociologists have paid little attention to issues of demography or family structure. They have been more interested in the topic of migration, particularly as it relates to the development of global capitalism. Marx was an early analyst of globalisation, arguing that the development of global capitalism divided the world into core industrial areas and peripheral agricultural areas that supplied the former with raw materials and labour power (Mac Laughlin, 1994, p.8). Ireland and other areas like the Scottish Highlands were for Marx, 'emigrant nurseries' that provided such labour. Thus, as outlined by Hazelkorn (1991, p.124):

> Whether permanent, casual or seasonal, Irish emigration [to Britain] provided a large reserve army of labour; its desirability was its mobility and willingness to enter employment, often unacceptable to British workers, and usually of an unskilled, low-paid nature.

In this sense the Irish and British economies were integrated into a single labour market, to the benefit of the latter economy. In the contemporary context, migrants from Eastern European countries constitute a 'reserve army of labour' within the EU. Ireland, the UK and Sweden were the only three member states that chose not to restrict free movement of labour in the aftermath of accession in

May 2004. As a result, they have been the prime destinations of workers from Eastern Europe. At present, 10 per cent of the Irish labour force is composed of non-nationals. The largest proportion of them (41 per cent) come from the EU 'accession states'; 11 per cent are from other EU countries excluding the UK; 18 per cent are from the UK; while the remaining 30 per cent are from outside of the EU (CSO, 2007).

Within the Marxist tradition Mac Laughlin (1994; 1997) is a social geographer who has perhaps made the most significant analysis of Irish emigration from the standpoint of social theory. He adopts a world systems theory approach to explaining nineteenth- and twentieth-century emigration, arguing that 'persistent and widespread Irish emigration is indicative of the peripheral *status* and not just the peripheral *location* of the Irish state in the world economy'. It can therefore only be understood by an analysis of the broader structural developments of global capitalism and the specific development of capitalist social relations within the country itself. 'It is . . . an intrinsically geographical and social class phenomenon in that it had clear geographical causes and social consequences which in turn structured and were structured by the regions which emigrants left behind and by the regions where they settled' (Mac Laughlin, 1994, p.45). World systems theory, according to Mac Laughlin, allows us to see emigration as a complex historical, geographical and social process that links the historical peripheralisation of Ireland to the development of industrial cores in the international economy.

Despite his global perspective, Mac Laughlin advocates that the best way to study emigration is at the local, community level and not on the more 'abstract national plains inhabited by statisticians, demographers and economists' (1994, p.54). This allows us to study the personal and social effects of emigration in detail. At the same time, Mac Laughlin is critical of behaviourist explanations — presumably those of historians such as Akenson and Guinnane, or of many popular commentators who focus on individuals' motives for emigration — which he sees as 'sanitised' and 'voluntaristic'. This point is echoed by Corcoran (1998, pp.137–8) and by Castles and Miller (1998, p.20) who see such accounts of migration as individualistic and ahistorical. This reminds us of the tension noted earlier between different approaches to explaining the migration phenomenon. A complete account would need to look both at the structural imperatives that drive migration and the meanings that individuals bring to their experiences.

Post-modern approaches

Post-modernist analyses of globalisation have shown a considerable interest in population and migration. The language of post-modern theory is replete with references to space and movement, and to concepts such as 'nomadism', 'fluidity of boundaries' and 'border-crossings' (Featherstone, 1997, p.240; Cronin, 2000). It is an approach that celebrates movement, diversity, cross-pollination and multiplicity of identities. The effect of the vastly increased mobility of modern populations is to break down traditional social categorisations. Featherstone (1997, p.241) suggests:

> The numbers of sojourners, refugees, and migrant workers means that 'the other' is no longer something to be searched out in exotic locations in the distant parts of the world by adventurers, literary travelers and tourists. The others work and live alongside us in the metropolitan areas. In effect, 'the rest is in the west'.

Furthermore, an appreciation of the issues of migrancy and mobility challenges the frameworks of sociology itself. As we have already seen, the discipline of sociology emerged as part of the project that saw the establishment of nation states and societies with(in) clearly drawn boundaries. The notions of 'society' and 'community' conjure up images of entities that are tied to location and where there is a strong connection between people and a particular space (country, town, suburb, street, and so on). An appreciation of the extent to which populations have always involved migrants, nomads and sojourners calls into question the perceived coherence of sociological and social categories. Writers on the Irish experience of migration have also begun to frame the analysis in terms of the fluidity and complexity of identity, space and everyday life (Kearney, 1990; Mac Laughlin, 1997; Corcoran, 2003).

Post-modern analyses extend the world systems approach into an analysis of globalisation. British sociologists Lash and Urry have shown how the experience of migration is part of the process of reflexive post-industrial development that is taking place in the Western world. Their analysis (1994, p.173) of migration into the United States shows how immigrants 'are concentrated in manufacturing, retail and low value-added consumer services in the information and control economies of the global cities' such as Los Angeles, Miami and New York. However, Lash and Urry point out that despite the globalisation of the migrant experience, the particular patterns across specific societies are highly variable.

Much recent analysis of global population flows tends to focus on issues of networks and clusters. For example, based on an analysis of Irish-born entrepreneurs in the United States, Corrigan (2006) highlights the importance of how emigrants and potential emigrants draw on social networks as a form of capital. This reflects what Irish people have long known about the emigration process: that human networks, based on kin, previous residence, occupation or education, are of key importance in shaping the decision to emigrate and the life chances of the new immigrant. Corcoran's (1991; 1993) analysis of Irish illegal immigrants in New York and of recent returners (2002b; 2003) reveals key aspects of this process.

POPULATION IN IRELAND

Ryan (1990, p.45) has argued that 'emigration is at the centre of the Irish experience of modernity'. It has been part of the process by which Ireland has been able to move from being a predominantly rural-based, agrarian society to an industrial state. Certainly the period of modernisation in Ireland has been accompanied by a constant stream of people leaving (and in many cases returning to) the country. The question is whether continual migration sustained or constrained the process or even had no effect on it at all.

Emigration in the twentieth century has been closely related to other population patterns; indeed it is inseparable from them. The forces that have led so many people to leave the country are derived from how families and communities have translated economic opportunities, property relations and religious and social attitudes into individual behaviour. The limits of economic opportunity available to, mainly, young people have led them to make decisions that have been shaped by the experiences of those that have gone before them. Others have felt compelled to escape the dominant frameworks of attitudes and behaviour that have governed religious, moral and social behaviour. The structures of families, the links that families have to property and opportunity and the patterns of birth and marriage: all have fed into people's decisions about where they can and should live.

Ireland's population pattern was, at least until recent years, often seen to be unusual or even unique in global terms. For example, in the first half of the 1900s, it was the only country in the world whose population *declined* (Geary, 1951, p.401), with its excess of emigration over natural increase. Furthermore, it was unusual in that more women emigrated than men. This combined with women's higher death rate (also unique) to produce a country with an unusual sex ratio of more men than women.

Though Ireland's fertility was unusually low by European standards in the latter half of the nineteenth century, it changed little during the subsequent century, while fertility rates in Europe plummeted. As a result, by the 1920s Ireland's fertility rates were, in the European context, unusually high. Even as late as 1987 Ireland's fertility rate was the highest of any developed country with the exception of the former Soviet Union (Coleman, 1992, p.56). It had the lowest proportion of first births and the highest proportion of births that were the fourth or subsequent child of the same mother. As a consequence the proportion of births to women over thirty was twice the Western norm. During the 1980s Ireland became the most 'youthful' country in the industrialised world, with almost a third of the population under fifteen. At that time it was the only developed industrial country that had net emigration. By the late twentieth century, Ireland was also unique in the Western world in prohibiting both divorce and abortion, though marriages were dissolved through legal separation and women did travel to Britain to procure abortions. One can conclude that, while individual aspects of Irish demographic history have been found in other regions of the world (Quebec, Bavaria, Puerto Rico, Spain), the specific constellation of features experienced in Irish society *has* been unusual, especially by European standards (Figure 6.1). The difficulty has been in explaining why this has been the case.

Whatever the past has held, in many respects the demography of Ireland is now rapidly converging with other European countries. Since the late 1970s there has been a marked decline in the fertility rate and in completed family size (Coleman, 1992, p.64). Nevertheless Ireland's birth rate (at 15.5/1,000 of the population) remains the highest in the EU (CPA, 2005), while mortality rates, though still slightly higher than in most EU countries, are also much closer to the European norm than they have ever been (see Chapter 10). Furthermore Ireland's former pattern of very late marriage has changed considerably and the age of marriage is now more in line with Western trends.

Coleman attributes the dramatic decline in fertility rates in Ireland to the widespread adoption of contraceptive practices, as Irish behaviour converges with that of the rest of the Western world (1992, p.73). This is seen by Coleman as evidence that Irish women are becoming more *modern* in their behaviour. Overall, he concludes that 'it looks as though the distinctive Irish fertility regime is finally over, and will join those of Quebec, Spain, Portugal and other Catholic countries as problems of recent history rather than those of the contemporary world' (1992, p.76).

Population patterns in Ireland have been affected historically by a number of factors, including:

- emigration
- the dominance of rural livelihoods and private property relations
- low levels of urbanisation
- low incomes
- the influence of the Roman Catholic Church.

Now the patterns may be being affected by trends such as higher educational levels, increasing costs of raising children for longer periods of time and the widespread entry of married women into the workforce. This shift can be seen to be explicitly linked to processes of modernisation and to reflect 'a modernised, literate, mobile, open society with a modern economy offering rewards to skills and education' (Coleman, 1992, p.74). But international comparisons suggest that there is no simple link between modernisation measures such as levels of workforce participation by married women and levels of fertility.

The social impact of Ireland's historically high rate of emigration has been profound. It has been argued that it facilitated the commercialisation of Irish agriculture; contributed to Ireland's deindustrialisation; and intensified

Figure 6.1 International trends over time in total fertility rates

	Total Fertility Rate				
	1970	1980	1990	2000	% decrease 1970–2000
Austria	2.29	1.65	1.45	1.34	41
Belgium	2.25	1.68	1.62	1.66	26
Denmark	1.95	1.55	1.67	1.77	9
Finland	1.82	1.63	1.78	1.73	5
France	2.47	1.95	1.78	1.88	24
Germany	2.03	1.56	1.45	1.36	33
Greece	2.39	2.21	1.39	1.29	46
Ireland	**3.93**	**3.23**	**2.11**	**1.89**	**52**
Italy	2.42	1.64	1.33	1.24	49
Netherlands	2.57	1.6	1.62	1.72	33
Portugal	2.83	2.18	1.57	1.52	46
Spain	2.9	2.2	1.36	1.23	58
Sweden	1.92	1.68	2.13	1.54	20
UK	2.43	1.90	1.83	1.64	33
EU-15	2.38	1.82	1.57	1.48	38
USA*	2.48	1.84	2.08	2.06	17
New Zealand*	3.18	2.03	2.27	1.80	43

Source: Crisis Pregnancy Agency Statistical Report 2005: Fertility and Crisis Pregnancy Indices. p.10. Dublin: Crisis Pregnancy Agency

Anglicisation and the eastward drift of political power (Mac Laughlin, 1994, pp.5–11). It has also been said to have altered power relations by removing young people from the society, so reducing the possibility of social or political change (Guiomard, 1995, p.190; Mac Laughlin, 1997, p.13). It placed power firmly in the hands of property owners but also consolidated the power of organised labour by removing much of the 'reserve army' of labour to elsewhere. Crotty (1986, p.79) argues that emigration gave Ireland:

> higher living standards than any other former capitalist colony. It gave it an unparalleled record of political stability and public finance rectitude. It created an intellectual and political void.

The changing patterns of Irish migration are discussed in more detail in the sections to follow.

ORIGINS OF IRELAND'S POPULATION PATTERNS

Though it has been a matter of great historical controversy, there now appears to be agreement that the distinctive features of Ireland's demography were established prior to the Famine, in the early nineteenth century. They included:

- late age of marriage
- high fertility within marriage
- a low level of births outside marriage
- an overall low rate of fertility across the population as a whole
- high levels of emigration.

Mortality rates, apart from the exceptional time of the Famine itself, were comparatively low, possibly, as Coleman (1992, p.57) suggests, through low levels of urban living and the 'safety valve' of emigration. After the Famine, the social reality of emigration tended to overshadow all other aspects of Irish demographic experience (Figure 6.2).

As the nineteenth century progressed, the demography of Ireland increasingly diverged from European patterns. In particular, it did not experience the same decline in fertility rates, partly because Irish couples, unlike most other Europeans, did not practice birth control. While, from the 1870s, most European populations began to practice contraception within marriage, the Irish generally did not, except to some extent in urban areas (Coleman, 1992, pp.59–61; Guinnane, 1997, p.273).

According to Akenson (1991, p.3), from the nineteenth century, the Irish became the 'most internationally dispersed of the European national cultures'. Post-Famine emigration was built upon an earlier history of movement — especially among Ulster Presbyterians — that stretched back to the early seventeenth century when the 'Atlantic economy' began to emerge (Kirkham, 1990). Even before that there was a long tradition of Irish people leaving the country's shores to found monasteries, fight in foreign armies, or take up seasonal work. While the numbers of Irish people leaving the country prior to the nineteenth century did not approach the levels of subsequent times (not least because transport technology was less advanced) those that left did help to set the trend for migration on a mass scale from the 1820s onwards.

It is estimated that 7 million people left Ireland for North America alone between 1600 and 1922 (Mac Laughlin, 1994, p.4), 4 million of those in the years from 1846 to 1925. Ireland was thus, along with countries like Russia, Italy and the Scandinavian countries, a 'leading European exporter of labour'. Emigration was at such a high rate in the wake of the Famine that it cancelled out natural increase and,

Figure 6.2 Ireland: natural increase and net migration 1880–2000

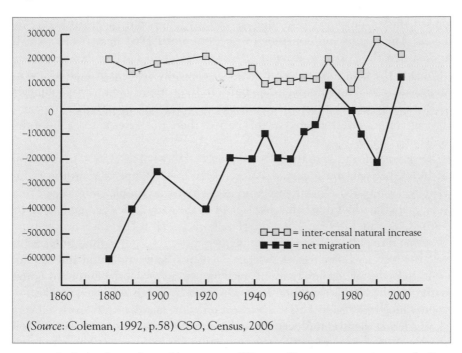

□—□—□ = inter-censal natural increase
■—■—■ = net migration

(*Source*: Coleman, 1992, p.58) CSO, Census, 2006

as a result, Ireland was the only country in Western Europe to experience a decline in population throughout the second half of the nineteenth century.

The demography of nineteenth-century Ireland was shaped by the patterns of livelihood and property, in particular landholding (Guinnane, 1997, p.284). Of special importance was the dominance of small farmers and peasants, enhanced through the land purchase legislation enacted by the British government in the late nineteenth and early twentieth centuries. Demographic patterns were also, as Guinnane reminds us (1997, p.252), a reflection of world economic conditions and Ireland's place in the British Empire and the world economy. Ireland was a major provider of labour and personnel for both the British imperial system and the emergent societies of North America. In return, emigration provided an important input to the home economy, especially through the earnings of seasonal labourers. For example, Mac Laughlin (1994, p.16) reports that 'Scottish money' — remittances sent back from Scotland by young Irish emigrants — accounted for up to a quarter of the cash income of poor families in the west in the period prior to the First World War.

POPULATION IN INDEPENDENT IRELAND

Overall the population of the island of Ireland as a whole shrank from 8.2 million in 1840s to 4.2 million in 1926, a decline of 48 per cent (Courtney, 1995, p.48).

But Irish independence did not bring an end to emigration as had been hoped. Indeed after the effects of the Great Depression and the Second World War had passed, the stream of people leaving the country returned to nineteenth-century levels. The population continued to decline until 1961 apart from a small increase in the post-war years of 1946 to 1951. This decline can be clearly related to the failure of the country to economically develop in such as way as to provide a livelihood for its inhabitants. In the period 1926 to 1961, numbers of those in agricultural employment fell by over 272,300. As only 101,800 non-agricultural jobs were created in this period, there was a net loss of jobs of the order of 170,500.

Levels of emigration in the 1950s approached those of the 1880s: from a level of 16,600 per year in the period 1926 to 1936 to 42,400 per year in the 1950s (Drudy, 1995, p.75). With fourteen in every thousand people emigrating every year, more than half those that left school in the early 1950s had emigrated by 1961 (Guinnane, 1997, p.279). For Hazelkorn (1991, p.125) such people were 'reacting rationally to severe economic decline and labour surplus at home as well as widening differentials in welfare payments' between Ireland and Britain.

In Ireland itself fertility rates diverged increasingly from the European norm, with only the Netherlands and Iceland — and in North America, Quebec — approaching Irish levels. This was a reflection of the fact that Irish levels fell very slowly during the twentieth century while those of other Western countries fell sharply. At the end of the 1950s the Irish pattern of late marriage began to break down and this inevitably impacted on fertility rates. By 1970 Ireland's fertility rate was the highest in Europe (Figure 6.1). Despite its already high levels of fertility, Ireland, like other Western countries, experienced a baby boom in this decade. It was not until the early 1970s that fertility in Ireland began to drop sharply towards European levels; a fact reflected in the sharply declining proportion of fourth and higher order births (Coleman, 1992, pp.61–7).

A number of reasons have been suggested for the demographic change that appears to have brought Ireland 'into line' with the core European societies. These include, not surprisingly, the increased availability and use of contraception and (via the Irish Sea) abortion. The 1970s saw a high level of political and legal action (spearheaded by women's groups and individuals including later President Mary Robinson) aimed at removing the legal impediments to the availability of contraceptives (Hug, 1999). The demand for contraceptives was probably the result of a complex set of factors, but research in the European context suggests that these included the increased costs of having children, improved education, the erosion of traditional moral and religious strictures, increased female workforce participation, and the political and social liberation of women (Coleman, 1992, p.75).

While emigration continued in independent Ireland, there was a marked change in the destination of emigrants. From the mid-1930s Britain became the main destination as opposed to the United States, partly following a tightening of entry regulations there. While 1876 to 1921 saw 84 per cent of emigrants go to the United States and only 8 per cent to Britain, by the period 1946 to 1951, four-fifths were emigrating to Britain (Hazelkorn, 1991, p.125). It is estimated that, in the period 1890 to 1990, over 2 million Irish people emigrated to Britain, two-thirds of whom stayed (Ryan, 1990, p.46). In the 1960s there were over a million Irish-born people there, making the Irish the largest ethnic minority group in Britain. The destinations within Britain changed during that period, with a substantial shift southwards. Scotland and the north of England no longer attracted substantial numbers. Emigrants followed the shift of economic balance to the south-east of the country, particularly London: by 1971, the Irish-born made up nearly 4 per cent of London's population (Ryan, 1990, p.48). The shift to Britain, being more easily accessible to Ireland, meant for many a change in the *experience* of emigration as pointed out by Geary in the early 1950s: 'very large numbers now return on holidays and a considerable proportion of those who go come back after a year or two' (1951, p.402).

The immigration of large numbers of Irish provided Britain with a convenient labour pool, thus reducing its dependence on workers from ex-colonies or the developing world. Britain has never had to develop a 'guest worker' system like that in Germany, France or other European countries. Those who emigrated from Ireland were largely unskilled, often from rural backgrounds. The 1954 *Commission on Emigration* revealed that three-quarters of male emigrants were of this category while 90 per cent of women were classed as domestic labourers or other service workers, though were more likely to work in bars, restaurants and hotels than in private homes. There was also a small but significant number of skilled professionals, doctors and engineers, for example, who could not secure employment in Ireland and constituted a 'brain drain' (Hazelkorn, 1991, p.128). Mac Laughlin suggests that, by the 1960s, 'Irish graduates with qualifications in engineering, medicine and law were probably regarding Britain and Ireland as an integrated labour market' (1994, p.28). The growth in the service industries in the 1960s saw an increase in the number of Irish emigrants moving into white-collar work such as nursing, teaching and office work. This coincided with the shift in focus towards the south of England and away from the more traditional industrial areas of the midlands and the north.

IRISH POPULATION IN THE AGE OF GLOBALISATION

As suggested earlier in this chapter, Ireland has long been recognised as part of a global economy and culture and this has been a central element of 'Irish identity'. In recent years there has been an intensification of this discourse. From cultural theorists to media personalities, all have a view about how the particular development of Irish population patterns has reflected our increasing integration into a global society.

In some ways, contemporary demographic patterns in Ireland are becoming increasingly similar to those of Western Europe and countries like Australia. Since the 1980s a number of distinctive patterns have emerged in the majority of Western countries and the *second demographic transition* (Courtney, 1995, p.42) describes this emergence. Ireland has been seen as a late entry to this transition, like other Catholic countries such as Spain and Portugal. The trends related to the second demographic transition include:

1   *marriage*
    fewer legal marriages
    a rise in cohabitation
    later age of marriage
    higher rates of separation and divorce
    higher rates of second and subsequent marriages
    more homosexual unions.

2   *fertility*
    smaller families
    later motherhood
    more voluntary childlessness
    more single-parent families
    more 'only children'
    more children born outside legal marriage.

3   *ageing*
    people living longer
    better health in later years
    more 'old elderly' (those over 75)
    later retirement (for some)
    longer periods of retirement.

While Irish society appears at last to be converging with Western trends, in other ways the country's demographic profile remains exceptional. For example, while most other European countries are faced with the challenge of an ageing and increasingly dependent population over the next thirty years, the opposite is true in Ireland. Indeed Fahey and Fitzgerald (1997) argue that the country is now entering an unprecedented period of 'demographic advantage'. According to the Central Statistics Office (CSO), in the period 1971 to 2002 the population of the Republic of Ireland has grown by almost one-third to reach nearly 4 million. This increase largely took place during two periods: the 1970s when the population grew by 390,000, and the period from 1996–2002, when the population increased by almost 300,000. In 1971 almost half the population was under 25 years. The number in that age group has declined as a proportion of the population to 38 per cent. This reflects a number of demographic changes, including a reduced birth rate; increasing life expectancy; and increasing inward migration (Hourihane, 2003).

Many of the demographic changes now taking place reflect the changing position of women in Irish society which has been expressed in legislation, social attitudes, economic activity and sexual behaviour. The number and proportion of births outside marriage has risen considerably. While the rate of just over 30 per cent is lower than that of the Scandinavian countries (where over half of births are outside of formal marriage), the UK or Australia, it is now considerably higher than in many European states, such as Italy, Switzerland and Germany (Council of Europe, 2001). This bald statistic is difficult to interpret as many children may actually be born to couples who are cohabiting but are not actually married (Fahey and Russell, 2001). It has also been suggested that the relatively high number of non-marital births reflects a changing social climate in which there is much less pressure on pregnant young women to get married. Eighty-four per cent of respondents in a national survey agreed that in today's society it is acceptable for a woman to rear a child as a lone parent, without a stable relationship with the father (Rundle et al., 2004, p. 18). The dramatic increase in the number of married women in the workforce has probably contributed to an increase in delayed childbearing, a further decline in completed family size (the process commenced in the 1960s) and an overall decrease in fertility in recent years.

An increased emigration flow reflected the parlous state of the Irish economy in the 1980s, in particular the contraction in employment in indigenous manufacturing industries such as textiles and engineering and the inability to convert new investment into jobs. Despite a considerable expansion in the developing service industries (109,000 new jobs from 1981 to 1993) the period saw a surge in unemployment in Ireland with the rate doubling from 10 per cent (126,000) in 1981 to 17 per cent (230,000) in 1993 (Hazelkorn, 1991, p.126; Drudy, 1995, p.75). The situation did not improve in the early 1990s as 175,000 left the country's shores (about 33–35,000 per annum) between 1991 and 1996, two-thirds of them aged 15 to 24 (Corcoran, 1998, p.140). In 1997 the levels of emigration began to decline again. In that year 29,000 people left the country and the figure further decreased to 18,500 by 2004 (Mac Éinrí, 2006). Unemployment and poor economic conditions at home were a significant 'push' factor in emigration while 'pull' factors related to the strength of host-country economies and the nature of their regulation of immigration.

For Hazelkorn the continuation of the emigration flow accorded with the globalisation of the Irish economy. Drawing parallels with the government of Turkey in the 1960s and 1970s, she suggests (1991, p.131) that 'Irish governments facilitated emigration as a means of alleviating social and political tension, a possible means of providing additional skills and experience, and as a source of income through remittances and tourism'. Skill shortages in host countries such

Figure 6.3 Emigration from and immigration to Ireland, and net migration rates, 1995–2004

Emigration from Ireland

	1995	1996	1997	1998	1999	2000	2001	2002	2003	2004	Total
UK	13,300	14,100	12,900	8,500	11,200	7,200	7,800	7,400	6,300	4,900	93,600
EU	5,100	5,100	4,100	4,300	5,500	5,500	5,600	4,800	4,300	3,400	47,700
USA	8,200	5,200	4,100	4,300	5,300	4,000	3,400	4,800	2,500	2,800	44,600
ROW	6,600	6,800	7,900	4,100	9,500	10,000	9,500	8,500	7,600	7,400	77,900
Total	33,200	31,200	29,000	21,200	31,500	26,700	26,300	25,500	20,700	18,500	263,800

Immigration to Ireland

	1995	1996	1997	1998	1999	2000	2001	2002	2003	2004	Total
Irish	17,600	17,700	20,500	23,200	26,700	24,800	26,300	27,000	17,500	16,900	218,200
UK	5,800	8,300	8,200	8,300	8,200	8,400	9,000	7,400	6,900	5,900	76,400
EU	3,200	5,000	5,500	5,800	6,900	8,200	6,500	8,100	6,900	10,600	66,700
USA	1,500	4,000	4,200	2,200	2,500	2,500	3,700	2,700	1,600	1,800	26,700
ROW	3,100	4,200	5,500	4,500	4,500	8,600	13,600	21,700	17,700	14,900	98,300
Total	31,200	39,200	43,900	44,000	48,800	52,500	59,100	66,900	50,600	50,100	486,300

Net migration

1995	1996	1997	1998	1999	2000	2001	2002	2003	2004	Total
−2,000	8,000	14,900	22,800	17,300	25,800	32,800	41,400	29,900	31,600	222,500

(*Source:* Bartley and Kitchin, 2007, p.238)

as the United States, UK and Germany continued to provide a market for the export of Irish workers (Figure 6.3). As the nature of economic activity has changed — from labour intensive to capital intensive to knowledge intensive — so the demand for labour has changed. The development of 'global cities' as powerhouses of economic activity (for example, London, an increasingly important emigrant destination) has also helped to shape the decisions of intending migrants (Skeldon, 1997, p.187; Lash and Urry, 1994).

Changes in the nature of labour demand mean that emigrants may now be more skilled than previously. According to Hanlon (1991, p.53), who has studied the emigration of Irish accountants, the 'upwardly mobile middle class were the most likely emigrants'. The NESC report of 1991 showed that a third of emigrants in the 1980s and 1990s were already employed full-time prior to departure.

Hazelkorn (1992, p.128) similarly argues that, compared with those of the 1950s, more recent emigrants tend to be better educated, more urban, increasingly male and 'predominantly young, single and mobile'. A large proportion of graduates from the third-level education sector emigrated during the 1980s — up to two-thirds for some courses. Many subsequently returned during the 1990s, including a high proportion of those with third-level education (Sweeney, 1998, p.105).

Corcoran (2002a) suggests a model (Figure 6.4) for interpreting the impact of class differences on emigration. Highly educated emigrants — the professional or transnational elite — tend to be individualist and enjoy a considerable degree of personal agency in terms of their life plans and career choices. In contrast, the more traditional 'reserve army' of Irish emigrants, whose role was to fill the gaps in the secondary labour market of global cities, are much more constrained. Their decision-making is frequently contingent and inadequately thought through. They gravitate very much towards their ethnic group, where informal networks facilitate their entry into the labour market. They may be subject to a variety of constraints ranging from prejudice and discrimination to the vagaries of the host-country system of immigrant regulation.

Figure 6.4 Emigrant typology

process of migration	'reserve army' emigrants	professional elite
decision-making	contingent	reflexive
migratory context	ethnicisation	self-actualisation
migrant persona	situational ethnicity	flexible subjectivity
migratory experience	structural constraint	personal agency
(*Source:* Corcoran, 2002a)		

'Reserve army' emigrants make decisions that are primarily determined by the prevailing economic conditions. Furthermore they are likely to be constrained in terms of opportunity structures because of low or non-transferable skills. Their professional counterparts make decisions that tend to be reflexive or based on an ongoing and self-conscious evaluation of personal and professional goals. The context of reception in the host country is also different for each group. The 'reserve army' emigrants tend to be absorbed quickly into the Irish ethnic niches in the labour market. Furthermore they tend to live in the same neighbourhoods and congregate in the same bars. In contrast, the professionals tend to reject both symbolic and substantive ethnicity, preferring to make their way as individuals without unduly advertising their Irishness, particularly in the workplace. While the 'reserve army' emigrants find that to survive in the host country they must often develop an ethnic persona in a variety of strategic situations, the professional elite are busy deploying their flexible subjectivities across a range of work and leisure arenas. Finally, Corcoran argues that the experiences of the 'reserve army' emigrants most closely mirror those of previous generations of Irish emigrants (and Central European immigrants in Ireland today) bounded as they are by structural constraints in the form of economic and social conditions as well as legal barriers. The Irish professional elite, in contrast, embody many of the attributes associated with modern individualisation. Rich in cultural capital and attuned to information and communication structures, they apply themselves assiduously to the task of self-actualisation.

The notion of the 'diasporic hero' (Gray, 1997, p.228; Corcoran, 1998: 136) has emerged: those elite individuals, often tied into the global media industries (Frank McCourt, the Corrs, Terry Wogan, Roy Keane, Gloria Hunniford, and so on) who are able to 'sustain their own unique biographical narratives in the context of a myriad of possibilities and choices'. As Corcoran suggests, we are encouraged to accept and celebrate the successful emigrant or agent while we fail to acknowledge the existence of the other, the marginalised, less successful emigrant. 'Such a characterisation of emigration as a beneficial experience for the best and brightest functions as a soothing anodyne, assuaging any doubts we may have about the fate of those who leave Ireland without credentials, prospects, or marketable skills' (Corcoran, 1998, p.138).

INTERPRETING POPULATION

Given the centrality of population to social change (and stasis) in Ireland, it is hardly surprising that it has generated numerous and complex interpretative discourses. As in other countries, population has been the object of political debate and intervention. The debate around population is closely related to other social topics such as the rural-urban divide, changes in family structure and the growth of suburbia.

Since the nineteenth century, emigration has been seen as an Irish 'problem' (Delaney, 1998, p.25), but the nature of the problem has varied considerably over the years. Within nationalist discourse, emigration was seen as a problem caused by an external force: British colonialism. Nationalists ignored the role of indigenous property and placed the blame for emigration in the hands of the English and the 'ranchers'. According to this 'narrow nationalist' viewpoint, landlordism was the sole cause of emigration and emigrants were victims of alien oppression by 'tyrants' who drove the Irish as exiles from their 'happy home' (Mac Laughlin, 1994, p.21). Contemporary nationalist literature portrayed emigration as the product of 'alien' rule and suggested that self-government would solve Ireland's social and economic problems and thus lead to the end of emigration. As a result, the issue of emigration was a key part of the campaigns of Irish political leaders such as O'Connell, Parnell and Pearse (Delaney, 1998, p.25).

Attitudes to Irish emigration have been shaped not only by ideas of nation-hood, but also by ideas of social class. Ryan (1990, p.50) makes the point that emigration was seen negatively by the rural petty bourgeoisie, where ideologies about land and 'blood' were perhaps strongest (Mac Laughlin, 1997, p.22). Amongst other groups emigration was strongly linked to notions of nation-building and bourgeois respectability. Counter to the popular nationalist argument, Irish and British Malthusians saw emigration as a natural and rational response to overpopulation in Ireland, and as a facilitator of rural modernisation. By the middle of the nineteenth century such an approach had become part of bourgeois Irish nationalist ideology. Emigration was seen as a way of removing the 'weaker' elements of the population (ideally far away to America) and thereby strength-ening the stronger and more 'manly' indigenous population.

After independence, and a recognition that the problem had not gone away with the British, the discourse on emigration had to change. A contradiction emerged between the private-property-oriented policies of successive governments since independence, and their condemnations of emigration (Delaney, 1998, p.28). Fianna Fáil was the most vocal of the political parties in its opposition to emigration, making heard the concerns of its western and small-farmer constituency. This was also reflected in its 'self-sufficiency' economic policy of the 1930s and 1940s. For its leader, de Valera (Dáil debate 17 February 1937, cited in Delaney, 1998, p.30):

> The aim of the Irish government [is] not to provide facilities for the emigration of our people to the states of the British Commonwealth or elsewhere. Its aim is to concentrate on utilizing the resources of this country and so improving the conditions of life here that our people will not have to emigrate, but will be able to find a livelihood in our country.

Emigration became increasingly important as a political issue during the 1930s and in the wake of the Second World War, becoming a key feature of the Dáil campaign of 1948. That year the widespread concern about the issue saw the establishment of the statistics-oriented *Commission on Emigration and Other Population Problems*. There was much concern about emigration of young women and there were even proposals put forward for a ban on the emigration of females under twenty-two.

The most recent changes in Irish demographic experience have, not surprisingly, further influenced the political discourse around population. As Fahey (1998a, p.51) suggests, the 'normalisation' and 'convergence of Irish demography towards European patterns . . . has lent substance to the image of Ireland as a modernising, developing nation . . . the demographic recovery . . . has signalled a new vibrancy and has helped justify the positive rhetoric which now dominates political discourse'. In contrast to the image of an ageing Europe, Ireland's nation of 'Young Europeans' (a popular slogan used by the IDA to attract TNCs to the country) is perceived as active and dynamic.

But the modernisation of the Irish population as expressed in our participation in the second demographic transition has also been seen to present threats. In particular:

- the dramatic changes in the nature of family structure
- the volatile discourse around sexuality
- the shifts in the role and status of young people
- the intense debates around reproductive rights
- the challenge of a multicultural society.

These have generated a powerful conservative reaction (see Chapter 16) that perceives demographic change and the associated attitudinal shifts not as progress but as decline.

In a period of economic growth, or boom, even, emigration has to a certain extent lost its position on the political and social agenda. Mac Laughlin argues that since the 1960s emigration has been sanitised and de-nationalised, now seen in technocratic and administrative terms and not as a national political issue.

A MULTICULTURAL IRELAND?

Multiculturalism has become a familiar term in societies such as Canada, Sweden, Australia, the United States and Britain, but can have very different meanings and resonances. In Canada and Australia it tends to have positive overtones and reflects official discourses about the need for those societies to meaningfully recognise the cultural diversity brought about by long histories of immigration. In the United States and Britain, the term tends to be far more politically charged and tends to refer to the struggles of minority groups (most specifically Black, and, in Britain, Asian) in conflict with a majority white culture. In Ireland it is not clear what people are referring to when they talk about multiculturalism, though generally the term seems to embrace elements of both of these meanings. In addition 'interculturalism' has become the favoured term amongst government and activist groups. This issue is discussed further below.

In recent years Ireland has experienced a phenomenon that has been largely absent for most of its recent history: substantial *immigration* (Figure 6.3). In the year to April 2002, 47,500 people came to live in Ireland (CSO, 2002a). Immigration is now as important a factor as natural increase (births minus deaths) in determining the growth in the Irish population. An estimated 10 per cent of the population is now foreign-born. There have also been important changes in the origins of immigrants to Ireland: they are becoming increasingly diverse. As Mac Éinrí (2001, p.52) points out, until the mid-1990s the major sources of immigration were to be found amongst former Irish emigrants (popularly termed 'returnees' or, more poetically, 'homing pigeons' (Fitz Gerald, 2002, p.66) and British people who came to Ireland either for 'counter-cultural' reasons, or as retirees. The only significant alternative source was amongst the employees of TNCs (often American, Japanese or German nationals) who relocated to Ireland as a result of their employment. By 2002, while returnees still made up 38% of immigrants (down from 55% in 1999), 35% of those moving to Ireland came from outside the EU or the USA, up from 12% in 2000 (Mac Éinrí, 2001, p.54; CSO, 2002a).

Another relatively new development has been the Irish state's new-found interest in facilitating specific types of immigration, often of a temporary nature, to address labour-market shortages. This includes, as suggested by Lash and Urry (1994), workers at both the 'top' and 'bottom' ends of the labour market. Thus over 18,000 short-term work permits were issued to nationals of over 120 different countries in 2000. While some of these were for skilled, managerial and technical workers, the majority were for jobs in the catering and service industries. For instance, in the last quarter of 2006, 28 per cent of workers in the hotels and restaurants were foreign nationals, while 13 per cent of construction jobs were filled by migrant workers (CSO, 2007). The countries most represented were Latvia, Lithuania, Czech Republic and Malaysia (Mac Éinrí, 2001, p.87). Such workers typically have limited rights, and the administration of the temporary work-permit system has some strong similarities with the 'guest worker' approach of countries such as Germany and Switzerland, which has had severe negative impacts on immigrant workers, and their families, in those countries (Castles and Miller, 1998, p.222). The work-permit system was largely overtaken by the opening of Irish borders to workers from the ten new accession countries that joined the EU in May 2004. Since then, tens of thousands of Poles, Latvians and Lithuanians have registered for PPS numbers in Ireland, although the actual number of new member-state immigrants working in Ireland in 2005 was just under 70,000. This is because many of those who registered stayed here only temporarily or, in fact, simply registered and returned home (*The Irish Times*, 25 November 2006). As the economist Martin Ruhs has pointed out, 'we need to know the facts about the volume, composition and process of migration to Ireland' (*The Irish Times*, 26 September 2005). We have limited information about the experiences of immigrants in the formal (and informal) economy, and we have virtually no information on those migrants who come to Ireland as dependents.

As Castles and Miller (1998, p.212) point out, the experiences of immigrants are significantly shaped by the policies and practices of the state. As Ireland has historically been a country of emigration rather than immigration, it is perhaps understandable that it has had a very poorly developed immigration policy in contrast to 'immigration societies' like Australia or the UK. According to Mac Éinrí (2007, p.238) Ireland is now faced with the difficulty of 'constructing immigration and integration policies against a background of a rapidly changing picture, limited experience, an often less than positive attitude toward difference, and a largely mono-cultural tradition'.

This was exemplified in the Citizenship Referendum held in 2004, when a large majority voted in favour of a constitutional amendment to remove the automatic right to citizenship of a person born in Ireland. The political debate surrounding the issue was largely framed in terms of a threat to national identity and a perceived (though unfounded) crisis in maternity hospitals, issues amplified through extensive media coverage (Breen, et al., 2006). As Fanning (2002) shows, this negative attitude has long roots in the history of the Irish state. This stance has impacted negatively on those that have come to Ireland, in a period when migration activity has seen a dramatic shift. Policy responses have been reactive and piecemeal and generally have been in response to perceived crises, especially in relation to asylum-seekers and refugees.

The academic response to Ireland's new demographic reality has also been diverse and is still developing. The changed situation has stimulated a considerable amount of commentary and has opened up new areas of sociological analysis and research (see, for example, MacLachlan and O'Connell, 2000; Farrell and Watt, 2001; Fanning, 2002; Rolston and Shannon, 2002; Lentin and McVeigh, 2002). Maguire (2004), for example, has shown how first-generation Vietnamese immigrants are transnational in the sense that they identify more with Vietnam rather than Ireland. They do not speak English and therefore do not communicate with Irish people. The second generation express a more 'hybrid identity', caught as they are between two cultures, Irish and Vietnamese. The question of belonging raises itself for second generation immigrants. They perceive themselves to be Irish, yet they are always questioned as to where they come from. In many cases the voices of immigrants themselves are being heard in the academic literature (such as Sinha, 2002; Mutwarasibo, 2002; Wang, 2006; Kropiwiec, 2006). The launch of a new academic journal, *Translocations*, in 2006 provided another space for discussion of migration, 'race' and social transformation issues. Other key themes include statistical analysis of immigrant flows; discussions of the phenomenon of racism in its many forms; policy analysis (or analysis of the impact of policy vacuum); the media response to immigrants; anti-racism; issues of identity, gender, religion and disability; the connections between responses to Travellers and to immigrants; and the implications of increased immigration for Ireland's health, education and social services.

There is not space to discuss all these issues here. We will rather conclude this section with a brief examination of some key academic and policy discourses that have emerged in the attempt to understand the new direction that Irish society has taken. Much of the discussion is couched in terms of the concept of 'racism'. The most immediate concern is with negative responses to immigrants: in terms of individual prejudice, biased or inflammatory media coverage and physical attacks, but also with what is termed 'institutional racism', that which is embodied in the policies and practices of organisations, especially state bodies (Fanning,

2002, p.180). There has been considerable debate as to whether Ireland is a racist culture: Greeley (1999, p.155) argues that international attitudinal research reveals the (southern) Irish to be 'the most tolerant people in the English-speaking world', while both Aniagolu (1997) and Rolston and Shannon (2002) trace a long history of Irish racist attitudes and practices, particularly in terms of the role of Irish people within the British Empire. Farrell and Watt (2001, p.13) stress that it is important to address the issue in a holistic rather than reactive way:

> reducing a discussion on racism to a discussion on migration and asylum policy can have the, albeit often unintentional, effect of reinforcing the myth that the only people in Ireland to experience racism are recent migrants and that ethnic and cultural diversity in Ireland is as a consequence of recent migration.

This draws attention to the need to look at the historical roots of racism in Ireland, including anti-Semitism (see Chapter 14), attitudes towards Travellers and towards Irish people of colour before the most recent development of large-scale immigration.

As previously mentioned, the term 'multiculturalism' has commonly been used to discuss the changes that are taking place in Irish society as a result of immigration. Thus, for example, Fitz Gerald (2002) speaks in positive terms of the Irish 'multicultural economy', where immigration by both 'homing pigeons' and non-Irish is helping to produce a favourable demographic balance that will help to stimulate future economic growth. Here Fitz Gerald is referring to little more than cultural diversity. This is what Fanning (2002, p.179) identifies as 'weak multiculturalism' where 'the imagery of diversity proliferates but where the aim is to manage diversity rather than contest inequalities'. Fanning sees this approach as typifying official responses in Ireland: there is a focus on 'liberal democratic rights', but little attempt to seriously address underlying structural inequalities and manifestations of institutional racism. Weak multiculturalism is an individualistic response to difference.

It is this concept that Farrell and Watt (2001, p.26) are presumably referring to when they assert that multiculturalism is an 'outmoded concept'. They favour the term 'interculturalism' which requires that 'we focus attention and become aware of the accepted norms within the dominant culture. . . . The development of an intercultural approach implies the development of policy that promotes interaction, understanding and integration among and between different cultures and ethnic groups'. Interculturalism is what Fanning refers to as 'strong multiculturalism' — a multiculturalism that overtly addresses issues of structural inequality and institutionalised racism. For Fanning, by contrast, the term 'interculturalism' has contradictory meanings. Inasmuch as it is used by the state and its institutions (such as the education system, An Garda Síochána) it refers to a very weak form of multiculturalism. On the other hand, when mobilised by activist groups (particularly grass-roots Traveller organisations), interculturalism has been used in the sense of a strong multiculturalism that overtly challenges the status quo.

It emerges from this brief discussion that use of terms such as multiculturalism and interculturalism (and connected concepts such as 'racism' and 'integration') are, in the Irish context, both confused and hotly contested — as they are in many other societies. This is reflected in Lentin's (2002, p.228) analysis:

> Multiculturalism is a 'portmanteau term' for anything from minority discourse to postcolonial critique, from municipal and governmental anti-racism programmes to ethnic diversity as prominently manifested in foodscapes (as in Thai curries and Japanese sushi joining burgers, pizzas and Indian and Chinese takeaways as quintessentially 'Irish' foods in contemporary Ireland), from black music to the commercial appropriation of 'the black' and 'the east'. Multiculturalism is not a single doctrine, does not characterise one political strategy, and does not represent an already achieved state of affairs. It is not a covert way of endorsing some ideal, utopian state. It describes a variety of political strategies and processes that are everywhere incomplete.

There is no doubt that the debates over the meaning of the concepts of multiculturalism and interculturalism will be an important part of the continuing sociological analysis of the phenomenon of cultural diversity and inequality in Irish society.

CONCLUSION

In this chapter we have attempted to explore some aspects of Ireland's rather exceptional demographic experience. In many ways it forms one of the more atypical aspects of Irish society and it is perhaps surprising that, apart from some interest in emigration issues, and more recently issues related to immigration, Irish sociologists have not paid more attention to population. Furthermore, in a context where population profiles tend to be fairly stable (at least in the developed world) Ireland is perhaps unusual in the volatility of its demographic experience. In the space of a very short period of time, Ireland has transformed from being a country of emigrants to a country of immigrants. Tens of thousands of new immigrants have made their homes, some temporarily, in towns and cities throughout Ireland. It is unquestionable that new immigrants have helped to stimulate the economy, and their absorption into the labour force has had no visible net impact upon the employment of Irish people. But as Fitzgerald (*The Irish Times*, 25 November 2006) points out, immigration has not been without its problems:

> Inevitably, a minority of employers have sought to take advantage of some of these foreign workers, many of whom are unfamiliar with our labour laws and minimum pay . . . In less unionised sectors, immigrants may have to depend

upon our labour inspectorate for protection against exploitation and that part of our public regulatory apparatus is currently grossly under-staffed.

It is crucial that we begin to think about immigrants to Ireland not just as a 'reserve army of labour', but as rights bearers. But to do this, the terms of the 'immigration debate' would have to be transformed. Ireland is now faced with a unique and historic opportunity. The country is well placed to embrace tolerance and diversity as hallmarks of our society, to uphold the rights as well as the responsibilities of new immigrants and to promote the principles of multi-culturalism from national to local level. The question is, does the state have the courage to take up that challenge?

So, does Ireland's convergence with the rest of Europe, its 'coming of age' in the demographic stakes, signify the arrival of a truly 'modern' society as is often suggested? Guinnane, from the more measured perspective of history, draws our attention to how some features of Ireland's nineteenth-century demographic experience are re-emerging in contemporary demographic trends across the Western world; for example, late age of marriage, delayed childbirth, high rates of non-married people. He concludes (1997, pp.282, 283) that:

> The Irish grew increasingly to organise and to conduct their lives in household units that were not centred on a married couple. The same is increasingly common in the modern world. Why? . . . increasingly men and women seem to think marriage is not worth the sacrifices it entails. In this respect the post-Famine Irish were very modern.

This telling passage indicates not only the importance of determining the social bases of people's population experiences but also the complexity of the links between them. While Ireland's demographic profile may be increasingly conventional in comparative terms, what is certain is that it will continue to retain the capacity to surprise.

7
Inequality, poverty and class

Irish society is often thought of as a classless society. Irish people tend to treat one another fairly informally, preferring, for example, to use first names even with relative strangers rather than titles and surnames. Holding a certain job or speaking with a particular accent is not widely regarded as entitling a person to special respect. Irish social life is characterised by an egalitarian ethic that rejects attempts by some groups to claim social honour from others. There is also a widespread belief that opportunities for social betterment have increased and that anyone can study hard, get good educational qualifications and move into a better position in society if they want to.

This does not mean that people have no sense of inequality as a part of Irish society; rather, inequality tends to be understood in terms of a gross differentiation between the majority — the 'more or less middle classes' — and an 'underclass' made up of the poor, the long-term unemployed, substance abusers and marginalised groups such as Travellers. Kieran Allen (1999, p.39) has described this picture as 'the duality of a contented majority versus a socially excluded minority'. He argues that inequality is ideologically articulated by key opinion-forming groups as 'a residual category' — a feature of life that applies only to the socially excluded, to 'them', not to 'us', the included, no matter how unequal the terms of our inclusion may be. Public discussions of class inequality in Ireland tend to be framed overwhelmingly in terms of the 'social problems' of poverty and social exclusion.

Thus, while the issue of social class has been central to European sociology and its analysis of capitalist modernity, we cannot take for granted that it is as important in Ireland or that it operates in the same ways. We therefore open this chapter with two questions:

- What place, if any, does class occupy in the self-understanding of Irish society?
- How has class been understood and researched through Irish sociological analysis?

Irish sociology has made some major contributions to the *empirical* uncovering of inequality in Irish society, most notably through ESRI-based research, but also in the work of individual researchers such as Hout and Jackson (1986) and Millar (1998). Strongly influenced by the work of British class analysts such as Goldthorpe, this research has interpreted questions of class and inequality in very specific terms, suggesting that they are best addressed through a focus on *occupational stratification* and *social mobility*. These researchers see the task of class analysis essentially as describing the patterned stratification of the occupational structure and inter-generational movement across it and identifying the individual and social-structural factors that can explain these patterns. Using this approach, they have been able to show that despite common-sense assumptions to the contrary class inequality is and has been a highly significant feature of Irish social organisation. According to Whelan and Layte (2007), earlier research on social mobility has shown Ireland to be characterised by comparatively low levels of absolute and relative mobility. Gross opportunities for upward mobility were less than in other European countries and disparities in opportunities between those from more and less favoured backgrounds were wider. How, if at all, has recent economic development associated with the 'Celtic Tiger' altered this picture? Whelan and Layte conclude that while absolute mobility increased during the 1990s and into the 2000s, relative mobility and equality of opportunity remained stable over time (Whelan and Layte, 2007, p. 85):

> the occupational playing field remains substantially tilted in favour of children from more advantaged households even as the flow of children from working-class origins into middle-class positions has automatically increased. However, there is evidence of a reduction in such equality over time.

SOCIAL MOBILITY AND INEQUALITY IN IRELAND

Analysis of class and inequality in Ireland has taken place against a background of significant and rapid social change — especially occupational and locational change. Breen and Whelan (1996, p.4) suggest that, when asked to think of their society as a class society, the discomfort that many Irish people experience derives at least in part from a belief that the large-scale economic change of the past four decades has destroyed the 'old order' organised around inequality and has ushered in a new order in which equality of opportunity has greatly expanded. They note that many sociologists across the world have thought about inequality in the same way and have taken for granted that economic growth, especially industrialisation, has inevitably been accompanied by increased social mobility.

It was widely argued that high levels of mobility in industrial societies were a consequence of a shift towards *universalism*. Where universalistic criteria were used to assess and value individuals, the social position that a person attained over the life course would be based not on their ascribed or innate characteristics but on their own achievements. This is a core belief within the ideology of modernisation whose impact on Ireland is discussed in Chapter 3 and elsewhere in this book. Societies that have greater mobility may not be more equal overall, but they are thought to have greater *equality of opportunity*. Modernisation theorists expect industrialised societies to be more open, socially fluid places where talent and performance, not inherited advantage, determines people's life chances. A key aim of the class analysis carried out by ESRI and related researchers since the 1970s has been to test, question and, increasingly, to challenge such assumptions.

The approach to class that they have developed is often labelled 'neo-Weberian', but this is a misleading and perhaps inaccurate description. In many ways it would be more appropriate to call it 'neo-Durkheimian'. The influence of Durkheimian thought on this body of research is revealed in a number of ways, from the researchers' commitment to the ideal of an 'open', meritocratic society to their understanding of 'equality' as meaning equal opportunities rather than equal rewards (Baker, 1997). We find in their work neither the sense of tragic irony that runs through Weber's analysis of struggles over power, nor the radical democracy of Marx's conception of a classless society as one organised around the principles of 'from each according to capacity, to each according to need'.

The ESRI research has concerned itself particularly with the study of social mobility. Social mobility can be understood in two key ways (Whelan, 1995, p.336):

- as *structural mobility*: a consequence of changes in the occupational structure itself
- as *relative social mobility*: the chance or 'odds', compared to others', of moving into a different class to the one into which they were born

Structural mobility may be linked, for example, to expansion in service-sector jobs as a result of developments in technology and the labour process in industrialising societies, or to a decline in the numbers of small-scale family businesses and thus of occupational positions inheritable through the family. Both processes increase the importance of education as a means of competing successfully in the job and livelihood market.

In the first half of the twentieth century, opportunities open to Irish people depended heavily on whether their family owned property such as a farm or small business. Those set to inherit a position in a family enterprise could stay in Ireland. The rest generally had to emigrate or enter the religious life or, if they found work in Ireland at all, it was often as a result of family contacts and connections; not many positions were available to those who had only educational qualifications to rely on — a process graphically illustrated by McNabb (1964) in the *Limerick Rural Survey*. By the mid-1980s the pattern had changed dramatically. Nearly three-quarters of males at work were employees in businesses owned by others, that is, non-family ownership (Breen *et al.*, 1990, p.57). There was an increase in the numbers of men in the managerial, skilled manual and white-collar areas, with marked declines in unskilled and semi-skilled occupations (Whelan, 1995, p.332). The transition from recession, emigration and large-scale unemployment that characterised the 1980s, to the boom and labour shortages of the 1990s, is described as 'dramatic' by Whelan and Layte (2007). They point out (Whelan and Layte, 2007, p.67) that these processes contributed to a significant upgrading of the class structure:

> The available evidence shows that the proportion of Irish people in professional and managerial occupations has grown substantially since the 1970s and, if anything, this trend has intensified over the past decade. At the same time, the proportion of the population in low-skilled occupations has fallen steadily. As a consequence, the majority of Irish people are in jobs involving better conditions and prospects than those of their parents.

The shift out of agriculture has been central to changes in class structure and to structural social mobility rates in Ireland. In 1961 half the gainfully employed men in Ireland worked in farming; this had decreased to a fifth by 1981 (Whelan 1995, p.332). Late and rapid industrialisation meant that the transition from agricultural to industrial and service employment did not follow that of the core capitalist economies. Whereas societies such as the United States and Britain saw a shift of workers from agriculture to industry and then to service occupations, the weak development of industrial employment in Ireland saw those displaced from agriculture leaving the country — and exiting the class structure — through emigration. In other words, those displaced by modernisation in Ireland came to make up a significant, and largely subordinated, element of the British class structure (Hazelkorn, 1991).

Over a period of fifty years the occupational structure in Ireland has changed from one dominated by self-employment and small family enterprises to one dominated by employee status in larger enterprises. Recruitment is now based primarily not on family sponsorship but on educational credentials, though kinship connections often remain crucial in finding out about available jobs (Allen, 1998, p.193).

As a result of the shift in the structure of the Irish economy towards one based on industry and service provision and the decline in agricultural employment, enough room opened up at the 'top' to allow considerable mobility into the professional and managerial class from other classes, including farming and urban working classes. This is what Whelan and Layte (2007) identify as the increase in absolute mobility. But this does not mean that the relative advantages enjoyed by families with privileged positions in the earlier class structure have disappeared. In Ireland, absolute mobility rates (measuring the 'inflow' into given classes) may have increased substantially, but relative mobility rates (measuring 'outflow' from class of

Figure 7.1 Social class groups by sex 1991 and 2002

	%	%
Men		
Prof, manag, employers	22.6	34.6
Clerical	11.8	10.5
Farmers	16.9	11.0
Skilled manual	24.9	24.4
Semi-skilled manual	9.2	10.4
Unskilled manual	10.9	7.7
Agricultural	3.7	1.1
Total	**100.0**	**100**
Women		
Prof, manag, employers	27.0	37.3
Clerical	21.7	27.8
Farmers	11.8	6.0
Skilled manual	18.4	12.1
Semi-skilled manual	9.1	9.8
Unskilled manual	9.5	6.2
Agricultural	2.6	0.9
Total	**100.0**	**100.0**

Source: Whelan and Layte (2007)

origin or the extent to which individuals are able to move up or down the class ladder) have remained remarkably unchanged over time (Breen and Whelan, 1996, p.171; Whelan and Layte, 2007). It is *relative* social mobility — discovered, for example, by comparing the occupational level attained by a son with that of his father (more recent work has included daughters, but not mothers) — in which mobility analysts in Ireland have been particularly interested.

This relationship is of interest to mobility analysts because the degree of association between a person's class of origin and their current class position contributes to the measure of social fluidity in a society. What mobility research seeks to uncover is how much social fluidity exists in one society in comparison to another. Measuring mobility is important, according to Breen and Whelan (1996, p.169), as 'restrictions on mobility opportunities are a crucial mechanism by which resource and constraint differences between families become perpetuated across generations'. In other words, when mobility opportunities are blocked or constrained, what might otherwise remain simply economic differences between individuals are transformed into membership of identifiable *social classes* with distinctive lifestyles and unequal life chances.

In the late 1980s 'outflow' from class of origin remained surprisingly limited. Over half the children of managerial and professional fathers were themselves in the managerial and professional class; among working-class men, 70 per cent were themselves the children of working-class men. In comparison to other Western European countries, the Irish figure for immobility is comparatively high, but what further marks out the Irish experience is the 'extremely low level of upward mobility from the working class to the professional and managerial class' (Breen and Whelan, 1996, p.169). While, in terms of the types of people that become professionals and managers, Ireland *appears* quite an 'open' society, this appearance 'turns out to be consistent with very substantial inequalities of opportunity associated with a persistence of the underlying pattern of relative advantages' (Breen and Whelan, 1996, p.172). In other words, the 'classlessness' of Irish society is, in this respect anyway, something of a myth.

Those born into the upper class enjoy a number of advantages — ownership of property or capital, social status or prestige and access to influential social networks, the opportunity to obtain educational credentials — that allow them to avoid downward social mobility. The distribution of these 'class resources', Breen and Whelan (1996, p.174) note, 'shows virtually no change over time'. As Clancy (1995, p.487) remarks:

> It would appear that, since social destinations are so closely related to social origins, the middle classes have perfected the process of passing on their 'achieved status' from one generation to the next. The reproduction of achieved status in an apparently meritocratic society seems to have replaced the inherited privileges of an ascriptive society.

Recent research by the ESRI however has pinpointed an increase in absolute mobility in Ireland and a smaller increase in relative mobility, suggesting that in the years of the economic boom Irish society has become more open. Whelan and Layte (2007, p.84) suggest that as the labour market tightened in the late 1990s, and more workers reached a minimum educational threshold, employers had to rely on criteria such as performance-related attributes that, it appears, have been to the advantage of those from less favoured backgrounds. Some degree of social fluidity appears to have thus been introduced to the Irish class system, despite its overall stability.

Our discussion has concentrated on social mobility among Irish men, but what about Irish women? Whether their positions in the occupational structure are influenced more by their social class background or their gender is a highly controversial issue. Crompton (1998, p.19) suggests that it is very hard to combine both class and gender in a single analysis of inequality, as 'the persistence of the gendered division of labour . . . continues to create apparently insuperable obstacles to the development of a single classification which would encompass both men and women'.

Mobility analysis in Ireland suggests that while class of origin strongly influences the occupational achievements of women as well as men, class and gender also interact to produce some distinctive outcomes for women. Women working outside the home still tend to be found in a restricted range of occupations, primarily professional and managerial, white-collar and semi-skilled manual classes; they are largely excluded from farming, petit bourgeois, technician and skilled manual occupations (see Chapter 8). Women remain largely excluded from the inheritance of productive property, such as agricultural land (P. O'Hara, 1998). 'Over time, women have upward mobility levels that are similar or even greater than men's, but they display substantially higher downward mobility rates' (Whelan and Layte, 2007, p.76). Women also change class through marriage and are somewhat more likely to do so than men are to change class through employment. Overall, Breen and Whelan conclude, what most determines one's life chances or eventual position in society is not one's gender but the class or occupational position of the *family* into which one is born. This is evidenced in research carried out by Harmon and Denny (reported in *The Irish Times*, 21 September 2004) on the trajectory of Leaving Certificate students from 1998 to 2001. The authors found that children from better-off backgrounds who have a range of social and economic supports in place such as access to grinds and private school education consistently get the highest marks in their Leaving Certificate (see Chapter 8). Indeed the distribution of marks 'mirrors the distribution of income' in Irish society.

The work of the ESRI researchers has been of great importance in challenging assumptions complacently made about the decline of inequality as Irish society 'modernises'. Increasingly this research has turned its attention away from a simple focus on father–son occupational mobility to address more problematic issues in the study of inequality, such as:

- gender differences in mobility
- the emergence of the two-career family and the problems it raises for analysis
- how far the problems of a socially-detached underclass can be understood through measures of inequality based on positions within the labour market.

Nevertheless the empirical perspective on class inequality remains rather narrow. It has little to say about social or cultural dimensions of class, nor about classes as historical agents of social change.

Rather, Breen and Whelan (1996, p.2) think of 'class' primarily as 'sets of structural positions' within the economic structure. While in theory understanding how these structural positions may form into groups that possess a distinctive socio-cultural identity is important, how this might happen is hardly addressed in this research. And despite their challenges to the underlying assumptions of modernisation or industrialisation theory, they replicate some of them. For example, the analyses produced from this research tend to have a strong 'meritocratic' bent. The distribution of class positions within Irish society, while noted, is taken to be a less interesting phenomenon than relative mobility between these positions. This is because the latter is 'taken as an indicator of the degree of equality of opportunity or "openness" in a particular society' (Breen and Whelan, 1999, p.329). The implication is that inequality in occupational positions is in itself acceptable. What is unacceptable is for access to higher or better rewarded positions not to be 'open' to everyone (see also Lynch and O'Riordan, 1999, for a strong critique of a similar approach to meritocracy in education).

Baker et al. (2004, p.3) have developed an alternative theory of equality that challenges the ingrained power and privilege of elite groups in society. They treat egalitarianism radically as 'a practical project of developing new ideas, restructuring social institutions and achieving social change'. They suggest that one way to reduce class inequalities in society is to adapt a corporate welfare system in the economy that would promote equity in terms of wage and working conditions both within firms and between larger firms and their smaller counterparts across other industries (2004, pp.90–91). The primary mechanism through which this might be achieved would be through reducing wage differentials. This would be a far more radical approach to economic restructuring than simply redistributing wealth through the taxation system.

For Breen and Whelan, relative social mobility is the most useful measure of the level of inequality in Irish society. Other ESRI-linked work considers inequality in other terms, such as 'income inequality', the distribution of income across families and social groups in Ireland. This issue is central to much of the work done by both Nolan and Callan on levels of poverty in Ireland, where the measure used to estimate rates of poverty is in fact a measure of income inequality. For example, this is the basis for the three 'poverty lines' developed by Callan and Nolan (1988), where households are defined as being 'in poverty' when in receipt of an income that is either 60 per cent, 50 per cent or 40 per cent below the average household income in the state. (A commonly used poverty line in Ireland, also adopted by EU bodies such as Eurostat, is based on a figure of 50 per cent of average weekly industrial earnings. Other poverty lines may be based on the level of payments for various social welfare benefits, such as Social Welfare Allowance). The existence of large numbers of households whose income falls so far below the average indicates substantial inequality in the distribution of income across society.

Hardiman (1998, p.130) argues that the distribution of wealth in Ireland is highly skewed. She ranks Ireland among countries like the United States, the UK and Switzerland in the extent to which wealth is concentrated in the hands of a small minority of the population. According to Nolan and Maitre (2007, p.27), 'the spectacular economic growth in the past decade has seen the gap in average income between Ireland and the richer OECD countries narrow dramatically'. But analysis of income trends during Ireland's boom period reveals that rapid growth has not greatly affected the Irish ranking in terms of income inequality: Ireland has a high degree of economic inequality in comparative terms after the boom, just as it did beforehand.

Poverty

Poverty, class and social inequality are closely linked issues. Indeed, the early sociologists were drawn to the question of class partly as a desire to explain the incidence and persistence of poverty in industrial society. But there is much debate about how to define poverty and how this is done can have significant effects on how it is perceived and managed in society. Callan and Nolan (1998, p.147) point out that 'no single measure of poverty commands universal acceptance or is appropriate for all purposes', but the most common perception of poverty in Ireland, both from 'common-sense' and sociological perspectives, is that of *relative poverty*. This conceptualisation of poverty relates to the acceptable social standards within a society. Ireland contains few people living in the *absolute poverty* experienced at times in some developing countries, but much of the population remains in situations where they are denied many of the attributes of an acceptable social life. This is expressed clearly in the Irish government's National Anti-Poverty Strategy (NAPS), outlined in 1997 (NAPS, cited in Callan and Nolan, 1998, p.147):

> People are living in poverty if their income and resources (material, cultural and social) are so inadequate as to preclude them from having a standard of living which is regarded as acceptable by Irish society generally. As a result of inadequate income and resources people may be excluded and marginalised from participating in activities which are considered the norm for other people in society.

It is this understanding of poverty that underpins the establishment of the poverty lines (see above) as a means of measuring the phenomenon. Equally important, suggest Callan and Nolan (1998, p.148), is the distance by which people are located below the poverty line, that is, the *depth of poverty*. Both measures conceptualise poverty in terms of a lack of money and wealth — 'economic poverty' (Atkinson, 1997, p.10) — but more recently the concepts of *deprivation* and, in particular, *social exclusion* have come to the fore both in sociological thinking and policy debates. Each of these terms attempts to capture how deficiencies and inequalities of wealth and income combine with other aspects of power and social interaction.

Deprivation can include other deficiencies in people's lives, such as the lack of a cooked meal each day or a warm coat in the winter. The notion of 'exclusion' may relate to broader deficiencies, for example, an individual or household's inability to socially interact; to exercise political power; or to access services and facilities, perhaps because they cannot afford a telephone or they have no access to transport. A person may be poor but not deprived or excluded, and vice versa, though in practice there is usually considerable overlap between the two. 'Social exclusion' often serves as no more than a convenient euphemism for 'poverty', being a term that is less politically charged than the latter.

Overall there is much debate about how to measure poverty. Poverty statistics, like those for unemployment (Allen, 1998), are politically sensitive: a government may choose one set of figures, interpreting them in a certain way, while a lobby group may derive a completely different picture using a different measurement, or even draw opposite conclusions from the same set of figures. Atkinson (1997, pp.16–17), for example, has demonstrated how 'optimists' and 'pessimists' can each draw solace from the figures that relate to the decline (or growth) in poverty in Ireland during the 1990s, depending on whether ESRI or EU measurements are adopted. Furthermore, the picture can be changed quite considerably depending on whether households or individuals are taken as the unit of analysis. The main source of recent research data in Ireland is the Living in Ireland survey (Callan et al., 1996), which has been in progress since 1994 and is based on information derived from interviews with 4,000 households. This has provided ammunition both to those who assert that poverty in Ireland has increased and those who see an improvement in the situation. But it has made available a wealth of data about patterns of income and expenditure in the population that expands our understanding of the forms of inequality found in Irish society.

Nolan and Maitre (2007: 38) note that the numbers falling below relative income thresholds derived as proportions of average incomes have risen over the course of the economic boom:

> taking the commonly-used relative income poverty threshold of 60 per cent of median (equivalised) income, for example, about 16 per cent of persons were below that level in 1994 but in 2001 the corresponding figure was 22 per cent (see Whelan et al., 2003 for details). This reflects the fact that social security support rates, though they increased a good deal more rapidly than consumer prices, lagged significantly behind the very rapid rise in incomes from work and property. This meant that the impact of the boom in bringing very substantial numbers from unemployment into work was more than offset by the numbers of long-term pension recipients (notably the elderly) who fell below such relative thresholds.

Substantial numbers of people in Ireland therefore continue to experience deprivation and exclusion as a result of inadequate financial resources, but there has been a marked shift in the types of individuals and groups that experience poverty. Poverty in Ireland is found decreasingly among the retired or elderly and increasingly among the unemployed (and consequently families with children). This contrasts with the situation in some other EU countries where the retired make up a much larger proportion of those in poverty, as do those in work — the 'working poor'. In Italy and France in the late 1980s, this group made up nearly a third of those in poverty (Atkinson, 1997, p.15). Factors such as disability and changes to family structures also have the capacity to significantly affect the incidence and experience of poverty. Ireland now fares worse in relation to overall levels of poverty than some of our EU partners, such as the Scandinavian countries, Belgium and the Czech Republic, but better than others such as the UK, Portugal and Italy (Nolan and Maitre, 2007).

Changes in the groups experiencing poverty reflected increases in unemployment up to the mid-1990s, and changes in social welfare and superannuation (pension) policies and levels of payment. Long-term unemployment had previously been a particular problem in Ireland, with a greater proportion of the unemployed falling into this category — without a job for over a year — than in other EU or OECD countries. A significant proportion of the long-term unemployed have been out of a job for over three years. Such people typically lack educational qualifications or marketable skills. This would suggest that poverty is clearly linked to class; yet class theory has been rarely used to explore poverty in Irish sociology.

In summary, the work of the empirical class researchers has been very significant in challenging facile assumptions about the disappearance of 'class divisions' in Irish society. The painstaking research of Whelan, Breen, Nolan and others has provided extensive quantitative data about the extent of persistent social inequality in Ireland, though we have already seen that such data is open to differing interpretations and 'spins'. But the dominance of particular themes — the treatment of inequality as a poverty issue and the identification of class inequality with occupational inequality — has meant that many other important questions to do with class in Irish society have hardly been raised, let alone answered. To counter the narrow focus of much Irish work on class, we now illustrate some of the diverse ways that sociology has addressed and discussed the idea of class, before returning at the end of the chapter to look at some less well-known, but often most illuminating, accounts of class and class processes in Irish society.

WHAT IS 'CLASS'?

All known societies are characterised by forms of social inequality and by sets of meanings that seek to explain, justify or obscure such inequality. There are many ways to explain, even to justify, inequalities of opportunity and outcome. Age, gender and, at times, ethnicity are important factors. But in all modern societies, wealth, income, education and social esteem or status are always of key importance. 'Class' is widely used by sociologists in discussion of these kinds of inequality.

Despite some suggestions that, both as a social issue and as a useful sociological category, class is no longer relevant (Crompton, 1998, p.9; Lee and Turner, 1996), most sociologists agree that the texture of people's lives, the shape of society and the essence of social inequality continue to be determined to a considerable extent by the ownership of property, the distribution of power and rewards and the nature of people's livelihoods. Furthermore, as Savage (1995, p.16) points out, it is only in recent times that the methodological and theoretical sophistication of sociology has begun to provide high-quality substantive information about class inequalities in modern societies, not least, as we have seen, in Ireland. But if we argue that class difference remains central to understanding society, what do we mean by class?

Class carries a number of broadly accepted separate meanings:

- It can refer to a system whereby people are grouped according to their common economic position, especially as those positions give access to differential rewards in the shape of wealth, property, income or power.
- It is widely understood as an expression of people's lifestyles, in particular how they consume and how they express themselves through certain styles of consumption.
- It is seen by many as a matter of social esteem, prestige or status — a measure of social standing within a particular society.

These three sets of meanings obviously overlap to an extent but they also give rise to differing implications and understandings. Given its centrality to an understanding of society, the definition and analysis of class has been a highly contentious issue within sociology. Not least, there is a complex interrelationship between class and other social and analytical categories such as gender and ethnicity.

Class can be understood on a number of different levels. At the *macrosociological level* sociologists may analyse the structural features of inequality. Why and how is it that societies continue to manifest broad patterns of inequality? How are these structures of inequality reproduced over time and how is this related to the activities of broad social groups and interests? What are the implications for macrosocial outcomes such as health, welfare or development? At the *microsociological level* of analysis, sociologists may ask questions about how class is experienced, for example, within the workplace or the household; how do attitudes and values relate to class and how are these expressed through social interaction? A focus on the broad social structure may help to delineate consistencies and patterns that endure over time and set limits to social action, consciousness and change. An analysis of the minutiae of everyday activities and relationships may allow us to focus on the dynamic living out of social structures, in other words, to capture something of the 'lived experience' of class. The greatest challenge for class theorists and analysts is to combine the two levels of understanding: to show how people's everyday lives and experiences are tied into, or appear to be disconnected from, the broader structures that shape societies.

Is 'class' merely a descriptive category and a way to categorise certain aspects of social experience? Or should classes be seen themselves as social actors, as a motive force in history? This has been a central issue in debates between different sociological perspectives on class and it raises questions about the importance of a temporal or historical dimension in class analysis. Sociologists who think of classes as social movements that can shape historical outcomes generally emphasise an understanding of the particular class formation as a key element in the class analysis of a society. To understand *class formation* means to grasp how the class structure has been shaped by and has emerged from a history of relationships between classes. In contrast, positivist (see Chapter 1), or what are often misleadingly called 'neo-Weberian', approaches to researching class tend to be *categorical* or *taxonomic*: they slot people into positions or 'boxes' and then locate these positions in relation to a social hierarchy, such as a hierarchy of occupations. Like analysts of class formation, positivists think of classes as having an objective reality — they are empirically observable and measurable — but their reality is as a social category rather than a historically acting collective subject. Those who adopt a more interpretative approach in sociology are more likely to define class as a set of meanings that structure individual actions and social space, the complex but invisible patterns of relationships between groups and individuals.

We can conclude then that 'class' contains a very complex set of ideas. It can embrace many aspects of social life, from inequalities of wealth, property and income to the work people do, the education they receive and the housing they occupy, their values, attitudes and political beliefs and practices and even the art, literature and mass media that they produce or consume. Furthermore, these dimensions overlap and interact. How we understand class is also fundamentally determined by the particular theoretical lens that we use to examine the phenomenon.

THEORIES OF CLASS

It is common for introductory presentations of class theory to begin with a contrast between three broad perspectives:

- functionalist
- Marxist
- Weberian.

Functionalist analyses can be described as basically 'common-sense' understandings of inequality. They see inequality as normal, indeed functional, for society. Thus, 'inequality in complex societies [is] rendered legitimate via an emerging consensus of values relating to the societal importance of particular functions . . . such theories incorporate a moral justification of economic inequality' (Crompton, 1998, p.7). In other words, social inequality is not only inevitable but morally defensible. The existence of unequal material rewards provides incentives for socially desirable behaviour such as innovation, business development and the creation of wealth; and it is further claimed that there is a consensus across society that disproportionate rewards for such innovators and wealth creators are justified and legitimate. Simply put, functionalists argue that it is both necessary *and* desirable that surgeons and company directors have greater wealth and income than cleaners and bus drivers.

Marxist analyses of class, on the other hand, are sharply critical both of the basis of the class system and its social effects. For Marx, productive activity or work was central to human experience and society. The central division in all societies is based on people's relationship to the material basis of production. In capitalist society this is highly unequal. Productive property like land, railways or factories is held and controlled by a small group of owners — the bourgeoisie — while the vast bulk of the population owns no capital assets and has only their labour power to sell — the proletariat. These two classes have diametrically opposed interests: the bourgeoisie in maximising the profit they can make from the labour of the proletariat; the workers in maximising the return to themselves on their labour. The struggle over these interests is termed 'class conflict'. It is on the basis of this inequitable system of organising production that, for Marxist sociologists, social inequality is founded. For Marxists, the wealth of company directors is directly at the expense of their employees.

The nature of capitalist society has changed considerably since Marx was writing in the nineteenth century and, accordingly, Marxist sociologists have developed more complex and sophisticated analyses of class while retaining the fundamental elements identified by Marx. Theorists such as the American sociologist Erik Olin Wright have expanded Marx's analysis of work-based inequality to embrace other dimensions of the productive process; for example, the power to control others through the organisation and management of work; access to specific types of skills or credentials that workers can use to bargain for a bigger slice of the cake. There is little Marxist-influenced class research in Irish sociology. Most Irish class analysts understand themselves to be Weberian or neo-Weberian in their theoretical perspective, but this is achieved largely by selectively emphasising some aspects of Weber's theory at the expense of others.

Weberian approaches to social inequality have focused very much on the issue of status but, for Weber, the key struggles in society were over the issue of *power*. These struggles were not limited to the economic realm and could include struggles in relation to authority, political influence or the determination of social standing and respect. The three key aspects of power identified by Weber were economic power, prestige and political power. They are summed up in the trio: *class*, *status* and *party*.

Like Marx, Weber related class to the distribution of the means of production and to the economic market. He too emphasised how the majority of people have only their labour to sell on the market — whether that labour equates to manual strength, dexterity or the intellectual and organisational abilities that were gaining importance at the time Weber was writing — and how this placed them in a very unequal position compared to those who owned capital. For Weber, however, classes were not self-conscious groups with a specific political interest as they were for Marx; rather, they were categories or collections of workers of a given type (it is this aspect that may lead people to label stratification research as 'neo-Weberian'). Self-consciously organised groups with political goals fell more in line with Weber's second category, *status groups*.

For Weber, status is based on social prestige. A status group has been defined as follows (Cuff *et al.*, 1998, p.51):

> a collection of people who recognise themselves as equals, who look upon one another as equally worthy, and who look up to and down on other social groups. A status group involves shared understandings, mutual recognition among its members and, of course, acknowledgement from its superiors and inferiors of its standing in the general scale of social position.

Status groups are characterised by a shared culture or belief in cultural distinctiveness: Weber was particularly interested in religious or ethnic divisions in a society as a basis for their formation. More recently, status has been linked to the consumption of particular sorts of goods. Indeed, class theory has come to be differentiated between Marxists, seen to be interested in *production* (and associated issues such as work and the organisation of the labour process), and Weberians, associated with an emphasis on *consumption* (and related issues such as culture, education, housing and so on). In this sense, status represents the ability of those who share a similar class position to convert their economic (or political) advantage into symbolic markers of cultural superiority: having the right sort of house, car or fashion clothing (see Chapter 16).

Finally, *party* is the term used by Weber to denote the role of political power in shaping social inequality. In other words it concerns the ability of groups to organise for their own ends. Much status group activity characteristically takes the form of *social closure*, attempting to limit access by outsiders to the cultural characteristics that form the basis of a claim for superior status. This might mean a refusal to accept people of certain religious beliefs; to prevent outsiders from becoming proficient in the language of the high status group; or to impose quotas to restrict access to high status educational qualifications such as in law or social work. The success of social closure practices is influenced by the relationship that the group has to political power structures. Like Marx, then, Weber understands inequality as being significantly shaped by the nature of the formal political system in a given society and by relations to the state. Weber's ideas cannot be reduced to a simple hierarchy of occupational positions but, unfortunately, in the guise of 'neo-Weberian stratification theory', this is how they are often presented.

Class theory has always been difficult to pin down because of extensive debates in social theory and rapid change in the contours of Western society (Crompton, 1998, p.13). There are numerous varieties of class theory and analysis and not enough space here to explore even a fraction of them (see Crompton, 1998; Devine, 1997; Lee and Turner, 1996, for comprehensive discussions). In talking about the analysis of class in contemporary societies, it is important to be aware of the changes taking place in the nature of global society: shifts that have variously been described as the movement towards a post-modern world of 'disorganised capitalism' (Lash and Urry, 1994). In particular, the perceived decline of class politics, the break-up of traditional social divisions and categories and the emergence (at least in popular discourse) of groups such as yuppies, slackers and downshifters have provided challenges for class analysis.

There is a growing popular interest in the impact of status in society. Alain de Botton, the Swiss-born philosopher, has mapped the human preoccupation with relative standing in his bestseller, Status anxiety (2004). Similarly, Michael Marmot in his 2004 book, Status syndrome, explores how status helps to shape the general well-being of senior civil servants. He argues that there is a discernible downward gradient from high-status individuals (and their partners), who tend to live longer, healthier and happier lives, to those of even fractionally lower status. According to Marmot, while we all enjoy the gratification that can be derived from being admired and respected by others, high status also impacts on individual life chances. The dividend is two-fold: people who enjoy high status tend to be very socially integrated, and research has shown that the denser one's social networks the better for one's overall well-being. Furthermore, the higher your status, the more likely you are to exercise control and autonomy over your job and lifestyle. Such autonomy is important as it increases the potential for realising wants and choices and acts as a bulwark against the kind of debilitating stress that makes us physically or mentally ill.

Wilkinson's (2005) work on the epidemiological implications of inequality makes a similar point. Drawing on a wealth of research material, Wilkinson argues that social status and respect matter, and the psychological damage done by being ranked as low status has negative consequences in terms of general health and well-being. The greater the equality in a society, the greater the overall life expectancy. The United States is the richest and most unequal country, with the lowest life expectancy in the developed world. This is worrying for Ireland, for while recent economic growth has made a substantial contribution to social progress, many stubborn social problems remain. A 2005 NESC (National Economic and Social Council) report, The developmental welfare state, argued that although absolute per capita levels of social spending have increased, in real terms deep social inequities remain. For example, the report identified continued educational disadvantage, homelessness, long-term dependence on social welfare, area disadvantage and the situation of the Travelling community.

The analyses of the classical social theorists, developed during the triumph of modernity and subsequently elaborated by generations of sociologists, retain a great deal of relevance in understanding today's societies. Combining in particular Marx's and Weber's ideas, we argue, following Wright (1989), that the explanatory and theoretical power of class analysis can be found in how it links three key elements of social life:

- *material interests* — the means of maximising economic welfare; in our type of society this relates very much to power, wealth, status, property, income, education and work.
- *the lived experience of everyday life* — a very broad term that may embrace numerous aspects of people's existence; of particular relevance, perhaps, in the study of class, are aspects of life such as work, family, values and consumption.
- *the capacity for collective action* — how people may act together in the world based on their membership of a broader social entity; once again, this is a very broad set of ideas. Collective action may take the form of gang warfare, social movements or a range of activities related to people's material and social circumstances, perhaps based on what they perceive to be 'class' issues. Examples may include industrial action, political behaviour or forms of social protest.

Theories of class, then, can be said to operate on at least three levels:

- as a theoretical understanding of how social structures operate to constrain the possibilities of social action
- as an understanding of the nature of everyday life in terms of how its practices and patterns reflect and are constrained/endowed by social structures
- as an understanding of the strategies and organisational arrangements that groups use to represent themselves and to establish their symbolic boundaries and vision of the world.

However, these analytical ideas have some complex implications in terms of sociological understanding and analysis.

Structure and agency and the class debate

Arguments about social class in sociology have been very much influenced by ongoing debates in social theory, in particular that known as the structure and agency debate. This debate contrasts theories that suggest that social structures determine human action with those that focus more on the potential of individuals and groups to shape their own destinies. Like most perennial debates, this one is unlikely to be resolved but it remains essential to understanding much about how social class has been, and continues to be, used within sociological analysis.

The 'structure' side of the debate owes much to the influence of Marx. It is undeniable that Marx stressed the key role of the economic dimension in shaping human history and contemporary society. Many readings of Marx deduced that cultural and social phenomena could in effect be read off from an understanding of the economic and production relationships within society, including the class structure. As a result, many Marxist theorists, in particular those calling themselves 'scientific Marxists' (for example, the writers Althusser and Poulantzas, prominent in the 1970s), paid a great deal of attention to the theoretical definition of class groupings within capitalism, but they did not devote similar attention to how people actually experienced (or did not experience) class in everyday life.

Structuralist approaches to class have much in common with functionalism, despite their very different pedigrees. They tend to emphasise the power of society and to underplay the ability of human actors to influence events. Both approaches also tend to be teleological, in other words, they assume a particular end-point in advance. Not surprisingly many sociologists of class have been highly critical of structuralist accounts. Interestingly these critics also draw on the Marxist legacy, but have tended to emphasise the humanist side of Marx's writings (especially those that he completed earlier in his life which were in fact published after his death) rather than the more materialist analysis found in later works such as the celebrated work *Das Kapital*.

Writers in the humanist Marxist tradition included the Hungarian, Lukács, and the Italian, Gramsci. Each of these was to have a very significant influence on thinking about capitalist society and class, particularly in Europe. Each stressed the importance of politics and ideas in the formation of class. In many ways they attempted to address the question that had haunted Marxism: if it was in the interests of the workers to overthrow the capitalist system, why did this not occur? Lukács stressed the role of *reification* — a concept drawn from Marx. This is the process by which people see the world as an independent object rather than an outcome of their own actions. At its most extreme, reification results in fatalism and a belief that nothing can be changed via human action; more generally it means that people tend to accept the world as it is, not believing that they can effect a difference.

Gramsci is best known for his concept of *hegemony*. This notion builds on Marx's ideas about the role and nature of ideas in class society. For Marx, as famously stated in his book *The German ideology*, written in 1846, the dominant ideas in society are the ideas of the ruling class. Gramsci devoted much of his writings to trying to explain how this process took place, focusing in particular on Italian society. The struggle for hegemony in society, the intellectual domination of debate and interpretation, is a key element in the class struggle. We can see in the work of both Lukács and Gramsci part of a larger debate about how the struggles for power and influence between competing class groups are experienced, at least partly, as battles over meaning, understanding and the nature of social reality.

The ideas of the French sociologist Pierre Bourdieu, who died in 2002, have been increasingly influential amongst researchers on class. Like many modern social theorists, Bourdieu attempted to reconcile the objective and the subjective sides of human societies (Cuff *et al.*, 1998, pp.322–7). This led him to devote considerable study to cultural phenomena and to attempt to combine an analysis of the production and consumption of culture (in education, the mass media and in high and popular culture) with an understanding of class that draws heavily on the work of both Weber and Marx.

Bourdieu's writings try to link issues of consumption with economic and social power (see Chapter 16 for more detail). A key concept that Bourdieu developed is that of *cultural capital*. This refers to the existence of dominant and socially legitimated ideas about what is culturally valued and desirable in our society, for example, art house cinema (as opposed to *Pirates of the Caribbean*), literary fiction (as opposed to the works of Cecelia Ahern), fine art exhibitions (as opposed to greyhound racing) and gourmet food (as opposed to burgers and chips). Bourdieu believed that the power of the bourgeoisie is based both on economic wealth and income *and* on possession of 'cultural capital, the forms of cultural distinction that privileged middle-class groups can embrace and pass on to their children by giving them the right "disposition" to perform well in the educational system' (Heath and Savage, 1995, p.278). Thus, the privilege of middle-class groups is maintained partly through the passing on of property (housing, shares, money); their greater access to success in the education system; and their ability to engage in exclusionary and valued forms of cultural activity. Of course access to all three types of scarce resources is often overlapping and mutually reinforcing.

As class theorists have attempted to address the issues raised by the structure and agency debate, we see that they are also led to raise questions about how people actually experience and 'live' class. But success in integrating questions of culture and lifestyle into class theory brings its own problems. Too great a focus on issues of lifestyle can cloud an awareness of how class is structured by unequal access to resources, power and control. The challenge for a sociological analysis of class is to incorporate both aspects of the phenomenon.

SYMBOLS AND STRATEGIES OF CLASS

Marxist theorists argue that classes are formed *within* and as a result of class struggle. A key debate in class theory and analysis has been the extent to which classes 'act' in their own interests (Crompton, 1998, p.16). For some Marxist theorists a class will, by definition, act to defend its own interests within the realm of class struggle. From a Weberian viewpoint such action is possible, even likely, but not inevitable. Either theoretically or empirically, it is very difficult to establish relationships between class position, class consciousness and class action or social mobilisation. It is untenable to simply read off observed behaviour from a theoretically specified 'base': for as Cloke and Thrift (1990, p.169) point out, 'people whose earnings and relations with capital production are similar will not necessarily share a corporate consciousness, interest or inclination for action.' To analyse collective action requires an understanding of how issues and projects are collectively articulated and expressed and how groups are mobilised as a result.

Many class analysts make a distinction between class awareness and class consciousness. *Class awareness* refers to the extent that people identify with a particular class grouping in terms of lifestyle, attitudes, patterns of consumption and so on. It does not mean recognising the group as a class; indeed for middle-class people it may require a belief that class itself does not exist and that it 'is all down to the individual'. In other words (Breen and Whelan, 1996, p.3):

> Class awareness involves a shared awareness and acceptance of a common style of life among the members of a class; it does not imply recognition that the attitude, beliefs and styles of life that members of this class have in common signify a class affiliation, that there are other classes with different attitudes, beliefs and patterns of behaviours.

Class consciousness thus means a recognition that classes exist and that one is a member of a particular class distinct from other classes.

While much class theory is concerned with macrosociological issues of social structure, mass political and industrial movements, historical development and large-scale social change, it is clear that class analysis also applies to the level of 'everyday life'. How people daily live out class relationships is of importance for at least two reasons. Class concepts can help us to better understand people's day-to-day experiences of inequality and powerlessness; similarly, an insight into people's everyday lives can contribute to an understanding of how class groupings are produced and reproduced and how class consciousness, ideologies and class-related attitudes are sustained.

To an extent we all live in what Mike Allen (1998, p.11) terms the 'partitioned society'. 'What defines us' in the class sense, he suggests, is 'the total segregation of all life's hopes, chances and experiences.' He is indicating how modern (especially urban) life allows us to circumscribe our experience so that it obscures our direct experience of inequality. This provides us with a feeling of control over our own lives, or self-determination. But the capacity to feel in control of one's life is itself unequally distributed. For example, it is frequently dependent on access to privacy. As Allen (1998, p.32) says, there is a sharp contrast between the lack of basic privacy accorded to recipients of state benefits (for example, queueing for the dole) and the privacy demanded by the wealthy and powerful when tribunals of inquiry or the Revenue Commissioners are attempting to investigate their financial affairs.

Everyday experiences of class awareness or of social inequality may also be shaped by relationships to space. Class and inequality are often related to neighbourhood and 'community'; territory, residence, distance, space and movement help to shape people's experiences of class, inequality and poverty. In larger urban settlements, neighbourhood segregation may render social relationships and groups more homogenous and class and status more clearly delineated. In other words, people are 'sorted' by class, wealth and income into particular neighbourhoods and suburbs (Fahey, 1998b). Once there, they tend to interact to a large extent with others of similar background and class identity. In smaller rural settlements, despite substantial material inequalities and social exclusiveness, there may be more informal and friendly contact between relatively wealthy and poorer people. People of different classes may interact as neighbours or be linked by personal ties of work, kinship or friendship. Indeed, regular interaction in a variety of institutional contexts may lead to a social and psychological desire to ignore or deny social inequality. Residence in a smaller community may increase the likelihood of class mobility, affect class solidarity and consciousness and lead to a more flexible set of class distinctions.

CLASS FORMATION, CLASS CONFLICT AND THE LIVED EXPERIENCE OF CLASS IN IRELAND

We have argued that the interest, usefulness and explanatory power — indeed, the value of class analysis — depends on how well it links three key elements of social life: the structured distribution of material resources; the lived experience of everyday life; and the capacity for collective action that groups exercise. We conclude this chapter by asking how well Irish sociology has succeeded in addressing these dimensions. We focus briefly on some Irish studies of class that differ in approach to those of occupational stratification or income inequality initially discussed.

We look first at attempts to relate *class formation* and *class mobilisation* to Irish material or cultural conditions in order to understand how these processes are shaped by the distinctive history and economic and political location of a given society. We understand class formation to refer not only to the emergence of new classes in a society but also to how existing classes are reproduced or indeed change over time. Crotty (1983) argues that the 'capitalist colonial' relationship between Ireland and Britain in the late nineteenth century, in encouraging the development of a particular sort of small-scale agrarian-based economy, contributed to 'the embourgeoisement of the periphery and the proletarianisation of the core'. Those Irish who emigrated to Britain because they were surplus to the requirements of agriculture in Ireland became landless and propertyless labourers while those who stayed to work in Ireland became owners of small property.

The importance of property is stressed by Hannan and Commins (1992) who emphasise the persistence of a 'vibrant, small-scale landholding sector' in Irish society right into modern times. To them this represents a major challenge to the position of modernisation theorists who maintain that industrialisation tends to make all developing societies more alike (see Chapter 3). They argue that the remarkable endurance of such a 'pre-industrial' property-holding class into the 1990s has been ignored in most analyses of contemporary Irish society (1992, p.87). The dispersion of small property ownership across a substantial section of the population renders the Irish class structure and experience quite different to that of many other modern societies (Fahey, 2002a).

Hannan and Commins are interested in this class of small property owners for two reasons. First, they want to understand why this class has adapted so successfully to 'the modernisation of the country's economic and social structure' (1992, p.79). Second, they want to contrast it with the fate of the urban working class which, they say, has been far less successful in this regard. To explain the success of the small property owner involves an examination of both the individual and collective strategies used by this group. Individually, households with land have been able to work out a range of 'survival strategies' that in many cases allowed them to move out of full-time farming into multiple sources of income generation, which has often provided a better gross household income. This class has also been adept at taking advantage of opportunities for social mobility, particularly through education, for their children (see Chapter 8 and P. O'Hara, 1998). Collectively, it has not only enjoyed considerable favouritism from the Irish and EU states (in relation to state industrialisation strategies, as agricultural producers and as land-owners) but has also displayed a remarkable capacity to organise politically in pursuit of its own interests. In nearly all these ways, there is a strong contrast with the urban working class whose members' chances of employment and upward mobility have been consistently much poorer over recent decades.

Hannan and Commins's treatment of class in this analysis is quite limited. They have little to say about class consciousness or even class awareness among this social grouping. They do not locate the small property-owning class clearly in any relationships with other classes in Irish society, preferring to focus on contrasts between classes, nor is the formation of this class explained through tracing its position in the class structure overall. Small property owners are presented as competing for state benefits with the urban working class, but independently of them. Despite these omissions Hannan and Commins's analysis remains interesting as it shows how the dynamics of Irish societal development have been shaped by historically distinctive processes of class formation.

A second way to look at class formation and mobilisation in Ireland has used an approach that emphasises classes as formed in and through their relations with other classes, usually, though not always, in relations of struggle and conflict. This is the *political economy approach* (Curtin et al., 1996; Tovey, 1999a; 2000) and has been applied in particular to the issues of rural development (and under-development) and rural poverty. It offers a strong contrast to the dominant spatial approach to these topics, that treats poor people essentially as 'people who live in poor places' (Pringle et al., 1999). While not wanting to deny that where people live can bear upon their social and economic opportunities, the political economy approach tries to understand poverty as 'a dynamic condition, that is, produced out of, maintained and/or changed by dynamic processes in society in general' (Tovey, 1999a, p.97).

The political economy approach argues that the situation of disadvantaged groups is best analysed through an examination of their relations with other classes or groups. In the case of rural poverty, for example, the disadvantage of small farmers or landless labourers has been produced by how *other* classes have pursued their own interests. The progressive marginalisation of smaller producers since the 1850s has occurred not as an accident of location but as the outcome of strategies used by larger farmers (Crotty, 1974) and the food industry (Tovey, 2000) to secure and increase their own profits and place in society. Curtin *et al.* (1996) argue that the class position of 'family farmers' across the developed world must be understood in terms of their relationships with an increasingly globalised and integrated food industry, control of which (even in Ireland where it has historically been dominated by farmer co-ops) has progressively shifted away from primary producers towards the distribution and retailing end of the chain. Thus, rural social classes can be seen, like urban industrial ones, to be formed in their relations with other classes and, in particular, in relation to the owners and managers of industrial capital. At this point, from a political economy perspective, the understanding of rural poverty intersects with and becomes part of the understanding of poverty and exploitation among urban industrial workers.

The Marxist or materialist theme that underpins the political economy approach contrasts markedly with the 'neo-Weberian' orientation of most Irish class analysis. Marxist concepts, approaches and positions have also influenced ethnographic accounts of the *lived experience of class* in Irish society. A Combat Poverty Agency funded study, *Against all odds*, was based on an in-depth examination of 30 poor families living in urban and rural areas. The authors, Daly and Leonard (2002), highlighted how inadequate resources and lack of basic necessities curtailed people's everyday lives. The high level of ill-health among adults, children and young people in the study — there were health problems in two-thirds of families — reaffirms the link between low income, poverty and ill-health. Insufficient money, insufficient capacity and resources to change their situation and insufficient public service provision exacerbate problems relating to health and well-being. Most households, for example, had no money left over in a typical week. Many households were in arrears on regular and basic expenditure such as rent, electricity and telephones. Families' contact with voluntary and community organisations was extensive and vital in supporting families to cope. While people appreciated the assistance, some expressed unease about having to rely on 'charity'. Parents' main concern was that a lack of amenities such as a local playground, or their inability to afford leisure activities, would make their children more susceptible to involvement in joyriding or drug use in their local communities. People generally lived in fear. People living in disadvantaged housing estates are not only likely to become victims of crime, but to anticipate this as part of their daily lives (Daly and Leonard, 2002). By EU standards, Ireland has amongst the highest rates of child poverty, even though it has fallen in recent years.

Figure 7.2 Per cent of children living below national poverty lines

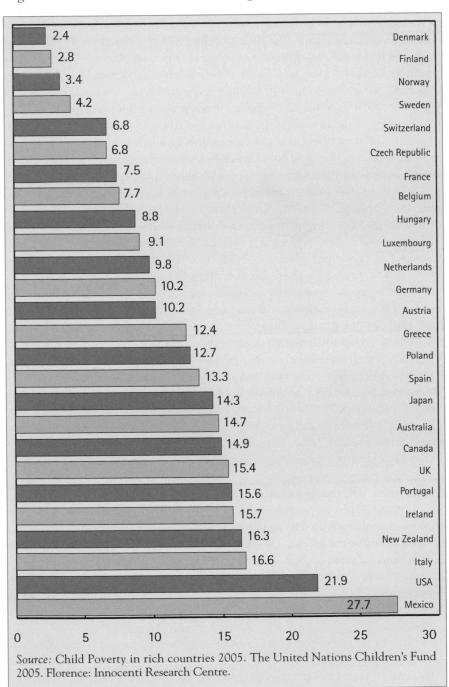

2.4	Denmark
2.8	Finland
3.4	Norway
4.2	Sweden
6.8	Switzerland
6.8	Czech Republic
7.5	France
7.7	Belgium
8.8	Hungary
9.1	Luxembourg
9.8	Netherlands
10.2	Germany
10.2	Austria
12.4	Greece
12.7	Poland
13.3	Spain
14.3	Japan
14.7	Australia
14.9	Canada
15.4	UK
15.6	Portugal
15.7	Ireland
16.3	New Zealand
16.6	Italy
21.9	USA
27.7	Mexico

0   5   10   15   20   25   30

Source: Child Poverty in rich countries 2005. The United Nations Children's Fund 2005. Florence: Innocenti Research Centre.

In research carried out in the town of Ennis, Curtin and Ryan (1989) examine the relationships between class, occupation, lifestyle, leisure and social interaction in an attempt to provide a more holistic account of the lived experience of class. They compare, in particular, the periods of the 1930s and the 1980s. In the former, class difference was clearly marked in a number of ways that were immediately intelligible to Ennis residents: 'on the streets one could judge with some accuracy a person's occupation by his style of dress, and from his occupation determine the type of house he lived in and in which quarter of the town it stood' (1989, p.129). Clearly demarcated class positions were reinforced through everyday activity and, of particular interest to Curtin and Ryan, the social clubs to which Ennis men typically belonged. Ranging from elite clubs for the bourgeoisie to labour clubs for the working class, these institutions provided both a location for leisure activity (most working-class houses were too small to allow for this) and, on occasion, for class-based political activity. In the 1980s most of the town's 'clubs' had disappeared and leisure activity had shifted towards, on the one hand, the domestic space (that is, in front of the television) and, on the other, to pubs in the town, which reflected to some extent the class and gender-based divisions previously provided by the exclusive clubs. The changes in everyday life, structured by employment, education and place of residence, were implicated in many complex ways with issues of class, gender and age. While inevitably partial and impressionistic, this research provides an important parallel to the occupational stratificationist approach outlined at the start of this chapter.

Conflicts within communities over proposed development can sometimes bring everyday understandings of class into sharper relief. Corcoran (2002a) explored this process in relation to a proposed docklands development project in the Dublin north inner city. In 1998, the first proposal submitted for the development of fifty-one acres of the brown-field site on the north side of the Liffey emerged from a property consortium, led by Treasury Holdings. An American-based architect designed a twenty-six building complex for the site, including a national conference centre, apartment blocks, office buildings, hotels, parkland and the refurbishment and change of use of several listed buildings and structures. Partial planning permission was granted by Dublin City Council in the first instance, but this decision was appealed by a range of parties, including the local residents, the DDDA (Dublin Docklands Development Authority) and the development consortium. As a result of the unprecedented scale of the scheme and the interest it had generated, an oral hearing was conducted by An Bord Pleanála in the Spring of 2000. In July of that year, An Bord Pleanála rejected the bulk of the scheme, granting planning permission for the National Conference Centre only.

The hearing on the Spencer Dock development project provides some insight into how the idea of the city can become the focus of contested claims. Conflicts between commercial interests (the Spencer Dock Development Company) and community values (Docklands residents' associations) were largely grounded in arguments over the significance of place. On the one hand, the proponents of the scheme argued that the development would represent the most comprehensive urban project in the history of the state. The scheme was defended on economic grounds, with the suggestion that since Dublin was already part of the global information economy, it could capitalise on growth in that area by providing commercial buildings such as those proposed in the Spencer Dock scheme.

On the other hand, the residents (and a variety of other interested parties and groups) opposed the development on the basis of its architectural inappropriateness, excessive scale, environmental impact, disregard for the past, and social implications for the community. Oral testimonies by docklanders give us an insight into the importance of place in the everyday, taken-for-granted life of the city's historic working-class neighbourhoods. The residents' representatives employed a territorial, place-based identity as a basis for their political mobilisation. The communities chose to represent themselves symbolically as a cluster of urban villages, linked through a powerful sense of place attachment to the locality. They argued that their neighbourhood retains a powerful sense of place, grounded in a shared historical past, working-class culture and a web of familial ties. The proposed development was viewed as a threat to the neighbourhood, so defined. Furthermore, in affirming the sense of a place-bound identity in the urban villages of the docklands, residents quite self-consciously rejected the aestheticisation of place. They argued, for example, that their streets and homes were not part of some 'Jim Sheridan film set. They are homes where people were born, parents died, brothers and sisters emigrated to America and Australia' (Submission 16 to Spencer Dock oral hearing, 10 February to 14 March 2000). Here the residents demonstrate their felt need to distinguish between their lived experience of the character and tradition of their place, and its cultural representation in global space. The docklanders mobilised around the sense of place attachment, identifying the docklands as a geographically distinct place with a particular relationship to the city and the skyline. In addition, they made representations to the oral hearing about the significance of their neighbourhood as a repository of Dublin's literary and historical heritage.

Furthermore, opposition to the proposed development crystallised around the clash between the global and the local, with the Treasury Holdings plan viewed as a kind of battering ram of globalisation that ultimately threatened to obliterate the 'local' in Dublin. Local docklands opposition to the proposed development may therefore be interpreted as a questioning of the city's new globalised status, neatly summed up in the term 'the Manhattanisation of Dublin'. Among docklanders and their supporters, there appears to be a growing awareness that unfettered development that ignores the vernacular of the city can only lead to a Dublin that is much the same as anywhere else and, therefore, a nowhere place. The concerns expressed over the course of the oral hearing clearly indicate a desire for Dublin to retain its character, to respect working-class communities and traditions and not to succumb to placelessness through the importation of mammoth American-inspired architecture.

Perhaps the most detailed and theoretically developed analysis of class from an ethnographic perspective is that of Australian anthropologist, Chris Eipper (1986). His study focused on the town of Bantry in Co. Cork in the light of the impact of Gulf Oil, a multinational oil company that had established an oil refinery in Bantry in the mid-1960s. Eipper's analysis of local community interaction sought to examine the changing nature of class domination in Irish society in its local, national and international forms. Although he treats the lived experience of class as a key issue for understanding local social life, Eipper does not believe that class and class processes can ever be fully understood if they are treated as purely local. At the same time, he argues, class cannot be treated, as has sometimes been the case in locally based studies, as no more than 'external factors' that provide a 'context' for local experience. Rather, what Eipper calls the 'nexus between church, state and business' (the 'ruling trinity' that provides the title for his study) is forged and operates *simultaneously* at the local and national level (1986, p.3). We can only understand 'how class worked in Bantry' if we link this up to 'how it worked in a number of other places too'. Eipper's approach is ambitious in that it tries to look at the macro and the micro at the same time, unusual in sociological analyses of class. It also tries to keep in sight both issues of structure and of agency. As a result, Eipper has perhaps been the most successful at constructing a theoretical perspective on class in Ireland that integrates the three key dimensions of class analysis: interests, cultural meanings, and political action.

To develop this perspective, Eipper makes an essential distinction between two ways that people can act in their relations with others: as 'acting subjects' and as 'social agents'. 'Class,' he argues, 'has to be analytically grasped as both an ideological encounter and as a material condition' (1986, p.12). Class is understood as a material condition when we treat people's behaviour as a result of the material constraints under which they operate; or the economic location they occupy; or as an expression of their pursuit of material self-interest. But the problem is how to translate abstract categories of class, such as capital or wage labour, into substantive classes that have cultural and political histories, such as the bourgeoisie or the working class. To understand social experiences 'in all their lived complexity' we cannot 'satisfactorily treat people as merely personifications of economic relations . . . the actual flesh and blood people who empirically relate to one another in real life' relate to one another 'as persons' (1986, p.12). They are formed by social and cultural experiences as well as by economic position. Their interaction is shaped by notions of status and social honour, in turn expressions of the dominant ideological beliefs about the types of persons and ideas that are entitled to respect and deference. Eipper, then, argues that class analysis has to combine the analysis of two forms of class relationship:

1   People act as the 'social agents' or representatives of economic class locations, for example, as the representatives of the interests of owners of capital.
2   They are acting subjects, real people living a distinctive way of life within a given social habitat.

Both ways of acting involve struggles for power and control, particularly for control of people's class consciousness 'which is the acme of class struggle, of class formation' (1986, p.14).

Eipper uses these theoretical concepts to produce an analysis of class and power relationships in Bantry before and after the arrival of multinational capital in the area. As we have already suggested, he sees Irish society as dominated by a ruling bloc comprising church, state and business. He examines closely both the personal power exercised by each of these groups in Bantry life, historically and contemporaneously, through the clergy, politicians and local business elites, and, at a national level, the relationships between the church 'as a corporate body', the state and business institutions, particularly as these involve the control of 'development' and its ideologies. But spanning both these levels is a third form of class power: 'the impersonally instituted authority of corporate property, of capital accumulated and organised on a world scale, as a more imperious version of class domination than that confronted in the analysis of the ruling bloc dominating Irish society' (1986, p.203). This is the class power of multinational corporations. The penetration of this global form of class power into Irish society, Eipper argues, leads to the subordination of local and national class processes to international ones (1986, p.203):

> At Bantry, Gulf Oil was able to subordinate all other objectives to its pursuit of profit. If it enhanced the profits and the power of the local business people it did so only by creating an affluent and assertive industrial proletariat, and if it enhanced the wealth, privilege and prestige of the local bourgeoisie, it did so only by making a vassal of it. And . . . nationally, it does seem reasonable to suggest that the growing penetration of the national economy by foreign capital will have analogous consequences.

As is the case with the Dublin docklands development, the arrival of Gulf Oil in Bantry not only signalled a realignment of class forces, locally and nationally, but also a reconstruction of the dynamics of social change in Irish society. In future, the capacity of classes to reproduce themselves and their relationships with other classes would increasingly be mediated by and dependent upon the class interests of global capital.

This point is made in the urban context by Benson (2007) in her exploration of the process of gentrification in the traditional working-class community of Ringsend in Dublin. Benson argues that Ringsend, as a deindustrialised space in a prime location close to the city centre, has become ripe for development as a neighbourhood oriented towards the needs of middle-class professionals. Apartment blocks have been built on sites once dominated by industry and not only represent a shift to a post-industrial landscape, but also a shift in the social and spatial relationships that were embedded in Ringsend as a particular place. The marketing of these new apartment blocks draws on Bourdieu's notion of *distinction* in order to appeal to the consumer desires of prospective buyers (see Chapter 16). Ringsend is no longer the domain of Dublin's traditional working class. Rather the process of gentrification represents a new phase of capital accumulation in the city that excludes the working class on many levels: economic, social and cultural. The emergent forms of community that exist in the new apartment complexes differ from the everyday understanding of the practice of community by Ringsenders. For the old-timers, community is grounded in co-presence and locality, while for the newcomers community is not necessarily place-based: social networks and attachments extend well beyond the reach of Ringsend. Benson (2007) concludes that the sustainability of Ringsend as a neighbourhood with a particular history, landscape and social fabric is not contingent on integration but on ensuring the vitality of a mosaic of co-existing micro-communities.

CONCLUSION

The work of Eipper and other researchers discussed in the last section reminds us that class analysis is not only about uncovering the extent and distribution of inequality or poverty (or even wealth) in society, but is also an attempt to understand social dynamics, and the emergence and trajectories of distinctive cultural worlds of being. As Eipper argues class is not a static category, but a historical one. It is linked inevitably to social change: classes change society and social change alters classes and their relations. As Eipper (1986, p.11) points out: 'it is not the evolution of classes as such, which explains change, but the evolution of the processes forming classes; it is the processes which create classes more than the classes themselves which are important.'

The primary emphasis of class analysis, from this point of view, should be on processes of class formation. The key to understanding class formation is class struggle. But the ultimate goal of class struggle is to control class consciousness or, more broadly, those cultural understandings that help either to reproduce or to suppress class formation and mobilisation. Class analysis must then also concern itself with the cultural realm and how it shapes the experience both of individuals and collectivities. Irish sociology has gone a long way in addressing and explaining the sources of inequality in Irish society, but the analysis of social processes as class dynamics retains considerable scope for futher development.

8
Education

Education stands at a central point in our discussion. On the one hand it is about the creation of particular forms of knowledge, and how certain understandings of life and society are generated, transmitted and debated in Irish society. On the other hand education is intricately bound up with questions about modernity: it is seen as a key to modernisation and a driver of social, economic and personal change.

Any sociological analysis of education faces an institution of great complexity. The activity of formal education involves a huge proportion of Ireland's population — an estimated one-third of the people (Drudy and Lynch, 1993, p.ix). 'Education' is an umbrella term that covers a broad range of activities and sites from pre-school to primary and post-primary, through to third-level and adult education. It can also include public- and private-sector training and even extend to processes of self-education that take place outside of any formal structure. Furthermore, many other activities, from tourism to sport to the mass media, also have a significant, and sometimes quite self-conscious, 'educational' component.

The range of actors and institutions involved in education is similarly broad and includes children and parents; students and lecturers; pupils and teachers. Of major importance also are the personnel and institutions within the state — in the bureaucracy of the Department of Education and Science and in the numerous official bodies involved in education, from the school inspectorate to parents' groups and third-level accreditation bodies. Education is intricately connected to other institutions such as the world of employment, law, the mass media and social administration. Like many of the aspects of society discussed in this book, 'education' as a separate field of analysis is constituted at an abstract level while the social reality of education is in many ways inseparable from the totality of the fabric of social life.

Education is also closely connected to the concept and the project of *modernity*. As Clancy (1995, p.467) points out, this is for at least two reasons. First, education stands for our ability to develop society in ways that can lead to the betterment of populations: through economic growth; spiritual enlightenment; aesthetic appreciation; and social progress. As a consequence the measurement of educational development, in terms of, for example, levels of literacy, numbers of schools or the output of scholarly articles, is often used as a way to measure social development more generally. In Ireland our success as a Western European economy is often linked with our 'educated workforce' and high levels of cultural achievement. Second, education reflects modern humanity's urge to shape nature through the application of rational knowledge: through learning about and knowing the world we can better control it. Education can thus contribute to a more efficient use of physical resources, for example, through better farming practice, and can also help in the creation of a more ordered and rational society, through consumer education, civics and so on.

In this chapter we examine some key aspects of education that have been of interest to Irish sociologists. First we examine some of the mythology that has grown up around education. On the one hand, state institutions and the popular media trumpet our levels of educational achievement while, on the other, a range of international statistics indicate that Ireland compares quite poorly on a number of indices. We then provide a brief overview of the main sectors of education, focusing in particular on issues of management and control. The content of education is discussed: what is taught in schools and other educational sites, and why? We may be better able to answer these questions by exploring how educational outcomes and processes are related to issues of social inequality, of gender, class and ethnicity.

EDUCATION IN IRELAND: MYTH AND REALITY

Ireland presents itself, for example, in IDA advertisements, as a modern (even post-modern) country with a highly educated and literate population. Yet even a brief survey of some of the relevant statistics reveals a somewhat more complex picture.

Figure 8.1 indicates the proportion of the population with upper secondary education (that is, to Leaving Certificate level or equivalent) in the OECD countries. We can see that Ireland, at 63 per cent, is below the OECD average of 67 per cent in terms of completion of upper secondary education. But the position has improved rapidly — in 1995 the comparable figure was only 47 per cent. In the younger age group, 25–34, we can see that Ireland is slightly above the OECD and EU average, but still very far behind countries such as Canada, the Czech Republic and Korea that, according to the statistics, have achieved almost universal completion of upper secondary education. Major problems and barriers persist in primary education, notwithstanding considerable investment in recent years: there are still numbers of schools operating in sub-standard accommodation, and primary class sizes are amongst the largest in the EU, with a quarter of pupils in classes of over thirty (*The Irish Times*, 6 February 2007). There remain major problems of adult literacy (see below) and comparatively few resources have been dedicated to tackling this issue.

Figure 8.1 Population that has attained at least upper secondary education (2004) *Percentage, by age group*

	25–64	25–34	35–44	45–54	55–64
		AGE GROUP			
Australia	64	77	65	62	49
Austria	80	87	84	78	69
Belgium	64	80	70	58	45
Canada	84	91	88	83	73
Czech Republic	89	94	93	87	82
Denmark	81	86	82	79	77
Finland	78	89	86	76	59
France	65	80	70	59	49
Germany	84	85	86	84	79
Greece	56	73	64	50	31
Hungary	75	84	82	76	57
Iceland	60	68	64	57	46
Ireland	**63**	**79**	**68**	**54**	**39**
Italy	48	64	52	44	28
Japan	84	94	94	82	65
Korea	74	97	86	57	34
Luxembourg	62	74	64	58	51
Mexico	23	25	25	21	13
Netherlands	71	80	74	68	59
New Zealand	78	85	81	77	64
Norway	88	96	92	86	78
Poland	50	60	49	46	42
Portugal	25	40	26	18	12
Slovak Republic	85	94	91	84	64
Spain	45	61	50	36	21
Sweden	83	91	89	81	71
Switzerland	85	89	86	83	79
Turkey	26	33	24	20	14
United Kingdom	65	70	65	64	59
United States	88	87	88	90	86
OECD average	**67**	**77**	**71**	**64**	**53**
EU19 average	**67**	**78**	**71**	**63**	**52**
Brazil	30	38	32	27	11
Chile	50	64	52	44	32
Israel	79	86	81	75	68
Russian Federation	89	92	95	90	72

OECD COUNTRIES (left margin label for rows Australia–United States)

PARTNER COUNTRIES (left margin label for rows Brazil–Russian Federation)

Source: OECD, Education at a glance, 2006
[Available at: www.oecd.org/dataoecd/47/51/37363421.xls]

Figure 8.2 Educational disadvantage league

Average ranking according to five measures of absolute educational disadvantage: reading literacy — age 15; maths and science literacy — age 15; maths and science achievement — year 8.

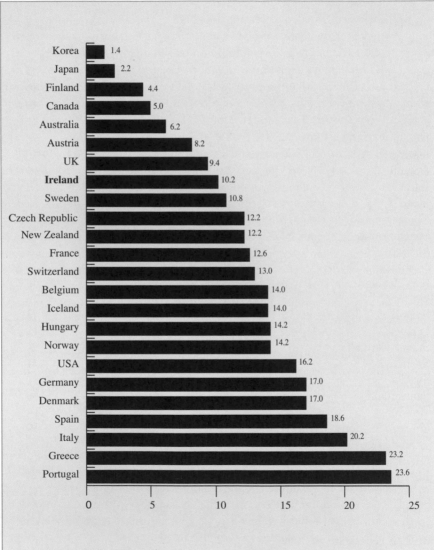

(*Source:* UNICEF, 2002, p.4)

Despite poor resourcing in some areas, Ireland generally performs well in international 'league tables' of academic achievement. For example a comprehensive UNICEF report of educational effectiveness in 2002 placed Ireland eighth amongst the OECD countries, significantly ahead of countries such as Denmark, Germany and the US (see Figure 8.2). Ireland appeared fifth in terms of teenage literacy, the highest placed of the EU countries, and eleventh in maths, well ahead of Germany, the US and the UK. In terms of *relative educational disadvantage* — how well the weakest students perform compared to the average — Ireland ranks about the middle of the table. Despite examination of a number of likely variables, such as student-teacher ratio, expenditure on education and parental ability, the report finds it difficult to explain the variation of performance between countries.

Wickham (1998) criticises aspects of Ireland's educational performance from another perspective, throwing cold water on the notion of the 'intelligent island'. He argues that though in Ireland 'we have a lot of education', we are far from being a 'learning society' (1998, p.82). In particular, the links and networks between education and industry need to be much better developed. In this criticism he is carrying on the long tradition that has existed since the late nineteenth century of calling for more 'technology' in Irish education (Drudy and Lynch, 1993, p.217). Ireland suffers, according to Wickham, from a highly academic approach to teaching and learning, as reflected in the focus of our secondary schools, exam system and universities. In contrast, our vocational education is too narrowly focused, aiming to meet the needs of firms and single industries like the computer industry, rather than the requirements of society as a whole. There is very little company-based training (unlike in Japan) and academic research is very poorly funded. All this adds up to a 'weak national system of innovation' and means that as a society and economy we are likely to remain dependent on others to do our thinking for us.

While Wickham is correct in highlighting the shortcomings of the Irish system, some of which, such as research funding, are now beginning to be addressed, he also reflects a rather narrow view of education in Ireland. For example, he pays little attention to the range of courses offered in the non-university third-level sector. Though often vocationally oriented, these offer a broad range of employment options, from the training of make-up artists for the film and TV industries to multilingual secretaries for the financial sector as well as the more familiar education of computer programmers and laboratory technicians. Furthermore, while he acknowledges the importance of the cultural sector, he does not recognise the importance of 'academic' knowledge in the development of growth and investment in this field. Such 'non-instrumental' knowledge is crucial to the development of industries as diverse as computer games, tourism and teleservices. If technical, scientific and rational knowledge are the hallmarks of modernity, it may be that a post-modern society and economy demands more in the nature of critical thought, creativity and flexibility.

It is now commonplace for educationalists, sociologists and policy-makers to make explicit the connections between education and the information economy. McBrierty and Kinsella (1998, p.8) assert that 'knowledge, information and associated skills have displaced labour as the primary source of productivity and competitiveness.' A feature of recent Irish economic growth has been the rapid rise in industrial productivity (comparable to the 'Asian Tigers' of Taiwan and South Korea). While there is considerable disagreement over the causes for this phenomenon, a key role is attributed to the influence of expanded education.

The arguments over the extent and nature of education give some indication of its centrality not only to economic growth and development, but also to the creation of national identity, personal fulfilment and the institutionalisation of power. As a major institution in Western societies, including Ireland, it will always be at the centre of emotive and extended debates. We examine some of these debates in this chapter, but first we provide a brief sketch of the main contours of the Irish education system.

THE IRISH EDUCATION SYSTEM

It is conventional to divide the provision of education into four stages:

- primary education
- post-primary education
- tertiary education
- adult education.

We will keep this convention though it omits consideration of important aspects of the educational process, as suggested above, such as pre-school education and vocational training. The Irish education system provides a unique amalgam of state, religious and other interests. It is also dynamic: responding in different ways to changes in social attitudes; the strength and influence of other institutions; industry-based pressure groups; and competing 'expert' discourses, including sociological and educational research. This section therefore can provide only snapshot views of the system.

Primary education

The 1937 Constitution specifically acknowledges the role of parents in Irish education. It asserts that the family is the primary and natural educator of the child — Article 42.1 states that it is the inalienable right and duty of parents 'to provide, according to their means, for the religious and moral, intellectual, physical and social education of their children'. While a very small number of parents have claimed their rights under the Constitution and have opted for home-based education, virtually all children in Ireland are educated from an early age in national school; there are over 3,000 national schools in the state and only 60 non-state-funded primary schools (CSO, 2006c, p.115; Curry, 2003, p.81).

Despite the intention of those that developed the Irish national school system in the mid-nineteenth century, it rapidly became a *de facto* and *de jure* denominational system, with its denominational nature explicitly recognised and supported by the state (Curry, 2003, p.85). The churches secured the dominant position in the provision of primary education in the country and Ireland maintained a largely state-financed but religion-controlled system. This position of power has been actively protected by the churches and it is only since the 1970s that others, such as teachers and parents, have had any formal role in the management of national schools. Even this role remains heavily circumscribed, with effective power still in the hands of a heavily centralised government department, the patron of the schools (the local bishop) and industrial agreements between the teachers' unions and the state.

Church control of the primary school system only began to be challenged in the mid-1970s. In the face of both Catholic Church and state opposition, some parents sought to establish inter-denominational national schools. The first of these, the Dalkey School Project, opened in the late 1970s and it was followed by similar institutions, often having to operate out of unsuitable temporary premises, in towns like Sligo and Galway. A second challenge to church control has come from a perhaps unlikely source: the expansion of primary education through the medium of the Irish language, in the *gaelscoileanna*. Like the multi-denominational 'project' schools, these are managed by boards of people committed to a specific educational and social objective, rather than by nominees of the local Catholic or Protestant bishop.

The impact of these developments is reflected in the recent pattern of school establishment. Between 1986 and 1997 a total of 72 new national schools were approved by the Department of Education and Science. Only two of the schools established in this period were traditional Catholic Church controlled institutions. The remainder comprised 56 *gaelscoileanna*; 13 multi-denominational schools and one Muslim national school (*The Irish Times*, 21 September 1999). In 1999 the control of national schools shifted perceptibly away from church to state as the government announced that it was to fund capital development of primary schools fully, thus removing the reliance on church and parish funds. This has reduced the influence of religious bodies in primary education and allowed for the easier development of non-denominational schools: there were 41 of such schools in 2007 with more in the planning or development stages.

Post-primary education

Historically post-primary education in Ireland has been provided by a mix of church, state and other private bodies, with the first of these agencies being dominant. Participation rates in post-primary education have risen markedly since the introduction of 'free' secondary education in 1967. The sector serves about 340,000 (CSO, 2006c, p.111) students in a variety of school types: secondary, vocational, community and comprehensive. Though almost completely funded by the state, this level of education remains organisationally dominated by religious bodies, principally the Catholic religious orders. Of a total of 742 second-level schools, 403 are secondary, 247 are vocational and 92 are community or comprehensive (Department of Education and Science, 2007). The four types of school differ mainly in their ownership, management structures and funding arrangements, but offer a common curriculum determined by the Department of Education and Science.

Unlike most other European countries that have, or have had, a binary system of post-primary education, the greater proportion (around 55 per cent) of post-primary education in Ireland takes place in 'academically oriented' secondary schools. These are privately owned and managed institutions under the control of religious communities, boards of governors or individuals, but are formally recognised, funded and regulated by the Department of Education and Science. Vocational schools and community colleges educate just over a quarter of post-primary students. They are administered by and funded through the Vocational Education Committees (VECs) of local government. Community and comprehensive schools, containing about 16 per cent of post-primary students, are managed by boards of management of differing compositions: those of community schools are representative of the local VEC, religious communities, parents and teachers. Those of comprehensive schools represent the relevant diocesan religious authority, the local VEC and the Minister for Education and Science, with no input from the other partners in education, that is, students, parents or teachers.

There are significant differences between the privately owned secondary schools and the others in the sector. The former are far more likely to be denominational and single-sex while the latter are non-denominational (in the case of vocational schools) and coeducational (in the case of vocational, comprehensive and community schools and colleges). The secondary schools have a tradition of providing an 'academic' curriculum while the vocational schools have, in the past, had an explicit mission to offer 'technical' education. This distinction is overlaid by a class distinction: secondary schools (with a number of important exceptions) have been oriented towards a middle-class clientele with vocational schools being for working-class students. The more recently developed comprehensive and community schools and colleges aim explicitly to bridge this division — with varying degrees of success.

The 'points race' for access to third-level education has given rise to a significant private, unregulated post-primary education sector, as in countries like Japan and Italy. This manifests itself in private colleges catering to 'repeat' exam candidates (popularly known as 'cram schools') and in the provision of personal private tuition or 'grinds'. According to the Commission on the Points System (1999 p.100), 'a high number of students report attendance at grinds. This . . . raises very fundamental questions as to how students and their parents perceive the work of schools, particularly in fifth or sixth year.' Though small in comparison with the fee-paying sector in countries such as the UK, the United States and Australia, the emergence of private institutions at upper-second and third level is evidence of the incipient marketisation of Irish education.

As in the primary sector, the influence of the churches is starting to diminish in the post-primary sector, but for different reasons. The main causative factor is the decline in membership of the religious orders, such as the Christian Brothers and the Mercy Sisters, who had such a key role in the establishment and management of secondary schools and who also secured influence over community schools and colleges. Already a considerable number of Catholic secondary schools are under the direction of lay principals and this will increase greatly in the next two decades. The orders have begun to establish alternative structures that may permit them to retain a management role in such schools into the future (Clegg, 2003).

Tertiary education

Ireland has effectively, like many other Western countries, moved into a period of mass tertiary education. Almost two-thirds (approx. 60 per cent) of Leaving Certificate students now go on to some form of third-level education. In 2004/5 there were 134,000 full-time students enrolled in institutions funded by the Department of Education and Science. These include seven universities, fourteen institutes of technology and a number of other institutions, including teacher-training and some private colleges. Unlike some countries (e.g. Australia and the UK) Ireland has maintained what is known as a 'binary' system of higher education, with academic and professional studies in universities and vocational and applied studies in institutes of technology, though this distinction is becoming increasingly difficult to sustain. In 2006 there were 79,000 students enrolled in universities, 52,000 in institutes of technology and 2,500 in teacher-training and other public-sector colleges. This compares with a figure of just 21,000 full-time students in all tertiary institutions in 1965 (CSO, 2006c, p.111; Department of Education and Science, 2007).

Other important sectors include the Post Leaving Certificate (PLC) which in 2005 had almost 30,000 students (many of whom are 'mature age' students) in approx. 225 institutions (Watson et al., 2006) — one of the fastest growing parts of the Irish education system, as pointed out by Lodge and Lynch (2004, p.14) —

catering in particular to women. Another important sector, based in the institutes of technology, is apprenticeship. However, of the over 7,000 apprentices in 2000, only 50, or less than 1 per cent, were women (Lodge and Lynch, 2004, p.15). Added to these figures are those attending a number of private colleges (including a considerable number of international students) and those who travel to other countries (mainly the United Kingdom) to study.

Adult education

Adult learning has been one of the more neglected elements of educational provision in Ireland — not least by sociologists — but is now one of the most rapidly growing; it is estimated that in 1996 there were at least 1,000 community-based education initiatives or groups in the country (Department of Education and Science, 1998, p.21) and Aontas, the adult education body, has estimated that in 2007 there are over 300,000 Irish people involved in adult education, from community-based education programmes to evening courses. In recent times it has begun to acquire a higher profile, particularly in relation to economic and community development. Lynch (1997, p.118) suggests that there are complex causes behind this expansion, but 'the greatest of all is probably the changing trends in thinking among educationalists, a movement both physical and psychological . . . a movement for education to go out into the community, rather than the community coming to it'. Adult education is now seen as 'the route to empowerment for many marginalised groups in modern Irish society', including those in poverty, substance abusers and those suffering from educational disadvantage (Connolly, 1997, p.40). Women in particular are central to the provision and use of many aspects of adult education. Adult education is seen by many as an opportunity for people to make up for the poor educational provision of previous years, and to move beyond the considerable inflexibility of the Irish school system (Hannan et al., 1998, p.127). But the sector remains heavily underfunded and has a low political profile compared to other aspects of education.

As Slowey (1987, p.118) points out, the adult education sector is highly diverse and it may be misleading to talk about it as a 'system' at all. It continues to reflect its origins in 'the labour movement, church activities, university extension, women's associations, scientific and literary groups and community activities'. As a consequence the range of activities that fall under the rubric of 'adult education' is vast, from the person completing a PhD with the Open University to the community activist undertaking training in advocacy skills and the retired person learning how to make their own wine. The motivations for engaging in adult education may include social involvement and contact, acquisition of specific knowledge and skills, general self-development and a means of assessing one's potential (Slowey, 1987, pp.131–3). For women in particular adult education may also provide an opportunity to move out of a purely domestic role and to (re)enter the paid workforce.

Notwithstanding the extreme diversity of the adult education field, there is now greater interest in the concept of *lifelong learning*, where the process may be as important as the outcome. This is not a particularly new concept, and Ó Buachalla (1974) was talking about 'permanent education' more than three decades ago. The Irish government has argued for support for lifelong learning on the basis that it can address six key areas: consciousness raising; citizenship; cohesion; competitiveness; cultural development; and community building (Department of Education and Science, 2000). It has yet to be seen whether the policy rhetoric is accompanied by practical outcomes and whether there is a real appreciation of the barriers to access, including funding, accreditation and childcare, that actively militate against wider participation in adult education.

A major problem that has emerged in Ireland in recent years, and that challenges dominant concepts of the modernity of Irish society, is that of adult literacy, or the ability to communicate adequately in certain situations. A series of OECD surveys (the International Adult Literacy survey, carried out in 1994–1998) have shown that Ireland has significant literacy problems compared with most other OECD countries (OECD/Statistics Canada, 2000). In the 1998 survey, Ireland was placed amongst the lowest of the twenty countries studied, ahead only of Slovenia, Portugal, Poland and Chile.

The 1995 OECD survey indicated that a quarter of Irish adults were restricted to the most basic literacy tasks (finding simple information in a text) compared with just 6 per cent in Sweden and 10 per cent in the Netherlands (cited in Department of Education and Science, 2000, p.34). The survey showed that literacy barriers were closely linked to poverty, lack of educational qualifications, unemployment, older age and lack of participation in any form of adult education. Lack of literacy skills may lead to a reluctance to accept promotions at work or to access social welfare benefits fully though, according to the most recent international literacy survey (OECD/Statistics Canada, 2000, p.72), Irish people were amongst the least likely to say that their opportunities at work had been affected by literacy issues. In addition, literacy problems in childhood, reinforced by negative educational experiences, often lead to a generalised lack of self-esteem and self-confidence.

Literacy problems may also provide a very real barrier to the first steps of the adult education ladder, in particular for those already otherwise disadvantaged. As Lynch (1997, p.119) remarks, it is ironic that 'those who lack the necessary literacy skills to get one foot on the first rung of the educational ladder are in fact amongst those who suffer most from marginalisation and exclusion.' The OECD survey (OECD/Statistics Canada, 2000, pp.50–51) has indicated that there are strong connections between low levels of literacy, low levels of involvement in voluntary organisations and low levels of participation in adult education: this suggests that literacy problems may be associated in important ways with patterns of social exclusion.

While it is difficult to obtain information specifically about mature students, there is evidence that while participation of such students is low compared to comparable countries, it is beginning to become a more important aspect of higher education. All tertiary institutions now actively recruit such students to at least some of their programmes, with the consequence that the number of new entrants to third level aged 23 years or over has increased to over 9 per cent in 2004 (O'Connell *et al.*, 2006, p.28). In Ireland, 4 per cent of 30–39 year olds in are enrolled in education, compared with 14 per cent in Australia and 16 per cent in the UK (OECD, 2006, Table C1.1). Like other adult learners, mature students at colleges, universities or institutes of technology face numerous barriers: financial, logistical, domestic and regulatory (Lynch, 1999a, pp.187–214).

THEORETICAL BASES FOR THE STUDY OF EDUCATION

We have seen that the Irish education system is both large and complex. It involves a great proportion of the population and consumes vast resources. But what is it for? And how should we understand it? This is where the differing theoretical orientations towards education come into play. Reflecting as they do the broader shapes of sociological theorising (discussed in Chapter 1), they sometimes differ sharply as to how we should interpret the educational enterprise. There are also some important areas of commonality between them, as we shall see.

A *functionalist analysis* of education focuses on how it contributes to the stability of society. The education system, from primary school to third level, is seen to have a range of functions. These include a socialisation and training function, providing people with the basic and more developed skills required to operate effectively within society (such as literacy) and more specialised skills that support the functioning of the economy (such as computing skills). Schools and other educational institutions are also a key location for the creation and maintenance of national and cultural identities. This function is perhaps most starkly illustrated in the US system, where the teaching of national symbols, songs and historical narratives is particularly overt, but this process is mirrored in all societies. Education also has a major allocative function, based on the notion of meritocracy: it functions to distribute jobs and social positions to individuals based on their capacity, abilities and performance. In this way the education system is an essential basis for social stratification in society. A further set of functions — the integrative functions of education — include the maintenance of language communities and the development of social networks.

Like most manifestations of functionalist thinking, its place in educational sociology has been sharply criticised from conflict and interpretative viewpoints. But, like other functionalist arguments, it continues to have great resonance with common-sense accounts of social life and, as it does not challenge to any extent the existing power relationships within society, it enjoys considerable support among governments, policy-makers and many researchers.

One of Max Weber's main concerns in the analysis of Western society was the spread of *rationalisation* — the development of calculative and technical ways of thinking about the world that are most clearly expressed in science and economics (see Chapter 1). Though Weber did not deal at length with the issue of education in his work, it is clear that the themes underpinning his analyses of social life are of considerable relevance to an understanding of this topic. For example, his analysis of bureaucracy and bureaucratic systems of societal management stressed the importance of particular forms of rational, specialised and disinterested knowledge. This type of knowledge may be contrasted with 'magical' or religious knowledge, and with the notion of 'cultivation', whereby a person is socialised in a more general way for a particular station in life.

In modern societies the acquisition of specialised knowledge becomes a key to social standing and, increasingly, to wealth and power. Members of society are able to perceive the importance of such knowledge and to pursue it. Access to education becomes a crucial aspect of personal development and, inasmuch as resources are scarce, is of benefit to those individuals and groups that can gain access to specialised knowledge. In Ireland a *neo-Weberian approach* to education, which sees education very much as a resource that individuals and groups can access to varying degrees, has been influential. Drudy and Lynch (1993, p.39) argue that a neo-Weberian approach 'also draws our attention to concepts such as power, domination and authority; to the conflict over economic resources and rewards; to the competition for status and prestige; to the struggle for control; and to the role of bargaining, negotiation and compromise'.

Whereas a neo-Weberian approach stresses the choices and strategies that social groups may adopt, the *Marxist approach* to education reflects an economically determinist position. Clancy (1995, p.469) points out that both functionalism and Marxism, as varieties of structuralism, share a determinist, macrosociological view of education. The main difference is in the normative assessment of the situation. The Marxist approach focuses on how the education system operates as an institution for the creation and transmission of social inequality and the maintenance of the class system. Schools are seen as a site for social control, both through the overt activities of reward and punishment and through the 'hidden curriculum' that stresses and rewards punctuality, obedience and respect for authority — the very attributes required of a productive workforce. The school, for Marxists, is also a site for the transmission of capitalist ideology, in particular, values related to private property, nationalism and individualism. Of those theorists operating within a Marxist or neo-Marxist paradigm, perhaps the most influential in the last quarter century has been Pierre Bourdieu. Bourdieu moved away, to some extent, from the mechanistic determinism of more traditional Marxist arguments about education. He emphasised the cultural sphere and the notion of 'cultural capital' as a significant source of inequality.

A *feminist analysis* focuses on gender inequalities within education. The main issues for feminists here are the sexism of both the hidden and overt curricula; discrimination against girls and women within the education system; the male control of educational institutions and other aspects of gender inequality. Early feminists saw education as having the potential to radically transform the nature of gender relationships and to provide women in particular with a means to redress discrimination against them in public and private spheres. Later feminist research recognised that entering the institution of education was insufficient in itself to bring about wholesale social change. They argued that not only were girls and women disadvantaged in terms of access, but that the system was a key site for the creation of dominant ideologies about masculinity and femininity. The school was therefore not an arbiter and transmitter of neutral knowledge, but a mechanism for the maintenance of patriarchal social relations. More recently feminists have enthusiastically adopted post-structuralist theories in an attempt to better understand the operation of discourse and the creation of subjectivities within the educational field. This has led to a fundamental critique of the philosophical basis of schooling and of knowledge, as well as analysis of educational processes and practices.

An *interactionist approach* to education is microsociological and focuses especially on what happens within the classroom or other educational sites. In other words, it emphasises the importance of the process of *schooling* itself. There is a concern with the meanings and interpretations that people bring to social situations, including those related to education. Interactionist and other interpretative approaches argue that structuralist approaches to education, whether functionalist or Marxist in nature, ignore the realities of teaching and learning. Post-structuralist approaches are also highly critical of the notion of the participants in education being viewed as fixed identities. They emphasise the processes of personal growth and development that occur within the system and point out that identities are multiple and dynamic, rather than singular and static. This approach pays a great deal of attention to issues of language and discourse. The overall thrust of these types of sociological approach is away from *determinism*. The experience of education can be neither read off from notions of ability or attitude nor deduced from class, gender or ethnic position. Rather it is something that needs to be examined in detail, in context and with an openness to its dynamism and capacity for change.

One influential approach is *rational action theory* that suggests that people make calculations about the value of education to themselves or their children. While this approach emphasises the capacity of people to make choices about the paths and options available to them, it can be said to largely ignore broader patterns of inequality and meaning that shape the choices that people face. Of greater importance since the late 1970s, especially within the British sociology of education, has been *resistance theory*. This approach suggests that oppositional behaviour of some within the education system (most importantly, working-class students, especially males) is a rational response to the situation in which they find themselves. It tries to combine the determinism of structuralist theories of education with the voluntarism of the more interpretative approaches. Resistance theory grew out of the work of ethnographers who closely studied everyday behaviour in schools — especially the work of writers at the University of Birmingham, such as Angela McRobbie and Paul Willis, whose 1977 book *Learning to labour* has been one of the most cited books in British sociology and cultural studies. While resistance theory does help to make sense of the rejection of education by a significant minority of those within it, it does little to point towards an alternative. Fagan (1995, p.94) concludes that, '[while it] certainly draws a more politically enabling picture of early school leavers, and does not construct them in positions of subordination, it leaves them without a political strategy or political project for emancipatory social change'. Lynch and O'Riordan (1999, p.92) are more positive. They suggest that resistance theory:

> has identified spaces and places for challenging unequal social relations through education. It has enabled people to see beyond the limits of structures and to identify modes of thinking and analysing which can facilitate change. It has offered hope for change which is important in and of itself.

But they point out that most resistance theory is developed by middle-class people on behalf of marginalised groups and not *in conjunction with* such groups or individuals themselves.

Post-structuralist approaches focus very much on the role of language in the creation and power of definitions of educational reality. An early example in Ireland was the work of Denis O'Sullivan (1989; 1992) who examined how the American economist Dale Tussing helped to shape the discourse of Irish education in the late 1970s. A more recent and extensive analysis of Irish education that has consciously adopted a post-structuralist viewpoint has been that of Honor Fagan (1995). This study attempts to deconstruct the discourses that constitute the social category of 'early school leaver'. Fagan outlines and deconstructs the dominant discourses within education, including the sociology of education itself. Through her post-structuralist approach she aims to question the assumptions made of existing 'realities' and furthermore how sociology itself constructs the objects of its analysis. The political aim is to open up alternatives to how issues are posed and so to shape the action that flows from analysis. The 'early school leaver' is shown to be constructed within a range of powerful discourses, each of which seeks to explain the phenomenon. These include the genetic discourse that sees educational problems as inherited; the 'cultural deprivation' discourse that locates the problems in working-class culture; and the structuralist Marxist discourse that sees the issue as a reflection of the power of capital. Each of these discourses serves to disempower and oppress its object — those that leave school 'early'. Fagan argues for what she terms the 'political discourse': one with a radical and emancipatory aim that seeks to actively change the situation, not just to describe or explain it.

The post-structuralist approach favoured by Fagan (see also Ryan, 1997) has a distinctive methodological approach. It combines extensive but selective use of the 'voices' of the researched, with a complex and dense theoretical exegesis that seeks to make sense of the phenomena being analysed. It is as if the complexity of the social world is reflected in the very language being used to talk about it. It is not surprising that it is a mode of discourse that is deeply unattractive to policy bodies and government agencies who seek clear, concise information that appears to incorporate common sense with a scientific style of presentation. Thus, while a post-structuralist approach challenges the orthodoxies of education on many fronts, it has had as yet had little impact on the policy-making or management processes around Irish education.

Education and modernity

Concluding a review of Irish educational development in the period 1945 to 1960, Sheehan (1979, p.70) suggested that it was 'part of the transformation of Irish society which began in the early 1960s'. In this he was reflecting the common view that ties the phenomenon of education ineluctably to the processes of development and modernisation. The project of modernity is, among other things, a project about changing knowledges and identities. It is about the population becoming 'modern' in its attitudes and values as much as in the country's economic growth or infrastructural development. The institution of education, along with that of the mass media, is seen as a key to this change process.

Fahey (1992b, p.386) points out that education was the largest single area of expenditure of the newly independent Irish state and that primary schooling in particular 'was a major instrument in the political consolidation and rejuvenation of independent Ireland . . . [state] influence was central, extensive and ambitious in at least some of its objectives'. The modernising effects of education were complex, however, and sometimes contradictory. Among other things they led to a significant reordering of the relationships between children, families and the state. One effect was that children, rather than being seen as an immediate labour asset, were more likely to be regarded as dependants and as an investment for the future.

A key moment in Irish education was the publication in 1965 of the *Investment in education* report (Department of Education, 1965). The product of OECD experts, this report, in the words of Luke Gibbons (1996, p.83), 'set out to remove the school from the sacristy and place it in line with the need for greater technological change in Irish society'. It was positioned very much against the background of the programme of industrialisation and the opening up of the Irish economy and was centred on the notion of manpower planning (Kelleghan, 1989, p.204). The report helped to shape the future of Irish education and, through giving greater impetus to nascent trends, contributed to an expansion of the system and to issues such as social inequality and educational effectiveness being placed on the political agenda. Overall, however, the report was part of a pragmatic rather than an ideological response to the educational challenges raised by a modernising society. Even when potentially controversial initiatives such as comprehensive schools were mooted, they were discussed within existing political and social discourses of localism and control and not in the fiercely ideological context typical of many other Western countries (O'Sullivan, 1989).

The influence of education in relation to modernity is seen as manifold. Curry (2003, p.79) points out that the Irish national school system was very important in the development of mass literacy — a literacy, it must be pointed out, that in many parts of the country entailed the replacement of the Irish language by English as a symbol of modernity. Education has also, more recently, been viewed as a key to change in political attitudes. Political scientist Tom Garvin (1998, p.154) suggests that 'mass education of a kind not available to previous generations has accelerated the detraditionalisation of Irish political culture.' This has seen a decline in traditional Catholicism and in militant republicanism, each commonly associated with the 'old' Ireland. Garvin further sees an effect on power relationships within Irish society: 'the old peasant deference to clerical authority, partly derived from a popular perception of priests as educated men who could be trusted because they were on your side, has faded' (1998, p.152). These examples reflect a very broad and influential discourse that explicitly links changes in Irish society and culture to the impact of education.

Drudy and Lynch (1993, p.85) suggest that 'having one of the highest retention rates in education in the EC [European Communities], Ireland is fast becoming a sophisticated, well-educated, industrialised society in which rational rather than traditional authority holds sway.' Within such a modernising society, expectations of teachers and of schools have steadily expanded: they should now play an explicit socialisation role in terms of assisting students' personal and social development and in implementing various community and health education projects. Schools have become a significant area for intervention through government programmes to combat social disadvantage, promote healthy lifestyles, prepare young people for a labour market that requires information-based skills and to promote values of citizenship and political responsibility. Schools have also been given the task of addressing broader patterns of inequality in society, including those of class and gender; these issues are discussed later in this chapter.

The changing roles of education and the demands placed on it by other societal institutions are reflected both in Irish government policies and in the broader approach of the EU to education. For example, an EU Commission White Paper on Education and Training underlined the role of schools in human resource development and recommended that the education system be viewed as a critical element of the economic infrastructure of member states (Commission on the Points System, 1999). Similarly, a Commission White Paper on teaching and learning explicitly links education to the development of modernity. It argues that education is wedded to the 'dawning of the information society and the relentless march of Science and Technology' (cited in Department of Education and Science, 1998, p.17). Most recently the Irish state has turned again to the OECD (2004) to map out a direction for educational investment: this time in relation to research and the expansion of 'fourth-level' or postgraduate education. This activity is seen to be crucial to Ireland's future development as a 'knowledge society'. These documents are representative of a discourse that has permeated and shaped Irish education at least since the *Investment in education* report.

It would be a mistake, however, to assume a clear and unambiguous link between education and the project of modernisation. While education has been associated with the development of scientific rationality, specific types of interpersonal relationship, achievement orientation and a facility with technology, it has also provided an arena for the maintenance of attitudes, behaviour and relationships that have been seen as barriers to the development of a modern sensibility. Thus Ó Buachalla (1974, p.355) has remarked that 'it often appears in educational systems as if the rate of change and innovation is frustratingly slow — education seems to follow a haphazard pattern of development — with huge inertial resistance within systems inhibiting long-term adaptation and reform.' Given the multiple social demands placed on education, this complexity and institutional inertia is hardly surprising.

THE SOCIOLOGY OF EDUCATION IN IRELAND

Though there has been some history of sociological research into education in Ireland, until the 1990s public debate in the area was largely the preserve of historians and economists. Sociological analyses tended to be rather narrow and instrumentalist and a review of the field by Drudy in 1991 identified the dominant approach as functionalist and positivist. Research tended to be very much shaped by the predominance of policy-related issues and there was a lack of independent research funding. This tended to severely circumscribe educational discourse and, in the vivid terminology of O'Sullivan (1992, p.434), alternative viewpoints were notable by their absence: 'to utter the unsayable is to invite marginalisation, exclusion or communicative dismissal.' This lack of theoretical diversity led, according to Drudy (1991, p.110), to 'considerable paradigmatic insulation and lack of debate on the nature of the educational system and its relation to other major social institutions'. In other words, there was little impact on educational sociology from the broader theoretical and methodological debates within the sociology discipline, in particular in relation to more interpretative and critical approaches. The dominant interest was very much in the relationship between socio-economic status and educational attainment. A more critical approach has since developed that has focused on the nature and role of the educational system and its relationship to the state (Drudy, 1991, p.112) and on people's attitudes about aspects of the system, but there is still a dearth of research within the Irish sociology of education that can tie together the experiences of students, teachers, families and the broader community.

Despite the limitations of many sociological analyses, the discipline has been of major importance in exploring the relationship between education and society though, for a variety of reasons (Kelleghan, 1989, pp.202–5), it is difficult to relate research directly to policy outcomes. It has been crucial in expanding thought about education and schooling beyond the psychologistic interpretations that dominate much educational discourse (Lynch, 1999a, p.3). In Ireland it has provided comprehensive data with which activists and policy analysts can push for reforms to the provision of education, particularly for disadvantaged groups. It has provided educators with an alternative to individualistic and fatalistic accounts of school 'failure'. On the other hand it has done little to incorporate any input from the 'objects' of research. In this sense the sociology of education has, like much sociological discourse, been a 'colonising activity' (Lynch, 1999a, p.40). It has had little space for the voices or interests of children and young people, the main consumers of education. For example, research by Lynch (1999a, pp.217–59) has identified the lack of democracy *within* schools as a key issue for students, but this has never been the focus of large-scale, government-funded research, nor is it likely to be.

The ESRI has been a major site of sociological research into Irish education. In common with its programme of research into socio-economic inequality (see Chapter 7), it has largely adopted a so-called 'neo-Weberian' focus (Drudy, 1991, p.112; Drudy and Lynch, 1993, p.39). It sees social inequality as an outcome of the skewed distribution of resources in Irish society, such as property, skills and credentials, and adopts a largely pluralist model of the state (see Chapter 4). The ESRI has focused on the two main issues that have dominated the international literature: the relationship between social inequality and education (especially as this relates to questions of intergenerational social mobility) and the links between gender and education, including such issues as subject choice, coeducation and exam performance. ESRI research tends to be highly quantitative (cf. Smyth, 1999) and policy-oriented; indeed it has contributed significantly to recent educational policy documents.

For critics such as Lynch the major shortcoming of Irish educational sociology is that it has failed to challenge the broader structural issues of poverty and class inequality. Research such as that carried out by the ESRI and the Education Research Centre at Drumcondra tends to focus on the distribution of chances within the existing, unequal and hierarchical, system. Within this dominant liberal model of meritocratic individualism (Drudy and Lynch, 1993, pp.49–50), issues of class or gender are not analysed as 'generative forces of action' within the education system but as attributes of individuals. This shortcoming has been replayed more recently in the shift of theoretical interest from issues of inequality to issues of 'difference', and a concern for other types of disadvantage based on ethnicity, culture and gender. Lynch (1999a, p.29) argues that this shift further marginalises fundamental issues of inequality.

The challenge of responding to these issues is taken up by Fagan who, as previously indicated, is one of the small number of Irish sociologists of education to adopt an overtly post-structuralist research strategy. Fagan's approach is to present a text based on interview material garnered from her subjects through what she terms (1995, p.95) 'a modernist social-research framework' and then to analyse it through alternative 'readings' or theoretical frameworks. The aim is twofold: to examine the usefulness of various widely-used theories, such as reproduction theory and resistance theory; and to provide a range of alternative ways to analyse the social reality in question. A major issue for Fagan is to move beyond theoretical analysis. For her, while the theoretical approaches discussed above do something to illuminate the experiences of early school leavers (her research focus) they are fatalistic with regard to outcome. They reflect 'a prevailing logic that shows *how it is* and gives us an understanding of *why it is* the way it is' (1995, p.121) — but go no further. Fagan's aim (like Lynch, 1999b) is to develop an emancipatory politics out of her sociological analysis of education — a 'cultural and pedagogical politics of early school leaving'.

More recently a major contribution to the sociological analysis of schooling in Ireland has been the extensive study conducted by Lynch and Lodge (2002). This attempts to address some of the positivistic shortcomings that these authors and others have identified in prior Irish educational research. The study focuses on the key educational institutions themselves — the schools — and aims (2002, p.1) to 'explore the inside life of schools, in classrooms and staffrooms, in corridors and recreational spaces where students and teachers live out the practice of education on a daily basis'. This involved interviews with teachers and pupils; analysis of essays written by pupils; and, crucially, observation of the social interaction that took place in the classrooms, playgrounds and meeting rooms. While observation of teaching practices is an important part of the training of teachers, such micro-level analysis is rare in the Irish sociology of education. Lynch and Lodge then attempt to locate this micro-level interaction within a macro-level theoretical framework that addresses issues of power and control as central in Irish education, not least issues of structured class and gender inequality and injustice.

The move within the Western sociology of education from 'class' to 'difference' may represent an avoidance of the most intractable issue in education, arising perhaps from a frustration with reformist approaches as well as reflecting a response to the demands of marginalised groups. In other words, three decades of educational reform, including the development of comprehensive education, widespread coeducation, extensive curriculum reform and changes in teaching practice have left patterns of class inequality in education largely unchanged.

Lynch and Lodge's research attempts to show how and why the class basis of Irish schooling has been maintained, as well as other inequalities based on gender, ability and ethnicity. They also draw attention to the importance of 'affective relationships' of caring, interdependence, solidarity and belonging, though unfortunately they did not explore this aspect in the research (2002, p.12). An important aspect of their extensive study (discussed in more detail later in this chapter) is that it focuses on issues of power and justice in schools: issues that normally tend to be neglected or sanitised. Thus they raise a key question (2002, p.2):

> if all students are not treated with equal respect and enabled to develop their capabilities to the full, this raises important moral questions about the right of the State to confine people in an institution that may have enduring negative effects, be that culturally, economically or socially.

This important research challenges many aspects of both the common-sense and sociological understandings of contemporary Irish secondary schooling.

DEFINING KNOWLEDGE: SHAPING THE CURRICULUM

The content of the curriculum — what is taught — is a key site of struggle in education. In Ireland this was particularly the case within the primary system. Historically the national schools were the locus of a battle over the hearts and minds of Irish children between the colonial state and the Catholic/nationalist opposition to it. According to Clancy (1995, p.473) 'issues of moral socialisation took precedence over issues of technical socialisation', and the teaching of subjects such as Irish, history and religion assumed great importance in the independent state.

Many critics (though few sociologists) have drawn attention to the religious domination of the Irish education system. It is certainly true that Irish schools have to an extent been saturated with religion: religion may be 'fully integrated into the rest of the curriculum and . . . the ethos and "hidden curriculum" fully reflect the religious ideals of the school' (Clancy, 1995, p.476). While the visual symbolism of religion continues to mark many Irish schools, the extent to which religion permeates the curriculum is variable. There is evidence (an Irish National Teachers' Organisation survey of 1996) that teachers are becoming resistant to their religious role in national schools, with a majority of 60 per cent wishing to relinquish it (*The Irish Times* 21 September 1999). Similarly, religious ideas and ideals no longer permeate the content of what is taught. As Drudy and Lynch point out (1993, p.82), greater numbers of students now study:

scientific, commercial and technological subjects, which teach students to seek empirical proof for the existence of phenomena, to maximise profit, and to rely on technological solutions for human problems. Such principles are very much at variance with a faith based on dogma or belief in the efficacy of divine intervention for the resolution of human difficulties.

Apart from religious ideas, the education system seeks to inculcate a number of other qualities and values: key among these is that of achievement. As Clancy (1995, p.470) suggests, 'the differentiation which teachers make between students within the school prepares students for the differential allocation in the labour market.' The demands of the labour market are directly (in the gearing up of the Institutes of Technology to respond to 'skills shortages' identified by industry) or indirectly fed through to the education system. Through this process the value placed by the labour market on particular subjects reflected in the status or rewards accruing to different occupations shapes the evaluation of particular types of knowledge. The limited fields of endeavour that are recognised by the system are then further narrowed according to notions of ability. Ability is reduced to one's performance according to a set of standardised tests: ultimately the exam-based Leaving Certificate. There is little or no recognition that 'ability' is discursively created, dynamic, contingent and shaped by broader issues of class, ethnicity, age and gender.

Clancy alerts us (1995, p.479) to the growing *instrumentalism* of the Irish education system. The official discourse on Irish education has come to be suffused with a concern for labour-market issues and competitiveness to the detriment of more humanist concerns. Do business and industry have too much influence over what is taught and learnt through the Irish education system? Clancy suggests that it is not just a matter of successful interest groups but that the discourse of education itself has shifted from its humanist base: 'the growth in provision and take-up of economically utilisable subjects on the post-primary school curriculum reflects the centrality of economic self-interest as a cultural value' (1995, p.480). Similar trends exist in the tertiary sector where the language of 'total quality management', with its emphasis on 'benchmarking', 'best practice', 'stakeholders' and the student as customer, has come to dominate policy- and decision-making (Skilbeck, 2001).

A Marxist approach to education looks critically at the content of the curriculum. It sees the focus on achievement as an ideological process that helps to underpin the logic of the capitalist system. There has been little such critical research examining the assumptions that underlie the curricula of Irish education or how they reflect the interests and views of the powerful in Irish society. This conclusion is hinted at by Clancy, very much a mainstream sociologist of education, though he does not mention capitalism *per se* when he says that the educational system is 'an instrument of cultural domination; its real function is best understood in terms of the need for social control in an unequal and rapidly changing social order' (1995, p.471).

Lynch (1999a, p.260) argues more fundamentally that because of the power of ruling-class male social groups, 'only particular forms of knowledge have been legitimated within education.' These are forms of knowledge that are based on linguistic and, to a lesser extent, mathematical skills and abilities. Other competencies and qualities, such as artistic and creative ability, caring and empathetic skills, kinetic (movement) skills, lateral thinking and what Lynch terms 'personal intelligences' (1999a, p.275) are routinely neglected or ignored by the examination system that dominates Irish education. Lynch finds this deeply ironic (1999a, p.260) as:

> the educational institution has, in certain respects, become cut off from many of the lifeworlds and labour markets which it serves at the very time that educational credentials are being used more than ever to select and satisfy people within the labour market.

In other words, in a time when cultural diversity and creativity are becoming key economic resources in themselves, it can be said that education is in some ways becoming less functional for Irish society. This also applies to the skills required for 'love labour' — increasingly required activities of caring, nurturing and looking after others.

McSorley's (1997) Clondalkin study suggests that the content of the curriculum is unattractive and irrelevant to working-class students. Fagan's (1995) findings are very similar. She points out that the education system completely fails to reflect the reality of students from poor families. Thus 'by not using the life experience of the young people as a basis from which to educate, and by not linking the background of the young people to the curriculum, the curriculum is irrelevant and meaningless' (1995, p.100). The result is a very high level of conflict between students and teachers and also between families and teachers.

GENDER AND EDUCATION

Gender is central to the experience of education. People's experiences of 'being a boy' or 'being a girl' are shaped in many ways by the experience of schooling (Ryan, 1997). Here we indicate how the education process is crucial to the social construction of gender (itself discussed in some detail in Chapter 9). Drudy's (1991, p.115) review of Irish educational research suggests that gender has only become an issue since the 1980s. Since that time there has been a considerable amount of sociological research on gender and education in Ireland but this has tended to take place within a limited number of institutional contexts and from a rather narrow theoretical position. Lynch (1999a, p.135) points out that the dominant discourse in the Irish sociology of gender and education has been the liberal feminist discourse of *equality of opportunity*. In other words, it has been about identifying barriers to equality of opportunity within existing structures rather than challenging them in any fundamental way. Lynch suggests that there has been 'no substantive analysis of mainstream compulsory education in terms of its pedagogical, organisational or curriculum practices from a critical feminist standpoint' (1999a, p.134). Nor, it must be said, has there been any extensive analysis of the relationship between masculinity and education. Perhaps ironically this has only now started to occur as girls have begun to significantly outperform boys in public examinations. Overall, it can be said that the orthodoxy of hierarchical and meritocratic educational structures and discourses has not been effectively challenged.

Given that educational research has, as we have seen, tended to 'work within the system', there has been a tendency, reinforced by positivist models within social research, to measure 'equality' through indicators such as the number of women participating in particular educational courses; the number of men and, especially, women in non-traditional areas; or the number of images of men and women depicted in texts (Lynch, 1999a, p.135). In addition, though we have an increasing quantity of information about gender in Irish education, this is rarely combined with a sensitivity to issues of class or ethnicity.

Historically Irish women have a history of high participation in second-level education (partly due to a lack of alternative employment opportunities). Males and females are now equally represented in many aspects of education, with females now making up a slight majority (in the range 51 to 55 per cent) at post-primary level (Lynch, 1999a, p.141). Women have increased their level of participation in third-level study and now comprise 54 per cent of new entrants, claiming the majority of entry-level places in universities (at nearly 60 per cent), 'other colleges' and (especially) teacher-training colleges. They now make up the majority of entrants in all fields of study except for 'engineering, manufacturing and construction studies' (O'Connell *et al.*, 2006, p.23; 30). Rates of participation across socio-economic groups are similar for males and females. Girls now outperform boys in virtually all subjects in second-level public examinations (Junior and Leaving Certificates), including applied mathematics and engineering, though the perception of 'male' subjects (such as technical drawing) and 'female' subjects (such as home economics) persists and is reflected in the distribution of exam candidates in these areas. (Lynch, 1999a, pp.142–3).

As pointed out by Lodge and Lynch (2004, p.13), gender issues in education are 'very complex' and range across questions of access, curriculum, 'affective' issues of human relationships and major issues related to power. There is a growing body of research in Ireland on such issues, and the strong positivist framework in relation to the sociological research on education is being expanded into more critical and micro-level analyses. The next section of this chapter briefly explores some of the issues related to gender and education that have been of interest to Irish sociologists.

Education and farm women

One part of the Irish population that has been particularly successful at accessing education, especially third level, is the farming community, where participation rates are higher than for all other groups except for the managerial and professional class. Patricia O'Hara's research into the educational experiences of farm children, and the associated strategies of farm mothers, is an interesting illustration of how education intersects with broader gender, familial, demographic and economic processes.

Within the demographic and economic constraints of Irish farming, maternal support for children's education must be seen as a key element of the reproductive role of farm women. In an industry that promises only limited opportunities for economic survival, education is seen as a means to secure an off-farm livelihood. According to O'Hara (1998, p.136): 'farm women are the key architects of farm families' efforts to secure for their children desirable occupations outside of farming'. Women are the key influence over children in the goal of maximising educational opportunity.

In the period 1961 to 1971 the participation rate of farm children in second level education increased from 28 per cent to 55 per cent (P. O'Hara, 1998, p.137). By the early 1980s over two thirds of farmers' children were completing the Leaving Certificate, compared to little over half this for the children of the urban working class. By the late 1980s over three in ten of farmers' children that completed the Leaving Certificate went on to third level. Even on the smallest and poorest of agricultural holdings participation rates in third level were high. By 1992 very nearly half of farm children went on to full-time higher education, more than double that in 1980 (P. O'Hara, 1998, p.137). Farm children had the highest rate of participation in the then Regional Technical Colleges and the second highest rate (after professionals and managers) in universities.

Farm families were very adept at securing education grants: 'it seems that farm families, accustomed to dealing with eligibility criteria, form-filling and other bureaucratic procedures associated with EU and state aid to farming, have been quick to grasp the opportunities which state grants for third-level education, and latterly the EU Social Fund, afforded their children' (P. O'Hara, 1998, p.138). In addition, farm mothers actively support the education of their children in a number of important ways, for example, by supervising homework and attending parent–teacher meetings. There is evidence that on dairy farms the labour input of farm women generates crucial income for the support of children's education (P. O'Hara, 1998, p.146).

As previously mentioned, the proportion of farm *daughters* accessing third-level education is particularly high. As O'Hara remarks 'it is clear that farm families make exceptional efforts to educate their daughters' (1998, p.139). She argues that education was, and is, an important means of escape from the limited occupational opportunities offered by rural areas, and was also a way to avoid the patriarchal structures of Irish family farming. Educational success can offer rural women a measure of financial independence they could rarely achieve on the farm, given the male-dominated patterns of property transfer that persist in rural Ireland. O'Hara (1998, p.147) suggests that 'mothers' commitment to education for their children can be interpreted as a strategy of resistance to their own subordination within family farming and to farming as an occupation.' While clearly the specific experience of farm women cannot be extrapolated to all of Irish society, their experience reveals the importance of examining the mechanisms whereby educational choices are enacted and the specific cultural and economic contexts within which they are made.

Coeducation

Sociologists have demonstrated that educational institutions are key sites for the construction of gender identities. The work of researchers such as the Australian post-structuralist sociologist Bronwyn Davies (1990) has shown that gender is being formed from very early on in the education process, that is, in pre-school or play group. There is some evidence that, by the time they reach second-level school, girls have a poorer academic self-image (Lynch, 1999a, p.142). While high levels of stress have been identified in both male and female students, especially in exam classes (Hannan *et al.*, 1996, p.199), levels appear to be particularly high in all-girls secondary schools, perhaps related to the strongly academic focus combined with a strong emphasis on the personal formation of students in particular directions (Lynch, 1999a, p.229).

There has been considerable debate about the merits of coeducation in terms of its 'overall' benefits and whether it favours boys, or girls, or both. While Ireland has had a long history of segregated single-sex schooling at post-primary level, now the majority of pupils (about 70 per cent at primary level; 62 per cent at post-primary) are educated in coeducational environments (Lodge and Lynch, 2004, p.16). This applies particularly to those in the vocational, community and comprehensive school sectors. It has been argued that girls suffer from coeducational schooling, especially as they have been shown by some research to receive less attention and encouragement from teachers than do boys (Lynch, 1999a, p.143). A study carried out in Irish schools by Emer Smyth and Damien Hannan (1997) sought to examine the effects on girls of coeducation, in particular, whether a shift to non-segregated schooling adversely affects their educational and occupational achievements.

According to the authors of the study (1997, p.10), coeducation changes the patterns of interaction and the 'engenderment' of schools. As Lodge and Lynch (2004, p.17) point out, the unusually large (in international terms) proportion of young people in Ireland who are educated in single-sex settings means that many 'cannot avail of the day-to-day learning about gender relations that takes place in coeducational environments'. International research remains inconclusive as to who benefits from coeducation; it is a very complex issue that requires careful disentanglement of the multitude of factors that shape students' school experiences. These include the social background and prior ability of students; school history, management, ethos and organisation; policies of selectivity of schools; and coeducation itself (Hannan et al., 1996). The Irish research, which examined performance in Junior and Leaving Certificate examinations, showed that after other factors had been taken into consideration, the effects of coeducation on performance were minimal and were certainly less important than other factors such as social class and ability. One finding that did stand out was that girls in coeducational settings underperformed in the area of mathematics. While this finding will take further research in the Irish context to explain, it is suggested that this may be the outcome of dominant ideas among pupils, teachers and parents about the gender appropriateness of certain subjects. This applies in particular to the range of subject choice that is made available in the first place. Boys' single-sex schools are much less likely to offer subjects such as Home Economics and Music, whereas girls' schools rarely make available subjects such as Technical Graphics or Materials Technology (Lodge and Lynch, 2004, p.17). This inevitably shapes the subsequent third-level options available to students, as reflected in the comparatively low numbers of males who enter health and welfare related courses and the significantly lower number of females who opt for technological programmes at this level. Given the central importance of educational experiences and qualifications, these patterns clearly have a major impact on the career pathways of males and females.

Schools and sexuality

There has been little research in Ireland that addresses the issue of sexuality in schools, yet schools are highly sexualised locations. A small-scale study by Ryan (1997) focused on the experiences of girls attending six coeducational schools in the Dublin area, towards developing an understanding of how sexuality is involved in the development of gender identity in the school context. The research revealed the importance of 'reputation' and how it is understood in different ways for boys and girls. Girls reported that they had to be seen to be attractive and interested in sex, but not so interested that they could appear to be 'easy' or branded a 'slut'. On the other hand, they could not appear to be too uninterested in sex or boys, for fear of being branded 'frigid', 'stuck up' or 'lesbian'.

Other small-scale research by Inglis (1998b, pp.145–6) had similar findings, though these are presented in a more optimistic context. He concludes that 'pupils may be far more experienced and adventurous in their sexual attitudes and practices than either the teachers or the parents believe. Sex has become part of their lives. It is a central aspect of their everyday relations ... sexually active is seen as being the norm.' Young people gained information from the mass media and (occasionally) from parents, but the main sources were friends and siblings. Teachers, and especially religious personnel, were generally seen as being irrelevant. The key issues for students were related to what to do in situations like 'relationships, bad experiences, being drunk and having unprotected sex' (1998b, p.138). The main fears, especially for girls, were pregnancy and 'getting a reputation'. But Inglis found evidence of ultimate female control: 'there was a sense that while avoiding pregnancy and a reputation was a girl's responsibility, girls ultimately had the final say as to what would and would not happen sexually' (1998b, p.143).

In 2004 the Crisis Pregnancy Agency commissioned the first major research study of teenage sexuality in Ireland (Hyde and Howlett, 2004) and this confirmed the findings of the earlier small-scale research. The research revealed the complexity and difficulty that contemporary Irish school-goers face in negotiating sexual mores and discourses. Though the research was carried out in schools, the schools themselves do not figure significantly as sites for sexual interaction, and perhaps there was a lost opportunity to explore this challenging topic: for example there is a reference (2004, p.65) to the role of mobile-phone texting in teenage encounters that would repay further research. The research was largely pessimistic about the discourses of sexuality that operated in Irish schools: sex was largely for the benefit of males, a rigid 'double standard' operated, and much confusion and ignorance about sex was apparent. The research revealed (2004, p.60) that friend-ship networks, even in large cities, tended to be very close and intense, and that this helped to emphasise the regulatory power of 'reputation' for both boys and girls.

Like Ryan (1997, p.32) Hyde and Howlett found little evidence that the dominant educational discourse had any place for positive images of female sexual desire or agency. The dominant discourse was one of 'protecting' girls from dangerous male sexuality. This aims to render girls as passive and also as responsible for all teenage sexual behaviour. Nevertheless the research suggests (2004, p.79), following Inglis, that teenagers have become more liberal about sexuality in recent decades. This shift may, they suggest, be:

closely related to young women's increasingly 'liberal' stance in relation to sexual intimacies. At a broad level, it appears to be the agency of young women, facilitated through the processes and knowledge acquired in their social circle, primarily through friends and the media, that has redefined and re-shaped adolescent sexual norms.

If the research on heterosexual relationships and behaviour is limited, we know even less about the experiences of gay and lesbian young people in schools. What has been recorded, which is largely retrospective reporting of people's past experiences, is described by Lodge and Lynch (2004, p.37) as less than encouraging. They say that the research 'identifies isolation, depression and loneliness among students because of their sexual orientation. These experiences are coupled with a fear of being known to be different, regarded as deviant or living in fear of being rejected or beaten.'

Lodge and Lynch (2004, pp.37–38) report that many lesbian and gay young people have experiences at school that impact on their academic success: they may suffer from harassment, stress, depression or even violence and this may lead them to achieve less well academically or even drop out of school. Furthermore, the identity of gays and lesbians — whether pupils or teachers — is rendered almost invisible in the curriculum: it is just not talked about. For example, in areas such as SPHE (social, personal and health education) or RSE (relationships and sexuality education) there is a 'silence round sexual orientation' and universal hetero-sexuality is assumed. Even where the curriculum is supposed to address issues of homosexuality, this is avoided. Thus, for example, Lodge and Lynch (2004, p.39) report research that indicates that: 'not a single second-level school had completed the sexual orientation component of the RSE programme.' They conclude that 'the silence that surrounds sexual orientation in the education sector is reflective of a discomfort around sexual issues in general that has characterised Irish society over a lengthy period' — a discomfort that they trace to the religious control of Irish education.

Both Ryan and Lynch, in separate research exercises, have observed behaviour in Irish schools that they would define as sexual harassment, including verbal denigration and unsolicited touching of female students and teachers. Ryan argues that there is no acceptable framework within schools for dealing with such abuse or harassment. Lynch (1999a, p.236) argues that 'gender inequality was not part of most students' daily vocabulary-of-analysis' and thus harassment was neither identified nor recognised in the institutions concerned. Hyde and Howlett also call for an overt focus on issues of gender and sexuality in schools, and remark (2004, p.46) that in a school where a gender studies programme was offered, attitudes to gender and sexuality appeared to have changed.

We outline in Chapter 9 the neglect of issues of masculinity within Irish sociology. The same critique can be made in the area of education, for much the same reasons: there has been little examination of the specific experiences of boys or of the construction of masculinity through the practices and discourses of Irish education. Lynch (1999a, p.233) has suggested that in boys' schools she studied, 'the equation of superior masculinity with physical prowess and sport was particularly evident in schools where sporting success was central to the school's sense of identity.' There is a perception that (especially working-class) male peer groups adopt a culture that is hostile to education. A cultural milieu of this type was described in Britain in Willis's *Learning to labour* (see above), but there has been no equivalent Irish study. A similar milieu is described in Fagan's analysis of early school leavers, but this does not make any particular attempt to bring gender issues to the forefront.

At the primary level, Lodge (2005) has examined the gendered nature of 'middle childhood' (that is around the age of 7–8 years) within the school environment, in particular the school playground. She found that while many of the children exhibited 'stereotypical' patterns of play and friendship, 'others (of both sexes) had more ambiguous gendered styles of behaviour and interaction' (2005, p.181). Nevertheless most play was sex-segregated, with most boys being involved in football (the highest status activity) and 'apparently haphazard games of chasing'. Play between the sexes was generally sexualised, in the form of 'kiss-chasing'. The gendered patterns were, in the school studied by Lodge, reinforced by broader institutional structures of sex-segregated education. It may well be that children in a less sex-segregated environment might exhibit different patterns of gendered behaviour. Indeed the most popular boys in the group studied reflected less stereotyped, more 'androgynous' behaviour that embraced both skills at sport but also 'kindness to peers and a willingness to engage in games played by girls' (2005, p.188). This suggests that gendered identities in schools are perhaps more malleable than is generally perceived.

EDUCATION AND CLASS INEQUALITY

> What is remarkable about the debate about class inequality in education … is its almost ritualistic character. While there is probably no single subject that has been researched in as much detail as class inequality in education, there have been no serious attempts at policy level to radically alter the class outcomes of education (Lynch and Lodge, 2002, p.38)

As outlined in Chapter 7 there has been a major shift in the class basis of Irish society. Where formerly property was the main determinant of social wealth and position, this has now been at least partly replaced by the ability to secure wages or salary in a competitive and dynamic labour market (Breen and Whelan, 1996, p.98). As a result there is now a closer link between educational attainment and labour-market position. A key concern of sociologists of education, in Ireland as elsewhere, relates to how schools operate as a selection mechanism for future occupational positions: how do people acquire the qualifications that will provide them with the means to access scarce resources in the future?

There is now a considerable body of Irish sociological research that examines issues of educational opportunity and economic and class inequality. According to

Lynch and O'Riordan (1999, p.93) this, as with other educational research, has been from within a positivist framework. They argue that the 'equality empiricists' have dominated the debate around educational inequality, framing it within a 'liberal political perspective and a broadly functionalist sociological tradition'. Within this approach the problem of class inequality in education is defined as a lack of opportunity to move upwards within an already class-stratified society. Lynch and O'Riordan conclude that, while this 'liberal model' helps to show how educational resources within the existing system are (mal)distributed, it does little to challenge the hierarchical nature of the system itself. It fails to critique the content and objectives of education and the broader systems of inequality that shape the nature and priorities of the system. For Lynch (1999a, p.252), 'while distributing more education to those groups who want it is crucial, it may also be necessary to change the education system itself to take account of the differences which various groups bring to that system. Schooling needs to recognise and respect difference if it is to treat all people with equality of respect. It cannot assume that all people will fit the one mould.'

As indicated by Lynch and O'Riordan, the Irish 'equality empiricists' (largely located within, or connected to, the ESRI) have produced a sizeable body of data in relation to the links between social inequality and educational participation and outcomes. This research continues a process of research that has been taking place in Ireland since the mid-1960s (Drudy and Lynch, 1993, p.141). The government-sponsored *Investment in education* report published in 1965 (carried out by economists, not sociologists) revealed the links between educational and class inequality. The considerable investment in education that took place in the wake of this report (including the introduction of 'free' secondary education) led to a growth in educational participation, but this was not equitably distributed across the population. Research by Clancy (1982; 1988) during the 1980s showed that in terms of access to tertiary-level education, investment in secondary education had actually contributed to an *increase in inequality*: those favoured in class terms were better able to make use of the new educational opportunities that had been opened up.

Research into (male) social mobility in Ireland by Whelan and Whelan (1984) also demonstrated the links between education and class. It suggested that access to educational opportunity was a major factor in the 'inheritance' of class inequality and that this pattern was particularly marked in Ireland, at least during the 1970s. Subsequent research by Breen and Whelan on data from the late 1980s revealed that little had altered: a 'modest' change for men and none at all for women. They concluded (1996, p.126) that:

> Despite increasing overall levels of educational attainment the pattern of educational social fluidity has remained unaltered. There is a continuing strong link between class origins and educational attainment.

This can be seen clearly from the data presented in Figure 8.3. Over half the children of those in the 'higher professional' social group leave school with five or more Leaving Certificate honours; only 4 per cent of those with parents who are unskilled manual workers enjoy the same outcome. The implications for further study and employment are clear.

The relationship between educational attainment and subsequent labour force outcomes has also endured and exhibits, 'a relatively straightforward pattern . . . whereby class origins are largely translated into educational qualifications which then determine the distribution of relative chances of access to the more desirable classes' (Breen and Whelan, 1996, p.126). Overall, while investment in education in Ireland has led to an increase in educational attainment and performance at all levels, the differentials between classes have not diminished. Rather the increased emphasis on education as a mechanism for social advantage has seen the already advantaged groups in Irish society further secure their position.

A HEA report (TWG, 1995), drawing on the work of a number of sociological researchers, has identified three crucial schooling transition points at which the effects of socio-economic background are particularly significant. The first of these relates to whether a student continues in school long enough to take the Leaving Certificate or becomes an 'early school leaver'. While one-fifth of all students left school without reaching Leaving Certificate level, only 3 per cent of those with higher professional backgrounds failed to make this transition compared with almost half of those from unskilled manual backgrounds. This pattern is long established. Research by Rudd on early school leavers in 1966/7 (cited in Clancy, 1995, p.484) revealed that the 15 per cent of students who left after primary school (note the change in measurement) were predominantly from the unskilled/semi-skilled working-class and farming groups. One determinant of early leaving is reading ability, which has been shown to be linked to social-class background. McSorley (1997, p.39) reports large differences between children who attended schools in outer-suburban Clondalkin and inner-city Dublin, where 19 to 35 per cent of children were two to three years behind in reading ability, and those at school in Rathgar, a wealthy suburb, where no children were below their expected ability for age. The implications of leaving school without qualifications are severe. There is a strong relationship between lack of qualifications and unemployment. In 1993, 78 per cent of those without a formal qualification remained unemployed after leaving school; this figure dropped to just 30 per cent for those with a Leaving Certificate (Allen, 1998, p.199). Of those unemployed in 1997, 63 per cent had not completed secondary education (Department of Education and Science, 1998, p.25).

A second key educational transition relates to the level of achievement of those who remain to complete the Leaving Certificate. Here the level of achievement varies widely according to socio-economic group. As Smyth and Hannan (1997, p.16) point out 'most of the difference between schools in average Leaving

Figure 8.3 Educational performance and family background

Family background	No qualifications %	Junior cycle %	Senior cycle		
			Level 1 Pass LC %	Level 2 Up to 4 hons LC %	Level 3 5 hons or more LC %
Unskilled manual	16.2	31.2	29.4	19.0	4.1
Other agricultural	12.3	24.7	27.9	22.2	10.7
Semi-skilled manual	9.9	28.4	33.9	22.4	7.1
Other non-manual	7.7	21.7	29.4	32.4	8.7
Skilled manual	5.9	18.1	30.6	35.9	9.4
Intermediate non-manual	3.5	11.9	20.2	46.2	17.9
Farmers	2.7	13.9	20.2	46.5	16.7
Self-employed, managers	1.8	7.8	17.0	46.7	27.2
Salaried employees	1.6	4.7	21.8	44.7	26.7
Lower professional	0.4	3.4	10.2	45.4	40.1
Higher professional	0.0	2.9	6.8	37.0	52.9
Low status	9.0	22.6	30.1	30.3	8.0
Average	5.7	16.3	24.0	37.4	16.7
High status	2.0	9.3	17.1	45.2	26.3

(*Source*: Department of Education and Science, 1998, p.27)

Certificate performance is due to differences in the social background and prior performance characteristics of their pupils'. While fewer than one-third of those from unskilled and semi-skilled manual backgrounds attained at least two grade Cs at higher level, over three-quarters of those from the higher and lower professional groups did so. This raises many issues in relation to the 'neutrality' of the examination system as a measure of 'merit'. As Smyth and Hannan (1997, p.15) indicate (Figure 8.4) the constellation of factors shaping 'exam performance' is complex.

The third transition relates to the destinations of those who successfully complete the Leaving Certificate. Research by UCD economists Harmon and Denny (reported in *The Irish Times*, 21 September 2004) shows that the average Leaving Certificate points achieved by a student from a 'professional' background

Figure 8.4 Factors that may influence exam performance.

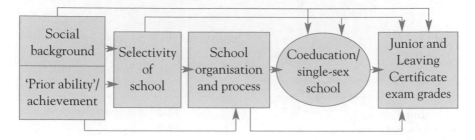

(*Source*: Smyth and Hannan, 1997, p.15)

is 363, compared with 260 from an 'unskilled' family of origin. O'Connell *et al.* (2006), who have succeeded Clancy as the key researchers in this field, show that while 87 per cent of students who complete the Leaving Certificate at a fee-paying school go on to third level, this figure is just 55 per cent for those in vocational schools (2006, p.70). This leads them to remark (O'Connell *et al.*, 2006, p.65) that:

> social selectivity in access to higher education is a cumulative process. Retention in the second-level system and performance in the Leaving Certificate are important determinants of entry to higher education, and . . . retention and performance are in turn heavily influenced by socio-economic background.

While overall participation in third-level education has increased dramatically since the 1970s in Ireland, as in most Western countries, very significant differences in terms of social class persist. The work of O'Connell *et al.* (2006) shows that the trend identified in Clancy's earlier research has been largely sustained. They conclude that patterns of entry to higher education by socio-economic background reflect both continuity and change: the more powerful social classes are still favoured, but participation across the board has increased, with the important exception of those from a non-manual (i.e. service and clerical) background (Figure 8.5). This leads them to observe 'a trend toward improved equity of access to higher education' (2006, p.9). The research also points to the increased complexity of the concept of 'social background' and the difficulty of collating and interpreting data in this regard. In particular there has been a major decline in the number of 'manual' workers who have college-aged children, reflecting the overall restructuring of the Irish workforce in recent years (O'Connell *et al.*, 2006, p.44). Nevertheless the fact remains that the children of higher professionals and farmers are over-represented in higher education, skilled

Figure 8.5 Estimated participation rates* in higher education
by fathers' socio-economic group (new classification), 1998
and 2004

	1998	2004
Employers and managers	0.65	0.60–0.65
Higher professional	1.11	1.25–1.36
Lower professional	0.63	0.59–0.65
Non-manual	0.29	0.25–0.27
Skilled manual	0.32	0.60–0.50
Semi- and unskilled	0.23	0.33–0.40
Own account workers	0.39	0.60–0.65
Farmers	0.65	0.82–0.89

Source: O'Connell et al, 2006, p.9.
* Participation rate (ratio) reflects the share of HE entrants from a particular social
background to the share of that group in the total population. A ratio higher than 1
indicates a higher participation rate than would be expected on the basis of share of the
population; a ratio of less than 1 indicates a lower participation rate than would be expected.

manual workers and managers/professionals are fairly equitably represented, while
non-manual workers and semi- and non-skilled manual workers are not equitably
served by higher education (O'Connell et al., 2006, p.47).

Such differences may be expressed in spatial terms: admission to third-level
education is just 4.5 per cent for students from the Dublin suburb of Clondalkin, but
it rises to 54 per cent for those from the wealthy area of Rathgar (McSorley, 1997,
p.39). The Dublin region, with its high concentration of working-class people, has
the lowest participation rate in tertiary education, while the western counties, such
as Galway, Sligo and Leitrim, have the highest. Clancy (2001) indicates that these
patterns have been consistent over the period of his analysis, though O'Connell et al.
(2006, p.9) have found some evidence of increasing participation rates in areas such
as Tallaght–Firhouse and Finglas–Ballymun. For those that make it to college, Clancy
found significant social-class selectivity between different types of institution and
within institutions, between fields of study: the elite groups are disproportionately able
to access the elite courses such as law, medicine and dentistry. Institutes of
Technology, while they have been crucial to the widening of educational access
(especially outside Dublin), are disproportionately accessed by the less well off. This
leads Clancy to warn (2001, p.177) that 'what is essential is that a concern for
equality of opportunity requires us to monitor not just the overall admission levels but
also the differentiation within the third level sector'.

A final set of barriers may exist for those who wish to engage in adult education.
There is consistent evidence (Drudy and Lynch, 1993, pp.261–7; Department of

Education and Science, 1998) that those already disadvantaged in the education process, such as early school leavers, are also excluded from adult education. Barriers to participation include financial constraints, lack of childcare provision, entry requirements and lack of appropriate information and guidance. Thus, suggest Drudy and Lynch (1993, p.262), adult education has not become a viable 'second-chance' option for the majority of those that have already been let down by the education system.

Given that such disparities have been long recognised in Ireland and that the state has made some attempts to increase equality of opportunity through its funding mechanisms and policy decisions, why is it that access to education remains so skewed by social-class background? There have been a number of explanations. Some of these locate the causes of inequality in cultural factors, others in the economic sphere, while others are more focused on the content and nature of the educational process itself.

In a study of young people who had dropped out of the primary and post-primary school systems in the outer Dublin suburb of Clondalkin, McSorley (1997, p.2) reports that home-based factors related to poverty, parental separation, unemployment, imprisonment, chronic illness and addiction are 'pivotal', as are parental attitudes and behaviour. McSorley suggests that parents in deprived areas such as parts of Clondalkin, who are socially and economically very disadvantaged, tend to 'lack the economic, academic and emotional resources to ensure their children are up, fed, dressed, with homework properly done and uniforms, books and lunch all ready in time for the school day'. Long-term and intergenerational unemployment, addiction problems and familial conflict each contribute to a breakdown in structure and routine that is inimical to academic success.

Many of the parents interviewed in the course of McSorley's research said they had 'hated' secondary school and had left as early as possible, without any qualifications. Of those interviewed, only 6 per cent had a qualification as high as the Intermediate Certificate and 59 per cent had left after primary school (the average age of respondents was thirty-three years so most of these parents would have had available to them the 'free' secondary education system introduced in the late 1960s). These parents now have far more positive views about primary school, seen as participatory and welcoming, than they do about secondary school, which remains an 'alien environment'. This may relate to the low levels of expectation that these parents have for their children: less than a third expect that their children will complete the Leaving Certificate (McSorley, 1997, p.27).

Many of McSorley's findings reflect earlier research carried out by Fagan (1995) who explored the lives of some inner-city 'school drop-outs'. Absenteeism was a major contributory factor to school failure — whether this was 'going on the hop', as described by Fagan's respondents, or missing school with parental knowledge and consent, as McSorley found to be widespread in her Clondalkin study. Parents sometimes actively encourage their children (especially girls) to stay away from school. Pupils often have to look after ill parents or siblings and may miss large amounts of school at times of family bereavement. Fagan (1995, p.48) argues that school drop-outs are typically 'surrounded by a community of early school leavers', including their peers, parents and others. There is little positive orientation to education; rather, an instrumental approach to work. The opportunity to gain an independent income is highly valued, both by school students and their families.

There has been considerable resistance to culturally based analyses such as those sketched above. It has been suggested that they do no more than reflect the particular sets of assumptions and values that (almost universally middle-class) researchers bring to the research process (Drudy and Lynch, 1993, pp.149–51). Lynch (1999a, p.112) offers evidence, provided by community activists, that working-class communities and parents do value education highly. Fagan (1995, p.83) remarks that a deficit account assumes a deficiency on the part of the individual, family and community. Clancy (1995, p.489) argues that there is a need to move away from such culturalist accounts: for him it is more important to examine the class-based nature of the education system itself: 'instead of focusing on the class characteristics of those who succeed and those who fail it is appropriate to examine the class characteristics of the educational experience at which they succeed or fail. This reorientation in approach represents an important development within the sociology of education'. The implication of this approach is that if there is large-scale failure within a system, it pays to look at features of that system itself.

Bourdieu's theory of *cultural capital* places a discussion of cultural factors within the broader context of the class-based nature of the education system. For Bourdieu cultural capital refers to the ideas, practices and artefacts that are highly valued in our society. There is some evidence that particular forms of cultural expression are favoured in schools and that more advantaged students have greater cultural capital through access to resources like private tuition, books, computers, leisure activities and travel (Drudy and Lynch, 1993, pp.156–7). Though Bourdieu's theories have had some impact on Irish educational research, there has been much debate over their usefulness. In particular, it is argued that such an approach can divert attention back to the cultural aspects of students and families and away from the broader question of economic inequality.

Critical researchers argue that such economic barriers remain the most important determinants of educational success. Drudy and Lynch (1993, p.161) suggest that poverty is an educational issue that has been neglected. The voice of the poor is effectively excluded from debates about educational inequality. Poverty makes it more difficult for working-class students to maximise any advantages that the system can offer. Furthermore, parents experiencing poverty find it difficult to experience a positive relationship with the education system. For Lynch (1999a, p.240) the persistence of poverty challenges the notion of choice in relation to access to education: 'those who have resources can exercise choices and those without resources generally cannot, or have relatively restricted choices depending on the area they live in.' McSorley's research (1997) indicates that teachers in Clondalkin schools perceive the problems of early school leaving as being connected with poverty and related social factors. The unemployment rate in the local-authority housing estates in the Clondalkin areas studied can be as high as 73 per cent.

In addition to culturalist and economic accounts, a third set of arguments relates to the organisation of schools themselves: the *school effects approach* (Smyth, 1999). This involves the study of a variety of schools to determine whether, and how, the organisation of the school as an institution has an important impact on the academic and social development of its pupils. The issue of 'school effectiveness' is a controversial and complex one, brought into focus through the activity of governments, particularly that of the UK, where school performance has become a contentious political issue and there is an increasing marketisation of education. Rigorous and regular school inspections, the compilation of performance indicators and the newspaper publication of 'league tables' for British schools has helped to generate a climate for a considerable academic 'school effects' literature (Smyth, 1999, pp.1–11). Similar processes are finding their way into the Irish educational system, though not without considerable resistance, not least from teachers. But it is very difficult to say what makes an effective school. A school that is effective in one area may not be in others. The criteria for measurement are highly contentious.

Smyth (1999, p.215) reports that gender, class and age remain as key predictors of pupil performance in Irish schools. But aspects of the organisation of schools are important: 'school matters'. For example, the practice of 'streaming' students according to a measure of ability is shown by Smyth (1999, pp.31–6) to have an overall negative effect. It increases the inequality of outcomes and reduces overall average marks, particularly at Junior Certificate level. Restriction of subject choice also has negative effects. It is better to allow students to sample the maximum number of subjects and to optimise the possibility that they will choose subjects they like. Smyth also reports that an enhanced level of participation in school management by the various groups — students, parents and teachers — involved in the schooling process leads to increased school effectiveness. The benefits of a clear and consistent disciplinary environment are demonstrated, as are those of positive teacher/pupil interaction and provision of feedback by teachers to students.

McSorley (1997, p.1) reports that in north and south-west Clondalkin over a third of the school-going population is absent on any given day and more than half the population leave school by age fifteen. Part of the reason, she suggests, is that 'the academic content and organisational structures of school do not meet the needs of poor and disadvantaged pupils.' Many early school leavers come into direct and frequent conflict with the structures, ethos and everyday practices of school. They have discipline problems, poor relationships with teachers, experience of bullying, a perception that there are 'too many subjects' of limited relevance, too much homework, and a view that school is 'too hard' and 'boring' (McSorley, 1997, p.31). Clondalkin parents report that the middle-class value system that typified schools was a major contributory factor to poor teacher/pupil and teacher/parent relations. Parents questioned the purpose of the education their children were receiving and wanted them to do more practical subjects such as typing and car mechanics. Fagan (1995, p.103) suggests that the education system actively colludes in absenteeism by not dealing effectively with the issue. She argues that a genuine response would entail a radical examination of the aims and objectives of education: 'obviously the problem is so pervasive, indeed structural, that to tackle it would be to call the whole educational system into question.'

The milieu of the working-class school itself is a cause of educational inequality. Research by McSorley and Fagan shows that there is an institutional devaluation of working-class culture within educational institutions. We have seen Fagan's remarks about the gulf that exists between the conventional academic curriculum and the reality of life for poor and many working-class pupils. The lack of respect for the culture of students was reflected in a lack of respect by teachers for pupils (which was reciprocated). According to Fagan (1995, p.19), for some of her respondents ongoing psychological battles and psychological torture occurred in the classroom. As a consequence, for the pupils placed in the lowest-grade class and where there is no hope of them progressing at school, no respect is felt for any teachers whatsoever, and so indiscipline reigns and the teacher is the enemy (Fagan, 1995, p.19). The outcome was a repertoire of resistance that spanned 'bunking off', 'messing' in class, through to open violence against teachers and school property. Ultimately, concluded Fagan, the response available to pupils alienated from the system was 'extremely destructive as opposed to culturally creative' (1995, p.119).

For Lynch and Lodge (2002) issues of class pervade the educational project, but are rarely named as such. Rather class differences and processes in education are euphemised as 'disadvantage' or 'social exclusion' and are individualised as the attributes of particular persons. Lynch and Lodge identify a range of sites where class differentiation and the exercise of power and control take place: this includes the macro-level of economic policies that fail to challenge inequality seriously; processes of selection and choice in relation to schools; streaming and other ways of categorising pupils in schools; and differential patterns of interaction in classrooms. As well as easily observable factors such as fees, 'voluntary' donations, uniform and transport to school, they point to some of the more subtle ways in which schools are marked in relation to class (Lynch and Lodge, 2002, p.48):

The social class project of a school was visible in many ways, most conspicuously in the quality of the school environment, including the quality and range of school facilities. It was also visible in more subtle ways; in the types of sports and extra-curricular activities promoted in the school; in the presence or absence of prospectuses; in the quality of design work, printing and paper used for year books, magazines and prospectuses; in the images presented of 'successful' past pupils; in the types of plays/musicals that were staged (if at all); and in the language used to describe events.

ETHNICITY AND EDUCATION

Irish educational settings are increasingly marked by ethnic and cultural diversity. This provides challenges for educators and is also beginning to be recognised in sociological and educational research.

The negative educational experience of Travellers is beginning to attract more sociological and policy attention, though there is a lack of reliable data in this area. According to Kenny (1997) one-third of primary-school-aged Travellers are 'fully integrated' into primary schools, one-third have specialised support or classes and a third remain outside the formal educational system. Nevertheless Lodge and Lynch (2004, p.94) report that: 'even though many students are formally enrolled (in primary schools), their attendance is low in many cases. When attendance levels are low and when school drop-out is a common problem, then it is almost inevitable that attainment levels are low also.'

This then impacts on the mainstream post-primary system where participation by Travellers in most aspects is very low (Figure 8.6). The formal education system (especially second level) is seen as negative by many Travellers for a number of reasons: feelings of 'difference' and discrimination; lack of flexibility towards nomadic lifestyles; the higher levels of family responsibility of Traveller girls and the potential role of the education system in undermining Traveller culture (Lodge and Lynch, 2004, p.96). The perception of likely discrimination or hostility is borne out in Lynch and Lodge's findings in relation to settled secondary students' attitudes: they report that 'deep-seated prejudice towards Travellers was encountered across most of the schools . . . many students were quite willing to express their dislike and antagonism towards Travellers in public' (2002, p.138). Nevertheless this was not universal and the discriminatory discourse was challenged by some students, especially those who had actual contact with Travellers in educational settings.

For Kenny, improvement of the educational experience for Travellers depends on proactive change within schools: 'if education provision, from the central policy-makers through to the local classrooms, were informed by principles of anti-racism and inter-culturalism, the need for special support for Travellers would be pared back to its true extent, because at least an alien school programme would not be confounding the difficulties confronting Traveller children' (1997, p.66). The necessity for Travellers to be involved at the planning and policy level is echoed by Lodge and Lynch (2004, p.98). Similarly, it will be important for Travellers to become involved as providers of education — as teachers and other education staff — in order to help to develop more appropriate educational pathways and practices.

Figure 8.6 Distribution of Traveller students in mainstream post-primary schools

School year	First Year	Second year	Third year	TY*	Fifth year	Sixth year	PLC	Total
2000–01	531	319	183	27	67	38	13	1,178
2001–02	582	397	220	31	86	49	16	1,381
2002–03	650	482	272	26	102	62	14	1,608
2003–04	626	527	341	44	113	63	15	1,729

*Transition year.
Source: Lodge and Lynch, 2004, p.95

The phenomenon of substantial immigration to Ireland (see Chapter 6) also has major implications for the education system, as does the development of an international education industry. O'Loingsigh (2001, p.115) states that there is a lack of recognition of cultural diversity within our existing system. This is reinforced by existing structures: for example the denominational aspect of the primary school system. The need to respond to ethnic diversity will require a change of management structures, of 'school ethos', and of the level of resourcing. For example, there is virtually no teaching of 'mother tongue' languages to immigrants or the children of immigrants, despite the existence of legislation in the Education Act that indicates that cultural and linguistic diversity must be recognised. An intercultural education system is required, suggests O'Loingsigh (2001, p.119) that is:

> not about integrating ethic minorities into our culture so that they become 'more Irish than the Irish themselves' but rather about educating people about tolerance, human rights, democracy and, most of all, respect for difference.

Given the rigidity of the Irish school system, in particular the continued power of the church, it is unlikely that the education system will change rapidly to address the issue of multi- or interculturalism.

Lynch and O'Riordan (1999, p.122) point out the important fact that educational disadvantage within Irish society can only be fully understood in terms of the advantages enjoyed by others. They argue that:

The financial, cultural and educational experiences of working-class students need not, in and of themselves, create educational inequality; what creates inequality is the fact that others have differential access to resources, incomes wealth and power which enables them to avail of opportunities presented in education in a relatively more successful manner.

In very many ways the education system has been structured by the advantaged in order to maintain their position. As well as operating within a system that reflects their economic and cultural interests, wealthier students are able to purchase on the private market goods and services (grinds, computers, books, foreign travel) that give them an educational advantage. They enjoy better study conditions and experience fewer pressures to take up part-time or full-time work.

The facilities and opportunities available to more advantaged groups in education relate to how the process itself is perceived. Allen (1998, p.202) makes the point, for example, that whereas training for the long-term unemployed is seen as a 'social cost', similar education provided for graduates is defined as an 'investment'. Such analysis may help to explain the consistent enactment of education policies (such as 'free fees' in secondary and more recently third-level education) that disproportionately benefit the already well-off (Clancy, 1995, p.485); and the neglect of areas (in particular, primary and adult education) that have a greater capacity to lead to social equality.

Lynch and O'Riordan (1999, p.122) argue, 'those whose own class are the definers of what is culturally and educationally valuable in the first instance are strongly positioned to be the major beneficiaries of educational investment'. Historically in Ireland there is a strong discourse, supported by church and state, that favours academic education. Academic education, translated into high Leaving Certificate honours, can be used by the advantaged to gain access to prestigious third-level and professional courses in fields such as law, medicine and dentistry; thus social and economic power is maintained.

As pointed out earlier by Lynch and Lodge the inequalities in Irish education have proved remarkably durable and knowledge about their existence has not led to a significant movement for change. There have been a number of initiatives in recent years, such as the development of the Leaving Certificate Applied, the 'Breaking the Cycle' and 'Early Start' programmes and the Home/School Liaison Scheme, yet these have done little to change the broad picture of educational inequality (MacVeigh, 2006). The work of Lynch and her colleagues over the last two decades points to a much more stringent critique: one that would see a fundamental questioning of what education is for. This would then entail a questioning of the nature of our economic and social systems. As we suggested at the beginning of this chapter, education is indeed in many ways central to how we understand Irish society.

9

Gender, sexuality and the family

The most significant development in the discipline of sociology in the last three decades has been the rise to prominence of gender issues. This is related to two key processes:

- the reconstruction of Western (and also non-Western) societies in terms of occupational structures, secularisation and demography as outlined elsewhere in this book
- the rise of the modern women's movement and the permeation of feminist and gender-oriented discourses into all aspects of social life.

Similarly, many of the major issues of public and private social and political debate in Ireland for the past thirty years have related to issues of gender, sexuality and the family. The country has been convulsed by a series of conflicts around the, often linked, issues of contraception, adoption, abortion, censorship, homosexuality, sex education and divorce. In addition, the abuse of children and women — physical, sexual and psychological — has come to prominence in the media and the legal and welfare systems. These revelations and debates have placed sex, gender, the body and the family at the centre of arguments that have also brought into play discussions of morality, freedom, personal integrity, authority and control. For many participants and observers these conflicts and exposés have been central to the question of modernity and Irish society. For many, the vigorous public arguments over issues of the family, sexuality and gender are indicative that, for better or for worse, Ireland is becoming an increasingly modern society.

There are at least three common viewpoints about how relationships between men and women have changed in Ireland over the last three decades. One view is that there has been a huge amount of positive change and progress. Commentators point to the election of Presidents Mary Robinson and Mary McAleese and the prominence of women politicians such as Mary Harney, Mary Lou McDonald and Mary Hanafin; female sportspeople such as Sonia O'Sullivan and Derval O'Rourke; and the appointment of women as judges in the High Court and the Supreme Court. They may also cite the exposure of abuse against women and children, the conviction of the perpetrators and the calling to account of the institutions of church and state; the increasing involvement of men in housework and childcare; the cultural prominence of women artists, writers and musicians; and the huge shift of women into the paid workforce and into formerly male-dominated occupations. They may draw attention to the achievement of legal equality for men and women; the gradual development of women's health services, childcare services, coeducational schools and youth groups; and so on. To such commentators these factors are often seen as further indicators that Ireland is becoming a 'modern European state'.

A second view is essentially opposed to the first, stressing how *little* has changed in Ireland and how much gender inequality and differentiation remains. This view propounds the continued real discrimination against women in many areas of employment and social life; women's inferior position with regard to wealth, property and income; the continuing economic dependence of women and children on men; and the continued existence of widespread violence inflicted by men upon women and children. We may be reminded of the fact that the higher echelons of Irish social institutions such as the law, medicine, the media, the churches, business and government continue to be dominated by males; of the persistence of stereotyped images of masculinity and femininity within our culture; and of the failure of society and government to respond to key issues such as child-care, abortion, care of older people and other social concerns.

A third and developing view is that the nature of gender inequality is changing and that increasingly *men* are disadvantaged within Irish society. This argument points to men's poorer health status and shorter life expectancy; to the academic weakness of boys and suggestions that the educational environment has become 'feminised'. This approach can be summed up in the popular phrase: 'boys are the new girls'. There is concern over males' higher level of exposure to violence and to their high tendency towards suicide and road trauma. Men have campaigned against their perceived marginalisation within the new forms of family and over legal decisions in relation to custody of and access to children. Overall, there are concerns over the inability of men to adjust to changes in society, education and the workplace and to develop new models of masculinity. The existence of these three sets of views (and others) — which in turn may all overlap and coexist — indicates something of the complexities of the gender issue.

Despite the emergence of gender as a significant category of analysis in global sociology, and the importance of gender-related social issues in Irish society, it has tended to be played down in many texts dealing with Irish society (O'Connor, 1998, p.6). But, increasingly, gender issues have underpinned important areas of sociological research in Ireland including, for example, rural life, education and religion (discussed accordingly throughout this book).

The topic of gender is open to discussion and analysis from any number of vantage points. In recent decades important gender-based geographies, histories, cultural studies and psychologies have emerged, along with numerous studies from within other disciplinary areas, that have attempted to examine the position of women and men in the context of Irish society and its institutions. Of equal importance, there has been a concerted effort to change the paradigms within which we think about society, to move away from a male-centred or androcentric way of looking at the world and to adopt a view that reflects the experience of all people. We would argue that, within this re-thinking of the world, a sociological perspective is important and that the tools offered by sociology can provide us with useful knowledge about how society's structures, institutions, discourses and processes have helped to shape the relationships between men and women and how these relationships have been interpreted. Conversely, a focus on the experiences of commonality, difference and inequality within gender relationships is a crucial part of any thoroughgoing sociological analysis.

This chapter is not an attempt to produce a comprehensive sociology of gender in an Irish context. There are already excellent volumes that do that in far more detail than we can attempt here (see especially Byrne and Leonard, 1997; O'Connor, 1998; Galligan, 1998a). There is a small but growing literature in Ireland on issues pertaining to men and masculinities (e.g. McKeown *et al.*, 1999; Keohane and Chambers, 2002; Ferguson and Hogan, 2004; Cleary *et al.* 2004; Schubotz and Rolston, 2004). A special issue of the *Irish Journal of Sociology* (14(2)) explored a range of contemporary issues including socialisation, education, land, fatherhood and suicide from a masculinities perspective. In this chapter we limit ourselves to:

- outlining the conceptual basis for a sociological examination of gender
- providing an overview of how issues of gender have been related to Ireland's development and identity
- examining some issues in relation to gender and work, family and power
- exploring some aspects of the sociological study of sexuality in Ireland
- reviewing some aspects of the emergent field of Irish masculinities studies.

In summary, in other parts of this book we discuss how gender relates to issues of:

- agriculture and industrial development (Chapter 3)
- education (Chapter 8)
- health (Chapter 10)
- crime and deviance (Chapter 11)
- consumption (Chapter 16)
- the emergence of the women's movement (Chapter 17)

Additionally, gender as an analytical category makes its presence felt in a more diffuse way throughout all chapters of the book.

SEX AND GENDER

It is important, and useful, at this stage to address some questions of definition. In particular, the differentiation between the concepts of *sex* and *gender* is important in the development of a sociological understanding of the relationships between women and men. Sex is commonly held to refer to the differing physical attributes, genital arrangements, chromosomal structures, reproductive systems and secondary sexual characteristics such as distribution of body hair, breast development and so on. Sex gives rise to two categories: *female* and *male*. Gender refers to the *meanings* that arise out of sexual classification; and to the socially constructed experiences and identities that arise from assumed sexual differences. The clues to such gender identities are found in the physical attributes of sex and in a whole gamut of qualities and activities, ranging from social attitudes to style of dress, work performed, or emotional make-up. The categories that gender gives rise to in Western societies are *feminine* and *masculine*. Masculinity and femininity are constructs specific to historical time and place. They are categories continually being formed, contested, reworked and reaffirmed in social institutions and practices (as well as a range of ideologies). Amongst these conflicting definitions, there is always space for negotiation and change. Here we will maintain a focus on gender as it is the socially constructed categories of masculinity and femininity that concern us. For simplicity we will use the terms 'men' and 'women', and 'female' and 'male' — though we are aware that these tend to emphasise 'natural difference' more than we would like.

THEORISING GENDER

Sociobiology

There is a strong set of ideas, found both in common-sense and academic theories, that the differences between men and women are founded on a 'natural' basis. Writers point to *biological* differences such as those found in brain structure, hormones or body size, shape and strength. Men, for example, are typified as aggressive and goal-driven and women as submissive and emotional. It is argued that such differences provide an explanation, and often a justification, for differential outcomes in regard to sex roles, occupational segregation or inequality. The search for 'natural' explanations may be particularly intense at a time when the common assumptions about gender relationships are under threat.

It seems we have moved on from a time when women were seen to be naturally weak, emotionally unstable and believed to have smaller brains than men, but the belief in a direct biological basis for gender difference and inequality persists. The most recent research in this area tends to focus on genes (for example, a gene for 'aggressiveness') and on the nature of hormonal influences. But for sociologists there can never be a simple or automatic link between any biological basis and social outcomes: even the most extreme of biological variations must be mediated by social processes. Nevertheless the interdisciplinary perspective known as socio-biology has sought to explain certain aspects of human social behaviour — including those aspects related to gender difference — in biological terms. Sociobiology has always been intensely controversial as there is a fine line between explaining differences in terms of a biological basis and *justifying* them in these terms. When the differences concerned are expressed as social inequalities, this becomes a highly emotive field.

Patriarchy

The concept of patriarchy has come to refer to the systematic patterning of society in such a way that men dominate, exploit and oppress women (O'Connor, 1998, p.7). For O'Connor (1998, p.13) a variety of everyday taken-for-granted practices reflect and reinforce patriarchal control, including practices and processes within the family; in interpersonal relationships; within the paid and unpaid workforce; in consumption; and in the bureaucratic structures of the state and the economy. The problem with patriarchy is that it appears to be both universal and timeless. Though a number of matriarchal societies have been identified through anthropological studies and although some societies, such as hunter–gatherer societies, appear to display less gender inequality than our own, all known societies can be seen to be patriarchal to some extent. As patriarchy has been identified as a universal quality of extant human societies, it has been criticised as an essentialist and fatalistic concept that adds little to our understanding. For sociologists it is a description rather than an explanation. It is certainly the case that all societies are differentiated by gender and have been dominated in various ways by men. The question is, *why?*

Sociological theories

It can be argued that theories derived from sociobiology *and* theories of patriarchy are non-sociological, in that they are *essentialist*. In other words, they fail to examine how gender differences are created and expressed through social processes. Conversely, sociological theories attempt to trace how gender difference is constituted within particular types of social institutions, processes and historical contexts, and to explain why it is that gender inequality exists and is reproduced within society. There are many varied sociological theories of gender, including broad-brush theories in relation to the historical origins and global experience of gender inequality; middle-range theories about how gender is structured in and through social institutions like the family, the educational system and the state; and micro-level theories that seek to explain how gender is constructed through and shapes phenomena such as conversation and everyday social interaction. Furthermore, sociological theories reflect the full range of political positions that exists in relation to gender, from conservative and reactionary to radical and revolutionary. It is therefore very difficult to summarise and convey the diversity of sociological approaches to gender. Here we can only briefly mention the main theoretical stances that sociologists adopt in relation to gender issues.

For *functionalists* gender relationships and differences are seen as crucial to the effective functioning of society. Gender differences serve an integrative function in society: they help to bind members together. Thus, masculinity and femininity are seen as a complementary set of roles that span the family (in particular), the public sphere and the workplace. Women are responsible for the domestic arena, for the management of family life, and the socialisation of children; while men are to be found in the public sphere, the world of paid work and making connections to the broader world outside the family. Socialisation, for functionalists, is among other things the preparation of people for the 'proper' fulfilment of such sex roles. Males are brought up to be rational, competitive and instrumental; females to be affective, empathetic and co-operative. Subsequent social interaction reinforces these gender scripts and sanctions are brought to bear on those that do not clearly reflect the appropriate role. Society discriminates against 'masculine' women or 'feminine' men and those who step outside the proscribed gender-appropriate activities. See, for example, Liston's work (2002) on women in sport in Ireland. Liston found that male participation in sport generates sporting capital (cf. Bourdieu). Sport exemplifies a cluster of values and expectations that are coterminous with our ideas about ideal masculinity. As a result, non-conformists (women, gay men) do not fit in. Overall, women in sport tend to be valued for their femininity more than their sporting prowess.

While functionalist approaches (which share many assumptions with socio-biology) are little in favour with contemporary sociologists, they clearly continue to have resonances in everyday life and popular culture. Many jokes and throwaway remarks relate directly to the 'proper' roles of the sexes while, perhaps more seriously, stereotypes in relation to the appropriate behaviour of males and females may adversely affect individuals' progress through the education system, employment and in public life. The functionalist concept of 'sex role' continues to be very widely used, often in a non-critical way, in analyses of social phenomena.

Within Marxist thought the oppression of women is an aspect of class conflict and antagonism. Marxists point to the discrimination against women and the consequent low cost of female labour (for example, in the textiles or contract-cleaning sector) as a means of further exploiting the working class. In addition, the unpaid work of women within the nuclear family allows the next generation of workers to be *reproduced* at a lower cost to the forces of capital. More broadly, the family is also a key site for the inculcation of ideologies favourable to capital: the family, and in particular women, who bear the brunt of this work, teaches children to be obedient, productive, healthy and communicative, the very values necessary for an efficient labour force. These sets of ideas have been brought together in sociology in *social reproduction theory* — an approach that argues for a systematic connection between the subordination of women and capitalist economic exploitation (Connell, 1987, p.43).

Whether such reproduction takes place in ways that 'suit' capital is always contingent: always open to question. The family equally has the capacity to become a site of *opposition* to capitalism, and the relationships between men and women are constantly reworked and redefined, not pre-set by the nature of the capitalist economy. Similarly, it is debatable whether gender inequality *does* favour capitalism. As we saw in Chapter 1, a key historical feature of capitalism has been that it breaks down what are seen as traditional relationships and structures and reconstitutes people as workers and consumers. In many respects the development of capitalist social relationships has seen a greater level of equality between men and women. If we think of how changes in the position of women have created new sources of educated workers and enthusiastic consumers, we can see how higher levels of gender equality can be of great service to capital.

Feminist sociology is usually associated with the second-wave feminist movement. (The 'first wave' is usually taken to refer to the suffragist movements of the late nineteenth and early twentieth century, but of course this does not mean that organised women's movements or systematic feminist thought did not precede this.) While always being concerned with the issue of gender inequality and particularly its relation to women, there are many varieties of feminism: it is by no means a homogenous movement or system of thought.

It is common to divide modern feminist thinking into three main strands: liberal, socialist and radical feminism. Each overlaps with social theory in other fields: thus, socialist feminism shares many assumptions with Marxism; radical feminism with libertarian thinking. Similarly, intellectual currents in feminism are inextricably linked to competing political positions and strategies within the women's movement. For example, radical feminism is strongly connected to small-scale social movements and alternative lifestyles; socialist feminism to trade union activity; and liberal feminism to parliamentary politics and 'femocracy'.

Liberal feminists are concerned to uncover the immediate forms of discrimination against women and to fight for legal and other reforms to overcome them. They tend to focus on mainstream methods of bringing about social change, such as political lobbying, use of the media and working through existing political, business and bureaucratic structures. A good example in the Irish context would be Women's Aid, a voluntary organisation that provides support and information to women and their children who are being physically, emotionally and sexually abused in their own homes. It is self-defined as a feminist, political and campaigning organisation committed to the elimination of violence against and abuse of women.

Socialist feminists argue that women's oppression is both an aspect of capitalism and of patriarchy. An end to the current nature of capitalism does not in itself mean an end to the subordination of women, but is an essential part of it. The full liberation of women from oppression will also require a struggle against the control by men of private and public institutions. Socialist feminists often work through smaller left-wing political parties and groupings, trade unions, social movements and in academia and the media.

Radical feminists see male control of all women through patriarchy as the main problem. They argue that women must struggle to free themselves from the control of male institutions. They are most likely to work through women-only groups. Forms of action may span conventional lobbying techniques to innovative forms of protest such as the long-running Greenham Common anti-nuclear weapons protest in 1980s Britain. Each of these approaches to feminism finds a reflection in the work of feminist sociologists.

In the 1990s a body of writing arose that challenges what it sees as the orthodoxies of Western feminism, including the established divisions between the strands outlined above. Known as 'the new feminism' it rejects the oft-quoted precept that 'the personal is the political' and attempts to move feminism away from what it sees as 'lifestyle' politics and back into the public sphere. A key proponent of the 'new feminism', British writer Natasha Walter, suggests that the former approach has led feminism to a 'dead end'. Thus, she suggests, the feminist focus on women's cultural and sexual behaviour has not led to the expected radical changes. She argues (Walter, 1998, p.4) that:

> Feminism has enunciated many, too many, critiques of dress and pornography, of poetry and film-making, of language and physical behaviour. It has sought to direct our personal lives on every level. And yet women have still not achieved fundamental equality; they are still poorer and less powerful than men. Rather than concentrating its energy on the ways women dress and talk and make love, feminism now must attack the material basis of economic and social and political equality.

The rise of the 'new feminism' expresses the tensions of a movement that has achieved remarkable success but which has still to fully challenge the underlying realities of entrenched gender inequality. For Walter (1998, p.6) the new feminism is, above all, materialist: 'it concentrates on the material reality of inequality, and allows women to live their personal lives without the constraints of rigid ideology.' As such it may represent a return to much of the style and substance of earlier models of feminism, particularly those found in the trade-union movement and among socialist feminists.

Lumby argues (1997, p.169) that it is hard for young women in particular to find a place in the institutionalised feminist world, as it leaves no space for how women's experiences might differ along age, ethnic, class and cultural lines. She argues that, like traditional philosophy, institutionalised feminism 'relies on the strategies of saming (women are the same) and othering (women are different from men) to construct identity'. The new feminism aims to tap into the concerns of younger women (and men), to draw on the vibrancy of popular culture (including fashion and music) and to make use of the new communications technologies of a globalising world: 'riot grrrls, guerrilla girls, net chicks, cyber chix, geekgirls, tank girls, supergirl, action girls, deep girls — this is the era of DIY feminism' (Bail, 1996, p.3). Inevitably the new feminism has had to confront suggestions of a 'sell-out' to patriarchy and capitalism, and a lack of political purity. The debate between traditional and new feminists is a vigorous and challenging one for feminist thinking. Within sociology it may lead to a shift away from the concern with cultural issues of sexuality and representation and towards more mainstream sociological concerns with the structures of social inequality.

In response to the development of the women's movement and stimulated by the increased reflexivity of (post-)modern society, there has been a recent interest in the nature of *masculinity*. There has been a recognition that changing models of femininity may give rise to changes in the imagery, understanding or experience of masculinity. For a long time within society, and within sociology, masculinity has been 'invisible'. As British social psychologists Edley and Wetherell (1995, p.2) suggest, 'masculinity has been regarded as the standard case, the usual pattern, synonymous with humanity in general.' Historically men have had the capacity to define 'normality'; it is women who have been positioned as deviations from the norm and femininity that has required exploration and explanation. Thus, gender studies have tended to focus very much on women's experience and studies of men *as men* have been until recently comparatively rare.

For Edley and Wetherell (1995, p.5) the new focus on masculinity and the experiences of men can be explained at least partly by changes in the nature of economic relations and production, in particular the shift towards knowledge-based industries and new patterns of work. These have combined with changes in the structure of families (see below) to radically alter the position of men within society. The traditional image of the male breadwinner labouring in the male-dominated workplace of farm, factory or office now has a diminishing resonance in reality. Edley and Wetherell argue that a comprehensive understanding of contemporary masculinity requires an interdisciplinary approach, one that combines a sociology of men with a social psychological understanding of male subjectivity and an appreciation of the discourses within which masculinity is defined and framed within our culture. In reviewing how masculinity has been constructed over 2000 years of history, they conclude that it is 'a story, not of smooth transitions, but of struggle and bitter dispute' (1995, p.7).

The failure of sociologists to adequately analyse the nature of masculinity has impoverished our understanding of gender as a whole. For McKeown *et al.* (1999)

a full understanding of Irish masculinity is necessary to trace out, and to intervene in, fathering practices in Ireland. Drawing on research within the feminist tradition and from the rapidly expanding body of international research into masculinity, they place the practice of fatherhood within the context of the law, the 1937 Irish Constitution, psychoanalysis, work and, perhaps most interestingly, the division of domestic labour within the home. While the analysis and conclusions that McKeown *et al.* arrive at are in some ways controversial (for example, in their call for a constitutional amendment to protect paternal rights), they have provided a useful contribution to the understanding of gender relationships in Ireland. We return to masculinity studies at the end of this chapter.

RESEARCHING GENDER

The emergence of the second-wave women's movement and of feminist analysis has been instrumental to the development of an extensive sociology of gender. The research agenda has been extremely broad, as indicated above. But a gender-oriented sociology has not just been about opening up new or neglected areas of analysis; it is also about *doing* sociology differently. It has seen a concerted attempt to develop ways to generate sociological knowledge and understanding that lie outside of, and provide an alternative to, the 'malestream'. As a result there has been much debate within sociology as to whether such a thing as a feminist research methodology can exist: are there particular ways to do research, and to analyse the findings, that can avoid the biases identified in 'malestream' research? Taken further, are there ways of doing research that can reflect and develop the feminist ethos of gender equity?

There has been much debate over the possibility of a feminist research methodology. It has been suggested that feminist research should be reflexive, participatory, egalitarian, qualitative, action-oriented and critical of conventional methods and research tools. Millen (1997, p.15) suggests that feminist research is 'a politicised framework for the understanding of knowledge, and charges *all* researchers, male and female, to examine the role of sex and gender in society and to ensure that androcentric norms are not incorporated into their work'. The debate about feminist research methodology centres largely on whether it implies simply a particular focus on and sensitivity to gender issues — sometimes called (pejoratively) the 'add women' approach; or whether feminist research involves a wholly different paradigm — the development of a feminist epistemology or system of knowledge. This divergence of views is illustrated in a brief debate that took place in the pages of the *Irish Journal of Sociology* between two Irish feminist sociologists: Ronit Lentin and Evelyn Mahon.

For Lentin (1993, p.120) feminist research methodologies (for they are multiple) are those that '[make] visible the lived experiences of Irish women or which have included the researcher's lived experience and reflexivity as part of the research process and findings'. Feminist research can include any type of research method (interview, survey, discourse analysis and so on) but — for Lentin — to be feminist it must be *reflexive*. In her research into gendered responses to the Holocaust, this meant 'including [her] own intellectual and emotional autobiography' (1993, p.122). The aim of such a feminist methodology is the transformation of the discipline of sociology from the inside: by an outsider. The totality of such feminist interventions, suggests Lentin, has led to the creation of a new *feminist research paradigm* within sociology. Underpinning this paradigm are the following principles: 'feminist research draws on women's own interpretations of their own experience, relates them to the way in which the society in which we live is constructed and reflexively includes the researcher in all stages of data collection and data production' (1993, p.124). Feminist research, she claims, requires a shared experience of oppression between sociologist and subject; conversely, 'traditional research' involves and expresses an inequality of power between the researcher and researched. Ultimately, adoption of a feminist research paradigm means that the gap between 'academic feminists' and 'Irish women they seek to empower' is narrowed. A brief survey by Lentin of a selection of extant research reports assesses their feminist research credentials on the basis of whether they 'make visible real women'. She suggests that through either a lack of resources or a desire to be accepted by mainstream sociology and funding agencies, Irish feminist researchers have largely failed to adopt what she has defined as a feminist research paradigm.

This position is strongly rebutted by Mahon. While for Lentin feminist research is research carried out by avowed feminists, for Mahon it is research that is underpinned by a *feminist theoretical perspective*; it can thus be carried out by men as well as by women. She argues that feminist research is more than merely rendering women's lives 'visible' (after all, *Hello* magazine does this rather effectively); rather, it is a process whereby the sociologist depicts 'the social processes by which [women's] lives are constructed and reproduced in a way which has generally led to their oppression or unequal treatment in society' (1994, p.166). It is research that rejects the assumption that male experience is universal. For example, the feminist challenge to class theory has meant that sociologists of class can no longer define a woman's class position simply by reference to her husband's. In addition, Mahon rejects Lentin's position that the feminist researcher must share in the oppression of the subject. She argues that an academic detachment *is* possible and that it is not necessary to have experienced a situation personally in order to be able to understand it. Overall, she is arguing for a more positivist and theoretically informed, and less emotive and grounded, approach to feminist research. The substantial and complex issues related to feminist research methodologies are explored in considerable detail in a subsequent edited collection (Byrne and Lentin, 2000). The editors argue that 'feminist research methodologies are being fruitfully utilised in student training and education, in action-based community settings, and in post-graduate, academic and some policy research in Ireland' (p.6).

GENDER, HISTORY, IDENTITY

So far in this chapter we have teased out some of the contours of the diverse sociological approaches to gender issues and have given an indication of the complexity and sophistication of these views; as already mentioned, it is impossible to condense this discussion into a simple outline of the 'sociology of gender'. We now examine some aspects of Irish society through the lens of a gender perspective. Topics have been selected that may help to illuminate some of the other concerns identified, in particular the nature of Irish 'modernity'. The changes that have taken place in Ireland, over at least the last three decades, have often been reflected in or shaped by the changing relationships between women and men.

An understanding of contemporary gender relationships in Ireland requires consideration of how such representations and identities have developed over time. In a sense, all history is a history of gender, in that gender is implicated in all human activity. But it is also the case that until comparatively recently historical writing tended to focus disproportionately on the experiences of men: women (and children) were marginalised or remained completely absent from written accounts (O'Dowd and Wichert, 1995). As a result, the lived, day-to-day experience of Irish women has been overlooked and its importance played down.

The writing of history is in many ways a search for identity, an attempt to develop a coherent narrative that embodies the character of a people. In turn, 'history' becomes part of the context within which gender relations are lived out in the contemporary world and is therefore crucial to a sociological understanding. A number of writers have attempted to trace the historical and discursive connections between gender, sexuality and 'Irishness'. In common with Nash (1997, p.108) they argue that different versions of Irish national identity have prescribed 'certain kinds of gender and sexual identities for Irish men and women. These gendered representations . . . impact upon the lives of women and men and influence their opportunities and constraints in work, education, political activity, personal relationships and senses of themselves.' One of the tasks of the sociologist is to try to interpret the nature and directions of such 'impacts' in contemporary Irish society.

For Ronit Lentin (1998, p.11; 1999) the construction of Irishness has been 'disturbingly gendered'; the definition of Irish citizenship that has emerged since independence has actively marginalised women and indeed has sought to erase all expressions of difference. Thus, for example, the 1937 Irish Constitution has been labelled by Lentin and other analysts as a conservative document that assigns a subordinate role to women. It places women essentially as wives and mothers within the context of the family. The model of femininity it espouses is 'passive, private and domestic'. Most notoriously, Article 41.2.1 of the Constitution, which recognises the special contribution to Irish society of women 'within the home', has been identified as a patriarchal statement about the 'proper' place of women in Irish society. It closely reflected Catholic Church teaching at the time it was written, but continues to exert an influence over policy and law.

A number of writers have argued that the *land* of Ireland — the central motif of our history — has been viewed historically in a gendered way: as a feminine entity (see Lentin, 1999, pp.5–7). Ireland is not unique in this regard. Similar arguments have been made for other national landscapes, including those of Australia (Schaffer, 1988) and of Sweden (Åberg, 1999). The geographer Catherine Nash suggests that the land of Ireland has been depicted as female in a number of traditions and contexts that range from old Gaelic representations to colonialist viewpoints to nationalist myths (such as Dark Rosaleen, Caitlín ní Houlihán and the *aisling*). To nineteenth-century English colonialists, Ireland (and its people) was typified by 'supposedly . . . feminine characteristics of sentimentality, ineffectuality, nervous excitability and unworldliness' that rendered it incapable of self-government; in contrast, for Irish nationalists 'avowals of heroic masculinity were made alongside the celebration of dependent, passive, domestic and selfless Irish femininity' (Nash, 1997, p.114). In such discourses of nationhood 'Ireland is raped, seduced or married and in turn features alternatively as virgin, wanton woman, bride, mother or old woman' (1997, p.116). For O'Connor (1998, p.84) the images of 'Mother Ireland' and 'the self-sacrificing Irish mother' — dominant images within Irish nationalist discourse — 'reflect and reinforce men's fear and loathing of women', though this provocative point is not developed any further.

Nash goes further and argues that the historical perception of the land as feminine, especially within Irish nationalism, is linked to how the femininity of Irish women has been constructed. She suggests that there are 'traditional associations between nature, land, fertility and femininity' (1997, p.110) and that these are reflected in women's legal, social and ideological position. For example, beliefs about the sanctity of Irish womanhood were converted into the regulation of cultural forms such as fashion, film, literature, music and dance. 'Foreign notions' of sexual equality, it was said, undermined the home and native honour towards women and degraded Irish women (Nash, 1997, p.115). The idea that the gendered imagery of Ireland as a country is linked to the formation of gendered identities among its people is an intriguing one, but it needs to be further understood through research. One of the problems with such analyses, from a sociological point of view, is that they tend to essentialise both femininity and masculinity.

It is only recently in Ireland that sociologists have begun explicitly to grasp the relationships between gender and *ethnicity*, though this has been a key issue for the study of gender in the United States, Britain and Australia. Studies (for example, Lennon *et al.*, 1988; Buckley, 1997) of Irish women in Britain have led the way, bringing attention to the ethnic minority status of Irish people in Britain and drawing out some of the implications of this in terms of inequality, racism and the complexities of personal and social identity. Ronit Lentin has sought to focus on the inherent racism of the dominant constructions of 'Irishness', such as that expressed in the 1937 Constitution, and, closer to home, within Irish sociology and women's studies. For her, 'the assumption that to be Irish is to be Roman Catholic (or, in a very limited sense also Protestant) settled and white, has not been adequately challenged by politicians, social scientists or the media' (Lentin, 1999, p.9). Lentin mounts a strong argument that narrowly defined conceptions of 'Irishness', for example, as expressed in the Constitution, serve to deny full citizenship to ethnic minority women, such as refugees and asylum seekers, Travellers, Muslim and Jewish people, and Black-Irish people.

Lentin has focused in particular on the issues of minority ethnic groups, including the Travellers (the issue of whether Travellers constitute a separate ethnic group is a highly controversial one: see Chapter 17). For Lentin Travelling women have been 'occluded in Irish sociological and feminist studies of women and citizenship, which often do not problematise the term "Irish women" and tend not to engage with the thorny question of difference' (Lentin, 1998, p.13). She points out that in Ireland Traveller women are 'excluded from full access to political, but mostly civil and social citizenship' (1998, p.14) — this includes feminist political and academic projects. Lentin is highly critical of Irish feminism in this regard: 'at worst, "white" sedentary Irish feminism discusses racism as if it is the problem of the racially excluded' . . . 'at best [it] tends to "speak for" racialized Irish women' (1998, p.18). Tannam (1999, p.31) points out that policy and academic texts on gender in Ireland tend to ignore the experiences of migrant women and those of minority ethnic groups. The rapid change that Ireland is now undergoing, particularly its transition to a multi-ethnic state, means that analysis of gender in Ireland needs to examine the specificity of Irish women — and men — of varying ethnic identifications and, inseparable from this, the nature and practice of racism in Ireland.

Recent research in Ireland has problematised women's invisibility in migration studies. Indeed, Carla de Tona's work on Italian women in Dublin argues that the silent presence that characterises migrant women 'is not the outcome of their existential condition, but the means through which the discrimination of their condition is perpetuated' (2004, p.315).

Angeline Morrison has explored notions of Irish identity in the context of women of mixed-race backgrounds living in Dublin. She found that their readings of their own bodies (and thus identities) as 'black' had largely to do with the way white, racialised Irish society read them (2004, p.365). Furthermore, people had difficulty accepting their 'Irishness'. In other words, for these women race was a category imposed on them and, in the racialised consciousness of the majority population, they could not really belong. Visible racial and ethnic signifiers often serve as the focus for a 'moral panic' as was the case in Ireland in 2004, when concerns about so called 'maternity tourism' were expressed by the government and amplified by the media (Breen et al., 2006). The concerns centred on the perceived increase in pressure on maternity hospitals because of rising numbers of births to non-nationals. According to Luibheid (2004, p.335) in an era of accelerated globalisation the Irish government requires new strategies to construct the nation as a sovereign space. She argues that discourses and practices targeting child-bearing asylum-seeker women, and culminating in the 2004 Citizenship Referendum, provided the government not just with an opportunity to reassert national boundaries, but also with the means through which to generate 'new modes of racialisation and racial hierarchies within Ireland'.

The issue of gender is inextricably tied up with questions of identity and difference. In Ireland, as elsewhere, the constitution of personal and social identity is a complex and highly dynamic process. It is suggested by many that in Ireland key components of our identity can find their explanation in our colonial history, the nature of our land(scape) and how we conceptualise others. It is further suggested that ideas about identity are translated into specific forms of social practice. We have outlined some of the arguments that have been put forward to link these questions in an Irish context, but would suggest that, while the arguments are fascinating, there remains much work to be done within the Irish sociology of gender to explore such connections.

THE FAMILY

The family, in Ireland as elsewhere, has been identified as 'an important symbol of collective identity, unity and security' (O'Connor, 1998, p.89). It is seen by many — including many social scientists — as the 'natural' basis for society. It has also risen to prominence in commercial, political and social policy rhetoric, with much attention being given to 'the family' in political campaigns, media advertising and social policy initiatives, where it stands for themes such as 'parental care, whole-some meals and morals, conjugal eroticism and sibling responsibility' (Robertson, 1991, p.166). An understanding of the family is also central to any discussion of gender relationships, for it is through this institution, and others, that our experiences and understandings of gender and of sexuality are formed and mediated.

As the term 'family' has risen to prominence in public discourse, however, it has become more problematic and opaque. While for marketers of cars or breakfast cereals it has positive connotations of nostalgia and emotion, for economists and bureaucrats it may give rise to negative perceptions of 'tradition'. The rationalist economic discourse of modernity tends to focus very much on the *individual* as worker and as consumer, and perhaps as citizen. There is much focus on individual rights and actions in 'the market' and the family is seen within this context as somewhat anachronistic and limiting: as in 'family business', 'family farm' or 'family obligations'.

Such a focus on the, implicitly male, individual has allowed questions of oppression and inequality of, and within, families to be largely ignored. But as Robertson (1991, p.158) points out we need to understand the family as the locus of much of what we define as social behaviour. Thus, 'if we are interested in such things as economic performance and social status, the interaction of life-cycles within the domestic group is much more informative than the life-cycle of each individual.' An understanding of the family is basic to a sociological understanding.

In Western societies there has been much debate over competing definitions of 'the family'. It is now widely accepted that there are many variations from 'the norm' of the nuclear family of married heterosexual couple plus children. For example, Irish social welfare policy and practice has now begun to recognise the validity of families based on cohabiting (not married) couples or lone parents (O'Connor, 1998, p.90). There is far less agreement — in Ireland and elsewhere — over the possibility of families based on homosexual unions, for example, such arrangements have no validity under Irish legislation governing inheritance. In 2006 the High Court rejected an action taken by a lesbian couple aimed at having their Canadian marriage recognised as valid under Irish law or securing the right to marry in Ireland. Dr Katherine Zappone and Dr Anne Louise Gilligan argued that the state acted unlawfully and breached their constitutional rights to equality, marriage, property and family. The High Court dismissed the case on the basis that the Irish constitution does not allow for same-sex marriage (*The Irish Times*, 14 December 2006). In Ireland and other Western countries, the range of family types is becoming increasingly diverse, including 'blended families' that result from a number of relationships involving different partners; single-parent families; and groups of unrelated people living together in 'family-like' arrangements. There is also an increasing number of people living alone.

While diversity of family types is not new (Irish history speaks of a number of types of domestic arrangement), the challenge to traditional conceptions is seen by many as further evidence of modernity. For example, the trends in relation to single parenthood, where increasingly women choose to bring up children without a permanent male partner, have been said by Irish sociologist Pat O'Connor (1998, p.122) to suggest a new 'marginalisation of men within the family'. For O'Connor this trend implies a 'radical challenge to our ideas about the family and to the cultural and social construction of heterosexuality'. Similarly, the greater acceptance of divorce and remarriage in Ireland signals a change in what can constitute a valid family arrangement. At the same time the more limited notions of the 'traditional' family continue to receive active support from many, if not the majority, in Irish society. In particular, most men, and women that are not working outside the home, tend to have more traditional views in relation to the family (Galligan, 1998b, p.118). Such views are often expressed in self-conscious opposition to perceived changes in Irish society. Defence of a particular view of 'the family' is central to conservative thinking everywhere.

Crucially, the family is implicated in relationships of power and inequality in Irish society. It is an important mechanism through which economic inequality is maintained and property rights are transmitted. It also provides a basis for access to, and success within, the education system. The family as a set of relationships is a major conduit for the transfer of property, particularly through the inheritance of farm businesses and residential property. But property rights are unevenly distributed *within* families: many forms of property are male-dominated and owned.

The experiences of women and men in Irish families may be shaped in important ways by the broader social relationships within which a family is located. Involvement in paid work, for example, may help to determine who has the 'power' within families while at the same time women *and* men tend to underestimate and devalue the importance of unpaid work both 'inside' and 'outside' the family (P. O'Hara, 1998, p.87). There has been a considerable body of research in Ireland into the decision-making processes within family units, particularly in relation to farm families. A seminal work in this area was Hannan and Katsiaouni's (1977) analysis of farm families 'in transition'. This work was overtly informed by modernisation theory and sought to examine how traditional patriarchal structures within Irish farm families were being replaced by more modern negotiated roles, as rural families increasingly converged with urban ones.

Recent research into the lives of rural women by Pat O'Hara (1998) places such decision-making more specifically within the economic and gender-based power structures within which farm women find themselves. Thus, 'the weight of culture, tradition and family ideology in rural Ireland clearly identifies the farm family as a patriarchal structure where the interests of men (fathers and sons) supersede those of women and daughters' (1998, p.114). Male power is significantly reinforced by men's legally supported domination of property ownership. In O'Hara's study fewer than a fifth of farms were jointly owned by husband and wife and this usually only happened where a woman brought land to the relationship. As has been found in Britain (Symes and Marsden, 1983), the more 'modern' or commercially oriented a farm business is the more likely it is to be structured along 'traditional' gender lines. However, in terms of house ownership on farms, there appears to be a move towards a more gender-equitable relationship, with family homes being placed in both names. According to O'Hara (1998, p.118) this reflects 'more egalitarian ideologies of marriage' and the financial resources that a woman working off-farm can bring to the family.

By 2000 half of all couples in Ireland were dual earners (Russell *et al.*, 2004), though the institutional and cultural context has not kept pace with this change as evidenced by unequal domestic power relationships, poor childcare provision and lack of support for women in the public sphere. In everyday discourses, the Irish mother continues to occupy the role of primary carer and life-giver, leading to pressures and tensions in the attempt to manage both work and domestic spheres. A government agency's campaign to promote hygienic food in a hygienic environment very deliberately played on women's insecurities about failing as 'mammys'. This was possible because, while women's lives have changed dramatically in recent years, institutional change and cultural shift has been much slower. Thus, according to Collins (2006, p.98):

Women are torn between an ideology that contends that women should be in the workforce and an ideology that contends that women should be in the home. These contradictory pressures leave women feeling they are never good enough either as workers or mothers. In the family this leads to the well-known phenomenon of 'compensating' children with consumer goods for not spending enough time with them. In the home this means that women try to compensate for their absence by ensuring that it is a safe environment for their families. This, I believe, is behind the rise of anti-bacterial products, as women try to ensure a 'germ-free' home, and behind the anxiety about the safety of food.

Demographic trends are both a reflection and a determinant of ideas about gender and family. Ireland, like many other Western countries, has seen a major change in the nature and structure of the family unit in recent times. This set of changes has been referred to as the 'second demographic transition' (see Chapter 6). Key trends include: a marked decline in marriage, birth and fertility rates; later age of marriage and first childbirth; increased ex-nuptial births; smaller completed family size and an increase in the number of people remaining single. For writers such as Galligan (1998a, p.27) such changes reflect the modernisation of Irish society, a growing level of secularisation and a more assertive attitude among women in relation to family formation. It is also possible that the wider economic transformation in Irish society is continuing to exert an effect. Fahey and Layte (2007, p.165) have argued, for example, that 'rising living standards and expanding opportunities for women seemed to have encouraged greater numbers of women to start a family and have at least one or two children, even though the same economic forces seemed to have been a deterrent to having the large numbers of children of the past'.

By 2006 births outside marriage made up nearly a third of all births in Ireland, and lone parents (including separated and divorced parents) now head one in seven of families. There is evidence (O'Connor, 1998, p.120) that the majority of lone parents have to an extent chosen their situation and, overall, enjoy routine parenting tasks and the independence of single parenthood. At the same time, lone parents form a significant proportion of those in poverty, they continue to face discrimination and face particularly high barriers when it comes to (re)entering the labour market, for example, poor transport and childcare facilities and the poverty traps created by the social welfare system (Leane and Kiely, 1997).

Family relationships represented a key issue for the women's movement that emerged in Ireland in the 1970s. In particular, many feminist activists, as in other parts of Europe, especially the Mediterranean countries, focused on family law reform. Such challenges took place in a society that had developed a highly conservative view of the family and gender, buttressed by the institutions of church and state (Galligan, 1998a, p.91): the role for women as spelled out in the

Irish Constitution of 1937 has already been mentioned. There had been minimal legal reform in Ireland in relation to the family prior to the early 1970s. Feminist pressure groups such as AIM focused on (Galligan, 1998a, p.95):

- the protection of married women's property and other interests within the family
- opposition to discrimination against married women
- changes in the legal machinery of family law
- the legal status of separation and divorce.

For Galligan, voluntary groups such as AIM brought Irish family policy 'out of the Victorian age to a respectable stage of enlightenment comparable to similar policies in most European states in the late twentieth century' (1998a, p.105). Overall, while family policy in Ireland has not seen a fundamental restructuring of the family, it has seen an incremental improvement in the human rights of women and children within marriage.

It is very important for sociologists to remember that the family is a *dynamic* concept. In Ireland we have seen within a relatively short time a considerable shift in the nature and understanding of the family unit. There is evidence that the extended family was the norm within Irish rural society. Movement to urban and suburban areas does not necessarily mean that the extended family unit has disappeared, but it may be experienced in different ways, perhaps facilitated by the telephone, Internet and the car. In looking to the future we can begin to discern some important changes, for example, a rise in numbers of single-person households; considerably smaller families; the rise of the one-child family; increasing levels of lone parenthood; more gay and lesbian couples; and more voluntarily childfree people. What will the broader social effects of these changes be? and of other shifts in our society, such as the changes in the nature of jobs and careers? and what of the possibility of an extended lifespan and more 'active ageing'?

GENDER AND WORK

The last three decades of the twentieth century saw significant changes in the relationship of Irish women and men towards the labour market (see Chapter 7). But the world of work remains a key site for the expression of gender difference and the positions that men and women hold in the labour market are a major determinant of wealth, income, power and status. Work itself is a major element of personal identity and influence over well-being and is a complex and contentious concept. Common-sense understandings, reflected in many public discourses, assume that work means 'paid work'. Such conceptions underpin, for example, the statistical measurement of work; social welfare policies and procedures; childcare provision; and employment policy. Furthermore, the notion of paid work in Ireland is further narrowed to 'full-time paid work' and there has been little recognition of part-time, casual or seasonal work. O'Connor (1998, p.191) argues that 'male work norms' have been taken as typical. But it is clear that what we think of as work has the potential to embrace a much wider range of human endeavour: all the work arrangements listed above, as well as unpaid work of various sorts — caring for others, voluntary work, domestic labour (housework) — and work carried out on a reciprocal basis (such as repairing a neighbour's car). Such is the gendered nature of work that we often associate men with paid work in the public sphere and women with unpaid work in the home; but it should be obvious that such a distinction holds little meaning, and says more about dominant ideologies in Irish society than about how people spend their time and energy.

While work is difficult to define, it is apparent that at least paid work is changing quite radically in its forms. Thus O'Hearn (1998, p.103) points to the following trends:

> Irish work has undoubtedly become more casual and less secure since 1985. In industry and services alike, more and more employees have flexible status like part-time, temporary and fixed-contract work. This is partly a result of newly created jobs that are on flexible terms. But it is also the result of large numbers of employees who have been shifted from full-time permanent status to more flexible terms.

The types of work relationships listed by O'Hearn are sometimes termed 'atypical' in relation to the traditional norm of a full-time, life-long job. But such forms of flexible, casual, part-time, contract-based and insecure work are becoming more widespread. Historically, women have been more likely to be involved in these atypical arrangements, which now account for between a fifth and a quarter of all jobs in Ireland (O'Hearn, 1998, p.105).

The contemporary nature of work in Ireland has inevitably been shaped by the patterns of economic development that have taken place since the late 1950s, as discussed in some detail in Chapter 3. The Irish economy has seen a rapid and large-scale expansion of the service industries, ranging from financial services to tourism and catering, and there has been extensive inward investment by TNCs and other firms. This economic change has influenced the development of the Irish labour market, not least in relation to gender. For example, Crowley (1997, p.81) suggests that how TNCs operate in Ireland 'maintains both Ireland's dependent status in the international economy and the increasing feminisation of that dependency'. In particular she highlights how the bulk of work for women in TNCs has been low paid and low skilled. This situation is perpetuated by no-union policies or 'sweetheart deals' with unions which do little to challenge gender inequality in the workplace. Crowley argues that as the TNCs have 'capitalised upon the already existing patriarchal order within Irish industry' (1997, p.86) they have done little or nothing to raise the status of women in Ireland. Such a position

Figure 9.1 Ireland and EU: employment rate, 1996–2006

% of population aged 15–64				
	Ireland		EU 25	
Year	Men	Women	Men	Women
1996	67.5	43.2	:	:
1997	69.1	45.9	70.2	51.1
1998	71.1	48.1	70.6	51.8
1999	73.6	51.2	71.0	52.9
2000	75.7	53.2	71.2	53.6
2001	76.2	54.0	71.3	54.3
2002	75.0	55.2	71.0	54.7
2003	74.7	55.3	70.8	55.0
2004	75.2	55.8	70.9	55.7
2005	76.2	58.0	71.3	56.3
2006	77.3	58.8	:	:

Source: Central Statistics Office, Women and Men in Ireland 2006, Dublin CSO

assumes, of course, that employment in the paid workforce in itself brings no benefit to women — a highly debatable position. Furthermore, things may be changing: while the employment of young women in unskilled jobs was certainly the strategy for TNCs that came to Ireland during the 1970s and 1980s, the nature of TNC operations in Ireland since the 1990s may have led them to focus more on skilled labour and on 'pink-collar' information-based jobs, such as in call centres.

The factors that shape the involvement of men and women in the labour market reflect both 'supply side' and 'demand' factors (Smyth, 1997, p.63). Changes in the nature of the family; in social attitudes; in educational participation; and in social infrastructure have helped to make more labour of particular types available. At the same time, changes in the economy and in the productive sector have led to demands for new kinds of worker and different skills and attributes.

In 1926, 60 per cent of women who were gainfully employed worked either in agriculture or in domestic service (Beale, 1986, p.140). Just one in ten worked in industry. Women who had paid jobs were predominantly young and single, though there was a significant proportion of women within the urban workforce who were never married. From 1932 to 1973 married women were formally and legally excluded from the public service through the so-called 'marriage bar'. From the 1930s to 1961, as emigration took its toll, the paid female workforce in Ireland actually diminished. Many women left the country to take up service-sector and industrial jobs in Britain and elsewhere.

The period 1951 to 1991 saw a seven-fold increase in the number of married women in the paid workforce. For O'Connor (1998, p.188) this is 'one of the most dramatic changes to have taken place in Irish society over the past twenty-five years'. The majority of mothers now work outside the home (CSO, 2006b). So marked has been the shift of women into the labour market that sociologists in Ireland and elsewhere now talk about the 'feminisation' of the workforce; 90 per cent of the increase in employment in the EU since 1971 has been in women's employment (O'Connor, 1998, p.214), particularly in the burgeoning service sector.

Factors that increase the 'supply' of women's labour and which have been seen by many to underpin their increased participation in the workforce include better education, declining fertility rates, and the capacity to earn higher wages. The 'opportunity costs' of staying at home to mind children or do housework (in other words, the income foregone) have greatly increased, especially as education levels have risen (Smyth, 1997, pp.65–6). Other factors that have increased the supply of female labour have been the removal of many of the social and legal barriers to women's employment, for example, the elimination of the public-sector marriage bar. Married women's work has also become more visible. Often it was hidden in the overall labour of a small family business or farm, but now it is more likely to be in the paid workforce as an employee. The result of such changes, as we have seen, has been a significant increase in the number of married women in the Irish labour market. The dramatic increase in female participation in the labour force means that the female employment rate stands at 59 per cent, which is close to the EU target of 60 per cent by 2010 (CSO, 2006b and figure 9.1). Given the abject failure of the Irish state and society to support women's participation in the labour market, such as minimal childcare provision, very low participation by men in household labour and discriminatory tax policies, this increase is quite remarkable.

It is not enough to focus on the factors that have increased the 'supply' of female workers; we must also look at factors that have shaped the demand both for women's and men's labour. These factors are inextricably bound up with the change in the Irish economy since the late 1950s. The expansion of manufacturing and service industries within the Irish economy as part of broader global trends has contributed to the expansion in women's employment opportunities. Many of the jobs in the new electronic, light engineering, pharmaceutical and manufacturing industries attracted to the country were taken up by women. The huge growth in the service industries, in particular, retail, tourism, financial services and community and personal services, has also been a stimulus to the expansion of female employment. Conversely, the manufacturing and agricultural industries that traditionally employed mainly men have declined. These facts challenge the way that the Marxist 'reserve army of labour' thesis has been applied to women. Marx argued that there are groups of workers who have a marginal attachment to the labour force and who can be drawn in or driven out of employment as the economy expands or contracts. Thus, it has been suggested that women (especially married women) are brought into the labour force as necessary and can be easily dispensed with in times of restructuring or recession. However, this theory was not borne out in the Irish recession of the 1980s, when female employment continued to increase (Smyth, 1997, p.71).

Of key importance in understanding issues related to gender and work is the concept of *labour-market segmentation*. Sociologists argue that there is not a single labour market; rather, the demand for labour is segmented in a variety of ways. Most simplistically, there is a primary or 'core' labour market of relatively highly paid, secure, skilled jobs that offer promotional opportunities and other benefits (for example, teaching); and a secondary or 'peripheral' labour market that, conversely, offers low security, demands flexibility, has low pay and benefits and little or no career structure (for example, restaurant work). There is also segregation *within* industries. There is much debate about the extent to which employers and employees (particularly through unions) can shape these differentiated labour markets.

There has been no systematic study of labour-market segmentation in Ireland and it is therefore difficult to gauge how men's and women's workforce experiences are determined by this process. There is some evidence that women are more likely to work in peripheral industries, such as textiles and the clothing sector, while men are more likely to be found in core industries such as printing and brewing (Smyth, 1997, p.73). But the location of specific industries within the 'core' or 'periphery' in this way is highly problematic. It is perhaps more useful to examine *occupational segregation*: the extent to which men and women are concentrated within particular sorts of occupation and whether the labour market is effectively divided up into 'men's jobs' and 'women's jobs' (see Figure 9.2).

Occupational segregation in Ireland has been very marked. In 1992, 77 per cent of working women were to be found in the services sector (EU average 71 per cent). They were further concentrated in four occupational groups:

- commerce and finance
- professional and technical
- services
- clerical.

A number of occupations are highly feminised: including childcare, primary education, health care, clerical work and personal and domestic services. Women

Figure 9.2 Occupations with highest segregation

Male dominated occupations	Females as a percentage of total	Female dominated occupations	Males as a percentage of total
Plasterers	0.2	Secretaries	1.3
Carpenters	0.2	Receptionists	2.9
Bricklayers	0.3	Housekeepers	4.0
Roofers	0.4	Educational assistants	4.4
Rail construction workers	0.4	Child minders	4.9
Mechanical plant drivers	0.5	Nurses	8.3
Builders	0.6	Radiographers	8.8
Vehicle body repairers	0.6	Care assistants	8.9
Motor mechanics	0.7	Sewing machinists	9.3
Sheet metal workers	0.8	Hairdressers and Barbers	11.1

Source: CSO 2002 Principal Socio-Economic Results

remain concentrated in low-pay sectors of the economy and are frequently found in low-paid, part-time, insecure and 'low-skilled' occupations.

The significant expansion of 'modern' industry in the economy may not have altered the situation. In a study of the electronics industry in the south-west of the country, Barry and Brunt (2002) concluded that little had changed in relation to gender-based job segregation:

> Occupational segregation on the basis of gender remains a key characteristic associated with the employment structure of the multinational electronics industry in Ireland. Operatives, who comprise the majority of those employed within the industry, are predominantly women, while professional, scientific and managerial positions are held predominantly by men. In general the majority of female workers are young, single and childless. . . . A high proportion has not received formal training at third level, to develop skills specifically tailored for the electronics industry. This provides for the emergence of a pool of cheap female labour for the region . . . classified as semi-skilled, [who] remain in the lowest paid categories and have little chance of engaging in upward mobility within the occupational hierarchy of the firm (2002, p.37).

While equal pay has been an Irish industrial issue since it was first debated by the Irish Trade Union Congress in 1917 (Beale, 1986, p.145), it has yet to become a reality. According to McGinnity et al. (2007), some narrowing of gender differentials in pay rates has occurred between 1987 and 2000. More recently, the CSO has estimated that female hourly rates of pay now stand at 85 per cent of males (CSO, 2006b). Many women are trapped in low-pay industries like catering or cleaning or are concentrated at the bottom of hierarchies in higher paying industries like law. At the same time, women are over-represented in the professional/technical area, partly reflecting their major role in the health-care and education industries. While the extent of occupational segregation has diminished somewhat over the past three decades, the process is complex. Some areas have become more homogenous (for example, primary teaching, banking) whereas others have become more diverse (for example, law, accountancy). Why have these patterns persisted? It is certainly the case that stereotypes about certain kinds of occupation remain: 'male' occupations are seen as dirty, physical, to do with power and strength (Carey, 1997) while women's occupations express aspects of femininity such as 'caring', dexterity and communication skills. These clearly relate to broader gender stereotypes.

It is still the case that very few women are found in senior management. In the boardrooms of the nation's private and state companies, men dominate, as they do in the trade union movement, even in unions (such as nursing and the retail trade) in sectors that mainly employ women. While education and health employ the highest proportion of women, with close to an 80 per cent share of the total at work in these sectors, few are at senior level positions. For example, women account for 84 per cent of primary school teachers but only 51 per cent of primary school managers (CSO, 2006b). The glass ceiling is still very much part of the Irish business and administrative worlds.

The links between paid and unpaid work are important: both in how unpaid work obligations (like looking after children or elderly relatives) can impact on availability for paid work; and how the experience of paid work is shaped by parallel non-paid work obligations (from delivering children to school to minding children when they are ill). Leonard (1997, p.120) says that 'because of modern industrial society's preoccupation with formal paid labour as the purest form of economic activity, the economic value of forms of labour which exist outside this limited definition tend to be underrated.' Leonard argues that unpaid 'caring' work is differentially valued along gender lines. Thus, cooking a meal for an older relative (typically done by a woman) is virtually 'invisible' and is rarely seen as work whereas servicing a car for the same relative (typically done by a man) is far more easily identified as such. Informal work is carried out within a gendered network of expectations and obligations. Therefore, 'women's motivations for engaging in informal helping networks [are] closely bound to culturally defined rules regarding gender specific obligations both within and outside the household' (Leonard, 1997, p.122). Such work remains undervalued by men and by society.

In some similar ways, other areas of women's work are structured by the relationships with unpaid work. Daly's study of women cleaners (cited in

O'Connor, 1998, p.204) showed that respondents' attitudes to work were based on their identities as housewives rather than employees. O'Connor concluded that this identification was of disadvantage to the women concerned: 'they saw themselves basically as housewives, and saw their skills as personal, indeed often female characteristics. They effectively colluded with the devaluation of their work' (1998, p.205).

GENDER AND THE PUBLIC SPHERE

When we talk about women's power we are still talking about potential rather than reality. (Walter, 1998, p.3)

As we said earlier, conflicts over gender, sexuality and the family have been a significant part of the Irish political and public discursive landscape for at least the last thirty years. For many people the shift towards modernity in Ireland is symbolised not only by the development of the economy and the physical infrastructure, but also by how people think, talk and act in relation to moral issues. Often, in Ireland, this means issues related to gender. Thus, as Jenny Beale argued (1986, p.184): 'as Irish society has industrialised and urbanised, and as traditional values and ways have been challenged and questioned, every aspect of women's lives has been subject to scrutiny and change.' For Beale the image was one of progress, of overcoming the barriers to women's full equality in Irish society. Nearly two decades later, the picture is perhaps more complex. While many of the challenges faced by the women's movement have been addressed, the more intractable issues related to gender remain. Galligan, in an analysis of women's political mobilisation in Ireland, points to an apparent contradiction: 'there is little doubt that the role of women in Ireland today is very different to the social role and function assigned to their mothers, even if attitudes towards that new role remain staunchly traditional' (1998b, p.106).

Furthermore, in Ireland as elsewhere, the direction of change is being questioned. Is 'having it all' in a consumer heaven the aim of Irish people — particularly women — or does a more equal opportunity to work and to consume only serve to paper over the deeper layers of inequality within Irish society, such as occupational segregation, family violence and the unequal burden of domestic labour and childcare? Discussion of gender and family issues in the public sphere continues to reflect the long-term issues of gender inequality, and the unresolved uncertainties of moving rapidly towards a post-modern society. It is often around gender- and family-related issues that the tensions and connections between the personal and the political are made most apparent, whether in relation to, for example, state support for home births; responses to male youth suicide; or the policing of domestic violence.

It would be superfluous here to list the many public debates — usually heated, often sensationalised — that have taken place over such issues as child sexual abuse. They are very well known to all people in Ireland through saturation media coverage and continual public and private debate. The very frequency and ubiquity of such debates, scandals and revelations are evidence to many people of the speed and depth of the processes of modernisation within Irish society. Peillon (1998, p.117) suggests that 'through these crises Ireland is being propelled, at an incredible pace, into what Anthony Giddens has called *high modernity.*' Irish people are being forced, through the sheer speed and depth of change, to adopt a thoroughly modern stance of reflexivity, to be increasingly self-conscious about the sort of changing society they inhabit. It is thus hardly surprising that, as suggested by Foucault, our society has become highly involved in perpetual talk of gender, sexuality and morality.

From the 1930s to the 1960s women in Ireland suffered from legal discrimination in a broad range of areas, including employment, property rights, family law, inheritance, social welfare, taxation and access to, and protection of, the law (Galligan, 1998a, p.30). The legal system explicitly and implicitly favoured men. As a consequence the key issues for the Irish women's movement (and for supportive males) have been equal pay; the reform of family law; issues in relation to contraception and divorce; male violence; and childcare — items on the agenda of most Western feminist movements.

The early second-wave feminist movement in Ireland was not particularly radical in its challenge to prevailing social and political values compared to the women's movement of many other countries of the West. But given the conservative nature of Irish society, the limited liberal agenda of the majority of Irish feminists was seen by both public and politicians to be a radical challenge to established tenets of public policy. The strategies and outcomes of the Irish women's movement had less in common with the more advanced movements of northern Europe and Britain and much similarity with those of countries such as Greece and Italy (economies with a strong agricultural sector and powerful institutionalised churches) and the United States (with a comparatively small public sector) (Galligan, 1998a, p.54). As a result, according to Galligan (1998a, p.29), 'women's public participation [was] clearly predicated on traditional social attitudes reinforced by the ideology, institutions and structures of an authoritarian Roman Catholic Church and a conservative, nationalist State.'

Women are under-represented in decision-making structures at both national and regional levels. Only 14 per cent of TDs in Dáil Éireann are women, while they account for just 34 per cent of members of state boards and under 20 per cent of members of regional and local authorities (CSO, 2006b). The reasons for women's comparative lack of success in the political sphere (a feature by no means unique to Irish society) are complex and not easily explained or remedied. They may include direct political party discrimination against female candidates; timing of political meetings that pay little attention to women's domestic obligations; male networks of political power and influence; women's lack of power in other fields that 'produce' politicians such as business, law and the unions; and male-dominated political agendas that may be of little interest to women.

While women's success in Irish party politics may be limited (though still highly significant) they may have a more enduring level within local, grass-roots and community-based politics, the emergence of which has been an important part of the Irish political scene over the last decade. While Galligan suggests that 'the nature, quantity and outcomes of women's public activities at grass-roots level have yet to be analysed in any form' (1998a, p.58), she points out that the experience in Ireland parallels that of other European countries. Such involvement tends to be 'specific and issue-driven', for example, in the areas of adult education and drugs issues. 'It is seen as an end in itself, not necessarily the start of a broader level of political involvement, as the dearth of women in local politics does not reflect the extent of women's participation in local political activities' (Galligan, 1998a, p.59). This also suggests that the highly adversarial and ritualised nature of local politics may have little attraction for publicly minded women.

While local government yet fails to be attractive, across the EU women are actively becoming involved in locally oriented bodies such as the area-based partnerships. But even here they may find that they are marginalised by men, especially when it comes to formally powerful roles within such organisations. Geddes (1998, p.106), in a study of such partnership bodies across the EU, reports that 'women play active and prominent roles in many local partnerships, but are much more likely to be community representatives and project leaders than partner representatives on partnership boards or management committees where policy decisions are made . . . in most local partnerships formal and active equal opportunity policies are conspicuous by their absence.' He suggests that even when a partnership is focused on issues related to women, women are not necessarily dominant in the decision-making process. In Ireland there has been an attempt to address the gender inequality in partnership organisations. Local partnerships have been directed by the government to have at least 40 per cent female representation on management boards. This requirement may be difficult to meet due to a lack of women in senior positions in partner organisations (health boards, farmer organisations and so on) but in the Tallaght Partnership, for example, 41 per cent of board members are women, an outcome aided by the presence of strong, local women's networks (Geddes, 1998, p.106).

Despite the barriers facing women within both the formal and informal political processes, it is apparent that the specific raising of gender issues and input by women have had significant effects on the form and the content of political debate and policy-making. Thus, suggests Galligan (1998a, p.21), the 'mainstreaming of feminist priorities has made a significant contribution to the increased output of public policies with a women-centred focus in modern times.' If nowhere else, this is reflected in the support that women's groups have received from the state. For example, by 1993, 600 groups were receiving financial support from the Department of Social Welfare alone (Galligan, 1998a, p.60). At the same time, the women's movement is experienced and expressed very differently within groups that are experiencing racism, poverty and social exclusion. Movements around gender, despite the sometimes universalising nature of their object, can be as exclusive and divisive as any social or political movement. Lentin, among others, has argued (1998, pp.6–7) that:

> Most studies addressing citizenship and Irish women . . . presume a homogeneity of 'Irish women' and of feminist struggle, and fail to address the impact of both racist discourses and the multi-tiered access to citizenship on women of ethnic minorities.

In other words, mobilisation around the categories of gender can occlude other important divisions and differences in Irish society.]

SEXUALITY

In the words of Oliver J. Flanagan TD: there was 'no sex in Ireland before television' (Tobin, 1996, p.68). Similarly, sexuality is a topic that has been virtually ignored within Irish sociology (Inglis, 1998d). This neglect is unfortunate because, since at least the early 1960s, debates over a range of issues linked to human sexuality have formed a key element of Irish society and of gender relationships. There is a commonly held perception that attitudes towards sexuality have seen a marked change in Ireland in recent years and, as Beale (1986, p.87) argues: 'it is over issues to do with sexuality that the conflict between traditional and progressive forces in Irish society can be seen most clearly.' As with constructions of gender more generally, our understandings, experiences and attitudes about sexuality are socially shaped — by the media, the education system, religious institutions, the family and social interaction with others.

'Sexuality' is not an unproblematic term. Like 'gender' it is a social construction. We find not only one sexuality but multifarious sexualities, discussion of which could fill a whole chapter of this book and more. In many ways sexuality permeates every aspect of our lives, though often in a subconscious or unremarked manner. It is built into how we experience aspects of life such as education, work, leisure and the media. Inasmuch as we can perceive it as a unified field of practices, attitudes and institutions, it is, as British social historian (or historical sociologist) Jeffrey Weeks points out, 'an *historical* unity which has been shaped by a multiplicity of forces, and which has undergone complex historical transformations' (1989, p.ix). In other words 'sexuality' is a diverse field of experience and behaviour that is brought together at certain times through a common body of language or discourse. There are many such discourses that help to mould our understandings of sexuality. Among the most powerful are those generated from within the family, the education system, medicine, popular culture and the churches. In Ireland the legal and political systems have also been very important as debates about various aspects of sexuality have irrupted into the public sphere.

One of the few Irish sociologists to have looked in any detail at the issue of sexuality is Tom Inglis of UCD. He has discussed the nature of Irish gender and sexual relationships within the context of the sociology of the Catholic Church in Ireland (see Chapter 14) and in relation to the development of (and reaction to) sex education programmes (see, in particular, Inglis, 1998b). A key aim of Inglis's research is to 'break the silence' in relation to Irish sexuality and to question our assumptions. He is especially concerned (1998b, p.3) about the ignorance of many Irish people on the topic and suggests that the failure of Irish people to confront the issue of sex leaves them lacking in confidence and competence.

Inglis's theoretical approach to the analysis of sexuality is founded in the work of French writers Michel Foucault and Pierre Bourdieu. The former theorist has been particularly influential in the development of analyses of the relationship between sexuality and modernity. Sexuality, for Foucault, is not a 'natural' or timeless universal expression of human desire. Rather, it is actively created through *discourses* derived from professional knowledge, social institutions and everyday understandings. Such discourses shape how we think and talk about sex and this, according to Foucault, is something that people in modern societies do all the time. He argues in the first volume of *The history of sexuality* (1980, p.35) that 'what is peculiar to modern societies . . . is not that they consigned sex to a shadow existence, but that they dedicated themselves to speaking about it *ad infinitum*, while exploiting it as the secret.' Knowledge about sex, as about other things, is for Foucault a *site* of struggle, power and control. It is indeed the case that in Ireland the link between sexuality and the desire to control others has been very strong, whether expressed in the realm of family relationships, in the school or in the public sphere.

Contrary to Oliver J. Flanagan's belief, talk about sex did not emerge in Ireland only in the time of modern communications technology. Foucault points out to us that sexuality in the past was not so much hidden or repressed, but talked about in a different sort of way. As Inglis suggests (1998e, p.102) in 'traditional' Ireland 'sex was real and demanding and it was rigorously inculcated in every church, school, hospital and home in the country.' This was a discourse that linked sex to ideas of sin, control, danger and regulation. As constituted by the churches (especially, but not only, the Catholic Church) and the state, sex was a powerful force that needed to be curtailed, particularly within the institution of marriage.

In a fascinating discussion, Inglis has analysed the historical role and influence of the 'Irish mother', in particular how this has helped to shape attitudes to sexuality in

Ireland. The basis of this process was laid in the nineteenth century with the restructuring of the rural economy towards pastoral farming (see Chapter 3). As women lost their productive role — for example, as weavers and spinners — they were increasingly confined to a powerless domestic position. A new basis of power was built through an 'alliance' between Irish rural mothers and the modernising Catholic Church, which was worked out as follows (Inglis, 1998e, pp.198–9):

> The domination and control of women by the Church, and the necessity for women to ally themselves with that dominating power if they themselves were to have any power, led to their high level of marital fertility which, in turn, created the need for postponed marriage, permanent celibacy and emigration among their children. These practices were encouraged by the mother in the home through a devotion to the Church, a rigorous sexual morality, and a physical and emotional distance from her children. It is this scenario, re-enacted over the generations, that is the essence of the dialectical relationship of power between Church and family in modern Ireland.

The implications of this 'alliance' for the shaping of sexuality in Ireland were manifold. Inglis suggests that priests gained control of the sexual life of mothers by their portrayal of women as 'weak, fragile beings who must be protected (by the priest) from the sexual viper that lurked within them'. The church imposed a strict discipline of sexual morality. Women were encouraged to feel ashamed of their bodies. The discourse of the church penetrated their everyday lives as the Catholic confessional became a site for the interrogation of women about their sexual feelings, desires and activities. Inglis suggests (1998e, p.188) that 'sex became the most abhorrent sin'. Indeed, it came to dominate the notion of sin itself. On a broader plane, Inglis sees mothers as having an essential role in the 'civilizing process' (as defined by German sociologist Norbert Elias). The modernisation of Irish society was reflected in the extension of disciplines of cleanliness, control and obedience into the Irish family and the key instruments of this process were the church, the school and the mother. The home, along with the school, became a site for supervision and surveillance by the church. The mores of the church and the practices of priests provided a powerful model for child rearing, as mothers imitated the social and moral perspective of the religious. 'Through an imitation of their celibate lifestyle, their body discipline and morality [mothers] inculcated a sexual and emotional repression which was crucial to the attainment of postponed marriages, permanent celibacy and emigration' (1998e, p.193).

In modern Ireland we now talk about sex in very different ways, with a complex range of public and private discourses that embrace 'news reports, feature articles, documentaries, panel discussions and talk radio' (Inglis, 1998b, p.148). The nexus of sex and religion has been at least partly broken and 'desire and fantasy [have been] liberated from the cells of sin' (Inglis, 1998e, p.103). The church itself has also learnt how to talk about sex in the new language of 'relationships', if not yet of pleasure. There is now a multiplicity of competing discourses that relate to issues of modernity, the public sphere and sexuality. For Inglis (1998b, p.150) modern Ireland is now witnessing a conflict between two main opposing belief systems. One set of beliefs is based on traditional Catholicism and links contemporary manifestations of sexuality to materialism, consumerism and liberalism. Such a view sees modern expressions of sexuality as being intricately linked to the process of producing, buying and exchanging commodities. The other discourse of sexuality reflects 'a modern, or indeed post-modern, secular society based on liberal individualism'. It claims to be open about sexuality and to be non-judgmental about people's private and intimate behaviour or about depictions of sexuality in the media. The existence of these two powerful and competing discourses can, as Inglis (1998b, p.150) says, give rise to a particular contradictoriness in Irish experience. He remarks:

> It may well be that a characteristic of our open, democratic, pluralist society is that children are expected to be able to reconcile these contradictory images and, on a Sunday morning, move from watching Madonna on MTV to praying in church to images of Our Lady.

Overall, Inglis argues that Irish attitudes to sexuality have changed for the better, with an increased self-confidence (1998b, p.146):

> There is no longer the same shyness, embarrassment, guilt and shame about being sexual. There is not the same sense of fear that used to be a characteristic of Catholic Ireland. Sin and damnation seem to be a thing of the past. Being sexually active is the norm.

As Inglis has remarked (1998e), the context in which we understand Irish sexuality has changed markedly and this is bringing about an attendant change in attitudes. Two reports published by the Crisis Pregnancy Agency in 2004 illustrate the changing nature of sexual attitudes and, at the same time, point to the continuity of more old-fashioned ideologies about 'good girls' and 'bad girls'.

A report on sexual attitudes by Rundle et al. (2004) focuses on a national sample of 3,000 men and women aged 18–45. The vast majority were sexually active and 80 per cent regularly used a method of contraception. Non-use of contraception was generally associated with older age, lower educational level, lower social class and casual relationship status. Forty per cent of men and 26 per cent of women admitted that drinking alcohol had contributed to having sex without contraception. Nearly one quarter of participants (23 per cent) agreed that if a woman carries condoms while not in a relationship it gives the message that she is looking for sex or is 'easy'. This theme is visited also in a report for the agency carried out by Murphy-Lawless *et al.* (2004) which utilised a qualitative approach to explore the attitudes of young women to sexuality and fertility issues. Generally, the young women interviewed feel there is greater openness in Irish society, that women's roles have evolved, and that women have more life choices now. But the researchers still found a very strong discourse about women having sex outside of relationships being labelled in a certain way:

> I think, like, well for young people say around my age, I think the attitudes are still very backward like. Especially when it comes to men our age like, they still brand women 'slags' like, for sleeping around, and men 'studs', that's still very much alive (Nurse, 26, small city).

> And I think women still feel, well in my experience anyway . . . women still feel carrying condoms at times will make them be perceived as kind of easy, or expecting to have sex or something (Community worker, 29, small town).

Furthermore, the greater openness and loosening of gender roles also brings greater confusion, as Inglis has argued, and as this respondent illustrates:

> I think there is more openness, you are able to discuss the very fact you are a sexual being, and things like the ability to enjoy sex. But there's also a sort of a level of insecurity and discomfort about that . . . there are more 'shoulds'. You should enjoy sex. You should want to have it a lot, or more than you did. There's also the kind of *Cosmopolitan* culture that I think is going around, where young girls are under pressure to be a certain type of woman (Teacher, 30, Dublin).

The Crisis Pregnancy Agency has gone some way towards producing comprehensive accounts of sexual behaviour in Ireland, a topic that was long a neglected one.

Inglis does point to a major issue when discussing sexuality, one that applies to any attempt at discovering sociological knowledge: he reminds us that most individuals are skilled social actors and know how to talk about sexuality (or any other topic) in terms of what is deemed appropriate in any social situation. Thus, 'how young people talk about sexuality varies according to whether they are a couple being intimate, in a group, in a classroom or with their parents'. Thus, in a sense, people's sexual identities are *plastic*. They are, to an extent, shaped by social situations and by competing definitions. Similarly, a man who has sex with another man may not identify himself as 'gay', but he may be labelled so by powerful discourses of the law, medicine or popular culture.

While Inglis reflects a liberal optimism about sexuality, some Irish feminists have stressed the complexities and contradictions inherent in its practices, especially where it concerns women. O'Connor (1998, p.177), for example, indicates the distinguishing features of sexuality as experienced by young Irish women: an emphasis on active heterosexuality; continuing problems over the availability of contraception; the tangled concept of 'love'; the experience of sexual harassment; the stigmatisation of abortion; powerful and contradictory messages around body imagery; an emphasis on sex as a consumer product; and the pressures against 'saying no'. She points out (1998, p.180) that 'there is considerable pressure on young women to be sexually active but little acceptance of the need to locate the conception in the wider context of social responsibility.' For women 'love' can be a source of both power and vulnerability — a veil that hides the power within a relationship or a means of achieving a measure of equality. Unfortunately, the slowly developing sociology of masculinity in Ireland has yet to provide a similar critical analysis of the challenges that modern patterns and discourses of sexuality provide for Irish men.

Masculinities

Victor Seidler (1988) has explored the concept of masculinity and its development within the Western Enlightenment tradition. The Enlightenment bequeathed a vision of masculinity that equates reason with authority and that resulted in the devaluing of emotion. Authority ultimately was based around the concept of the father. During the Industrial Revolution, this image was elaborated on to include the good provider role. Fathers were to inhabit the role of aloof and distant *pater familias*, the disciplinarian who left matters concerning family to his dutiful wife. Medicine and psychology colluded in legitimating and inculcating this image of appropriate masculinity, in the process labelling non-conformist masculine behaviour — such as homosexuality — as deviant. Indeed, how society responds to and shapes homosexuality is of importance not only for gays and lesbians, it is crucial to the formation of sexualities more generally. Homophobia, or fear of homosexuality, is a potent force in the development of dominant modes of masculinity and femininity. McKeown *et al.* (1999: 23) show how *hegemonic masculinity* (a term coined by the Australian sociologist Connell) is created and at least partly sustained through homophobia:

> At a public level the hegemonic definition of masculinity still values power which is exercised — mostly by men — in such a way that alternative ways of being and viewing men are closed off. Within this exemplary form of masculinity, qualities and practices of care and nurture are subordinated and associated not merely with femininity but, at worst, with gayness — a form of masculinity which is constructed as the worst thing a man can be.

Indeed, gayness is seen as a negation of manhood and this is translated into anything that can be seized upon as evidence of feminine behaviour: involvement in domestic work, particular popular cultural choices or ways of walking, talking or dressing. Similarly, homophobic responses to lesbianism help to shape dominant notions of femininity. Moane (1997, p.88) argues that:

> [Homophobia] is damaging to all women because [it] involves extreme negative images and views of women, and induces fear in heterosexual women about their own feelings of affection for other women. The label 'lesbian' has been used as a weapon to silence and intimidate women who speak out assertively or defiantly, and as a label to express an anti-feminist position.

It is not surprising then that Inglis (1998b, p.98) links Irish gays and lesbians to a 'radical attitude to sexuality': one that challenges existing conceptions of gender, family and sexuality. The emergence of gay and lesbian sexualities into Irish public life has served to disrupt patterns of sexuality and gender relationships that have developed since the famine period. Similarly, lesbian and gay activism has challenged dominant discourses of national and cultural identity.

In Ireland, as elsewhere, gays and lesbians have been very much involved in the processes of building a community. While we discuss some of the problematic issues around the concept of 'community' elsewhere (see Chapter 5), it is notable that, particularly since the foundation of the Irish Gay Rights Movement in 1974 and the formation of separate lesbian organisations in 1978, Irish gays and lesbians have sought to develop a way to express and celebrate their sexuality — and to defend their rights — that is specifically Irish while also having a global context.

It is only very recently, as we pointed out earlier in this chapter, that masculinity has moved centre stage in gender studies. This is partly as a result of the women's movement and the reconceptualisation of fatherhood that has followed in the wake of attempts to develop more egalitarian models of family formation and child-rearing. Instead of focusing on binary oppositions between men and women, the trend now is towards exploring masculinities and femininities. The literature on masculinity in Ireland is limited but growing. In her introduction to the special issue of the *Irish Journal of Sociology* on masculinities, Cleary (2005, p.1) quotes aptly from Harry Ferguson: 'while men were and are everywhere in Irish society, little attention was given to them as men, as gendered subjects.'

A 2001 NESF report on lone parents contained a chapter detailing the experiences of non-resident fathers, who hitherto tended to be written out of analyses of lone-parent families. A small study of non-resident fathers, conducted as part of the preparation of that report, identified a number of key issues affecting the development and maintenance of a fathering role after a relationship has ended. In particular, the research identified the contingent nature of fatherhood for young, marginalised men in Dublin. These fathers' experiences were compared to those of fathers who occupied estranged, committed and activist father roles. Key factors that militate against fathers maintaining an active role in their children's lives are identified. While the experiences of fatherhood vary across different categories of fathers, the majority of them aspire towards and value their fathering role, but their capacity to adopt a positive fathering role is affected by a range of institutional, economic and social barriers (Corcoran, 2005).

Weeks (2005, p.64) argues that the new narratives of masculinity that are emerging 'speak of vulnerabilities as much as of power. They speak of fear and anxiety as much as of strength'. One Irish study (Cleary, 2005) that exemplifies this transition was carried out with a group of men who had engaged in suicidal behaviour. It revealed how socialisation of young men into traditional masculine roles inhibits their capacity to share their feelings with others, often with devastating consequences. According to Cleary (2005) non-disclosure of distress emerged as a key issue in examining pathways to suicidal action. Disclosure of difficulties was viewed as un-masculine, as implying weakness, and this was associated with feminine or homosexual-type behaviour. According to Cleary 'constant performative work . . . was required to project an image of strength and to conceal growing levels of distress. When extreme, this challenged their sense of coherent self-identity' (2005, p.155). For these men, the pressure to conform to traditional modes of masculinity was so overwhelming that they could not be true to themselves.

Others studies of masculinity have focused on its changing role within popular culture. The image of the 'child-centred father' has become a mainstay of contemporary advertising and nowadays men are almost as likely as women to be sexually commodified in the selling of consumer goods. Indeed, as women have become more dominant in the economy, both as the producers and consumers of goods and services, men have been portrayed more often as goofy, female-dominated losers. The markets for men's clothing, personal products and even plastic surgery have exploded and men are coming under increasing pressure to conform to gender stereotypes. The playbills at rugby internationals regularly carry advertisements for facial creams alongside the more traditional 'male' products. 'Metrosexuals' such as David Beckham — who combine both feminine and masculine qualities – take up acres of newspapers and magazine space. Popular culture, in other words, is representing to us the fluidity and indeterminateness of notions of masculinity and femininity.

Sociology of childhood

Until relatively recently, children tended to be neither seen nor heard within mainstream sociology. Traditional views of the socialisation process reinforced the notion that children, in the context of their families and personal communities, play a passive role. Newer literature within the field of sociology of childhood has challenged traditional passive conceptualisations of the child and argued for an interpretive reproduction approach. Such an approach holds that 'children are active, creative social agents who produce their own unique children's cultures while simultaneously contributing to the production of adult societies' (Corsaro, 2005, p. 3). Corsaro argues that childhood, as an embedded part of the social structure, is interrelated with other categories like social class, gender and age groups (2005, p. 3). A growing concern of Irish sociologists is how 'good' an experience childhood is in contemporary Ireland. Research suggests that children and families who are rich in social capital and sociability receive considerable social support and access to valued resources. The mechanism through which economic capital underpins and interacts with social capital gives rise to social inequalities in society.

Several studies in recent years, particularly those emanating from the Children's Research Centre at TCD, have raised questions about what kinds of resources are present in the family and in the community that will help bring about successful outcomes for the child. Likewise, the sociological literature on childhood is concerned to elucidate the benefits that a child brings to the family and community of which they form a part. It is increasingly acknowledged that sociologists must move beyond the strictures of a narrow 'family structure effect' in trying to understand the everyday, lived experience of Irish children, since wider community, neighbourhood and structural effects will have an important bearing on their quality of life. This is particularly important for children in special situations — children with special needs, children with different ethno-racial identities, poor children — because they have to manage 'their difference' from others in their schools and communities on an ongoing basis.

Morrow (1999) has pointed out that much of the research focusing on issues such as family life and well-being has taken a top-down view of the effect of parents on children and the ability of parents to invest in their children's well-being and future. A more active conceptualisation of children, she argues, 'would explore how children themselves actively generate, draw on, or negotiate their own social capital, or indeed make links for their parents, or even provide active support for parents' (1999, p.751). Thus the emphasis is now on the transactional nature of the relationship between children, family, neighbourhood, community, media and culture because we allow for the fact that each has the capacity to influence and to be influenced by the other. As Kelley et al. (1997, p.305) argue, we should view children not simply as objects of adult socialisation, but rather as young people who are 'competent reporters of experience'. Crucially, the longitudinal study of Irish children currently being undertaken under the auspices of the National Children's Office is premised on the principle of children as active agents with the capacity to define their own situations.

Leonard (2006) has carried out research into children's experience of growing up in North Belfast, in an interface area where Catholics and Protestants live close together, but demarcate their own territories through a variety of symbolic means. One of the most striking features of the research was the tendency for the children to describe their daily lives in terms of growing up Protestant or Catholic. This badge of identity was employed more frequently than either gender or class. Leonard points out that the surrounding environment in which the children live their daily lives is highly segregated on the basis of religious identity. The majority of children did not have any friends from the other religious community and a substantial number had never interacted socially with anyone outside of their own religious grouping, demonstrating the closed nature of their immediate social world. The research revealed the ongoing presence of sectarianism in the daily lives of children in the interface area. Leonard cites research carried out by Paul Connolly that found that, from as young as three years of age, children are able to identify and negatively evaluate the other religious group and this process becomes more prevalent once children enter the segregated school system that characterises Northern Irish society. The children's narratives revealed a propensity to denigrate members of the other community. They tended to define themselves socially and symbolically (through the use of jewellery, hairstyles, clothing and body piercing) in terms of members of 'in-groups' and 'out-groups'.

But children also recounted some contexts in which they were able to produce more diverse identities. Some children spoke of interacting with the other religious community while on holidays outside of Northern Ireland, or even at a skateboarding venue in the city centre of Belfast. Leonard thus concludes that even in highly constrained circumstances, children possess the ability to construct a range of identities, identities that are negotiated and renegotiated across different spheres of interaction. Nevertheless, while the children in the research demonstrated the capacity to exhibit multiple identities, sectarianism still played a key and central role in the formation of their local identities.

Research that takes children's lived experience as the point of departure has the capacity to broaden our understanding not only of the social world of children, but of the important sociological forces that shape that world. In turn, such research allows us to see children as agents in their own right, whose actions and reactions help to shape the social context of childhood.

10
The body, health and illness

Our everyday understanding of the body is that it is an organic entity, or perhaps even a machine or system, that is subject to occasional breakdown and gradual deterioration. When we think of our own body, or of health and illness, we tend to think in individual, personal terms. The contribution that sociology makes is to emphasise the social nature of the body and of the processes and conditions that we call health and illness.

For example, our likelihood of contracting hepatitis is partly an effect of the robustness of our immune system and our exposure to a particular virus, but it is also shaped by our:

- age
- sex
- gender
- occupation
- geographical location
- lifestyle, including our behaviours in relation to sex and drugs
- previous involvement with medical systems (especially blood transfusions)
- knowledge and attitudes.

The same applies to any other form of illness or wellness, from our chances of having a trim, taut and terrific body to our likelihood of developing malaria. All are the result of social processes.

This chapter commences with a brief discussion of the emergent discipline of the sociology of the body, for without human bodies there is no health or illness. It then outlines the main concerns of the sociology of health and illness, emphasising how the varying theoretical perspectives brought to bear influence the choice of object of study. We argue that the biomedical model of health remains dominant and in an Irish context continues to shape much of the sociological analysis of health and illness and the policy initiatives that are often based on such research. Finally, we look very briefly to the future, for ours is an era of dramatic change in the fields of medicine and the sciences of life and the body. What is the role for sociologists as society grapples with the social and ethical challenges of the Human Genome Project, cloning and transgenic transplants?

THE BODY

Whilst sociologists often speak of individuals in abstract terms (as agents, actors, role-players and so on) there has been a strong shift in recent years towards recognising the social importance of the body — hardly surprising in a culture seemingly obsessed with *physical* bodies — with interests ranging from dieting to working out, from fashion to cosmetic surgery. Furthermore, as society becomes increasingly interested in the possibilities of 'virtual' entities, there is also an increased focus on the corporeal, whether through technology, health or sport.

Sociological interest in the body is comparatively new. Sociological thinking has long emphasised the 'cultural' and consequently the 'natural' — including the body — has long been played down. There has even been considerable hostility towards approaches like sociobiology and genetics which have sought to incorporate biological processes into social analysis.

Recent sociological interest in the body has been stimulated by a number of factors (Nettleton and Watson, 1998, pp.4–7). First, recent times have seen a *politicisation* of the body. Two groups have been of particular importance here. Feminists have focused very much on how women's bodies have been controlled and abused in a range of cultures. Works such as *Our bodies, ourselves* (Boston Women's Health Book Collective, 1973) and analyses of childbirth and eating disorders have critically examined how women's bodies are shaped by social factors and practices such as the medical industries, advertising and the fitness industry. Similarly, disabled groups have focused on how society discriminates against those that stray in any way from the dominant view of the 'normal' body.

Second, *demographic change*, particularly in relation to the ageing or 'greying' of the population in Western societies, has led to new issues. Increased lifespan has led to the emergence of new sets of questions. The incidence of some diseases, such as cancer and stroke, has increased while there are important issues related to the quality of life in later years. Many of these are directly linked to the body and its functioning. Ultimately, there are social and sociological questions related to death and the issue of euthanasia.

Third is the rise in *consumer culture*. There is a hugely increased focus on the body as part of this development. On the one hand, the body is a staple of advertising imagery and questions are constantly raised about the effects of images portrayed in the media. On the other hand, the body itself has become a major site of consumption: from cosmetics, fashion, diet and fitness to plastic surgery, tattoos and body-piercing.

Fourth is the effect that the development of *new technologies* is having on our bodies and our experiences of them. Again there are many areas of change here. New surgical techniques, including organ transplants, artificial body parts and cosmetic surgery, lead us to question the boundaries between humans and technology. One writer (Hayles, 1995, p.321) suggests that up to 10 per cent of the

American population may now be considered cyborgs — part human, part machine — in as much as their bodies are partly made up of pacemakers, plastic hips, penile implants, silicon breasts, artificial skin, stomach staples or transplanted corneas. There are other areas of technological development that can only be listed here but which may have as yet unforeseen impacts on our personal and social lives: smart drugs (to improve memory or intelligence); genetic manipulation; cloning; dietary supplements ('nutriceuticals') and transgenic implants (the use of animals' body parts).

Finally, the development of *communications technologies*, in particular the Internet, but also technologies such as digital cameras and computer viruses, have helped to raise questions about the nature of the 'virtual' and the 'real'. In an age where a person can adopt multiple personas on the web or continuously retouch their own family photograph album, the physical body may become a touchstone of 'reality' and authenticity. This may increasingly be the case as other aspects of our identity — such as nation, class and religion — become less salient or defined.

Overall, we are now far more *reflexive* about our bodies. Rather than a vehicle (or encumbrance) for action that is taken for granted, our bodies are now sites of activity: always open to monitoring, improvement, alteration and concern (Jenkins, 1999). We no longer adopt a fatalistic approach to our bodies but expect to be able to assert a greater degree of control. This translates into a wide range of behaviour: from working-out and dieting, to yoga and aerobics, to cholesterol tests and pap smears. Our heightened consciousness of our bodies has undoubtedly driven the continual expansion in the field of 'health' described below.

There is now a considerable sociological industry that focuses on the body (Nettleton and Watson, 1998, p.2), much of it pitched at a very abstruse and abstract level and often with little analysis of how the body operates in everyday life. However, the renewed interest in the body and the self has stimulated new insights into the sociology of health and illness, calling into question particularly the assumptions made of many of its routine categories. The challenge for sociology now is to combine the new critical approach to the body with empirical analyses of how people view, use and feel about their bodies within a range of social settings and structural situations.

THE SOCIOLOGY OF HEALTH AND ILLNESS

A major aspect of our embodied existence is the health or illness that we experience — individually and socially. Whereas the sociology of the body has tended to be neglected, there has long been an interest in medical sociology and in the sociology of health and illness. This can be traced back to Durkheim's work on suicide which in many ways provided a model for the sociological study of illness and became one of the bases for the specific social science discipline of epidemiology.

Medical sociology has given much in the way of support to the medical industry by supplying data about patterns of disease and in attempting to deduce causal relationships from such observations. It has also provided an interpretation of the 'sick role': the process whereby people adopt the role of 'patient'. Such a role requires the stripping away of many of our everyday beliefs and practices and allows us to expose ourselves to unquestioned subservience to professional instructions, outside observation of humiliating bodily practices and invasive medical examinations and procedures. In return we can claim the status of 'patient' and escape adherence to many of the norms of society, such as daily work, a cheerful countenance and appropriate dress. The sick role concept has been widely used in the training of doctors and other medical personnel.

The sociological analysis of health and illness has now moved beyond epidemiology and analysis of the sick role to embrace numerous aspects of social life. This reflects the increased interest in the body as well as the expansion of 'health' to embrace an ever-increasing proportion of our everyday life and behaviour. According to Porter (1997, p.15), 'the rise of sociology in health care can largely be explained by the gradual demise of . . . the "biomedical model" of health and illness [see below] which saw health and illness as a purely mechanical, physical matter.' It is now recognised that issues of health and illness can not be reduced to malfunctions of the individual body or the prevalence of germs or other causes of disease (though these of course are and remain factors). Rather, there is now a recognition that health and illness are social entities — a sociology of health and illness is therefore necessary. Such a sociology can investigate many aspects of the medical field.

Sociology allows us to investigate patterns of health and illness. This embraces the branch of social research known as epidemiology. Epidemiology is the side of medical sociology that is closest to the medical professions themselves. It tends to use a positivist and highly quantitative approach focusing on rates of illness or other factors, attitudinal research and the use of control groups and other aspects of scientific research. It has had an important role to play in the contemporary shift within the health services towards 'evidence-based practice'.

Sociology has much to contribute to an understanding of the experience of health and illness. Here both quantitative and qualitative techniques are used. How people define and experience pain, for example, has much to tell us about how they may or may not respond to the provision of health-care services. Similarly, the exploration of how women have experienced childbirth and the medical interventions associated with it has helped to alter how maternity services are being provided.

The sociology of health and illness has also contributed a great deal to our understanding of the medical industries and the medical professionals and other workers that operate within them. It has often been critical of the professions, laying bare the ways that professional groups create and sustain relations of power and domination over others in society, particularly through legitimated monopolies of knowledge and practice such as the right to issue prescriptions or sign sickness certificates. Moreover, it can teach us a lot about how professional groups attain and maintain their privileged status.

Interpretative sociology has much of interest to say about how health care is provided, in particular how members of the various groups involved in the practice of health and illness, such as doctors, nurses, patients and administrators, interact in ways that help to define each others' roles and the nature of health and illness themselves. Discourse analysts, drawing on the work of writers such as Thomas Szasz (1961) and Michel Foucault (1973), have explored how the discourses of health are created and maintained through institutions such as hospitals, clinics, asylums and popular medical books. This approach emphasises the social constructedness of health and illness. Some of the most radical critiques of medical practice and medical knowledge stem from this approach. Categories such as 'health', 'madness' and 'sick' are called into question and revealed to be fully social in nature. Medical knowledge is shown to be a particularly powerful form of discourse, and this approach is critical to an analysis of the 'medicalisation' of modern social life.

THE BIOMEDICAL MODEL

The most powerful discourse within the field of medicine remains the biomedical model of health. This model dominates current thinking about wellness and illness as it appears in people's everyday beliefs and attitudes, in the practices of most health workers and in medical research and policy-making. The model holds that health and illness are caused by identifiable factors such as bacteria, viruses, toxins, chemical imbalances, genetic disorders or physical accidents. These factors can be identified most effectively by trained and professional personnel according to standardised tests and diagnoses. They can then be treated to varying degrees of success by specific practices, drugs and techniques. Medical research is a process of cumulatively discovering more about the causes of disease and ill health and, as society develops, medicine will gradually identify and cure an increasing number of ailments and conditions. At the same time, 'folk' knowledge, traditional cures and superstitions will become increasingly less prevalent. As a result, the welfare of people in developed societies will gradually improve, longevity will increase and people will suffer less.

This is a very powerful discourse and one that appeals both to health consumers and to the medical industry. It supports the position of medical professionals, gives hope to patients and predictability to policy-makers. It justifies the activities of drug companies, medical researchers and builders of hospitals and other health facilities. It also aligns very well with the theories of modernisation. It is a discourse taken so much for granted that it is very difficult to challenge or subvert.

Tucker (1997, p.31) suggests that 'it is one of the characteristics of the modern biomedicine that it has hegemonic designs and it has consistently discredited, marginalised or suppressed other systems or practices.' These include 'folk' medicines, 'alternative' medicines and other approaches, some of which have nevertheless managed to become more 'respectable' and have been admitted to the field of 'real' medicine, for example, chiropractic, acupuncture and meditation.

Tucker reminds us that medical knowledge, like all knowledge, is socially constructed. The answers to health challenges are not just out there waiting to be discovered by scientists, doctors and researchers. Rather, medical knowledge is intrinsically tied up with social factors such as class, religion, gender difference and the interests and activities of commercial and political interest groups. This helps us to understand, at least partly, why so much money has been channelled into the development of drugs like Viagra, while across the world millions of children die every year from diarrhoea.

The biomedical model tends to be individualistic; thus the Department of Health and Children's women's health policy targets cigarette smoking as the greatest threat to women's health, rather than poverty, discrimination or the nature of the workplace (O'Donovan, 1997a, p.160). Similarly, dietary advice is applied to the individual patient, rather than being aimed at the food industry as a whole.

What might be the alternative to the biomedical model? *Holism* is often cited. This term can have various meanings, and the boundaries between 'biomedical' and 'holistic' medicine overlap and are hotly contested. A holistic approach can apply to the individual where a broader range of systems, including the 'biological, the energetic, the psychic, the interpersonal and the spiritual' (Tucker, 1997, p.42) are brought into view. More broadly holism encompasses economic and political as well as biological and environmental systems; it reflects the idea that health and illness are not simply biological phenomena but are socially produced. Tucker (1997, p.42) argues for a holistic medicine that does not privilege single explanations or therapies, which he contrasts with the 'reductionism' of the biomedical model. He suggests that:

> The emergence of a holistic paradigm will require not only a change in the practice of medicine and health care, but also in the knowledge system and the model of science on which it is based. It will also require changes in the institutional fabric of health care.

What might this mean in practice? Perhaps it might be to provide the consumers of health care with more information, thus leading to greater choice of therapies. Such an approach is advocated in policy documents such as the Department of Health and Children's strategy document *Quality and fairness* (2002b, p.132). It may mean giving greater recognition and support to alternative medicine and therapies, such as homeopathy, herbalism or shiatsu. Or it may mean paying greater attention to social and environmental issues such as air pollution, workplace hazards or dietary intake. The spiritual dimension is also seen as important. This may mean providing ways for people to have more 'meaning' in their lives.

The end result of a holistic approach may be to enhance the health of the population, but it may also serve to increase the level of surveillance of people and to extend the reach of medical dominance into ever more areas of everyday life. This is suggested by O'Donovan (1997a, p.159), who argues that broader dissemination of medical information leads to an 'intensification of biomedical hegemony'. Similarly, the adoption of 'alternative' therapies may result in a replication of the biomedical model, particularly as practitioners strive to become 'professionals' (the case of chiropractic illustrates this).

The conflict between biomedicine and holism is intense, but also complex and dynamic. It is clear that one of the strategies used by professional medical groups has been the active exclusion of many forms of therapy and practice. In Ireland as elsewhere, the history of the medical profession as we know it today has been the marginalisation and negation of 'folk' practices such as bonesetting, herbalism and faith healing. The discourse of biomedicine has achieved great power, and its supporters can hold up great achievements and point to any number of 'medical marvels'. However, popular choices seem to favour an increasing number of 'alternative' therapies, and many medical problems are dealt with through a broad variety of means of self-medication (MacFarlane, 1997) or attendance with 'alternative' practitioners (Tucker, 1997, p.31). Belief in the power of faith healers remains high, with 75 per cent of the Irish population reportedly expressing support for their efficacy (Ward, 2002, p.75). It seems clear that both models of health and illness will continue to contend for public and official support.

DEFINING HEALTH AND ILLNESS

While we can usually say of ourselves that we are feeling well or sick, health itself is a difficult concept to define (Blaxter, 1995). In its 1946 Constitution, the World Health Organisation defined health as a 'state of complete physical, mental and social well-being', but this understanding poses as many questions as it answers and seems to set up an impossible ideal — few of us could claim such a state for ourselves. Indeed, survey research has revealed that up to 95 per cent of the population experiences some sort of ill health in any two-week period (MacFarlane, 1997, p.17).

In many respects health and illness are relative terms and thus very difficult to define. Furthermore, definitions are often dependent on the criteria and normative frameworks used by the observer. While the existence of a broken arm may be fairly unproblematic, conditions such as obesity, depression or hyperactivity are far more open to interpretation and, as Cleary (1997, p.195) suggests, even for the understanding of 'diagnosis-specific data', methodological and conceptual considerations are crucial. Post-modern theorists, building on the work of writers such as Foucault, further problematise the notion of health. As Fox (1998, p.11) suggests, 'all definitions [of health] have a politics associated with them; all try to persuade us to a particular perspective on the person who is healthy or ill.'

Medical policy-makers and epidemiologists use the term 'health status' to refer to the present state of illness or wellness in a community. It can be described in terms of 'rates of death and illness in a community, the prevalence of good and poor health practices, rates of death and disease (chronic and infectious) and the prevalence of symptoms/conditions of well-being' (Doorley, 1998, p.17). Health status can be defined and measured by an outside observer, perhaps an 'expert' such as a doctor or dietician, according to various criteria. Similarly, it can be based on the self-reported health-related perceptions of a person — physical functioning, emotional well-being, pain and so on. In reality it is difficult to combine both measures.

We have seen that it is very difficult to define health or well-being in any sort of holistic way. As a result, those that seek to measure such entities tend to use simpler indicators such as life expectancy; incidence of and/or death rates from specific diseases; availability and provision of specific health services. In terms of capturing the complex state that may constitute health, these are obviously fairly crude and indirect measures. However, there is a strong desire to establish and measure health in terms of these sorts of indicators. These include the desire to compare countries according to their health status; the need to inform health policy and expenditure; the ability to measure progress in a certain direction; and a way to anticipate future health needs (Doorley, 1998, p.18).

The most common indicators of health status used are life expectancy; death rates; morbidity rates (that is, rates of incidence of certain diseases); patterns of lifestyle; and self-perceived health status. Ireland continues to lag behind many countries in the availability of such data, especially at the localised level. This has made it difficult to analyse health patterns in Ireland; to identify causal patterns (for example, links between pollution levels and health outcomes); or to inform policy-making in a critical way.

Life expectancy

Life expectancy is seen as one of the most important of health measures. It is widely used to compare countries (for example, in United Nations reports) and to measure 'progress' in a country, especially in terms of its modernisation. It is calculated by applying the death rates within a five- or one-year age group, and within each sex from the population under study, to a hypothetical birth cohort of 100,000 individuals (Doorley, 1998, p.20). Compared to other countries of the European Union (Figure 10.1), life expectancy in Ireland is on the low side. For men in 2002, life expectancy was at 75.1 years, below the EU15 average of 75.8

Figure 10.1 Life expectancy at birth, European countries, 2002

Country	Males	Females
EU15	75.8	81.6
EU25	74.8	81.1
Ireland	**75.1**	**80.3**
Northern Ireland	76.0	80.8
Austria	75.8	81.7
Belgium	75.1	81.1
Denmark	74.8	79.5
Finland	74.9	81.5
France	75.6	82.9
Germany	75.6	81.3
Greece	75.4	80.7
Italy	76.8	82.9
Luxembourg	74.9	81.5
Netherlands	76.0	80.7
Portugal	73.8	80.5
Spain	75.7	83.1
Sweden	77.7	82.1
UK	76.6	81.0
Cyprus	75.5	79.1
Czech Republic	72.1	78.7
Estonia	65.3	77.1
Hungary	68.4	76.7
Lithuania	66.3	77.5
Latvia	64.8	76.0
Malta	75.9	81.0
Poland	70.4	78.7
Slovenia	72.7	80.5
Slovakia	69.9	77.8

Source: CAO 2004; For Germany: Federal Government Statistics Office press release available at www.destatis.de/presse/englisch/pm2004/p4860022.htm; for UK inc Northern Ireland: National Statistics Online available at www.statistics.gov.uk/cci/nugget.asp?id=168; Cyprus: WHO figures but above the average for the expanded EU25 of 74.8. The position for women was less sanguine, the Irish figure of 80.3 below both the EU15 average of 81.6 and the EU25 figure of 81.1. In all countries of the EU women outlive men, though in both Ireland and other countries the gap is slowly narrowing.

While Ireland's performance could be seen as relatively poor in EU terms, there has been quite positive recent movement in the figures, with Irish people's life expectancy rapidly increasing by 2.1 years for males and 1.8 years for females in the period 1996–2002. Looking further back, we can see quite a dramatic improvement in Irish people's life expectancy — the figures in 1960 were just 68.1 for men and 71.9 for women. At the turn of the twentieth century (1902), a man or a woman, if they survived to the age of 25, could then expect — on average — to live to just 63 years of age. In 2002 (the most recent period for which figures are available) a 25-year–old can expect to survive until 76 (men) or 81 (women). (CSO, 2004a). This extension of life has major implications, for example in the area of retirement and pensions, as well as in relation to health status and lifestyle.

The causes for Ireland's poor performance relative to other EU countries are likely to be complex, but may be related to lifestyle factors (such as diet, smoking, accidents); prevalence of certain diseases and conditions (such as Ireland's high rate of spina bifida or heart disease); and variations in the extent and efficiency of the delivery of certain types of health services (e.g. the level of cancer screening services).

Causes of death

Figures on the major causes of death are often used as an indicator of the health status of a society and even of its success in becoming developed. The reasons why people in a society die, and the stage of life at which they die, are determined by social factors. Thus, in 'less developed societies' major causes of death are likely to be infectious diseases (such as measles, typhoid, malaria) and malnutrition; in more 'advanced' societies wealth, improved diet and sanitation and access to medical treatment means that such causes of death are far less likely. People, living longer, then succumb to the 'diseases of modernity' such as heart disease, stroke and cancer.

In Ireland there have been major changes in the pattern of mortality in the past six decades. There has been a *decline* in deaths from infectious diseases such as influenza, measles and tuberculosis and an *increase* in deaths from cancer and cardiovascular disease (including heart disease and stroke) (Devlin, 1997, p.19). There has also been a decline in deaths attributed to 'senility' as the coding of causes of death has changed over the years (see Figure 10.2).

Figure 10.2 Causes of death in Ireland 1947 and 2005

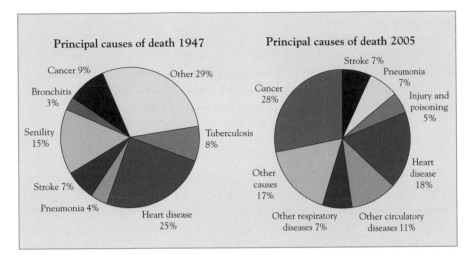

(*Source*: Devlin, 1997, p.14, CSO, 2006a)

Morbidity

Morbidity data relates to the level of 'illness' in society. As we have seen, 'illness', unlike death, is open to interpretation and contestation, thus the data is far less reliable. Furthermore, the collection and collation of such data is dependent on cases coming to the attention of the formal health services, which occurs with only a minority of medical conditions. Some, such as cancer, almost inevitably involve contact with the health services, therefore data are quite good; others are legally notifiable (such as certain infectious diseases) and again, the information is relatively reliable; others, especially 'minor' ailments such as influenza or muscle sprains, are far less likely to be recorded or measured.

A more effective method of gathering data about morbidity is the health experience questionnaire, where people are asked about their health-related experience and activity over a defined period of time (for example, 'the last month'). A number of internationally recognised questionnaire instruments have been developed and these allow for international comparisons. One of these, used in the United States, UK, Scandinavia and Germany and to a limited extent in Ireland, is called SF36 (as it comprises 36 questions). It reflects once again the complexity of what we term 'health', and attempts to capture this by measuring eight health concepts that are relevant across all social groups, including (Doorley, 1998, pp.24–5):

- limitations in physical activities because of health problems
- limitations in usual role activities because of physical health
- bodily pain
- general health perceptions
- vitality (energy and fatigue)
- limitations in social activities because of physical and emotional problems
- limitations in usual role activities because of emotional problems
- mental health (psychological distress and well-being).

PROVISION OF HEALTH SERVICES

As in relation to health and illness, data on the provision of health services is also highly complex, open to interpretation and contestation and difficult to gather. However, there has been a long tradition of comparing countries on the level of services provided. The level of provision, in terms of numbers such as total and per capita health spending, hospitals, hospital beds and doctors, is one of the key pieces of information that is commonly used to measure the 'development' of a country.

Figures in relation to health services need to be placed in context. For example, the period from 1980 to 2000 saw a drop in the number of acute hospitals in Ireland and a reduction in bed numbers from 17,665 to 11,832. This represented a per capita decrease from 5.1 beds per thousand population to just 3.1/1000 (Department of Health and Children, 2002a). It would be a mistake to interpret such figures as merely an indication that the level of health service provision in the country had dropped. Some would interpret this as reflecting the rationalisation of acute hospital services and a parallel shift of resources into 'community-based care'. Others see it as a process of 'cutbacks' of services. The danger of relying on raw statistics, for Ireland as for any other society, is revealed.

The expansion of the health field over the years has meant that the health services provided by the public and private sectors have also developed. These range from the supply of drugs and medicines to the provision of many 'social services' such as care for children and the elderly, through to the delivery of acute hospital care. The range of services provided by the Health Service Executive (HSE), the body that since 2005 has been responsible for the delivery of health services in Ireland, is illustrated in Figure 10.3.

HEALTH, ILLNESS AND SOCIAL CHANGE IN IRELAND

The sociology of health and illness in Ireland needs to be understood against the background of the significant social changes discussed elsewhere in this book. For example, there have been significant changes in fertility patterns, family size and composition and marriage rates. There have been substantial changes in the

Figure 10.3 Health service functions of the HSE

Programme area	Types of services
Primary, community and continuing care [PCCC]	General practitioner [GP] services Community-based health (eg dental, ophthalmic, aural services; maternity and infant care; public health nursing services – eg family planning, pregnancy, counselling) Personal social services: • older persons • children • disability services • mental health services • social inclusion
National Hospitals Office [NHO]	Resource allocation, service delivery and performance management of 53 acute hospitals
Population health [PH]	Promoting and protecting the health of the entire population and target groups, with a particular focus on health equalities • health intelligence and data gathering • environmental health services • immunisation • infection control

Source: HSE corporate websites

relationships between women and men and between adults and children. The involvement of the state in people's everyday lives has greatly increased. There have been dramatic alterations in the nature of work people do and how they spend their leisure time. There have been changes in the food people eat, the drugs they use and the natural and built environment. All of these factors have at least the potential to impact significantly on how we see and use our bodies and how we experience health and illness.

There has also been a huge expansion in the health infrastructure. The Department of Health was established in 1947 and since then there has been a development of public and private health provision that has been broadly in line with that of other Western countries. Ireland has developed a 'mixed' health system based on public and private funding; in this way it is similar to other European countries such as France and Austria.

The changes in patterns of health in Ireland since the foundation of the Department have been striking. Life expectancy for females has increased from to 62 to 80 and for males from 61 to 75. Infant mortality has plummeted from 68/1000 to just 6/1000, one of the lowest rates in the world, and maternal mortality, once frequent, is now a rare event. Beyond the statistics are the changes in attitudes, approaches, institutions and practices that have made for a greatly increased quality of life (Robins, 1997, pp.5–6):

> Fifty years ago many citizens with mental illness or mental handicap, elderly and infirm persons in need of care, unwanted and deprived children, outcast unmarried mothers, were being cared for *en masse* in large institutions of mainly nineteenth-century origin. Patients of little means needing basic medical care were subjected to the discriminating and restrictive requirements of the Victorian dispensary doctor system. Those of modest means requiring hospital treatment received no support from the state and often had to face intolerable financial burdens. Persons who were functionally, economically and socially disadvantaged by long-term disability were ignored, written off by society, with little effort made to integrate them in normal living activity.

By all these measures, the improvements in our health-care system have been dramatic. For many analysts they are a clear reflection of the fact that Ireland has become a fully 'developed' society. The patterns of disease and mortality in Ireland resemble those of other Western nations and are very different to those of the 'developing world' where mortality levels are higher and deaths from infectious diseases are the main cause of death.

More recent trends have started to reflect the significant changes that have taken place in Irish society and the broader international trends in how health care is delivered. Many of these reflect the pressures created by the expansion of the health field; the increased costs dictated by new medical technologies, procedures and drugs; the demographic challenge of the ageing of the population; and the increased incomes of an expanding range of health professionals and ancillary staff.

One response to increased costs that also reflects significant changes in the concepts underpinning suitable modes of care has been the shift from institutional to 'community' care. This trend has been particularly noticeable in those areas previously structured around large residential institutions, such as mental health and care for young people, but it has also begun to change the way that health care is delivered to the aged and to other groups. The change reflects many sets of ideas in the health-care field and, according to Saris (1997, p.218), there exists:

a broad political consensus, encompassing such diverse elements as policy-makers interested in reducing the profile of 'big government' and utopian visionaries valorising the 'community' as a place of refuge from a heartless 'society', formed around the proposition that the time had come to close down these big institutions.

Community care is not without its controversies. Feminists, in particular, have pointed to the fact that 'care in the community' very often means care by women, whether family members or often very poorly paid female staff. In the area of aged care, for example, fewer than 1 per cent of home helps in Ireland are men (O' Donovan, 1997b, p.150). Community-based services are seriously under-resourced, patchily provided and of low status, often focused on the 'needy' and the 'down and out' (Edmondson, 1997, p.162). Much of the work is, like domestic labour, not seen by health-care managers as 'real work'. Rather, 'care has been constructed . . . as charitable non-work provided by philanthropic women to their less fortunate neighbours' (O' Donovan, 1997b, p.153). Community care may be an opportunity to respond to health needs in a more holistic way, but at present it remains very much the poor relation of institutionalised health care.

There has been an increase in the numbers and varieties of health professionals, paraprofessionals and 'wannabe' professionals. Doctors, surgeons and nurses have now been joined by dieticians, physiotherapists, chiropractors, acupuncturists and medical social workers, not to mention foot reflexologists, iridologists and a whole panoply of 'alternative' therapists. There is a burgeoning of specialists in all areas as medical knowledge becomes increasingly rationalised and fragmented.

The increasing rationalisation of medicine has seen a greater level of evaluation, performance measurement, research and monitoring built into the health-care system (M. Butler, 2002). Increasing public and private resources are being channelled into health care and there are increasing demands for accountability within the system involving concepts such as 'casemix' and Diagnostic Related Groups whereby health systems are funded on the basis of identifiable and measurable conditions and practices. Moves in this direction may represent a shift in power from autonomous professionals to managers and bureaucrats, though there is a high level of collegiality and common purpose among management and practitioners within the Irish hospital system. Furthermore, the increasing attempt to rationalise medicine runs counter to the holistic philosophies that are becoming increasingly influential.

Worldwide, medicine is increasingly experienced as 'big business' — a highly profitable one at that. The United States represents one extreme and its largely private health-care system consumes a greater proportion of financial resources than any other in the world. There are numerous opportunities for profit-making in health care:

- fees-for-services for private practitioners (often working in publicly funded hospitals)
- health screening and tests
- pathology services
- health insurance
- drug and appliance manufacture
- private hospitals, clinics and nursing homes.

Some have characterised this as the 'medical-industrial complex' (Davis and George, 1993, p.185). The medical and health-care industries provide significant employment in Ireland. According to the Industrial Development Authority (IDA, 2007), fifteen of the top twenty-five of the world's medical technology companies have operations in Ireland: transnational corporations such as Abbott, Boston Scientific, Johnson & Johnson and Tyco Healthcare employ over 26,000 people. The pharmaceutical industry is also very large: international companies such as Wyeth, Pfizer and GlaxoSmithKline have over eighty facilities in Ireland, employing over 17,000 people and generating over US$34 billion of export income annually. Six of the world's ten most popular prescription drugs are produced in Ireland.

Social inequality and health care

Despite the continuing expansion of medical services and infrastructure and, at least in terms of the biomedical model, an improvement in average health status, health and illness in Ireland are still very much determined by inequalities of class, gender, ethnicity, wealth and power. Sociologists have long had an interest in such inequalities — and in seeking to explain them.

Class

Our knowledge of how health and illness are related to social inequality is an outcome of social epidemiology. Such research has consistently indicated (for example, Wilkinson, 1996; Collins and Shelley, 1997; Nolan and Whelan, 1997; Balanda and Wilde, 2001; Burke et al., 2004) that in advanced industrial economies like Ireland, the UK, Australia and the United States, poor health status is associated with variation in social class. Class difference has been shown to be related to overall mortality, infant mortality, disability and morbidity (Burke et al., 2004). Poorer than average health has also been shown to be strongly correlated with unemployment (Nolan and Whelan, 1997). The data reported in Balanda and Wilde (2001, pp.29–31) indicates that with the sole exception of cancer of the kidney, all 64 other causes of death revealed a higher rate in the 'lowest' social class compared with the 'highest'. In many cases the variation is

Figure 10.4 Relative rates of dying from various causes, comparing highest occupational group with lowest occupational group (Balanda and Wilde, 2001)

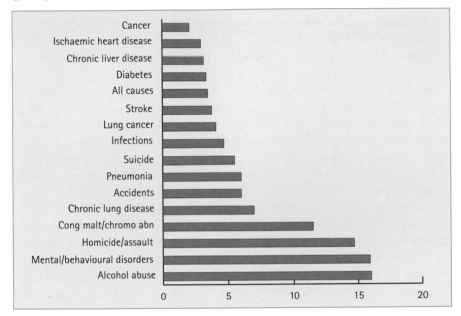

Source: Burke *et al*, 2004, p.22

startling: those in the 'lowest' class are fifteen times more likely to die from homicide; six times more likely to die from respiratory disease; and seventeen times more likely to die of alcoholism.

Negative health factors and indicators associated with poorer and less powerful social groups include, but are not limited to:

- higher levels of chronic physical illness
- higher levels of perinatal mortality
- more financial problems that directly impact on health
- higher levels of smoking and drinking
- lower levels of breastfeeding
- lower levels of consumption of fruit and vegetables
- lower levels of exercise.

(Burke *et al.*, 2004, p.23–29)

Burke *et al.* (2004, p.28) point out that health inequalities in Ireland can be dated back at least to early nineteenth-century reports that showed death rates among children in poor districts to be higher than in wealthier areas. Despite economic growth, political change and the extensive development of the health services, such types of differentials have largely persisted, as indicated by numerous studies and reports (Burke *et al.*, 2004; Tussing and Wren, 2006). As Burke *et al.* conclude in an overview conducted for the Public Health Alliance:

> In Ireland, people who are poor and excluded get sick more often and die younger than people who are better off . . . Health inequalities are shown to exist when any measurement of income or wealth is used, i.e. socio-economic status, social class, poverty lines, deprivation, income and wealth indices, and levels of education (2004, p.22).

That such inequalities (Figure 10.4) persist reveals much about the structured inequality of Irish society. The 'causes' of such differences are briefly explored later in this chapter.

Ethnicity

In many societies a correlation has been demonstrated between ethnicity and health status. Such relationships may be asserted to be biological (for example, sickle cell anaemia in African-Americans) or are recognised as the outcome of inequalities of wealth and power, discrimination and racism. The relationships are often complex. Ethnicity and class interact with each other as well as with other social factors such as age, gender and place of residence.

One group that has been identified in Ireland as having particularly poor health status is the Travelling community. According to the Department of Health and Children (2002c), life expectancy and general health status amongst Travellers are considerably lower than the general population, though lack of good quality or recent data can make comparisons problematic: the last comprehensive statistical analysis of Traveller health took place in 1987, though the Department of Health and Children is currently (2007) involved in a comprehensive all-Ireland Traveller Health Study, which will provide up-to-date knowledge about Traveller health. It is clear, however, that Travellers die more frequently as a result of stillbirth, perinatal mortality, infant mortality and from SIDS (Sudden Infant Death Syndrome) (Department of Health and Children, 2002c, pp.24–6). The main cause of Travellers' inferior health status is to be found in poor living conditions, social exclusion and racism. In addition, health services have not been well adapted to the specific needs of Travellers; in particular they have not adequately responded to Traveller culture and how it may shape perceptions of, and responses to, ill health and health services (McCabe and Keyes, 2005). Consultations with Traveller communities and organisations prior to the new health study indicated common sets of issues: individual prejudice and institutional discrimination; unsuitability of services; lack of confidence, education and support within Traveller communities; the changing roles of Traveller men; lack of trust;

incidence of stress, depression and mental health problems. The consultative process also indicated the desire of Travellers to be centrally involved in the shaping of the understandings and discourses of Traveller health (Institute of Public Health in Ireland, 2007).

The significant level of immigration into Ireland (Chapter 6) has given rise to considerable ethnic diversity. There has been little sociological research into the health needs and possible health inequalities that impact on new ethnic groups (Hyde *et al.*, 2004, p.82). It is likely that the health experience of ethnically defined groups may be influenced by cultural patterns that shape how the body, illness and health are conceptualised and expressed, the relationships between such groups and the existing health services, and how these may be shaped by cultural practices related, for example, to religion, language or models of gender-appropriate behaviour. Immigrants to Ireland also make a significant contribution to the health workforce and this will add further complexity (NCCRI, 2002)

There has been an interest in the health status of Irish people living abroad, particularly in Britain (Williams, 1996; Walls, 2006). It is only relatively recently that the Irish have been recognised as an 'ethnic group' for the purposes of public policy in the UK. Williams reports that, though data on the Irish-born in Britain is very difficult to interpret, data on second and subsequent generations of the Irish community reveals higher than average mortality rates (1996, p.59). A recent report (Walls, 2006) points out that the Irish are the only significant immigrant group in Britain whose health status has diminished following immigration. They exhibit higher rates than the 'white British' of cancers, coronary disease, stroke, accidents and suicide, amongst other conditions. The inferior health status of the Irish in Britain can be linked to the economic and cultural structures associated with migration. As migration is such an important aspect of Irish society, the implications may be profound.

Gender

Health status is clearly patterned by gender, in Ireland as in most other countries. Gender issues in health remain controversial and cannot be separated from broader questions about gender, power and inequality. On nearly all indicators, the health status of men is worse than that of women (Richardson, 2004, pp.11–27). Men have higher death rates at all ages, from babyhood to older age groups; they are more likely to die in accidents, from suicide, and from diseases like heart disease and all cancers, except those of the skin, the breast and the reproductive organs. In fact, the only other causes of death more likely to apply to women in Ireland are meningitis, congenital malformation of the nervous system, and diseases of the skin and of the musculoskeletal system, such as rheumatoid arthritis and osteoarthrosis (Balanda and Wilde, 2001, pp.29–31). Moreover, in recent times the male suicide rate, already higher than the female, has increased sharply in many Western societies including Ireland. Irish males are now nearly four times more likely to end their own lives than are females (Balanda and Wilde, 2001, p.164).

However, the statistics do not necessarily reflect the whole picture. As Kelleher (1997, p.vii) points out:

> While women do live longer they also have a poorer quality of life as they age than men, bear the inequalities found in every society in the world more than men, carry the hidden un-prestigious and extensive responsibility for the iceberg of health need in every country, and strive throughout to bear and rear new generations of people in a complex and unjust world.

Furthermore, Irish women have rates of certain cancers (colon, breast, larynx and oesophagus) and ischaemic heart disease that are among the highest in the EU (Mahon, 1997, p.88; WHC, 2006). This may be attributed largely to 'lifestyle factors' (diet, smoking, lack of exercise) and inadequate screening and preventative health strategies.

Irish sociologists of health and illness have attempted to identify and account for gender-based disparities in health status. Since 1997 a statutory body, the Women's Health Council (WHC), has carried out substantial research with a view to advising the government on women's health issues. There has been far less attention paid to men's health issues, though more recently the specific health issues that pertain to men have been placed on the agenda (Richardson, 2004).

Research carried out by the WHC has pointed to the complex relationships between health, gender and inequality. The Council has pointed out (2003, p.19) that 'women in less well-off socio-economic groups have consistently been shown to be at the greatest disadvantage with regard to many aspects of health'. Yet the same report admits (ibid.) that 'it is still almost impossible to say with any certainty how many women are disadvantaged, and in turn to gauge the extent of any health inequalities that may exist'. Unequivocal measurements of 'health', as we have seen above, are difficult to obtain, and the allocation of women to occupational, class or income categories is also fraught with difficulty (see Chapter 7).

The WHC points to a number of particular categories of women who are likely to suffer disproportionately from ill-health as a consequence of their overall economic and social disadvantage. One of these groups is carers in the home. The WHC (2003, p.23) points out that carers 'have been found to receive little social, practical or financial support from formal health services, despite their common experience of isolation, reduced social interaction, high levels of strain and psychological distress, and compromised health status.'

Another group of women that suffers relatively poor health is women with disabilities, largely due to their exclusion from the labour market. Physical and social barriers to accessing health services — from poorly designed buildings and equipment to lack of sexual health awareness — compound such inequalities. Other categories of women more likely to suffer ill-health or difficulty in accessing services include older women, lone parents, lesbians, women who are homeless, rural women, drug and alcohol mis-users, asylum-seekers/refugees and Travellers.

Specific men's health issues may relate to particular health problems that are unique to them, such as prostate or testicular cancer or, of perhaps greater sociological interest, to how the social construction of masculinities may shape males' experiences of health and illness. Richardson (2004, p.3) argues that the former approach, which tends to focus on the 'differences' between men and women, is problematic, and that men's health needs to be addressed in its own right, with recognition that men's health, like women's, is patterned by issues of age, sexual orientation, ethnicity and social inequality. It is also shaped by experiences of maleness and expressions of masculinity: Richardson calls for less of a focus on the 'health' aspect of men's health and for a more critical assessment of 'men'.

Richardson (2004, p.6) points to how 'men's health' has been 'hijacked' by the popular media (particularly websites and glossy magazines) and redefined as a largely aesthetic issue, of how to become and remain physically attractive (to women or other men) through the use of products and services provided by the pharmaceutical, fitness and cosmetics industries. The focus of such a discourse is inevitably on individual strategies of self-improvement and bodily maintenance and grooming, rather than on the social determinants of men's health. While men are considerably more likely to suffer ill-health, from involvement in traffic accidents to diseases of the respiratory system, they perceive themselves to be healthier than women, and are less likely to make use of health services. As Richardson (2004, p.21) states: 'even where knowledge and awareness of health issues is high among men, the assumption cannot be made that this will impact on health behaviours.' The reasons for this apparent mismatch are inevitably complex, but may reflect complex relationships between the body, health, vulnerability, control and masculinity.

Contemporary Irish constructions of masculinity may manifest themselves in patterns of behaviour that may contribute to poorer health outcomes for males. Examples include high levels of alcohol consumption (see Chapter 13) which contribute to increased incidence of conditions such as cirrhosis of the liver, alcohol-related cancers and psychiatric illnesses, and involvement in accidents and violent incidents; men are also less likely to eat 'healthily', with much higher consumption of fried foods and meat/fish than women; they are also twice as likely to use illegal drugs (Richardson, 2004, pp.16–19).

The complexity of issues related to gender remind us of the difficulty of defining health, especially as the biomedical model is increasingly open to critique. On the basis of the indicators used by health managers and policy-makers, men are more unhealthy, but feminists in particular have drawn attention to how women's experience of ill health is broader, more diffuse and more hidden. There is a message here: sociological analysis of health and illness needs to reflect the difficulty and complexity of the issues involved and avoid simplistic interpretation of statistics that may be misleading, or partial, or both.

Women have an important role as health-care providers, particularly within the home, where much primary health care takes place. This is a dual role: maintaining good health of family members through, for example, food preparation and maintenance of hygiene standards; and direct provision through caring for others and mediation with health-care services. Within Irish society, there is a strong expectation that women, especially female family members, will take responsibility for health-care tasks. Further, the caring role is 'intricately bound up with definitions and conceptions of femininity' (Hodgins and Kelleher, 1997, p.43).

The unpaid (and low-paid) work of women as health-care providers is reinforced by community care policies that have seen a shift in emphasis away from the institutional delivery of some forms of health care like psychiatric care and care of the chronically ill. It has been shown that 'care in the community' usually means care by families and more often than not care by women (MacFarlane, 1997, p.19). The assumptions made of this gender division of labour underpin the perception of the nursing profession. Conversely, women are under-represented in senior and well-paid positions within the health services: just three of the eleven members of the Board of the HSE are women and while women comprise 80 per cent of employees in the health service, only 29 per cent of medical and dental consultants are women (CSO, 2006b, p.10).

Causes

It is one thing to say that social inequality and health are related. It is another to tease out the many factors that help to create and sustain this relationship. Thus, in relation to unemployment (Nolan and Whelan 1997, p.103):

> It is extremely difficult, with the types of data usually available, to distinguish the role of different factors, or to isolate the impact of unemployment *per se* from that of the broader socio-economic background from which those experiencing unemployment generally come.

In the UK, the wide-ranging *Black Report* (Townsend and Davidson, 1982) offered four main explanations for the observed relationships between class and health:

- *artefactual data* — the findings were a result of how the data was collected and the limitations inherent in this
- *selection* — healthier people, as a result of their better health, were able to get better jobs or otherwise move into higher social class groups

- *materialist explanations* — health was affected by material deprivation, including poor housing, poverty, pollution, hazards at work
- *cultural explanations* — class shaped certain lifestyle factors such as alcohol and tobacco consumption, diet and exercise.

The conclusion was that the last two explanations were the most likely; similar conclusions have been reached in other studies. In Ireland, the Kilkenny Health Project found that levels of smoking among unskilled and semi-skilled manual workers were almost twice those of non-manual workers. In general it found 'an association with social class for smoking prevalence, alcohol consumption, prevalence of obesity, [measurements of blood pressure] and [health] knowledge levels, but not for mean cholesterol levels or light leisure activity' (Collins and Shelley, 1997, p.92).

It must be emphasised that the links between broader beliefs and attitudes, knowledge of health factors and everyday behaviour are very complex. Key sets of beliefs relate to whether or not one feels susceptible to particular conditions, in control in everyday situations and how one can reasonably behave in social settings. This may influence, for example, a person's decision whether or not to give up smoking, notwithstanding their knowledge that it is a health hazard. It is important not to fall into a 'blame the victim' mentality when addressing the issue of 'lifestyles'. Morris (1995, p.136) reminds us:

> These behaviours plainly are embedded in the social structure. When questions are asked not merely how people behave but why they behave as they do, 'lifestyles' provide no release from the need to confront that structure — which also has so many other effects on health.

Furthermore Wilkinson (1996; 1999; 2005) has argued that the most important factor in determining health inequalities is not differential exposure to material hazards and risks (in particular low income), but rather the level and nature of social inequality and cohesion. Thus 'in more egalitarian societies, where differences in incomes and in social status are smaller, the average health standards of the population may be substantially improved . . . [egalitarian societies] also seem to be more socially cohesive' (Wilkinson, 1999, p.257). Putnam (2000, pp.326–335) makes a similar argument in relation to the influence of what he calls social capital on health. According to this argument it is the stress and psychosocial damage caused by relative inequality and low levels of social interaction that is the key to ill health. Given that Ireland has a comparatively high level of economic inequality (Barrett *et al.* 2000, p.132) but also arguably a high level of social interaction and community cohesion, the determinants of health inequalities will inevitably be complex. This is an approach to health status that will repay further research in the future. Meanwhile, others suggest that health inequalities are more directly related to material deprivation, for example to poor diet, housing, physical environment and access to leisure pursuits. Cumulative deprivation throughout the life-course may also be significant, including such factors as low birthweight, poor educational attainment and subsequent poor or hazardous employment conditions (Hyde *et al.*, 2004, p.71).

We have seen that the health field has expanded greatly in recent times. The concerns of modernist reformers were with ameliorating the health impacts of industrialism as these related to the incidence of infectious diseases, workplace hazards, poor housing and other social factors associated with mass society. Post-modernism sees an interest, both among sociologists of health and policy-makers, in other issues, particularly those to do with identity, rights and culture. An example may be found in the response of activists, sociologists and policy-makers to the issue of female genital mutilation (FGM), a practice widely carried out by some of the peoples of Africa and the Middle East. While the standard Western response to FGM has been one of horror and a 'high moral tone' (Shaughnessy, 1997, p.123), the issue is shown to be highly complex, involving a range of sexual, health-related, political, religious, economic and social factors. Any attempt to address the issue requires a sophisticated and multi-faceted social understanding. Once again, we see a tension between the rationalist, positivist approaches to social issues that tend to be favoured by policy-makers, and the more speculative, interpretative and complex approach of much of contemporary sociology.

Policy responses to inequality

Hederman O'Brien, reflecting the arguments of Wilkinson (above), reminds us that once a certain level of income is attained in a society ill health is usually a reflection of economic and social inequalities (1998, p.81):

> Neither the total amount spent on health services nor the availability of sophisticated procedures will, of itself, offset the decreasing health standards and mortality rates of those at the bottom of widening differentials in a prosperous society.

The implication here, one that has been recognised in other societies (see Morris, 1995), is that any attempt to tackle the persistent links between health and inequality *must* include action on broader issues of social inequality such as poverty, unemployment and gender discrimination. Doorley (1998, p.38) concludes that a better distribution of economic resources would probably be the most effective way to reduce inequalities in health. The health sector thus needs to be more vocal in advocating stronger social policies to achieve this. However, these aspects of social inequality are deeply entrenched in Irish society.

One of the difficulties of responding to issues of social inequality is expressed in the paradox described by Bunton (1998, p.25):

> The analysis of social policy process has become increasingly important in contemporary health care, especially due to an increased emphasis on the enhancement or promotion of health rather than simply the treatment of illness. Yet at the same time the possibilities for coherent social policy are being increasingly restricted and our conceptions of social policy have undergone considerable change.

In other words, the extent to which the state can influence outcomes in society is increasingly open to challenge. The idea of a single one-size-fits-all 'health policy' can be seen as a highly modernist notion — it is assumed that social life is predictable, rational and relatively homogenous (or predictably heterogeneous). All these assumptions are now called into question in Irish society.

Social policy is increasingly being determined by supranational bodies, in particular the agencies of the EU. Many of the factors that help to determine the notion of health are under the control of multinational corporations, for example, in the drug, tobacco, food, insurance and health-care industries. There have been significant changes in the organisation of work and employment that have rendered problematic the way that health care is funded. There is an increased heterogeneity of population and behaviour: Ireland is witnessing increasing ethnic and cultural diversity and there has been a rise in 'alternative' lifestyles, medicines and therapies, many of which are widely dispersed (MacFarlane, 1997). Within consumer culture there is an increased emphasis on personal choice and the object of health care may now be seen as the 'customer', rather than the 'patient'. Furthermore, thanks to the availability of medical information on the Internet, the patient/customer is now likely to be highly informed (or misinformed) about their condition and treatment options.

It is also important to consider changes in the nature of the organisations and institutions that deliver health care. There has been much criticism of how Irish health-care systems are managed. For example, McKevitt (1998, pp.44–5) argues that in Ireland the delivery of health services is typified by a 'strategic deficit' and by 'poor performance measurement systems, inadequate professional supervision and underdeveloped management capability'. Given the highly complex and conflicting nature of health-care institutions, detailed and intrusive management and policy-making are indeed difficult. The model that appears to be emerging in Ireland as in other similar countries is one of facilitation and support for a range of diverse activities (McKevitt, 1998, p.60). The emergence of the Health Service Executive in 2005 can be seen as an attempt by the state to manage this diversity better.

Irish health-care institutions

There is extensive evidence that most health-care issues are dealt with by people themselves, without reference to formalised health-care services such as doctors and hospitals (MacFarlane, 1997, p.18). Therefore health-care institutions only come into play in relation to specific events, conditions and situations. It should therefore be remembered that health-care institutions represent only one, albeit important, part of the health-care story.

The Irish health-care system is based, like that in most Western countries, on a mixture of public and private funding. It is difficult to identify accurately how much of the funding is 'public', but it may range from 75–90 per cent. There has been considerable debate in Ireland in recent years in relation to the so-called 'two-tier' health system, which sees differential services available to three categories of persons: those with private health insurance (about 50 per cent of the population); those with medical cards (about 30 per cent of the population); and those with neither of these (the remaining 20 per cent) (Wren, 2003; Tussing and Wren, 2006). Public spending in Ireland on 'health' (which as we have seen includes some functions that in other countries would be defined as 'environmental services' or 'welfare services') is at a level that is 94 per cent of the EU15 average (Tussing and Wren, 2006, p.64), behind countries such as Germany and Denmark but ahead of the Netherlands and Italy. Health care is expensive and consumes about a fifth of total government spending or about 9 per cent of GDP — a figure that has remained fairly constant since the late 1990s (Tussing and Wren, 2006, p.62; T. O'Hara, 1998, p.4).

The period since the early nineteenth century has seen a continual expansion in the provision of institutionalised health services. The first institutions were the workhouses, established in 1703; county infirmaries followed in 1765 and these provided the basis on which the public health services were subsequently developed (O'Shea, 1998, p.55). Among the earliest country-wide systems was that of asylums for the insane, first developed in the early nineteenth century as part of the general process of 'civilising' the country (Saris, 1997, p.214). Voluntary hospitals date back to the early eighteenth century. Jervis Street Hospital, now part of the Beaumont Hospital in Dublin, opened in 1718 (O'Shea, 1998, p.54). The churches, especially the Roman Catholic Church, have been actively involved in the development of health services since the 1830s. Public health services in the community as we understand them today started in 1878 with the appointment of dispensary doctors and in 1925 county medical officers (O'Shea, 1998, p.55).

The Department of Health was established in 1947 and subsequently expenditure on health care expanded rapidly until the fiscal crisis of the 1980s. There was a sharp decline in spending in real terms during the 1980s but since then there has been a gradual shift back towards expansion, though spending on health has not kept pace with the expansion in the economy or the population. Health policy and the structures that stem from it have increasingly been driven by expert groups within and outside government, in particular since 1995. There is now a highly technocratic approach to the development of health-care services. This can be perceived in the highly managerialist structures of the HSE.

The public system now plays 'a major role in the provision and funding of services, the regulation and setting of standards for inputs to the health system and in recent times [there has been] an increasing emphasis on setting standards and objectives' (T. O'Hara, 1998, p.4). Despite the establishment of the HSE, it is still apparent that the management and planning of the health-care system is not fully centralised, rather as T. O'Hara (1998, p.5) suggests:

> a combination of government, Department of Health and Children, advisory and executive agencies and voluntary organisations all play a role in service delivery and development, though their degree of power and influence varies.

Medicalisation

One factor driving the global expansion of health services is medicalisation: the process by which an increasing range of events and conditions are defined as being of interest to medicine. Many conditions, previously taken to be non-medical, are now grounds for consulting a doctor. Forms of behaviour previously seen as deviant are now defined as medical problems: bad behaviour by children is now hyperactivity or attention deficit disorder; shoplifting is kleptomania. Occasionally the process can operate in reverse, for example, alcoholism is decreasingly likely to result in admission to psychiatric institutions in Ireland and more likely to be viewed as the result of personality or social factors.

The critique of medicalisation is most closely associated with the work of writers such as Thomas Szasz, Ivan Illich and Michel Foucault. Szasz (1961) was sharply critical of the regimes of psychiatry, in particular how psychiatric terminology and practice were being used to respond to social problems such as crime and poverty; Illich (1976) was critical of the whole medical industry/ bureaucracy and highlighted the perverse role of medicine in *creating* illness and injury (iatrogenesis) through inappropriate and incompetent interventions; Foucault saw the institutions, techniques and discourses of medicine, along with the penal and other state systems, as a means of surveilling and controlling populations. The level and efficacy of such surveillance has only increased as holistic medicine has become more favoured. A whole range of lifestyle, social and even spiritual factors is now taken into account and subjected to comment, intervention and control. This has contributed to the expansion of medicalisation.

One part of life that has become increasingly medicalised and has attracted the attention of many sociologists is that of childbirth (Hyde *et al.*, 2004, pp.210–216).

The discipline of obstetrics excluded and marginalised traditional midwifery practices, in particular through the monopolisation of specific technologies such as forceps. In the process female practitioners were replaced by men (McDonnell, 1997, p.70). The male-dominated profession of obstetrics has used a powerful discourse of risk and safety to exercise control over both women giving birth and midwives. It is argued, for example, that doctor-controlled hospital births are 'safer' than midwife-controlled home births, though evidence for this is contentious to say the least (Hyde et al., 2004, pp.214–215). In an Irish study Hyde (1997) shows not only how medicine has 'taken over' the process of childbirth itself, but argues that the medical profession also makes moral judgments on the circumstances of pregnancy, particularly in relation to 'unmarried mothers', and justifies these on medical grounds. This then affects the interpretation of events such as post-natal depression or whether or not a baby should be given up for adoption. In Hyde's study, women were seen to be unable to decide what was in their own best interests, so medical staff, particularly 'paternalistic' doctors, attempted to impose processes and activities (like seeing a social worker) upon them. This was related to class and age. Hyde concludes that, along with other discourses such as economics and religion, 'medicine at least plays a part in the maintenance of social order around social arrangements for childbearing' (1997, p.123).

More recently there has been a focus on the shift from medicalisation to what has been termed 'biomedicalisation' (Clarke et al., 2003, cited in Hyde et al., 2004, p.208). This refers to the extension of medico-scientific control from the 'external' world to the internal, molecular and genetic level of the human organism. Scientists and medical researchers, in particular through the development of the human genome programme, increasingly have the ability to manipulate and determine 'life' itself. Genetic screening and gene therapy, if pursued within the current socio-political structures of medicine, are likely to re-focus attention onto individual responsibility for health and well-being, at the expense of more structural social and environmental factors (Hyde et al., 2004, pp.207–210).

Professionalisation

The issue of the professionalisation of health care is very much linked to that of medicalisation. Professionalisation is the process whereby an occupational group is able to claim special status for itself, for example through access to special knowledge or training, a monopoly over certain practices and the ability to exclude competing groups. The outcome is a greater measure of prestige, power and income. By the early twentieth century medicine had achieved dominance of the health field in North America, most countries of Europe and Australia (Daniel, 1998, p.209).

Medicine has been able to create and sustain its professional status through a variety of strategies. The key process is that of *closure*: the ability to keep others out of the field of operation of the professional group. The most effective way to do this is through a process of registration, backed up by legislation. This requires the state to give legal backing to a range of occupational practices (Davis and George, 1993, p.209):

- access to restricted substances (for example, prescription drugs)
- direct access to clients (fees-for-services)
- control over content of education and training
- self-regulation
- control of all others in the field.

Strategies to secure public acquiescence with the claim for professional status have largely been made through appeals to science and reason, according to the biomedical model. At the same time, the knowledge must retain a level of opacity and mystique as to render it inaccessible to others.

The development of professional power does not rest only on securing rights over knowledge and practice — it is also crucially based on interactive relationships such as *trust*. As Daniel points out, if we do not accord a doctor or nurse trust they have little power over us. Of course, the relationship of trust is built very much on the types of knowledge that are at stake (1998, p.212):

> The complexity with which the expert [doctor, specialist] deals is typically baffling and alarming in the risks it poses. Trust reduces the client's apprehension of external complexity and uncertainty by substituting an inner confidence in the simplification of control held out by the expert.

Many of the accoutrements of professional practice — the framed degree in the consultant's office, the letters after the name, the calm demeanour, the conservative dress — are props that aid in the building of a trusting relationship. At the same time numerous distractions, such as disagreements over appropriate care, personal or social factors (such as ethnicity, dirty fingernails) or situational factors (a run-down office, a rude receptionist), can rapidly erode the relationships of trust that are so difficult to create. Access by clients to alternative sources of information, for example, health information on the Internet, can also threaten the trust relationship. Trust is also sustained by the discipline itself: our belief in medicine as a rigorous, *scientific* practice that strives for the most effective outcome; and its *ethical* basis, our belief that a doctor will not intentionally harm us.

Nursing

In contemporary Ireland a particularly interesting site for the observation of professionalisation in medicine is the field of general nursing. The process of professionalisation has created an opportunity — and a dilemma — for this key group that accounts for 40 per cent of the Irish health workforce (Dwyer and Taaffe, 1998, p.237). Nursing is an almost exclusively female occupation — only 8 per cent of nurses are men. Indeed, it has been one of the few secure professional careers open to women until very recently. Irish nurses have historically been recruited from middle-class and farming backgrounds and are well educated. Religious orders have played a very significant role in the development of nursing and in recruitment and training.

While medical practice has become the dominant profession within the health-care system, nursing has historically been subordinated. Unlike most doctors, nurses work under supervision, for wages and for fixed hours, usually in a fixed location. They lack real autonomy. They have also faced considerable gender discrimination and stereotyping within the workplace and the industry. As Davis and George remark (1993, p.210): 'the emergence of nursing as a full-time occupation has occurred within a framework of gender inequality which has led to the subordination of nursing in the health-care occupational hierarchy, and resistance to attempts to change it.' McCarthy (1997, p.176) reflects on how Irish nursing has been affected by the particular vision of femininity espoused by the founder of modern nursing, Florence Nightingale:

> It is true to say that Ms. Nightingale's ideas of vocation, discipline, diligence and obedience lived on in Irish nursing up to the 1970s and some remnants may still remain. They were perpetrated through an outdated method of education which included personal training and schools of nursing set within the hospital culture. The effects can be seen within the profession itself and in social appreciation and expectation. They have affected professional growth, and inhibited roles, education, accountability and management.

Historically, nurses have been largely excluded from management and policy-making positions but more recently have sought to escape such subordination by adopting a strategy of professionalisation.

The dramatic changes in recent times in the nature of nursing have contributed greatly to the thrust towards professional status. There has been considerable specialisation, with the emergence of numerous specialties within nursing, such as critical care, midwifery, oncology, anaesthetic and A and E (accident and emergency) nurses, to name just a few. Nurses now work with highly expensive and sophisticated technology, with complex medications and procedures and with a high level of autonomy and decision-making ability.

The changes in nursing have led to efforts to change the nature of nurse training, now increasingly carried out through the third-level education sector, and to develop an autonomous body of nursing knowledge, including a sociological component (Porter, 1997). This has not been without its difficulties, given the hostility of the existing medical professions and the lack of development in the field in the past. The shift towards the creation of a professional discourse for nursing has been accompanied by an increased use of industrial muscle. Unthinkable in the past, nurses have increasingly threatened and carried out industrial action, and have resolutely pursued their claims through the industrial relations systems.

There are signs that the professionalising efforts of nursing are beginning to pay dividends. This may mean an increasingly professional and managerial role for nurses and there is some evidence that this is taking place in the Irish health system (Dwyer and Taaffe, 1998, p.250). In 1998 the Irish government published the *Report of the Commission on Nursing*, a response to increasing industrial unrest in the nursing sector. Its recommendations in relation to a range of matters, from grading to education and training, have subsequently been implemented. Nursing education is now at honours degree level, professional clinical pathways have been established and nursing is increasingly represented in the management structures of the HSE. The development of an indigenous body of theoretical knowledge has proven to be more problematic: Hyde *et al.* (2004, p.246) claim that this 'represents the single most difficult challenge for those aspiring to full professional status for nurses'.

However, while there is evidence of some success in raising the power of nurses, the strategy has created some of its own difficulties. The change in the status of nurses may mean some dilemmas for the emerging profession (McAdam, 2004). The shift in educational status may mean that the traditional hierarchies within medicine will need to be confronted. Will university-trained nurses be content to adopt the subordinate role of their hospital-trained predecessors, or will the improved status of nurses mean the emergence of additional levels of assistants and technicians, as is already the case in many countries? How will patients respond to nurses that may be more focused on technology and management than on the more traditional caring skills? Will the emerging discourse of professional nursing simply ape the biomedical model, or will it provide for a more holistic and patient-centred model of health care?

FUTURE CHALLENGES

During the last fifty years the major social questions in relation to the body, health and illness in Ireland have changed dramatically. In the 1950s the issues were about the control and eradication of infectious diseases such as TB and polio. The major challenge was to build a modern public-health infrastructure on the base of an often-despised system that had grown out of the workhouses of the eighteenth and nineteenth centuries. The major challenges for medicine in the years to come are posed by new medical technologies ranging from human genome marking to artificial body parts grown from embryonic stem cells. The challenges are financial and ethical and have the capacity to fundamentally alter our notions of the body, health and illness and the very nature of the self.

In the Irish context, particular ethical challenges have been raised by the way that technological advance has led to a redefinition of 'life' in the areas of the 'conceptive technologies' (for example, IVF) and the life-sustaining technologies (for example, life-support machines). Such technologies force us to consider issues about life, death and medicine that were formerly implicit. They 'reorder the boundaries between culture and nature and they raise fundamental philosophical questions about biological contingency. They alter the concept of the body itself' (McDonnell, 1997, pp.71–2). When life is dependent on a respirator, how then do we define death? Questions then arise about the right to die and the possibility of a 'good' death. Similarly, reproductive technologies raise legal, ethical and social dilemmas in relation to motherhood, the role of women and the nature of the human embryo.

Another major challenge relates to the management of the health-care system. International trends reflect a tendency for the proportion of national resources consumed by health care to expand. In some ways Ireland benefits from this trend: the spectacular success of the impotency drug Viagra in 1998 (the main ingredient for which is manufactured in Ringaskiddy in Co. Cork) is but an indicator of the substantial income industries located in Ireland derive from global health-care expenditure. But the spiralling costs of health-care provision also place strains on the Irish exchequer and there are major challenges in delivering efficient and effective health care to an ageing population. Increased efficiency and rationalisation may lead to a depersonalisation of health care, with the emergence of what Ritzer (1996, pp.43–5) terms 'assembly line medicine' — offering 'Docs-in-a-box'.

The dual tendencies of holism and biomedicine will continue to contend for public acceptance and support. The acute hospital sector, increasingly sophisticated and high-tech, will demand a growing share of resources. At the same time, people are increasingly turning to alternative therapies and practitioners. There are demands for a community-based approach to health that embraces a more preventative role, focusing on health promotion rather than cure. It is likely that trends towards 'self-care' will continue to intensify, with an ever greater interest in dietary matters, cosmetic surgery and exercise regimes. There is also an increasing recognition that control of environmental factors, from noise pollution to farm chemicals, is crucial in the maintenance of health. Overall, shifts in public images of health will also provide challenges of shifting resources, and a threat to the entrenched power and status of some professional groups, as well as providing opportunities for the emergence of new types of practitioners, such as physical therapists and various types of counsellors. Health, illness and the body will continue to provide a fascinating area of research for sociologists. And sociologists have the potential to shape a health-care system that is of benefit to all.

11

Crime and deviance

For many Irish people one of the most significant perceived social changes over the past thirty years or so has been in the extent and nature of crime. This chapter explores that perception. Discussing the topic from a sociological perspective allows us to raise some questions about change in Irish society, as well as about how sociologists and others more directly concerned with problems of order and social control, think about and define crime. A sociological approach challenges much of the received wisdom in this field, especially in relation to the apparent increase in crime rates. It also questions the very definition of crime and raises issues about the links between crime and social inequality.

Crime has long been of interest to sociologists, not only because it is recognised as a major social issue, but also because it reflects much about the condition of society itself. This insight goes back at least to Durkheim, who was particularly interested in examining rates of crime and how they varied between different societies or in the same society at different times. He argued that the rate of crime in any society reflected the balance it had managed to achieve between *individualism* (encouragement and approval of efforts towards individual self-realisation) and *social regulation* (the imposition on the individual of group rules and values). In theory, a society that has got the balance right would display a 'normal' rate of crime. In practice, however, most societies have abnormal levels of crime — either too low, when there is too much regulation of the individual by society, or (something we are probably more familiar with) too high, when individualism becomes uncontrolled.

Durkheim's ideas remain very influential in the sociology of crime. He reversed the common assumption of criminologists that we need only study 'social factors' as part of the 'explanation' of crime; he stressed that crime itself was profoundly social. He also demolished the idea that societies can ever be crime-free or that this is even a meaningful aspiration to have. He introduced the counter-intuitive idea that it is just as important to study a very low crime rate in a society as it is a very high one. We suggest that this is a very useful insight if we are trying to understand recent patterns of crime in Irish society.

Durkheim's interpretation of crime rates is queried by many other sociologists even when they accept his core idea that the nature and extent of crime in society is a good indicator of social, cultural and economic conditions. Many suggest that crime rates are best seen as an indicator of social inequality, where high crime levels reflect high levels of inequality. This is not to suggest that there is a simple relationship between the two variables: as we show below, the links between crime rates and social inequality are complex and sometimes contradictory.

Sociological research on crime in Ireland has to date been quite limited though with a marked increase in research since the late 1990s. Most research takes the form of analysis of official crime statistics and is mainly concerned to establish levels of crime and how they change over time. To a lesser extent, researchers have also tried to show how crime is socially distributed in Ireland in terms of both criminal actors and victims of crime. Very little research has been published on other dimensions of the crime issue, all of which have now become major public issues within Irish society, such as white-collar crime, the operation of the Irish criminal justice system, the routine policing practices of An Garda Síochána, the operations of the courts or the social processes of imprisonment. This situation seems likely to change for the better as there now appears to be a greater willingness amongst such institutions to facilitate research and to open themselves up to public enquiry and debate.

These developments may indicate some profound changes in the beliefs in contemporary Irish society about the nature of authority and how it should be exercised. In this chapter we address a more limited set of issues to do with crime, primarily relating to crime rates. These are used as a basis to examine some aspects both of Irish society and of how sociologists study crime. (O'Mahony, 2002, provides a comprehensive overview of issues in relation to crime and justice in Ireland.) We have stressed at a number of points in this book that, given Ireland's position as a culturally and economically dependent society, it is important for Irish sociologists to deconstruct or reflect upon the practice of sociology itself. Thus, much of our discussion deals with the complexity of the notion of crime and the various ways that it has been researched and studied.

CRIME IN IRISH SOCIETY

We open with a fairly straightforward discussion of the extent of crime and of recent trends in relation to crime in Irish society. It is often said that crime is a serious social problem in Ireland — is this claim accurate, or is it more true that it is the *fear of crime* that is a serious and increasing social problem? These questions are difficult to answer, the more so because data on crime in Ireland is limited. The key source has been the Garda Síochána *Annual report on crime*. Like all official statistics on crime, this is subject to a number of ambiguities (see below) that make its interpretation quite problematic. However, the official crime statistics are exhaustively discussed in McCullagh (1996) and O'Mahony (1993), who draw some guarded conclusions.

Figure 11.1 Indictable crimes in Ireland, 1950–2006

Year	Indictable/Headline Offences and Murders Recorded	
	Indictable/Headline Offences Recorded	Number of Murders
1950	12,231	9
1955	11,531	4
1960	15,375	3
1965	16,736	7
1970	30,756	11
1975	48,387	23
1980	72,782	21
1985	91,285	25
1990	87,658	17
1995	102,484	43
2000	73,276	39
2001	86,633	52
2002	106,415	52
2003	103,360	45
2004	98,964	37
2005	102,258	62
2006*	103,710	66 *provisional

(# The term 'indictable' was replaced by 'headline' in 2000. The range of offences covered is broadly similar.)

Source: http://www.cso.ie/statistics/headline_offences.htm

In recent years around about 600,000 offences per annum have been 'known to the gardaí'. Over 80 per cent of these (half a million) are 'non-indictable offences' — misdemeanours not thought serious enough to warrant trial by jury but which can be summarily dealt with by a district court. While these crimes are generally not seen as serious, they can include offences that have a major impact, such as drink-driving, joyriding and some assaults (O'Mahony, 2002, p.111). The majority of summary offences are traffic offences like speeding and driving without tax or insurance. Of approximately 100,000 'indictable offences' recorded annually since the early to mid-1980s, over 95 per cent have been property crimes. Some of these 'offences against property with violence', such as burglary, robbery or arson, might be regarded as relatively more serious but still did not include violence against people. No more than 2 per cent of all crimes recorded were 'crimes against the person' — murder, manslaughter, rape, wounding and assault. The figure for indictable or 'headline' crimes remained fairly stable at just over 100,000 per annum for the period 1995 to 2005 (Figure 11.1). As O'Connell (2002, p.117) notes, this is against a background of a steadily increasing population over the same period, so that in effect the per capita rate has declined. While there has been concern in relation to the rise in the homicide rate (O'Connell, 2002, p.120), the official statistics suggest that violent crime is at a very low level in

Ireland. The statistics indicate that the level of violent crime is about half the US rate, a third of the EU average and a quarter of that for Denmark or England and Wales (O'Mahony, 2002, p.111).

We might conclude that, contrary to the impression given by much public and political commentary, Irish crime statistics do not give great cause for alarm, but it is noticeable that when experts on crime make that sort of claim in public they are generally received with hostility. Most Irish people appear to be committed to the idea that to have any crime at all is a cause for alarm. The widespread expectation that we should be trying to, and could, achieve a crime-free society can itself be treated as an appropriate object of research. It seems plausible to suggest that the genuine indignation many Irish people express over the level of crime is linked to the powerful view of Irish society as a *community*, or 'community of communities' (see Chapter 5). Thus to rob or steal from others is an offence against neigh-bourliness that threatens collective solidarity and undermines our self-construction as a homogeneous cultural group (Irish media focus on the alleged criminality of refugees reflects this, as pointed out by Pollack, 1999). But there has been very little research carried out into the beliefs and interpretations about crime held by ordinary Irish people, so this argument must remain somewhat speculative.

To return to our focus on official statistics, it might be argued that a real justification for public concern about crime is afforded by the observable trends. These indicate that, in the three decades from the 1960s to the 1990s, there was a significant and quite dramatic expansion in the quantity of recorded crime. Thus, as indicated in Figure 11.1, the number of indictable offences rose from about 15,000 in 1960; to 31,000 in 1970; to nearly 73,000 a decade later. By 1995 the levels had reached those that currently pertain. Thus we can see a ten-fold increase in the serious crime rate over the forty years from 1955 to 1995, at a time when the population increased by just 25 per cent. But in the period 1995–2005 the population rose by nearly 18 per cent while the incidence of reported indictable crime rate was virtually unchanged. When the change in population is taken into account, crime rates have been remarkably stable over the period 1981–2005, notwithstanding fluctuations and variations in relation to particular types of criminal activity.

Many people argue that even if crime itself has not been increasing greatly in the last ten years the real problem and cause for concern is the growth in *violent* crime. O'Connell (2002, p.120) notes about a 50 per cent increase in homicides: the average annual rate from 1972 to 1991 was about 34; this increased to an average of nearly 51 for the years 1995 to 1998. This level has been maintained for the period 2000–2006. Therefore we can see that trends in both homicide and serious crime more generally have remained quite stable. Compared to other European countries, rates for homicide (Figure 11.2) and serious crime (Figure 11.3) are still very low (as with all crime statistics, such figures need to be treated with a considerable degree of caution: the definition of 'serious crime' in particular may vary considerably across states). Yet in two periods, the mid-1990s and the mid-2000s, there have been strong public perceptions of a dramatic escalation in crime. These may be related to high-profile 'gangland killings', but also to periods of strong political and media interest in crime (McCullagh, 2004).

Figure 11.2 Homicides per 100,000 people — Europe

	2000	2001	2002	2003	% change 2000–2003
Albania	17.5	14.9	11.7	12.6	–28
Armenia	4.2	4.0	3.6	3.7	–12
Austria	2.3	1.9	2.1	1.8	–24
Belgium	6.5	7.2	7.7	8.4	28
Bulgaria	6.5	6.2	5.5	5.3	–18
Croatia	6.7	6.1	6.0	5.3	–21
Cyprus	1.5	2.0	1.0	3.5	141
Czech Republic	2.7	2.3	2.3	2.3	–17
Denmark	4.0	3.7	3.9	4.1	4
Estonia	13.7	12.0	11.4	12.4	–9
Finland	9.8	10.7	10.2	9.2	–6
France	3.9	4.2	4.3	3.9	0
Georgia	9.6	10.5	10.4	10.6	10
Germany	3.8	3.5	3.5	3.4	–11
Greece	2.7	2.6	2.2	2.3	–13
Hungary	3.5	4.0	3.6	3.8	7
Iceland	1.8	2.1	1.7	0.3	–81
Ireland	**1.4**	**1.4**	**1.4**	1.3	–7
Italy	3.9	3.8	3.9	3.9	0
Lithuania	10.9	10.4	8.6	10.3	–6
Luxembourg	13.9	11.2	13.5	12.9	–7
Malta	2.1	3.1	4.3	3.3	60
Moldova	9.3	9.3	9.0	7.6	–19
Netherlands	10.9	11.0	11.2	11.4	5
Poland	3.7	3.7	3.4	3.0	–20
Portugal	...	...	...	...	...
Romania	5.7	6.1	5.4	5.1	–11
Russia	21.7	23.0	22.2	21.9	1
Slovakia	2.6	2.4	2.4	2.7	2
Slovenia	4.0	3.2	3.9	2.9	–28
Spain	3.0	3.1	3.2	3.2	9
Sweden	...	...	...	...	...
Switzerland	2.2	2.4	2.9	2.5	13
Ukraine	...	...	...	...	...
UK: England & Wales	3.0	3.3	3.5	3.3	...
UK: Northern Ireland	10.2	12.8	16.5	9.0	...
UK: Scotland	13.7	15.6	17.8	16.2	18
Mean	6.6	6.6	6.6	6.3	
Median	4.0	4.0	4.1	3.9	
Minimum	1.4	1.4	1.0	0.3	
Maximum	21.7	23.0	22.2	21.9	

(*Source:* WODC, 2006, p.39)

Both O'Mahony and McCullagh, however, looking at trends in violent crime over a longer time period, argue that the claim that Irish society is becoming increasingly violent or crime-ridden is unfounded. Describing the pattern of trends in 'crimes against the person' from 1973 to 1991, O'Mahony (1993, p.36) points out that it would be more accurate to say that levels of violent crime in Ireland prior to 1995 had been very low:

> The graph has the rough shape of a hump-backed bridge, indicating that the number of such crimes climbed steadily for the first half of this period and then as steadily declined in the second half. The total of such crimes was 1,655 in 1973 and rose to a maximum of 2,478, almost exactly 50 per cent more, in 1981, but then progressively declined to a figure of only 1,435 in 1991. Astoundingly and totally contrary to the current public perception of crime and views on the prevalence of violence and brutality, the figure for 1991 is the lowest for any year in the whole study period. According to these figures there appears to be less violent crime against the person today than for a long period past.

Further evidence that Irish crime rates do not reflect a major social problem might be found in comparisons with other societies in Europe. Cross-cultural or comparative analyses of crime patterns, pioneered by Durkheim at the end of the nineteenth century, were relatively neglected during most of the twentieth century and have only recently begun to command attention and support again. Comparative researchers nowadays are much more aware than Durkheim was of the difficulties attached to official statistics in general and the particular problems of trying to compare statistics across countries that have different ways of counting, categorising and recording crimes (O'Connell, 2002). Nevertheless, it is fairly safe to conclude that from 1950 on, and particularly since around the mid-1960s, most European countries experienced a steady increase in the level of crime. Ireland is not in any way exceptional in this. In 1950, Sweden and the Federal Republic of Germany, for example, already had official annual crime rates of around 2,000 reported crimes for every 100,000 in the population, while England and Wales, France and the Netherlands had rates of around 1,000 per 100,000 population. By 1988, Sweden's crime rate had risen to around 11,000 per 100,000 population and in the other four countries the rate was around 6–7,000 with France having the lowest rate (Heidensohn and Farrell, 1991). If we put the Irish crime figures into this context, it is clear that our rise in crime started from a much lower level (around 430 per 100,000 population in the 1950s) and — at around 2,700 offences per 100,000 people — is still much lower today than in many European countries (Figure 11.3). While most Irish sociological discussions of crime focus on explaining the rise in crime rates since the 1960s, perhaps what most needs to be explained, or what is most exceptional about the Irish case, is the comparatively *low* level of crime that has persisted throughout this period, despite an overall rise in European crime rates.

Figure 11.3 Offences per 100,000 population — Europe

	2000	2001	2002	2003	% change 2000–2003
Albania	150	122	142	165	10
Armenia	396	379	401	369	−7
Austria	6906	6428	7260	7881	14
Belgium	9747	9481	9886	9784	0
Bulgaria	1773	1769	1780	1729	−2
Croatia	1550	2197	2273	2424	56
Cyprus	575	592	622	944	64
Czech Republic	3812	3494	3630	3490	−8
Denmark	9447	8837	9145	9013	−5
Estonia	4189	4270	3918	3968	−5
Finland	10259	9964	10017	10343	1
France	6352	6808	6865	6605	4
Georgia	253	330	352	369	46
Germany	7622	7734	7902	7976	5
Greece	3496	4153	4409	4158	19
Hungary	4446	4607	4173	4110	−8
Iceland	6613	6512	6735	6018	−9
Ireland	**1933**	**2259**	**2743**	**2634**	**36**
Italy	3822	3741	3852	4236	11
Lithuania	2254	2174	1999	2352	4
Luxembourg	5200	5092	5778	5728	10
Malta	4364	4065	4326	4489	3
Moldova	864	854	819	697	−19
Netherlands	8207	8476	8825	8530	4
Poland	3278	3597	3635	3799	16
Portugal	3515	3583	3753	3983	13
Romania	1576	1518	1393	1237	−21
Russia	2012	2033	1739	1906	−5
Slovakia	1645	1722	1985	2067	26
Slovenia	3363	3719	3839	3810	13
Spain	2307	2534	2582	2377	3
Sweden	13615	13304	13790	13995	3
Switzerland	3729	3775	4184	4481	20
Ukraine	1159	1061	958	1188	3
UK: England & Wales	9917	10552	11220	11241	...
UK: Northern Ireland	7125	8275	8399	7515	...
UK: Scotland	9912	9879	10032	9639	−3
Mean	4524	4592	4740	4736	
Median	3729	3741	3852	3983	
Minimum	150	122	142	165	
Maximum	13615	13304	13790	13995	

(*Source:* WODC, 2006, p.37)

Explaining trends in crime: modernisation or expanded capitalism?

The increase in crime in Ireland, which started around the late 1950s and soared dramatically during the 1970s, came just as Irish society was starting to modernise and, particularly, to industrialise. Sociologists argue that this is more than a coincidence, that modernisation inevitably brings a rise in crime. In a sense, increased crime is the price we have to pay for the affluence and individual freedom we enjoy in modern society. But sociologists vary considerably in how they explain the connection between modernisation and rising crime.

One argument is that it is the experience of change itself — especially when rapid and externally imposed as in many developing societies — that leads to increased crime. Change produces social disorganisation, with disruption of societal values and of the institutions and methods of social control. In the transition from a 'traditional' to a 'modern' society, the shared values that maintained order formerly are eroded but new values have not yet developed to replace them. As a consequence there is no consensus about how people should behave. As people become more mobile, especially as they migrate from rural areas into cities, the old institutions of family, church and local community lose their capacity to restrain behaviour while new institutions of control are not yet fully established. Social dislocation is widely experienced as old jobs disappear and people have to move in search of new ones. In other words, modernisation, like any type of social change, brings into being a temporary (though possibly quite long-lasting) period of social disorganisation when people are left without clear values or controls; it is therefore not surprising that during this time the crime rate soars.

Behind this account we can detect some interesting underlying assumptions. It assumes, for example, that people need to be closely guided and regulated by society if they are to behave in a moral or sociable way — left to themselves they are naturally anarchic and violent. This is a powerful argument that turns up very frequently in discussions about crime not just in sociology, but also in mass media treatments of crime. But does it really make much sense of either the European or the Irish experience? In Europe, as we have seen, rising crime rates occurred in most countries from the 1960s but they have been particularly marked in those that, from an Irish vantage point, we would regard as already modern, and advanced. This is odd, for if rises in crime are associated with the *transition to* modernity, the crime rates in these countries should be levelling off and stabilising, to reflect a new 'organisation' of values and a social control system that reinstates social regulation.

Moreover, the Irish experience of industrialisation and economic development in the last fifty years has not involved massive *social disorganisation* — certainly not in comparison to the experiences of many 'late industrialising' societies. In Ireland industrialisation was dispersed throughout the countryside rather than concentrated in cities. Dublin's population did grow substantially, but this was due more to indigenous growth than to massive immigration from rural areas; those who did in-migrate from the countryside were mainly educated people moving into secure middle-class jobs. Irish society did experience rapid social change, but not the social disorganisation or breakdown of 'the traditional social order' that could satisfactorily explain the rapid rise in crime. Only certain groups in the population did, perhaps, experience severe dislocation: those who emigrated (and who have long made up a disproportionate number of prisoners in British jails) and the urban working class whose jobs disappeared as older industries declined, and who were moved out of the centre of Dublin as parts of the city were redeveloped during the 1970s economic boom. Disorganisation theories *may* help to explain the predominance of youths from new outer suburban estates who passed through the criminal justice system in the 1970s and 1980s, but they do little to explain general trends in crime over the period.

It is interesting in this context to compare Ireland and a number of post-Communist countries in Europe. These countries saw a surge in official crime rates — in a more compressed time period than was the case in Ireland — after the fall of Communism at the end of the 1980s. Attempts to explain this rise by sociologists and criminologists living in these countries have also drawn heavily on theories of social and cultural disorganisation (Parker, 1993). While these experts are well aware of the oppressive nature of the state security apparatus during the Communist era, the restrictions on citizens' rights of movement within or across borders and the highly developed powers of surveillance, what comes through in their accounts is in many cases almost a nostalgia for the controlled and organised nature of social life in that earlier period, with its much lower rate of crime. Parker reports similar accounts from police and justice officials and from Czech politicians, people for whom the change in regime had in many cases meant a loss of security and certainty about their work, and often also a loss in social power or status. His study helps to remind us that explanations for crime often reflect the situation and concerns of the person doing the explaining as much as any objective features of the crime rate. Regret for the loss of some aspects of the past, or fears about the future, seem particularly likely to give rise to theories that treat change in itself as responsible for pathological rates of crime.

McCullagh (1996) discusses an alternative explanation of the connection between modernisation and rising crime rates (put forward originally by Rottman, 1984) that is concerned less with the fact of social change in itself and more with the type of society that we are changing into at the time. This has been called a *social structural explanation* (in contrast to a 'social disorganisation' one) as it emphasises that the modernisation of society brings into being a new social structure, one that is organised in particular around *property*: ownership of property, social status based on property and careers in relation to property. Modernisation in Ireland opened up a range of new, legitimate career opportunities in Irish society during the 1960s and 1970s based around the production, sale, advertising, management and protection of property. But it also opened up a range of *illegitimate* career opportunities to do with property. In modern, urban, industrial society, property has become more widespread, more visible, more transportable and more desirable, so that opportunities and motives for property crime inevitably increase. This explains why even in highly developed societies the crime rate continues to rise. Property keeps on expanding, taking on new forms and becoming more highly valued in these societies.

In addition to showing how the new society is structured around property, we need to address the issue of *inequality* in access to property. Modern capitalist society has been described as a society that systematically encourages every person within it to aspire to property ownership, to a higher standard of living and increased consumption; but at the same time, as it is so unequal, it systematically prevents certain groups within the society from realising these aspirations in legitimate ways. These conditions — which the American sociologist Robert Merton, following Durkheim, called 'anomic' — seem to provide the best possible chance of producing rates of property crime that are very high and that are particularly associated with the lower working class. Note that this way of explaining crime in society rests on rather different assumptions about human nature to those of the disorganisation thesis. It assumes that people are not naturally aggressive and selfish, but that these qualities are fostered in them by an anomic society — one which encourages people to believe that only wealth and consumption can give their lives meaning and worth but which nonetheless denies many of them the chance to ever achieve these goals. As a consequence, issues of income distribution, and particularly access to employment opportunities, may have a particularly important role in shaping the nature and extent of crime in modern societies.

The social distribution of crime in Ireland

Merton's *anomie theory* of crime rests on the claim that most crime is committed by the most marginalised and excluded people within the capitalist class system. It prompts us to ask how crime is socially distributed in Ireland, that is: what sort of people, typically, are victims of crime and what sort of people are perpetrators? The media often suggest that the main victims of crime in Ireland are the elderly and poor, perhaps particularly old people living in rural areas. We might think that crime is largely a matter of the disadvantaged preying on the disadvantaged as people in poor areas are attacked and robbed by their own neighbours or by those from a similarly deprived social background. A victim survey by Breen and Rottman (1985) indicated that the common perception was mistaken: they found crime to be an overwhelmingly urban phenomenon, concentrated in Dublin. The most likely to be victims were those in the higher social classes (self-employed or white collar employees), generally younger (young middle-aged) and located in middle-class housing estates. These trends were supported by a subsequent survey (Watson, 2000) that also indicated specific gender patterns of victimisation: women were the most likely to be victims of theft, while men were more prone to being assaulted. Crimes related to vehicles helped to push the age profile of victims towards middle-age (being more likely to be car owners) but when this factor was removed from the analysis, it emerged that younger people (under 25) were disproportionately victimised. About a fifth of victims were institutions (mainly small businesses), while the other 80 per cent were individuals. The former were more likely to suffer from repeat victimisation. Similar patterns emerged in the most recent victimisation survey carried out by the Central Statistics Office (CSO, 2004b). In addition it was indicated that non-nationals had a higher experience of being victims of crime: not surprising as they tend to be in the younger, more urban categories.

It is less easy to describe the typical 'victimiser'. We have no 'self-report surveys' in Ireland that ask people to report if they have ever been involved in criminal behaviour; and the reports compiled by An Garda Síochána only give details on the minority (less than one-third) of crimes that result in detection and a conviction. A small number of studies exist that can shed some light on this; for example, Rottman's (1984) analysis of people 'apprehended' for indictable offences in the Dublin Metropolitan Area, while not fully generalisable, provides some striking information. Rottman found that most of these people were male (84 per cent), generally very young (one-quarter were under sixteen and a further half between seventeen and twenty), economically extremely marginal (80 per cent of the seventeen- to twenty-year-olds were unemployed and the rest were in unskilled or semi-skilled work) and drawn from very specific locations in Dublin that were at that time places of great physical and social deprivation.

O'Mahony's (1993; 1997) research on the inmates of Dublin's Mountjoy prison produced a picture of the 'typical Mountjoy male prisoner' — supported by subsequent research by Dillon (2001) — that is quite similar to the above: he is a little older than Rottman's group of 'apprehended offenders' (early to mid-twenties), from a large family, an early school leaver (probably having dropped out of school before the legal minimum leaving age), who has been unemployed for most of the period since and, when employed, has had unskilled and poorly paid work. Typically, Mountjoy male prisoners come from urban areas, especially from the Dublin inner city or from one of the poorer outer suburban areas such as Crumlin or Ballymun. Subsequent studies of other groups in custody have revealed similar patterns of deprivation, including family breakdown, school problems and substance abuse, amongst other factors (Kilkelly, 2006, pp.11–13). While we have to consider the possibility that some of these characteristics explain better why the person is in prison than why he broke the law (see below), it may be safe to conclude that typical offenders in Ireland come from extremely disadvantaged and marginalised groups.

The picture that emerges from both the official statistics and the small amount of available research could be summarised as follows: the bulk of the crime committed in contemporary Ireland is still relatively small-scale property crime and the property attacked is mainly that of younger middle-class people, while those who attack it are very young males from working-class backgrounds who have little chance of integrating into stable and rewarding jobs and lives. We might be tempted to conclude that in a society where the state has generally intervened to redistribute resources from those with little to those with quite a lot, crime offers an alternative resource redistribution from those with quite a lot to those with very little.

Explaining Ireland's low crime rate

To the social disorganisation and social structural theories outlined above, McCullagh (1996, pp.133–42) has added a third way to explain how crime is linked to processes of change and development. He argues that the pattern of change is best understood as a process not simply of the expansion and institutionalisation of capitalism, but of dependent development (see Chapter 3). He argues that *dependent development* has influenced Irish crime patterns in a number of ways. First, it generated new levels of affluence in Irish society that in turn, as Rottman argued, produced new opportunities for crime. Second, it created a group in society who are prepared to take advantage of these new opportunities (1996, p.136):

> As development has proceeded, increasing numbers of young working-class people have been marginalised to positions of almost permanent unemployment and disadvantage. In such situations crime becomes a mode of economic and social survival.

McCullagh emphasises that the opportunities created were not only opportunities for 'conventional' working-class crime. The increase in business activity as a result of development also created new opportunities to engage in white-collar and business crime. The issue of white-collar crime is very important and is discussed further below. Here we note only that McCullagh sees the increase in commercial and business crime as related to a third characteristic of dependent development — the weakness of the state. McCullagh (1996, p.135) suggests that peripheral and dependent development turns the state into 'a broker for international capital' with 'a deferential stance towards multinational companies'. Such states adopt a relaxed attitude to the regulation and policing of incoming corporations, for example, in the area of environmental pollution. The Irish state, McCullagh argues, was already finding it difficult to regulate the behaviour of indigenous business, making it doubly weak in the face of commercial crime.

McCullagh recognises that this explanation has not been tested out in any detail by research. Nevertheless, compared with the modernisation perspective, and even the 'development of modern capitalism' perspective of Rottman and Merton, it does promise a better grasp of how features specific to the Irish experience of development may have shaped the nature of crime in Irish society in recent decades. But it remains rather unclear in McCullagh's discussion just what it is about Irish crime rates that can be explained by the dependent development theory — a rise in the rate of crime? or a low rate of crime compared to countries whose development has not been constrained or formed by dependency? Arguably, the concept of dependent development *can* explain rather well why the crime rate in Ireland, despite marked increases in recent decades, remains consistently *low* compared to many other developed societies.

For example, societies that have experienced dependent development are often characterised by high rates of emigration: they import capital from core societies but export labour to them. Irish emigration statistics vary inversely, in an almost perfect correlation, with Irish crime statistics. When emigration rates are high, as in the 1950s or the second half of the 1980s, crime rates fall; when emigration rates are low, as in the 1970s or the late 1980s/early 1990s, crime rates increase. An explanation may be that crime rates tend to be related to the proportion of the population that is under approximately twenty-five years of age: when this is high, for example, if emigration outlets are blocked, the crime rate increases. This again suggests that crime is largely something engaged in by the young (or at least, young men) and that most people, given reasonable opportunities in life, 'grow out of' crime as they age.

There is a second and rather different way that McCullagh's argument could be used to explain why Ireland has a low crime rate. The rule-breaking behaviours that he suggests are encouraged under dependent development, particularly given the presence of a weak state, include breaches of health and safety or environmental regulations; illegal or marginally legal business and banking schemes; and corporate and individual strategies for tax evasion. In Ireland until very recently these have generally either not been treated as criminal offences or, if criminalised, have not been policed or prosecuted with the same vigour that is applied to 'ordinary' crime, even when practised on a fairly large scale and/or leading to considerable social harm. Thus, a rapid increase in these types of behaviour will not show up in official crime statistics and they will continue to reflect a society that appears much more consensual and orderly than it actually is.

This argument indicates the major problems that exist in how crime is defined and measured and casts doubt on whether crime rates, as measured by official statistics, are in any way meaningful phenomena for the sociologist to study. We explore some of the issues involved in the next section of this chapter but, before leaving this discussion, it may be worth considering a country that has attracted a good deal of attention from sociologists of crime in recent years, precisely because of its rather low official crime rate. If we wish to understand crime in Irish society, we might find it illuminating to draw comparisons not with America, or even with core countries in Europe, but with Japan. Though Japanese development history may not easily be summarised as dependent, many discussions of Japanese economic performance since the 1950s stress its distinctive cultural underpinnings. This distinctiveness is also widely seen as relevant to understanding its low levels of crime.

Bayley notes that the rate of serious crime in Japan is less than one-third that in America. For him this raises questions about how 'this orderliness has been achieved' (1991, p.169). Modernisation theory cannot explain it, for Japan is as 'fully as modern as the United States, transformed equally during the last century by processes of urbanisation, industrialisation and technological development'. It has a similar, if more historically recent, democratic political structure; and its legal system, if generally more lenient than the American, is very similar to it in form, 'hardly surprising since the Japanese system is the product of American reform after World War II, overlaying earlier borrowings from Germany and France' (1991, p.170). So what might explain the different levels of crime in the two societies?

Bayley suggests two highly significant features. First, Japanese society is more egalitarian, at least in terms of the distribution of wealth. The average income per capita is about the same in both countries but there is a much greater gap between high and low incomes in America than in Japan. Second, Japanese culture is characterised by 'mechanisms that are peculiar to Japan in their strength and extensiveness' (1991, p.172) which inhibit the impulse to crime. Bayley summarises these as 'propriety' (the voluminous and detailed rules about what is proper behaviour in every social situation that make the Japanese 'compulsively watchful about decorum'), 'presumption' (by that he means the acceptance of the presumptive right of immediate social groups — particularly family, school and workplace — to tell the individual how to behave, with the result that 'fitting in is the ultimate discipline in Japan') and 'pride' ('discipline is maintained in Japan because people take enormous pride in performing well the roles demanded of them'). Ultimately it is the 'cultural dynamic' constituted from these three mechanisms that for Bayley provides the strongest explanation of Japan's low crime rate. He acknowledges that from an American point of view, the low level of crime may be achieved at too high a price: as Durkheim earlier suggested, crime rates may be seen as 'pathologically low' as well as 'pathologically high' in the sense that they are the outcome of a degree of collective regulation of the individual that would be unacceptable to Western observers socialised within a culture that values individual self-determination above all else.

Bayley's analysis of crime rates in Japan suggests that Irish crime researchers might usefully investigate what it was about Irish cultural arrangements in the 1950s and 1960s that so effectively inhibited the impulse to crime. Moreover, such an approach might still pay dividends in addressing and explaining our current crime situation. But it would be important to bear in mind, as Durkheim originally argued in developing his concept of anomie, that such inhibitions are likely to be experienced differently in different social groups and may well bear much more heavily on lower than on higher social strata.

SOCIOLOGICAL APPROACHES TO CRIME

Of all the subjects that sociologists study, crime is particularly difficult to introduce in a simple way. It has generated much debate within sociology itself and within other disciplines with an interest in the area (like law, psychology, criminology) — not just about the empirical facts involved but about the concept of crime itself, how it should be defined and how it can be researched. Crime is also, as we noted above, an important political issue and there is always much public concern and talk about crime, which has helped to shape how sociologists have addressed it.

One way that sociologists have tried to clarify the topic, and to move away from a simple echoing of public concerns, has been to develop the concept of deviance. What is the relationship between deviance and crime? The former is a broader concept: it refers to behaviour that deviates from or breaks *any* social rule, whether of politeness (how close you should stand when having a conversation, not talking with your mouth full); of self-presentation (dress so that others can tell what gender you are); of property (do not take what does not belong to you); or of sexual orientation (do not become sexually involved with young children or with members of your own sex). It is obvious that deviance is an extremely wide concept — whenever we identify a social rule, we can identify behaviour that breaks that rule. Crime refers to a subcategory of deviance; it is behaviour that breaks a particular type of social rule, namely, those rules that in our society have been enshrined within and given the force of criminal law.

Studying crime as a social problem

Until the 1950s most sociologists took for granted that what they should study was, simply, crime: all they had to do was discover what sort of behaviour was prohibited under the criminal law of their country, and that defined what they were studying. Moreover, most early researchers in the field were motivated by a desire to respond to public concern about crime. The public defined crime as a major social problem about which something should be done, so sociologists and criminologists set out to study this social problem in the hope that, if they could discover its causes, they could help society to control or even eliminate it. Effectively, they allowed the public — or more accurately, the more powerful and vocal groups among the public — to define their topic and set their research agenda for them.

Much of this early work started from the assumption that crime is something done by *criminals*. As a result, what sociologists ended up studying was groups of convicted criminals, arguing that the cause of their criminal behaviour lay within the individuals themselves, something that made them different from other, law-abiding people. If they could find what it was that made criminals *different*, that would be the key step towards a solution to the problem of crime. The 'causes' that researchers looked for varied considerably and have been the subject of much lively debate. In the nineteenth century, it was common to look for *physical causes* of criminality. Thus, phrenologists argued that criminality could be detected in the shape of the skull or the size of the brain (Gould, 1997). This approach still manifests itself from time to time, for example, in the search for genetic differences between 'criminals' and 'normal people'. Other researchers looked more for *psychological defects*: people who took illegal drugs were (and indeed still commonly are) thought to suffer from personality defects of various sorts, such as a poorly developed super-ego, or excessive narcissism; or were people with 'addictive personalities'. Sociologists were particularly likely to look for defects in the *socialisation* or childhood upbringing or environment of the criminal.

What is striking about these approaches is that they all located the cause of crime as an individual defect or pathology within the individual criminal. They assumed a difference between people who break criminal laws and those who do not — or who have not been discovered to have done so. And it is in that simple point that the weakness of this approach to crime is revealed. People who break criminal laws do not equate with convicted criminals. Furthermore, it would be impossible to find any group of 'ordinary conformists' with whom we could compare convicted criminals because any selection from the general population is bound to include at least one person who has broken a criminal law but has not been charged with an offence. Nearly everybody in the ordinary law-abiding population has broken some law at some time in their lives.

Just as convicted criminals — that is, people with a *public identity* as a criminal — are not the same as 'all those in society who break the criminal law', we need also to note that official statistics on crime, such as those produced annually in Ireland by An Garda Síochána, do not include all crimes committed (O'Connell, 2002). The gardaí can only report a crime that is known to them, which generally means that some member of the public has told them about it. But the public is much more likely to report some types of crime than others — victim surveys indicate that people are more willing to report car-thefts, for example, than house burglaries, and that in general how likely they are to report any sort of theft depends on whether the objects stolen were insured and whether the insurance company insists that the police be informed. Also what people are prepared to report changes over time; rape and child sex abuse, for example, are much more likely to be reported nowadays than even ten years ago, while a couple of generations ago they were reported very rarely indeed.

Official statistics on crime, then, are not a simple snapshot of what is happening at a point in time, but are the outcome of a complex series of social interactions and processes (Tuthill, 2005; WODC, 2006). First, a member of the public has to report to the gardaí that a crime has been committed or the gardaí themselves need to detect the commission of a crime, a fairly rare event except for public order and traffic offences. Then the gardaí have to record the crime as a crime, and in many cases this does not happen, for a number of reasons. For example, for a long period 'domestic violence' was not treated as a crime. The reported crime may for administrative reasons be aggregated with a number of others. A crime may be detected and recorded as 'cleared up' or it may be 'written off' when a suspect admits to a number of crimes. The Director of Public Prosecutions may decide not to bring a case to court or a judge may dismiss a case for lack of evidence or on a legal technicality. Given this complex set of processes, we may conclude that what official statistics measure is not the 'rate of crime' in society, but rather the outcomes of a complex process of reporting and recording of crime. They tell us more, perhaps, about what other people do in responding to a crime than about what criminals do.

If official statistics only include a selection of all 'crimes' committed (and we are taking the perhaps unjustifiable step here of assuming that 'crime' has an objective existence outside of the processes that define it), it seems that official statistics on *criminals* (which tell us things like their age, gender, social class, or place of origin) are even less reliable. To 'officially' become a criminal, a person has to pass through a series of stages from arrest, to preparation of a case against them, to court appearances, and finally a guilty verdict and the recording of a conviction. At each stage there is a high drop-out rate which happens for a range of reasons that may have little to do with whether the person actually committed the offence or not. Moreover, those who come to the attention of the gardaí or are arrested or convicted are not a random sample of all criminal law breakers but a specific select social group: generally young, male, unemployed and from particular locations within urban areas. The *social* characteristics that distinguish these people from the rest of the population are far more striking than any alleged physical or psychological 'defects' they might carry.

Other objections can be made to studies of crime that equate it simplistically with breaking the criminal law: crime is, as was suggested above, a social construct. Criminal laws are not fixed or static — they vary between societies and change, sometimes quite radically, over time in the same society. What counts as a crime is thus *relative* to a particular time, place and culture. If the assumption that criminals are different from conforming people is hard to sustain, so is the assumption that crimes (and criminals) resemble each other. Why should burglars have anything in common with those who live off immoral earnings, or illegal phone-tappers share anything with rapists, other than that they have all been found to have broken a law? Similarly, if our concern is with behaviour that does *harm* to society, there is little reason to confine ourselves to the study of crime since much harmful behaviour is not criminalised and, in addition, there are 'crimes' that most people would feel are not really very harmful (such as keeping a dog without a dog licence). The criminal law produces a very narrow and biased measure of 'harmful rule-breaking': it concerns itself primarily with the sort of harmful behaviour the poor or the powerless are likely to engage in (particularly rather petty property theft) but is much less concerned with the sort the rich and powerful, or even the 'respectable', engage in.

Studying deviance as part of social order

For such reasons many sociologists largely abandoned the concept of crime and defined the object of their study as *deviance*. They set out to investigate any sort of rule-breaking that arouses public disapproval (for not all rule-breaking does) whether or not it was criminalised. The impetus for research was increasingly derived from within sociology rather than from the real or perceived demands of governments or policy-makers. The research effort was aimed at further understanding the problem of *social order*: how did people manage their social relationships; how did they make their social world meaningful and intelligible? In short, how was society organised in a routine, regular way so that we can usually explain what has taken place and what might happen next? Rule-*making* is obviously an important element in our attempts to make society 'orderly', but so is handling and dealing with rule-*breaking*, and the concept of deviance was a means towards researching these issues.

But the switch from 'crime' to 'deviance' did not deal with all the difficulties that faced those working in this area. Almost immediately they had to confront the issue of whose disapproval counts — if some members of society strongly disapprove of a certain type of behaviour (for example, sex before marriage) but others do not, should we regard the behaviour as deviant or not? Should sociologists simply endorse the view of the more 'respectable' and more powerful groups? It also became apparent that the same rule-breaking behaviour might be disapproved of and therefore deviant in one set of circumstances, but tolerated and therefore not deviant in another. For example, if you help yourself to stationery in a shop you are stealing, and deviant; but if you do so at work where such pilfering is seen as a perk of employment, you are not deviant. In grappling with such problems, sociologists of deviance, particularly those known as *labelling* theorists, made an interesting discovery: crime and deviance are not characteristics of individual rule-breakers, but result from the *reaction* of others to the rule-breaker. Whether they ignore, tolerate, disapprove or punish is crucial in determining whether someone achieves the social identity of a deviant, or criminal, or continues to live a life that is to all outward appearances one of conventional conformity.

This approach emphasises that deviance is *socially constructed* — partly from what the rule-breaker does (or is thought to have done) and partly from how others respond to that behaviour. There is no point then in searching for the causes of criminality *within* the individual. Personal characteristics might help to explain why a person broke a rule in the first place, but to explain how they went on to become a (labelled) criminal we must also investigate how society responds to and treats this sort of rule-breaking. This response, as noted earlier, can change over time and different subgroups may respond in different ways. If you smoke marijuana in one type of social setting, you may very quickly find yourself arrested and charged; in another type of setting you may be ignored. Deviance is the result of interaction between rule-breaker and witness and not merely the result of what the rule-breaker does.

A new research agenda on crime

Thinking of deviance as socially constructed led sociologists to develop a new and interesting research agenda. They asked:

How are official crime statistics created?
How do police practices influence how levels of crime are measured and announced to the public?

How is a small group of 'criminals' produced from a much larger initial pool of rule-breakers?
Is there something about the social background of 'criminals', or about how they present themselves to others, that leads police to suspect and arrest them, a jury to convict them and a judge to imprison them when others may escape these processes?

Does it make a difference to their future career if a rule-breaker is dealt with by the police, or by another agency such as psychiatry or social work?
In the United States the problem of illegal drug use is regarded as primarily the property of the police and is dealt with by lawcourts and prisons; in the Netherlands, substance abuse falls in the field of the medical and welfare agencies and is dealt with in different ways. Do these variations make a difference to the rule-breaker in terms of the sort of commitment she or he may develop to a further career in crime?

Increasingly we can bring into the picture the whole issue of *social control* — how society handles and manages crime — as well as the issue of crime itself.

CRIME AND INEQUALITY

Most research on crime, including much sociological research, takes for granted that crime is somehow connected with poverty, disadvantage or powerlessness. Some of the more interesting sociological theories of crime, such as Merton's reworking of Durkheim's anomie theory, provide us with convincing accounts of why criminals are drawn overwhelmingly from the most deprived groups in society. But sociologists of deviance have raised a number of questions about this presumed connection. Labelling theorists ask whether the poorest in society are the most prone to breaking the law, or whether they are the most prone to being *caught*: identified and publicly labelled as law-breakers. Marxists ask how we should understand the law in capitalist society: does it extend equal rights to all, or is it partisan and biased, primarily concerned to protect the interests of the powerful? Box (1983) and McCullagh (1995) suggest that sociology should ask not 'who commits most crime?' but 'who causes most social harm?' It may then find that much severely harmful behaviour is not even defined as crime or, if so defined, offenders are not subjected to criminal charges, proceedings or punishment. The behaviour that is most likely to escape the criminal justice system is white-collar crime.

White-collar crime in Ireland

The term 'white-collar crime' was coined by American criminologist Edwin Sutherland (1961 [1949] p.9) to refer to 'a crime committed by a person of respectability in the course of his occupation' in order to make a profit for or otherwise benefit his company or employer. It is also referred to as occupational crime — to differentiate it from 'street' crime. It may take a number of forms: there are crimes committed for personal gain, which a person can only carry out because they hold a particular occupational position. A teller may defraud a bank; a dentist carry out unnecessary dental work; or a farmer may claim subsidy payments for animals that he does not own. A second form of occupational crime (that originally defined by Sutherland) is that committed in the course of an occupation in order to benefit or further the corporate goals of an employer; this is now often called corporate crime. There are many crimes related to tax evasion, insurance fraud, breach of employment law and price-fixing: in some cases the line between such crimes and 'accepted business practice' can be difficult to discern. Further types of white-collar crime refer to those carried out by states (McCullagh, 2002): whether at a high level (such as the French government's bombing of the Greenpeace ship the *Rainbow Warrior*) or by state officials in the course of their employment (such as a planning official taking a bribe from a property developer).

McCullagh (1995, 1996) suggests two reasons why sociologists should be particularly interested in white-collar crimes. First, they are primarily 'crimes of the middle class' — not usually committed by people in disadvantaged or socially excluded situations. Second, they are crimes that are mainly marginal to public consciousness — our imagery of typical crimes or criminals does not usually embrace respectable businessmen engaged in fraud, negligence or misleading practices. Societal response to harmful or criminal behaviour varies greatly, so that while certain types of property theft receive great public attention and disapprobation, others are hardly noticed. McCullagh (2002, p.165) points out that the lack of public consciousness of white-collar crime in Ireland means that there is still very little information on its nature or extent, either within the Garda Síochána crime statistics or in the literature of sociology or criminology.

This situation may be changing rapidly. In Ireland, as in other countries such as Australia, public awareness of political and police corruption, industrial negligence, commercial fraud and professional malpractice is growing rapidly. In Ireland, this new public consciousness dates back at least to the discoveries of the so-called Beef Tribunal, set up in May 1991 to investigate claims of malpractices within the Goodman Group of beef-processing companies. It was alleged that these companies enjoyed excessive favours from the government and state departments. The Tribunal found evidence of occupational crime: the group was found to have '[abused] public funds on a large scale' by 'systematically taking meat that it was deboning under contract for the EC intervention system, meat that belonged to the EC, and packing it for its own commercial contracts with, for instance, the Tesco supermarket chain in England' (O'Toole, 1995, p.264). It also discovered evidence of corporate crime: the group '[contrived] to cheat the public of taxes' (O'Toole, 1995, p.281). However, no member of the Group was convicted of any criminal offence: indeed the only person prosecuted was a journalist, Susan O'Keeffe, for refusing to reveal her sources. Since the late 1990s the public proceedings of three further tribunals of inquiry, the McCracken, Moriarty and Flood/Mahon tribunals, and the Dáil's Public Accounts Committee, have reinforced public concern and anger over white-collar crime. Yet crime continues to be routinely portrayed in the popular media, and even in much academic discussion, as intimately connected with, and explained in terms of, experiences of poverty, disadvantage and social marginalisation.

How does this happen? McCullagh identifies three processes that operate to emphasise working-class crime and conceal or play down middle-class crime. First, the process of *law-making*. How laws are made has the effect of sanctioning some kinds of harmful behaviour while ignoring others. For McCullagh (1995, p.412) 'in Ireland the law has been written in such a way that the anti-social behaviour of those in business, corporate and commercial positions is inadequately regulated, or where it is regulated, it is generally not done so through the criminal law.' He illustrates this through a discussion of the Bantry Bay disaster of 1979, when a tanker discharging oil blew up and fifty people were killed. The subsequent inquiry into the disaster showed that these deaths were 'avoidable' yet no related criminal prosecutions ever followed. More recent examples, such as the outcome of the Beef Tribunal, appear to support his case.

The second process is that of *law enforcement*. Even where white-collar crimes are defined in law as crimes, enforcement tends to be selective and considerably less energetic than in the case of 'street' crimes. McCullagh notes that while the average larceny recorded by An Garda Síochána in 1993 involved less than £500 (€635), we find examples of corporate frauds that involve at least ten times that amount where criminal offences have been identified, but no prosecutions have followed. Tax evasion is a type of white-collar crime that is widespread among companies in Ireland but, though listed as a serious crime on the statute books, until recently few resources were put into policing it. Criminal sanctions have been used extremely rarely against corporate tax evaders and very few have been imprisoned. For McCullagh (1995, p.420) 'the situation with tax evasion can be summarised as being a common activity where the chances of non-detection are still significant and the risks of being criminally adjudicated are relatively minor.'

The third process is that of the *court system*. Research into the decision-making processes of Irish courts suggests that white-collar criminals, even in crimes aimed at personal benefit, such as embezzlement, are relatively unlikely to be convicted. If they are convicted, they are less likely to receive a prison sentence, or to have to serve it, than working-class 'professional' criminals are. Overall, McCullagh (1995, p.424) concludes, while there is 'compelling evidence that corporate and white-collar misbehaviour is a significant problem in Irish society', it can also be shown that it is systematically dealt with in a different way to working-class criminality. Middle-class crime largely escapes 'the stigma of criminality', and so has quite different effects on the future life of the offender and on the public perception of the seriousness of the offence. As McCullagh remarks (2002, p.158) 'there is a stark contrast between being a statistic in a health and safety report and being photographed coming down the steps of a courthouse in handcuffs'. The production of working-class crime as the major social problem in Irish society is thus as much the achievement of the criminal justice system, and of those that create and sustain it, as it is of working-class criminals.

Earlier we suggested that, if we wish to develop a comparative perspective on Irish crime, useful comparisons could be made with Japan. Setting aside the complex statistical and definition problems alluded to above, Japan appears to have relatively low levels of conventional crime but quite high levels of white-collar crime. If Japan's low levels of conventional crime are the outcome of powerful cultural dynamics that inhibit deviance, how is it that middle- and upper-class groups can often escape their hold?

Kerbo and Inoue (1990) suggest that the explanation may lie in some aspects of Japanese social structure. They argue that the top of the Japanese power structure is occupied by a relatively closed, interlocking circle of three elites: the corporate elite, the national bureaucratic elite and (the weakest of the three) a political elite organised around the then ruling Liberal Democratic Party. The corporate elite consists of the most powerful business executives, who are closely linked, 'especially through intercorporate control of corporate stock' (1990, p.141) plus members of the big professional associations that, representing these businesses, 'organise business pressure and political activities to an extent probably considered illegal' elsewhere. The bureaucratic elite consists of career civil servants and administrators who, though relatively low paid, enjoy considerable power and respect; many retire early to top corporate executive positions. Kerbo and Inoue (1990, p.143) note that the ruling elites do not share a privileged class background and have little 'old upper class family wealth in Japan'; rather, they have 'come up from relatively humble origins' as a result of 'sponsored mobility that is channelled through elite universities. The "old school ties" are extensive'.

Can the existence of a group very like Mills's 'power elite' (see Chapter 4) explain the high levels of corporate crime in Japan? Kerbo and Inoue suggest that it can, for two reasons. First, the inner circle of power is very hard to break into: executives of smaller business are locked out of the big money deals and find themselves having to compete ruthlessly and often illegally if they want to break in. Second, the elite group is relatively free from formal pressures to make them accountable to other groups in the wider society. The importance of mobility through sponsorship means that white-collar crime in Japan is *collective* rather than individual in orientation. Corporate leaders who engage in illegal activities are often protected and their activities covered up or concealed by subordinates. Subordinate groups will make efforts, sometimes illegal, to enhance the position of their leaders as this enhances the position of the whole group. It can thus be argued that the same cultural dynamic that helps to reduce conventional crime levels in Japanese society operates, in the circumstances of the commercial upper and middle classes, to *increase* the likelihood of, and provide justifications for, white-collar crime. The power structure in Irish society is clearly not identical with the Japanese; yet there are enough similarities, perhaps, to make research into the nature and relationships of Irish business, administrative and political elites a useful way forward in understanding white-collar crime in Ireland.

WOMEN AND CRIME

We noted earlier that much sociology of crime aims to identify and explain the links between criminality and social factors such as class, age or location. Yet as Heidensohn (1989) points out, if you wanted to find just one characteristic to predict which children were most likely to become criminals in adult life, you could not do better than to choose *gender* as your explanatory variable. Yet until the mid-1980s, gender issues in relation to crime were scarcely mentioned at all in sociology. The blind spot in relation to women probably had much to do with the fact that the sociology of deviance, like most sociology, was until very recently carried out almost entirely by men. But it also owed much to the fact (as we have seen) that crime was studied as a social problem. Since female criminals were few, they did not merit study. But the study of women and crime (within a context of greater sensitivity to gender issues in general) can reveal a great deal about the nature and operation of the criminal justice system. In particular it helps to develop our understanding of social control.

Women feature quite rarely in official statistics on crime: in the early 1980s it was predominantly men (84 per cent) that were apprehended by Dublin gardaí for indictable offences. The further we move on through the criminal justice system, the fewer women appear. For example, the *Annual reports on crime* show that around 10 to 15 per cent of those convicted of offences in any year are women (Bacik, 2002, p.135). This varies by type of offence: about a quarter of those convicted of larceny are women but this falls to just 2 per cent for those convicted of 'offences against the person' or 'offences against property with violence'. Women are also most unlikely to be imprisoned for crime or to spend long periods of time in prison. As O'Mahony points out (1993, p.101), around 6 per cent of those committed to prison in recent years have been women; and women constitute around 2 per cent of the total daily average of people in prison, suggesting that on average they get shorter sentences than men.

Studies from elsewhere in Europe, where similar gender patterns have been found, show that, when charged by the police, women are more often first-time offenders than men and that very few of them indeed could be called 'professional criminals'. One sociologist has remarked that the world of organised crime can hardly be described as an Equal Opportunities Employer, and another that in general crime is 'a field of endeavour in which women could be said to have underachieved'. More seriously, how might we explain the under-representation of women in official statistics on crime? Many of the classical explanations that were formulated to explain male involvement in crime become less convincing when we look at women. As we have seen, for example, there is often said to be a link between crime and poverty. But are women not poor? Is there something about how women respond to and manage poverty that is different from men and is less likely to lead into crime? High crime rates are also often associated with powerlessness, but women in general occupy positions in society of even less power than men.

There are two possible ways to respond to this problem. One takes the data at face value and tries to find differences in the social experiences and positions of men and women that would explain their very different patterns of involvement in crime. The other is more critical of the official statistics and suggests that perhaps they indicate not the 'real' extent of women's involvement in rule-breaking, but the interaction processes between women rule-breakers and those who witness and respond to their rule-breaking. Perhaps there is something about these processes that systematically leads to women's rule-breaking being less obvious; or more tolerated; or less likely to attract the attention of official agencies of control. Perhaps women are treated more leniently; are less likely to develop an official criminal record; or be sentenced to go to prison. If any or all of these were true, we might conclude that women engage in a lot more rule-breaking than official statistics reveal.

Labelling theory has been important in exploring the links between gender, crime and deviance. It argues that deviance is a *social role* imposed on some in society, often for reasons that have less to do with behaviour than the sort of person they are. For labelling theorists, the labelling of someone as deviant (thief, prostitute, drug abuser) is often precipitated by *contingencies* — aspects that are contingent (accidental) to the rule-breaking act, such as where it occurred, in front of what audience, or what sort of person the rule-breaker appears to be. Gender is a characteristic of people that is generally highly visible and socially significant, in the sense that we are always aware of, and respond to, the gender of a person we are interacting with. It seems most likely that gender will enter into the labelling process that leads to the social creation of criminals in our society.

Research on this topic does to some extent confirm that people who witness rule-breaking are influenced by the gender of the rule-breaker in framing their response (McCullagh, 1996, Chapter 4). Women are generally not seen as serious rule-breakers and are less likely to be reported to the police; the police are less likely to proceed to charge them; and there is less public fear of women criminals so police and judges can respond in a more lenient way. But this appears to be true only where the offence involved is fairly trivial; and there is considerable debate over whether we should summarise the treatment of women offenders in terms of leniency at all.

Some sociologists have argued that women offenders benefit from the fact that the criminal justice system tends to be staffed primarily by men who have been taught to take a chivalrous and protective attitude towards women; others interpret the situation very differently. For them, if women sometimes escape labelling for an offence that a man would have been labelled for, this is not evidence of a chivalrous attitude but shows that women, here as elsewhere in society, are not taken seriously by men. But what most women experience at the hands of the criminal justice system, it is argued, is not more lenient treatment but treatment that *differs* to that received by men. Sometimes it is less severe, but sometimes more so.

For example, in the case of juvenile offenders, British and Australian studies show that girls whose behaviour is 'unruly' are more likely to be put into institutional care than boys. In Ireland one study indicates that girls are twice as likely than boys to be placed in secure care (cited in Kilkelly, 2006, p.15). This is usually justified by magistrates on the grounds that girls need 'care and protection'. This indicates that such girls are seen to be at risk of immorality as well as crime, whereas boys in the same situation are only seen as at risk of crime. Studies of adult criminals also suggest that the courts often respond on the basis of their gender role rather than or in addition to their actual offence. A woman offender who is a mother with dependent children, or who has a husband to be sent home to, may be given a non-custodial sentence where a male offender would have received a prison sentence. On the other hand, women whose lives do not accord with conventional gender roles, even those who are victims of rape, often experience harsh and punitive treatment by the police and the courts.

This suggests that the criminal justice system is a patriarchal institution that both acts on and helps to reproduce gender stereotypes that reinforce men's dominance over women in the society as a whole. A growing body of research (see Heidensohn, 1989; Walklate, 1995) reveals the existence of deeply rooted patriarchal assumptions and beliefs about women among British police officers, magistrates and judges. These include assumptions that women are emotional rather than rational; are unlikely to plan crimes but are easily led into supporting other criminals; and that what they say is unreliable or untrue. There is as yet no comparative research on the Irish criminal justice system, but we should not necessarily take for granted that similar attitudes exist here. Moreover, in most though by no means all cases the outcome for women of the operation of such assumptions does tend to be less punitive in conventional terms.

When we recognise how the criminal justice system may be biased in relation to gender, we can see how it may also be involved in the reproduction of class inequalities and in some contexts inequalities of national or ethnic difference. As we saw in our discussion of white-collar crime, so it is with crime and gender: we cannot treat the operation of the criminal justice system as if it were purely a reaction to crimes committed in society, but must recognise that it is involved in the creation of patterns and trends in relation to crime and in the social constitution of deviance.

This is a most important outcome of recent work on women and crime. But even allowing for the fact that women are less likely to be labelled as criminal than men, they do also appear to be less likely to break rules in the first place. That still needs explanation. One very promising line of argument here suggests that we should investigate the different patterns of informal social control to which men and women are subjected. Women and girls appear to be subjected to more extensive informal policing within the family, school, by neighbours, by colleagues at work and by strangers in public places. If, in everyday social life, men were treated the same way as women, the prisons would be virtually empty and the police and judiciary idle (Heidensohn, 1989). But what we learn from studies of women and informal social control might suggest that law and order achieved in this way could come at too high a price. It is useful to end as we began, by reminding ourselves of Durkheim's view that crime rates can be 'abnormally' low, as well as 'abnormally' high.

Part III

Cultural change

Introduction

For Welsh writer Raymond Williams (1976, p.76), who has traced the history of the term 'culture', it is 'one of the two or three most complicated words in the English language'. In Part III we make an attempt to get to grips with this complex entity and to start to explore some aspects of Irish culture from a sociological perspective.

For sociologists, culture refers primarily to the way of life of a people, social group or historical period. It includes two main elements: *ideas*, for example, from philosophical systems, values and rules for behaviour through to concepts and perceptions in everyday use; and *material artefacts*, such as tools, works of art, furniture or food. Culture is often contrasted with *nature* — the progress of human civilisation is thought to involve a process of overcoming our natural instincts and replacing them by obedience to learnt rules. Williams shows how the concepts of culture and *civilisation* are linked, and that in everyday life 'culture' is most likely to be used in reference to intellectual and artistic activity.

But sociologists do not confine their understanding of culture to the so-called high culture of classical music, fine art and serious literature; they are as likely to study pop music, TV soaps, street murals or John Grisham novels — often referred to as popular culture. Increasingly the line between the two is becoming blurred through, for example, techno versions of Handel's *Messiah*, the annual media hype over the Man Booker Prize and blockbuster exhibitions in museums and galleries.

At its broadest, culture embraces the customary ways that people behave towards each other, This is the territory of everyday rituals, from religious wedding ceremonies to buying a round in the pub. It also includes the *meanings* and interpretations that people attach to social relationships and to the world in which they live. Material objects are part of culture insofar as they have been created for a purpose, or reflect a set of meanings, and they are meaningful to their makers and users.

Though sociologists usually separate structure and culture, as indeed we have in this book, in reality they are closely interrelated. The process of structural change we call industrialisation is as much about change in meanings and ideas as it is about technological change. Tools and technologies carry social meanings that help to shape the process of industrialisation. For example, many European farmers of the 1950s and 1960s bought tractors, even when their farms were too small or their land too mountainous to use them profitably, because they had been persuaded that the modern farm is a mechanised one.

The patterning of inequality in Irish society is also at least partly a product of ideas and meanings, for example, about how valuable to society different occupations are and what sort of rewards their holders deserve. To study society as culture, then, has always been a part of sociology, though often a rather peripheral and neglected part. This may be due to the sway of positivism — it is hard to capture meaning through quantitative or statistical methods. As a consequence, the sociology of culture has been seen as less than scientific, its findings less able to be generalised and of less social or political utility. Yet without a sociology of cultural meanings we cannot obtain a sense of *social process*. We may know how the social structure fits together but not how it works — how it comes into existence, how it shapes, constrains or facilitates particular sorts of action and interaction, or how it may be changed or discarded over time.

The influence of post- or late modernity and its analysis has led to a welcome surge in the sociological analysis of aspects of culture. The discipline has been strongly influenced by the currents running through cultural and media studies, feminism and literary theory: disciplines that all take culture seriously — perhaps sometimes *too* seriously. This also reflects the increasing social and economic importance accorded to culture. The period is witnessing the burgeoning of the 'culture industries' — tourism, media, retailing — and concomitant policies, and politics as culture becomes the field of real struggles over power and resources. Furthermore, there has been an explosion of 'identity politics', based on the cultural values of ethnicity, sexuality and lifestyle. It is no surprise that issues of culture threaten to edge out structural themes of inequality within international sociological thought.

In Chapter 1 we argued that sociology has long been preoccupied with the analysis and interpretation of modernity. That modernity involves not just changes in social structure but also specific processes of cultural change was apparent in the work of the classic social theorists. As Durkheim drew attention to the emergence of individualism as the new morality, Marx predicted the growth of alienation and commodity fetishism. Theorists of urbanisation, from Tönnies to Simmel, understood the transition to urban life as a profound alteration in the meanings we attach to our relationships and our sense of self. Perhaps most famously, Weber envisaged modernity as deeply shaped by cultural processes of increasing rationalisation, secularisation and the loss of mystery and enchantment.

Weber, in particular, provides some guiding ideas with which to approach culture and cultural change. But we find again that the specificities of Irish experience are not always easily subsumed into dominant sociological interpretations. Bell (1991, p.90) remarks:

European sociology developed historically alongside capitalist modernity as an attempt to grasp the dimensions of this emerging order. In a sense, classical sociological theory is a persuasive narrative about capitalist modernisation. As we know, this narrative has been less convincing when applied to the Irish experience.

Despite such divergences, we also discover that apparently unique Irish experiences have universal dimensions that may be illuminated by a broader sociological vision. Post-modernism has opened sociological awareness to the odd, the non-standard or deviant in human social experience so that these no longer have to be marked as 'failures of modernity'. In an Irish context, this perspective can be something of a liberation. But it needs always to be accompanied by sociological interest in the standard and the norm, in what is seen to be socially normative and legitimate.

We open Part III with a popular if perennial question: does Ireland have a distinctive, homogeneous culture? If so, has it been changing over time, perhaps becoming less distinctive? Development of this idea inevitably leads us into a discussion of nationalism itself as an ideology that has played a large part in shaping modern Ireland. The belief that Irish society is united around a single shared culture can also lead us to overlook cultural differences within the society. We introduce the idea of *cultural politics* to suggest that culture can be an arena of power struggles and conflict as well as a basis for social unity and cohesion. Our discussion moves from a concern with the content of culture at the start, to a concern with cultural practices and cultural processes. In our analyses of national culture, popular culture, religion and media we hope to explore both these aspects and to raise some questions, at least, about what it means to be Irish today.

12

One nation, one culture?

What makes a person Irish? Is it because they carry an Irish passport or because they were born in Ireland? Must they speak Irish, drink Guinness, be Catholic, or play camogie or hurling? Must they live in Ireland, or is it enough to be one of the 40 million across the globe that allegedly claim an 'Irish identity'? These are questions that have become both less and more important in late modernity. As the world dissolves into a single global culture and the cultural products of global capitalism pervade our daily lives, what continued relevance can specific national cultures retain? At the same time, as our economy increasingly turns on the production and consumption of meanings and images, possession of a national culture, if only to sell to tourists, film-goers or airport shoppers, may be of crucial importance.

In this chapter we explore aspects of Irish cultural and national identity. We open our analysis with a discussion of nationalism and the idea of nation: a topic often neglected in English-language sociology texts. We trace connections between modernisation, language, culture and nation and examine how these have worked themselves out in an Irish context. We then examine the importance of the state in relation to the nation, developing some of the points made in Chapter 4. Finally we look critically at various meanings of 'culture': one of the most complex terms in the lexicon of the social sciences. The chapters that immediately follow explore further aspects of cultural expression in the fields of popular culture, religion and the media.

Giddens (1985) has sought to reinstate the centrality of the nation as part of modernity and, as we see below, other sociologists have developed interesting analyses of nationalism and the construction of nationhood. Yet it remains that sociology has problems with nationalism. It sits uneasily alongside the universalising, rationalising modes of thought that have long pervaded the discipline. As a result nationalism is often seen as a minor, peripheral or deviant element in the modern world: something of an embarrassment that can and should be disregarded or dismissed as no more than a defensive reaction to modernity. In contrast to this, here we hope to show that its analysis is a key towards understanding contemporary Irish society.

CULTURE AND NATION IN IRELAND

To return then to our opening question: what is it that determines Irishness? In the twenty-first century we regard ourselves as living in a world of separate nations, each of which is marked out by its own distinctive culture, shared by the majority of its population. Thus, membership in the 'Irish nation' is often thought to mean displaying a culture that is recognisably Irish. But what are the particular cultural characteristics that give us our national identity? This is where the issue becomes far more complex. One feature is that such characteristics are quite malleable, according to the situation concerned. They may relate to quite minor aspects of interaction, such as how close a person stands to another, how they pitch their voice or the sort of jokes they make; at other times they may refer to the historical or cultural knowledge a person displays — a 'real Irish person' ought to recognise Cromwell's phrase 'to hell or to Connaught' or know who Seán Óg Ó hAilpín is. The variability of shared culture is an issue that we return to later in this chapter.

Initially, we focus on two aspects of national culture that many would agree on. First, the cultural characteristics that underpin our national identity are usually thought of as basic, inherited characteristics that are ascribed rather than achieved. No matter how hard someone from outside the nation tries to 'become' Irish it is usually impossible for them to do so perfectly. Second, of the cultural attributes that may define nation and identity, the most important in the Irish case are commonly identified as language and religion. The Irish nation has often, at least until the last decade or so, been described as 'Catholic and Gaelic'. It is this particular religious inheritance and connectedness with a specific linguistic and cultural past that is believed to constitute us as a separate and distinctive nation.

Territoriality, or connection with a particular space and place, is also a key to defining national identity. The Irish historical experience of emigration and diaspora, as we saw in Chapter 6, has distinctively shaped our understandings of what it is to belong to the Irish nation, but also makes it eminently possible to be Irish and to live outside of the territory of Ireland. Portable cultural attributes appear to be given more significance, in the Irish case, than spatial location and attachment; thus we are able to think of John F. Kennedy, Grace Kelly or former Australian premier Paul Keating as in some way Irish even if they spent by far the greater part of their adult lives outside the country, or indeed even if they had never visited Ireland at all. As a corollary, many people living abroad who have no direct connection to Ireland may think of themselves as 'Irish' — though often vicariously (Negra, 2006).

Modernisation and national culture

Those for whom a nation is defined by a shared and distinctive culture often argue that maintenance of national difference depends on a degree of isolation from, or a barrier against, intercultural contact. A distinctive language or to a lesser extent a separate religion, helps to provide such a barrier. This is based on the assumption that nations emerged through a process of separation and differentiation. It is often taken for granted that the absence of contact between social groups allowed distinct cultures to form and develop and, conversely, that the increased international contacts that typify the modern world threaten the survival of unique national cultures. For example, some of the concern currently being expressed about immigration to Ireland springs from a fear that this will dilute Irish cultural distinctiveness.

Modernisation theorists generally welcome the merging of separate national cultures and identities into international and supranational ones, whereas this is generally a cause of regret for nationalists. For modernisation theorists the process of modernisation sees societies becoming more alike, structurally and culturally. The theory suggests that to develop economically, societies must first detach their populations from local, 'divisive' loyalties (to kinship, community or minority languages) in order to establish a shared national culture as the basis for the nation state. The values of this national culture then increasingly converge with those of the advanced societies and ultimately give rise to a shared 'world culture' in which nationalism and national cultural barriers are no longer significant.

How useful is this thesis as a way to understand Irish national culture? Has it become less distinctive as Irish society modernises? Earlier we suggested that two major cultural markers of the Irish nation have been the Roman Catholic religion and the Irish language. If the modernisation argument is correct, we might expect to find a pattern of decline in both in recent decades.

In Chapter 14 we examine in detail aspects of religion in Ireland. One issue we discuss is whether Irish society has become more secularised in recent decades: has the influence of religion declined? Modernisation theorists largely agreed with Weber that modernising and industrialising societies are also secularising ones. For Weber 'the disenchantment of the world' — the triumph of scientific and economic rationality over magic and mysticism — was a central feature of modernity. But at first sight Irish society appears to be an exception to the secularisation thesis. Religiosity is still a salient feature of Irish life and remains a key to our culture and behaviour. Fahey (1992a) argues that if we locate its origins in the aftermath of the Famine, rather than in the late 1950s, the 'modern era' in Ireland has been marked by growing church power and influence. Inglis (1998a, pp.249–59) makes his point more explicitly: through its control of the institutions of education, health and welfare and its influence over family structure and interpersonal relationships, the Catholic Church has had a pivotal role in the process of modernisation of Irish society. Though the Church's influence may have waned, the Catholic agenda continues to resonate in Irish society (see Chapter 14). In 2006 a group of mainly Catholic intellectuals and journalists established the Iona Institute, a non-governmental organisation dedicated to strengthening civic society. In particular, the Institute aims to be an advocate for marriage and religion in contemporary Irish society.

For Irish nationalists, language has been just as important as religion. While sociological research on the Irish language has been ongoing for some time, it is rarely addressed in sociological debates nor accorded any relevance to an understanding of contemporary Ireland (exceptions include O'Reilly, 1996; Watson, 1997; and Hourigan, 2001). This neglect, we suggest, could profitably be reconsidered. It seems to be related to a general lack of interest within Irish sociology, until quite recently, in issues to do with culture, but may also be an indication of Irish sociology's commitment to modernism, which finds great difficulty in seeing minority languages and their speakers as other than deviant and exceptional.

Language and modernisation

A modernisation perspective encourages a belief that modernising societies become linguistically homogeneous: within them everyone will eventually speak the same language or, at the very least, linguistic differences will decline as a significant source of division and conflict. If a minority language does, exceptionally, survive, it will be in those parts of the society that have been more isolated from cross-cultural contacts and have remained more traditional in their economic and social practices. But as soon as these areas modernise, the language will disappear there as well.

At first sight, this thesis might seem to adequately describe the fate of the Irish language. Since the middle of the nineteenth century, Irish culture has been transformed by an extraordinary language shift from Irish to English. By the 1960s Irish survived as an everyday language mainly in rural communities along the western seaboard that could easily, if inaccurately, be described as traditional and isolated. As these communities have been incorporated into modern Irish society (particularly its mass media) it is often argued that the language is now disappearing there (Hindley, 1990).

Nevertheless, Irish is not dead. According to the 2002 census, 1.57 million people (or over one-third of the population in the Republic of Ireland) can speak Irish and 10 per cent of the people in Northern Ireland claim to have some knowledge of Irish. The number of children receiving an education through Irish has increased noticeably in the last twenty years. For the school year 2006–7, there were 163 gaelscoileanna (Irish-medium schools) at primary level and 38 at post-primary level in the 32 counties outside of the Gaeltacht region. Approximately 33,000 pupils attend these schools (www.gaelscoileanna.ie). Most English speakers in Ireland today know some Irish and, like religious affiliation, the Irish language is still regarded as a central element in Irish national identity by a large majority of the population (Ó Riagáin, 1988; Language Planning Advisory Committee, 1988). Outside of Gaeltacht areas, and increasingly in some of the Gaeltachtaí as well, Irish tends to be used most by people in higher social class positions and with higher educational qualifications and Irish speakers tend to be most numerous in the larger cities and towns. According to Foras na Gaeilge, which promotes the Irish language, new immigrants have demonstrated an interest in learning and speaking the language. A group of immigrants has recently formed an organisation, iMeasc, to promote the Irish language among people coming to Ireland (www.gaeilge.ie).

The proportion of Gaeltacht households that receive a government grant on the basis that their school-going children are fluent in Irish has declined in recent years to a low of 25 per cent (*The Irish Times*, 6 January 2003), but this should not be taken as a valid measure of public community use of Irish in these areas. Irish speaking has become significantly de-territorialised in recent years: campaigns to establish both Raidio na Gaeltachta and Telefís na Gaeilge (now TG4) drew important support from urban, eastern and largely middle-class Ireland and from national organisations such as Conradh na Gaeilge and Bord na Gaeilge as well as from the Gaeltacht Civil Rights Movement (Gluaiseacht) and later social movements in Gaeltacht areas (Hourigan 2001; Watson 1997).

These points suggest little support for the modernisation theorists' argument that the culture of modernising societies becomes more homogeneous and that minority languages and other minority cultural elements fade away. Modern Irish society remains bilingual — a feature it shares with many other societies in Europe that contain two or more distinct language groups (such as France, Spain, the Netherlands, Belgium, Italy, Switzerland, Finland). Worldwide, bi- or multi-lingualism is the normal condition of social groups and societies, rather than the exception. Furthermore, the rise or decline of any language is not a 'natural' phenomenon that occurs without human or social agency, as the modernisation thesis tends to suggest. The relationship between a majority and a minority language is not one of modernity versus backwardness but one of power.

This is reinforced by a significant EU report on minority languages. It defines minority language groups as those (Euromosaic, 1996, p.1 [italics added]):

> marked by a specific language and culture, that exist within wider societies and states, but which lack the political, institutional and ideological structures which can *guarantee the relevance* of these languages for the everyday life of members of such groups.

The report indicates that the most enduring languages are those that have the support of a state, even if that state is located in another territory (thus Dutch/Flemish in Belgium benefits from the position of Dutch as the official language of the Netherlands) or have benefited from policies of decentralisation or regionalisation (for example, Catalan, in Spain). State support for Irish, though limited, is similarly a crucial factor in explaining the survival of Irish speakers as a social group. Backing for the Irish language television station TG4 has been a major contribution towards 'guaranteeing the relevance' of the language. Correspondingly, the lack of a genuine policy of supporting Irish language programmes on RTÉ over many years was a clear signal to the Irish people of the irrelevance of the language.

The Euromosaic report makes a key point about the salience of theories of social change like modernisation theory. It argues that conceptions of modernity, especially the assumption that cultural and linguistic homogeneity are essential for a nation to develop, have acted as significant factors in 'minoritising' certain European languages. This has particularly been the case for those languages that were not incorporated into the national discourse of economic development. In other words, those languages that did not find expression within the structures and processes of development lost out as they increasingly became perceived as being excluded from the project of modernity. The decline of linguistic diversity has been part of this project across most of Europe but it has failed, inasmuch as 'minority languages' survive. The twist now is that European governments and the EU are finding in such languages a resource for cultural diversity: increasingly they are recognised as part of Europe's 'cultural capital'. In accordance with the Official Language Act 2003, official Irish language services are now available in the Republic of Ireland, and, in the context of the European Charter for Regional or Minority languages, such services are available where there is a demand in the North of Ireland. Irish was awarded official status within the EU as a result of sustained public pressure in 2005, ensuring the language has equal status to other European languages (www.gaeilge.ie).

We have suggested that the fate of a distinctive linguistic culture is shaped by the policies and practices of states, but it is also important to recognise how they may be shaped by cultural processes. Speaking Irish appears to have gained a certain cachet among certain class and age groups in Irish society — the last time it was perhaps as fashionable was just prior to the establishment of the independent Irish state, though for rather different reasons. In late modernity, individuals appear to develop a heightened concern about self-realisation and identity; they pursue a 'project of the self' (Giddens, 1991) and look for distinctive ways to express and symbolise an authentic individuality. This creates new circumstances where choosing to speak Irish acquires a range of new cultural meanings; it might even be described as 'post-nationalist' (McCrone, 1992) in that it no longer articulates an identity based on membership in the collective Irish nation, but rather a highly individualised way to 'be Irish' where difference is as important as sameness in the elaboration of identity.

If Irish society is bilingual, what of the English language in Ireland? The modernisationist argument that cross-cultural contacts erode national cultural differences can be applied here too, and perhaps be seen to be a better fit. Some observers have argued that, in the past twenty years or so, English as spoken in Ireland, particularly by urban middle-class groups, has become much less distinctively 'Irish' in both accent and idiom than it was in the past. Tovey et al. (1989) suggest that we have come to share the same standards for 'good English' as are used by the English themselves and that middle-class Irish people can 'pass' very easily into English society as a result. Others see 'Hiberno-English' as developing into a 'mid-Atlantic' variety of English that is as easily assimilated into American as English ways of speaking. There is a certain playfulness in how the English language has been manipulated through local accents, lexicons and dialogue. For instance, the cultural resonance of the so-called DARTspeak (or Dortspeak) — a particular idiom associated with South Dublin residents (the DART suburban train line runs through the region) — is evidenced in the popularity of the fictional character Ross O'Carroll-Kelly. The creation of journalist Paul Howard, O'Carroll-Kelly has a weekly Sunday newspaper column written in DARTspeak and has published several books. 'Good English' is further challenged by the rise of text language, especially among young people. Irish people have the distinction of being the most frequent texters of all national groups across Europe.

Such trends, if real, could be interpreted as a shift from national distinctiveness towards a more modern, global culture. But for now we must conclude that the question of whether Ireland is losing its national cultural distinctiveness is clearly not an easy one to answer. The example of language suggests, in fact, that the idea that the Irish people have a unitary national culture to 'lose' does not reflect the situation very well — we have at least two main linguistic cultures, one Irish-using and one English-using, and a growing number whose first language may be Romanian, Polish or Mandarin. The barrier to analysis may be to assume that every nation must have a separate, shared culture that differentiates it from other nations, and that we should be able to identify and define this culture in an exact way. This assumption can be traced back to ideas about the nation that shaped the emergence of nationalism as an ideology in the nineteenth and early twentieth centuries.

The idea of an Irish nation

If nations are based in separate cultures, then nationalism simply expresses pre-existing cultural differences between groups. Earlier we suggested that such differences are thought to have emerged from earlier periods of cultural isolation. Sociological studies of nationalism question these ideas. They ask how people could become aware of their own culture as something distinctive, if they had no contacts with other cultures. If people lived only within their own group and never encountered strangers, they would probably have no concept of 'a stranger' and, equally, no concept of 'ourselves' or 'my own people'. We only realise that we share a distinctive culture when we encounter people who have a different one.

This argument, first developed by the Norwegian anthropologist Barth (1969) has been applied by Tovey et al. (1989) to an analysis of Irish culture. Barth develops the argument that our sense of cultural or national identity develops largely through reference to others. In identifying what 'we' are, we contrast ourselves with what those in another group — 'they' — are like. In this process, selected aspects or symbols of our lives are positioned centrally to our cultural or national identity — usually those items that most clearly differentiate us from the group with whom we are making the comparison. Our national identity is thus *constructed* from cultural elements that we choose to treat as significant markers of difference. This process is often linked to social and political struggles, providing a way of drawing boundaries around the groups involved. Thus, an increase in cross-national contacts should lead to, if not increasing differences between cultures, at least an increasing belief in and emphasis on difference.

In applying this approach to Irish national identity, we note that the association of the Irish nation with Gaelic culture and Roman Catholicism occurred primarily in the nineteenth century in the context of increasing political and economic integration into the United Kingdom. We thus compared ourselves most directly with the British, especially the English. Religious affiliation was an obvious cultural marker, given the decline of linguistic difference. But Catholicism became a defining symbol of Irishness not just because a religious difference existed. In Ireland the Catholic Church was greatly expanding its role (for example, establishing a Catholic secondary school system) and, while distancing itself from nationalist politics, was very alert to any challenge to its authority from the colonial regime. But events in England were also relevant. In the second half of the century it experienced waves of anti-Catholicism. In the struggle between Ireland and England it was not only the Irish who were concerned to assert their national identity. The English nation was also being constructed, forged around the symbols of Empire, the Anglican Church and the English language and its 'glorious literature'. The nation in Ireland was defined by prioritising those elements of culture where the contrast with the emerging English nation was clearest. Inevitably, Irish nationalists would see the restoration of the Irish language and the celebration of Catholicism as essential to Irish nationhood.

Nations, therefore, are not derived from cultural essences but are the invention of nationalists. They are what Benedict Anderson (1983) in a celebrated phrase refers to as 'imagined communities': idealised visions of contemporary social relationships based on particular interpretations of the past. In imagining it as a community, nationalists assert that those within the nation share a deep sense of solidarity with even those fellow-nationals they never meet and with past generations from whom they claim biological or cultural descent. Nationalists imagine the nation as having distinct boundaries and that people belong clearly to a single nation and know which nation is their own. Nationalists also imagine the nation as having a right to self-determination, to independent self-government. In this view the nation is a set of ideas and beliefs and nationalism is an ideology. Nations are produced by 'thinking nationally'.

This argument contrasts sharply with the belief that nations existed prior to nationalists, whose role was to bring them to our attention. Early nationalists included scholars and antiquarians who saw themselves as uncovering and returning to public awareness a heritage that belonged to a particular people, or nation. Following Anderson, we can interpret such actions as the *invention of a past*, to provide a social group with a sense of pride in their identity and a feeling of collective solidarity. The Gaelic scholar Douglas Hyde, for example, argued that Irish men should stop wearing trousers (an English dress custom) and return to the 'traditional' Irish dress of knee-breeches. He saw himself as uncovering a forgotten national tradition in dress but could equally be said to have invented a traditional past or heritage in order to help realise a future Irish nation (see Chapter 13 for more on distinctive Irish patterns of dress).

Anderson says that nations 'move up and down history'. They are not, as nationalists may claim, primordial 'givens' that have been in continuous existence since the beginning of history — this long historical existence is *also* imagined. In 'thinking nationally' we make connections with past events — the Great Famine, the Act of Union, the Flight of the Earls, the coming of St. Patrick — that seem to explain some feature of our present situation. Imagining the nation is to a large extent a matter of constructing myths: myths of origin, for example, that recount how the nation was founded. Even if revisionist historians point out that nationalist interpretations of history are 'mistaken', the myths generally survive as their task is to help us to make sense of the present and future, not the past. Dublin may or may not have been 'founded by Vikings', but the claim that it was helps to explain the feeling of many Dubliners that they are different from the rest of the Irish people.

Nationalism as ideology: the nation and the state

What is an ideology, and how is it related to culture? At the most general level, an ideology is a set of beliefs, or a belief-system, that shapes how people understand their social world and how they organise it. Ideologies are often implicit and can only be discovered by careful analysis of what people say or write. They are part of what sociologists examine when they examine culture. But there are major philosophical differences between sociologists in how they use the term 'ideology' (Thompson, 1984). Marxists use it to describe what they see as false or 'mystificatory' beliefs: they might label the belief that we live in a democracy ideological, if in fact all the important political decisions in Ireland are made by a ruling class. Others use ideology to simply refer to a systematic set of ideas (or a 'world view') that is important in shaping social institutions: the belief that jobs should go to the best qualified (not 'who you know') is widely shared in Ireland and could be called 'an ideology of meritocracy'. Sociologists of education (for example, Lynch, 1999a) might ask how this ideology has influenced the organisation of the Irish education system.

Our discussion of the concept of nation suggests that it is constructed through an ideology of nationalism. Key analysts of the phenomenon (Anderson, 1983;

Smith, 1986; Hobsbawm, 1990; Gellner, 1983) have argued that ideologies of nationalism are particularly associated with the nineteenth-century development of industrial society and the centralisation and consolidation of political power into the modern state. They focus particularly on how powerholders within a territory could assert their rule over other groups, dissolve existing cultural differences and divisions (especially through the establishment of a universal education system) and construct the image of a unified citizenship that consented to a single system of laws — a process referred to in one famous study as 'turning peasants into Frenchmen' (Weber, 1976).

A striking feature of nationalist ideology in this period, often contrasted with contemporary or 'new' nationalisms, was its inclusiveness (Delanty, 1996). The goal of nineteenth-century nationalists was to build a society in which citizenship would be available to all social categories and would transcend all 'partial' identities of class, ethnicity, religion or region (Rex, 1996). Successful construction of a nation in these terms required, more than anything else, the legitimation across the entire territory of a single language as that of state authority and civilised society. This ideal has turned out to be far more problematic than was expected: language conflicts have persisted or reappeared in virtually all modern nation states.

Nationalism has not just been an ideology used by existing territorial rulers to enhance their legitimacy. Many *new* states, including the Republic of Ireland, have come into existence as a result of the imaginings of nationalists. Here too, the state has played a large part in realising nationalist aspirations towards a shared national culture and solidarity. Nationalism has been a particularly useful ideology for new states. Their legitimacy is greatly enhanced if they can present themselves as 'nation states' — if their territorial borders appear to coincide with the cultural boundaries of the nation. Thus, new states commonly adopt the symbolism and mythologies forged by nationalists before independence and associate these with all possible state or public occasions. Indeed, in most contemporary societies, whether old or new, it is the state that creates the nation not, as nationalist ideology claims, the other way around.

Important tools for nation-building are mass education and the mass media. In a national education system, new generations of students can be socialised into a common culture, language and values and thus increase their sense of national belonging. The strong presence of the national flag and anthem in American schools can be seen as meeting the need of a federal state, built on continual immigration and with strong ethnic tensions, to constantly re-create a shared national identity. Irish language and history were used by the new Irish state in a similar way. While education through Irish has since declined, the rule that all Irish children must learn some Irish at school remains state educational policy. It is sometimes said that the place given to Irish within the education system reflects how a group of Irish linguistic nationalists captured and maintained control over the state after independence. But it can equally be argued that the Irish state captured (and some would say almost killed) the language, recognising its centrality to the creation of a new shared culture that would underpin loyalty to the new political regime (Kelly, 2002).

The mass media has also played a key role in the construction of Irish national identity (see Chapter 15). When the Free State government first set up Radio Éireann in 1926 it was given a clear remit to 'contribute to the project of building the Irish state and nation' (Kelly and Rolston, 1995, p.565). According to Barbrook (1992), the evolution of broadcasting media in Ireland was informed by two key principles: the preference for state involvement over a commercial alternative and the self-conscious mission to nation-build and foster Irish culture. The broadcasting service was put under the direct control of the Minister for Posts and Telegraphs and he took for granted, as evidenced in his reports to the Dáil, that it had a political, economic and in particular a cultural role: to confirm the separate identity of the new state by frequently broadcasting in Irish and by giving significant space to coverage of GAA All-Ireland finals. Its remit was also to contribute through its educational programs to agricultural, industrial and commercial development in the country. In later years the role of television was admitted to be far more ambiguous: a reality not lost on Éamon de Valera who, as he launched RTÉ television on New Year's Eve 1961, referred both to the power of the media to 'build up the character of a whole people' but also its capacity 'to lead through demoralisation to decadence and dissolution' (Savage, 1996, pp.xi–xii), reflecting papal teaching of the time.

Nation states and state nations

The problem of securing loyalty to a new set of state institutions has been experienced by all post-colonial states, but O'Dowd (1992) argues that relationships between nation and state are particularly problematical in Ireland. This is because, although the legitimacy of the Irish state rests on its claim to represent the historic Irish nation, the nation is not coterminous with the population of the Republic of Ireland, and the boundaries of the state arose out of struggle and coercion rather than as a 'natural' manifestation of a boundaried cultural unit. Not unexpectedly, then, in recent years there have been concerted attempts by elites in the Republic to redefine national identity and to construct a new national consensus that 'aims to have the state shape the "nation" rather than vice versa' (1992, p.35).

The 'new national consensus', according to O'Dowd, involves predominantly three elements. First, it implies a willingness to 'postpone indefinitely' any resolution of 'the national question', in effect to dismiss the claim of older nationalists that state and nation must coincide if the former is to have any legitimacy. Though it should be noted that the peace process in Northern Ireland is continuing apace and that while the idea of a coinciding nation and state is off the agenda, linkages are developing between North and South in a multiplicity of ways. Internally the composition of key social organisations, such as the Police Service of Northern Ireland, are being transformed in line with the contours of the nation rather than the now discredited Northern state. Second, it switches the focus of political attention towards the EU, accepting that the nation state is no longer the only significant unit. And third, it seeks to build a consensus among Irish people around economic and social development rather than in terms of shared nationality. The development of a range of state institutions, including national media; professional and voluntary associations; and research bodies, has consolidated an Irish 'public' whose identity derives from membership within the Irish state. Thus, argues O'Dowd (1992, p.36), 'the Irish Republic is increasingly portrayed as a "state-nation" rather than as nation-state.'

As the Republic of Ireland state replaces the Irish nation as a source of identity for the population, the identification of peoplehood with a common culture undergoes some interesting changes. On one hand, it is now possible to exhibit cultural traits (an interest in soccer, or even in cricket) that would once have called into question one's 'Irishness'. On the other, new movements arise that try to re-create a sense of national identity outside the state. The move to identify and preserve items of 'national heritage' might be regarded as a new expression of nationalist ideology within Ireland but, according to McGrath (1996, p.41), this process can be problematic:

> How heritage constructs a particular identity in a country which does not have an agreed national history has generated considerable contention and criticism . . . the landscape is a product of history, a testimony to the work of successive generations of people and nature; but the process by which history is translated to people living in the present is not a neutral activity.

Disputes that have emerged in recent years have frequently pitted the modernist desire to enhance and extend the road network against the desire of preservationists to respect local heritage and the vernacular landscape. Such disputes have arisen aver the route of the M3 motorway and its impact on the historic Skyrne Valley and over the extension of the M50 and its impact on the ruined Carrickmines Castle (McDonald and Nix, 2005).

Slater (1993) has investigated how the landscape of Co. Wicklow, now widely regarded as an essential part of Irish heritage, derives its current form from the activities of eighteenth- and nineteenth-century landlords guided by a visual ideal of 'the picturesque'. This idea came originally from the Romantic movement in European painting, where landscapes earlier thought to be threatening and aw(e)ful were redefined as sublime, and painters sought to arrange their material so that they could incorporate a contrast between the sublime and the beautiful:

high, rugged mountains against gentle, harmonious, smoothly flowing foregrounds. The Wicklow landlords physically altered the landscape to accord with these ideas, going so far as to remove any signs of tenants' existence at strategic viewing points. Thus, 'picturesque' locations such as Lough Tay, that we now claim and value as part of Irish heritage, were constructed to literally erase from the image the human social relationships that constituted agrarian Ireland (Brett, 1996, pp.39–51). The translation of landscape into heritage may thus impose a constructed national identity on people without their realisation. And while the contemporary drive for the construction of heritage may have started out as a movement to re-create a sense of communal identity that had little to do with the state, it has now become part of state policy in terms of both economic development (particularly tourism) and education.

SUBCULTURES, COUNTER-CULTURES AND 'CULTURAL POLITICS'

Many sociologists, particularly modernisation theorists, have shared with nationalists the belief that societies are or should be, broadly speaking, culturally homogeneous. They have assumed that societies cannot be integrated and orderly unless they are held together by consensus on some central values and ways of doing things. But sociological research consistently reveals cultural difference *within* society. So how can sociologists best understand and explain this apparent contradiction? Often they have recourse to the concept of subculture.

This concept implies the existence of a dominant or major culture. It suggests in effect that there is a set of values and beliefs that is shared by most people and which is essential to the harmonious working of society, but that some 'subgroups' may display a certain amount of variation from the cultural norms. For example, the dominant culture of modern industrial societies places particular emphasis on the values of achievement — hard work, long-term career planning, accumulation of material possessions — but we can find groups within these societies who behave in ways and hold views that do not conform to these values.

The American sociologist, Talcott Parsons, was one of the first sociologists to write about a distinctive 'youth culture'. He said that teenagers commonly develop ideas and ways of behaving that emphasise leisure and play over hard work, and hedonism and immediate gratification over long-term aspirations. Parsons saw youth culture as a *subculture*, in the sense that he thought it was a transient stage in the lives of young people that did not jeopardise the dominant culture. It was a subcultural element that society could accommodate and that even contributed to social order in the society as a whole. Parsons explained that modern societies develop youth subcultures because young people within them are required to go through an extended period of education and training. Adult status is deferred for much longer than in pre-industrial societies, and this creates tensions between young people and other adults (such as their parents and school teachers) on whom they are dependent. The youth subculture provides a way to deal with these tensions as well as a way that young adults can gradually separate from their families and move into the world of their peers.

Since Parsons's time, 'subculture' has been widely used to refer not only to transient groups but to culturally distinctive ones that are permanent features of society — religious or ethnic minorities, for example, or social class groups. In Ireland some research in relation to Travellers suggests that beliefs and customs that exist within that community — for example, in relation to marriage and the role of women — are a variation on those in mainstream Irish culture, but are not so different as to constitute a separate culture (they resemble, rather, an exaggerated version of the dominant culture of an earlier period). However, some (including some Travellers) contest the label 'subculture', claiming that Travelling People in Ireland are a distinct *ethnic group* (or 'nation') with a separate and distinctive culture of their own (see Chapter 17). This alerts us to some difficulties in the use of the term 'subculture': the decision to define a group in such a way is to an extent a political and ideological one.

As increasing numbers of subcultures were studied, sociologists began to make a distinction between a subculture and a *counter-culture*. If subcultures are variations on the dominant culture, we need a different term for groups that more completely oppose dominant societal values and meanings. The term 'counter-culture', introduced for this purpose, represented a first step in recognising that culture not only unites societies but can also divide them and be a source of conflict.

It is not always easy to decide if we are dealing with a subculture or a counter-culture. Youth culture at times appears subcultural — when, as Parsons suggested, it operates to relieve the tensions of adolescence and to give young people a space from which to integrate into an adult world. But at times youth culture appears to be counter-cultural, and to form a basis for the emergence of social movements that challenge the dominant values of society. Similarly, the distinctive culture of working-class groups can be seen as an adaptation of mainstream values and beliefs, or as a counter-cultural expression of values that are opposed to those of the dominant classes.

Many sociologists have abandoned the assumption that a single dominant culture holds society together. They assume that societies are naturally diverse and ask instead *how* some groups can establish their own customs and values as normal, so that those of others are seen to be subcultural deviations from the norm, less worthy of respect. The diverse cultures found in a society tend to be placed in a hierarchy and to establish a high position for one's own culture is part of an ongoing struggle for power between different groups. Weber first referred to social groups whose power derives from the prestige accorded to their culture as *status groups*. In Irish society, the metaphorical 'Dublin 4' is a status group at the top of the cultural hierarchy, while refugees are a status group at the bottom; the Anglo-

Irish Ascendancy is a status group that was once at the top but is now, perhaps, downwardly mobile. Weber believed that conflict between status groups is as important as class conflict. He was drawing our attention to the fact that it is not only the ownership of property that confers power, but also the possession of superior cultural credentials.

Pierre Bourdieu, whose work we discuss in more detail in Chapter 16, combined Weber's ideas with insights from Marx to develop a theory of culture as a kind of economy or marketplace. It is a marketplace where people use cultural capital rather than economic capital. They bring to their exchanges with others certain cultural attributes — an upper-class accent; an Oxford degree; fluency in Italian; knowledge of W.B. Yeats — that they know will secure the respect and admiration of others in a particular social context. Such respect and admiration can in many cases be converted into economic wealth or social power. For example, there is now considerable status in society accorded to 'celebrities'. Some celebrities have a particular talent or ability, such as a good singing voice, the ability to act, or to model high fashion. Yet, perhaps as a result of the multiple media platforms now available, it is possible to become a celebrity without having any particular ability. Some celebrities are now famous for being famous. Paris Hilton, heir to the Hilton fortune, came to public prominence when a video of her having sex with her boyfriend was released on the Internet. Hilton used her new-found notoriety to promote first herself, then a range of products and commodities that bear her imprint. Now, when she makes a personal appearance, as she did in Grafton Street in 2006, the area is cordoned off. Similarly, reality TV programmes such as *Big Brother* have created overnight 'stars' of rather ordinary people who are fêted (or reviled) for their very ordinariness.

Bourdieu says people come to acquire cultural capital largely through their social class background and educational experiences. In general, the most valuable cultural capital is that associated with a high level of education and a cultivated upper-middle-class background. But there are 'cultural markets' where other sorts of cultural capital — such as celebrity status — can command a high return. The value of any cultural attribute is an outcome of social strategies to secure it. Bourdieu suggests that those who possess cultural capital constantly strive to keep the price of their possession as high as possible, for example by ensuring that a particular accent or a particular educational qualification is handed on within an exclusive social circle.

Cultural divisions: the rural and the urban

Following Weber and Bourdieu we can see the development of cultural patterns as a history of struggles over taste and 'distinction' (Bourdieu, 1984). A similar contest has taken place between urban and rural cultures in Irish society.

Rural–urban conflicts have been central to cultural politics in Ireland, but it is important to trace who evokes this distinction, under what circumstances, for what purposes and with what results. Such contrasts are often used by groups in pursuit of political or social campaigns. Movements to rescue rural society, or to stress the values of urban living, occur at particular points in time, and adherents select particular meanings for 'rural' and 'urban' which they promote to the powerholders in society.

Appeals to the rural–urban divide are a familiar part of Irish culture. On the one hand, the Irish Farmers' Association tries to engender a sense of threat from urban Ireland in order to maintain its members' solidarity in the face of increasing rural diversity and differentiation; on the other hand, urban trade union leaders and politicians in search of an easy target construct rural Ireland as a privileged receiver of EU and Irish state supports, thus making it in some way responsible for unemployment and poverty in Irish cities.

Political scientist Tom Garvin (1982) has developed the thesis that in the early decades of independence the new Irish society was rather exceptional, in European core terms, as it was dominated by an elite based in and oriented towards rural society. In the early Irish state the urban centre was unable to impose its interests and values on the society. The template for the new 'real Ireland' was constructed from elements that were not only rural, but based on western, small-scale, family farming, rural areas. For Lincoln (1993, p.206) the consequences were as follows:

> The reality is that Dublin has rarely featured in recent history as a place meriting special attention. Its role as capital has seldom counted as a matter of any material consequence, still less as a locus of Irish 'culture' in which people should have pride. Dublin has enjoyed an ambiguous relationship with the country of which it is capital and the urban culture which it represents has seldom been viewed as something of value.

This ambiguity was, for Lincoln, the outcome of colonialism. Dublin was the centre from which a colonial administrative class ruled the rest of Irish society, and it constructed the city to suit its own cultural conceptions. When colonialism ended it was inevitable that the colonised would respond by overthrowing all things urban. But Lincoln traces the 'anti-urban emotional thrust of Irish nationalism' even further back, to the work of Thomas Davis, himself a member of the colonising class. Davis probably learnt his anti-urban rhetoric from English culture rather than from the Irish dispossessed, since anti-urban sentiment and a romantic view of the rural as a 'green and pleasant land' was a strong element in English Victorian ideology (Offer, 1981). It seems unlikely that in Ireland this idealisation of the rural was accepted by everyone, even in the early years of the new state, in the uncontested way that Lincoln suggests. For example, emigration rates from rural areas, particularly among rural women, suggest that rural life was seen by many ordinary people as something to be escaped from at the earliest possible opportunity.

Contesting narratives about the contribution of rural life to 'making the nation' are found in many newly post-colonial societies with substantial rural populations. As Vandergeest (1996, pp.283–4) suggests:

> Because the national culture and history is invented, different nationalists may not agree on what constitutes the core culture. There are often important differences between groups of intellectuals and their selection and inter-pretation of traditions that they feel exemplify national culture.

For one group of intellectuals, national identity is associated with the continuity of urban culture or with central rule such as a monarchy, with the result that rural villages are seen as places that need to be modernised and civilised in order to become part of the nation. Others, in imagining the nation, 'look to a natural history based in the countryside and in tribal or rural cultures, as typified by the Romantic movement in Europe and more recently by oppositional movements in Asia' (1996, p.284). Recovery of an authentic national identity requires recovery or re-invention, codification and defence (against modernisation or Westernisation) of the traditions of rural life. Vandergeest comments that 'both are descriptions of rural areas as seen by urban people, and they both simplify rural life by associating the village with a more primitive or pure past' (1996, p.280).

In the early decades of independence the culture of rural Ireland was elevated to a position of prestige and symbolic importance in the new society. Politicians, church leaders, writers, artists and film-makers agreed that the real Ireland was rural Ireland, while urban life and culture were often regarded with suspicion as 'foreign' to Irish ways. But since the 1960s it has been urban culture that has increasingly established itself as the expression of the real (modern) Ireland, while the rural has been labelled backward and traditional.

Urbanisation is more than a shift in regional population balance and the concentration of population around Dublin. It is a state of mind. It refers to how the political balance has tilted from the rural to the urban as urban areas increasingly attract infrastructural resources, gain access to the media and influence state policy and public debate. It reflects how Irish national identity is constructed and how we understand and represent ourselves. The 1970s and 1980s were marked in Ireland by a strong tendency towards historical, political and economic revisionism — perhaps the first manifestations in Ireland of a 'post-modern' sensibility — as sacred cows were slain and established myths were cast aside. Where the rural had been constructed as the revered heartland of the real Ireland, leading groups in the society began to promote the idea of a European Ireland. The features once valued as rural were recast as 'peasant', 'peripheral' and 'uncivilised' — summed up well, for example, by the slang term 'culchie'. Farmers in particular came to represent and stand for the traditional Ireland from which Europe would help us to escape (ironic, since Irish farmers were probably the most 'Europeanised' group in Irish society and gained disproportionately from EU membership).

With increasingly urban patterns of residence and occupation we would expect Irish culture to have changed since the 1960s. But what has changed is not just the culture but the prestige accorded to two different cultures in Irish society. Urban status groups have been able to claim for themselves much of the prestige — the 'cultural capital' — of modernity, despite the efforts of some rural status groups (for example, developed farmers) to contest this. In contemporary Ireland, to be urban has become the cultural norm. New modes of urban living are taking shape, such as the reclaiming and reshaping of inner-city neighbourhoods, the spreading of suburban estates, and the increasing concentration of commuters in peripheral towns. The suburb has emerged as the dominant urban form in Ireland over the last half-century. Indeed, it can be argued that Ireland is becoming increasingly ex-urbanised, as many of these new forms of suburban living appear to be both post-rural and post-urban. They are post-rural in the sense that vast housing estates, shopping malls and leisure complexes are colonising more and more of the countryside, threatening the sustainability of a 'rural landscape'. They are post-urban in the sense that the relocation of work, consumption and leisure facilities to the edge of the city, and indeed into small towns, reorients suburbanites away from the metropolitan core. Although we have emphasised here the urban/rural distinction, it is arguable that Ireland is increasingly a suburban society.

For Bourdieu, cultural politics have material consequences. As urban Ireland has asserted its cultural dominance, beliefs about ownership of and rights to the rural countryside have changed. Rural land is no longer regarded solely as the private property of the farmer but also as part of the 'national heritage' to be conserved and enjoyed by an increasingly urban population. Ownership of rural land remains concentrated in the hands of farmers and continues to constitute a major form of wealth, but the conservation movement has helped to shift its control towards urban people. From this perspective, conservationism can be seen as an ideology that advances the interests of a particular status group in Irish society — a largely urban, well-educated, but property-less group. It advances a claim to power based on possession of scientific and technical knowledge, against the claims of rural property owners.

It must also be acknowledged that many farmers, recognising the value of their lands for development purposes, have sold their land for the development of suburban estates, enclaves and dormitory towns. The conservation movement strongly opposes such sales because of the visual impact on the landscape and the infrastructural implications (McDonald and Nix, 2005).

Creating the appearance of cultural unity

Classical social theorists were very much interested in the fate of cultural difference in modern societies. Generally, they were agreed in predicting that differentiated identities would diminish. Marx, for example, thought that the development of capitalism threatened to reduce human beings to little more than 'quantities of labour power' without social or personal identity; Weber feared that human beings might be allowed to be 'economic actors' only, in rationalised societies; while Durkheim, even though he recognised that modern society is distinctive in its 'cult of the individual', saw that a collapse of collective solidarity could leave individuals with no identity in common other than their essential humanity. But much recent sociological debate has been about, not the decline but the survival or revival of difference and division. For Floya Anthias (1999) the late modern world is one that has experienced both the proliferation of difference and its increasing celebration. She argues that concern with difference is not the same as concern with equality: whereas sociological theorising about class was founded on a modernist belief that inequality, social exclusion and marginalisation should and could be removed from society, contemporary theorising about difference is based on a post-modernist belief in the value of diversity for its own sake and as a necessary condition for authentic self-realisation.

This turn towards the analysis of difference has been powerfully encouraged by developments within feminist sociology, where there have been lively debates on the virtues of pursuing 'gender equality' for women as against trying to reconstruct social relations and institutions to better fit the 'different' life experiences and world views of women. Within feminist sociology also the problems associated with essentialist use of the category 'women' to represent all women, have been widely debated. An interest in difference has also been encouraged by sociological recognition of contemporary ethnic conflicts and issues.

In this chapter we have argued that sociological analysis has the ability and indeed the responsibility to investigate both aspects of difference and the forces that attempt to instigate greater homogeneity. While societies may be culturally diverse, there are strong forces within them that aim to sustain the appearance of cultural unity. Among these forces are nationalist ideologies and the activities of different status groups as they struggle to represent their own culture as *the* national or modern culture.

CULTURAL UNITY AND DIVERSITY: MODERNITY AND POST-MODERNITY

Much of this chapter has been preoccupied with teasing out the associations between national identity and shared culture, and with the connections made by sociologists, modernisation theorists and others, between increasing cultural homogeneity in society and the process of economic and political modernisation. We have put forward a number of ways of thinking about the concepts of nation and culture while trying to avoid the suggestion that they must somehow coincide. We pointed out, for example, that nations are culturally diverse and that uniformity is an ideal, or ideology, articulated by nationalists in their attempts to legitimise the nation state as the natural basis for an international political order. We suggested that ownership of the national (in the sense of the normal or legitimate) culture is a valuable asset that different groups in society struggle and compete with each other to achieve and retain, using various strategies to further their aims. In particular, we emphasised that cultural differences within a society are not neutral but are inevitably ranked in a hierarchy of social worth and prestige, where the capacity to represent one's own culture as the real or modern culture of the society as a whole can make a material difference to the situation of the group to which one belongs.

Behind much of the discussion is a further issue that struggles for recognition: the idea that achieving cultural homogeneity is not just evidence that a society is modernising, but is in fact part of the project of modernity itself. It is only with the development of theories of post-modernity that sociology has begun to take stock of modernity and to start to understand how deeply sociology itself has been imbued with the values, goals and world views that characterised a quite specific period in world history. The ideologues of modernity — not just nationalists, but other intellectual elites committed to the universalising values of democracy, meritocracy and science — believed that the way forward for the world was through the reduction of cultural difference and the gradual eradication of particularistic and divisive minority cultures. The rediscovery and re-evaluation of cultural pluralism, a central feature of post-modern thinking, is both a rejection of the project of modernity and a recognition that that project did not, and could not, succeed.

Theorists of post-modernity see in the pluralisation of cultures and meanings an image of the contemporary world. In everyday life, they argue, people encounter a range of cultures and must routinely deal with cultural difference as normal. This is part of our growing sense of living in a global society. Our everyday consumption — food, technology, fashion, sport — is increasingly globalised: and more likely to originate outside of than inside Ireland. Yet our primary concerns — family, housing, work — remain rooted in our own local and national society. This may produce a peculiar combination of experience — simultaneously global and local — that distinguishes the contemporary era quite sharply from that of preceding generations. In this pluralistic world, post-modernists suggest, people have abandoned faith in overarching, comprehensive, *objective* explanations of their experience. The ideologies of the modern era — of social change as progress, so important to the early sociologists — can no longer explain the shape of history as we move into the post-modern world. The world has become *relativised*: all perspectives and cultural meanings are equally valid, and all have become interchangeable.

Durkheim suggested that modern societies differed from earlier ones in the value placed on individualism. In post-modern society, belief in individual self-realisation turns into a quest for personal identity. In a pluralistic world the question 'who am I?' becomes increasingly important, and increasingly difficult to answer. Some people turn to psychotherapy, looking for an answer in their own psychological biographies; others find an identity through consumer choices or in particular lifestyles. In recent years, as we noted earlier, there has been some increase in the use of the Irish language by urban people in Ireland; according to the post-modern thesis, they are adopting Irish not because they are convinced by a nationalist 'grand narrative' or perspective on history but because this lifestyle choice offers them a sense of personal identity.

Perhaps ironically, in a globalised world, attachment to local place and local culture offers a sense of personal rootedness. A study of new Irish suburbs demonstrates the continuing relevance of place attachment and its perceived importance to quality of life. Data gathered by Corcoran et al. (2007) bears out Rustin's argument that much of human experience does not transcend but rather continues to be bound by time and space constraints: 'even though mobility and choice of place has grown, territorial locations remain nodes of association and continuity, bounding cultures and communities' (quoted in Robins, 1993, p.310). But it may be too soon to say if this is a phenomenon that can be sustained, particularly given the potential of new technology and the Internet to create virtual communities that are no longer place-bound. Post-modernity as a perspective in sociology is still ambiguous (as it would be) as to whether it describes a new type of society, which comes *after* modern society, or whether it is describing a new state of mind where we can reflect on modernity and see it in a much clearer light. The rebirth of interest in minority languages (and other forms of ethno-cultural difference) is evident not only in some middle-class groups in Ireland, but right across Europe. It may be the end of nationalism as an ideology, and so the end of modernity; or it may be the start of a nationalist rebirth, in a new social context, and thus the next instalment of the modernist project. Watch this space!

13

The culture of everyday life

[Everyday life] is work, hard work, in all the senses of the term — whether physical, economic or ethnomethodological. The fact of this work, of this concrete activity in specific situations, must be played up if we, as social scientists, are not to transform the people we meet into automatons, passive cogs in impersonal machines. The machines make conditions . . . the people make their own lives, for themselves, the members of their households, kin and networks of friends and acquaintances. However overwhelming the constraints that frame the people, they must still perform the rest of their days, and, in the process, produce a particularity, a difference that the casual glance may miss (Varenne, 1993, pp.112–3).

The last chapter revealed the complexities that surround the notion of 'culture'. As Western societies, including Ireland, experience continued economic growth and an ever-greater involvement in the knowledge-based economy, emphasis on matters of culture increases. At one level, we now spend more time in 'cultural activities', from watching sport to visiting museums or eating in restaurants. Increasingly people also make their livelihoods in such areas — the 'culture' industries — and the economic potential of culture has attracted more interest from business and policy-makers (Howkins, 2002). Reflexively, as (post-)modern people, we are often engaged in thinking about, talking about and reading about our 'culture'.

Culture refers not only to a set of practices that take place in the 'public' world, but also to the texture of everyday life within households, families and workplaces. But the public and the private are not clearly demarcated social spheres of existence: they overlap and interpenetrate. A family meal out in a restaurant, for example, is both a 'private' and a 'public' event; part of culture, as defined by the cultural industries of tourism or catering, but also culture in terms of the patterns of people's everyday life. Going out for a meal is also one of the ways that we as tourists or visitors may sample, locally or abroad, the culture of a society that is not our own.

It is this combination of ideas about culture that we aim to investigate in this chapter. The title reflects a concern with two areas that are usually analysed separately in sociology: 'popular culture' and 'everyday life'. The idea of 'the culture of everyday life' (Fiske, 1992) is an attempt to reflect on both at the same time. We do this through an examination of three aspects of life that have been relatively ignored by Irish sociologists: fashion and dress; food and eating; and pubs and drinking. We have selected these through our own interest and because there is some (though not much) sociologically relevant information available. These activities and aspects of life do not, of course, exhaust the reality of people's everyday lives, nor capture their full 'particularity' as Varenne suggests in our opening paragraph. We could also very valuably look at aspects of everyday life such as work, commuting, housing, shopping (discussed briefly in Chapter 16), tourism or waste, to name just some areas that justify (and need) more sociological analysis in the Irish context. Most of what we say here will be suggestive rather than in any way conclusive.

CULTURE

In Chapter 12 we did not clearly define 'culture', but examined various manifestations or interpretations of it, including: language; dress; taken-for-granted knowledge; patterns of social interaction; religion; feelings of territoriality; shared values and beliefs; and conceptions of normality. Following Williams (1976, pp.87–93) we can identify three ways to define culture — these interpretations have evolved over centuries of use of the term. The first is culture as a process of intellectual, spiritual and aesthetic development. In this sense the term is similar to our concept of 'civilisation'. We might contrast our society with that of the Dark Ages, when people in general were not exposed to fine art or literature, or indeed to what we now regard as 'good' table manners. We might see a person who had received a good upbringing and education and who was knowledgeable and discerning as 'cultured'. This is a highly normative concept of culture.

A second interpretation reflects an 'anthropological' understanding: what Williams refers to as the 'particular way of life . . . of a people, a period or a group, or humanity in general'. It is in this sense that we might talk about the 'Maori culture of New Zealand' as a set of practices and attitudes typical of that people, such as language, dress, foodways, religion, kinship patterns and so on. This is the concept of culture that underpins our discussion in Chapter 12. Use of this concept may well involve debates about authenticity and boundaries: does our conception of Maori culture embrace the fact that Maoris now speak English, use mobile phones, make and export wine and play rugby? How far can the idea of a Maori culture, or indeed of an 'Irish culture' stretch?

The third interpretation of culture pointed to by Williams is that of culture as 'works and practices of intellectual and especially artistic activity'. This is a widely accepted concept of culture as reflected in the work of cultural practitioners, such as painters, musicians or architects. Thus under the heading 'culture' the government publication *Facts about Ireland* (Department of Foreign Affairs, 1995) lists, amongst others, the work of poet Nuala Ní Dhomhnaill and architect Michael Scott, and illustrates artefacts such as a painting by Roderic O'Connor and a statue of harpist and composer Turlough O'Carolan. There are vigorous debates as to what can, or should, be included in this definition of culture: especially if it is a matter of providing financial support for such activities.

The broadest conception of culture derived from the above definitions would embrace 'everything' that a people does or thinks: as such it dissolves as a useful concept. So we might wish to limit the boundaries of culture, but so inevitably the debate begins. Eating chips from a paper bag may not be 'cultured' behaviour according to the first definition; it may certainly be seen as a distinctively Irish way to behave (which the Irish also share with some other cultures); and it is unlikely that you could get a government grant to do it, unless it was part of a piece of 'performance art'. It is not really possible to pin down what 'culture' means: it may be more instructive to be aware of how the concept is being deployed in a particular context, and why people are using it.

Popular culture

Drawing on the concept of culture, sociologists have further sought to identify a field that may be termed 'popular culture'. As we have seen, the second part of this term is difficult enough to define: to go further and try to mark out particular aspects of culture as 'popular' is to add further problems. The concept is malleable, contested and may or may not even be useful, but this does not mean it is not widely used. A variety of interpretations of popular culture has been used in research and analysis: a useful checklist of these approaches is outlined by Storey (2001, pp.5–16).

One way to think about popular culture is 'simply culture which is widely favoured or well liked by many people' (Storey, 2001, p.6). Therefore if a book sells 100,000 copies in the Irish market, or a soft drink sells fifty million cans across the EU, we might think of it as 'popular'. This concept, while helping us to think about what popular might mean, has certain problems. First, we need to define a threshold over which the product in question has to pass (1,000 or a million downloads of a song, for example?). Second, is the quantitative measure sufficient: just about everyone in Ireland eats potatoes — does this make them an item of popular culture?

A second way to think of popular culture is to define it in relation to its opposite — 'high culture'. High culture may include such phenomena as opera, sculpture, or arthouse films, contrasted with a popular culture based on pop music, graffiti art or glossy magazines. This distinction relates to Bourdieu's concept of cultural capital (see Chapter 7) wherein the 'value' of cultural practices is established through oppositions to other practices. Thus, he suggests:

Distinction and pretension, high culture and middle-brow culture — like elsewhere high fashion and fashion, haute coiffure and coiffure, and so on — only exist through each other, and it is the relation, or rather, the objective collaboration of their respective production apparatuses and clients which produces the value of culture and the need to possess it (Bourdieu, 1984, p.250).

The distinction between these two types of culture may be made on various grounds: one might be 'difficulty' — a book that is easy to read might not be seen as literature; another might relate to complexity — a restaurant meal may be more elaborate than fast food; or the distinction may lie in the context in which an artefact is created or consumed: the original *Mona Lisa* in the Paris Louvre is high culture; a poster of the same image on the wall of a flat in Galway is popular culture. This distinction may be very difficult to pin down in practice: Marilyn Monroe's films can be unambiguously thought of as popular, but what of the images of that same star in the art of Andy Warhol?

Storey (2001, p.8) also suggests that popular culture may be thought of as 'mass culture'. This view sees popular culture as the 'lowest common denominator', deliberately designed to appeal to the maximum number of people. As well as being contrasted with high culture, mass culture is also defined in opposition to 'authentic' folk culture, cultural expression that emerges organically from 'the people'. Thus a boy-band such as Westlife is seen as a cynically-produced and marketed product no different in essence to washing powder; a rock or folk group that has emerged through years of touring and struggle (such as U2) is seen to be superior. This view is potentially condescending and dismissive of popular taste, but it may also draw attention to the processes whereby mass media and cultural industries package products — from music to food — for particular markets and audiences.

A further definition of popular culture, according to Storey, is based on Gramsci's notion of *hegemony* (see Chapter 7). Gramsci developed this term to explore how dominant groups in society could intellectually and culturally dominate others. The Gramscian approach to popular culture commonly sees it as a 'site' where dominant and dominated groups struggle for power and where dominated groups are able to express 'resistance'. Thus, just because a cultural product is created and distributed by a powerful entity (for example a TNC like Sony), this does not mean that the corporation has the power to determine how it is publicly consumed or interpreted, nor what resistant uses people may make of such products. Similarly 'new feminists' (see Chapter 9) have argued that women and girls can use the products of a sexist society (toys, clothes, cosmetics) to make their own cultural statements that may not be what the creators had in mind (see Rand, 1995, for an extensive discussion of how Barbie dolls have been used in such ways).

Finally, an understanding of popular culture may be shaped by theories of postmodernism, as outlined in the introduction to Part 3. Postmodernism, in line with its dismissal of 'grand narratives', does not see a distinction between high and popular culture. In our contemporary world, the lines between art and entertainment, culture and commerce, authenticity and artifice are so blurred that the categories are fatally compromised. As Storey remarks (2001, p.13) 'for some this is a reason to celebrate an end to elitism constructed on arbitrary distinctions of culture; for others it is a reason to despair at the final victory of commerce over culture'.

Culture then, whether in general or 'popular', is a complex concept and may express a variety of relationships between people, objects and meanings. Often the concept is overtly or covertly normative, seeking to talk about how things *should* be, and suggests that certain ways of doing or being are 'better' than others. This is to enter territory replete with discourses of criticism and evaluation. From a sociological stance, it may be of more interest and value to examine how culture is *lived* in a real sense. This points us to the concept of *everyday life*. Such an approach may shift us away from an interpretation that sees culture as predominantly a set of texts or meanings, and return us to a more materialist interest in how 'things' are used and produced, as well as consumed, in people's day-to-day interaction.

Briefly, the *sociology of everyday life* can be thought of as an area where 'the study of forms of social behaviour and social interaction [in] . . . everyday social settings and the analysis of more general social processes and relationships meet and intermesh' (Bennett and Watson, 2002, p.ix). The second part of this definition relates to the macrosocial concerns that much of this book has been concerned with. But the idea of the 'everyday' calls for further unpacking. It may relate to the routine and familiar, literally things that happen 'every day' like shopping or eating. As Bennett and Watson (2002, p.x) point out, it also relates to the 'ordinary' things that ordinary people do, rather than the activities of the wealthy and powerful. In this sense everyday life is closely linked to the second meaning of culture outlined above: the taken-for-granted ways of doing things within a society. It also connects with many notions of 'the popular'.

Everyday life also relates to the notion of the 'public' (Bennett and Watson, 2002, p.xi). This interpretation connects us to the idea of *civil society* (see Chapter 5), understood as that part of society outside of the state and the family. In contemporary times the 'public' is synonymous with the ordinary people of society going about their daily business. We think of public opinion or public transport: each relates to everyday, non-elaborated ways of doing and being — reading the newspaper or taking the bus — carried out in company or in interaction with others. Again, the notion of public is closely related to the many of the concepts of popular outlined above.

But the study of everyday life can reveal a more oppressive aspect. Foucault has analysed modernity's ever-increasing processes of *surveillance* of the ordinary person. This involves modern forms of discipline, such as the school, the asylum, the hospital and the prison: sites of institutional power within society intensely concerned with observing, recording and attempting to control and change the everyday life of the individual. This process does not only take place in easily identified institutional settings: today our movements on the street are monitored by CCTV; our supermarket purchases are logged through 'loyalty cards'; and our telephone or Internet communications are tracked by ever more sophisticated electronic systems (Lace, 2005). The process of surveillance has, ironically, strong roots in sociology: much of the social science of the nineteenth century (such as that reflected in the SSIS, see Chapter 2) was concerned with gathering information about the everyday lives of the poor and the powerless in order to 'govern' them better.

In combining the perspectives of popular culture and everyday life, we can develop a framework that might allow us to understand and analyse people's routinised and informal activities, for example in relation to dress, food or drink. Each of these, as suggested, is part of our normal taken-for-granted daily activity, connected closely to ideas of domesticity and home, but also fundamental to our public being in the world. Wearing clothes, consuming food or visiting the pub are never just private personal activities — they are intensely social and are shaped by complex social forces. They relate strongly to the second conception of culture: that of the 'particular way of life' of a people. But in a globalised consumer society (see Chapter 16) our lives are at least partially shaped by commercially-produced, often branded products that are heavily design-laden and so intimately connected to popular culture. Thus a pair of jeans can no longer be just an item of clothing, it connects to a broader set of meanings to do with youth, music and image. A ready-cooked 'Thai' meal is linked to visual representations through advertising, travel brochures, film or restaurants. Contemporary everyday life is intricately bound up with the products of popular culture. We may ask whether it is possible any more to create an 'authentic' everyday culture within a world that is saturated with media, products and consumerism. Or can we do little more than take the ingredients provided to us by the modern capitalist economy and recreate them in our own ways, as far as we can?

It is within this matrix of meanings and questions that we outline some salient features of everyday life in Ireland. Our discussion is limited by the available material. An analysis of everyday life ideally calls for an ethnographic approach that involves a close *in situ* study of social practices — the 'concrete activity in specific situations' referred to by Varenne (1993, p.112), but this type of research is sorely missing within Irish sociology. We will encounter versions of it in the material below: for example in Corrigan's analysis of clothing, or Curtin and Ryan's analysis of pubs. Unfortunately, though in-depth community studies have been a strong feature of sociological research in Ireland (see Chapter 5), such studies have tended to overlook the everyday cultural phenomena that we discuss here: perhaps clothing, food and drink are so taken-for-granted that sociologists, and even anthropologists, do not really 'see' them, especially when they are looking for evidence of community, class or power.

FASHION AND DRESS

Perhaps more than any other element of consumer culture, clothing is the most efficient at announcing one's status to the world. At a broad level anyone will be able to read some useful social information from dress. At a narrower level, others will be able to read more complex messages from the same items. The street theatre of dress has not one audience, but many (Corrigan, 1997, p.176).

There has been comparatively little written about the sociology of fashion or of clothing in the Irish — or indeed international — context. As Corrigan (1988, p.vii) points out, there has been a long historical tradition of social and political commentary on dress and its relation to society (clothing as meaning), but little analysis of what people actually wear on an everyday basis (clothing as objects). But what people wear has long had social significance, and many social movements, not least feminism, have focused on 'what not to wear' as a significant theme. Clothing is held to act in some ways as a mirror to society; for example female fashions are thought to say something about women's position in society; economists have even produced serious studies that correlate economic cycles with skirt lengths.

There has been considerable interest in the nature of fashion; somewhat less in the making of clothes themselves; and very little in people's experiences of choosing, wearing and using clothing. There has been a tendency, as with many popular cultural phenomena, to separate studies of production, of interpretation and meaning and of consumption. The first may be studied by economists or industrial historians; the second by those in cultural studies or semioticians; the last by sociologists or even market researchers. This division of labour ignores the key roles to be played across the field by technological change, marketing, industry structures and so on in determining what gets worn by whom. As Entwistle (2000b) argues:

Precisely what styles are deemed 'in fashion' depends on the circulation of meanings woven around clothes by a whole range of agents — fashion colleges and students, designers and design houses, tailors and seamstresses, models and photographers, as well as colour forecasters, fashion editors, distributors, retailers, fashion buyers, shops and consumers.

Entwistle reveals, for example, the powerful influence of the small number of industry personnel who decide which colours are going to be 'in' for a particular season. This influences what textiles manufacturers produce, the garments designers create, and ultimately what is available to fashion commentators and those who purchase clothes in the shops.

A full study of clothing and fashion, as of any other type of cultural product, would analyse the 'system of provision' that ties consumption to production to meaning-creation in complex ways (Fine and Leopold, cited in Entwistle, 2000a, p.209). No Irish sociologist has yet attempted such a task though, as we see below, McCrum (1996) does discuss some key elements of the Irish 'fashion system'. Our brief discussion of the sociology of fashion and dress in Ireland inevitably draws upon a small number of diverse, discrete and suggestive sources: a complete and systematic analysis of this fascinating topic is yet to be carried out.

Fashion

> Fashionable dress is dress which embodies the latest aesthetic, it is dress which is defined at a given moment as desirable, beautiful, popular. In articulating the latest aesthetic, and in making available certain kinds of clothes, fashion provides the 'raw material' of daily dress, produced by a multitude of people operating across a variety of sites (Entwistle, 2000b).

Corrigan, an Irish sociologist now working in Australia, is one of the few that has taken seriously the sociology of fashion and dress. He notes that in eighteenth-century European society clothing was used in a public way to demonstrate status and occupation. We still see traces of this in how hospital workers' uniforms clearly symbolise the wearer's place within the medical hierarchy. The emergence of mass industrial and urban society in nineteenth century Europe saw an emphasis on how a person's individuality and character could be revealed. The result was not, as might be expected, a greater individuality in dress, but rather a concern for uniformity. It was now thought that clothing reflected what a person was *like*, rather than their social position. There was thus a concern to control public appearance: 'people started to dress in a very uniform and unindividual way, fearing that an unusual button or cuff would betray them as deeply flawed and deviant creatures' (Corrigan, 1997, p.161). The twentieth century saw further change with a greater desire to express individuality through clothing. It was now believed to reflect the creativity and style of the person who wore it.

The factors associated with changes in fashion and dress are inevitably complex, and relate to technological development; broader values related to the body and its display; economic change; and to trends in other areas of production and consumption, for example in relation to housing, transport and family structure. Sociological analysis of fashion attempts to connect broad societal change with the visible changes in what people wear. Key writers, who remain influential within the field, include Veblen and Simmel. Bourdieu, who had such an intense interest in the sociological meaning of material culture, has had comparatively little to say on dress, which is perhaps surprising given its intensely symbolic nature. Most recently the English writer Entwistle has sought to systematically draw together sociological work and theory in the field.

The sociological interest in fashion can be traced to the seminal analysts of modern consumption and everyday life: Veblen and Simmel (Sweetman, 2001, pp.61–5). For Veblen, writing at the end of the nineteenth century, trends in fashion and dress within modern society were shaped by the phenomenon of 'conspicuous consumption'. Wealth was expressed both through the quality of material, but also in the way that clothing was distanced from what might be required for everyday physical labour. Thus the starched white shirt and shiny top hat (for men) or the corset and high heels (for women) were indicators that the person did not — indeed *could not* — engage in the manual trades or domestic work. For Veblen, dress was associated with social difference, most specifically with class distinction.

For Simmel fashion is also closely linked to class (Corrigan, 1997, p.170). It reflects a tension between the desire for conformity and durability on the one hand, and peculiarity and change on the other. This tension helps to shape fashion and ensure constant change: there are those that are imitators and those that are specialists and risk-takers. It is also the desire of lower classes to imitate the fashions of the wealthy, and the desire of the latter to look distinctive and not like the lower classes, that constantly drives fashion forwards. This is the process that McCracken (cited in Corrigan, 1997, p.171) refers to as 'chase and flight'. Fashion helps to underpin social group identity and thus helps to solidify class differences. It 'brings together all those that have adopted the fashion of a particular class or group, and excludes those that have not. [It] produces similarity, union and solidarity within the group and the simultaneous segregation and exclusion of everyone else' (Corrigan, 1997, p.170). Social hierarchies are now arguably far more complex than in Simmel's time, with many drivers of fashion besides what is worn by the wealthy: as a consequence analysts of fashion find Simmel's approach less useful. But the contribution of both Veblen and Simmel to the understanding of 'how fashion works' has been influential within most subsequent sociological analysis of the phenomenon.

Bourdieu, in *Distinction* — his major work on consumption and everyday life — connects choices of clothing to social class, pointing (1984, p.201) to the rather obvious 'opposition between the suit, the prerogative of the senior executive, and the blue overall, the distinctive mark of the farmer and industrial worker'. The distinction can also be seen (amongst both men and women) between the wearing of formal 'top coats' amongst the dominant classes, and the more likely jacket or raincoat amongst workers or 'junior executives'. He is also significant in connecting fashion to how different social groups inhabit and use the body: this is an important if neglected aspect of fashion and dress (Entwistle and Wilson, 2001).

For Bourdieu, echoing earlier theorists, there are tensions and ambiguities within fashion and its connections to unequal social relationships. These help to stimulate innovation and change, as struggles for dominance amongst social groups are refracted through the symbolic oppositions of the fashion world. Fashion is based on the orchestration of struggles within the industry itself, between old/new; classical/practical; expensive/cheap; old/young and so on; and also on conflicts between those with power, and those without. Thus the established holders of power are associated with classical, tasteful and expensive clothing, and with established labels or designers; those challenging or up-and-coming within the social hierarchy are associated with the 'new', the 'young' and the avant-garde (Bourdieu, 1984, p.233). There are clear echoes here of the high/popular culture dichotomy: 'haute couture' is akin to fine art, with expensive materials, painstaking attention to detail and its own arcane language. Mass produced clothing is a cheap imitation of this: a disposable product produced for a mass market, shorn of the more outrageous elements of high fashion, aimed at the 'lowest common denominator'.

Unlike many of those who focus on interpreting the symbolism of fashion, Bourdieu does make some attempt to find out about what is actually happening at the everyday societal level — mainly through questionnaires about (French) people's practices and attitudes. Thus he is able to discover (the perhaps not very surprising fact) that women who do not go out to work use less make-up; but also that those 'higher' in the social hierarchy have a greater degree of confidence about their looks. This is important, suggests Bourdieu, as increasingly the way we look is an important aspect of cultural capital that we bring to the workplace:

> the interest the different classes have in self-presentation, the attention they devote to it, their awareness of the profits it gives and the investment of time, effort, sacrifice and care which they actually put into it are proportionate to the chances of material or symbolic profit they can reasonably expect from it. More precisely they depend on the existence of a labour market in which physical appearance may be valorised in the performance of the job itself or in professional relations, and on differential chances of access to this market and the sectors of this market in which beauty and deportment most strongly contribute to occupational value (Bourdieu, 1984, p.202).

As in his other analyses Bourdieu attempts to connect a highly structuralist account of culture with patterns of social inequality and interaction. The result is some very suggestive discussion of what clothing and fashion might mean in an unequal capitalist society.

Entwistle suggests that while Veblen, Simmel and Bourdieu have been important in the development of a critical sociology of consumption and fashion their analysis is now out-of-date and does not adequately reflect how fashion now operates in society. They each produce a symbolic analysis of fashion, where it can be 'read' like a text. But, Entwistle argues, fashion cannot now be reduced to the expression of a single societal theme (such as class distinction) but is a system made up of complex and sometimes contradictory elements. It is now, she suggests, 'the outcome of a range of intersecting practices: market and economic practices, labour relations and practices, technological developments and a range of more "cultural" practices such as marketing and design' (2000a, p.227). Maynard (2004), in an analysis of fashion and globalisation, suggests that clothes themselves may be becoming less important as signifiers of 'being fashionable', with greater importance being attributed to contemporary consumer goods. She suggests (Maynard, 2004, pp.41–2) that:

> wealth and position are more likely to be indicated by accessories, such as shoes, bags and watches, by the stylishness of owning the latest technology, by grooming, by the level of fitness, travel opportunities, membership of a gym, real estate, or even by owning intangible luxuries such as perfumes, rather than simply clothing alone.

As Maynard shows, on a global scale there has been a blurring of high fashion and 'street fashion': fashion no longer 'trickles down' from the 'upper echelons' to the lower social classes; it is as likely to 'bubble up' from the street, to cross over from popular music, to emerge from art colleges. It is increasingly fragmented and flexible, with numerous fashion niches and no clear overall direction. At the same time mass retailers — in Britain Marks and Spencer and the Burton group sell a quarter of all clothes between them — have considerable power in (literally) shaping what people wear (Entwistle, 2000a, p.225). Entwistle (and other writers such as Sweetman, 2001) also stress the importance of linking fashion and dress to the body: in all cultures the body is always the 'dressed body'. This draws our attention to clothes as objects that are worn, a point made strongly by Sweetman (2001, p.66):

> When I wear a suit I walk, feel and act differently, and not simply because of the garment's cultural connotations. . . . but also because of the way that the suit is cut, and the way its sheer materiality both enables and constrains, encouraging and demanding a certain gait, posture and demeanour, whilst simultaneously denying me the full range of bodily movement that would be available were I clad in jogging-pants and a loose fitting t-shirt.

Fashion in Ireland

Fashion can be seen in two ways: as a specific style of dress in vogue at a particular time and place (as in '1920s London fashion') or as a specific industry — the fashion industry — that as Entwistle suggests embraces designers, manufacturers, distributors, retailers and commentators. The concept of an 'Irish fashion industry' is a relatively recent one, and has attracted only two significant historical studies (McCrum, 1996; O'Byrne, 2000) and no extensive published sociological analysis.

For O'Byrne (2000, pp.9–13) the Irish have for much of their history had 'little or no distinctive style of dress'. He suggests that this may be because Irish people lack a sense of fashion or style, based on what he terms their 'visual illiteracy', 'innate conservatism' and lack of 'discipline'. Together these might add up to a more casual or less reflexive attitude to appearance. He argues that indigenous styles of clothing have, apart from in some isolated areas of the western seaboard, been obliterated by British ways of dressing. Thus 'as a rule, the inhabitants of Ireland dressed no differently from their nearest neighbours across the Irish sea'. The trade policies of the British government, which for a long period construed Irish manufacturers as rivals, did nothing to help the development of an indigenous Irish industry (McCrum, 1996, p.2).

Conversely, O'Dowd (1990) suggests that until the twentieth century there was much about the clothing of those on the Irish west coast and elsewhere that was 'particularly distinctive': including garments such as the black woollen shawl and the hooded cloak; the Aran Islands *crois* or belt; *troigthíní*, trews or soleless socks; and pampooties, a type of shoe. According to O'Dowd (1990, p.7) 'it was clothing that was essentially uninfluenced and unaffected by high fashion and almost totally dependent on the availability of local resources and locally produced fabrics. Imported materials were only slowly adopted in areas near the large urban centres and by those who could afford to buy them'. McCrum (1996, p.xiii) similarly draws attention to distinctive aspects of the Irish clothing industry, including the key roles of fabrics like weatherproof wools and linen. She also argues that the Irish fashion industry has been distinctive and very successful for the size of the country.

This concept of traditional or 'authentic' dress is a complex one. In the nineteenth and early twentieth centuries Gaelic nationalists (paralleling the Russian revolutionaries) attempted to instil nationalistic modes of dress, drawing on the once typical clothing of the Irish rural dweller. O'Byrne (2000, p.13) notes that such attempts to 'recreate what was believed to be native Irish dress' met with resistance, indeed derision, from the people; even Pádraig Pearse was sceptical, suggesting the proposed costume for men (which included trews) was 'fatal to . . . dignity' (quoted in Dunlevy, 1989, p.176). More recently we can note that the 'traditional' Aran sweater dates only from the twentieth century (O'Dowd, 1990, p.8) when designers produced a highly elaborated version of the sweaters —

originally introduced by British visitors — worn by fisherman and farmers of the west coast. Further elaboration came from Continental Europe via returned emigrants from Boston (McCrum, 1996, p.6). This specific garment is now closely associated with Ireland and Irish culture. Brought to worldwide attention in the 1960s by the Clancy Brothers ballad group, it remains a popular item on the tourist market. There are 65 outlets in France selling it and other 'traditional' Irish clothing such as tweed caps (O'Byrne, 2000, p.170), not to mention numerous tourist shops the length and breadth of Ireland itself. To add a further twist, O'Byrne (2000, p.165) shows how the Irish designer Cuan Hanley has produced a contemporary 'simplified' version of the Aran: completing the circle by designing a garment that looks remarkably like the original sweater. In clothing as in other aspects of Irish life it can be unwise to take categories of 'traditional' and 'modern' at face value.

It is argued by the fashion industry that the image presented by the Aran sweater is no longer appropriate to a 'modern' Irish society. O'Byrne (2000, p.170) remarks that 'just as dry stone walls and white-washed cottages do not reflect the reality of Ireland in the new millennium, nor do Aran sweaters and tweed jackets provide an accurate view of Irish fashion today'. The irony is that numerous Irish fashion designers, from Sybil Connolly in the 1950s to Lainey Keogh in the 1990s, have drawn upon this discarded heritage in order to create an 'Irish' niche in the global fashion industry. O'Byrne sees the Irishness of the indigenous industry not in its motifs or fabrics, but in a specific set of ('traditional') skills and workmanship: he suggests (2000, p.171) that 'the survival of these skills, perhaps more than anything else, is what sets Irish fashion apart'.

O'Byrne also looks to the success of the formerly 'peripheral' Belgian fashion industry as a model for Ireland, but admits that there is nothing, apart from the personnel involved, that is identifiably 'Belgian' about it. It is part of a larger global, or at least European, industry. Ireland is a small player in this industry, but fashion — like other image-based cultural industries such as film, popular music and tourism — has a growing economic influence. At the same time the production of actual clothes, as opposed to designs for them, 'barely exists any longer' (O'Byrne, 2000, p.168). The global economy has seen most aspects of the textile industries relocated to countries with lower labour costs.

Dress

Irish people are the ones who never wear raincoats. We don't like planning and we don't like reality (Hourihane, 2000, p.99).

While there has been some interest in describing and accounting for the Irish fashion industry, and the historical development of costume, there has been virtually no interest in the phenomenon of everyday dress. For example, while

O'Byrne illustrates his account of Irish fashion with numerous images of Irish designed clothes, all are worn by models: there are no pictures of what ordinary Irish people wear on a daily basis. We know little of how people live out this central aspect of their everyday lives.

Corrigan (1988) points out that most sociology of clothing focuses on its symbolic aspect, rather than its uses in everyday social interaction: particularly as objects that are purchased, stored, worn and exchanged in a variety of social contexts. In research carried out in Dublin in the early 1980s, Corrigan sought to discover how people used clothing as part of their everyday lives. His sample embraced only a small number of families, but his findings are suggestive of people's complex relationships towards clothing and, through clothing, to each other.

Corrigan encouraged people to talk about the contents of their wardrobes and then, through repeated interviews and other interventions, sought to discover how items of clothing were linked to social relationships across and within families or groups of friends. He found that age, class and gender emerged as key 'sartorial variables' (1988, p.71). It also emerged that the amount and variety of clothing available to people had increased considerably since the 1950s, when young people's clothing would have been confined to school uniform, 'Sunday best' and a nondescript outfit for everyday wear (Corrigan, 1988, p.125).

People surveyed by Corrigan were generally happy to talk about their clothing, often linking particular items to specific people ('that skirt was a present from my sister') or to a specific phase of their life ('I wore that shirt when I was at college'). Gifts of clothing emerged as a significant element of people's wardrobes, and it was here that Corrigan focused, exploring the rationale for and consequences of gift-giving behaviour. He also systematically analysed patterns of exchange of clothing items, including transfers of 'cast-offs', and the 'borrowing' and 'stealing' of clothes amongst families and friends.

Not surprisingly he found that clothing could be implicated in relationships of conflict and power: in particular between mothers and daughters — indeed a 'state of war' could ensue between these family members in relation to what was worn, when and where. Typically such conflicts centred on issues of taste, appropriateness and 'niceness': as in when clothes were too revealing, not matching, or inappropriate for age or weather conditions. This is how Corrigan describes aspects of this relationship:

> There are two phases of the mother-daughter relation: an earlier one where the mother, her direct family or friends act as more or less exclusive sources of clothes; and a later one (after about age 13) where daughters *refuse* clothes bought or made by the mother, sometimes begin to take clothes the mother acquired for herself, and almost invariably begin to swop clothes with non-familial girlfriends of their own age (Corrigan, 1988, p.116).

The males in Corrigan's sample were far less likely to share or exchange clothing: indeed effort went into ensuring the separateness of their clothing from fathers or brothers.

In a study of the lives of low-income families, Daly and Leonard (2002, pp.123–129; 138–9) also explore the importance of clothes in everyday life, especially of children. They stress how for many children, wearing the 'right' (fashionable, brand name) clothes and (especially) footwear was socially very important. Not to have the appropriate clothes or runners could and often did lead to bullying in school, which in turn could contribute to academic under-achievement and early school leaving. The pressure to purchase expensive branded clothing had real implications for everyday life, diverting resources from other purposes and creating strain within families. It also, in some cases, determined the friendship networks that could be built and sustained. Clothing was seen very much as a mark of distinction between children. They sometimes devised stratagems to deal with this situation, as reported by one 14-year-old respondent (Daly and Leonard, 2002, p.139):

> Well, there's about four [types of runners] you'd be alright with: Adidas, Nike, Ellesse and Reebok. Sometimes when my ma can't afford any of these, I try and get ones with no name. Having ones with no name is better than having a crap name. You can pretend with ones with no name. Sometimes I make them all dirty so that it looks as if they're designer but you can't see the name right or I would cover up my feet so that it's hard to see the name.

Another child sewed brand name labels onto non-branded clothes in order to conceal her disadvantage. In a very real way, the clothing of the children in this study literally marked them out as poor and relatively powerless.

Sociological analyses of fashion and clothing are not well developed in Ireland. The work of Corrigan shows that such as an analysis can reveal complex and fascinating information about social relationships, and the more recent research by Daly and Leonard indicates that issues related to clothing are not peripheral or frivolous: how people dress and how others respond have real social consequences. The development of sociological theory in relation to fashion, dress and the body (Entwistle, 2000a; Entwistle and Wilson, 2001) suggests that there is great scope for further research in this field within the Irish context.

FOOD AND DRINK

Inglis (2002, p.27) has suggested that 'Irish people are becoming more rational, circumspect and educated about the pleasures of food and drink. They want to explore different tastes, products and services, and to eat and drink in new places'. In this they are probably no different to other cultures, where a diversification of food and drinking practices is taking place. Inglis suggests that such changes are related to modernisation of Irish society. But what can we say about modernisation and food? On the one hand there is a strong view that the shift towards a more cosmopolitan and 'adventurous' diet is a modernising tendency. Yet other already 'modern' societies (such as Australia, UK, USA) have seen similar trends in relation to diversification of food and drink behind which are common factors: the activities of the food industry, global migration and travel. It is worth examining the issues of food and eating in a little more detail.

Food and eating

At the most banal level, consumption of food is a fundamental aspect of everyday life: if we don't eat we die, and hunger has been said to be amongst the most powerful of psychological drives. To a large (though perhaps diminishing) extent everyday social life is structured around meals and mealtimes; similarly, the preparation and consumption of food has been identified by anthropologists as a fundamental basis of sociality. Along with dress, religious belief, language and kinship, food provides a key marker of cultural identity.

Sociological examination of food and eating reveals a field of great complexity. Topics for discussion range from the systems of provision within which food commodities — such as chicken or sugar — are produced, distributed and consumed; the symbolic meanings of food within families, communities, nations and the media; the connections between food and social inequality; the structure and meaning of meals or 'food events'; the nature of food choice; questions of nutrition, diet and health; and the complexities of food, gender and ethnicity (Beardsworth and Keil, 1997). The list is as broad as the discipline of sociology itself.

Contemporary Irish food systems mirror in many ways those of other Western economies, and particularly those of English-speaking nations such as Britain and Australia. While a number of food systems intertwine and cross-cut at local, regional and national levels, the power of multinational retailers and distributors is increasingly significant. The activities of such corporations have long been exposed to critique from sociologists and other social scientists but, until the recent eruption of food scares — in relation, for example, to salmonella, e coli and BSE — such critiques found little acceptance. Now sociological critiques of food systems find a deeper resonance in a society that is increasingly sceptical of globalisation in general and has some suspicion about the food it eats.

Food systems underpinned the earliest development of a global society: driving the migrations of early peoples and the explorations of sixteenth-century explorers and colonisers. International food regimes, based on the exchange of commodities such as meat, grain, sugar and slaves, formed the basis of global trade circuits that intimately tied the increasing consumption of tea, jam and white bread in nineteenth-century Ireland to the lives of plantation workers and farmers in India,

Australia and the Caribbean. Now Ireland has some food multinationals of its own (Kerry Foods, IAWS, Fyffes) that span the world and compete with giant TNCs such as ConAgra, Nestlé and Cadbury-Schweppes.

But in whose interests are such developments? Tovey (1982) calls into question the transformation of Irish dairy co-ops into major food corporations. Organisations that had been established to develop solidarity and welfare for Irish farmers now provide stock market gains and profits to non-rural 'dry' shareholders. It is arguable that Irish farmers have lost out in the development of the Irish food industry. How does it favour the farmer in Dingle if Kerry Foods becomes one of the world's largest producers of artificial flavours: manufactured in factories off the New England Turnpike in the USA? Schlosser (2001), in his analysis of the American fast food industry, reveals that the welfare of farmers, workers and consumers does not head the agenda for giant food corporations. Similarly there is extensive evidence (Norberg-Hodge et al., 2000) that the global food system poses an increasing threat to both the economies and the ecologies of the South.

Sociologists are increasingly interested in the question of food choice. Filling a major gap in historical analysis, we now know a substantial amount about the history of Irish food, at least until the early part of the twentieth century. It is a remarkable feature that the Irish diet as described in the law texts of the seventh and eighth centuries (Kelly, 1998, pp.316–359) is not fundamentally different to that consumed in the eighteenth century (Clarkson and Crawford, 2001) or reported in recent food consumption surveys. Regardless of the massive changes that have taken place over the last fourteen centuries, the Irish diet is still to a significant extent based on milk, grain, legumes and meat — with potatoes, tomatoes, sugar, tea and coffee amongst the most important contemporary additions.

What we eat

Across all income groupings, large amounts are spent on sweets, soft drinks, biscuits, crisps, sauces and creams, cakes and buns and tea (Friel et al., 2004, p.9).

Is a sociological interest in food choice anything more than intellectual voyeurism — a desire to know what the people next door are having for dinner? Or, more worryingly perhaps, could a managerialist interest in food and eating form the basis of an intensified monitoring and surveillance of the population: a desire to pry into people's everyday lives to ensure they are 'doing the right thing'? More promisingly, can it form the basis of a critique of existing food relationships: a way to challenge the power of the global food players?

In Britain the state-funded Economic and Social Research Council sponsored a major interdisciplinary study of food choice entitled *The Nation's Diet*. In a summary of the findings Murcott (1998, p.2) reported that food choice is of interest to: 'government departments, in sectors of the food industry, by professionals in health, in education and in catering, and many more'. Furthermore, it is 'a question that is self-evidently open to social scientific investigation'. It is also clear that the term 'food choice' itself is open to numerous interpretations and methodological approaches.

Nutritionists have an abiding interest in food choice. Increasingly they have moved away from crude measurements of food consumption towards methodological approaches drawn from sociology and anthropology. Such methods include food consumption diaries; analysis of household purchases; food frequency questionnaires; and in-depth interviews (Roos and Prättälä, 1999). Not surprisingly these methods reveal that food choice is shaped in many ways by questions of age, gender, ethnicity and class. This calls into question the biomedical basis of the nutritionist approach (see Chapter 10) which tends to focus on intakes of particular nutrients, such as minerals, vitamins or, more recently, antioxidants or amino acids.

In Ireland there is a slowly increasing knowledge about the basic facts of food consumption. The *North/South Ireland food consumption survey* indicates that in some respects the Irish diet has changed little since the nineteenth century, with the staples remaining potatoes, dairy products, bread and tea — items consumed every week by over 90 per cent of the Irish population. But not surprisingly this basic menu has been supplemented with a broad range of food items from bananas (consumed by 27 per cent of respondents) to yoghurt (eaten by just one person in six) (Irish Universities Nutrition Alliance, 2001, pp.16–17). The survey also revealed that 4 out of 10 of the population are 'overweight', and that the prevalence of obesity has increased sharply since 1990, especially amongst men.

There are major ethical questions to be asked in relation to the food that people choose to eat, and these inevitably concern sociologists. For example, who has the right to dictate what people 'should' eat? There is a long tradition of telling people, usually the poor, how to conduct their lives, and sociologists have sometimes colluded in this disempowering activity. In particular, is it correct to focus on individual choice and behaviour when the choices that people can make about what to eat are so powerfully shaped by the interests of food corporations? As Schlosser (2001, pp.139–140) shows, the public had to be encouraged to embrace the hamburger as an ideal food; then when it was found that chicken could be produced at half the cost of beef, the Chicken McNugget was energetically promoted.

A challenge for sociology is to link the use of food in everyday life to the broader conception of the *food system*. Such an approach can link practices in relation to food to broader questions. For example, a study of how and why people increasingly choose to eat 'organic' food has the capacity to connect with questions about food regulation and issues of risk and trust (Share, 2002). The study of genetically modified [GM] food also links with issues about the practice of science, the influence of global TNCs over our food, and broader ethical questions about 'nature' and the human manipulation of life. Perhaps these are the most crucial questions that sociologists can ask about food: involving as they do a genuinely fundamental change in the nature of what we put into our mouths and our bodies.

It is widely acknowledged that contemporary food systems are dominated and shaped by giant multinational corporations. Schlosser (2001) demonstrates how the American meat industry is controlled by a handful of firms, as is the French-fry industry, the lettuce industry and so on. Dixon (2002) reveals similar trends within the Australian and global chicken industries. Ireland is moving along a similar trajectory, for example in the dairy, supermarket and alcoholic drinks sectors, each of which is dominated by a small number of large firms. It is arguable that such oligopolies and oligopsonies are unhealthy for the quality and diversity of our food and drink. Similarly, they may not be good for those who work in the food industry, as the reported situation of some of the immigrant workers in Ireland's mushroom industry has suggested ('In Need of Rescue from Unscrupulous Bosses', *The Irish Times*, 12 November 2005).

How has 'the sociology of food' responded to such questions, and how might it link to our discussion in Chapter 2 of approaches within Irish sociology? In a review of the field Beardsworth and Keil (1997) point to the functionalist, structuralist and developmentalist approaches to food. In a later overview, Atkins and Bowler (2001) add the semiological, feminist, post-structuralist and post-modern. Each approach now commands an extensive bibliography and an expanding literature of its own.

Functionalist analyses of food and eating are most usefully placed within the 'managerial' approach. The most commonly manifest version of this approach is in the language of nutrition. As a quasi-medical discourse nutrition has attracted a remarkably low level of critical attention. The ubiquitous food pyramid and the positive qualities of monounsaturated fats, dietary fibre and antioxidants have entered the popular consciousness with little apparent resistance. When a particular food element, such as monounsaturated fat, is shown to be less (or more) beneficial than had been previously thought it is rare that the nutrition discourse itself is called into question. Coveney (2006) has shown how the 'nutrition landscape' is closely reflected in what he terms the domestic 'homespace'. Increasingly people voice their food choices in the language of the nutritionists: it is perhaps not for nothing that their study of diet is often termed 'surveillance'.

Critical sociological approaches to food span a variety of positions. Drawing on marxist theories of globalisation and commodity capitalism, food systems theorists such as Marsden (2000) outline the international networks of surplus accumulation and exploitation driven by TNCs and their political allies. Translated to the local level, such critical analyses examine the connections between diet, inequality and health (Friel and Conlon, 2004). Feminist approaches, not surprisingly, draw attention to gender inequalities in food provision, consumption and distribution, in particular within families and other domestic units. The critical approach also embraces the many ecological analyses of food systems, such as the developing 'food miles' critique (Norberg-Hodge et al., 2000).

Studies of food consumption patterns from a wide range of countries suggest links between social class and the sort of food that is eaten (Warde and Tomlinson, 1995; Crotty, 1999). An interesting aspect is the apparent influence of conceptions of 'healthiness' of food on consumption patterns by class (and by gender). Most studies indicate that the diet eaten by wealthier households corresponds closely to whatever is 'the nutritionally approved orthodoxy of the day' (Mennell et al., 1992, p.54). In the 1980s when health experts urged people to reduce their intake of salt, sugar and saturated fats and to increase their intake of fibre, 'so a class-gradient is observed in the use of items such as skimmed milk, vegetables and brown bread' (1992, p.54). There has long been an acceptance that higher income groups are more likely to consume fresh fruit and vegetables (Warde and Tomlinson, 1995, p.248), though evidence from the Slán survey (National Nutritional Surveillance Centre, 2003) suggests that in Ireland, for men at least, this relationship may be altering, with a significant increase in fruit and vegetable consumption amongst men in 'lower' social classes.

Sociologists and policy-makers have coined the phrase 'food poverty' to describe how food and diet may express relationships of inequality (see Chapter 7). As Friel et al. (2004, p.3) point out, 'food poverty is multidimensional, referring not only to the lack of access to a nutritionally adequate diet but also to the related impacts on health, culture and social participation.' Food poverty may relate to the absolute lack of food or, more commonly in Western societies, to the lack of availability of a 'healthy diet'.

As suggested earlier, judgments about food are often shaped by issues of morality, taste and even disgust or fear. Thus it may be difficult to assess the adequacy or quality of people's food intakes. For example, Belasco (2006) has pointed out how, in Western societies, discussions about food and social welfare inevitably assume the centrality of meat (and especially beef) in the diet. This tendency is reflected in a study of the costs of healthy eating in Ireland (Friel et al., 2004), where suggested 'healthy' diets presuppose daily meat consumption. This presumption is of course open to critique from a vegetarian perspective. It reminds us that matters of nutrition are social as well as scientific questions (Coveney, 2006).

Notwithstanding such factors, Friel et al. (2004) provide a useful insight into the complexities of food poverty in Ireland. They construct daily menus for hypothetical low income groups (two parents with two children, single parent with child, lone older person) based on 'typical' habitual dietary patterns and adjusted to reflect the recommendations of the 'food pyramid'. The costs of providing such a menu from different types of retail establishments (such as big supermarkets like Tesco, 'symbol' stores like Centra or 'hard discounters' like Lidl) are calculated using real-world prices. The choice of brands (national versus home brand) is also brought into the equation. The accessibility of different types of retail outlet is considered (cheaper large stores are often only accessible by car).

Based on their calculations, Friel *et al.* (2004, p.23) come to some disturbing conclusions, especially for those living exclusively on social welfare payments. They suggest that 'two adults with two children, a single mother with one child and an older person living alone, dependent on social welfare benefits as their only source of income, would have to spend 69 per cent, 80 per cent and 38 per cent respectively of their social welfare entitlements to eat healthily'. This finding suggests that exhortations to those on low incomes to eat healthy food (for example in relation to the 'obesity epidemic') are misguided. Rather, for low-income groups, the money available to spend is a major influence on food choice, and public health measures in relation to nutrition must also address questions of the distribution of wealth and income. Planning issues in relation to location and type of retail outlets are also important: the most easily accessible shops are the most likely to stock expensive and unhealthy foods (such as biscuits and snackfoods) and least likely to stock fresh fruit and vegetables.

Echoing the work of Friel and her colleagues, Daly and Leonard (2002, p.57) found that Irish low income families were very constrained in the choices they could make about food, in particular about what variation or innovation in food purchasing could take place. What was bought was what 'would be eaten'. They concluded that 'the extent to which people lived out their family's poverty through practices relating to strict controls around food shopping and diet was very striking'.

The *playful/intellectual* sociological approach to food has been heavily influenced by the structuralist and semiotic approaches of Lévi-Strauss and Barthes. The latter's semiotic analyses of food, especially in his celebrated *Mythologies* (1973) have spawned many imitators, from systematic semiological analyses to weekend supplement journalism. This approach underpins the work of the increasing number of sociologists who study food for its own sake, rather than to provide the sort of directly 'useful' knowledge offered by nutritionists. At its worst such an approach offers little more than an extension of the vast body of writing about food that ranges from recipe books to restaurant reviews — with little that is systematic or theoretically informed. At its best this approach can open up useful debate and provide valuable information about how people think, talk and feel about food; and how emotional and practical considerations can underpin food choice. For example, Collins (2006) analyses the campaign by Safefood — the Food Safety Promotion Board — to encourage Irish women to guard against Christmas food poisoning. Pointing out that in that in December 2004 no reported food poisoning was caused by Irish women in the home, Collins connects the food safety advertisements with the Good Friday Agreement, changing global notions of hygiene, and the changing role of women in Ireland.

As such she critically assesses an increasingly dominant conception of food as risk in contemporary societies — including Ireland.

Irish sociologists have tended to neglect the area of food. We know comparatively little of how people choose, obtain and consume food, and in what settings. We do not know how taste is defined and experienced in the everyday lives of contemporary Irish households. A critical approach would also address the encroaching power of the major food-related companies operating in Ireland, such as IAWS, Glanbia or Campbell Catering/Aramark. Increasingly the power to influence the production, distribution, retailing and serving of Irish food is being handed over to the major global food companies, such as Tesco, Diageo and Unilever. It is most likely that this process will see a transfer of power away from the consumer and the independent producer towards the corporation, and away from the local state to the multinational regulators such as the World Trade Organisation. A critical sociology of Irish food, that addresses such processes, might allow for some sort of public response.

PUBS AND DRINKING

Alcoholic drink has long been seen by both external and indigenous observers as central to Ireland's social life and sociability. While there has been much debate over whether, statistically speaking, Ireland is a heavy-drinking country or not, the evidence points to a long history of alcohol consumption and to its central place within the culture (Molloy, 2002). Indeed the consumption of drink and the influence of alcohol in Irish society appear to have been rapidly increasing since the early 1990s. But, as with other aspects of popular culture and everyday life, the world of alcohol and its main site of consumption, the pub, have been neglected by Irish sociologists: Inglis (2002, p.31) can validly assert that we still 'await a major social study and history of this important social institution'. Ireland is not alone in this regard: in the British context Watson (2002, p.191) has similarly remarked on the paucity of sociological analysis of the public house and of drinking. Drawing on available evidence, this section attempts to throw some light on this important aspect of Irish everyday life.

Watson (2002, p.190) suggests that 'public drinking "houses" of one kind or another have been important sites of social, political and economic exchange in almost every type of society'. Ireland currently maintains over 8,750 pubs — one for every 450 of the population (Molloy, 2002, p.78) — a figure that compares with 21,000 in 1838 and 17,300 in 1896, though the definition of the pub has changed somewhat in the interim period (Competition Authority, 1998, p.29). Until the mid-twentieth century pubs performed many economic and social functions, from locations for trade and commerce, to transportation nodes, to bases for political and community-based organisations. In more recent times most of these ancillary activities have been transferred to other specialised entities, while pubs have increasingly been incorporated into the broader leisure and tourism industries.

In Ireland, as in many other societies, pubs and alcohol have been seen both as a social problem and as an expression of national identity. Sociological research has tended to reflect this dual perception: analysis focuses either on 'problem' drinking, and its links with poor health, delinquency and other social problems, or on the role that drinking and alcohol play in relation to group, community or ethnic identity. A third sociological (and anthropological) tradition seeks to explore the pub itself as a site of social interaction, one that is shaped by broader structural elements such as gender and class.

Irish social studies of pubs and the drinking of alcohol include a number of contributions by anthropologist Tanya Cassidy (1997; 1998); histories of the pub by Kearns (1996) and Molloy (2002); and studies of Irish Catholic temperance (abstinence) organisations, including a history of the Pioneer movement by Ferriter (1999). Given the centrality of pubs and drinking to Irish social life, they have been less than adequately reflected in studies of Irish communities, though community studies, most notably those by McNabb (1964), Brody (1986), Curtin and Ryan (1989) and Peace (2001) provide some information about the social meanings of public alcohol consumption. Analysis of drinking and pubs in other cultures somewhat similar to our own, for example England (Whitehead, 1976; Burnett, 1999; Watson, 2002), Australia (Fiske et al., 1987) and New Zealand (Fairweather and Campbell, 1990), can help us to understand the Irish experience in a comparative context, as can an understanding of the drinking practices of elements of the Irish diaspora (Stivers, 2000).

Alcohol

Ireland has been unusual in its expression of extremes: a culture of teetotalism coexists with one of high drink consumption, there is both 'abstinence and excess' (Ferriter, 1999, p.166). Throughout the twentieth century at least the society maintained a high level of abstinence and as a predominantly Catholic country was unusual in this respect — teetotalism or temperance usually being associated with Protestantism. Conversely it has also been suggested that heavy drinking was a response to the authoritarianism of a Church-dominated culture (Inglis, 1998a, p.170). It could be said then that Ireland, like many other societies, has a contradictory and ambivalent attitude towards alcohol: 'drink was both a pleasure and a curse, but the tirades against alcohol led to ambivalent attitudes and ambiguity as to whether it was a good or a bad thing' (Inglis, 2002, p.33).

Surveys of consumption indicate the increasing importance of alcohol within contemporary Irish society. Coniffe (1993) has argued that it is very difficult to accurately compare alcohol expenditure across societies, but trends within one society can be instructive. In the 1950s it appeared that Irish alcohol consumption

Figure 13.1 Alcohol consumption 1960–2004, OECD countries

	1960	1970	1980	1990	2000	2001	2002	2003	2004
Australia	9.4	11.6	12.9	10.5	9.8	9.6	10.0	9.8	...
Austria	10.9	13.9	13.8	12.6	11.1	10.8	11.0	11.1	...
Belgium	8.9	12.3	14.0	12.1	10.3	10.3	10.7	10.7	...
Canada	7.0	8.8	10.7	7.4	7.7	7.8	7.8	7.9	...
Czech Republic	...	...	11.8	11.3	11.8	11.8	11.9	12.1	11.5
Denmark	5.5	8.6	11.7	11.7	11.5	11.4	11.2	11.5	11.4
Finland	2.7	5.8	7.9	9.5	8.6	9.0	9.2	9.3	9.9
France	...	20.4	19.5	16.0	14.2	14.5	14.7	14.0	...
Germany	7.5	13.4	14.2	13.8	10.5	10.4	10.4	10.2	10.1
Greece	...	...	13.2	10.7	9.5	9.3	9.2	...	...
Hungary	8.2	11.5	14.9	13.9	12.0	13.2	13.3	13.2	...
Iceland	2.5	3.8	4.3	5.2	6.1	6.3	6.5	6.5	6.7
Ireland	**4.9**	**7.0**	**9.6**	**11.2**	**14.2**	**14.5**	**14.3**	**13.5**	**13.6**
Italy	16.6	18.2	13.2	10.9	9.0	8.6	8.6	8.0	...
Japan	5.0	6.1	7.1	8.0	7.6	7.6	7.6	7.6	...
Korea	...	...	...	9.1	8.9	7.9	8.5	8.6	8.3
Luxembourg	13.1	15.6	16.8	14.7	15.4	15.3	14.7	15.5	...
Mexico	...	...	3.4	4.9	4.8	4.8	4.6	4.6	...
Netherlands	3.7	7.7	11.3	9.9	10.1	10.0	9.8	9.7	...
New Zealand	5.3	9.8	11.8	10.1	8.9	8.8	9.2	8.9	9.2
Norway	3.4	4.7	5.3	5.0	5.7	5.5	5.9	6.0	6.2
Poland	6.3	8.0	8.7	8.3	8.3	7.8	8.1	8.1	...
Portugal	17.2	17.9	14.8	16.3	12.9	12.3	11.5	11.4	...
Slovak Republic	6.9	12.8	14.5	13.4	8.9	8.7	8.8	7.4	9.4
Spain	14.6	16.1	18.4	13.5	11.5	11.5	11.2	11.7	...
Sweden	4.8	7.2	6.7	6.4	6.2	6.5	6.9	7.0	6.5
Switzerland	12.1	14.2	13.5	12.9	11.2	11.1	10.8	10.8	10.7
Turkey	0.9	1.1	1.8	1.4	1.5	1.4	1.4	1.5	...
United Kingdom	...	7.1	9.4	9.8	10.4	10.7	11.0	11.2	11.5
United States	7.8	9.5	10.5	9.3	8.3	8.3	8.3	8.4	...

Source: Definitions, Sources and Methods per country: www.irdes.fr/ecosante/OCDE/812010.html

levels were low in the European context (Department of Health and Children, 2002d, p.28). This may have reflected high levels of abstinence, as well as demo-graphic and economic factors. Ferriter (1999, p.203) suggests that in 1961 middle-class Dubliners spent more on drink and tobacco than they did on housing, but a more careful examination of statistics suggests that the bulk of this expenditure was on tobacco. There was a marked rise in spending on alcohol over the second half of the twentieth century: the Household Budget Survey indicates that expenditure on alcoholic drink amongst urban households rose from 1.1 per cent of total household expenditure in 1951–2 to 5.5 per cent in 1994–5 (CSO, 2000).

The two decades from 1980–2000 saw a dramatic increase in alcohol consumption in Ireland, as indicated in Figure 13.1. This was at a time when per capita consumption in other countries was relatively static (e.g. Denmark, the UK) or declining (e.g. Italy, Australia). By 2001 Ireland had, together with France, the highest per capita alcohol consumption in the OECD (save for Luxembourg, where figures are distorted by cross-border and tourist traffic). The rate of consumption has since declined slightly, but Irish people are still amongst the heaviest drinkers in the world. The reasons for such a rapid increase are not easy to discern, but may be related to the relative youthfulness of the Irish population and a sustained period of economic growth.

A number of community studies have found that Irish attitudes towards alcohol consumption and alcoholism have been tolerant. Drink is seen to be 'essential as a means of initiating social contact, especially with strangers' (Ferriter, 1999, p.205). Peace (2001, p.75), in his study of 'Inveresk' (see Chapter 5), found that those who suffered from drink problems were 'looked after' by the community. More broadly, the central role of alcohol and pubs, in Irish oral and literary culture, and as part of the built environment, needs hardly to be stressed: they can truly be said to be 'part of what we are', from Flann O'Brien's celebration of the 'Pint of Plain' to the marketing of Dublin's Temple Bar.

The pub

> Drinking . . . is essentially a social act, subject to a variety of rules and norms regarding who may drink what, when, where, with whom and so on. Drinking does not, in any society, take place 'just anywhere', and most cultures have specific, designated environments for communal drinking (SIRC, 1998).

In Ireland three-quarters of alcoholic drink is consumed within the confines of a public house, or pub. An understanding of the pub is therefore crucial to an understanding of Irish people's relationship with alcohol. The pub is also central to Irish sociality and society. We can agree with Watson that the pub is something of an 'icon of the everyday' to which most people can relate. Pubs have much to do with habit and repetition: as expressed in the term 'regular'. They may offer a real sense of continuity, regularity and order that is 'fundamental to [a] sense of place, of time and of security' (Watson, 2002, pp.188–9). In Irish society pubs have been closely related to everyday community life. Conversely, perceived threats to the institution of the public house, whether through drink-driving legislation, the banning of tobacco smoking or changes in licensing laws, are often seen as an attack on the community or on popular practices.

The American sociologist Ray Oldenburg (1999) has stressed the importance within modern societies of the so called 'third place'. This is a location that is *not* work and *not* home: rather a public place where people can easily meet, relax and interact. Such locations include not just pubs, but coffee bars, hairdressing salons, internet cafés, public libraries, amusement arcades and other similar but culturally specific locations. They are typified by their open, democratic nature, informality and ubiquity. For Oldenburg they are a major contributor to the maintenance of social capital and of healthy community life. His study of the 'third place' laments its passing in contemporary American society (echoing the concerns of Putnam, 2000 — see Chapter 5).

Pubs are one of a number of such 'third places' — which in Ireland in the past also included 'spirits grocers' (grocery shops that served alcohol, often frequented by women) and social clubs (which may or may not have facilitated alcohol consumption) — that have long provided a non-domestic social space (Kearns, 1996, p.23; Curtin and Ryan, 1989). For Kearns (1996, p.3) the pub is both the 'epicentre' and 'a true microcosm of social life, reflecting the socio-economic ethos of its host community'. Thus the pub both helps to create and to reflect the society around it. Historically Irish pubs, particularly those outside urban areas, tended to combine the sale of alcohol with other businesses, such as grocery sales, under-taking, drapery and so on that further increased their social influence (Lambe, 2001; Molloy, 2002, p.77). Furthermore, publicans have played a central community role, for example in providing financial services in the form of credit or loans. According to Kearns (1996, p.3) the pub has also served as a social support mechanism for men: an environment where 'they can openly share personal feelings about domestic life, work, health, finances and phobias'. Indeed, it may be argued that the pub shared many attributes with the church: the snug was often referred to as the 'confessional' and the barman as the 'curate'.

The pub provides for a particular type of freedom within modern industrial society. It was memorably described by the researchers of Britain's Mass Observation team in 1943 as 'the only type of public building used by large numbers of ordinary people where their thoughts and actions are not arranged for them' (cited in Watson, 2002, p.201). Socially, pubs occupy a space somewhere between 'work' and 'home'; indeed the pub's function, according to Fiske et al. (1987, p.5), is to 'mediate their opposition by a complex set of repudiations and incorporations of both'. The pub can operate as a 'home away from home' or as an extension of the workplace, but also contains elements that are opposed to those locations. Indeed it has often been seen as a threat to the stability of both these institutions and has been heavily regulated as a consequence.

For Fiske et al. (1987), speaking of Australian experience, the pub provides a strong symbolic alternative to the home, for example in its décor and in its acceptance of deviant behaviour, such as swearing or drunkenness. In Ireland the gloomy and functional ambience of pubs was noted both by McNabb (1964, p.233) in rural Limerick of the 1960s (though he found the local farm houses generally uninspiring too) and by Curtin and Ryan (1989, p.137) of urban Ennis pubs of the 1980s. But in both Australia and Ireland, as pubs have changed (in part to attract female customers) they have moved closer to the image of the home: with TV sets, carpets, food and familiar adornments. For Fiske et al. (1987, p.10) this may change the symbolic function of the pub: the 'erosion of the boundary between home and pub threatens to make the pub no longer a specialised privileged space, where anti-social behaviour is sanctioned.' Indeed there is now greater official pressure on publicans to restrict drunkenness on licensed premises.

While pubs may be seen as many things, they are pre-eminently places where alcohol is consumed. This helps to define the 'meaning' of pubs. Furthermore, they have tended to be associated with the consumption of particular types of alcohol, and in English-speaking countries, including Ireland, that drink has tended to be various forms of beer. Fiske *et al.* (1987, p.16) suggest that as a drink beer 'is cheap, egalitarian, masculine, social and, when drunk in pubs, significantly differentiated from both home (family/wife) and work (boss)'. This is not to suggest that in Ireland the consumption of spirits (in particular whiskey) has not also been important. But until relatively recently alternative, more 'domesticated' drinks, such as wine or coffee, were not an important element of Irish pub consumption.

Gender

> Pub culture is very important to men, particularly as their roles are challenged in modern society, often by women . . . where else, if not to the pub, have many men to go to relax? (Psychiatrist Patricia Casey, quoted in S. Butler, 2002, p.90.)

Watson (2002, pp.199–200) argues that: 'what goes on in the pub is not separated from other areas of life but inextricably involved in it. Social relationships in the pub are intimately linked to social relationships outside and play a key role in reinforcing men's position of control and dominance in relation to wives and girlfriends'. Sociologists have noted that pubs have tended, until recently, to exclude women and also that they may be associated with gendered attitudes and behaviour that have operated to maintain male power: for example, through joking and wordplay that is specifically demeaning to women (Whitehead, 1976; Curtin and Ryan, 1989).

In many cultures, including Ireland, the pub has been recognised as a masculine domain. Thus McNabb (1964, p.233) reports that in rural Limerick of the 1960s: 'a respectable woman would never set foot inside one of these places unless there is a grocery shop attached. She certainly never drinks in the local bar'. According to Molloy (2002, p.80) women were effectively excluded from most Irish pubs until the 1970s, and even then 'it was still common to see women and children sitting waiting outside a pub while husbands and fathers were drinking inside'. In 1989 Curtin and Ryan noted that Ennis pubs remained an almost exclusively male preserve. A consequence of the male domination of pubs has been the lack of adequate social spaces for women and children, though both Brody (1986, p.162) and Curtin and Ryan note the importance of other 'third places' (though they do not use this term) such as the shop and the church.

There are strong links between pubs and masculinity. Taking the first alcoholic drink in a pub is seen as a 'coming of age'. In 1960s rural Limerick 'a young man was initiated when he took his first drink in a public house. This was a sign that he had grown up, and was acceptable to the male community' (McNabb, 1964, p.236). Similarly Curtin and Ryan (1989, p.140) draw out the manifold connections between the workplace, the pub, sport and the development of what gender theorist Connell (1987) would refer to as 'hegemonic masculinity' (see Chapter 9).

Female drinking has been almost universally negatively perceived. From time to time there have been moral panics about female alcohol consumption. Thus in the 1950s 'pioneers writing about women were utterly unambiguous in asserting that females succumbing to drink were infinitely worse than drunken men, particularly in the context of the home' (Ferriter, 1999, p.168). Women were traditionally confined to the snug or the lounge and until the 1980s it was not unusual for pubs to refuse to serve women a pint of ale or stout, as opposed to a half-pint 'glass'. More recently, particular concern has been raised about young women's consumption of 'alcopops' and other spirit-based drinks.

Despite such societal disapproval, a commonly noted trend has been the recent feminisation of drinking spaces. Women are now welcomed into pubs and the nature of the spaces themselves has changed to accommodate this new market (Molloy, 2002, p.80). They have become increasingly domesticated:

> pubs have become carpeted and furnished. There are soft furnishings and household artefacts, magazines and newspapers, children's areas and tiled washrooms, all replicating, on a grander scale, elements of home and family life (Watson, 2002, p.209)

Associated with such changes there has been an increase in Irish women's alcohol consumption (Cassidy, 1997, p.447), probably related to increased disposable income as well as to changes in women's status and the availability of new styles of drinks. There have been significant changes in types of drink consumed, with a shift towards lighter beers (lagers) and white spirits, especially vodka (Molloy, 2002, p.81). Consumption of such drinks was initially associated with women, but they have found increasing acceptance amongst males as well, suggesting that there has been a significant 'feminisation' of drinking.

The pub as site of interaction

> When individuals enter a particular pub they are purchasing far more than a particular product, such as a drink or a meal. They are also purchasing an experience or ambience, which is associated with desire, and the creation and expression of identity and lifestyle. What is important is not so much the actual

products that are consumed but the meanings attached to those products (Watson, 2002, p.207).

Pubs, not surprisingly, are the site of extensive social interaction. Much of this is overwhelmingly 'everyday' and routine, as revealed through participant observation (Mass Observation, [1943] 1987; Fairweather and Campbell, 1990). Aspects of pub life that have drawn sociologists' attention have been practices of reciprocity and ideologies of egalitarianism and, linked to these, pubs' distinctive oral culture.

The ideology of egalitarianism and reciprocity in Australian pubs has been extensively discussed by Fiske *et al.* (1987). Kearns (1996, p.24) reports that the 'rounds system' was well entrenched in Ireland by the nineteenth century. Though it is certainly not unique to Ireland, Inglis (1998a, p.170) sees in the strict rounds system evidence for Ireland's 'rule-bound' culture — part of a broader subservience to church and state. Egalitarianism, as expressed through such drinking practices, is for Inglis an expression of the desire to be accepted in the wider group. He maintains (1998a, p.172) that pub drinking in Ireland has been closely associated with social control and that this is at variance with other European cultures where alcohol is seen as a vehicle of celebration and relaxation. The rounds system may also be seen as an aspect of mutual aid and obligation, mirroring but outlasting similar relationships within the sphere of production (see Chapter 5).

Irish pubs, like those in Britain and New Zealand, have been noted for their particular type of oral culture — termed 'slagging' in Ireland. This activity may be interpreted as an egalitarian, levelling process, where pretentiousness and selfishness may be challenged; alternatively it may be seen as an exercise of power, where a particular world view is enforced through verbal sanctions. In the *Limerick Rural Survey* McNabb (1964) deplored the process of 'taking a rise out of some person' and saw it as damaging to the (male) community. Inglis (1998a, p.172) sees in this process 'not so much a social problem but rather a practice by which the drinking group is maintained'. For Inglis the traditional rural pub, with its dominant group of bachelor drinkers, was an associate of the Church in the enforcement of a repressive social regime designed to protect private property and the family. Kearns (1996, p.34) however is more positive and argues that 'within the social dynamics of the pub each regular becomes valued for his distinctive personality and contributions to the group'. He is speaking of Dublin rather than rural pubs — there may be key differences between the two yet to be drawn out by sociologists.

For all sociological analysts, the pub is recognisable as a semi-public but highly regulated social space with its own codes of behaviour. Pubs, like the world within which they exist, are hierarchical and ordered. These arrangements can be expressed in the differences between pubs (Curtin and Ryan, 1989) and also through the geography of pubs themselves, for example as reflected in seating arrangements. Thus, according to Kearns (1996, p.33) 'the most coveted social niche in the life of many Dubliners is their status as a 'regular' in their local pub . . . regulars are the privileged pub elite. They form an inner social circle as secondary groups defer to them in seating and conversational status'. Campbell and Phillips (1995) report similar findings for rural New Zealand pubs.

Curtin and Ryan, in their study of clubs and pubs in Ennis, argue that pubs both help to constitute and to reflect class inequalities. They detect (1989, p.137) a 'distinct class pattern in their usage', and are able to identify 'middle class' and 'working class' pubs, as well as a minority of 'mixed' ones. People are drawn to specific pubs on the basis that the pub offers a 'forum for [the drinker's] particular cultural and leisure interests'. Echoing the findings of Mass Observation in 1940s Britain, they also conclude (1989, p.138) that the local pub 'takes on the character of a semi-exclusive "club" where the "inner circle" or regulars are clearly distinguished from casual patrons'. The parameters that define the clientele of a particular pub are strongly shaped by those in the workplace, and reflect broader ideas about group identity. The sets of meanings that define 'working class' and 'middle class' pubs emerge from the interaction between customers and the environment:

> the discreet middle class bar, where the clientele speak in low educated tones of lofty issues, only recreates for the worker the formal rules of the workplace. He is not barred from these pubs and he can afford to buy his drink like the rest, but he cannot participate fully nor does he want to. 'Public' places such as pubs and lounge bars in this way become class specific according to 'informal' codes which are just as effective in shaping the character of social life in the town as were the 'formal' codes associated with 'members only' clubs of the 1930s (Curtin and Ryan, 1989, p.142).

Contemporary patterns

There have been significant changes in both the extent and style of alcohol consumption and the nature of the pub in the years since the early 1990s, a number of which have been alluded to above. The pub, and the use of alcohol more generally, is now increasingly associated with, to use a term popularised by Lash and Urry (1994, pp.57–59), 'reflexive consumption'. In other words both pubs and their customers are increasingly self-aware of the 'meanings' of the activity of going out (or staying in) for a drink, and pay much greater attention to the symbolic aspects of the process. In the mid-twentieth century Irish drinkers generally drank one of a small range of products from a nondescript glass; contemporary imbibers may select from a dazzling array of beers, wines, spirits, ciders, mixed drinks or even waters, often drinking straight from a bottle that bears a well-designed, highly visible and fashionable label.

There has been a rise in the so-called 'themed pub': both in terms of the phenomenal global popularity of the 'Irish pub' and in relation to the emergence of highly-symbolised pubs serving niche markets. While themed pubs are not new, the numbers of them have increased greatly in numbers in recent years (Brown and Patterson, 2000). They are analysed briefly by Slater (2000, pp.255–6) who points out that 'there are bars for young professionals, family bars, student bars, gay bars and sports bars. The market in Ireland and beyond is being segmented in ways similar to other consumer sectors, such as tourism and magazine publishing'. While the emergence of more heavily themed pubs such as those described by Slater may be a new phenomenon, we have already seen that particular pubs have long been associated with social groups that are shaped by gender, class, age and occupation.

More novel, certainly, is the rise of the constructed 'Irish pub' as a global commodity. As Molloy (2002, p.91) reports:

> you can now order a traditional Irish pub from firms such as the Guinness-owned Irish Pub Company and the Irish Pub Design and Development Company, who will assemble your pub for you wherever you require. The second company offers six 'stylistic' choices: the cottage pub, the old brewing house, the shop pub, the Gaelic pub, the Victorian pub and the 'contemporary' pub.

By 2006 there were over 1,800 such 'Irish pubs' in 50 countries across the globe, including 400 in Germany, 300 in Britain and 200 in Italy, as well as in more far-flung locations such as Dubai and Nepal (Brown and Patterson, 2000, p.652; Kelley, 2006) and they must be counted as a highly significant aspect of 'Irish culture'. Brown and Patterson (2000, p.651) report that 95 per cent of 'country themed' pubs in the UK are 'Irish', easily outstripping 'Australian' or 'Scottish' pubs. Slater, in an analysis of 'Irish' pubs in Singapore and Brazil, shows how 'Irishness' is self-consciously and deliberately created and re-created within such pubs through an over-the-top combination of visual symbolism (old street signs, packets of Barry's Tea, posters of Irish writers, chamber pots), Irish music, festivals and food and 'Irish' behavioural characteristics of relaxed informality. This last aspect involves a type of planned spontaneity: 'designing the Irish pub seems to involve a necessary illusion: it should appear that no design has gone into it at all' (Slater, 2000, p.251). Indeed it is the planned nature of themed pubs — where, unlike in 'real' pubs, the *craic* is guaranteed — that is a major part of their attraction (Brown and Patterson, 2000, p.655; Kelley, 2006).

In the UK a major change in government regulation of pubs has led to substantial shifts in how they operate and has led them to target new markets in new ways (Chatterton and Hollands, 2003). In Ireland it could be argued that the *lack* of changes in regulation, and in particular the maintenance of existing licence numbers, has helped to shape the industry (Competition Authority, 1998). For example recent years have seen the emergence, particularly in urban areas that are undersupplied with pub licenses, of so-called 'superpubs' that can accommodate over 1,000 people. More broadly, pubs are now firmly part of the entertainment industry, and alcohol sponsorship underpins many aspects of Irish culture, from rock and pop music to the numerous summer festivals across the country. The comprehensive infiltration of Irish culture by the drinks industry has led to renewed concerns about economic, social and health impacts.

Pubs/drinking as social problem

> Public opinion on the question of excessive drinking is inconsistent. A generally expressed desire for moderation is not accompanied by a willingness to take the steps necessary to achieve it (Pioneer Father McGuckian, cited in Ferriter, 1999, p.251).

It could be said that in Ireland, as in many other societies, the conception of alcohol as a social problem has been shaped by what Room (cited in Cassidy, 1998, p.172) terms 'ambivalence'. In other words, a condemnation of alcohol is combined with an acceptance of its key role in society. The central position that alcoholic drink has within Irish culture has inevitably helped to determine responses to the social problems, such as alcoholism, poverty and drink-driving, that are associated with it. Such ambivalence is supported by the historic conflict between the drinks industries and those who have sought to regulate alcohol: sometimes referred to as the battle between the 'wets' and the 'dries'. In the past this conflict found expression in the struggle between publicans and drinkers and the temperance and abstinence movements; in contemporary times it is seen in the debates between the drinks industry and those involved in health promotion (Cassidy, 1998; S. Butler, 2002).

Social research has long been interested in the 'problem' of alcohol. In Ireland it was an early concern of the Statistical and Social Inquiry Society, discussed in Chapter 2: several papers on issues related to alcohol were read to the Society in the mid-nineteenth century (S. Butler, 2002, p.19). In the 1870s clear links were observed between poverty and alcohol abuse and in 1876, in order to establish Dublin weekend drinking patterns, police watched 210 pubs on a Sunday and enumerated the numbers and apparent social class of the customers (Kearns, 1996, pp.21–2).

Cassidy (1998) has traced aspects of Ireland's 'ambivalence' towards the control of alcohol in the drink-driving campaigns of the 1930s to 1990s. She has linked the changing discourses in relation to this ambivalence to the process of modernisation in Irish society and suggests (1998, p.165) that 'the public response to the problem of drinking and driving crystallises in many ways some of the essential features of the dynamic of modernity in Ireland'. This process is expressed through the government's attempts to challenge 'traditional' drinking practices, in particular the rounds system. From an earlier stage of ignoring the problem of drink-driving the state then adopted the 'Just two will do' campaign, which implicitly recognised that it was not socially possible for a person to have 'just one' drink in a social situation of reciprocity. Subsequent campaigns then moved to a stricter position, where the driver more or less had to abstain from drinking altogether. For Cassidy this change reflects a shift from the 'traditional drinker' to the 'modern drinker', who is also a 'reflexive drinker': 'such drinkers could now monitor their own behaviour and decide on what to drink and how much, according to the situation they found themselves in' (1998, p.170). The process is also one of removing the ambivalence associated with drinking and placing responsibility firmly on the drinker/driver. From this viewpoint, echoing the earlier position of the Pioneers (Brody, 1986, pp.173–4), a modern Irish person is one who abjures alcohol.

Ferriter (1999, p.249) points to the changing explanations for alcohol abuse: 'in the early 1970s prominent Irish medical figures . . . suggested causes of alcoholism, not in terms of distance from God, but in the context of the Irish physical disposition, innate inferiority complexes, and endogenous and manic depression'. This reflects an increasing medicalisation (see Chapter 10) of alcohol abuse. Shane Butler (2002) has examined in considerable detail the competing discourses in post-WW2 Ireland in relation to 'problem drinking' and alcoholism. In particular he has described in detail how two different approaches: the dominant 'disease approach' (associated with Alcoholics Anonymous) and the 'health promotion' approach, were reflected in Irish government responses to alcohol, and crucially, how these viewpoints related to the views of the medical and drinks industries. He argues that the former approach in particular contributed 'to a process of deflecting attention away from the wider context of drinking in Irish society' (2002, p.28).

Since at least the mid-nineteenth century there have been public and state concerns about a range of drink-related issues such as underage drinking, binge drinking, public drunkenness and violence, and linked issues such as suicide, alcohol's impact on the health system and public order. There have been numerous government reports on various aspects of the alcoholic drinks industry and culture, most of which have dealt with issues related to licensing, pricing and restrictive practices (Competition Authority, 1998, pp.4–7). More recently there has been a focus on health promotion and issues of 'alcohol-related harm', with a particular focus on 'binge drinking' (Department of Health and Children, 2004). There has been minimal input by sociologists into such enquiries; rather the expertise has been sought from economists, historians, medics and psychologists. If Irish sociologists develop an increased interest in aspects of everyday life, including the many social aspects of pubs and drinking, they may be in a better position to contribute to debates in these areas in the future.

Alcohol and modernisation

As with many aspects of Irish social life, the issue of alcohol has inevitably been connected to arguments in relation to modernisation. Alcohol, perhaps unsurprisingly, appears to reveal a range of contradictions in this regard. One perspective suggests that alcohol usage and modernity are counterpoised to each other: as a society 'modernises' it reduces its consumption of alcohol. There is evidence that this view has been prevalent in Ireland at certain historical points. The mid-nineteenth century interest of the SSIS in alcohol issues was inevitably part of its 'civilising' mission as it tried to align Irish social development with that of the remainder of the United Kingdom.

A century later, according to Brody, abstention was interpreted by some as an emblem of modernity. In *Inishkillane* attitudes to alcohol were linked to views about modernisation and the development of the community. Women and young people, in particular, were associated with abstention, in opposition to the dominant farmer sector of the population. For young men taking the Pioneer pledge was 'part of their identification with the forces opposing the traditional patterns of social life and social authority. . . . Alcohol is one issue on which the division between commitment to tradition and commitment to a newer consciousness can focus in everyday life' (1986, pp.173–4). Ferriter (1999, p.195) comments that such connections between attitudes to alcohol and attitudes to the Catholic Church, call into question some of the conventional Irish notions about religion, 'tradition' and 'modernity'.

In more recent times there appears to be a strong connection between economic growth and rapidly increasing alcohol consumption. Critics of the 'Celtic Tiger society' perceive the rise in drinking and in drink-related problems such as crime and disorder to be one of the negative side-effects of modernisation, alongside a general decline in community and family life. In the call for crack-downs on underage drinking, or on pub opening hours, it is possible to discern a call for a return to a more 'traditional' era: this is opposed by 'modernisers' who wish to bring Irish drinking patterns and facilities into line with those of 'Europe'. However, the dynamic history of alcohol consumption suggests that it is mistaken to make any simple association between drinking and economic growth, demography or social attitudes. As in most areas of Irish social life, the modernisation thesis begs as many questions as it answers.

CONCLUSION

This chapter has attempted to sketch out some of the key approaches to popular culture and to everyday life, and to suggest what an analysis of the 'culture of everyday life' in Ireland might look like. The point is made a number of times that Irish sociologists, like their colleagues in other societies, have tended largely to ignore the texture of everyday social life. When they have turned their attention to fashion, food or drink, it is more often to the symbolic aspects of these phenomena, rather than to the actual practices and attitudes of people as they make use of them in everyday social interaction.

It is arguable that a stronger ethnographic interest in the culture of everyday life would help to reveal a more comprehensive sociology of Irish society. But sociologists need to be aware of the tendencies within contemporary society that contribute to an ever-higher degree of moitoring and surveillance of people's everyday lives: whether directly as in CCTV and electronic data trails, or more insidiously through the operation of 'expert' discourses such as nutrition and health promotion. It may be that the development of an increased knowledge about how and why people drink, eat and dress in certain ways may lead to enhanced efforts to control these aspects of people's behaviour: whether by institutions of the state, professional groups, or private corporations.

It is also important to take note of the 'systems of provision' approach. Analysts of popular culture now stress that the use of artefacts in everyday life — eating a frozen dinner or wearing a pair of jeans — is just part of a longer chain of relationships that connects producers, marketers, distributors and 'meaning makers' of various types. Often, in an increasingly globalised world, these connections can span the globe, joining societies and institutions in increasingly complex ways. The culture of everyday life can be intensely domestic, but may also have wide-ranging ramifications.

14
Religion

If religion be the opium of the people, the Irish were addicts.
(O'Farrell, cited in Akenson, 1991, p.139)

Religion can be difficult to analyse sociologically, due to the emotive nature of the concepts involved. At the same time, it is arguably one of the key factors that affect Irish social life. Any sociological study of Ireland must reflect the importance of religion in the shaping of our contemporary society, its continuing relevance in terms of everyday social life and the still central role of religious institutions.

Remarkably enough, given its centrality to Irish social life, Irish sociologists, with some key exceptions, have failed to produce much description or analysis of the power of the churches in contemporary Irish society. Much of the sociological research has been carried out by the churches themselves and not surprisingly turns out to be less than critical of the institutions. Most critical analysis of the churches, and of the role of religion in Irish social life, has come from the pens of historians, novelists or visiting anthropologists.

A major limitation of Irish sociological research into religion is that it has tended to be highly positivist. It has, according to Inglis (1987, p.2) 'concentrated on gathering facts and data, usually through social surveys, and has avoided dealing with the larger, more general questions about the position and influence of the Church'. Conversely, as Akenson (1991) has argued, much historical research on religion in Ireland has relied on anecdotal and skewed sources of evidence, and has lacked rigorous statistical or comparative analysis. Thus, our knowledge of many aspects of the role of religion in Irish social life remains less complete than it could — or should — be. Most recently the apparent decline in the influence of the Catholic Church in Ireland may have led many people to discount its influence and to see religion as no longer of relevance. Yet it also apparent that issues related to religion are resurgent at a global level — not least as a consequence of conflict in the Middle East and elsewhere. It is likely that religion will continue to be of major interest to sociologists.

WHAT IS RELIGION?

Irish author Mary Morrissy provocatively addressed this question in an *Irish Times* article (17 December 1996) as she drew parallels between shopping and religion:

> It is the shopping mall that opens on a Sunday, at hours when most people in the 1950s would have been making holy the Sabbath day . . . in the next century — when surely most of our shopping will be done via a terminal from home — the shopping centre may well become the cathedral of its time. A place to be viewed as grandiose and lofty, impossibly old-fashioned and impractical and by then probably completely redundant.

Though Morrissy is not the first to note the similarities between cathedrals and shopping malls (such parallels became a cliché at the 2005 opening of the Dundrum Town Centre shopping mall in suburban Dublin), her remarks are certainly thought-provoking and may lead us to think about what exactly we mean by 'religion'. This is also a question that many of the early sociologists, in particular Durkheim and Weber, were drawn to.

What then are the key aspects of religion? They include the following:

- *sacred symbols* — the crucifix, the star, holy statues, the sign of the cross, and often certain colours such as red, purple and gold
- *rituals and special behaviour* — pilgrimages, prayers, hand and body movements
- *a feeling of reverence* towards and awe, even fear, of sacred symbols, practices, personnel and places
- *a community of believers* — a parish, congregation, sect, cult, religious order or religious community.

Symbols provide a key to the development of religion and to an understanding of what it might mean. They carry with them the emotional charge that arises from feelings of belonging — the excitement and fulfilment that comes from being part of a crowd or of an intimate group. Symbols and the rituals associated with them emphasise and develop group solidarity.

The distinctive contribution of sociologists has been to move beyond the common-sense understanding of religion as dealing with mystery and the supernatural and to emphasise its social nature. Thus, as Émile Durkheim pointed out in his 1915 work *The elementary forms of religious life*, one of the first sociological studies of religion, 'if in the midst of these mythologies and theologies we see reality clearly appearing, it is none the less true that it is found there in an enlarged, transformed and idealised form' (cited in Bocock and Thompson, 1985, p.1). Religious belief has a special nature and language but is clearly linked to underlying social patterns and structures.

The complexity of the religious symbolic universe may reflect the complexity of the society of which it is part. Functionalist sociologists stress how religious symbols (heaven and hell, good and evil) help to delineate the norms and values of society and how religious institutions and practices help to ensure adherence to those norms and values. They also show how religious symbols, and others including ethnic, 'racial' and linguistic ones, can be used to establish the boundaries of a society, thus helping to define who is 'in' and 'out'.

For Durkheim, a common feature of all religious systems is that they divide the symbolic world into the *profane* and the *sacred*. The profane is the matter-of-fact, everyday world that can be dealt with pragmatically, for example, the supermarket bread and wine that we may consume with our dinner. The sacred refers to aspects of the world that must be approached in a special, controlled and self-conscious way, with special sorts of behaviour and attitude, rituals and language — the bread and wine that appears and is consumed during a Christian communion ceremony. It is the meanings, actions and language that communities of believers enact around sacred objects, texts and places that helps to constitute religion.

Religions in modern societies, including Ireland, are the long-term outcome of historical processes that have seen the development of specialised and limited rites and cults into larger and more organised and institutionalised bodies of knowledge and practice. These processes include generalisation, abstraction, symbolisation and reification — all ways of organising knowledge about the cosmos — together with the development of specialised organisational and institutional structures such as churches, bodies of religious law, religious orders, seminaries and sacred works (Restivo, 1991, p.151).

THE SOCIOLOGICAL ANALYSIS OF RELIGION

The analysis of religion was of key importance to the early sociologists, both in terms of the influence and impact of forms of religious beliefs on society as a whole and in terms of the power and role of religious institutions in everyday social life. Restivo (1991, p.150) draws our attention to the important point that, from a comparative sociological perspective, religions reflect much about the nature of the societies where they are found. He suggests that the sacred realm is:

a sort of map of the social geomorphology, and the correlations between types of societies and types of religions illustrate the relationship between technological and economic development on the one hand and religious beliefs and institutions on the other.

Furthermore, religions are *active* instruments in the creation of societies. This approach to the relationship between belief systems and other aspects of social life can be found in particular in the works of Durkheim, Weber and Marx in relation to the development and evolution of religious belief.

Durkheim pioneered the functionalist analysis of religion as part of his broader attempt to develop a systematic sociology of modern society. For him the *functions* of religion include social cohesion, social control and providing meaning and purpose. Religion helps to maintain the boundaries of society and creates a sense of belonging, especially through shared participation in religious rituals and recognition of shared symbols. Religious bodies typically lay down standards of acceptable behaviour, of good and evil, and these operate to govern the behaviour of populations. Religions also tell stories that relate to the origins, history and purpose of peoples, and often speak of an afterlife. This helps to provide meaning and purpose for people over and above the mundane.

While Weber was not the first to connect religion and economic and social activity, his study of the links between Protestantism and capitalism was one of the most systematic. His work on the influence of religion, initially published in essay form in 1905 as *The Protestant ethic and the spirit of capitalism* and later expanded into a comparative historical sociology of world religions, was an attempt to study the development of religion from a historical viewpoint and to methodically explore its sociological fundamentals through the application of 'ideal types' to a mass of complex empirical material on religious belief and practice (Swingewood, 1984, p.151).

Weber did not posit a simplistic link between religion and economic activity; rather, he wanted to show that religious ideas were not mechanically linked to the economic structure but actively shaped how individuals lived out their day-to-day lives. His main concern was to explore how a set of beliefs about the world and the afterworld was linked to specific sorts of individual and group behaviour — beliefs that would ultimately underpin the development of the Western European capitalist economic system. The kernel of his analysis was how adherence to an ascetic form of Protestantism, specifically, Calvinism, led people towards a particular way of thinking about work, social values and social action.

Weber was moved to describe this particular form of Protestantism as it developed in Western Europe in the sixteenth and seventeenth centuries as 'the spirit of capitalism'. For here was found an emphasis on the deferral of gratification; on self-control; and on efficiency as a way towards salvation and away from eternal damnation. As it happened, these qualities were also those necessary for effective strategies of financial investment and capital accumulation (Swingewood, 1984, p.155):

> The spirit of capitalism is expressed in the rationalising attitude to life, in such maxims of conduct as be prudent, diligent, punctilious in repayment of debts and loans, avoid idleness since time is money, be frugal in consumption and so on. The spirit of capitalism is a social ethic, a structure of attitudes and behaviour closely identified with ascetic Protestantism and its associated religious sects such as the Puritans and the Calvinists.

Weber went on to carry out wide-ranging comparative studies of world religions in order to explore how religion, as one of the many factors that shaped societies, operated in a range of settings.

Weber's analysis has been much criticised, not least for its empirical shortcomings (see Swingewood, 1984, p.158). However, inasmuch as it emphasises religion as a crucial element in the development of society, it clearly has great relevance to Ireland for, as the historian Donald Akenson (1991, p.16) points out, during the last two centuries, it has been 'one of the most religiously sensitised nations in the western world'. Arguments similar to those of Weber have been mobilised from time to time in Ireland, especially in trying to explain why the (Protestant) north-east of the country industrialised while the (Catholic) remainder did not (see Akenson, 1991, p.18; Keating and Desmond, 1993; Garvin, 2004).

For Marx, famously, religion was the 'opium of the people': a cultural phenomenon that served to blind people to their 'real' needs. For him, religion in the form of sets of ideas or institutional structures ultimately served the needs of the ruling class in society. While Marx did not carry out systematic analyses of religion in the manner of Weber or Durkheim, his views have been influential and have helped to shape the anti-clericalism of many socialist movements.

Contemporary sociologists have paid less attention to religion, perhaps in response to the perceived secularisation of society (see below). In the Irish context Inglis (1998a; 1998d) has successfully harnessed the work of French sociologist Pierre Bourdieu to help explain the *habitus* or 'lasting, general and adaptable way of thinking and acting in conformity with a systematic view of the world' that underpins the unique position of the Catholic Church in Irish society. It is due to the development of such a habitus that many Irish people know almost instinctively how to behave in accordance with the tenets of their religion. It is, according to Inglis (1998a, p.11), 'embodied in the home, school and church [and] produces specific Catholic ways of being religious and ethical'. Furthermore, Bourdieu's concept of 'cultural capital', helps to show how being a 'good Catholic' in Irish society can translate into success at school, in the workplace, in business and political life and in the broader society.

Inglis's study of the nature of Catholicism remains the only systematic sociological study of contemporary religious experience in Ireland. It draws predominantly on the theoretical insights of Weber and Bourdieu to attempt to explain the still remarkable position of the Catholic Church in modern Irish society. For Inglis, the development of the modern institutional Catholic Church in Ireland has been a key element of the modernisation of Irish society — linked in the period since the Famine to both the emergence of a particular pattern of rural social structure and to the contemporary Irish form of the welfare state. He emphasises the role of women in the church, in particular as mothers, and traces the recent decline in church influence, which he puts down to a number of factors including the changing economic and social role of women and the growing influence of the media. A number of the themes delineated by Inglis are explored in the remainder of this chapter.

RELIGION IN IRELAND: FROM 'TRADITIONAL' TO 'MODERN'

In 1987, Inglis, in the first edition of his book *Moral monopoly: The Catholic Church in modern Irish society*, was able to say that Ireland was a particularly religious country: 'one of the first impressions of the country that marks it out as different from other Western societies is that the [Catholic] Church is a strong and active force in everyday life' (p.1). In the same vein O'Toole (1998, p.66) remarks that 'when it comes to belief in the existence of the soul, in life after death, in heaven, in prayer, the Irish score so much higher in surveys than the rest of the developed world as to seem not part of that world at all.' We can ask why, and how, has religion acquired such a central role in Irish social life?

With its tag as 'the island of saints and scholars' there has been a perception that in some ways Irish people are naturally religious. Inglis (1987, p.1) remarks that it is 'as if the Irish have always been a holy and religious people who are devoted to the Catholic Church'. Similarly there have long been notions that as a 'Celtic' people, the Irish have some sort of affinity with superstition, spirituality, magic and religious belief. We now see this view reiterated in much New Age writing and practice related to Celtic mythology (see, for example, Fay, 1997, pp.173–88). Sociological and historical analysis show that there was nothing natural or inevitable about the development of religious beliefs, practices and institutions in Ireland; rather, these can be understood as the outcome of many complex social factors.

There is within sociological thinking a tendency to see the development of Irish religion as reflecting a move from a 'traditional', highly devotional society to a 'modern', increasingly secularised one. But the modernisation approach may tend to oversimplify this process. In reality, the nature of religious belief and practice in Ireland has been very dynamic over the last two centuries and more, and its development has certainly not been unidirectional. For example, it was only with the rise of the Catholic middle-class in the late nineteenth century that Mass attendance grew from its mid-century rate of approximately 35 per cent to its turn-of-the-century level of 90 per cent (Miller, cited in Akenson, 1991, p.139). And, as we shall see later in this chapter, levels and styles of religious practice are continuing to change.

The picture that emerges from historical and sociological analysis is more complicated than a simple conception of modernisation would allow. For example, many of what may now be regarded as traditional aspects of Catholic Church practice were introduced quite recently, in the period from the end of the nineteenth century to the 1950s. Furthermore, much of what is now seen as modern or even post-modern in evolving religious practice, may represent a return to much older patterns of behaviour.

For example, historians of religion in Ireland highlight the existence of a 'folk religion', developed over a millennium, that pre-existed the development of the modern institutional churches as we recognise them today. In many respects, such as low attendance at formal religious events, a smaller gap between priests and people and a less centralised and dogmatic faith, this folk religion was closer to how many people see the modern churches developing. Some critics of contemporary religion, such as Kirby (1984, p.66), celebrate what they see as this more *authentic* expression of Irish spirituality:

> A more authentic, gentle, tolerant and yet demanding faith was lived by (our) ancestors which had a deeply developed social conscience, a healthy anti-clericalism and a complete absence of puritanism and prudery when it came to sexual matters.

Kirby suggests that the language of this pre-Famine folk religion reflected a more spiritual consciousness than that embodied in the 'stylised and sentimental prayer forms' associated with contemporary practice. It also embraced, he claims, a developed social conscience that expressed itself in everyday behaviour, for example, in respect for the poor and in a form of social organisation that appears to approach a form of primitive communism or communitarianism.

Many explanations have been suggested for the almost unequalled growth in power of the Catholic Church in Ireland in the period between the Famine and the 1980s, and the parallel growth in other organised religions (the Church of Ireland and Presbyterianism in particular) through much of the same period. There has been a great deal written on this topic, and space precludes an extensive discussion here. Historians and sociologists (see Kirby, 1984, pp.55–64; Akenson, 1991, pp.139–43; Fahey, 1994; Inglis, 1998a, pp.102–28; Keogh, 1998, pp.88–114) suggest a range of key factors (listed in Figure 14.1), some of which, it must be noted, can appear to be contradictory.

The Catholic Church that very successfully developed in nineteenth-century Ireland went on to wield extensive power in the newly independent state until very recently, as succinctly described by O'Toole (1998, p.70):

> The groundwork laid down in the nineteenth century was the basis for the Church's triumph in independent Ireland. Once there was an Irish state, it became the effective arbiter of social legislation, having a ban on divorce inserted into the Constitution, encouraging the introduction of draconian censorship of books and films, delaying the legalisation of artificial contraception until 1979, retaining largely unquestioned control over schools and hospitals funded by the taxpayer, resisting the slow development of a welfare state.

Figure 14.1 Factors affecting the development of the churches in post-Famine Ireland

- the decline of the landless cottier class (where older alternative belief systems were prevalent) due to the development of new land tenure arrangements before, during and after the Famine
- the nationalist political movement towards development of a separate national identity, where increasingly 'Irish' came to be equated with 'Catholic'
- the rationalisation of Irish society with increasing urbanisation and integration into a 'modern' and Anglophone society
- the growth of religious belief and practice as a response to rapid social change
- as part of the 'civilising process' in Western Europe, the increasing 'respectability' and 'gentling' of Irish society accompanied by the growth of moral discipline
- the successful centralisation and bureaucratisation of the various churches into more efficient administrative organisations
- from a class analysis perspective, the growth of religion suited both the British Empire and the Irish ruling class — as a distraction from class struggle and as a means of disciplining and controlling the working population.

It is common for critics to draw a pen picture of the 'traditional' (Catholic) Church in Ireland. This image is usually located somewhere around the 1950s — often seen as the heyday of the Catholic Church in Irish life, and often coinciding with the remembered childhood of the author in question. The 1920s to the 1950s has been identified as the age when 'devotional Catholicism' peaked and it saw the popularisation of practices such as pilgrimages to Marian shrines, the building of grottoes, the practice of Novenas and the development of sodalities (MacCurtain, 1997, p.247). It was also the time when the institutional church in Ireland was perhaps at its most influential (Fuller, 2005).

Thus, Kirby (1984, p.15) contrasts the early 1980s with a previous era when Ireland was 'a stagnant society, presided over by a repressive and sexually obsessed church, from which the young had to flee if they were to find any space to explore and satisfy their own needs'. Similarly, Inglis (1998a, pp.1–2) contrasts the situation in Ireland today with the memory of his own childhood devotions. As we have seen, the churches did have significant ideological and social power in this period.

There has certainly been a sea change in the nature and position of all the churches in Irish society in recent decades. The turning point is usually identified as the early 1960s, when change in the churches at the global level, as manifested, for example, in Vatican 2, combined with a period of unprecedented economic growth in Ireland and a new era of openness to international investment and influence. Kirby (1984, p.19) suggests that the new prosperity and growth in the country contributed to a new optimism for the future and a critique of the familiar institutions of Irish life, including the Catholic Church. Inglis (1998a, pp.231–8) identifies the media — not least RTÉ's *Late Late Show* — as a major instrument of modernisation and stimulus of change in the church. More recently exposure of the extent of child sexual and physical abuse within religious organisations (not just in Ireland) has been widely credited with a further weakening of the church's position. In the most recent period, substantial immigration to Ireland has seen an increase in some forms of formal religious expression, with the emergence of new religions (in the Irish context) such as African Pentecostalism and the Eastern Orthodox religions; the rapid expansion of others (such as Islam) and the rejuvenation of established groupings (such as the Church of Ireland in some parts of Dublin).

RELIGION, IDENTITY AND SECTARIANISM

The religious affiliation of the population (Figure 14.2) of the Republic of Ireland remains overwhelmingly Roman Catholic at 88 per cent in the 2002 Census, though this figure has declined significantly in the last decade; the 2006 Census is likely to reveal a further diminution in this proportion. In recent years there has been a large increase in those who do not identify with any religion, while there has also been a dramatic increase in the numbers who identify as Muslim and Orthodox. There has been something of a revival in the Protestant religions, with increases in the numbers of adherents of the Church of Ireland, Methodists and Presbyterians.

Prior to the recent increases, the decline of the Protestant religions in the republic, against the durability of Catholicism, had been perhaps the main feature of the Irish religious landscape. This decline has been attributed by historians to a number of factors, including: the return of British bureaucrats and servicemen and their families after independence; sectarianism directed against Protestants; lower rates of fertility amongst non-Catholics; the establishment of a theocratic Irish state; and the operation of the *Ne Temere* decree in relation to 'mixed marriages', whereby children were brought up as Catholics (Inglis, 1998a: pp.18–20).

Akenson (1991, p.xi) claims that 'the cultural differences between Protestants and Catholics are so central to modern Irish history that to evade them leaves a great black hole in the nation's story.' As he points out, the perceived 'fact' of difference between the two is taken for granted, in relation to both the Irish living in Ireland and the Irish diaspora. But it has also been agreed that the differences cannot be explained in terms of faith or belief alone (Akenson, 1991, p.12):

Figure 14.2 Religious affiliation in Ireland

Year	Total population	Roman Catholic	Church of Ireland (incl. 'Protestant')	Presby-terian	Methodist	Jewish	Other*	no religion	not stated
1901	3,221,823	2,878,271	264,264	46,714	17,872	3,006	11,696	–	–
	100%	89%	8%	1%	<1%	<1%	<1%		
1926	2,971,992	2,751,269	164,215	32,429	10,663	3,686	9,730	–	–
	100%	93%	6%	1%	<1%	<1%	<1%		
1946	2,955,107	2,786,033	124,829	23,870	8,355	3,907	8,113	–	–
	100%	93%	4%	<1%	<1%	<1%	<1%		
1961	2,818,341	2,673,473	104,016	18,953	6,676	3,255	5,236	1,107	5,625
	100%	95%	4%	<1%	<1%	<1%	<1%	<1%	<1%
1981	3,443,405	3,204,476	95,366	14,255	5,790	2,127	10,843	39,572	70,976
	100%	93%	3%	<1%	<1%	<1%	<1%	1%	2%
1991	3,525,719	3,228,327	89,187	13,199	5,037	1,581	38,743	66,270	83,375
	100%	92%	3%	<1%	<1%	<1%	1%	1%	2%
2002	3,917,203	3,462,606	115,611	20,582	10,033	1,790	89,223	138,264	79,094
	100%	88%	3%	<1%	<1%	<1%	2%	4%	2%

'Other' for years to 1946 includes 'no religion' and 'not stated'
(*Source*: CSO, 2004c)

> For at least a century and a quarter it has been commonplace for observers of
> Irish life to note that the differences between Protestants and Catholics in
> Ireland have nothing to do with religion *per se* and everything to do with
> divergent cultural traditions or with economic discrimination.

In other words, the relationship between religion and identity in Ireland has been,
and remains, a complex one.

From its earliest days, the independent Irish state began to define its people,
through the state apparatus and official discourses, in terms of 'Catholic' and 'non-
Catholic'. This dichotomy has always been attractive to commentators on Irish
social issues. As Akenson points out, such contrasts 'were easily drawn in the
nineteenth and early twentieth centuries and this was especially prevalent because
it was an age that was given to thinking about cultural differences in racial terms'
(1991, p.10; see also Gibbons, 1996, pp.149–63). Religious difference has become

a central theme in thinking and writing about Irish history and contemporary society, not least because of the continuing conflict in the North of the country.

Akenson's study of the historical differences between Irish Catholics and Protestants has gone a long way towards debunking many of the myths that have arisen about the two communities — both within Ireland itself and among the ethnic Irish of Australasia, North America and Britain. He focuses on a number of key areas where historians and sociologists have theoretically tied religion to other aspects of social life, specifically in relation to economic involvement, family size and structure and matters of sexuality and gender.

Akenson reports (1991, p.26) that differences in relation to family size emerged late and that present-day variations in family structure began from very small differences that emerged in the nineteenth and early twentieth centuries. Furthermore, there is evidence that the clergy of both religious groupings had similar attitudes to sexual morality; indeed, 'the image of the late nineteenth-century Catholic priest out beating the hedge rows for courting couples has become such a dominant motif that one forgets that the Protestant clergy had methods of enforcing sexual morality [for example, public shaming] that would have made the Catholic priests envious' (Akenson, 1991, p.36). Overall, based on available historical evidence, Akenson (1991, p.108) is led to conclude that, despite strong beliefs in Irish society about the social repercussions of Protestantism and Catholicism, there is:

> no empirically verifiable evidence that cultural factors caused a differentiation between the two religions on major social and economic axes. Neither in family structure, nor in economic behaviour, nor the treatment of women was there any compelling evidence for major differences, and, in some instances, there was positive evidence of fundamental similarities. What differences there were in these matters were much more plausibly ascribed to class than to culture.

Given these similarities, the interesting questions then are: how and why were the two groups so clearly differentiated? McVeigh (1995) argues that this process of differentiation can best be brought under the term 'sectarianism'. This is the process, familiar to nearly all Irish people, whereby religious differences are noted — through picking up clues from names, accent, school attended, sports played — then evaluated and sometimes acted upon in a way that is discriminatory.

The historical background of settler colonialism was obviously of key importance in the emergence of sectarianism: 'the triumph of the Protestant Reformation in England and its failure in Ireland meant that religion became the key signifier between settler and native — especially as second and third generation English and Scots planters became increasingly "Irish"'(McVeigh, 1995, p.626). By the nineteenth century, religion, politics and identity were inextricably linked in Ireland. As a result, non-sectarian politics such as that espoused by James Connolly became the exception that proved the rule.

Sectarianism — like racism — must be seen in structural terms not in terms of individual pathology. In other words, it is a quality of Irish society as much as of 'prejudiced' individuals. It has provided a means of institutionalising inequality and conservatism north and south of the border. The blatant forms of sectarianism in the North have been reflected in the South by a 'pluralist theocracy' (McVeigh, 1995, p.632) that recognised and entrenched religious difference. All major religious groups were explicitly recognised in Article 44 of the 1937 Constitution and they had high levels of control over 'their own' institutions, such as schools, hospitals and charities.

Sectarianism is about identity in the broadest sense of the term (McVeigh, 1995, p.627):

> Sectarian labels are about more than religion . . . they approximate more to notions of ethnicity — involving nationality, politics, culture, 'race', and boundary maintenance as much as faith and religious organisation. Religious identity . . . remains the main signifier of ethnic difference in Ireland.

But these identities are complex: what makes an 'Ulster Catholic' or an 'Irish Protestant'? Religious conviction and organisation is an important part of the story but what makes a Protestant a 'Protestant', a Catholic a 'Catholic' and a Jew a 'Jew' is determined by the interaction of historical, religious, social, cultural and political factors (Poole, 1997). Religion has operated in Irish society as an ethnic and cultural marker not necessarily related to beliefs or practices. Thus, suggests Akenson, 'it mattered not if an individual entered his church only to be baptised and to be buried, the life he lived between these two signal events was, in the eyes of those with whom he dealt, the life of either a Protestant or a Catholic' (1991, p.129).

Religious boundaries are both self-defined and other-defined. Each identity provides a positive evaluation of its own characteristics, plus a negative denunciation of the other side's: we're not like that lot! (Akenson, 1991, p.133). 'Otherness' was, and is, created and re-created through practices like endogamous marriage (marrying within the group, and discouragement of 'mixed' marriages) and segregated or 'denominational' education. It has only been by keeping themselves segregated in family life and by separating the young that it has been possible for religious communities — in Ireland as elsewhere — to develop and perpetuate unique world views and, at the same time, sometimes grossly inaccurate views of each other.

The harsh reality of sectarianism in the North is familiar to all. In the Republic, sectarianism was perhaps most vivid during the 1920s (Akenson, 1991, p.4):

> Mostly a rural affair, it consisted of hectoring, intimidating, burning and murdering isolated Protestants, most, but not all, of whom were owners of small town businesses or of relatively large farms . . . between early December 1922 and late March 1923 192 houses belonging to the Protestant minority in southern Ireland were destroyed. An outcome of the sectarian atmosphere that accompanied the establishment of the state was a reduction in the number of Protestants from 327,000 in 1911 to 221,000 in 1926.

It is also true that the sense of physical threat felt by Protestants in the South rapidly diminished as the state became more securely established. Meanwhile, at the political and cultural level, the first decades of the independent state saw an extension of Catholic hegemony that paid little heed to Protestant identity (Fanning, 2002, pp.39–42).

There is also evidence of considerable anti-Semitism within Irish society (Keogh, 1998). Fanning (2002, p.59) argues that the state's immigration policies were 'overtly anti-Semitic' in the period 1938–1956 and were aimed at producing a society that was 'without Jews'. He states (2002, p.63) that in Ireland Jews were perceived within the dominant discourse as 'enemies of the nation within a nationalism which drew upon religious sectarianism'. Both the Catholic Church and the Irish state, working in conjunction, expressed and put into practice anti-Semitic views.

Kirby (1984, p.52) suggests that the Catholic Church hierarchy, in its attitudes to issues such as desegregated education and 'mixed' marriages has continued to actively contribute to sectarianism, despite a rhetorical commitment to ecumenism. But in many ways the enthusiasm for division was shared by both 'sides' — each jealously guarding its own institutions, from boy scouts to schools and hospitals.

RELIGION, POWER AND SOCIAL INEQUALITY

Religion is always intertwined with structures of social inequality (Restivo, 1991, p.154):

> For the upper classes, it was a social activity intertwined with political ideologies and alliances, and a tool of oppression. For the lower classes, religion was a source of hope and release from the trials and uncertainties of everyday life. For the middle classes it was a source of rules about appropriate demeanour and deference.

There is a strong link in all societies between religion and power, including *political power*. The unity of religious and political power begins to decline in more technologically advanced and complex societies but the connections remain important, not least in Irish society. Religion has continued to be drawn upon by secular leaders in Ireland for legitimation and administrative organisation.

Religious personnel continue to be involved in political activity to shore up their own hierocratic (worldly) power.

In Ireland, the exercise of church power has taken place through ideological power (the power of belief systems), through the control of resources (land, property, health and education systems) and, it is increasingly being revealed, through coercive physical power (usually described today as 'abuse'). There has been relatively little attention paid in contemporary Ireland to these facets of power wielded by the churches: an element of the more general lack of critical analysis of religion alluded to earlier. Nic Ghiolla Phádraig (1995, p.597) has gone so far as to argue that the 'liberal critique of the church' serves to divert attention from other more important issues relating to inequality, such as the distribution of wealth. Pioneering work by Whyte (1971; 1980) analysed the often close relationship between church and state in independent Ireland, while Inglis (1987; 1998a) has usefully drawn attention to the vast institutional power and resources the Catholic Church retains to this day.

Gender and religion

Macionis and Plummer (1998, p.508) point out:

> All world religions are patriarchal. They have male gods at the centre of their cosmologies; favour men to be their officials on earth; and frequently devise ways of excluding women both from church and society. Many more recent sects and cults that are emerging seem to keep this patriarchal order.

Recent times have seen some change, most notably in Reform Judaism and most of the Protestant Churches (O'Connor, 1998, p.64). Some smaller groups, such as the Quakers, have always exhibited a high degree of equality of ministry (Wigham, 1992, p.53). The Roman Catholic and Eastern Orthodox faiths still strongly resist any moves towards equality, while the Anglican Church has seen deep divisions in some countries over the issue — especially in Australia and England.

O'Connor (1998) reminds us that most analyses of the position of women in Irish society ascribe a strong causal element to the structure and nature of the churches, especially the Catholic Church. O'Dowd (1989, pp.13–21) has outlined some of the key aspects of the evolving relationship between women and the churches in post-independence Ireland. He argues that 'to some degree all the churches shared an image of women's proper role, seeing it as familial, self-sacrificing and altruistic in the practical sense' (1989, p.13). In Catholicism, the Marian cult, which idealised motherhood while abjuring all manifestations of female sexuality, held sway. Catholic social teaching emphasised 'the family ideal, the family wage, and the natural role of woman as mother and home-maker'. This viewpoint is outlined at length in Inglis's (1998a, pp.178–200) discussion of the special role of the mother in the development of Irish Catholicism. The Protestant religions were more inclined to focus on the father as the senior figure in an economic and spiritual partnership.

O'Dowd (1989) lists a number of ways that legislation in the Free State put into practice elements of Catholic social teaching and this was accompanied by a range of other 'campaigns' and social initiatives, often (if not exclusively) aimed at women, for example, the campaigns against birth control or 'jazz dancing'. It can also be argued that the political-commercial-religious elite in Ireland has been a very male-dominated one and that this is reinforced by the existence of exclusively male elite schools and an exclusively male religious hierarchy.

The relationship between gender and religion in Ireland is not a simple one: while undoubtedly patriarchal, the churches did provide opportunities and support for women when there were few other avenues (Fahey, 1987). By 1941, one out of every 400 women in Ireland was entering a convent (cited in MacCurtain, 1997, p.248). Religious life was one of the only ways that women could access positions of power or responsibility in Irish society, for example, in further education or in management positions within the fields of education, social welfare and health. There was a contradictoriness in this position, well expressed by MacCurtain (1997, p.252):

> The image of the nun in midcentury Ireland (and elsewhere) was that of a docile and submissive figure clad in a black or white or blue sweep of garment with a medieval headdress who rarely raised her voice or eyes. Yet these same women were major players in church–state relations below the official level of the Catholic hierarchy. Owners and matrons of the main hospital systems in the country, they were entrusted by the state with the state's industrial schools and orphanages and with the responsibility of implementing the state's fragile and largely underdeveloped welfare policy.

At the level of the individual household and family, Inglis analyses in detail the role of the Irish (rural) mother in the development of the Catholic Church. His contention (1998a, p.199) is that:

> The domination and control of women by the Church, and the necessity for women to ally themselves with that dominating power if they themselves were to have any power, led to their high level of marital fertility which, in turn, created the need for postponed marriage, permanent celibacy and emigration among their children. These practices were encouraged by the mother in the home through a devotion to the Church, a rigorous sexual morality, and a physical and emotional distance from her children. It is this scenario, reenacted over the generations, that is the essence of the dialectical relationship of power between the church and family in modern Ireland.

This summarises fairly neatly Inglis's argument that the alliance of otherwise powerless mothers and the ever more powerful institutional church was the basis for the modernisation of Irish rural life and thus Irish society. The ascetic and constrained lifestyle enforced by a holy alliance of mothers and priests provided, according to Inglis's analysis, the conditions under which Irish property relations, occupational structure and demographic patterns altered in the post-Famine period. While Inglis's argument is fascinating, it is the case that similar discourses of femininity, rationalisation and control emerged in other societies where Catholicism was less influential, for example, early twentieth-century Australia (Reiger, 1985). Like Weber's suggestion of the link between Protestantism and the emergence of capitalism, Inglis's analysis of maternal power has the capacity to provoke interesting sociological analyses.

What of future relationships between gender and religion in Ireland? O'Connor (1998, p.67) suggests it is likely that religious institutions will maintain much of their current dominance, especially through their control of education; their linkages with middle-class religious pressure groups; and also inasmuch as they 'provide moral validation for the unpaid love and labour of the majority of Irish married women'. She also points to tensions, for example, in the gulf between Catholic Church teaching on birth control (a stern No) and Irish women's use of contraception (an enthusiastic Yes!). Similarly, increasing criticism is being voiced of the patriarchal nature of the church and the exclusion of women from any meaningful position in the church hierarchy.

Inglis (1998a, p.199) suggests that once women were able to access alternative sources of power through the workplace and public life (from the 1960s on) they were increasingly freed from the ideological power of the church. Gender issues have also been crucial in providing a site for oppositional discourses in relation to the church, in particular around matters of gender roles, reproduction and sexuality. While oppositional discourses to the hegemony of religion in Ireland have been few, Nic Ghiolla Phádraig (1995, p.598) suggests that *feminism* has been an important critical force, for example, through its central involvement in the various contraceptive rights, abortion and divorce campaigns.

IDEOLOGICAL CONTROL AND INSTITUTIONAL POWER

The extent of ideological control was and is reinforced by the churches' control of institutions such as education, health and social welfare and the generation of 'expert knowledge' such as medical discourses on childbirth or social studies discourses on attitudinal change.

A political discourse that focused on national identity based on difference from 'Protestant England' (and to a lesser extent Protestant Northern Ireland) helped to solidify the ideological control of Catholicism. There has been little organised (or even disorganised) anti-clericalism, unlike in France or Italy, for example. This has also been linked to the failure of left-wing politics to develop in Ireland (Mair, 1994, p.404). This contributed to the phenomenal institutional power of the church in Ireland. As Fintan O'Toole has remarked (1998, p.67):

> An Irish person was, and is, likely to be born in a Catholic hospital, educated at Catholic schools, married in a Catholic church, have children named by a priest, be counselled by Catholic marriage advisors if the marriage runs into trouble, be dried out in Catholic clinics for the treatment of alcoholism if he or she develops a drink problem, be operated on in Catholic hospitals, and be buried by Catholic rites.

O'Toole is describing the 'cradle to grave' welfare system that was developed by the churches, particularly by the Catholic Church, in Ireland during the nineteenth and twentieth centuries. The historical development of welfare institutions, and thus many of the service-delivery aspects of the Irish welfare state, is intrinsically tied up with the expanding role of the churches in Irish social life during this period. Indeed O'Toole suggests (1998, p.65) that in the Republic the Catholic Church became a 'surrogate state'. And, as Akenson (1991, p.109) points out, the institutions of the different churches were also an expression of their self-perceptions: they 'crystallised in social practice what the Irish people believed to be the proper relationship between persons of differing Christian denominations. The institutional structures were the mechanisms whereby the Irish-Catholic and Irish-Protestant people kept themselves apart from one another.'

Historically, the Protestant Churches had been involved in a number of philanthropic, educational and health-care institutions. After the repeal of the penal laws, and during the nineteenth and twentieth centuries, the Catholic Church became increasingly involved in a wide range of institutions from hospitals (for example, St Vincent's Hospital, Dublin) to homes for 'unmarried mothers' (the Magdalen Laundries), elite boarding schools (Glenstal Abbey) and borstals and residential homes for young people (for example, Letterfrack). The rapid growth of involvement in these institutions was facilitated by the large numbers of men and women entering the religious life (Kirby, 1984, p.56). This suited the state as religious labour was cheap or free, and the capital costs were met by fundraising from the flock and through 'dowries' brought in by the middle-class religious (MacCurtain, 1997, p.248)

For example, in education, a marriage of convenience was entered into between the emerging Irish state and the Catholic religious orders who already controlled significant elements of the education system. The existing denominational, single-sex schools provided a fertile ground for recruitment to the ranks of the religious, teaching costs were kept low through non-payment of full wages to religious staff and the school provided the sort of product desired by the state — young people schooled in orderliness, discipline, obedience and self-control (MacCurtain, 1997, p.249). The church offered the state continuity and stability and in return sought its support for continuity and stability in its own work (Nic Ghiolla Phádraig, 1995, p.609).

Though the operation of many religious institutions has now been opened up to critical examination, at the time of their operation there was little questioning of church control of welfare and educational institutions. As Nic Ghiolla Phádraig (1995, p.601) suggests, 'belief in the altruism of the religious running them and the fear of challenging the church together with ignorance of conditions and the inmates' lack of powerful connections isolated them from public scrutiny.' In the last two decades there has been an intense critique of such bodies, in line with trends in other Western countries. The critique has taken many forms, from films such as *The Magdalene Sisters* and TV series such as *States of fear*, to government reports (Madonna House) and statements by ex-'clients' themselves. The overall result has been a shift in the public perception of religious institutions in general.

More recent times have seen a decline of religious involvement in public institutions. The causes have been various but, as well as the exposure of abuses of power mentioned above, have included the sharp decline in vocations, especially in the religious orders; changes in church teaching about welfare and the role of the state (it had argued for the principle of 'subsidiarity', that the state should not undertake any functions that could be fulfilled by individuals or the local community — see Curry, 1998, p.10); the expansion of the state itself and its penetration into social affairs; and an increased demand for the professionalisation of services. Overall, Nic Ghiolla Phádraig (1995, p.617) argues that there has been a decline in the institutional power of the Roman Catholic Church in Ireland:

There are many spheres of Irish life over which the church has little or no influence. The mass media are the church's main competitors in the interpretation of Irish society. Public administration is outside the church's influence. The leading sector in Irish society and the one to which state policies are increasingly moulded is that of business and finance and transnational capitalism. Here again the church is inexpert and a nonplayer. There has been a growing distance between bishops and politicians with regard to social policy and family law.

Nic Ghiolla Phádraig points out that the very structures of the church are reflective of inequality: both through their hierarchical nature that centralises power, and their almost total exclusion of women from positions of power. So, despite the existence of 'a very clear radical movement' in the church (expressed most clearly in CORI), it has functioned to re-create the existing structures of inequality in Ireland. Nic Ghiolla Phádraig (1995, p.598) suggests that in Ireland the modern institutional church and the modern nation state developed simultaneously and 'gestated in mutual interdependence during most of the nineteenth century and into the twentieth'. The taken-for-granted intertwining of state and Catholic discourse was not threatened until the expansionist and consumerist economic policies of the 1960s (Fuller, 2005).

EDUCATION

According to John Curry (2003, p.77) 'the influence of the churches (especially Catholic) on the development of the [education] system is profound.' The churches retain to this day a central role in education in the Republic of Ireland, and this is recognised and supported by the state through funding and the ceding of organisational control to religious bodies. There are few other developed countries where explicitly religious schools are supported to such an extent. A number of sociologists see the religious control of education as the key to broader church power.

Schools are a major site of religious socialisation: operated through control over staffing, language, symbols, curriculum, physical environment and 'ethos'. Elite religious schools provide an analogous institution to the British 'public school' and are a source of intake for the professions, politics and business, while other schools (for example, those run by the Christian Brothers and the Ursuline and Presentation Sisters) aim to provide education for the children of middle-class and working-class families.

As in other institutional areas, the overt influence of the churches over education is waning, largely through a virtual drying up of the supply of religious to teach in or to manage church-owned schools. This was one of the reasons for the successful development of second-level community schools, despite Catholic Church objections (Curry, 2003, p.93). The church still attempts to operate as gatekeeper to the teaching profession at second level but does not have the same extreme level of influence as at primary level (where virtually *all* teacher training is still controlled by religious bodies). There is also increasing (though grudging) government support for multi-denominational primary schools, of which there are now 41 in the country, and Irish-language *gaelscoileanna* which are less directly under religious control. Another phenomenon is the significant number of Catholics attending elite Protestant-identified secondary schools such as the High School and Alexandra College in Dublin, or Newtown in Waterford (a Quaker school).

SECULARISATION

As we have seen, there is a general consensus that Ireland is, as expressed by Fahey *et al.* (2005, p.30), a place 'where religion and churches matter'. But there is also a strong view that the public power and everyday influence of religion in the lives of Irish people peaked at some time in the 1950s, and has subsequently been in decline (Fuller, 2005). This is the process that sociologists term secularisation. It is a term that until recently was almost synonymous with modernisation, but the persistent significance — indeed revival — of religion in ostensibly 'modern' societies, especially the United States, has led some sociologists to question the nature of secularisation as a process, or even its usefulness as an explanatory concept (Aldridge, 2000, pp. 89–122).

Secularisation has been defined (by Berger, as cited in Hornsby-Smith and Whelan, 1994, p.8) as 'the process by which sectors of society and culture are removed from the domination of religious institutions and symbols'. In its broadest sense, it refers to the increasing separation of the profane and the sacred, and the gradual downgrading of the latter, that has taken place since the Neolithic revolution and the development of agricultural societies. It suggests a 'disenchantment' of society (Weber's evocative term): a process whereby the spiritual and the supernatural come to play a lesser role in people's lives and may be replaced by more mundane, rational and scientific modes of thinking and expression. It is also often taken to refer more immediately to the decline of religious institutions in public life, for example a reduction in the public power of the churches and a decline in the status and prestige of religious figures. In terms more related to contemporary common-sense understandings of the concept, it can relate to a decline in participation in formal and informal religious activities, such as use of sacred objects, weekly church attendance or daily prayer.

There has been some debate about the extent of secularisation in Ireland, or what form it might take. The Moderator of the Presbyterian Church in Ireland, Dr Harry Allen, speaking in 1998, claimed Dublin to be 'one of the most secular cities in Europe, where vast numbers of people, especially those under 40, have no significant church connection' (*The Irish Times*, 3 June 1998). From the Catholic point of view, Cassidy (2002, p.18) argues that 'to an outside observer, there is little to parallel the dramatic changes that have marked the Irish faith profile in recent years, changes that have revealed the folly of presuming that Ireland was or would always remain a type of spiritual oasis in an increasingly de-Christianised Europe'. Cassidy sees the convergence between religious attitudes in Ireland and the rest of the EU as evidence of a modernisation process. Yet over nine-tenths of Irish people still see themselves as members of a religion; we see an increasing number of adherents for many churches in Ireland; and matters of religion still occupy an important place in public discourse. Some analysts have suggested that the 'public' aspect of religion has declined only to be replaced by more personalised, individualistic expressions, in line with contemporary consumer culture. Furthermore, as we have already noted in this chapter, religious belief, identity and practice are very complex entities and any attempt to 'measure' the extent of religious belief or practice is fraught with epistemological and methodological difficulty.

There have been a number of attempts by sociologists to address the issue of secularisation in the Irish context. The historical importance of religion in Ireland, combined with rapid social change in recent years, makes it an interesting test case for many of the theories about the relationships between religious belief and practice and social and economic change. Hornsby-Smith and Whelan (1994, p.5) suggest that, at the beginning of the 1980s, 'on a wide range of indicators considered, both parts of Ireland were far less secularised than any of the countries of western Europe', although there was evidence to suggest that generational change might be reducing the differences. For O'Toole, writing in 1995, Ireland remained 'exceptionally religious by the standards of the western world' (1998, p.66).

Ireland has thus appeared (as in many things) to be somewhat exceptional in relation to the links between religiosity and economic development. It appears to have experienced modernisation without a significant parallel secularisation process. It has been suggested that this might be a consequence of the links between religion and national identity, with all major religious groupings in both the north and the south of the island able to paint themselves as under threat from the 'other side', thereby retaining their attraction. Fahey *et al.* (2005, p.31) conclude that the 'complex role of religion in defining relations of dominance and subordination between competing cultural traditions ... has proved deeply enduring and has undoubtedly played a part in maintaining a central place for religion in Irish life.'

Others, including the sociologist priest Greeley (1999), have suggested that the enduring salience of religion in contemporary Irish society is not unusual, and that religion and modernity are not mutually exclusive. Typically this argument points to the United States, the quintessentially modern society that retains a very vibrant and expanding variety of religious institutions and practices. This perspective suggests that there is a fluctuating, rather than a simple linear, relationship between religion and other aspects of social change (Fahey *et al.*, 2005, p.31).

The period since the early 1990s in Ireland has been, as we have seen, one of intense social change. As well as sustained economic growth, urbanisation and suburbanisation and mass immigration, there has been a period of considerable upheaval in the churches — especially the dominant Catholic church. As in many other countries, there has been an exposure of decades of physical and sexual abuse, with linked cover-ups and legal and financial scandals. There has been a severe questioning of the doctrine of clerical celibacy, the demand for a greater role for women in the church and widespread questioning of religious doctrine in relation to contraception, divorce and other questions of sexual morality (Hug, 1999; Fuller 2002). There has also been a 'crisis' in Catholic religious vocations, and the church is unable to replace its ageing workforce. This has led many to suggest that even if Irish society resisted secularising tendencies until the 1980s, that the process has now gained considerable momentum and that Ireland is 'catching up' or converging with other Western European countries. One way to address this question is to examine aspects of religious practice in the Irish context, and to compare these with other societies.

Religious attitudes

An early source of information we have on religious beliefs and attitudes in Ireland is the survey data reported by Mac Gréil (1996). When asked if they saw their religious upbringing as a 'hindrance', very few of Mac Gréil's respondents said they did. But the importance of religion in one's upbringing appears to have become far less marked since 1972/73, when Mac Gréil carried out his initial survey. He suggests that there may be 'changes in the place of religion in the socialisation of the young . . . the religiosity of the homes and of the schools may be modifying somewhat'. He concludes that 'any rise in secularism in primary socialisation will inevitably result in a reduction in the perceived importance of religion in the growth and development of the person.'

Claims that Ireland is a secularised society, however, must confront the levels, very high by international standards, of fundamental religious belief. Thus, over 85 per cent of Mac Gréil's sample said they felt 'extremely' (25 per cent) or 'somewhat' (60 per cent) close to God, leading him to comment, once again, on the 'strong religious ethos of the population'. Cassidy (2002, p.22) reports from the 1999 European Values Study that 96 per cent of Irish respondents express a belief in God. Irish people also express a very strong belief (higher than in any other country surveyed, bar the Philippines) in core tenets of Christian religion, such as life after death, heaven, hell and sin (see Figure 14.3). (In their greater propensity to believe in heaven rather than hell, Irish people are like those in virtually every other country surveyed). Fahey (2002b) failed to find any support for the suggestion that Ireland was becoming increasingly atheist. These findings may be compared with the UK where only 21 per cent say they have no doubts about existence of God, and 26 per cent do not believe in God or do not know if He exists (Macionis and Plummer, 1998, p.517).

Figure 14.3 Acceptance of core Christian beliefs — Republic of Ireland

	Belief in God	Belief in life after death	Belief in heaven	Belief in hell	Belief in sin
1981 EVS	95%	76%	83%	54%	85%
1998 ISSP	94%	78%	85%	53%	—
1999 EVS	96%	80%	86%	54%	86%

EVS — European Values Survey
ISSP — International Social Survey Programme

(*Source:* Cassidy, 2002, p.23)

The extent of agreement with the Church diverges sharply, however, when issues related to moral teaching are explored. As Cassidy (2002, p.24) remarks, 'there is increasing evidence that Church teaching in key areas of sexual ethics is progressively less influential in determining lifestyle choices . . . on abortion, pre-marital sexual relations, extra-marital relationships and same sex relationships'. Thus, for example, the proportion of Catholic respondents (across all ages) who agree with the statement that 'abortion is always wrong' has declined from 74 per cent in 1981 to 51 per cent in 1999. By 1999 only 30 per cent of those in the 18–26 age group agreed with this view. According to an *Irish Times*/Market Research Bureau of Ireland (MRBI) opinion poll carried out in late 1997 (*The Irish Times*, 12 November 1997) only a fifth of Catholics follow the teaching of their church when it comes to making 'serious moral decisions', compared to 78 per cent who 'follow their own conscience'. This latter figure rises to 92 per cent for 18–36-year-olds. More than half of the people surveyed by MRBI disagreed to varying extents on the church's attitude to major moral and canonical issues, including divorce, contraception, priestly celibacy and women priests. Fahey *et al.* (2005, p.55) suggest that the conflicts over church doctrine, as well as the impact of church scandals, have contributed to a longer-term decline in confidence in the church that dates back to a period prior to the exposure of abuses in the 1990s. It appears, on balance, that Irish people are still very comfortable with the central spiritual claims of the Christian church, but are less likely to agree with its direction in other areas of life.

Religious practice

Another dominant strand in thinking and writing about the process of secularisation has been to focus on indicators of formal religious activity. After all, it is possible to believe one thing, but to do another. Again the work of Mac Gréil (1996) provides a useful departure point. He points out that any attempt to measure religiosity is necessarily limited and selective. For example, 'church membership', according to Mac Gréil, may be measured according to: participation in religious activity; commitment to religious beliefs and norms; acceptance by co-believers; and formal registration of membership. His own study aimed to measure only the first two of these factors. He suggests that 'levels of participation in Mass and in the Sacraments are generally accepted as basic measures of active [Catholic] Church membership'. At a deeper or more exacting level, 'various forms of pastoral and evangelising activity' are also important criteria, but these are more difficult to identify and are rarely measured.

Mac Gréil's research has been complemented by a number of surveys undertaken for the European Values Survey (Whelan, 1994; Cassidy, 2002; Fahey *et al.*, 2005), the International Social Survey Programme (Ward, 2002; Fahey *et al.*, 2005) and by frequent opinion polls undertaken by bodies such as the MRBI for media organisations and for the churches themselves. Taken together, the data indicates some fairly substantial changes in religious practices; but these processes vary considerably in terms of the sociological variables of location, class, gender and age.

Overall, surveys show that weekly mass attendance has declined from 87 per cent of Catholics, to around 65 per cent in the period 1981 to 1998 (Fahey, 2002b, p.51), to a reported 44 per cent in 2003 (*The Irish Times*, 30 September 2003). These levels may be compared to a European average of 30 per cent (O'Connor, 1998, p.61). Ireland, Poland and Malta are the only countries in Europe where monthly attendance at religious services exceeds 70 per cent (Fahey, 2002b, p.53). In Ireland the highest levels of Mass attendance are found in Connacht/Ulster and the lowest amongst those brought up in Dublin. Lower attendance is correlated with youth and with urban dwelling (see Figure 14.4). In Mac Gréil's opinion, urbanisation (especially residence in Dublin) is the strongest factor causing decline in church attendance. He suggests — in line with other analysts of secularisation from Durkheim onwards — that this may be due to a 'lack of community' in the city, though offers no evidence to support this. It remains the case, however, that church attendance is extremely high in Ireland by international standards.

Figure 14.4 Weekly church attendance by age, social class and rural-urban location, 1999–2000

Social class & rural-urban location	Age group				
	18–30	31–45	46–60	60+	All
Non-manual:					
Rural	61	69	86	94	76
Urban	24	42	73	91	49
Manual:					
Rural	32	63	78	85	63
Urban	13	45	78	82	50
All	27	56	77	89	59

(*Source*: Fahey, 2002b, p.52)

Prayer remains a popular activity, according to Mac Gréil, with nearly 40 per cent of people claiming to pray several times a day, and only 10 per cent praying less than once a week. Fahey (2002b, p.62) reports that only 9 per cent of Irish adults 'never pray', compared with 55 per cent in France and 48 per cent in Britain. Mac Gréil suggests that 'the practice of prayer on a regular basis must indicate a strong degree of belief'. The least likely to pray are those that are most educated and most urbanised. Mac Gréil surmises that there may be a decline in occasions like the family rosary or regular family prayers. This view is supported by Archbishop Dermot Clifford (*The Irish Times*, 5 November 1998) who suggests that 'family prayer would seem to be the victim of the modern age: television, telephones and the pace of life has squeezed out the family rosary.'

Confession has sharply declined as a religious activity, with over a tenth of Mac Gréil's respondents saying they never went. The MRBI figures show an even more precipitous decline in this activity. Mac Gréil suggests that this reflects a substantial change in the nature of Catholicism in Ireland that 'merits serious theological and pastoral examination'. There has also been some decline in what Inglis calls the 'magical' aspects of Catholicism: the use of religious medals, holy water, pilgrimages and retreats.

The least religious people, according to Mac Gréil, are those that are either tertiary educated or have incomplete secondary education, work in non-manual jobs, are Dublin-born, and are single males aged 21–35. These figures are borne out by the European Values Survey data reported in Fahey *et al.* (2005, pp.52–53). Conversely, the most religious people are primary-educated, well-off Connaught/ Ulster widows aged over 51. In fact, widows are so religious that Mac Gréil (1996, p.182) suggests that 'the religious practice of widowed respondents approaches that of those living a "regular life" in religious orders.'

Vocations have experienced a sharp decline in Ireland, as in the rest of Western Europe. The number of students training for the priesthood in the seminaries in Maynooth, Dublin, Thurles, Waterford and Carlow was about 220 in 1998. Two decades previously there were 600 studying at Maynooth alone (see Figure 14.5). However, as Mac Gréil points out, this is not due to parental resistance: the vast majority of his respondents would welcome their child becoming a nun or priest (presumably safe in the knowledge that — like being an astronaut — it is extremely unlikely to occur!).

Figure 14.5 Numbers entering Maynooth seminary

Year	No.	Year	No.
2006	26	1995	26
2005	19	1994	37
2004	28	1993	40
2003	19	1991	51
2002	20	1988	61
1996	18	1986	76
(*Source*: various media sources)			

THE DISENCHANTMENT OF THE (IRISH) WORLD?

The typical end-point of decline in religious adherence is not total rejection and indifference towards religion but a shift from strong and highly institutionalised attachment towards more intermittent and lukewarm adherence and towards various forms of privatised belief and commitment (Fahey et al., 2005, p.56)

A number of reasons for the decline in religious practice in Ireland have been suggested. One may be a general convergence with European and Western behaviour: figures are even lower for other Catholic countries like France, Spain and Italy. Second, the number and frequency of high-profile church-related scandals, while by no means unique to Ireland, have without doubt had a negative effect on the Catholic Church. These have ranged from the Bishop Eamon Casey case in 1992 to the numerous cases of sexual and physical abuse in church-run institutions, as well as individual cases of sexual and financial abuse. Third, the media has operated as a supplier of alternative value systems and also as an alternative way to pass time and socialise. Fourth, there has been a severe divergence between the churches (especially the Catholic Church) and much of the population in relation to social and 'moral' matters, such as contraception, celibacy, abortion and the role of women.

In 1984, Kirby was already seeing evidence that a 'major crisis' faced the Catholic Church. It had 'not yet awakened to the major challenge that faces it if it is to find any significant role for itself in the fast-changing Ireland now taking shape' (1984, p.10). It was, for him, a church that was unsure of what message it should preach and one that relied too much on a largely irrelevant set of principles and priorities. In asking Is Irish Catholicism dying? Kirby suggested that the secularising trend had been accentuated by a rupture between church and people, contributed to by the very organisational success of the church itself. The forms of the 'modern' Irish Catholic Church have actively contributed to this disenchantment: 'where the old was intimate with God and saw his hand in the things of the world, the new was stylised and sentimental encouraging a divorce between things spiritual and material' (Kirby, 1984, p.66). In 1978, a Working Party of the Catholic bishops had concluded that, 'for many the practice of religion is more a matter of law/routine/social pressure, rather than a result of intellectual or personal conviction' (Kirby, 1984, p.35). Does this mean that for many in Ireland religion has become a meaningless, ritualised practice?

Drawing on his interpretation of what was happening in other Catholic countries, Kirby argued for an activist role for the churches, with a shift in focus from policing private morality to one of public intervention in issues of public policy, such as poverty, overseas aid and ethics. It would challenge social and economic inequality and draw on the approaches of liberation theology in the developing world (1984, pp.74–83). He called for greater involvement by the laity, partly as a response to the decline in vocations, but also as 'the Church has little hope of addressing itself to the needs of the new generation of Irish people until it facilitates the laity to become involved at all levels of Church life' (1984, p.38). Harking back to the folk religion of earlier Ireland, he saw the desirable shape of the church as 'a community of ordinary Christians exploring their faith in ways which challenge them to a more socially committed life and a simplicity of lifestyle' (1984, p.13). This would find organisational expression in 'basic Christian communities' (1984, p.88), a direction echoed by other church writers such as Owen O'Sullivan (1997). Writing over a decade later, O'Toole sees a similar trajectory for the church, one where 'the Irish church in the year 2000 will look remarkably like what it was in 1800 — a focus for a relaxed but deep spirituality in which the broad culture rather than devotional and behavioural rules is what matters (1998, p.75). There is little evidence that such a change has occurred in this century; indeed the statistics reflect a growing disenchantment with and rejection of the central tenets of the Catholic church.

A similar story may not apply to other religious groupings. The 2002 Census indicated that many religions are increasing in the number of adherents, and that some such as Islam and the Orthodox religions are growing very rapidly. These figures are likely to show further growth when the 2006 census figures are available. Of course, these increases are largely due to immigration, rather than to a sudden enthusiasm for these new creeds amongst the indigenous population. There has been little published sociological research on such new religious groupings, though Mutwarasibo (2002) reports that over seventy new African churches had been established in Ireland by 2002.

Unless they are rejuvenated by the development of ethnically based faiths, the future for the mainstream, established Christian churches in Ireland may be to follow the route of the churches in other Western European societies and to 'adapt to a liberal society tacitly agreeing to provide religious services for a largely apathetic people' (Kirby, 1984, p.14). It has been suggested that many European societies are now witnessing the emergence of 'civil religion' (Bellah, 1967) or a 'social church' where people seek and use religious values and symbols without the social commitment involved — often referred to (pejoratively) in Ireland as 'à la carte religion'. For example, a former Moderator of the Presbyterian Church, Dr Allen, reported critically on 'social baptisms' among Spanish Anglicans, 'where families, suitably dressed, arrive at the church door, take photographs, and then proceed to the hotel for a meal, without ever going into the church. This also happens at confirmation time. They keep the custom but refuse the commitment' (*The Irish Times*, 3 June 1998). There is little evidence yet whether such practices are becoming widespread in Irish society.

THE FUTURE OF RELIGION?

There is much evidence that periods of rapid change lead to a greater level of religious activity. While economic, social and technological change has the capacity to undermine religiosity, for some, religious belief and practice provide a framework for responding to change. Given that there is evidence of rapid social and economic change in contemporary Ireland, how might the churches and religious practice change in the future?

This is a challenge that has been taken up in various ways by the churches in Ireland. In their attempts to respond to the threat of secularisation they have attempted to make themselves more relevant and in touch by involving themselves more in social and political issues, embracing the media and changing their practices. This may help to attract more people but it also risks blurring the sacred and profane, and demystifying the nature of religion. As Taylor (1989, p.3) points out, for religious regimes whose power and authority depends to some extent on the effectiveness of symbol and ritual, this can be a serious problem. Once the mystery has gone, what exactly is left?

One possible direction is a shift towards mysticism and New Age religions, such as a rediscovery of paganism (Fay, 1997). As the established churches become disenchanted and lose much of their mystery, perhaps there will be a greater attraction to more sect-like religious communities, and charismatic leaders may find favour over bureaucratic ones. Macionis and Plummer, (1998, p.522) report that it is estimated there may be as many as 20,000 new religious groupings in Europe alone. There is a possibility that such developments will embrace Ireland.

Catholicism and some of the other mainstream churches have at times incorporated mystical and personalised practices associated with the 'charismatic renewal' that borrow much from the evangelistic sects (Szuchewycz, 1989). The Catholic charismatic movement peaked in Ireland in the late 1970s. There is little information on the development of minority religions or cults in Ireland (but see Coulter, 1984) though public concern about them seems to have diminished compared to previous decades.

Another direction that the churches may take, which is of importance in countries like the United States and Australia, is to take a key role in the debate over emerging ethical dilemmas related to technological and social development. Many people are concerned about issues such as biotechnology, cloning, the human genome project, medical ethics, reproductive technology and the general direction of the development of scientific knowledge. At this stage, the churches have contributed little to the minimal public debate on these issues in Ireland. Similarly, there is a lot of concern about the effects of economic growth, particularly as it may lead to greater social inequality and a generally less caring society. There has been more of a response in Ireland to these issues, particularly through bodies like CORI, and the rhetoric of equality and social justice informs much of the language of the contemporary church at grass-roots level.

As Ireland rapidly becomes an increasingly multicultural society, the emergence of new ethnically based and globalised religions, such as the Orthodox faiths, Islam and Pentecostalism, will become far more significant. As in other countries of Europe, it is such religions that are the most rapidly growing. At the moment there is little apparent influence of the 'new' religions on the older, established ones, though heretofore almost moribund faiths such as Presbyterianism and Methodism have been invigorated by an influx of new worshippers, both as a consequence of immigration and a shift towards a less formal evangelical style. It is quite likely that as such faith groups expand their influence, there will be debates about their public role, for example in the area of schooling and the delivery of welfare services — areas where the established churches have had something of a monopoly.

An event that stimulated much debate about the nature of religious experience in the West, including in Ireland, was the remarkable global response to the death of Diana, the Princess of Wales. Though it has now become submerged under numerous consequent dramatic global media spectaculars, not least the attack on the World Trade Centre in 2001, this event raised the issue of what constitutes a religion, sociologically speaking. Boer (Re: Public, 1997, p.81) relates the death of Diana to the concept of civil religion — the process whereby there is a:

> dispersal of religious and mythic functions from the conventional religious institutions and into culture itself. In this process various bodies and institutions took on religious and quasi-religious functions that attempted to fulfil some of the religious needs that were no longer supplied by religious institutions.

It has been suggested that shopping and sport (Inglis, 1998c; Coakley, 1998) are perhaps among the new religions, suffused as they are with symbols, rituals and sacred sites.

Boer suggests that 'civil religion as a global phenomenon has been creeping, perhaps a little more slowly than other dimensions of culture, into the global arena, particularly through a global media that is able to transmit and present iconic figures to a world-wide audience.' Such iconic figures include Nelson Mandela, Mother Teresa, and Diana: described as (perhaps the first) 'civil religious saint'. The death of the latter two in the same week of 1997 only served to mutually reinforce their 'saintly' status. As McPhillips (Re: Public, 1997, p.88) suggests, 'there is little doubt that Diana's qualities of attentive motherhood, service to the poor and sick, personal frailty, innocence and humility have already become imbricated in a discourse of saintliness and even divinity.' If this is indeed the case, it is easy to see how her death had strong reverberations within Irish

Catholicism, where the image of the saintly Mary/mother figure is so powerful (Inglis, 1998a, pp.178–200).

Furthermore, as McPhillips further points out, the public response to Diana's death saw a (re)merging of the sacred and the secular. The funeral service itself combined elements of religion at its most formal, with celebrity schmaltz (via Elton John) and high emotion. The presence of sacred symbols was accompanied and outweighed by more prosaic and profane symbols, such as teddy bears, scribbled notes and ribbons. In effect it represented a combining of culture and faith, the sacred and the profane that harked back to earlier religious forms, not dissimilar to those called for by critics like Kirby.

More cynically, perhaps, the response to the death of Diana reflected the extent to which spiritual or religious expression has increasingly become commodified. Critics of the secularisation thesis have argued (Aldridge, 2000, pp.103–106) that it is liberal capitalist societies — such as the United States — that are most open to the growth of new religious forms, citing the Mormons and the Jehovah's Witnesses as examples of such dynamic religions. European societies, where the state is far more closely aligned with established religions, are less likely to see this type of religious entrepreneurship and consequent expansion. As in so many things, it will be interesting to see whether future religious change in Ireland takes us in the direction of 'Boston' or 'Berlin'.

15
Media

The relationship between the media and society has become an increasingly central concern within the social sciences. Media analysts pay attention to issues of ownership and control, the social organisation of media production, the nature of media audiences and the media's political and social effects. Historically, it has been a matter of some debate within media studies as to whether or not the media play an agenda-setting role with regard to the shaping of attitudes and the formation of public opinion. Early studies, for example, focused on elections and public health campaigns, and noted a correspondence (although not a causal connection) between the significance of issues as identified by the media and their salience to politicians and the general public (McCombs and Shaw, 1972; Blumler and Gurevitch, 1981; Cook *et al.*, 1983). These studies tend to overlook the fact that the priorities of three key constituencies — the media, the public and the policy-makers — may not coalesce but may, in fact, interact in complex ways and in different directions (Rogers and Dearing, 1987). While the media may not play an overt agenda-setting role, it is nevertheless deemed to be particularly effective because of its capacity to construct meanings, and to offer those constructs in a systematic way to audiences where they are likely to be incorporated, to one degree or another, into personal meaning structures (Gamson and Modigliani, 1989; McQuail, 2005).

The rise of 'new' media raise new concerns within the field of mass communication studies. According to Buckingham (2000), current debates about the perceived impact of new digital technologies in society tend to display the same sort of ambivalence that characterised earlier debates about the arrival of cinema, later radio, and television. These debates broadly fall into two strands: those that argue that new media technology have the capacity for dehumanization and a general dumbing down of culture, and those that see the technologies as tools for enhancing creative expression, communal bonding and individual self-fulfilment. The latter tend to stress the educative and interactive potential, for example, of personal computers that offer people new 'windows on the world'. In Ireland, as elsewhere, the mass media have become ubiquitous, pervasive and a part of our existence that is taken for granted. Young people in Ireland, for example, watch television an average of three hours per day, and those who have access to the Internet (the majority) use it mainly for email and to visit chat rooms (*The Irish*

Times, 20 September 2003). Three out of every five children between the age of eight and twelve own a mobile phone, with almost every child owning one by the time they reach sixth class (*The Irish Times*, 30 January 2006).

In some ways it is impossible to separate out 'the media' as a discrete entity within our society. Many of the issues and aspects of social life we have discussed in this book are permeated by the technologies and processes of the media. For example, our knowledge and understanding of crime is almost entirely determined by the media; the political process takes place largely through the newspapers, radio and television; our notion of ourselves as a modern society is expressed through advertising imagery, film and popular music; even the contours of class and inequality are reflected in the choices we make (and can make) about what sorts of films to watch, books to read, radio stations to listen to or music to download. Given the growing significance of the Internet and personalised Internet use in every day life, we increasingly have to think about audiences not just as consumers and interpreters of the media, but also as producers in their own right.

It is possible to apply a sociological imagination and critically examine the history, nature and development of media *institutions*, as organisations that pursue particular ends, from the creation of a national identity to the maximisation of profit. We can also analyse the content of media *messages*, whether they have obvious meanings that lie on the surface, or deeper, structural patterns that reveal themselves only through systematic processing and theorising. Furthermore, we can look at how people, as *audiences*, consume the media, and how they make their own sense of what they see on the screen, or read from the page, or hear on the dancefloor. The enormous success of Internet-based social networking sites such as Bebo and MySpace, and the YouTube website, demonstrate how the media and technology are helping to reconfigure how we construct and manage our personal identities.

SOCIOLOGY AND THE STUDY OF THE MEDIA

Despite how the mass media have insinuated themselves into every aspect of our daily lives, sociologists have perhaps paid them less attention than they might. There may be a number of reasons for this comparative neglect. First, sociologists have until recently tended to pay comparatively little attention to private aspects of everyday life, such as domestic work, food preparation and consumption, or everyday leisure activities. There has tended to be more emphasis on public aspects of modern society which were seen to be more important, such as work, politics and education. The mass media, as a part of life that is largely private, domestic and mundane, especially in terms of its consumption, have been victims of this emphasis.

Second, the mass media have been neglected in academic study as they fall on the wrong side of the high culture/popular culture divide. Apart from what is sometimes seen to be the more 'serious' side of the media (news, current affairs, politics and — because of its links with business and propaganda — advertising), the bulk of media output — soap operas, romance novels, chat shows, pop music — has tended to be viewed as trivial and unworthy of academic attention. There is also a strong gender division here. It is no coincidence that the media forms listed above are those that have tended to be consumed by, and associated with, a female audience.

Third, the mass media are very much a creation of two forces — technology and economics — that have tended to be neglected by sociologists, though with some notable exceptions. Sociologists, especially within the European tradition, have been demonstrably uncomfortable with analysing the commercial world of the media, except in critical terms; they are far more comfortable with the world of public service broadcasting. Similarly, and again with some important exceptions, sociologists have not examined in great detail the technological basis of our modern society. They tend to be more at home with texts (other people's and their own) than with machines, buildings or technological systems.

Finally, into the vacuum left by sociology, the analysis of the media has been largely taken over by other cognate disciplines, such as media studies, communications and cultural studies. The work in these areas draws inspiration as much from literary theory, philosophy and psychology as from sociological writers. In the United States, for example, the discipline of communications is heavily dominated by psychology while in Europe philosophy and literary criticism have provided much of the language for analysing the media. Given the well-established modes of criticism and analysis within these relatively new disciplines and inter-disciplinary fields, does sociology have anything distinctive to contribute to an understanding of the media?

We would argue that it is important to maintain a sociological dimension to studies of the media and that this can provide a useful complement to other approaches. In particular, sociologists can help to look at how people create, use and interpret the media; in this way they can balance analyses that tend to focus very much on the media as text, such as those derived from literary and film theory. Sociologists can make use of social theories and categorisations to examine how media processes are underpinned by relationships of power and inequality. According to Mary Kelly and Barbara O'Connor (1997, p.1), in one of the few published collections of sociological analyses of the Irish media, 'access to and mode of participation in [media] cultures are structured and limited by social class, by gender, by ethnicity; by location in space, and by generation.' Sociological analyses can also help us to understand how people use and interpret the media — how television, cinema, radio, Internet and other media forms are integrated into the textures of everyday life. One of the newest forms of multimedia to diffuse through society is digital game playing. According to Kerr (2006, p.128), digital games are now an intrinsic part of contemporary global flows of cultural goods, services and images. Digital games, which she suggests fuse digital technology and cultural creativity, should be seen as 'a socially constructed, dynamic and diverse cultural practice'. Kerr points out that a number of social factors, such as age, gender, race, income and class, act as a constraint on digital game players.

Given the ubiquity and pervasiveness of the media, there are many ways that they could be studied and analysed. Devereux (2003, p.9) points out that the media can be approached from a number of different and contrasting sociological perspectives that may focus on the following units of analysis:

- communication between senders and receivers
- media as industries and organisations
- texts as commodities
- texts as cultural products
- media as agents of social change and globalisation
- media as agents of socialisation and sources of meaning.

In this chapter we have chosen to follow a fairly conventional approach, in essence derived from mechanical concepts of the communication process. In this model (S→M→R) a Sender transmits a Message to a Receiver. In sociological terms we can think of these three elements as:

- the *producer* of the media message
- the message itself (or *text*)
- the *audience* for the message.

In reality, the process of communication is far more complex than this model suggests and engineering metaphors have not always been particularly helpful in understanding the human communication process but, for our purposes, it is useful to organise our survey of the media in this way.

Before looking at these three aspects in some detail, we start with a brief review of theoretical approaches to the media. We follow this with an overview of the development of the mass media in Ireland. In particular, we focus on the media in relation to the issues that have formed a key theme of this book: the experience of modernity and questions about the nature of development in Ireland. We then consider the three aspects of production, texts and audiences. We conclude with a discussion of the relationship between the media and the public sphere, and how the latter may be reconfigured in the future as a direct result of changes in media and technology platforms.

THEORETICAL MODELS FOR UNDERSTANDING THE MEDIA

There are very many theoretical models for understanding how the mass media 'work', which range from communication theories derived from engineering, to psychological and psychoanalytic models and a wide range of sociological theories that mirror the dominant perspectives within sociology. With limited space here we briefly outline some main points but for an exhaustive but accessible discussion of the numerous approaches, see McQuail (2005).

Functionalist sociological approaches to the analysis of the media tend to have much in common with the dominant perspectives in psychology. They aim to describe and understand what it is that people, and society, 'get out of' the media; in other words, what functions the media performs. In psychology this is known as the *uses and gratifications approach*. For functionalist sociology, the media have a broad range of functions in society. These include a *surveillance* function, whereby the media allow us to know what is going on around us, everything from the price of the latest mobile phone to the insurgency in Iraq and a *status conferral* function, whereby the media reflect high status individuals and groups in society, from Roy Keane to the latest *Big Brother* winner. The media also function to help *apply social norms*, partly through direct provision of information (for example, stop smoking campaigns) but also through the negative portrayal and censure of deviance, such as overeating or robbing banks. This is part of the media's broad function of the *transmission of culture*. This ranges from the socialisation of children (for example, through television programmes such as *Barney*) to the maintenance and passing on of national heritage (Irish-language programmes and films like *Michael Collins*). Finally, the media have been seen to have a *narcotising* function (or dysfunction) — they can flood society with too much information, thereby making it difficult for people to agree on norms and values or to know how best to act (Macionis and Plummer, 1998, p.587).

Criticisms of the functionalist approach and many of the psychological theories of the media centre on the fact that they tend to be highly descriptive. They are good at categorising and listing various effects and uses of the media. However, they are not very useful as a way to understand the crucial dimensions of power, conflict and inequality in relation to the media, nor are they very useful for understanding change. More critical approaches to the media have tended to dominate sociological work in the area, particularly those derived from Marxist and feminist perspectives. A key issue is the *political economy* of the media — in other words, who owns and controls the media institutions; how are media companies integrated into other forms of capitalist enterprise; and what are the relationships of power involved? A second focus is on the content of the media, especially in terms of *ideology*. How does the media provide a distorted or biased view of the world, and why might this be the case? Sometimes there is an attempt to link the two concerns: to show how particular patterns of media ownership and control lead to the dissemination of particular messages, but this is notoriously difficult to demonstrate. Furthermore, Marxist approaches to the media have paid little attention to audiences, that is, how media messages are consumed and interpreted. Much of the impetus towards an audience-focused study of the media has come from feminist research.

One of the first targets of the second wave feminist movement which emerged after the late 1950s was the mass media. In key texts of the women's movement, such as Betty Friedan's *The feminine mystique* (1963) and Germaine Greer's *The female eunuch* (1971), the imagery of advertising, and of women's magazines, in particular, was condemned. The use of blatant sexual imagery and demeaning images of women as barely intelligent 'housewives' has been a target of criticism and critique — a tradition that has continued in books such as Naomi Wolf's *The beauty myth* (1991). The subsequent rise of academic feminism within communication/media studies and sociology has seen a sustained critique not only of the media themselves but also of the paradigms, methodologies and concepts within which the media have been analysed. In particular, feminists have sharply critiqued the supposedly 'value-free' approach of much functionalist and psychological analysis. Similarly, they have criticised critical and Marxist approaches for their gender blindness. In their methodological and theoretical preference for qualitative approaches to research, feminist media analysts have brought new light to previously neglected areas of the media, such as audiences and education, and have given academic respectability to the study of previously derided aspects of the media such as the soap opera, the romance novel, pop (as opposed to rock) music and daytime radio and TV. There has been an interest in how the media are intertwined with other aspects of everyday life, such as eating, self-esteem and domestic relationships within families. Frequently, in feminist analyses of the media, there is an explicit attempt to link into broader questions of female oppression and potential, discourses of power and dominant sexist ideologies. For example, research on women's Internet usage has demonstrated that this medium offers a new means of expression for women who often feel marginalised within mainstream media. Cresser *et al.*'s (2001) exploration of e-zines found they offered women a unique medium for allowing creative expression, self-development, empowerment and affirmation. E-zines are seen to represent opinions of ordinary people that are not necessarily deemed newsworthy.

As in other areas of sociological investigation, the particular theoretical lens that is used will determine, to a large extent, the knowledge that is generated. In sociological studies of the media we can perhaps discern a pattern where a fascination with the power of technology has given way to a highly critical stance, to be in turn replaced by an acknowledgement of the complexity and diversity of the phenomenon being studied and the potential to shape technology in our own interests. This reflects how new media technologies themselves are received with various combinations of enthusiasm and fear, before they either fade away (CB radio, skywriting) or are assimilated into the textures that are taken for granted in everyday life (TV, mobile phones). The challenge for sociologists, then, is to analyse the place of the media in social life, without ascribing them a greater influence than they might merit.

THE MEDIA AND NATIONAL DEVELOPMENT

The mass media embrace a very broad range of institutions and activities, content and audiences. Traditionally, perhaps, they are seen to refer to newspapers, magazines, film, radio and TV. They may also expand to include book publishing; the recorded music industry; numerous aspects of advertising; digital games and arcades; theme parks; and, most recently, online services. In this section we examine very briefly some aspects of the development of three main areas of the Irish media: newspapers, radio and television, as these are the ones that have been given most attention by historians and sociologists. The potential for further research into the Irish media is great. The development of the media in Ireland has been very much tied up with the emergence of the nation state and with the 'identity' of that nation. The state has occupied an influential role in the development of the Irish media, for example, in relation to broadcasting policy. During the nineteenth century, newspapers were actively mobilised in support of nationalist and unionist politics; in the early part of the twentieth century, radio was central to the formulation of the newly independent state; film has been mobilised as a carrier of messages about national identity; and since the 1960s television has been seen as an overarching symbol and carrier of modernity. More recently, policy-makers have identified the Internet as a way of responding to the opportunities of an increasingly globalised world. Ireland is not unique in the fostering of such overt linkages: the media have been closely linked to the development of the state in societies as diverse as Nazi Germany, the emerging island nations of the South Pacific and developing economies such as Malaysia.

Despite this central role, the Irish state has not maintained direct control over the media in the manner that has been evident in many emerging nations. Rather, as Hazelkorn suggests, state policy towards the media has 'mimicked economic policy generally: the state filling the vacuum, promoting, regulating and deregulating sections for pragmatic, never ideological, reasons and in ways always beneficial to private interests' (1996, p.29). As long as private enterprise has been able to reflect the dominant ideological tenor of the country, the state has been prepared to allow it free rein. The government has become involved in the media industries only when there has been little capacity or enthusiasm in the private sector to participate. Then it has done so in ways that have ensured benefits flow to private business people and other powerful groups.

Pervading many of the debates about the mass media has been the issue of domination by outside forces and the extent to which the Irish media can, or should, be a means of fostering, developing or reflecting a distinctively Irish culture. Concern about the influence of British and American cultural products — particularly mass media products such as magazines, films, TV and radio programmes and popular music — has been long standing. It formed part of the early debates over the establishment of a national radio service (McLoone, 1991) and the creation of a national television service and was revisited in the 'Rainbow Coalition' government's *Green Paper on Broadcasting* in 1995 (Department of Arts, Culture and the Gaeltacht, 1995, pp.132–6). There is evidence that the early days of the Irish state saw a strong ideological element to media policy. The development of aspects of the media, for example some newspapers and radio and to some extent film, were tied to particular ideas about national identity and culture. In this regard the emerging Irish state was no different to others attempting to nation-build through 'imagining communities' (Anderson, 1993). As in many countries, the relationship between state and media has also involved religious bodies, and Inglis (1998a) has stressed the powerful influence of the Catholic Church, especially in relation to issues of censorship.

Newspapers

As a mass medium, newspapers have had a long history in Ireland, with the first newspaper being published in 1649, and the oldest in continuous publication being the *Belfast Newsletter*, founded in 1737 (Oram, 1993, pp.53; 105). The development of newspapers has been intertwined with social and political struggle. For much of their history, newspapers have been associated with particular political groupings or positions, or have reflected the concerns of economic and social interests. But, like virtually all other mass media in Ireland, the press is dependent on advertising, with at least 43 per cent of its income coming from this source (Rapple, 1997, p.70). More recently they have attempted to broaden their commercial appeal in response to competition from magazines, radio, TV and now online information services. But the market continues to be highly segmented, with particular newspapers targeting, for example, well-off business people, while others define their readership in terms of local communities.

An interesting example of the development of newspapers in relation to their social context is found in the now-defunct *Irish Press* newspaper group, which embodied the desire of many nationalists to break free from British cultural domination. This motive was one of those underpinning the foundation of the *Press* newspapers. In the 1920s Thomas O'Rahilly, a leading Catholic spokesman, asserted that 'in matters of the spirit we are becoming more and more England's slaves'. Publicity seeking support for the launch of the *Irish Press* claimed that 'the Irish people were in a condition of mental bondage, purchasing from their British former masters practically all the material which sustained their minds' (Curran, 1996, pp.8–12). The *Irish Press* was founded specifically as a communications medium for the Fianna Fáil party — in the face of hostility from existing papers

— and was 'central to [the party's] struggle for hegemony in the early 1930s' (Curran, 1996, p.8). The interests behind the paper were a complex mix of American supporters of the party, prominent members of the Irish bourgeoisie, local party organisations and activists and the leadership of the party itself, in particular Éamon de Valera. There was also tacit support from the Catholic Church, and the party used the church's campaign against popular British newspapers as a way to assist the development of the *Irish Press*.

According to Curran (1996, p.13), the *Irish Press* was a populist paper. In other words, it 'represented "the people" as a political category with interests separate and distinct from the pro-metropolitan interests of the "elite" in power'. It sought to channel working-class radicalism towards the Fianna Fáil party. In line with dominant Catholic thinking of the time, it presented rural culture as the 'authentic culture of the people'. It also had an early emphasis on and consciousness of the dependency of the news media on the news agencies of the core countries, in this case Britain, and pursued an anti-imperialist line. Thus, 'the guidelines for subeditors reflected a conscious determination to align the press with anti-imperialist and revolutionary movements elsewhere in the world, even to the extent of giving limited sympathy to the Soviet Union' (Curran, 1996, p.15).

As the independent Irish state developed, the *Irish Press* continued to reflect the position of Fianna Fáil, which was to become the dominant political force in the state. It attempted to appeal to the same coalition of interests as did the party: a sometimes uneasy mix of small farmers, the urban working class, indigenous industrialists and the nationalist political position. To many it reflected the voice of 'official' Ireland, with support for nationalist politics, the Catholic Church, rural life, the Irish language and private property. O'Brien (2001) has argued that the *Irish Press* ultimately was de Valera dominated rather than party dominated. He chronicles the disintegration of the relationship between the Fianna Fáil party and the newspaper. Over time the *Irish Press* company found itself alienated from its traditional readership base, in a modernising Ireland and a changing Fianna Fáil party. Its closure in the mid-1990s marked the end of 'the old certainties of Catholicism, nationalism and republicanism . . . replaced by the vulgarities of consumerism, pragmatism and a brand of consensual politics' (2001, p.230).

Ireland, despite the domination of the Independent News and Media group (see below), has a flourishing newspaper culture. At the national level, readers have access to a broad range of views from Irish and imported newspapers. There is also a strong local newspaper industry; local newspapers are very much tied to locale, with close coverage of affairs in specific parishes and neighbourhoods. Local newspaper publishers have been very assiduous in providing local coverage, with 'editionalising' to reflect particular markets in different areas or suburbs.

Radio

The foundation of Radio Éireann was based at least partly on a desire to escape the influence of British music-hall entertainment. Radio was perceived as a very important medium in the nation-building process. The national service was launched as 2RN in Ireland in 1926. According to Hazelkorn (1996, p.28), it was consciously modelled on the BBC formula for public service broadcasting. It was part of the civil service and was seen as a vehicle for promoting national sovereignty and cultural/religious identity. According to a historian of Irish broadcasting (Gorham (1967), cited in McLoone, 1991, p.4), Irish radio was:

> expected not merely to reflect every aspect of national activity, but to create activities which did not exist. It was expected to revive the speaking of Irish; to keep people on the farms; to sell goods of all kinds from sausages to sweep tickets; to provide a living and a career for writers and musicians; to re-unite the Irish people at home with those overseas; to end partition.

According to Kelly and Rolston (1995), Radio Éireann had a 'symbiotic' relationship with both the Catholic Church and the Gaelic Athletic Association (GAA), two of the more powerful institutions in the new state. Broadcasts of religious and sporting events helped to build radio audiences and also increased the influence of the institutions concerned. Radio was important in the preservation and subsequent repopularisation of Irish traditional music and also, in the 1940s and 1950s, for the development of Irish drama, with broadcasts of new plays by writers such as Brendan Behan, Austin Clarke and James Plunkett (Fallon, 1998, p.147).

As Brian Fallon suggests (1998, p.11), the process by which elements of 'culture' are used and appropriated are complex and not necessarily amenable to direction from the state or other powerful societal forces such as the churches:

> Ireland, badly in need of a developing national culture of her own, was hopelessly outgunned by external forces — mainly commercial — over which her leaders had little control, and few institutions or public bodies knew how to combat these forces effectively. Well-meaning but backward-looking people might call jazz 'jungle music', and Radio Éireann for a while held out against it, yet that did not stop the young from buying or listening to jazz records. If officialdom was hostile to swing music and the like, it was a simple matter to switch to the BBC Home Service and listen to Henry Hall. The clergy might storm from their pulpits on Sundays against the 'pagan' English yellow press, yet in nearby streets — sometimes, even, just outside the church gates — those same newspapers were on sale and doing a brisk trade. As for the popular cinema, it was of course subject to censorship, but in no way could it be

banned; it was a source of state revenue, and arguably it kept young people out of worse places, such as pubs.

RTÉ now serves a diversified and differentiated audience, in conjunction with local and national privately owned stations. Since the late 1970s, the dominant position of RTÉ has been challenged by these commercial radio stations, particularly at the local level. Independent radio was legalised in 1989, in the face of concerted opposition from the national broadcaster, after over a decade of almost unfettered activity by pirate radio stations that developed a loyal local listenership. Despite early financial and programming problems with stations such as Capital (Dublin) and national stations Century and Radio Ireland (now Today FM), plus the removal of a license from a Limerick station, local radio now appears to be in a very healthy state.

As of 2007 there are twenty-six independent local commercial stations and a further nineteen communities/communities of interest stations broadcasting in Ireland.

Television

Television arrived in Ireland at 7 p.m. on New Year's Eve 1961 though, for a short period prior to that, some enthusiasts on the east coast were able to pick up British TV signals (Tobin, 1996, p.63). RTÉ was set up under the Broadcasting Act 1960, which not only established the television service, but removed broadcasting as a whole from the direct control of the Department of Posts and Telegraphs. By 1966, 85 per cent of Irish homes had a television set (Sheehan, 1987, p.138).

The development of television in Ireland has been very important in relation to debates about modernity. In the 1960s a national TV network, like a national airline, became a very important symbol of development. In this regard, Ireland was no different to other similar European countries, such as Norway, that adopted TV at a similar time (Macionis and Plummer, 1998, p.586). Hazelkorn (1996, p.28) describes how TV in Ireland has been associated with modernising tendencies:

> The arrival of Radio Telefís Éireann in 1960 coincided with a phenomenal growth rate of economic change, transforming Ireland within a decade from an agricultural to an industrial society. Over the decades it has powerfully challenged traditional cultural forms and vented the aspiration of an emergent middle class, whose allegiances are increasingly attuned to Continental Europe, undermining the primacy of the countryside in national life.

For Inglis (1998a, p.92), similarly, television was a key instrument of modernisation. It 'brought the sophisticated, glossy image of urban life into the heartland of rural Ireland. It provided a constant reminder of what most Irish people were not'. For him, it was also instrumental in bringing about the gradual decline in the power and authority of the Catholic Church: 'the social process where moral discourse was limited to what was taught in the school, read in the occasional newspaper, heard on the radio and from the pulpit every Sunday, was changed by the little box which appeared in the corner of Irish homes' (1998a, p.93).

As in many countries (for example, Australia), the early days of TV saw domination by (and concern about) American programming, from *Mr Ed* to *The Fugitive* but, gradually, home-produced material became more popular, as the country developed the infrastructure and personnel necessary to create it. RTÉ came to produce an impressive amount of drama and other programming that often attempted to relate directly to the social changes that were taking place in Irish society (Sheehan, 1987). Of particular importance were debates over economic development and the liberalisation of family law (Kelly and Rolston, 1995, p.574). Ultimately RTÉ's public service remit has been somewhat compromised by its dependence on advertising, as this has inevitably limited its ability to push beyond the limits of popular taste. Inglis (1998a, p.232) sees the commercial element as very important and links the development of television to the expansion of advertising and the creation of a consumer society in Ireland. More recently RTÉ has tended to follow successful commercial templates from elsewhere, such as reality-type programming and talent-spotting shows. According to Corcoran (2004, p. 3), a strong public service broadcasting system remains the best hope for original Irish production, given the rather weak television economy and the unregulated commercial television system.

We have provided a very sketchy outline of some of the media development in Ireland. Each media form, of course, has its own detailed and complex history. In the three forms mentioned here, we can see a common involvement in issues of national identity. Such debates tend to be most intense in the period around and shortly after the introduction of a new medium, when provision is likely to be limited and the state is most involved. As the medium becomes more ubiquitous and as commercial considerations become more dominant, the medium often tends to become taken for granted. Few people, except for 'moral entrepreneurs' and perhaps media studies academics, get very worked up about what is on TV in Ireland today; radio is virtually ignored; and the most voluble public discourse is reserved for the new mass medium: the Internet.

Media and Irish identity

Kelly and Rolston (1995, p.563) suggest that the Irish media have had to tread a fine line between seeking 'to represent the existing socio-cultural worlds' within Irish society, and reproducing a particular version of cultural and national identity. They argue that the broadcasting media have been particularly successful in elaborating and developing a specific sense of Irish national identity without endangering social solidarity or losing touch with large sections of their listenership. But the elaboration has been 'within relatively narrow confines . . . defined by class, gender and elite interests within Irish society and by the existing consensus which favours these groups' (1995, p.576). Thus, RTÉ reflects a picture of the Irish as a homogeneous people that live in family households; are largely uninterested in intellectual debate or in high culture; share interests in sport, current affairs and a limited range of 'traditional' and popular forms of music; and are fond of chat. For Kelly and Rolston (1995, p.570), 'the united phalanx of nation, state and church, reproduced on radio, did not encourage the development of alternative cultural practices or of a class-based cultural critique. On the contrary, the all-encompassing concept of nation functioned to hide class differences, as well as those based on gender.'

A recent analysis of the re-vamped Angelus broadcast on RTÉ Television is an interesting case in point. While apparently modern, this newer Angelus relies on mythic and pre-modern versions of Irishness: 'it employs images of nature, craft labour, and reproduction to generate themes of the Irish as self-sufficient, hardy, unpretentious, industrious and intelligent' (Cormack, 2005, p.272). Cormack argues that these themes are rooted in a 'race memory' of Celtic Ireland that was promoted widely in the eighteenth and nineteenth centuries but which still resonates with Irish people today. Nevertheless she concludes that the attempts to link these themes to national identity in the Angelus broadcast are at variance with the spatial and temporal realities that now characterise Irish people's lives.

It is undeniable that the media have had an important part to play in the development of an Irish identity. Yet they have also been important in linking that identity to others in complex and sometimes contradictory ways. Thus, while the Irish media institutions have been an important element in the development of an indigenous 'Irish' culture, the same institutions can also be seen to have played an important role in the integration of Irish culture into a broader Anglo-American culture and its particular vision of 'modernity' which has become dominant in the years since the Second World War. The influence of this global culture is often seen in terms of cultural imperialism.

The media and cultural imperialism

Cultural imperialism is a concept that has come to prominence in the post-war period, particularly in the context of discussions about the media and their relationship to development and modernisation (see Chapter 3). The pre-eminence of Anglo-American media forms, from action movies and soap operas to advertising, has raised concerns about the effects that global (usually understood as Anglo-American) culture may have on local or indigenous cultures, especially in peripheral or semi-peripheral countries such as Ireland, Malaysia or Australia.

There are concerns that the world's cultural diversity could diminish (much as there are concerns about eco-diversity of animal and plant species) and that the result will be a homogeneous global culture. An optimistic view of this process is that the intensification of contacts and communications across cultural boundaries will produce a cultural melting pot from which may emerge a new global culture that is an amalgam of elements of the separate cultures it replaces. A more pessimistic, and more widespread view, is that the dominant Anglo-American culture may usurp the role of other cultural forms and become *the* worldwide culture.

Cultural imperialists take the latter, pessimistic view. They argue (for example, Sklair, 1995, p.151) that the culture of powerful countries is imposed on weaker countries in an exploitative way. Powerful First World countries have the capacity to impose their values and beliefs not only on poor Third World countries but also on wealthy industrialised countries such as Canada, Australia and Ireland. Global culture is then not the outcome of equal participation by all of the world's cultures but the result of dominant societies' imposition on other cultures and societies. While this thesis has focused on a whole range of cultural forms, from management theories to forms of wedding ceremony, the mass media are seen as the key channel for cultural imperialism (Street, 1997, p.75).

An influential proponent of the media imperialism thesis has been the American dependency theorist Herbert Schiller. During the 1970s his work created considerable interest in many countries, including Ireland, as people began to express concern about the extent to which 'foreign' media was displacing local or national indigenous media. He argued (1979, p.23) that transnational media groups (these would now include companies such as Sony, Philips, AOL/Time-Warner, Bertelsmann, Disney, News International, Reuters) should be seen as agents for 'the promotion, protection and extension of the modern world system and its leading component, the MNC [multinational corporation], in particular'. Global media work to open up, create and deliver global markets to other multinational corporations and through the manipulation of mass media audiences, transform these into loyal consumers of the products of the TNCs.

Though Schiller writes about transnational media corporations and dominance of the media by core areas of the world, it is primarily the US-based media TNCs he has in mind and which his theories have been most used to critique. 'Proving' the cultural imperialism thesis has been understood primarily as a matter of documenting the ownership of the global mass media and the origins of their content. If in a given society the media are found to be largely owned by US-based TNCs and/or if their content is found to originate primarily in America, this is seen as evidence for media and cultural imperialism. A world media system characterised by cultural imperialism will be found to be markedly asymmetrical; it will contain far more information flows from the centre to the periphery than the other way round — people in the periphery come to know a lot about the culture of the centre society but centre societies learn virtually nothing about the periphery. Moreover different peripheries will learn very little about each other. For example, in conflicts between Rwanda and Zaire during the 1990s, letters to the press in South Africa complained that while the South African media focused on news of entertainer Michael Jackson and then US President Clinton, it said little about what was happening in another part of Africa. Similarly, it could be said that in Ireland we know more about the weather in the United States, than we do about the politics of Denmark or Austria.

Schiller's approach stimulated much research that established the overwhelming extent to which the world media were penetrated by American-owned corporations and American cultural content. In the case of broadcasting, it suggested that global media flows were controlled predominantly by American and European TNCs, with formidable barriers facing outsiders who might try to gain entry to the system (Sklair, 1995, p.161). TNCs can 'dump' their products on Third world countries, including news items and programmes, while the flow of news from poor to rich countries remains very restricted. A study of international television flows in the early 1980s found large amounts of imported, mainly US, entertainment programmes in most of the sixty-nine countries surveyed, especially at prime time periods when advertising revenue is at its highest. While fears about the Americanisation of culture and the death of national/local culture as expressed by the cultural imperialism model continue to cause concern, other theorists have put forward an alternative *cultural integrity* model. According to this model, local cultures are resistant to an imposed global culture because of the integrity of local language, local social supports and other barriers of culture. Furthermore, analysts such as Appadurai (1996) and Featherstone (1997) have argued for a conceptualisation of globalisation in terms of flows that are not necessarily unidirectional.

Schiller's ideas prompted some research (Fahy, 1978) in Ireland that revealed the state of media dependency. As early as the 1940s three-quarters of all feature films screened in Ireland came from the United States, and a further fifth from Britain. The Irish experience was not very different from other European countries at the same time, where the proportions of American films screened ranged from 80 per cent in Belgium to 67 per cent in Spain. Even in countries that had their own film industries, like Britain and Italy, around two-thirds of all films screened were imported from America. In relation to TV, Fahy noted that in 1976, 59 per cent of RTÉ transmission time was made up of imported programmes, mainly sourced from the United States and the UK. Conversely, imported material made up only 2 per cent and 13 per cent respectively of United States and UK domestic TV schedules. In addition, of course, many (over 45 per cent) Irish TV viewers also had access at that time to a range of domestic British TV channels.

Data for radio and for newspaper readership appeared more hopeful. RTÉ radio had 73 per cent of the audience compared to, for example, 11 per cent for BBC Radio 2. RTÉ material was reported to be overwhelmingly Irish-sourced, though this may have concealed the real origin of programming, for example, most music material was recorded outside Ireland by non-Irish artists. Readership of Irish newspapers was also high — about two-thirds of adults claimed to see an Irish daily fairly regularly and about 88 per cent claimed to read an Irish Sunday paper. This compared with up to 12 per cent seeing English daily papers and about 40 per cent reading an English Sunday paper on a regular basis. Once again, this may conceal the real sources of information. Like all newspapers, the Irish press is heavily dependent on overseas-based news agencies, such as Associated Press (AP) and Reuters, for a very large proportion of news material. According to Fahy, Ireland was probably even more dependent on news agency sources than other small European countries due to the small number of foreign correspondents retained by Irish media companies.

Things have changed considerably since Fahy's research, but the direction of change is not easy to capture. A small but increasingly significant film industry has developed in Ireland, though the flow of material into cinemas that is not Irish or Anglo-American has probably declined. Irish audiences are increasingly fragmented. Multi-channel television, with a great many more channels than in the 1970s, is now available to most Irish viewers and this increase contains a greater choice of Irish-based stations, as well as many satellite and digital channels. The strength of Irish newspaper reading and radio listenership appears to be in decline, though again the field has been reinvigorated to a certain extent by new outlets, for example, *The Sunday Business Post* and expanding local and community radio, as well as national stations in Today FM and Newstalk 106. There has also been a boom in magazine publishing. Joint National Listenership Research (JNLR)(2006) showed that 85 per cent of the adult population listen to a mix of national, regional and local radio throughout the country. RTÉ Radio 1 remains the dominant single player in the market, garnering a 24 per cent share of the national audience; but listenership figures for regional and local radio continue to rise with a market share of just under 52 per cent in the key daytime (7 a.m. to 7 p.m.) period. The material used in radio programmes appears to have a higher Irish content than before as Irish performers have gained international prominence and distribution. In addition, the use of Irish foreign correspondents by newspapers and broadcasting news departments, in preference to the transnational news agencies, has increased.

It is difficult to be conclusive about the nature or extent of cultural domination in today's complex global mediascape. Ireland is saturated with media images derived from other cultures, as is the case for nearly all societies. Yet there remains a vigorous local media discourse, with strong and consistent audiences for indigenous products such as national and local newspapers, local radio and Irish-produced TV programmes. Furthermore, Irish audiences may have the capacity to interpret media messages from a range of sources through their own interpretative frameworks (see below). O'Toole (1997, p.171) suggests (pessimistically), 'for a generation that grew up on American television shows, America will always be interwoven with memories of an Irish homeland and an Irish childhood.' But it will always be the case that how Irish children (and adults) interpret *The O.C.*, *The Simpsons* or *Dawson's Creek* has at least the potential to be very different to the meanings derived in California. Furthermore, analysts of the Irish media now have to contend with a new factor: the undoubted success of some Irish media products within the global mediascape.

In particular, a recent collection of essays has focused on the valorisation of Irishness within American consumer culture. Irishness, it seems, can be invented, imagined and consumed as heritage and culture, while simultaneously acting as a marker of ethnic identity. As Negra (2006, p.4) observes: 'from the massive international success of the music/dance revue *Riverdance*, to the juggernaut of Celtic-themed merchandising, and the spate of Irish themed material on Broadway, Irishness, it seems, circulates every more widely in contemporary culture.'

How then are we to interpret the success of U2, Boyzone and Westlife, the Irish soccer team, *Riverdance* and Roddy Doyle on the global stage? Has this led to an increased national confidence and strengthened national identity, or has Irish culture been undermined by globalisation, understood as Anglo-American media imperialism?

MEDIA PRODUCTION

As mentioned at the opening of the previous section, the diversity of media forms makes it very difficult to generalise. This applies also to the processes and institutions of media production. Each form, whether TV, newspapers or recorded music, has its own organisational and institutional processes and forms and also specific technologies and occupational roles. For example, it is impossible to discuss together the work of journalists and sound engineers, without a comprehensive understanding of the newspaper and music industries.

Yet there are important commonalities about the processes that shape the various forms of media production. As media forms become established, there emerge institutional, industrial and regulatory processes that strongly influence the day-to-day production of media messages. A large media organisation like RTÉ or *The Irish Times* is in many ways like any other large bureaucratic organisation. The production of the evening TV news or an edition of a newspaper is the outcome of the work of many people, organised in an occupational structure where routines, work practices, bodies of knowledge and forms of technology that help to structure the final product are often taken for granted. In addition, there are legal controls and limitations, such as those presented by Ireland's powerful defamation laws, which may produce a 'chilling effect' on public discourse. At times, the structure and nature of the ownership and control of media organisations may have an important influence. It may be hard to demonstrate the personal intervention of a media tycoon like Rupert Murdoch or Tony O'Reilly, yet the particular company policies, management styles and individual preferences of media owners can shape the nature of the media product. We look briefly here at two aspects of the media production process: media ownership and the role of technology.

A feature of media ownership across the world is the *convergence* of formerly separate companies into large media conglomerates. Some of the names of these conglomerates are also familiar global brands, such as Sony, Disney and Philips; others may be less well known in the public arena (Viacom, Bertelsmann, Vivendi). The business pages of the press are full of stories of takeovers and mergers, as formerly nationally based companies like Eircom, Disney or Bertelsmann seek out 'strategic partners', joint venture opportunities or are involved in takeover bids. Increasingly, media companies are vying for control of the emergent players within the new media sector. Rupert Murdoch, CEO of News Corporation, who describes himself as a 'digital immigrant', purchased the highly popular Myspace.com online community for US$580 in 2005 (*BBC News/Business*, 19 July 2005). In 2006, Google, the Internet search engine, acquired YouTube, another social networking site whose content is uploaded by its users, for US$1.65 billion.

The convergence of media production operates at two important levels. On the one hand, there is the coming together of previously disparate companies into giant business conglomerates. A media conglomerate will typically embrace interests in the production, distribution and/or marketing of some or all of the following: film; video; TV; recorded music; book, magazine and newspaper publishing; business information and consultancy; satellite services; computer software, mobile telephony, and perhaps consumer electronics, toys or theme parks. Thus, it is now unsurprising for a particular media product — such as Madonna or *Star Wars* — to be produced and distributed through multiple arms of the same global conglomerate.

The convergence at the business level has been facilitated by technological convergence, especially through the development of *digital technologies*. Digitisation means that formerly separate technologies, such as computers, photocopiers, telephones and TVs, can now 'talk' to each other and, increasingly, can be combined to form new products. Similarly, digital production and recording has broken down the boundaries that previously existed between film, television, music or computer software. Any of these is now easily convertible into another, and new entities such as digital movies, computer games and the Internet are entirely new types of media that could not exist a short time ago.

There is considerable debate over the effects of the changes that have taken place. Critics argue that convergence may have similar effects to cultural imperialism; indeed, the two processes are often seen to go hand in hand. For example, the foreign ownership of most of the Irish telephony industry serves to reduce the capacity of the Irish people to control their 'own' telecommunications and media. Convergence is linked to the marketisation of the media industries, with a perceived reduction in the public service ethos that has typified European (and Irish) broadcasting.

On the other hand, it is possible to see how the processes of industrial and technological convergence can 'open up' the media. The emergence of giant conglomerates and the decline in the monopoly public service organisations may provide space for the development of smaller, 'niche' players in the interstices of the mega-media corporations. In Ireland, for example, there has been a huge expansion in the number of independent production companies in the TV, film and audio-visual fields. Furthermore, the digitisation and miniaturisation of production technology means that people can now make videos, publish books or produce music recordings, and even distribute them, without the need for a large production infrastructure like a record company, publishing house or film studio. Partly as a consequence of such technological change, but also due to financial pressures, public service broadcasters like RTÉ and TG4 are increasingly acting as facilitators and *publishers* of programming, with their core production activities being stripped back to such activities as news and current affairs.

Media ownership in Ireland

In Ireland, as elsewhere, newspapers, magazines and radio stations are increasingly owned by large conglomerates, often with other interests in areas such as the food industry or other branches of the entertainment industry. Furthermore, in Ireland, unlike in the US and Australia, there is no specific legislation in place to control media ownership. Little research has been carried out in Ireland into media ownership or the impact of cross-media ownership (where a company has interests, say, in newspapers, TV and telecommunications). Concern has been expressed from time to time about these issues and other effects of media monopoly, such as political interference and below-cost selling of newspapers. In 1995, in the wake of the collapse of the *Irish Press* group, the government established a Commission on the Newspaper Industry, but it found nothing to overly concern it, largely reflecting the viewpoints of the existing media players (Horgan, 2001, pp.160–2).

At the same time such is the pace of change in these dynamic industries that any account of ownership risks becoming immediately out of date, so this section will sketch out a snapshot of the media landscape as of early 2007. In Ireland, the public media sector has been dominated by RTÉ, embracing TV, radio, teletext, the *RTÉ Guide* and, until 1999, cable television distribution. RTÉ has also developed online media and is interested in digital broadcasting. The over-whelmingly important indigenous media player in the private sector is the Independent News and Media (INM) group, with international interests in a range of media including newspaper and magazine publishing; newspaper wholesaling and distribution, commercial printing, outdoor advertising, broad-casting, cable TV, telephony and the Internet. It has a dominant position in the Irish newspaper industry, accounting for two-thirds of all daily Irish newspaper sales and a large proportion of Sunday newspaper sales. It owns the highest selling daily newspaper, the *Irish Independent*, plus the *Sunday Independent*, *Evening Herald*, *Star* and *Sunday World*. The group launched a new daily freesheet, *Herald AM* in October 2005, and the *Polski Herald* which caters to Ireland's growing Polish community, was launched in November 2005. It also owns a number of regional weekly newspapers (including the *Kerryman* and the *People* newspapers). The INM group's Internet website, Unison.ie, supports 27 national and regional newspaper titles and is the leading news portal in Ireland, with almost 17 million page impressions per month (*INM Annual Report*, 2005).

The company is also a global media player with interests on three continents and a global workforce of 10,400. The INM group manages gross assets in excess of €4 billion. Spanning four continents and 21 individual countries, INM has market-leading newspaper positions in Ireland as well as Australia (regional), India, New Zealand, South Africa and the United Kingdom where it publishes the national title, *The Independent*, as well as being the largest publisher in Northern Ireland. The INM group publishes over 175 newspaper and magazine titles, operates 128 radio stations, and is a leading outdoor advertiser operator in Australasia, Hong Kong, Malaysia, Indonesia and across Africa.

In the past decade there has been a convergence between the UK and the Irish media industries. As we have seen, the Independent group has expanded into both Britain and Northern Ireland; in the other direction, UK companies such as Ulster Television (UTV), Granada and Scottish Radio Holdings have been at different times significant players in the media of the Republic. British media giant Emap is the owner of Today FM, Ireland's leading national commercial radio station, as well as owning FM104 in Dublin and Donegal's Highland Radio, the most popular local radio station in the country. TV3, the main private TV network, is owned by a British-German private equity company. Many British-owned newspapers, such as the *Daily Mirror* and the *Sun*, have a strong presence in the Irish market, producing 'local' editions with some 'Irish' content. It appears inevitable that given the common language and elements of culture, that the links between the media of the two countries will become closer.

Changes in media production

The technology of production has always been very important to an understanding of the media. Media institutions have frequently been open to rapid technological and industrial change, especially the broadcast media and the music industry. Change has perhaps been slower in book publishing and newspapers, due to different sorts of markets and, in newspapers, union resistance. But recently new text-processing and printing technologies have also brought significant change to these areas. Such changes are not just a matter of technological evolution. Typically they are tied up with conflicts over power. The titanic battles between Rupert Murdoch and the British newspaper unions were linked with issues of technological change as much as union strength. In Ireland there has been a history of conflict over technology in the main public media organisation, RTÉ.

In Ireland as elsewhere, public service broadcasters have been affected by the developments in broadcasting and communications technology. Partly as a result of such changes, partly as a response to increased competition in a less regulated environment, they have been forced to adopt the methods of commercial broadcasters, including new technologies and work practices. According to Hazelkorn, who has studied the changes in work practices in RTÉ, digital technology, in particular, has broken down the demarcations between journalistic, presenter and engineering skills. Some positions have been largely eliminated (sound operators, lighting electricians) while new areas have opened up, for example, for IT experts and multi-skilled engineers. Some jobs have been 'reskilled' — journalists, for example, are now more directly involved in the presentation/publishing process.

Overall, 'RTÉ has used a combination of early retirement, redeployment, retraining and alterations to staffing structures to effect the necessary cost efficiencies required by increased demands of competition and commercialisation' (Hazelkorn, 1996, p.33). With casualisation and flexibilisation of the workforce, more people can now make more programmes more easily. The changes have had differential gender effects. As in the newspaper industry, women have disproportionately benefited from the changes, with greater job loss in male-dominated 'craft' areas, like electrical work, and expansion on the 'creative' and administrative side, such as research. It is interesting that the 'newest' TV channel, TG4, is predominantly staffed by women (Horgan, 2001, p.181). These changes have broad implications for media in general. Hazelkorn (1996, p.37) highlights in particular the development of the 'independent production sector' as a key outcome. Increasing proportions of the output of public service broadcasters is undertaken by such companies. They are especially good at producing the relatively cheap and flexible 'infotainment' programmes (cookery shows, house and holiday programmes, entertainment news) which are currently so much a staple of TV programming.

MEDIA TEXTS

There are many ways to interpret and analyse media texts (Berger (1998) and Thompson (1990) provide excellent guides). Many of the methods, while adopted in full or partially by sociologists of the media, derive from the disciplines of literary theory, philosophy or psychoanalysis/psychology, and may be difficult to reconcile or combine with objective sociological knowledge of media institutions and audiences. Of particular influence has been the *semiotic approach* (Barthes, 1973) which attempts to interpret the media as a series of 'signs' that may relate in various ways to an underlying 'reality'. A more positivist approach is that of *content analysis* which ultimately involves categorising and counting various aspects of media messages, for example, how many and what sort of ads on RTÉ TV feature a female voice-over? Other approaches to textual analysis may focus on questions of *ideology* — how particular sets of signs, symbols and textual elements relate to broader issues of *power* in society; or on questions of *genre* — how does a particular TV show or magazine story fit in with the expectations that the audience has developed from previous exposure to similar media products? Here we look at three examples of textual analysis of Irish media forms: Sheehan's analysis of Irish TV drama; Barton's analysis of the Irish 'heritage' film; and Keohane's analysis of the music of the Pogues. While these do not reflect all the approaches outlined above, these examples have been selected as they each relate to some of the broader questions of development and identity discussed elsewhere in the book.

Television

Sheehan (1987) has carried out an extensive analysis of Irish television drama for the period from the launch of RTÉ in 1961 to the mid-1980s. Her aim (1987, p.6) is to develop 'an analysis of Irish television drama in terms of the underlying meaning of the stories being told and the emerging patterns of meaning, within the larger patterns of indigenous and imported television and within the development of Irish social history'. Sheehan's analysis comes very much from the point of view of literary criticism (1987, p.55). For example, she makes little attempt to understand the position of audiences, apart from some references to RTÉ's own audience research panel. She has little time for much of 'popular' television product, which she regards as 'aesthetically and psychologically immature, but by no means ideologically innocent' (1987, p.63).

Despite her elitist position, and her perfunctory dismissal of alternative interpretations (see Banks, 1990), Sheehan's is an interesting and valuable overview of the surprisingly large amount of TV drama produced by RTÉ. In current television schedules the individual TV play or, indeed, the mini-series of three to six episodes, is almost extinct; but during the 1960s and 70s in particular, television drama was a very important cultural form, and series such as *The Spike* (1978) and individual plays such as *The Ballroom of Romance* (1982) had a great social and cultural impact.

Sheehan draws on a number of approaches that typify much sociological analysis of media texts. She draws on the analysis of *myth* to explain why TV drama in general is important and attractive to audiences, and why it tends to follow certain forms. She overtly places her analysis of Irish TV drama within two main frames: the economic and social development of Ireland within the global economy; and the institutional structures of RTÉ as an organisation. For her, the restructuring of capital, as seen in the development of the information economy, is central to an understanding of how RTÉ drama output changed over the period. In addition she details the conflicts within RTÉ, which culminated in the late 1960s, over managerial control and the issue of cultural imperialism. The decline of a critical voice that was prepared to examine the changes taking place as Ireland modernised was linked to both these processes. In the later stages, international co-productions, with output aimed specifically at the international audience, shaped the sorts of topics that could be dramatised. In particular there was a strong emphasis on relatively non-controversial costume and historical drama.

Brennan's more recent work on *Fair City*, Ireland's most popular television soap opera, reveals the significant role of the serial in exploring personal and social problems like abortion, euthanasia, homophobia, racism and drug abuse. However, Brennan found that the diversity of social issues treated on *Fair City* was determined not so much by the creators, but by the production system itself (2004, p.67). Global and local transformations, he suggests, have reduced the professional autonomy and creativity of those who work on *Fair City*. Whereas in the past considerable prestige and power was attached to being a creator within the world of television drama, nowadays creators work on a production line, a process that Brennan describes as the proletarianisation of cultural production.

Film

Unlike Sheehan, Barton (writing a decade later, in 1997) draws explicitly on the theoretical basis of post-modernism to analyse recent developments in Irish film, in particular what she terms 'Irish heritage cinema'. Her analysis is stimulated by the release of what became the most popular (in Ireland) Irish-made film of all time, Neil Jordan's *Michael Collins*. Barton draws our attention to two implications that a post-modern sensibility towards film can produce. On the one hand, post-modernism in film involves drawing upon various images of the past to create a feeling of nostalgia, much as advertisements for Levi's jeans have drawn on images and music of the 1950s and 1960s. But, by playing around with technique, post-modern film can also draw attention to the *constructedness* of historical narratives — unlike realist cinema, which naturalises history. Unfortunately for Barton, the heritage film tends to follow the first of these approaches, thus producing a sanitised product for a global media market.

As in much of the film of Australia and Britain, there has been a strong emphasis in Irish cinema on historical and period drama — defined by Barton as 'heritage cinema'. The popularity of such films on the global stage (and of Hollywood films such as *Dances with Wolves* or *Fried Green Tomatoes at the Whistle Stop Café*) is based on the 'universal mood of nostalgia'. Irish heritage films reflect 'an "imaginary" past, a kind of glorious Celtic never-never land' — part of a 'desire to mobilise Irish myth in an international culture' (Barton, 1997, p.43). Film-maker Orla Walsh refers to this as the BBC image of Ireland: 'a fairy-tale Ireland, an *Into the West* kind of thing' (Sullivan, 1997, p.35). According to Barton such cinema does little to challenge conventional forms of storytelling; rather, it is conservative in structure and form, and politically and thematically cautious.

For Barton, the emphasis on the past may mean not having to deal with current issues. Citing the post-modernist theorist Jameson, she suggests that 'nostalgia for the past is often an unwillingness to come to terms with the present; in a society in which the reporting of child abuse, murder and marital violence is now a daily occurrence, there is a good argument for retreating into an imaginary state of grace, "the deliberate substitution of the pastiche, and imitation of past styles for the impossible invention of adequate contemporary or post-contemporary ones"' (1997, p.43).

Such conservatism may relate to the new imperatives guiding the arts in Ireland: 'the "theming" of Ireland' seen in the production of 'Irish pubs', heritage centres, Eurovision song contests and advertising geared towards tourists and potential investors. The desire to present the country as 'primitive and edenic' is closely linked to how the country is 'sold' by Bord Fáilte to tourists, through 'superb scenic landscapes; a quiet island with a relaxed pace of life; a distinctive heritage and culture; an absence of mass tourism; a friendly welcoming, convivial people; and a green, unspoiled environment' (Sheerin, 1998, p.45)

According to Barton (1997, pp.50–51) the rural romanticism and apoliticism of the heritage films is aimed at the '[British] Sunday evening television audience, the *Ballykissangel* viewer'. Such films are 'marked by a nostalgia for the past, for pastoral innocence; many of them are actually set in the past, the remainder are set in a rural Ireland which bears few traces of modernity'. A similar point could be made in relation to two box-office successes of the late 1990s that post-dated Barton's analysis: *In my Father's House* and *A Love Divided*.

Music

Recorded music has possibly been Ireland's most successful popular cultural export and we can easily highlight the international success of acts as diverse as traditional group The Chieftains and DJ David Holmes. A number of writers (for example, O'Connor, 1991) have suggested that music reflects in a particularly acute way questions of Irish culture and identity. Cork-based sociologist Kieran Keohane has analysed the music of the band The Pogues in terms of how it expresses particular aspects of Ireland's post-modern and globalised position. For Keohane, the music of The Pogues, a band that grew directly out of the Irish diaspora, is a 'pastiche' of styles and places, an example of the interface of the global and the traditional, and combines in a unique style elements of the folk tradition with punk. The content of the music is similarly complex, 'loaded with historical references and images which are carefully pieced together and linked to contemporary experiences, lending coherence and historical sense to the culture of the diaspora' (Keohane, 1997, p.296). In this way, the music of the Pogues illuminates the historical legacy of emigration, not in the romantic way that much historiography or heritage cinema does, but in its full complexity. Keohane argues

(1997, p.297), 'the Pogues' pastiche is more than simply a historically-informed text relating past with present. It is, more importantly, a medium and a device which subjects history and experience to a thoroughgoing radical critical examination.' Thus, it challenges not only romantic images of Ireland — unlike, say, the music of another band of the diaspora, the Saw Doctors — but also the mythical images of the metropolises of the core countries: it reveals the 'underside' of New York, Frankfurt and London, and how these global cities have been (and are still) built at least partly on immigrant and exploited Irish labour.

Sheehan, Barton and Keohane have each analysed aspects of the Irish media in relation to issues of national identity, globalisation and the 'proper' relationship between the media and the society it does (or does not) reflect. These remain key issues in relation to the media in Ireland, pervading both industry policies, for example, the 1995 Green Paper on Broadcasting, and critical responses. There are many who feel (as do all the above critics, to varying degrees) that the increasing globalisation of media production and distribution is a threat to our ability to tell 'our own' stories. The tendency, when producing for an international marketplace, is to provide what is attractive and non-controversial. But media producers will often respond, in the face of such criticism, that 'this is what the audience wants'. It is to audiences, then, that we now turn.

MEDIA AUDIENCES

Consideration of the media process indicates how important a knowledge of the audience is. We may claim that the producer of a media message has a certain intention or that a text has specific overt or covert meanings; but how people themselves interpret and understand media messages is of crucial importance if we are concerned about, say, the effects of the media, or how the media form a part of people's everyday lives.

Furthermore, the audience has been shown to be very important in the development of the media. Technologically oriented stories about the development of radio, television or other mass media tend to focus very much on the invention of the technology and its gradual development and dissemination into society. But as Sorlin (1994, pp.47–55) has shown, the audience is a significant part of the media development process. Thus, the audience for mass newspapers was built on a pre-existing market for news-sheets, privately circulated newsletters and so on; similarly, the development of the radio industry was greatly assisted by a community of amateur enthusiasts. More recently the Internet industry was largely developed by a community of computer programmers and individual users, who helped to develop browser software, search engines and other applications, that were subsequently picked up and commercialised by major companies. One of the most dramatic trends in recent years is the evolution of so-called Web 2.0, from the preserve of a small circle of dedicated bloggers and hard-core web users to the mainstream. Social networking technologies have proliferated across the Internet, changing the landscape of computer-mediated communications and reconstituting the audience as producers as well as consumers of content. As media and technology commentator Lillington puts it: 'from mashups to wikis, Flickr to Bebo, MySpace to YouTube, blogs to FaceBook, the web's hottest spot is where people converge to create and share their own content' (*The Irish Times*, 29 December 2006). An important question to ask is, what role is the Internet playing in the reconfiguration of social relations?

In recent years there has been a growth in the theoretical and practical importance of sociological audience research. This research has been driven by a number of concerns, especially those related to power (Kelly and O'Connor, 1997, p.3). They include:

- What is the power of the media relative to that of the audience; in other words, to what extent does the media itself determine how it is interpreted?
- How is interpretation and use of the media shaped by aspects of cultural identity, such ethnicity, age, class or gender?
- What are the responsibilities, if any, of the media to its audience(s)?

Researching audiences

All media companies are intensely interested in the topic of audiences. After all, as many critics have pointed out, the key role of the media institution is to *sell audiences to advertisers*. The company needs to know the size of its audience, its composition and nature (often seen in terms of consumers with particular levels of spending power) and, increasingly, *how* the audience consumes the product. Highly sophisticated methods of researching audiences have been developed by international companies, such as Nielsen, incorporating technology, for example, 'people meters' that measure exactly who is watching what and when on the TV screen. The technology is being continually developed, to enable it, for example, to track people's purchases (via packaging bar codes) and to link these to demographic categories and to particular advertising campaigns.

While demographics have been the main interest of the commercial media, psychological studies of the audience have dominated academic research in the area. As well as the uses and gratifications approach that has attempted to define and measure why people consume the media, there has also been a focus on the effects of the mass media, often on those perceived to be more susceptible to its messages, particularly children. Within this tradition there has been a great deal of interest in the issues of violence, health and welfare and, more recently, sexist imagery. Much of the research has been carried out using experimental techniques and questionnaires.

The most recent approach to audience research has been that based on the notion of the viewer or reader of the media as an interpreter of messages within a social environment, rather than a person with a particular mental orientation or a consumer within a demographic group. This approach often focuses on the 'fan' — the dedicated user of specific media products, such as comic books, *Star Trek* or romantic fiction. The methodology of research is usually ethnographic, in the sense that the researcher tries to get close to the experience of media consumption, and to enter the world of the media consumer. The data gathered is often rich and complex, though inevitably difficult to generalise to larger groups of media users. The interest in ethnographic and socially situated research reflects something of how we typically use the media: often less as a series of individual media events, but more as a continuous *flow* of messages, images and information, into which we may dip in and out during the day with varying degrees of attention (this point was first made by the British Marxist critic Raymond Williams). This aspect is vividly expressed by Sorlin (1994, p.43):

> The reception of the media, especially those that are broadcast, is akin to situations we experience daily, for instance at work, or when we are driving: moments of relaxation, of dispersed attention are interrupted by sudden tensions. Except when they read or watch very seriously, people are content to pick up a few segments from a continuous flow. But what has been absorbed, however partial it is, will be reused in other circumstances, in friendly conversations, at parties, in meetings at work and, likewise, the successive moments of the conversation with friends or colleagues will, alternatively, be exciting and cool. Information borrowed from the media and daily concerns will constantly overlap.

The concept of *mass* media implies a large and relatively undifferentiated audience. It is very much tied in to the development of the technologies of newspaper publishing, cinema, radio and, above all, television: technologies that have compressed time and space in such a way that very large numbers of people (up to several billion for events like the soccer World Cup) can experience the same messages and images at virtually the same moment. But to a certain extent the 'mass media audience' is a fiction, brought into being through the process of talking about, measuring or analysing it. In reality, people experience the media alone, in close domestic and family environments or in relatively small public groups. The media is thus, as Sorlin has suggested, inevitably linked with other aspects of our everyday social interaction.

Until relatively recently, sociologists and other academic analysts of the media — in Ireland as elsewhere — had tended to neglect the study of audiences, preferring to focus on media texts or, to a lesser extent, production processes and structures. There may be a number of reasons for this. First, it is far more difficult to research audiences. Media are above all *mass* media, consumed by very large numbers of people; but much of this consumption takes place in the domestic arena (generally the sitting room of the private home). To study audiences then requires that researchers gain access to a significant number of private spaces for an extended period of time. This is expensive and time consuming; it is far easier to focus research activity on a collection of video tapes or newspaper cuttings that can be easily and relatively cheaply analysed in the researcher's office!

Second, while media companies or their agents (market researchers, ratings companies) collect vast amounts of detailed information on audiences, this information is commercially very valuable and sensitive. Media companies are loathe to hand over even historical data to academic researchers, except for a very high fee. Third, and perhaps most crucially, the lack of audience research reflects some of the dominant concerns within sociology as a whole which we outlined in the first section of this book. As we have seen, sociology has been oriented towards the 'public' world of work, power and social issues. It has tended until recently to ignore or at least play down aspects of everyday life, including the domestic arena and popular culture. The mundane everyday activities of watching TV, listening to music downloads and reading newspapers have often been seen as relatively unimportant. It is really only with the influence of feminist sociology that the audience has come to assume the same level of importance as media institutions and the production of media texts.

A good example of the type of audience research that reflects such concerns is that of the British researcher Marie Gillespie, who has studied how television is part of the lives of a group of London Punjabi teenagers. She argues (1995, p.205) that 'TV talk, though it may seem esoteric and trivial, is an important form of self-narration and a major collective resource through which identities are negotiated.' In other words, how people think about, respond to and talk with others about what they see on TV makes up a part of their process of defining themselves and others. Given that people may spend more time watching TV every week than going to work, or being with family members, this is hardly surprising.

Gillespie's research is part of a group of studies that has shown how people across the world are able to make sense of global media products in their own ways. For example, Ang (1985) has studied how the US soap, *Dallas*, was watched by a group of women in the Netherlands; Gripsrud (1995) has traced the reception of another US soap, *Dynasty*, in Norway, while Miller and Slater (2000) have examined how the people of Trinidad have found new ways to express themselves through the Internet. Such detailed and culturally integrated consideration of audiences can address issues such as the extent to which indigenous or local cultures are 'undermined' by media, as the cultural imperialist argument would suggest. Gillespie finds that far from being a threat to British-Asian culture, programmes like the Australian soap, *Neighbours* — extremely popular among the young people she studied — are integrated into people's own lives in new and unexpected ways that help them make sense of their own lives and everyday cultural experiences.

Audience research in Ireland

For both theoretical and practical reasons, sociological audience research in Ireland has adopted a qualitative methodology, as opposed to the quantitative methods used by the media industry or the experimental methods favoured by psychologists. Qualitative audience research, according to Kelly and O'Connor (1997, p.3) can 'explore the rich cultural terrain at the interface between media, power and subcultural discourses and identities'. It (1997, p.4):

> requires in-depth analysis of the responses of (usually) a small number of individuals or groups to media texts, and an interpretation of these responses in the light of the socially situated culture or lifeworld of the viewer . . . although one of the limitations of this approach is the care needed in generalising findings to the population in general, the advantage is the access it offers to the local and everyday cultures and frames of reference which ordinary people bring to their reading of media texts.

In *Media audiences in Ireland*, Kelly and O'Connor (1997) provide a good overview of recent academic audience research, though 'qualitative research' has been interpreted as open-ended or semi-structured interviews with people *about* their media use; there is little evidence of observational or participative studies that attempt to establish *in situ* how people use the media in their ordinary everyday environment. Underpinning many of the studies is a concern with *power*: who has it — the audience or the media institutions? Is there a 'dominant ideology' at work, basically leading people to think in particular ways, or does the notion of the 'active audience' make more sense: where people can take what they wish from the media and interpret it in their own ways, even in an oppositional fashion? Kelly and O'Connor (1997, p.10) conclude that both these tendencies are apparent:

> The media confirm the ideological and symbolic power of some powerful and high status groups while weakening and disorganising those with little power. And yet it is possible for the latter to use the media creatively for their own psychological, pleasurable and cultural purposes. However the pleasures of the text can be highly seductive and hide the symbolic power of the media to confirm the status quo, in particular perhaps by its ignoring of voices and cultures 'from below' and its non-articulation of alternative and radical perspectives.

Three examples from Kelly and O'Connor's collection reveal different aspects of the power relationship between audiences and media institutions. They are briefly outlined here, in relation to the three questions about power raised above.

Media analysts have long had a concern with the power of the media relative to that of the audience, particularly in relation to those audiences perceived as 'vulnerable'. The greatest concern has been expressed in relation to the child audience. Margaret Gunning's research, carried out in 1995 and reported in 1997, focused on the response of a group of Dublin school children to their favourite programmes, *Baywatch* and *Den TV*. She aimed to focus on the *pleasures* of TV, rather than more negative aspects, and drew not only on sociological methods but on more psychoanalytically based theories derived from film studies, especially those that related to the pleasures of looking.

Gunning found that children have good knowledge of the constructedness of television shows, indeed, 'one of their greatest pleasures was in the deconstruction of the programme in terms of the set and the physical make-up of the characters' (1997, p.263). They enjoyed a recognition of the more 'subversive' meanings in *Den TV* and enjoyed the 'act of looking' in *Baywatch*. Overall, Gunning found the relationship between children and TV 'empowering', in contrast to some popular and academic conceptions. The children, she concluded, 'showed an ability to play around with the messages of the medium, whether in the form of playful imitation, or in the exhibition of their powers as critics in the deconstruction of its artificiality' (1997, p.266). As a result, she argues that debates on children and television must take into consideration the views of the audience, that is, the children themselves, who are not passive pawns of the TV industry.

The recognition that different audiences, and sections of audiences, can derive alternative meanings from media products is one of the key themes of recent audience research. It is now taken for granted that interpretation and use of the media is shaped by aspects of cultural identity, such as ethnicity, age, class or gender. In a study carried out in the mid 1980s, O'Connor analysed the responses of groups of people to a 1982 TV drama (*The Ballroom of Romance*) in terms of class and gender, and the intersection between the two. Responses to the film were shaped by the groups' differing genre preferences and the perceived relevance of the film (O'Connor, 1997, p.83):

> The full significance of the film for each group included not only their interpretation of specific scenes and sequences, but also their response to the film in terms of the pleasure which it afforded and the perceived relevance to their own lives. Because they inhabited different kinds of discourses and had access to different cultural competences, the viewing situation was framed in ways which differentially influenced the pleasures and meanings of the text. Or to put it another way, the groups had different ways of seeing the film based on different kinds of enjoyment, different levels of emotional involvement, and different points of engagement with the text.

The responses were complex, but it was apparent that, for example, men and women interpreted the film in different ways and derived various meanings from it. Men tended to focus more on the informational level — as an indication of what rural Ireland was like in the 1950s — whereas women had a more emotional response. There was also a difference in the response of working-class and middle-class viewers. Furthermore, a number of different patterns became apparent as determined by the intersection of gender *and* class.

Finally, there is a question as to whether, given the (limited) power that the media hold over the creation and dissemination of meanings, they have any responsibility to their audience(s)? This issue is linked closely to the concept of the 'public sphere' developed by the German social theorist Jürgen Habermas (see Chapter 5). For Habermas the public sphere was a place for discussion oriented towards the common good, untainted by commercial or governmental interests. The ideal location of the public sphere was, for Habermas, the coffee shops and salons of eighteenth-century Europe. The question can be asked whether the modern mass media allow — or should allow — such a space for disinterested public debate.

This is a topic that is addressed in Sara O'Sullivan's analysis of RTÉ 2FM's *Gerry Ryan Show* (GRS). She suggests (1997, p.167) that talk radio, of the sort found on the GRS, 'provides a rare opportunity for Irish audiences to participate in mass mediated debate and discussion'. She asks whether the show can be seen as part of the public sphere — or is it no more than entertainment, attracting listeners for RTÉ to sell to its advertisers? Might it have a democratic function, allowing for the raising of important issues or the influence of public opinion? An additional issue that is of great interest, given the success of TV shows like *Oprah* and even *Big Brother*, is the significance of the public discussion of what were formerly seen as 'private' matters, for example, sexuality, domestic relationships and personal opinions. This may be of particular importance in the Irish context, where so many recent political and social debates (over abortion, divorce, sexuality, child abuse and so on) relate to what might be seen as the world of the 'private'.

O'Sullivan identifies four types of call to the GRS which she terms:

- expressive
- exhibitionist
- service encounter
- troubles telling.

People call in to express views, to seek help, to offer support or to get things off their chests. She concludes that while the show allows for these sorts of expression, it does not encourage critical discussion of social and political issues. One reason is that access to the show is controlled by RTÉ staff: 'this control on participation makes it difficult to see how the show might have a contribution to make to the public sphere, where, in theory at least, access should be open to all' (1997, p.177).

Ultimately, the GRS is about entertainment, and this key production value shapes what can be discussed (and how). Nevertheless the GRS has dealt with serious issues such as child abuse and domestic violence and O'Sullivan suggests that it 'offers a space in the public sphere where matters of public concern may be discussed with others in similar situations' (1997, p.178). It provides a form of self-help for at least some listeners. While there is a concern that radio phone-in shows encourage talk at the expense of action, O'Sullivan concludes that 'calling the show is an important social activity, and . . . this form of participation might have consequences for Irish society, as well as for individual callers' (1997, p.185).

Audience research carried out in Ireland has uncovered similar data to that in other societies:

- People's responses to the media are complex.
- The media form an important part of people's lives but do not dominate it, as is sometimes feared by critics.
- People seek out what they enjoy in the media, use it to provide pleasure, a sense of belonging, company and something to talk about with their friends and workmates.
- What the media offer in terms of information is often limited and skewed. If people do not have alternative sources of data on a topic, the media will often provide their only information.

MEDIA AND THE PUBLIC SPHERE

One of the basic principles of democracy is the ideal of the public sphere, that notional space wherein the public formulate, debate and exchange opinion. Public opinion ideally is conceived as the outcome of the cut and thrust that occurs in the public sphere. There is now a widespread view that, while the democratic public sphere may be more necessary than ever, it is increasingly difficult to locate. The rise of infotainment programming and the concomitant 'dumbing down' of culture; the expansion in the number and range of media platforms; and the proliferation of news managers and news management techniques have combined to fracture the notion of a body politic, alienating us from the public sphere. Conglomeration, commercialisation and commodification characterise the media landscape today, with negative consequences, as former Minister for the Arts and Communications Michael D. Higgins outlines (2004, p. 139):

> The main tendencies in communications at the present time include convergence of technology, concentration of ownership in a number of international conglomerates and fragmentation of audiences. These tendencies occur at a time when the prevailing ideology guiding economic policy decisions

is one that places an emphasis on unrestricted market adjustments. The circumstances of these transitions are different from other historical shifts of the industrial era. It is very difficult to question, indeed identify, the assumptions upon which they are based. We are drifting into, rather than choosing, this new condition of our unfreedom — our existence as consumers rather than citizens.

In these circumstances, public service broadcasting is often held up as the last refuge of the public sphere, a far cry from Habermas's eighteenth-century coffee house, but an enduring forum nevertheless, for promoting reasoned argument and disputation. It is to the public service broadcasters that we repair when seeking balance, objectivity and impartiality in the reporting of the issues of the day. But public service broadcasting is no more immune than it has ever been to the machinations of its political masters: witness the unrelenting pressure to which the British Broadcasting Corporation (BBC) was subjected by the British government in 2003 over its coverage of the war in Iraq.

Politicians, and the 'spin masters' working on their behalf, to a greater or lesser extent, seek to control access, to shape 'their message' and to determine where and how that message is diffused. When public service broadcasting loses something of its reputation for independence, journalists baulk at covering 'difficult' and 'dangerous' stories, a chill wind blows through the newsroom and the audience inevitably is short-changed. Furthermore, public service broadcasting in Ireland and across Europe has come under increasing commercial pressure as technology delivers more and more media platforms. It has had to follow the market, resorting increasingly to programme-making of the infotainment variety. As Higgins has argued (2004, p.136): 'broadcasting now stands to be judged as a production space for commodified entertainment products rather than that public space where citizens listened and viewed to be informed, educated or entertained'. We now inhabit a world where time and space differences are being obliterated by the sheer flow of information through multiple media platforms. The notions of a 'national audience' and a 'body politic' are increasingly questionable in a media-saturated world.

According to Stevenson (1999), a number of key features shape the contemporary relationship between the public and the mass media. First, most of us, most of the time, engage with the media in privatised contexts where we are largely passive. The media's capacity to make us aware of common concerns (for example, the global news reach of the story of the September 11 attacks on New York) is mitigated to some degree by the comparative isolation in which we make our interpretations. There are fewer opportunities for people to pursue a collective response to either the terrorist attacks or to the US retaliation; we feel rather powerless and maybe even fearful a lot of the time. Fragmentation of the media audience means that rather than constituting a national audience of citizens, we are increasingly composed of targeted audience segments, delivered to advertisers and programme sponsors. At the same time Stevenson points out that the very fragmentation of the national audience makes it more difficult for governments and information managers to control and censor debate. The rapid expansion of new media made available by technological change means our public culture will become increasingly based on individual choice.

Second, the rapid development of media technologies has increased the volume of information available. But more information does not necessarily mean a better-informed citizenry. Indeed, Peillon (2000, p.181) has described how the use of public opinion polls and mass surveys by the political class, and increasingly by media professionals, enables it [the political class] 'to remain within the confines of a predictable public opinion in order to find its political action validated, justified'. The audience can become 'the news' through extensive use of opinion polls, exit polls, straw polls, email and so on. The delivery of information is now almost simultaneous, and a wealth of new interactive mechanisms is available to news producers and their audiences through the Internet. Indeed, the Internet helps to blur the distinction between producer and consumer since it facilitates two-way interactions. If one cannot source a story through the mainstream media, it is always possible to source it through the multiple outlets providing a range of alternative perspectives on the Internet, such as Indymedia.

Across Europe there has been an erosion of the commitment to public service broadcasting, as the commercial imperative comes to dominate. If there is no longer a place for public service broadcasting, is there a place for the public sphere? Even in countries like Britain where public service broadcasting has historically been strong, it has been subjected to a bruising. The Hutton inquiry in Britain may turn out to mark a watershed in terms of the relationship between government and public service broadcasting. The BBC, an institution trusted and respected all over the world, found itself under sustained criticism from government. Though accusations of a 'whitewash' quickly circulated in the media, polls conducted in the aftermath of the event showed that respondents were more inclined to believe the public service broadcaster than the British government. But most public service broadcasters now face an uncertain future. It may well be the case that the public will look increasingly to new digital technologies such as mobile phones and the Internet as a means to constitute a new kind of 'public sphere'.

Part IV

A post-modern society?

Introduction

Throughout this book, we have emphasised the links between the evolution of sociology and the parallel development of modernity. If there has been such a thing as the 'project of modernity', sociology has been very much part of it. It has sought to come to grips with perhaps the most rapid and far-reaching change in history, as human beings have adapted to urban living, routinised industrial employment, diminishing networks of kin and new experiences of time, movement and space. Much of our discussion has focused on the notions of development and modernity and has questioned how such terms and concepts have been applied to Irish society. We have tried to resist the tendency to submerge the Irish experience within a generic view of 'Western development', and to emphasise that the Irish experience is not merely 'deviant', but may have something to say about how we conceptualise and analyse social change.

If the nineteenth and the first half of the twentieth centuries were about the global spread of modernity, at least since the 1960s there has been an argument that we are now entering a new historical epoch: *post-modernity*. This is the time of 'post- . . . ': post-modern; post-industrial; post-capitalist; post-Fordist . . . ; each refers to a feeling that we are entering a new era and thus leaving something behind. Perhaps less clear is whether post-modernism refers to a way of being, a way of thinking about being, or both. We do not intend to delve into the genealogy or archaeology of the concept of post-modernity here. Rather, we will briefly signal some of the issues developed in the concluding part of the book.

If post-modernism is a way of being, there seems to be some agreement on what that might mean. A post-modern world is perhaps above all a world where *information* is the fundamental resource. Information is seen to underpin new forms of economy (in particular, so-called service industries such as finance, tourism and education); new types of relationships (those mediated through the mass media or the Internet) and new types of wealth and power (as in Foucault's couplet, power/knowledge, where each helps to constitute the other). Post-modernism is also about the compression of time and space, as the world of speed and mobility comes to dominate our social interactions and relationships.

The facilitator of the information age is *technology*, in particular, the technologies of communication and information — computer networks, jet travel, satellites, silicon chips. There tends to be a strong element of technological determinism in thinking about post-modernism. In the same way that the steel/coal/rail/electricity complex 'created' the world of modernity, post-modernism is seen to be at least partly the outcome of computers and allied technologies.

Post-modernism is also the age of *reflexivity*, a term we introduced in Part I. It is quintessentially a self-conscious and knowing age, whether expressed as an obsession with body and image; an increasingly self-referential mass media; or a sceptical and tentative social studies that is increasingly aware of its own implication in relations of domination and uncertain of the validity of its procedures and ideas. In post-modernism we may *know*, but we also know how *and* why we know and why we might not.

This leads us to the second position — that post-modernism is not really so much about changes in the real world, but in how we talk about and analyse that world. Here the key concept is the collapse in the validity of what are termed 'totalising narratives'; in other words, those types of knowledge that seek, and claim, to offer answers to the 'big' questions about our lives and society. The totalising, or grand, narrative is very much associated with modernity, where first the global religions, then the sciences, then Marxism and functionalism, and perhaps latterly economics, have provided an overarching framework for people to make sense of their society and lives.

In post-modernism, faith in grand narratives has declined as they collapse under their own contradictions. There has been a shift towards the local, the specific and the contextualised. We can only know what is happening in the here and now in relation to the particular object that we are studying for the moment. We can not generalise, for to do so is to do violence to the diversity of experiences and identities. Indeed, we can no longer assume that 'identity' is unified and singular. Post-modernism asserts that our identities are multiple; constituted through language (especially, for example, by the powerful discourses of the media, the law and medicine) and intimately related to and shaped by the circumstances that surround us.

Much of this is very threatening to sociological thought and practice. First, it challenges sociology's claims to be a grand narrative, and it is certainly the case that the broad theoretical schemas of functionalism and Marxism have fallen into disfavour. At their peak they claimed to be able to explain everything from art to sexuality: now they have often been replaced with eclectic theoretical approaches that may equally draw upon literary theory or psychoanalysis as on the categories of class, gender or ethnicity. Second, with post-modernism has come a suspicion of positivism, indeed, of evidence in general. So much of post-modern theorising depends on language and the play of language. Sociologists are far less inclined now to go out 'into the field'; they are often more interested in the analysis of documents, the deconstruction of visual imagery or the mining of a small number of in-depth interviews. Large-scale scientific survey research still goes on, but is rarely seen to have anything exciting to say at a theoretical or conceptual level. Third, the very concepts of society and nation, which we have seen to be so central to the sociological enterprise, have increasingly been called into question. Ex-British Prime Minister Margaret Thatcher's celebrated remark that 'there is no such thing as society' captured the post-modern mood, if not its politics. National borders dissolve into transnational entities like the EU or the World Trade Organisation (WTO), while simultaneously populations fragment into consumer groupings, ethnic enclaves and gated communities. The result, for post-modernists, is a world that is constantly in flux and impossible to pin down, whether by sociologists or anyone else.

It is from within such a context that we look back and trace some of the recent developments in Irish society that might help us to think through this putative new state of affairs. We have chosen to focus on three areas that we feel have much to tell us about how our society might be changing, and that reflect some of the developments within the field of sociology itself, as it seeks to come to terms with the (possible) new era.

Each of the three chapters deals, in a different way, with the shift in interest, both in the broad economy and within sociology, from matters of *production* to those of *consumption*. It is an intense focus on the latter that in many ways typifies postmodernity: this is a time in history when shopping has become the Western world's most popular leisure activity and when notions of choice and individual expression through the purchase of products and services has become a dominant discourse. Such ideas are not limited to the fashion world; they now infuse the language and practices of politics and protest. We see this in the phenomenon of new social movements, an emergent form of political practice that in many ways is more focused on the securing and expression of particular lifestyles and meanings than in obtaining power in the conventional sense.

We start this next section with an analysis of consumption, an area that — as elsewhere — has been comparatively neglected in Irish sociology. Following the format of previous chapters, we trace the interest in this aspect of life to the writings of earlier sociologists, especially Simmel, and then examine some aspects of Irish experience. We then go on, in the following chapter, to consider the nature of new social movements — a style of politics that, as we suggest, owes much to the triumph of consumerism in Western societies. It may be that such an approach to aspects of political change opens up possible new ways of interpreting contemporary Irish society. We conclude this section, and the book, with a specific analysis of an increasingly significant social movement: environmentalism. The environmental movement is not only a new social movement *par excellence*: it also has the potential to change how we think about both society and sociology.

16

Consumption

What is consumption, and why is it of interest to sociology? Consumption refers to how we use material objects, though the term also includes the use of services like having a haircut or going to the doctor and of facilities like transportation systems or landscapes. Consumption is a central part of everyday life. It has a great deal to do with how we meet our material needs but includes much more. How we consume goods and services makes up much of what we conceptualise as culture; for in consuming goods and services we consume culture and we also create and re-create it.

Given the key significance of consumption in our lives, the attention accorded to it by sociologists has been remarkably limited. While the term 'consumer society' has long been used to describe modern, capitalist society, its analysis has been left to economists and psychologists rather than to social theorists. But a sociology of consumption has begun to establish itself. This is linked to a renewed interest, among sociologists in general, in culture and processes of cultural change that is replacing earlier preoccupations with social structure and structural processes. This chapter outlines some of the key ideas in the sociology of consumption and examines what Irish sociologists have had to say about the topic in the local context.

THEORETICAL ANTECEDENTS

As we have stressed throughout this book, sociology developed historically as the study of modernity. This renders the lack of interest in consumption particularly odd as, for many people, increased consumption is the distinguishing feature of modern society. We can find a reason, perhaps, in how the early sociologists structured the understanding of modernity. The inheritance of Marxism is particularly important here for, in spite of Marx's emphasis on a materialist approach to history, he focused predominantly on just one aspect of the production and exchange of goods: that of production. While he saw capitalism as a system that encouraged people to consume and to 'fetishise' commodities, he helped to divert sociological attention away from consumption by arguing that the inevitable tendency of capitalism was towards the 'immiseration' of increasing numbers of working people, to the extent that this would provoke a socialist revolution.

Marx suggested that by the time capitalism had become fully established in the world the experience of the working class would generally be one of such reduced consumption that they would be unable even to buy the bare necessities of food and clothing, let alone the more optional goods from which a lifestyle and personal identity might be created. As far as the developed world is concerned, at least, this prediction has turned out to be wrong; but it meant that Marxist sociologists were relatively uninterested in, or unprepared to examine, the expansion of working-class consumption that took place.

Weber also helped, in a different way, to direct sociological attention away from the place of consumption in modern society. He argued that the development of capitalism was significantly shaped by the emergence, in early modern Europe, of a particular type of Protestantism (see Chapter 14), which he called 'ascetic Protestantism' to emphasise its stress on self-denial. Ascetic Protestants were committed to an ethic of hard work and success in their working lives, but saw this as a way to honour God, not to acquire a luxurious lifestyle. This encouraged Protestant businessmen to accumulate large amounts of capital that they reinvested in their businesses rather than spending it on themselves; many became wealthy capitalist producers but nevertheless lived domestic lives of frugality or, at best, modest comfort. The success of these businessmen encouraged others to follow their example. Weber thus provides a fascinating explanation for the growth in early modern Europe of a 'culture of capitalism' that, in promoting dedication to work and entrepreneurial success, substantially accounted for the spread of capitalism as an economic system. But he did not explain how, as capitalism developed and matured, the ascetic ethic of the early capitalists came to be replaced by the contemporary acceptance of consumption, or what we might call an ethic of consumption.

We commence this chapter, then, with an examination of how an interest in consumption has developed in recent sociology, despite the preoccupations of the founders of the discipline. We examine Veblen's early discussion of consumption, which continues to influence contemporary approaches, and the sorts of questions posed by the sociology of consumption (see also Chapter 13, for Veblen's contribution to the analysis of fashion). We are also concerned with how a sociology of consumption might be relevant to understanding Irish society. Although there has been research in Ireland on aspects of culture, and on attitudes to commodities like food and drink, or the landscape, a sociology of consumption is only beginning to develop. But we should not take for granted that the history of consumption or its significance in everyday life have been the same in Ireland as, for example, in Britain, where most of the work in this field has been done to date. An Irish sociology of consumption may help to question theories that have emerged from the core countries, and may also suggest new perspectives on the nature of social change and modernisation in Irish society.

FROM LEISURE CLASSES TO MASS SOCIETY

We noted earlier that Weber associates capitalist development with the repression of the desire to consume, rather than its expansion. In response Campbell (1987) aims to develop a theory to explain the parallel revolution in consumption. He initially confronts the question: why do we need an explanation at all? Surely it is natural to human beings to consume and all that can hold them back is a lack of resources? Even if modern patterns of consumption satisfy more than basic needs, have there not always been examples of greed and extreme desire for material possessions, in all societies? If so, then there is nothing peculiar about the place of consumption in modern societies.

Campbell argues that there is something significant to be explained. The behaviour of modern consumers is rather mysterious, in two ways. First, in the apparent limitlessness and insatiability of contemporary wants and of contemporary consumption: 'rarely can an inhabitant of modern society, no matter how privileged or wealthy, declare that there is nothing that they want. . . . It is a central fact of modern consumer behaviour that the gap between wanting and getting never actually closes' (1987, pp.37–8).

Second, as well as being continually renewed and re-created, wants are continually extinguished: 'a natural corollary of endless wanting is the high rate of product (and hence want) obsolescence' (1987, p.38). As a result, modern society is 'symbolised at least as much by the mountains of rubbish, the garage and jumble sales, the columns of advertisements of second-hand goods for sale and the second-hand car lots, as it is by the ubiquitous propaganda on behalf of new goods' (1987, pp.38–9). We could now add Internet auction site eBay and similar services to this list, including those that facilitate people in giving away their surplus possessions. Although we take these phenomena for granted, they are historically neither normal nor natural. In pre-industrial societies, consumption was governed by custom and tradition that set limits to the possible range of wants a person would have, though these were socially variable. We therefore need to explain how the specific pattern of consumption found in modern, industrialised societies developed and how it is maintained. Campbell surveys three theories of consumption in his search for an adequate explanation, and we now briefly review these.

The first approach he terms *instinctivist*. This explanation — familiar from economics — suggests a biologically based desire to consume. Human wants are seen to be inherent and 'triggered off' by goods that enter the individual's environment. Humans are thought to have a 'latent demand' for goods that is unleashed when new goods come onto the market. A problem with this approach is that it is unable to distinguish between biological *needs* (food, warmth, sex) and culturally mediated *wants* (diamonds, fast cars, Playstations). Nor can it explain how wants vary across societies or over time. In particular, it cannot address

Campbell's point that we can rapidly 'stop wanting' what are still perfectly usable — and to others, still desirable — consumer goods.

The second approach Campbell calls *manipulationist*. This sees consumers as compelled to develop wants by outside agents, particularly advertisers. This approach does not endow consumers with a pre-given capacity to seek out specific goods or satisfactions; rather, it treats them as passive objects of external influences. Campbell believes this approach overstates the power of others, even of advertisers, to create wants. While he does not wish to suggest we have *instinctive* wants that are independent of outside influences, he argues that we should not ignore the range of other cultural influences (churches, government agencies, kinship networks, family and friends) that help to shape our consumer behaviour. Much research suggests that consumers are not passive recipients of advertisements, they can actively discriminate between and evaluate the messages they receive. They can do this because they live in a world that has already been given meaning by their culture. Advertisers may try to exploit 'the desires and dreams of the consumer' (1987, p.47) but they do not create these in the first place, or at least, not in a cultural vacuum. It seems more plausible to say that what producers and advertisers try to manipulate are not the wants of consumers so much as the symbolic meanings that consumers attach to goods and products.

This idea is central to the third perspective identified by Campbell, which derives from the work of Thorstein Veblen. Veblen, remembered today chiefly for his book, *The theory of the leisure class* (1925), and his phrase 'conspicuous consumption', was an American sociologist who studied the 'new rich' in late nineteenth-century America. He was particularly interested in the processes whereby this group sought to gain social acceptance among more established elites. He argued that, among the wealthy, acts of consumption were a way to display, signal or lay claim to social status, as they reflected the level of wealth that the consumer possessed. Veblen suggested that commodities not only satisfy wants or needs, but also function as ways to convey meanings about oneself to others. Thus, acts of consumption are themselves signs or symbols; they belong to the cultural realm as much as to the economic.

While Veblen's own development of this idea was perhaps somewhat simplistic it has been very fruitful for more recent work on consumption. Veblen assumed that human beings are motivated above all else by the desire for 'emulation', that is, to compete with others in displays of wealth and prestige. He also assumed that the only significant cultural message contained in a commodity was its price: in purchasing a commodity a consumer is primarily sending the message to others, 'see how rich I am, that I can afford this!' But as Campbell points out, consumption goods also carry other meanings, particularly about taste and style, and these may have little to do with price. The overriding concern with price, and with 'conspicuous consumption', may be peculiar to newly wealthy groups that have acquired a new social position that they need to validate; but it may not be so important for those whose status is secure or who have no particular interest in upward social mobility.

Does Veblen explain for us why modern consumption has the character of restless insatiability? There is a partial explanation, perhaps, in his claim that humans strive constantly to emulate those higher up the status ladder than themselves. They must therefore be constantly prepared to change their consumption habits and styles. Those they emulate must also constantly invent new lifestyles or fashions in order to maintain their superiority. Thus, suggests one writer, 'drinking champagne or malt whiskey, once the preserve of the aristocracy, has moved down the social status ladder in this century, so that the upper echelons either cease to drink those drinks, or consume more exclusive and expensive vintages' (Bocock, 1992, p.127). This may explain the restless nature of modern consumption among those at or near the top of the social hierarchy, but it does not explain a significant feature of modern consumerism — that concern with consumption and style is now widespread across the *mass* of the population.

For Georg Simmel the answer to this question lay in the rapid urbanisation of Western societies: in the development of the modern city. Simmel is perhaps best known for his analyses of the contemporary urban human, in particular how people's behaviour has altered in response to living in a rationalised, depersonalised and busy city environment. The city constitutes a person who must develop a 'blasé outlook' — a calculated lack of interest in the numerous people one will share space with every day — whether at work, on public transport, or in the city streets. Consumption, then, is a way for people to reassert their identity and individuality in the face of the depersonalisation of modern life (Paterson, 2006, p.21). But this personal identity always exists in tension with that of the broader society: we wish to be individual but also to be accepted as part of the community. Thus what we see, as in the cycles of fashion, is 'a continual cycle of establishing the norm, challenging it, and thereby deriving a newly altered norm which hastily abandons the previously established norms' (Paterson, 2006, p.23). We recognise here the restlessness of consumption that Veblen alluded to. There is also clearly an antagonism between personal and societal or community needs: a conflict that we will see is present in contemporary Irish responses to consumption.

For Campbell, patterns of consumption can only be explained in relation to cultural movements that present as valuable and intelligible certain ways of behaving, while others are seen to be bizarre or irrational. The cultural movement that he sees as responsible for presenting modern consumer behaviour as the only good way to respond to commodities is the Romantic movement of the early nineteenth century. It was, for Campbell, this movement that introduced a new 'consumer ethic' into developing capitalist society. This ethic is expressed through romantic notions of sentiment, feeling, individualism and a commitment to pleasure. It manifests itself in a peculiar orientation towards goods: not a utilitarian one, but one that is typified by dreaming and anticipation and a shift in focus from having to 'wanting'. Consequently, 'goods are thought of as bridges to displaced meanings — bridging the gap between present lived reality and the set of ideals one keeps in mind', which may be 'a golden past or even a bright hope for the future' (Paterson, 2006, pp.24–35).

MASS CONSUMERISM AND THE AFFLUENT WORKER

Early sociological work on consumption, such as Veblen's, focused on the upper classes. It was not until the mid-twentieth century that sociologists began to ask questions about consumption behaviour among the industrial working class. They then tended to be primarily concerned with one question: does the rising standard of living and the increased availability of consumer goods, associated with industrial capitalism, lead to a blurring of class divisions within industrialised societies? Put more bluntly, do workers who experience affluence become more like middle-class people? The question was prompted in particular by the post-war boom in the British economy that led to rising wage levels for industrial workers, especially skilled workers in new industries. Compared with workers in the older, heavy industries like coal-mining and ship-building, it appeared that workers in the new industries turning out mass consumer durables were not only better off but seemed to be the forerunners of a new type of employee who no longer fitted easily into the traditional view of the industrial working class.

A major British study of such workers (Goldthorpe et al., 1968–9) set out to explore this question. It found that there were differences in lifestyle and consumption behaviour between workers in the old and new industries. The 'affluent workers' tended to be more home-centred, spent less time with other men in traditionally male pursuits such as football or the pub, were interested in spending money on the home (house decorating, domestic gadgets) and generally had at least one car in the household. But the authors of the study were not prepared to infer from this that 'affluent workers' were becoming more middle class. Their instrumental orientation towards work as a way to finance consumption, rather than as a source of personal satisfaction, had more in common with other members of the working class than with the middle class. What seemed to be happening was the emergence of a *mass consumer society* in Britain, where consumption patterns were being generalised across social classes rather than being sharply differentiated along class lines.

Such differences in lifestyle and consumption patterns were closely linked to the economic conditions in Britain at the time. They did not necessarily last into the 1970s and 1980s. Decline in older heavy industries such as steel-making, ship-building and coal-mining reduced the ranks of the 'traditional working class' and, in some regions of the country, led to reduced affluence, even in households where people worked in the newer industries. This helped to push consumption patterns back towards meeting basic needs. But it is probably fair to say, contra Marx, that the experience since the 1970s of the majority of people in developed capitalist societies has been one of gradually increasing affluence. The relatively well-paid who could make choices about consumption began to take for granted that their jobs could provide enough income not just to live, but to support a relatively affluent lifestyle (Bocock, 1992, p.133):

> This marked a move from the primary source of identity being based upon the paid work role a person performed, to identities being constructed around lifestyles and patterns of consumption. . . . The mode of consumption changed from one concerned primarily with basic material provision . . . to a mode concerned more with the status value and symbolic meaning of the commodity purchased.

'Conspicuous consumption' was moving down the status hierarchy as societies became more industrialised.

Most recent analyses of consumption have drawn heavily on post-modern theories of identity, in particular those associated with French writers such as Barthes and Baudrillard. These analyses focus strongly on how meanings are constructed in and through material goods and services and also stress the significance of consumption in everyday life: as Paterson (2006, p.30) suggests:

> in a late capitalist consumer society . . . meanings and signs are inextricable from, but not simply reducible to, the consumption and display of commodities; and the habitual, everyday use we make of them in constructing and maintaining aspects of our identity.

According to this view, consumption, as Simmel's approach suggested, is about expressing one's individuality within broader cultural patterns of similarity. Consumption, then, can be seen as a form of communication: 'this is who I am, not the same as you, but not so different either'. But at the same time our 'identity' is not a fixed entity, rather it may change according to the circumstances or social situations in which we locate ourselves; for example, our workplace identity may be quite different to the one we wish to express when out at the weekend. Modern consumption allows us to a certain extent to choose how we present ourselves, but this then raises further questions about authenticity — who or what we really are. As Paterson (2006, p.56) remarks: 'new identities may be bought and worn as if trying on outfits at the mall, to be discarded later . . . but in such a case you are *not* what you wear'. The tension between authenticity and artificiality is another one that we will see underpins Irish discussions about consumption.

CONSUMERISM AND CONSUMPTION IN IRELAND

This account of changing consumption patterns and meanings is based on the post-war pattern of economic development experienced by core capitalist countries such as the UK, the United States and Germany. Given the very different pattern of economic and social development in Ireland in this period, we would expect the Irish experience of consumerism to be rather different. There was no post-war development of large-scale consumer good manufacturers in Ireland. When a manufacturing industry did develop in Ireland during and after the 1970s, it was generally oriented to export markets.

Consumption processes in Ireland thus need to be understood in the context of the uneven development of global capitalism. This unevenness applies as much to the spread of modern consumption patterns as it does to the diffusion of modern capitalist economic relations. Dependency theory has provided a useful way to understand the processes of uneven development (see Chapter 3) and has been extensively used by sociologists to explain the Irish experience of development. But dependency theory largely concerns itself with how capitalism has developed in Ireland as a structure of production, and has little to say about how our position as a post-colonial or late developing semi-peripheral society in Europe may have shaped our practices or values in relation to consumption.

The dependency perspective suggests that incorporation into the sphere of multinational capitalism increases social divisions within the incorporated society. Penetration of TNCs into the economy creates a local elite of business people and others who help to manage or who supply professional or financial services to the TNC subsidiaries. This elite can enjoy a level of consumption not far below that of equivalent groups in core societies and, because of its cross-national contacts and networks, it may be very ready to adopt 'conspicuous consumption' values or to emulate international colleague groups in lifestyle and purchasing behaviours. At the same time, dependent development re-creates and expands a marginalised sector of society, condemned to poverty and exclusion from discretionary consumption. This analysis is very general and raises as many questions as it answers if we try to apply it to Ireland. The connections between dependency and consumption are generally discussed in the context of relations between the First and Third Worlds. They ignore uneven development *within* the First World, or the presence of semi-peripheral societies with distinctive historical trajectories on the margins of developed cores.

The nature of dependency analysis makes it difficult to account in any way for the consumption experience of the majority of the population in a society such as Ireland, that is, those who are neither part of the internationalising elite nor of the socially and economically excluded. Nor does it help us to trace the specific effects of trends such as increasing urbanisation and suburbanisation. Following Simmel, sociologists have tended to see a close association between consumption and urban settings. Cities are seen as particularly conducive to consumerism as they provide the best opportunities to obtain desired goods and services and also for displays of status associated with consumption choices. Urbanisation in turn is linked to capitalist development and industrialisation. Thus, less developed countries, with more rural populations, should be slower to develop modern consumption practices. Though Ireland remains more 'rural' than many other European societies, Dublin and a number of other cities do have long histories in relation to consumption, including a history of change and fashion (Brady, 2001; Findlater, 2001). It is wrong to assume that consumerism is a very new feature of Irish society.

One way to improve the usefulness of the dependency perspective is to investigate the specific nature of dependent consumerism. Sklair (1995, p.148) suggests an adequate understanding of modernisation requires an examination of two aspects of change: the first is a society's *transition to producerism*, the increased mobilisation of its people to work more productively. The second is a society's *transition to consumerism*, the increase in material consumption associated with a mass consumerist society. Dependent societies, it is argued, have less control over the management of their economy than do core societies. Similarly, we could say that dependent societies are less able to manage their own consumption behaviour. But what would this mean? — that they are less able to act to protect local consumption values, or to promote local cultural products and items? that they are more vulnerable to external evaluations of the status and prestige that stem from the consumption of certain goods, and so would have less confidence in indigenous status systems?

There is no reason that the development of consumerism should mirror that of producerism. We can suggest four possible combinations, that may identify different types of society within a core — periphery framework. The core societies of the world are high-producer/high-consumer societies; many 'underdeveloped' African and Asian countries are low-producer/low-consumer societies. Between these are two further possibilities: low-producer/high-consumer societies (perhaps in a process of decline from a former core position but continuing to finance a high standard of living from past colonial relationships); and high-producer/low-consumer societies, which put resources into the development of industry and capital, but institutionalise low wages. Sklair terms this last combination 'ascetic develop-mentalism' and suggests that China reflected this approach at least up to the mid-1980s. The concept negates the modernisationist argument that the low levels of consumption found in less-developed countries are the result of 'traditional' norms and constraints. The absence of mass consumerism in a society may not indicate poverty or a lack of economic resources, but it can reflect a specific ideological or cultural evaluation of consumption.

The concept of ascetic developmentalism captures rather well the era of economic self-sufficiency introduced in Ireland by the Fianna Fáil governments of the 1930s, 1940s and 1950s. While these governments urged restraint on consumption as part of a deliberate development strategy, it was also clearly more than that. The image of a lifestyle of modest comfort, combined with hard but healthy manual work, assumed the status of a distinctively Irish ideal. Limiting consumption was part of a broader strategy to establish cultural as well as economic and political independence from Britain, along with attempts to revive the Irish language and develop distinctively Irish dress codes. If British society was thoroughly urbanised, then it was the lifestyle of the frugal but relatively secure small farmer that was to symbolise Irish identity. If British society was charac-terised by materialism and consumerism, then Irish society would develop in the opposite way, through an emphasis on spirituality and non-material enjoyments.

For many Irish people ascetic developmentalism continued to dominate life into the 1960s, 1970s and even the 1980s. Taxation policies (high taxes on labour, low taxes on land and capital) and generous support for TNCs left much of the Irish workforce with relatively modest increases in their standard of living, despite continually rising levels of productivity at work and even despite increasing wages. But until the 1980s, restraints on consumption could retain some validity as a marker of Irishness; it is only relatively recently that the ideological legitimation for them was stripped of any conviction.

Recent sociological analyses of Irish consumerism (Inglis, 2002; Keohane and Kuhling, 2004b) address the tensions between the asceticism of the past and the contemporary enthusiasm for consumption. Inglis (2002, p.30) notes that formerly 'self-indulgence was a sin and pleasure had to be legitimated within an overall habitus of self-denial'. He sees the public expression of pleasure in consumption as a new feature of Irish life: one that is linked to the declining influence of religion. For Irish women, he suggests 'I'm worth it!' has replaced 'Lord I am not worthy' (Inglis, 2002, p.25). But he detects a residual lack of comfort with such conspicuous consumption. Keohane and Kuhling similarly remark on this unease, and ask 'why is there such a contradiction between what people are actually spending, and the generalised condemnation of over-inflated spending?' (2004b, p.47). The answer, for them, lies in an application of French sociologist Marcel Mauss's concept of the reciprocal gift relationship to contemporary Irish consumption behaviour. Mauss's theory sought to show how societies are held together by reciprocal relationships of obligation: partly cemented by the giving and receiving of gifts. Keohane and Kuhling suggest that such reciprocity is an important element of Irish culture, which stresses generosity to others as a basis of community; for example, as reflected in giving to charity, gift-giving at Christmas and in wedding ceremonies. Whereas before this system operated in the context of relative scarcity, it now takes place in a time of abundance: giving rise to high levels of expenditure, relative to other societies, but also to spiralling consumer debt. Nevertheless, unlike other critics, for Keohane and Kuhling (2004b, p.51) 'far from indicating the devaluation of traditional values of community, Irish consumerism shows paradoxically how the traditional value of community remains central.' But the 'combination of acquisitive accumulation and generosity, of possessive individualism and collective commitment' (2004, p.48) is ultimately destructive, as it does not allow for a more rational system of social redistribution to take place.

As Keohane and Kuhling (2004, p.47) point out, we still have few sociological studies of consumerism as it is experienced in everyday Irish life. The ethnography of French anthropologist Hervé Varenne (1993), based on ten months of living with his family in Ballinteer, Dublin 16, during the mid-1980s, is a source of partial but fascinating data. Based on participant observation of daily suburban life the Varennes draw a number of conclusions about the people they see around them. 'Greenhill' as they call their area, hovers ambiguously between successful middle class and struggling working class. It is difficult to decide whether the inhabitants have escaped poverty and small-town provincialism to realise a dream of social mobility, or whether they have 'traded the rich community life of small rural villages or dense urban neighbourhoods for isolation, loneliness, a kind of metaphoric death in an inauthentic world of rootless consumerism' (1993, p.102). 'The debate grinds on' Varenne adds, 'among the people of Greenhill themselves as the lawns get mowed, flowers planted, new carpeting put down and last but not least, mortgages get paid and new housing estates sprout up in the fields up the hill and down the road.'

What emerges clearly from Varenne's account is that the new consumerism of this type of life is not fully accepted by everyone and remains a source of confusion, guilt and defensiveness to many. As one of his respondents remarks (Meg Fleming, in Varenne, 1993, pp.115–16):

> There are a lot of women that haven't time for just sitting down with a child. I find in modern day, today, in Dublin especially, of course I haven't any views of anywhere else, because I haven't lived anywhere else, that they just really concentrate on the house. They have this idea of the perfect house but, I mean, my house is just a home as far as I am concerned. But you have this perfect house, carpet, furniture, fridge, washing machine, everything has to be there and number one child arrives when all this is done. This is the new, this is definitely, I am sure it's everywhere, whereas we did it all the other way. We had six children and never thought about the consequences. . . . Which would you prefer: wake up and say "I've got a pain". You go to hospital and they tell you you have cancer? Or would you prefer to sit at home with a carpet you don't like? Which I don't like. A day will come when you can replace it. Don't rush it.

CONSUMPTION AND CLASS

A central issue that has emerged in the sociology of consumption (already revealed in the work of Goldthorpe *et al.* (1968–9), discussed earlier) is the relationship between consumption and social class. Sociologists — and even more particularly, market researchers — have generally assumed that social class determines consumption patterns, or at any rate that if we know what occupational, educational and income bracket a person fits into we can fairly accurately estimate the consumer behaviour they will display.

Is class the main factor that shapes consumption patterns, or are there more significant divisions along other social lines such as gender, ethnicity or age? We mentioned earlier that the sociology of consumption has generally assumed that the modernisation process involves a move from low to high consumption levels, and that modern society is often conceptualised as a mass consumption society. A 'mass society' does not display marked differentiation between social classes, so one would expect only minor differences in relation to consumption patterns. Most people will watch the same television programmes, drive similar cars, dress their children in similar clothes, and so on. Studying consumption patterns in society then can be one way to examine how significant class differences remain for explaining social behaviour.

The relationship between class and consumption can also be reversed. Instead of asking if class determines consumption, we can ask whether consumption practices are part of what shapes and determines class position — the question asked by Goldthorpe et al. (1968–9). Most sociologists would now argue that differences in consumption may be as important as those in occupation or economic position in shaping the stratification system. To continue thinking in terms of class stratification in modern societies — even using that term in its broadest sense to include both economic and cultural meanings — we need to integrate discussions of consumption with those about class. Veblen has offered us one way to do this with his argument that consumption practices are used to signal and intensify class differences through an emphasis on variations in lifestyle and 'taste'. Later, we will see how the French sociologist Bourdieu has integrated this idea into an analysis of stratification in modern French society.

First, we need to discuss further the argument that in a modern 'mass' society consumption varies significantly by social class, and that class remains a very important cause of differences in consumer behaviour. Until the 1980s it was commonplace for researchers or advertisers to assume that the best way to understand consumer behaviour was to link it to a class analysis, distinguishing between classes on the basis of a combination of income level and occupation (Bocock, 1992, pp.134–5). Income level was assumed to correspond fairly closely with occupation, with the highest class (managers, administrators or professional workers) regarded as having the most disposable income and the lowest class (those relying on state benefits, casual workers) seen as having the least.

In practice, income (usually household income) appeared to correlate closely with the amount people spent on different consumption categories each week — food, housing, transport — and therefore how much surplus income they could spend on other goods, such as consumer durables (TVs, washing machines, DVD players) or luxury items (holidays, restaurant meals or wine). Bocock tells us that in Britain in the late 1980s, very clear patterns in relation to the consumption of a number of consumer durables were found across households from the highest to the lowest class. It was particularly clear in relation to luxury items like dishwashers (just under one-third of high professional and managerial households possessed one, compared to 1 per cent of unskilled manual households) and PCs (around 40 per cent at the top, down to 14 per cent at the bottom). On the other hand, 98 per cent of all households, regardless of class position, had a TV set and there was little variance across classes in the proportion owning a video recorder. Consumption of some goods had become 'mass', then, in Britain by this time, yet there were still large gaps between classes in terms of other goods. Whether this can tell us much about class processes in British society or not, it does clearly reveal the depth of income inequalities that continues to be part of British society.

What about Ireland? Research by the Combat Poverty Agency (Murphy-Lawless, 1992) suggests that similar differences exist here. A 1992 study compared the weekly spending patterns of two household types, one with an income of £200 to £250 (€250 to €320) per week, described as an 'average' family, and the other relying on unemployment payments. After paying for food and fuel, housing and transport, the 'average' family had 37 per cent of its income left over while the other family had 34 per cent. Out of this surplus each family spent about the same proportion on consumer durables and other goods (10 to 11 per cent). The family on unemployment payments spent a higher proportion of its income (but a lower absolute amount) on drink and tobacco than the 'average' family, but the 'average' family spent a much higher proportion on clothing, shoes and services of various kinds (mainly related to leisure and recreation, such as going to the cinema or out for a meal, getting clothes dry cleaned or hair cut, caring for a family pet). Neither family could be described as high consumers; even the 'average' family had very little surplus income after standard items in the family budget, such as professional haircuts, were accounted for. But they did have more than the other family, as one might expect, and used it on different forms of consumption.

A further study of the income and expenditure patterns of low income households was carried out in 2000 (Daly and Leonard, 2002). The researchers found that people often found it difficult to account for all expenditure: especially in relation to infrequent or unexpected outlays. On the basis of the information that was available, the findings to a large extent replicated those of Murphy-Lawless's earlier research. The main expenditure category was still food, followed by fuel and light, followed by cigarettes and alcohol (see Figure 17.1). Compared to average households, poor households spent a much greater proportion of income on necessities (Daly and Leonard, 2002, p.22).

Categorising class in terms, primarily, of income and, secondly, of occupation, seemed to work quite well, until recently, as a way to predict consumption patterns

Figure 16.1 Composition of average household expenditure in low income families

Areas of expenditure	Average weekly expenditure €	% of total income
Food	90.0	31
Rent/Morgage	30.0	9
Electricity + fuel	38.9	12
Loans + hire purchase	22.1	7
Children*	17.1	5
Cigarettes + alcohol	32.3	10
Telephone	8.8	2
TV/Video	3.8	1
Insurance (personal and home)	3.0	1
Other**	70.7	22
Average weekly household income***	325.7	100

* This includes expenditure on pocket-money, sweets, school lunches and transport.
** This includes expenditure on clothes, leisure and transport as well as income unaccounted for when spending was itemised.
*** This is the mean weekly household income. In those households where personal and household incomes differed, expenditure was calculated as a % of the total household income.

(*Source*: Daly and Leonard, 2002, p.21)

in different societies. Some lifestyle differences were also evident, particularly at the higher end of the social class system between, for example, professional people on one side and managerial or business personnel on the other, that produced some differences in consumer behaviour, but these were relatively slight and appeared to be declining in importance as educational qualifications expanded and access to older professional jobs became more open.

CLASS AND OTHER SOCIAL CATEGORISATIONS

Bocock (1992, p.138) argues that by the 1980s some market researchers (who seem to have been ahead of sociologists) were becoming dissatisfied with the results to be gained from using conventional class categories for consumers. They began to find that better predictions derived from the use of age-based categorisations — young adult, middle-aged, older people — instead of or as well as class. The idea that difference in lifestyle is found not only between classes but also within them, particularly between different age groups, began to attract sociological attention.

Among sociologists this connected with a long established interest in subcultures (see Chapter 12), particularly in the youth subcultures that had emerged since the 1950s. A striking feature of youth subcultures has been how they have been marked by internal divisions (mods versus rockers, hippies versus punks) that bear a relationship to social class (1960s rockers were working class, mods were lower middle class or in non-manual occupations) but are always expressed through differences in consumption styles: in clothing, haircuts, music, transport, use of leisure time. At the other end of the scale, there has been a growing recognition of the distinctiveness, in terms of both disposable income and consumption patterns, of older people (Bocock, 1992, p.141). This recognition is sometimes expressed through the concept of 'the Third Age'. It reflects the 'greying of society' that most Western societies are now experiencing. This has created a larger stratum of older people with reasonably good incomes (due to improved pensions) and considerable leisure to spend on consumption. It has also produced a certain awareness among older people themselves that they constitute a separate social group with distinctive interests and tastes.

Age is not the only categorisation that is widely used to understand consumer behaviour: gender is increasingly recognised as very significant. In a sense this has always been recognised by market researchers and advertisers but until recently their analysis of consumption in the general population was based on a narrow conception of the typical household which contained a nuclear family characterised by a simple division of labour. Adult male(s) were primarily concerned with providing the household income, while adult female(s) managed the disposal of that income. In other words, women controlled the consumption behaviour of households while men were seen as relatively marginal to the process. This image was underpinned by a model of the typical modern family as made up of a husband employed in paid work outside the home and a wife engaged only in domestic duties. It is mirrored in the 1986 Irish Consumer Research report *The Irish housewife — A portrait*. The housewife is the key target for business because she manages and negotiates household consumption, though ultimately her capacity to spend is limited by her husband's capacity to earn, that is, by his class position.

More recently gender has come to be recognised as a factor that is highly relevant to shaping lifestyle, and hence consumption. To some extent this reflects the decline of the 'typical household', the emergence of an increasing number of single-person households, and of women as individuals who work and consume in their own right. It also reflects the growing recognition of the involvement in consumption by men (Bocock, 1992, p.142):

Young men with reasonably well-paid jobs, or with a disposable income as a result of living with parents, were the first major target group in the youth market in the 1960s. However, as patterns of consumption and relative affluence have spread in the 1980s, older groups of men have become targets for consumption by advertisers.

As more women are drawn into the paid labour market, more men are opting to, or finding that they have to, share in the tasks of managing household consumption (McKeown *et al.*, 1999). At the same time, increases in family breakdown and divorce mean that increasing numbers of older and often relatively affluent men are establishing their own independent households and consumption patterns to go with this.

While the purchasing power of consumers continues to be largely determined by their occupation and economic position, it is increasingly clear that class in this restricted sense cannot provide a full explanation of how people use that power, or whether they use it at all. Between the capacity to consume an item and its consumption there intervenes a range of factors to do with taste, style and aspiration that may be more strongly influenced by age or gender than by class. This point has two important implications: first, social stratification is a more complex phenomenon than economistic accounts of social class have been able to reveal. Second, an adequate understanding of social stratification will have to integrate conventional class divisions with those associated with distinctive 'cultures of consumption' linked to gender, age, occupational status and quite possibly region, national identity and ethnicity. Since economic class does not determine all significant divisions in society, including divisions in consumption behaviour, we need to develop theories of class that can incorporate more than one dimension of stratification.

CONSUMPTION, DISTINCTION AND IDENTITY

The work of Weber may help. As we saw in Chapter 7, Weber distinguished between class and status as independent outcomes of the distribution of power in society. While he defined class primarily in terms of material resources or educational credentials, he related social status to the degree of social respect or esteem that people are accorded within society due to their social group membership. Status groups may be based on ethnicity, religion or profession, or may simply be groups that display a particularly valued lifestyle. For Weber most of the conflicts around inequality in modern society were the result of rivalry and competition between status groups, rather than between classes. Subsequent discussion of his ideas has generally focused on ethnic or professional status groups, but Weber's inclusion of 'styles of life' suggests that groups that are differentiated by patterns of consumption are also relevant to social stratification.

A problem with Weber's analysis is that having pointed out to us that status differences do not necessarily coincide with class differences, he offers little help in rejoining the two to construct a coherent picture of differentiation in modern society. But the challenge of reintegrating patterns of consumption into a theory of social class has been taken up by Pierre Bourdieu. Bourdieu starts from a Marxist position on class and locates the cause of social inequality in the social structure, especially the economic structure. But he adds to this a quite Weberian concern to understand differences between groups in terms of status.

Bourdieu's main work on this topic is *Distinction: A social critique of the judgement of taste* (1984), based on 1970s research into stratification in French society. One of Bourdieu's main purposes is to establish that 'taste' is not a purely individual or idiosyncratic quality, but is socially derived and socially utilised. Bourdieu says that the exercise of taste, as evidenced in patterns of consumption, is the main way that social groups distinguish themselves from one another. Here he is echoing ideas we have already seen in Veblen, but in emphasising the making of distinctions Bourdieu suggests that a focus just on conspicuous consumption is too crude to express the complexities of the stratification process.

Both Marx and Weber link class position to the ownership of capital. One of Bourdieu's major contributions has been to distinguish between two different types of capital that people may own — the traditional concept of economic capital, and his own concept of *symbolic* or *cultural* capital. While economic capital refers to material wealth, embedded in property, stocks, shares and money, cultural capital refers primarily to the various forms of intellectual resources that exist in society. These range from particular educational qualifications to the capacity to appreciate, critique or create new cultural forms and objects. Social groups differ, not only in the access they have to these sorts of capital but also in the extent that they esteem or aspire to either. Society is characterised by continual struggle, not just between groups in a stratification system but also over the stratifying mechanisms themselves — over whether knowledge or wealth, taste or property, should be dominant in differentiating individuals and groups and arranging them in a hierarchy of value.

Bourdieu is in no doubt that making distinctions along these lines is an important part of maintaining social inequality. They are part of how dominant groups try to retain their position. This process has necessarily become increasingly subtle and sophisticated in an era when consumption has become democratised and access to valued lifestyles and their material trappings appears to be open to broader sections of the population. Bourdieu's perspective, it should be noted, remains essentially structuralist: society is organised around the distribution of economic and cultural capital and the structural position an individual occupies greatly influences their capacity to choose between and adopt alternative lifestyles.

But Bourdieu is also emphasising that individuals are not entirely determined by structures. People respond to and act on the symbolic meanings attached to different commodities and different patterns of consumption, and develop beliefs and aspirations based on these meanings that are relatively independent of their structural position in society. Thus, in consuming, or in exercising taste in consumption, people create and establish differences between social groups, rather than simply expressing them. Thus, Bourdieu's work reveals to us how shopping reproduces society — or rather, how the act of choosing to purchase one consumption item instead of another contributes to the validation, or the disconfirmation, of a social structure based on status hierarchy. Whether Bourdieu can ultimately combine a structuralist emphasis with an image of the consumer as a creative and relatively autonomous actor is still much debated. But he has firmly established the issue of taste in the contemporary sociology of consumption, and other sociologists have adopted and developed this theme, particularly to see how taste and style are used by individuals to establish or create a specific personal identity.

For Bourdieu, judgments of taste in consumption are part of the learned and acquired habits of groups in different locations within the social class structure. They are also ways to create distinctions of status and to reproduce status stratifications within society; in other words, to create and reproduce social structure. But other writers have argued that in contemporary society consumption patterns have become so disconnected from class divisions that they constitute a virtually autonomous source of social differentiation and identity. With the advent of relative affluence for large sections of society, consumption has become a matter not just of meeting needs and securing material comforts but of lifestyle. This term connotes individuality, self-expression and self-consciousness in matters of style: 'one's body, clothes, speech, leisure pastimes, eating and drinking preferences, home, car, choices of holidays etc. are to be regarded as indicators of the individuality of taste and sense of style of the owner/consumer' (Featherstone, 1987, p.55). Society, it is argued, has now moved beyond the 'mass consumption' stage of the 1950s and 1960s; the emphasis in today's marketplace is not on providing consumer durables at affordable prices and standardised quality, but on providing the consumer with *choice*. The choices that consumers make are now central to their self-construction of a distinct social and personal identity.

Why the change? Post-Fordist arguments start from an analysis of change within industry (Kumar, 1995). New technologies and production methods emphasise flexibility in the use of labour and materials. In the area of marketing, strategies rely on the generation of brand loyalties and the establishment of minor, surface differences between essentially similar products. This gives industry a leading role in encouraging consumers to seek identity in differentiated consumption. But it tends to portray the consumer as a passive receiver of new products and marketing strategies. Other researchers argue that consumers themselves play an active, and sometimes uncontrollable or unpredictable, part in making decisions about consumption, and that they do this because they approach consumption primarily or increasingly as a matter of identity-construction (Lash and Urry, 1994).

Why should consumption be taking on such an important role in developed societies? One answer is that as a result of passing through the 'mass society' stage, we now live in a world where established class or status group differences have become blurred or have disappeared, so that they are no longer available as a source of personal identity. In a world characterised increasingly by what Giddens calls 'life politics', identity has to be sought and located in other arenas. Another answer goes back to Marx's analysis of the development of capitalism itself, and particularly to his suggestion that capitalism tends to devalue the experience of work. It deskills workers, removes any elements of craftsmanship from their working lives and allows them to be treated by employers as little more than commodities themselves, to be bought and sold on the labour market. The expansion of capitalism makes productive work an increasingly unsatisfactory source of personal identity. While work relationships are highly inegalitarian and constraining for most people, the marketplace becomes increasingly the place where people can experience themselves as free and equal citizens. Through exercising choice in our consumption practices we feel ourselves to be free; free to reconstruct what we 'really' are outside of the controls and constraints of work. Thus, there has been a shift in society 'from the primary source of identity being based upon the paid work role a person performed to identities being constructed around lifestyles and patterns of consumption' (Bocock, 1992, p.133).

We are now far removed from the explanation for modern consumerism that Campbell labelled 'instinctivist'. Far from seeing consumption as a way to meet a pre-existent human need, we see it as a form of symbolic communication, where meanings about identity and outlook on life are exchanged with others. Developing this idea, French sociologist Jean Baudrillard has insisted that we should understand consumption, in contemporary society, as primarily the consumption of symbols or meanings. In consuming meanings, moreover, we *become* these meanings. Identity, Baudrillard says, does not exist outside of or before consumption, it is constructed in consumption.

A T-shirt declares: 'I shop, therefore I am.' Shopping has become the second most important leisure activity in the US, after watching television (itself a form of preparatory shopping). This has stimulated much sociological interest, not just in the US, in the development of shopping and of the modern shopping mall. According to Langman (1992, p.43), the mall is 'the signifying and celebrating edifice' of consumer culture in the contemporary world. Renegotiation of 'shopping' from the satisfaction of basic needs in a local marketplace to a form of mass entertainment has been seen by others as one of the greatest achievements of modern capitalism.

Langman suggests that contemporary society is best described as 'amusement society'. Leisure is now central to the experience of selfhood, and shopping has become the pivotal leisure activity. Shopping malls are physically designed to promote various forms of loitering, parading and strolling as part of the consumption experience, as well as providing additional forms of entertainment (fun fairs, fashion shows). Contemporary shopping practice centres on strolling, browsing and 'grazing'. As the shopping mall becomes a leisure centre, those who visit it are likely to spend as much of their time gazing on the goods on display and fantasising about them as actually buying. As this redefined concept of shopping is transmitted around the world as part of a developing global capitalism, it is argued, increasingly, that populations of countries that have not experienced affluence are drawn into the fantasising mode as well. The post-modern understanding of consumption thus has implications far beyond the affluent elites of the world who can afford to purchase. At the same time, both overtly (through store detectives and security guards) and covertly (through physical layout and closed circuit TV), the mall is not open to everyone; it excludes the very poor and those with no capacity or inclination to buy.

Shopping in Ireland

In Ireland, as elsewhere in the developed world, retailing is both a major economic activity and an important aspect of people's lifestyles. According to Parker, of the Centre for Retail Studies at UCD, one in eight of the Irish employed population works in the retail or wholesale sectors (1999, p.69). It is also amongst 'the most dynamic of economic activities'. Crawford (1995, p.222) remarks that 'the history of retailing in Ireland remains to be written' (though see Brady, 2001; Findlater, 2001) and similar remarks could be made even more strongly in relation to the sociology: shopping has been virtually ignored by students of Irish society.

Kennedy (cited in Lambe 2001, p.207) reports that 'Ireland has always suffered from a plague of small shopkeepers' and we have indicated elsewhere (see Chapter 7) that Irish society has long featured a numerous and influential family business/small proprietor sector. In the nineteenth and for most of the twentieth century Irish shops were small and traditionally run in conjunction with pubs, sub-post offices or other service businesses. Shops in rural areas were the precursor of today's convenience store (Lambe, 2001, p.214) and were used on a frequent, often daily, basis. As a consequence they had an important social role, not unlike that enjoyed by pubs — a parallel noted by Brody (1986, pp.157–74). Thus the shopkeeper was an important person in the community, where:

> [extensive] contacts, combined with the physical location of the shops within the community, made them transmitters and receivers of information, news and gossip. These advantages, together with the significance of their economic role and strong kinship ties in the community enabled shopkeepers to enjoy an important social and political role, and to wield power and patronage at a local level (Lambe, 2001, p.222).

Irish retailing evolved slowly over the nineteenth and twentieth centuries, reflecting the increasing marketisation of society and improved systems of distribution, packaging and advertising (Lambe, 2001). Crawford (1995, p.223) suggests that the country saw a 'retailing revolution' in the period 1958 to 1988: stimulated by the arrival of the supermarket. In this period the number of supermarkets increased fourfold while grocery shops declined by 60 per cent. 'Family grocers' could not compete with the scale of the multiples' operations. They responded by forming collective voluntary groups that allowed them to achieve greater economies of scale and the result was that the relentless expansion of the supermarkets was halted by the late 1980s. By 1989 60 per cent of families used a major supermarket at least once a week for their shopping (Crawford, 1995, p.224). Small neighbourhood shops, especially those that will provide credit, remain important for many customers.

Parker (1999, p.70) has described the suburbanisation of shopping, particularly within Dublin. He identifies four stages to this process which involve the gradual shift out of city and town centre areas of the following types of retailers. Similar patterns can be determined in most Irish cities and larger towns:

convenience goods retailing — this saw the development of the first shopping centres. In Ireland the first was the Stillorgan Shopping Centre in south suburban Dublin, opened in 1966.

durable goods retailers, such as DIY stores and carpet sellers, moved into old factories or warehouse parks, in areas such as the Long Mile Road.

fashion retailers and other specialist shops — these were to be found in particular in new suburban shopping centres. This provided direct competition with more exclusive centre-city boutiques and department stores.

The fourth stage of development, currently being experienced, is the development of new styles of retail operation, often imported directly from Britain, continental Europe or the USA, such as outlet stores (such as that at Rathdowney, Co. Laois), big box outlets (such as Dixon's), warehouse clubs, petrol station forecourt stores, and retail parks (such as that at Dublin's Liffey Valley).

The latter two stages can be seen as the beginning of the 'malling' of Ireland, paralleling the processes alluded to above. This process has been analysed in the Irish context by Corcoran (2000). She suggests (2000, p.91–2) that 'since the 1960s Dublin has been turning itself inside out' as retail activity has shifted to the suburbs and the land along new motorways. Indeed, as Corcoran points out, 'the new shopping malls are predicated on a consumer class with spending power and access to private vehicles'. The development of shopping malls indicates a point where public and private interests can meet and collide. Thus the state has had a major role in underpinning new models of retail development, as in the Tallaght Town Centre. But the major beneficiaries are arguably property developers and the mainly British-based retail corporations (such as Tesco) that have seen Ireland emerge as a particularly profitable territory.

Overall there has been a huge expansion in retail space in Ireland. Most of this has been outside of the existing major urban centres, to the suburbs and 'edge city' locations. Such development has often closely followed road developments, with shopping centre and supermarket development linked, for example, to Dublin's M50 and also to bypasses of such towns as Athlone, Donegal and Mullingar. The attraction of such retail locations is outlined by Parker (1999, p.72):

> the M50 has provided rapid access around the city, enabling affluent and highly mobile suburbanites to extend their range of shopping choice to one or other of the larger regional-scale centres. By comparison to the effort involved in trying to access the city centre by private car and find (and pay for) parking, the ease with which the relatively free-flowing motorway leads to large-scale retail alternatives with extensive and free parking is considerable.

Other key trends in retailing, identified by Parker, include the continued strength of Dublin city centre as a retail location, particularly traditional shopping areas such as Grafton and Henry Streets, which have long been the most popular and prestigious shopping areas in the city (Brady, 2001). This is reflected in the very high rentals that can be secured by the owners of properties in such areas. This may be linked to another important trend — the internationalisation of Irish retailing. It is often remarked that a walk down Dublin's Grafton Street is little different to that of any British city, such is the dominance of British and other international retail brandnames. Parker (1999, p.72) reports that there are over eighty foreign-based retailers operating in Ireland. These include not just major supermarket operators like Tesco, but specialist stores like Richer Sounds and the Body Shop; discount supermarkets such as the German-based Aldi and Lidl; and major department stores such as Marks and Spencer. The influx of such global retailers is helping to change the landscape of shopping in Ireland — for example, in their demand for larger store premises.

The future of retailing in Ireland may be shaped by such trends. Others include the increasing cross-over amongst formerly separate areas of retailing. This is already happening in the UK, where Tesco has become a major petrol retailer while petrol companies are increasingly becoming involved in the supermarket and convenience store business. Other areas of change and development are in airport shopping, which has survived the removal of duty free sales for EU-based travel, and the establishment of new shops on third level campuses, on the

Internet and within entertainment sites such as museums. As Parker (1999, p.78) suggests:

> the major point about consumers' shopping behaviour is that historic behaviour patterns cannot be taken for granted. This is realised by the better retailers and past customer allegiances are not guaranteed and may become irrelevant.

Within the context of these structural changes to retailing, we must remember that the degree of affluence in a society and its distribution across classes continues to constrain the extent to which shopping and the shopping experience can provide a new source of individual identity. In addition, it is important not to uncritically accept the retail industry's drive to redefine shopping as entertainment: shopping is also *work* — obviously enough for those, generally young, female and poorly-paid who are employed in retail — but also for many consumers who must budget, list, drive, negotiate car-parks and shopping trolleys, and physically shift goods from place to place. For those without private transport the burdens can be considerable.

We may also question whether it is true that in late modern or post-modern society individuals lack a strong sense of identity and are therefore free (or forced, depending on your point of view) to construct one through shopping. In most developed societies, even if class is less salient than before, people still derive significant personal identities from where they live, and their cultural, ethnic and familial ties. In Chapters 5 and 16 we have seen how modern Irish society has been characterised by connections to broader social entities, whether communities or social movements: these may offer identities based in location, ethnicity, religious ideology or gender. Among certain social groups across the world identity may have come to depend very heavily on the exercise of consumer choice, but it would be a mistake to assume that this provides the only model towards which the rest of the world is inexorably moving. Unfortunately we have as yet scant sociological evidence in relation to the experiences and meanings of shopping itself for Irish consumers.

17
New social movements

In different parts of this book we have focused on culture and cultural change in Irish society. In Chapter 5 we argued that group identities can be considered part of culture, and that communities, for example, can be mobilised on the basis of feelings of common identity. In Chapter 12 we developed the notion of cultural politics to indicate that culture can be drawn upon as a resource, invoked and redefined by social groups as they struggle to achieve social status and to realise aspirations and interests.

In this chapter we aim to develop these ideas through a focus on the sociology of *new social movements* (referred to in this chapter as NSMs). NSMs interest sociologists as they seem to reflect new ideas about how to 'do politics' or bring about social change. It is widely claimed that in contemporary Irish society people have become apathetic about politics and lack interest in or respect for those who commit themselves to political activity. But the strength of social movements in contemporary Irish society, from community development to environmentalism, and from feminism to Rural Resettlement, suggests that it is the conventional, institutionalised form of party politics that people are perhaps apathetic about, and that many actively seek other ways to become involved in shaping Irish society. In this chapter we suggest how this development may be linked to cultural and structural changes within late modern societies. We suggest that the study of NSMs can reveal much to us about the nature of modern society in general, and specifically of Irish society.

THE SOCIOLOGY OF NEW SOCIAL MOVEMENTS

Why are sociologists interested in NSMs? One reason is that there appears to have been a strong increase in such new forms of collective political action across the world since the late 1950s. Collective popular action — such as the Solidarity movement in Poland — was a major element in the extraordinary fall of communism in Eastern Europe at the end of the 1980s. Prior to this, the emergence of the greens in Europe (especially Germany) during the early 1980s, the global anti-Apartheid movement of the 1970s and the civil rights, student and peace movements of the 1960s had played a major role in societal changes. More recently the environmentalist, anti-globalisation and anti-war movements have captured the public imagination, in Ireland as elsewhere. These events and experiences suggest that there has been a striking shift in how political action and change occur in late modern society. This might reflect other social and cultural changes, including in the nature of democracy itself. Certainly, in labelling these as 'new' social movements, sociologists suggest they are closely connected with features of contemporary society that mark it out from earlier periods of modernity.

If today's social movements are 'new', how do they relate to 'old' ones? The classic 'old' social movement that most sociologists have in mind is the labour movement that developed in the nineteenth century as a response to the onset of capitalist industrialisation. Many would regard this as the first modern social movement, as Tilly (cited in Scott, 1992) points out:

> People have, to be sure, banded together more or less self-consciously for the pursuit of common ends since the beginning of history. The nineteenth century, however, saw the rise of the social movement in the sense of a set of people who voluntarily and deliberately committed themselves to a shared identity, a unifying belief, a common programme, and a collective struggle to realise that programme.

The workers' movements were clearly class-based. In Tilly's view they emerged as class became the major dimension of social inequality in the early period of industrialisation. A feature of NSMs, then, is that they are *not* class-based. Even if most of their membership is drawn from a particular social class, their demands and goals are not confined to the interests of that class. The social identities through which they interpret society are more likely to be based on gender, age, ethnic/cultural identity or a particular vision of the 'good life'. Furthermore the 'newness' of such social movements compared to more traditional ones is defined, according to Goldblatt (1996, p.137):

> not only in terms of the obvious differences in goals and aspirations, but also of their site of political operation (civil society and culture over the state and politics), organisational structure (open, fluid and participatory), social composition (aligned along non-class cleavages), motivations to participation (morally and ideally as opposed to interest-based politics), unconventional forms of political activity (direct action, symbolic protest, mobilisation of public opinion) and core aspects of their ideological positions.

This is a very tightly packed list and we try below to examine its contents and explore some of their implications. For the moment, we note three important aspects of NSMs. The first has to do with how people are attracted to them and what they expect of their members. An NSM is more likely to have a loose organisational form that allows people to largely define their own degree of participation; and less likely to rely on the creation of formal hierarchies and defined official positions. The second is that NSMs tend to act and express themselves politically in ways that differ strongly from the conventional political behaviour of established parties, interest groups and lobby organisations. This difference stems at least partly from the fact that NSMs are less concerned to change political structures than to alter people's everyday culture and consciousness. The third is that NSMs are less concerned to achieve power or realise material improvements for a particular sectional group (as, say, a trade union may be) and more concerned with universal values and ideals. All these claims, as we see below, have been disputed, both as a general account of what NSMs are like and as applied to specific examples of such movements. But they retain the potential to illuminate features of contemporary society and particularly its political and cultural practices.

Sociologists debate and research NSMs as a striking aspect of contemporary social life, but their interest is also driven by an intellectual and theoretical curiosity. So, while they have sought to describe and explain a new aspect of modernity, sociologists have also developed a range of theoretical explanations to try to account for this phenomenon. The theoretical discourse around NSMs has had two major expressions: rather crudely these have been labelled the European and the American approaches. We open our discussion of NSMs with a brief outline of these.

EUROPEAN PERSPECTIVES ON NSMs

Habermas, critical theory and new social movements

European sociological interest in NSMs stems from a desire to identify agents of *social transformation* — particularly those actors who can bring about radical and emancipatory change in what is often seen to be an unequal, unjust and socially or culturally destructive modern society. Many theorists have been interested in NSMs in the hope that they might replace earlier class-based movements as agents of social change and might succeed, where those had failed, in overthrowing or transforming capitalist society.

Of particular influence has been the German sociologist and philosopher Jurgen Habermas. Habermas is one of the 'critical theorists' within German sociology that has sought to carry forward Marx's theoretical analyses of capitalist society by taking into account major changes in advanced capitalism unforeseen by the nineteenth-century theorist. For example, Marx expected that, as capitalism advanced, economic crises such as stock market crashes, depression and large-scale unemployment would intensify and inevitably precipitate revolutionary political change. Generally speaking, this did not occur, and critical theorists have stressed the extraordinary capacity of modern capitalism to contain and deal with such crises, without having to change itself in any radical way. Where Marx believed that capitalist exploitation would so impoverish the working class that it would ultimately force through revolutionary change, critical theorists have emphasised how capitalism has been able to 'buy off' the threat of working class political mobilisation, by a process of gradual but continual improvement in material standards of living and an integration of workers into an expanding consumerism.

As a critical theorist, Habermas has developed an analysis of late modern society that includes a deep interest in NSMs: could the youth, peace and ecology movements, for example, all prominent in Germany over the last three decades, be the collective forces to inherit the task of emancipating society? Habermas's (1987) analysis of contemporary society persuades him that NSMs are an outcome of and are now integral to the social structure of late capitalism. They may therefore be expected to play a significant role in helping it to change.

Habermas's analysis of late modernity owes much to Weber, perhaps even more than to Marx. He emphasises the idea that in modernity, the 'life-world' is increasingly subjected to 'colonisation' by the 'social system'. *Life-world* here means the sphere of everyday, immediate social experiences of individuals, their face-to-face relations with others particularly in the intimate domains of family, kinship and friendship. It is a world where we relate to others as people with minds and selves. When we communicate with others, we are constantly oriented towards the establishment of mutual understanding and, if possible, agreement. The *social system* is the external, impersonal world of institutions and formal role-relationships, particularly economic and political ones, that is organised through hierarchies of power and authority. Institutions operate on the basis of instrumental reason: they seek the most efficient means to achieve their goals, and this usually involves forms of domination and coercion — people are treated merely as objects and means to ends.

Following Weber, Habermas sees modern society as being characterised by a continuous expansion of instrumental *rationality* and is afraid that this is reaching the point where it threatens to take over relationships within the life-world — interpersonal relationships are becoming increasingly calculative and impersonal. The emergence of NSMs, then, can be seen as a response by the life-world to the threat of colonisation by instrumental reason. NSMs are movements 'to defend the life-world'. This explains why they possess some distinctive features when compared to earlier, more conventional class-based movements. In particular, it explains why they are typically less concerned with the instrumental pursuit of material goals and interests and more interested in finding new ways of living, of relating to others, of exploring identities and developing the self.

Touraine, social movements and post-industrial society

The French sociologist Alain Touraine has also investigated the relationship between social movements and their social context. He has been described (Scott, 1992) as a 'structuralist' as he suggests that social movements are determined by social conditions such as the class structure. He identifies two types of society where social movements are important:

- industrial society, where the main productive activity and source of social power is in manufacturing
- post-industrial society, where it is the production of knowledge, and the power derived from it, that is most important.

Since, Touraine argues, these types of society are structurally quite different, the social movements found in each will also vary.

Industrial societies give rise to industrial or workers' movements (Touraine, 1982) that develop around struggles in the sphere of work. These usually focus their demands on the state, for example, in demanding access to economic decision-making. As they succeed in their claims, they increasingly become part of the system of government and therefore less identifiable as social movements (see our discussion of corporatism in Chapter 4). In post-industrial society new movements emerge that are no longer concerned with the workplace or with accessing state power. They develop in civil society (the realm of social life that is neither primarily economic nor primarily political) and are mainly concerned with defending it against the state. In post-industrial society, according to Touraine, those who wield power are not the owners of material production resources but the controllers of knowledge — science, technology and the media. NSMs in post-industrial society aim to defend those subordinated to technological or knowledge control, that is, all ordinary citizens whose lives are governed by the decisions of a knowledge elite. They seek not to become part of that elite but to defend culture and civil society against it, so they are less concerned to organise themselves into effective lobbies or interest groups along conventional political lines and more interested in developing alternative lifestyles and ways to relate to knowledge and technology. Though following a different route, Touraine reaches much the same conclusion as Habermas: NSMs are qualitatively different from earlier social movements in both their ideology and forms of activity. At the same time, they play a similarly important role as mobilisers of collective action against the forces of societal domination and coercion.

While this account of NSMs is necessarily abstract, derived from a view about the nature of post-industrial society, Touraine (1983) has made a detailed study of the anti-nuclear movement in France and through this seeks to demonstrate the applicability of his model. Both the anti-nuclear and the ecology movements can be seen as expressions of resistance against the concentration of certain types of knowledge in state hands, and against the use of knowledge for purposes that threaten 'all citizens' and not just a certain section or class in society. Neither is 'political' in the sense of seeking access to state decision-making or of taking over state power. Touraine suggests that when these movements do become politicised, as in the formation of green parties, this is a deviation from their real nature and an indication of their failure — a point of view that has, understandably, been controversial.

Melucci: new social movements in the field of culture

The Italian writer Alberto Melucci is recognised as the key contemporary European theorist of new social movements. His original exposure to Catholic youth movements in post-war Italy, with its all-embracing focus on aspects of everyday life, led to an interest in the specifically 'cultural' aspects of the new types of social protest movement he saw emerging in Italy and elsewhere across the Western world during and after the student rebellions of 1968. For Melucci (1995) the key characteristics of new social movements are:

- The *centrality of information resources*: in an information society, access to and control over information, rather than over material goods, is the major source of power. New social movements thus aim to shape how meanings are created and circulated in society: they challenge mainly on 'symbolic' grounds.
- They are involved in *self-reflexive forms of action*: actions are not just a means to an end, but an end in themselves. Thus the form and appearance of a protest action may be as important as its 'practical' outcome.
- They have a *planetary dimension*: new social movements operate within global information flows, even when the actions themselves may be intensely local (for example anti-capitalist actions in Dublin are instantly relayed to a global Internet audience via services such as Indymedia).
- They express a particular relation between what Melucci calls *latency* and *visibility*: he suggests that alternative approaches to living are practiced by 'submerged networks'; it is only when these networks experience problems or issues that they mobilise publicly.
- The 'success' of NSMs must not just be measured at the 'political' level, but also at the 'cultural' level; for example, effects may be measured in terms of institutional change, the emergence of new elites and cultural innovation, but there are also less visible outcomes in terms of the creation of *new meanings* and the opening up of new challenges to the dominance of the 'allegedly neutral rationality' of those in power.

It is possible to see how Melucci's analysis is particularly applicable to movements such as the global anti-capitalist movement, with its strong focus on aspects of lifestyle (food, clothing, music, language) and highly visual events like colourful street protests and 'street parties'. But such social movements are also open to the critique that they are ultimately incoherent, fragmented and relatively powerless compared to the large, established, well-organised bodies of the state: an argument that Flynn (2006) makes in relation to Ireland's environmental movement (see Chapter 18). The value of 'lifestyle politics' versus the use of more traditional political strategies, such as lobbying, strikes or electioneering, is one that arises in relation to all contemporary social movements.

An important aspect of Melucci's work is that he is also interested in how NSMs may successfully operate for, as he points out, each is:

> the result of multiple processes, of different orientations, of a constructive dynamic which the actors bring about (or fail to bring about): in any case it is thanks to this dynamic that an action develops or fails to develop, evolves or is arrested, reaches its objectives or falls apart (1995, p.113).

Here he is drawing on American theories and approaches that seek to look more pragmatically at how social movements operate and what might make them effective. We now look at some aspects of this approach.

AMERICAN PERSPECTIVES ON NSMs

From the European perspective, NSMs are characteristically treated as harbingers of the future, not an attempt to escape into a romanticised past. They are seen as a response to critical issues in modernity, around contemporary forms of social organisation and ways of life, that moves us towards new types of society and social relationships. This interpretation is in striking contrast to that of functionalists, such as Smelser (1998 [1962]), who see oppositional social movements as indicative of a problem or failing in the social system — evidence of social strain. This view assumes that those who take part in such movements are rejecting the present in favour of the past: they are traditionalists who want to reconstruct pre-modern social conditions and relationships. There is a presumption that if whatever is malfunctioning in the system can be repaired, the strains that cause social movements to develop will be removed and the movements themselves will fade away.

American work on social movements has moved from functionalism towards an approach known as *resource mobilisation theory* (RMT)(McCarthy and Zald, 1977). RMT treats social movements as organisations and asks how they obtain the resources they need to function effectively. The main resource needed by a social movement is mobilisation itself: the emergence of large numbers of people who agree with the movement's ideas and aspirations and who are prepared to support it and take part in its campaigns. From this perspective, the main question that social movement researchers should pose about any particular movement is: how does it succeed in securing those resources? The answer will differ according to the movement and society being studied. Each has to be examined in its own right, without presuppositions about the sort of movement it might be.

If the European approach to NSMs has been characterised by 'grand theorising', the American approach has leaned in the opposite direction, emphasising the collection of data within a relatively restricted conceptual framework. But this does not mean it is without theoretical assumptions. One assumption is that social movements can be addressed as examples of *social organisation*: answers to questions about social movements are to be found in an analysis of one or more movement organisations, and how they generate attention, enthusiasm and support among target audiences, rather than, as is the case from the European perspective, an analysis of the broader society.

Thus, an RMT approach to the study of the environmental movement in Ireland would entail a study of the various organisations involved, such as Greenpeace and the Green Party on one side and An Taisce, Birdwatch Ireland and the Heritage Council on the other. The RMT approach has its advantages. If we can assume that the membership of the movement coincides with the membership of these organisations and that movement activities coincide with the organisations' activities, then we have a relatively clear picture of the boundaries and characteristics of our object of study. But to limit the concept of social movement so severely can mean we end up identifying it only with its formal, hierarchical, organisational structures. This leaves out all the fluid, unorganised, localised occasions in everyday life where the values and goals of the movement are put into practice. If Irish people, though not members of such organisations, start to recycle household waste, would we not want to include them in a study of Irish environmentalism?

A second major assumption of the RMT approach is that people are essentially rational and so participate in social movements for instrumental reasons; indeed, in certain ways it views a social movement as a business operation. It sees social movements as being most likely to mobilise people: when they aim at goals that are in the interest of many; when they clearly articulate these goals; and when they can convince people that a social movement is the best way to realise them. If the movement or organisation fails on any of these criteria, people will not recognise that their interests are at stake, or will favour other organisational forms, such as lobby groups or political parties, at the expense of the social movement. RMT does not distinguish between social movements and other forms of collective organisation. They are points on the same spectrum. People can move from one to another on the basis of a rational decision about which is more likely to be effective. There is a clear contrast here with the European approach to social movements, which sees them as a specific and unique type of collective action that requires theoretical interpretation.

It is unlikely that the RMT assumption about the instrumental rationality of movement participants stands up. Mobilisation as members or participants in social movements may stem from instrumental grounds, but this alone is unlikely to fully explain people's actions. I may discover a movement that looks likely to achieve something in my interest (say, a movement to increase the salaries and social standing of sociologists in Ireland), but if I can see that it will succeed without my participation, then I need not take part — the so-called 'free rider' problem. Others can make the running for me. If everyone thought like that, nobody would ever become involved. So it seems that a movement that can successfully mobilise support has to appeal to more than a person's rational understanding of their own best interest. If this was true of early social movements like the labour movement, which attempted to realise the interests of a specific section of society, then it seems even more likely to be true of NSMs that claim to speak for 'all the people'. For example, it may be in the interest of humanity as a whole to consume and waste less and conserve resources for the future; but for each individual in the present generation, to reduce present consumption levels may be to go against immediate self-interest. Thus, if people are to be mobilised by the ecological message, it must touch on something other than their instrumental reason.

Any account of how NSMs successfully mobilise resources must reflect how they appeal to a range of concerns: about identity; about new ideas and their practical expression; and about the rejection of conventional values and lifestyles. Indeed it can be argued that to treat NSMs as if they were a means to something else is to mistake their nature. Melucci (1989) suggests that people participate in NSMs and their activities as an end in itself: as a symbolic expression of dissent from the dominant culture. This may be why, for example, green activists do not necessarily choose the most 'efficient' way to organise to achieve a goal, if efficiency means adopting hierarchical or undemocratic structures of leadership or decision-making.

Synthesis

Recent discussions of NSMs have tended to integrate elements from both the European and American perspectives. Supporters of RMT have recognised not only the capacity of social movements to realise political objectives and instrumental goals but also the significance of the movements themselves as sources of cultural change and new symbolic meanings in society. Indeed, one of the most important achievements of NSMs, as Scott (1992, p.157) points out, is to redefine 'politics'. For example, they highlight new issues that the state should concern itself with, such as waste recycling, and others that it should withdraw from, such as censorship. Writers from the European tradition now recognise that the social structural or ideological characteristics of societies are not sufficient to explain the emergence and development of specific NSMs. They recognise that it is also important to examine the organisational factors emphasised by RMT, such as resources and concrete social and political contexts.

EXPLAINING SOCIAL MOVEMENTS

Why have NSMs and new forms of protest and opposition become such a significant feature of contemporary societies? There are three dominant explanations:

* post-materialism
* the idea of a 'new' middle class
* the argument that an important political shift in developed societies has provided space for new forms of political mobilisation and action.

The post-materialist thesis

The post-materialist thesis is associated with Inglehart (1977) who claimed that his large-scale attitude research (mainly among Americans) revealed that social values were, for some social groups, shifting from 'materialist' to 'post-materialist'. The main social group concerned was the young, well-educated generation that had grown into affluence and stability after the Second World War — the so-called 'baby boomers'. This group was less preoccupied with career advancement and the acquisition of wealth and more interested in the overriding goal of 'self-fulfilment'. Inglehart suggests that the growth of social protest movements since the late 1960s can be explained by generational change and the experience of affluence. At least among the highly educated, increased affluence has apparently led to an interest in 'non-material' forms of fulfilment that relate to social relationships, autonomy and self-realisation. This point reflects Touraine's concept of post-industrialism: the phase of modernity associated with the growth of higher education, expansion of the service sector and increased affluence.

The new middle class thesis

The post-industrialist thesis also underpins the second explanation for growth in NSMs — the new middle class thesis. It is suggested that changes in the class structure of developed societies in recent decades have inverted the relationship between class position and social unrest — these days it is not the industrial working class that joins in protest movements but the well-educated and professionally oriented middle class. Why should this be so? Post-industrialist theorists claim that late modern society is experiencing the emergence of a new middle class. Whereas the 'old' middle class based its position on the ownership of material wealth, the new middle class is made up primarily of 'knowledge workers', whose power derives from control of specialist or expert knowledge. In their working lives these workers may find themselves in conflict with members of the old middle class who are their employers. Knowledge workers aspire to significant autonomy in their work but the conventional employer still tries to control the workforce tightly. The employer wants to make a profit, whereas the new-middle-class employee is interested in the use of knowledge for its own sake. Many members of the 'knowledge class' work as professionals in public-sector employment. They also experience conflict between their desire for self-direction and the bureaucratic controls that the state seeks to enforce.

Some advocates of this thesis (see Maheu, 1995) suggest that the new middle class is the agent for a new round of class struggle, where it will challenge the 'old' class of entrepreneurs and managers. It is suggested that in this struggle the working class will play a conservative part, supporting the old class. This approach then sees NSMs as primarily *class-based*, like the old social movements. Others are less convinced of this and suggest that the new middle class tends to provide strong support for single-issue movements (such as the anti-nuclear or Third World solidarity movements), but is not generally oppositional.

The political thesis

The third explanation for the growth of NSMs focuses less on changes in social structures or values and more on the political arena. In many developed societies political parties have sought to shed their identification with particular classes or interest groups to become 'catch-all' parties (the British Labour Party under Tony Blair being a prime example). As a result, the social controls that political parties have traditionally exercised over their supporters are reduced, leaving citizens free to take up new political goals and new ways to engage in politics. At the same time, new forms of corporatist relations (see Chapter 4) have developed between powerful interest groups and the state, so consolidating power in the hands of elites. The policy-making process becomes less accountable to the general public, increasing levels of alienation and resistance among those excluded from it, particularly the well-educated, professionalised, middle ranks of workers. They are then more likely to reject existing forms of political involvement and to seek or invent new ones outside the conventional party-political system.

Giddens, emancipatory politics and life politics

British sociologist Anthony Giddens suggests an approach to NSMs that integrates most of the ideas we have discussed. He argues that late modern society is characterised by the development of a new type of *life politics* — a politics of the self — in contrast to the older *emancipatory politics* — a politics of resistance to exploitation, inequality and oppression (1991, p.211). The latter includes political movements that aim to free people from the residues of the past (in the shape of tradition) or from current inequalities of power and domination. It tends to mobilise those who already enjoy a degree of emancipation to work to remove such conditions from society in general. An emancipatory politics is thus, according to Giddens, a politics of 'others'. The mobilising principle common to all forms of emancipatory politics is a belief in individual autonomy as the greatest good. To free people from subjection to constraint and domination is to enable them to exercise autonomous control over their own lives and destinies. It is a characteristic assumption of modernity that this is a good thing. But emancipatory political movements say little about how people should use their autonomy; this is where life politics has something to offer.

If emancipatory politics is a politics of others, life politics is a politics of the self. Giddens describes it variously as a politics of choice, a politics of lifestyle, and a politics of self-actualisation. The emergence of such a politics, he argues, is a sign that societies are reaching the stage of 'high' or 'late' modernity, where most, if not all, members of the society enjoy freedom from material constraints, such as poverty and hunger, and from domination by other social classes or groups. The aim of life politics is to develop an ethics around the issue of 'how should we live?' (1991, p.215). One of its most interesting effects is to make the processes of 'doing politics' as important an issue as the outcomes. How we organise ourselves to protest is as important as whether or not we achieve specific goals. Giddens borrows from feminism the phrase 'the personal is political' to express this idea: our everyday life is intimately connected with how society is organised, and our everyday processes of identity construction and interpersonal relationships form the basis for wider social organisation. There are clearly links here with the work of Melucci, discussed earlier.

In a sense, we have now come back to where we started, with Habermas and the idea that NSMs are 'movements to defend the life-world'. For Giddens it is not so much that the life-world needs defending in late modernity, but that it needs to be expanded, developed and authenticated. We could say that NSMs are movements to add meaning to lives that have achieved a certain level of material comfort and legal freedom but lack a sense of authenticity and personal worth.

NEW SOCIAL MOVEMENTS AND IRISH SOCIETY

In the remainder of this chapter we draw on the ideas outlined above to examine the experience of NSMs in Irish society. We discuss three examples here and in Chapter 18 we focus on a fourth, the environmental movement. In two of these cases (the women's and environmental movements) studies exist that draw explicitly on social movement theories to understand the Irish experience. In the other two (Catholic fundamentalism, Irish Travellers), the claim that we are dealing with an NSM at all may be contested; they have not yet been examined within this framework by Irish sociologists.

Discussing these cases helps us to learn more about Irish society. To what extent do explanations for the emergence of NSMs, such as the thesis of the 'new middle class', apply to a late developing, peripheral or dependent society like Ireland? Are new movements here a response to or shaped by indigenous Irish conditions, or are they more an example of cultural imperialism or external 'modernising' input into Irish culture? At the same time, to discuss particular examples of Irish movements allows us to explore further the concept of NSM and the theories and assumptions that lie behind it.

The women's movement

Nearly all writers on NSMs point to a limited number of concrete examples: usually youth, student and peace movements, the ecology or environmental movement and the women's movement. The women's movement is generally regarded as an example of a 'classic' NSM. It has also been of great importance to developments in Irish society over the past four decades at least and no sociology of Ireland can ignore it. Some recent studies of the Irish women's movement (Mahon, 1995; Connolly, 1996; 2002; see also Galligan, 1998a) explicitly make use of the concepts and ideas of social movement theorists. Here we briefly examine the contrasting accounts presented by Mahon and Connolly.

Each writer agrees that the women's movement is a conscious, deliberate attempt to collectivise in order to bring about social change — with a focus on the political system as the target and with a key resource in the commitment and active participation of its members. Thus, each invokes a resource mobilisation perspective on the Irish women's movement. Connolly's analysis generally remains within this perspective. She treats the women's movement primarily as a set of social movement *organisations* and asks how they mobilised resources and ultimately achieved a degree of institutionalisation within the Irish political system (Galligan, 1998a, takes a similar approach). Mahon's discussion moves fairly quickly to circumstances outside of the women's movement and its constituent organisations; she emphasises the movement's wider social, economic and political context.

Each writer raises questions about characterising the women's movement in Ireland as a new social movement. Connolly argues strongly that it is not historically 'new'; we can trace the women's movement lineage back to the 1850s. She makes no theoretical distinction between 'old' and 'new' social movements nor does she adopt Giddens's distinction between emancipatory and lifestyle movements. As a result, Connolly may overstress the instrumental rationality and politicisation of the Irish and the international women's movements and underemphasise their symbolic or non-conventional methods of protest; she treats these as a result of exclusion from conventional institutional sources of power (1996, p.45). Other writers (for example, Oakley and Mitchell, 1998) have suggested that the international women's movement has embraced elements of both political activism and concerns about personal identity — that is, both emancipatory politics and life politics.

Another issue relates to the origins of the Irish women's movement: is it an indigenous phenomenon or, as opponents have sometimes labelled it, a cultural import? For Connolly, the Irish women's movement is 'organically' part of a global women's movement, but must also be recognised as Irish. We can only explain its resurgence in the 1970s by recognising that throughout the preceding fifty years or so — a period not at all conducive to feminist political success — a committed cadre of Irish feminists kept the movement alive, organised through bodies such as the Irish Countrywomen's Association (ICA) and the Irish Housewives' Association (IHA) (Connolly, 2002, p.25). Such organisations helped to form and maintain 'inter-movement networks' that provided a basis for organisation and mobilisation when the atmosphere once again became supportive. For Connolly, to say that the movement is distinctively Irish is to say that it is not *new*. This is a central finding of her research, and she argues that earlier research had overemphasised the significance for the contemporary Irish women's movement of external factors, such as the international Civil Rights and anti-Vietnam movements of the 1960s (1996, p.47).

Mahon also recognises earlier feminist movements but highlights the novel characteristics of the present one by referring to it as second wave feminism — 'an international phenomenon' that emerged in the United States and Northern Europe in the late 1960s and early 1970s (1995, p.677). What was internationalised, in her account, was not just the ideology of women's liberation but also the social structural conditions that enabled mobilisation to succeed among women exposed to it. She emphasises, in particular, the entry of large numbers of relatively well-educated women into the labour market.'Such women usually entered jobs that were poorly paid or less satisfying than those that men, without necessarily better qualifications, held. From these conditions emerged feelings of relative deprivation that provided fertile ground for recruitment by the developing women's liberation movement.

Thus, the conditions faced by women in Ireland who were not part of the older established women's networks, but who were to become mobilised in the movement in the 1960s and 1970s, becomes an important part of the explanation. The Irish economy at that time was not the same as that of the post-war United States. As a late industrialising economy, Ireland offered few opportunities for industrial work for women. There was no critical labour shortage in the 1970s and 1980s to draw women into labour force participation. Indeed, state policies such as the public-sector marriage bar discouraged women from aspiring to work outside the home. For Mahon what created fertile ground for an Irish mobilisation around feminist issues was: in the 1970s, the 'modernising influence' of EEC accession; in the 1980s, progressive changes in Irish women's education and labour force participation; and in the 1980s and 1990s, 'resistance to the EC's modernising influences' on the issues of divorce and abortion.

Mahon suggests, in summary, that once the structural conditions existed for the emergence of a women's movement, it developed more or less automatically. This is a common assumption in relation to NSMs that Connolly questions. Following RMT, she introduces the organisational resource issue as a major variable that intervenes between structural conditions and mobilisation. But Connolly has little to say about the structural changes in Irish society that Mahon sees as so relevant. While tracing the important links between earlier women's groups and the second wave feminist movement, Galligan (1998a, p.57) also stresses the close parallels between the development of the Irish women's movement and those in other Western countries such as Britain, Spain, Greece and the United States, for example, in the issues addressed by feminist groups and the issues that led to conflicts and splits within them.

The Irish feminist movement thus provides a good example of how varying social movement theories can produce different interpretations of reality. It also helps to bring into an Irish context some other issues that concern NSM theorists. For example, it questions how we define success for a social movement like the Irish women's movement. Does it reside in incorporation and institutionalisation within the boundaries of 'conventional' interest-group politics? Or does it reside in the achievement of changes in lifestyles and the establishment of 'submerged networks' that make up the wider social movement? Connolly (2002, p.12) suggests that both outcomes can be observed:

> beyond the local praxis of feminist groups, feminist politics and ideas promulgate the diffusion of wider cultural change in gender relations, across society in general . . . feminism has therefore had a pervasive, not unitary, mobilising effect across Irish society.

We can also pose the question: how significant has the women's movement been in Ireland as a 'modernising' influence? The next case we examine may shed further light on this question.

Catholic fundamentalism

In April 1981 an organisation came into existence that was to have a major and divisive impact on Irish society for at least the next ten years. This was the Pro-Life Amendment Campaign (PLAC), set up with the aim of having an amendment inserted into the Irish Constitution that would formally guarantee the absolute right to life of the human embryo from the point of conception. The background to this demand was the rapidly increasing availability of abortion in many European countries and, in particular, its recent legalisation in 'traditionally Catholic countries such as Italy and Spain' (Inglis, 1998a, p.83). PLAC succeeded in having the amendment carried in the Referendum of 1983 after a bitter and divisive referendum campaign. In 1986 the strength of newly reorganised Catholic fundamentalism revealed itself again with the defeat of a referendum to amend the Constitution to allow for divorce legislation. Further legal cases, campaigns and referenda saw further battles over 'moral' issues including abortion, divorce and homosexuality continuing into the mid-1990s.

Further details on the activities of Catholic fundamentalists over the period can be found in Inglis (1998a), O'Reilly (1992) and Hug (1999). We are less interested here in describing the events that took place than in developing an explanation for them — specifically one that is framed by the debates over NSMs. Both Connolly (1996) and Mahon (1995) regard the emergence or resurgence of Catholic fundamentalism as one of the major events that has shaped the Irish women's movement over the past decade. Connolly argues that it was a significant force that pushed Irish feminists towards more mainstream activities and organisations during the 1980s, encouraging them in particular to use the courts as an arena to struggle for women's rights. Catholic fundamentalism thus helped, argues Connolly, to make the Irish women's movement into a less radical, more diffuse and more institutionalised social movement (1996, p.68).

Mahon (1995) emphasises the divisive impact that the formation of the Society for the Protection of the Unborn Child (SPUC) and later PLAC had on the women's movement and how subsequent campaigns helped to mobilise women into taking a more active part in the debates, on both sides. To that extent, Mahon suggests that the clash between the women's movement and a revived Catholic fundamentalism empowered women generally, even while it helped to destroy the idea of a single 'women's movement' that could articulate values that all women, by virtue of their gender, could agree on.

How can we understand the social impact of Catholic fundamentalism in Irish society during the 1980s and early 1990s? We suggest here that one useful way to understand it is to treat it as an example of an NSM. This is not the orthodox viewpoint, which treats Catholic fundamentalism as an inherent part of Irish society that occasionally becomes more vocal and politicised. Thus, while the women's movement has generally been interpreted as a (new) social movement, Catholic fundamentalism is painted in as the ubiquitous background against which Irish women have had to struggle for equality. It is therefore not something that needs to be explained.

Nevertheless there have been sociologists who have attempted to explain the genesis and trajectory of Catholic fundamentalism. Connolly (2002, pp.163–165) treats briefly the emergence of the PLAC, which she refers to as a movement of the 'counter right'. She finds its origins in similar American movements that developed in the United States in the 1970s. She suggests that the PLAC 'rallied an alliance of conservative forces, which were generally opposed to changes in the status of women that occurred in a number of areas, in the previous decade' (i.e. the 1970s). This then developed into a 'highly-resourced counter-right movement' (2002, p.171). Connolly suggests that anti-feminist women were active in the movement and they have since gone on to be 'diversified into women's organisations associated with the counter-right'. We see here strategies of mobilisation amongst Catholic fundamentalists that mirror to some extent those within the women's movement itself. Indeed Connolly (2002, p.179) suggests that:

> the consolidation of a counter right movement (which encompassed SPUC [Society for the Protection of the Unborn Child], Family Solidarity, Youth Defence, Human Life Ireland, Mná na hÉireann and, more recently, the Christian Solidarity party and the National Party) is in fact a good indication of a cycle of success for the women's movement in Ireland.

The activity and considerable success of the counter-right Catholic movement prompts the question: is there something about how NSMs have been sociologically defined that prevents us from recognising religious fundamentalist movements as movements? Can a model of an NSM that has been developed to study movements like the women's, peace or environmental movements, make any sense at all of right-wing or conservative movements? We return to this question later to help us explore and develop the definition of an NSM. But we can also ask: why define Catholic fundamentalism as a social movement at all? What difference would it make to our understanding of Irish society — and of the role of religion and religious institutions in Ireland during the 1980s and early 1990s — to conceptualise the rise of religious fundamentalism in this way?

Journalist Emily O'Reilly (1992) has written a detailed account of the many and varied organisational forms, tactics and strategies used by the Catholic right in Ireland during this period. She interprets the phenomenon very largely as the achievement of a single individual, John O'Reilly (presumably no relation), 'a little-known state employee' who 'hijacked this country's social legislation for almost two decades' (1992, p.7) through his 'machinations on behalf of the conservative Catholic lobby' (1992, p.16). According to her, John O'Reilly was involved or instrumental in setting up a succession of Catholic fundamentalist organisations from the Irish Family League to PLAC, from SPUC to Family Solidarity, and including the Anti-Divorce Campaign of the mid-1980s and the second pro-life campaign of the early 1990s. In particular, she claims, John O'Reilly is a member of and has made maximum use of the organisational resources of the Knights of St. Columbanus, 'a patriarchal, secretive, Catholic, fundamentalist network of individual men who seek to exert power and influence through infiltration of hostile groups and organisations, anonymous lobbying, and the targeting of individuals hostile to their orthodoxy' (1992, p.20). O'Reilly quotes from a paper written by John O'Reilly in 1988 in which he argued that the Knights were particularly well placed to exercise secret influence over the direction of Irish society's development since 'an organisation or a group is never more powerful than when it influences events without itself being regarded as the initiator' (1992, p.29). Emily O'Reilly traces the concealed hand of the Knights within most of the Catholic fundamentalist organisations set up during the period, in particular PLAC. But behind the Knights we always find this single individual — John O'Reilly.

By contrast to this account of the remarkable influence of a committed individual, UCD sociologist Tom Inglis treats the public morality campaigns of the 1970s to 1990s (contraception, divorce, abortion, homosexuality, sex education) as a consequence of the activities of the Catholic hierarchy or of the Catholic Church as a whole. Though he concedes that it was only towards the end of the 1983 pro-life campaign 'that the clerical resources of the Church began to be used fully' (1998a, p.84), he nevertheless claims that an analysis of the campaign shows that 'the hierarchy used the full organisation of the Church to urge the laity to remain loyal to its teachings and to incorporate these into the political framework of the country' (1998a, p.87). In relation to the 1986 divorce referendum, despite describing 'the anti-divorce lobby' as 'not formally linked to the Church' he concludes that 'the referendum demonstrated the continuing ability of the hierarchy to set limits to the political sphere in Irish society' (1998a, p.90). Inglis's account is part of the dominant public discourse in relation to these events: that the Catholic Church continued to claim the right to exert power and influence over Irish society. The only difference was that, due to changes in circumstances and social values, it did so through relatively autonomous organisations of lay Catholics rather than directly through the church hierarchy.

Both these explanations — one individualistic, the other institutionalist — are conspiratorial accounts of social change, where appearances are deceptive and hidden interests work covertly behind organisational fronts. When dealing with a religious institution like the Catholic Church, this conspiratorialism is hard to accept. It implies that the church membership or *laity* plays no part except as pawns of the hierarchy or the Knights: they must be dupes who cannot see they are being manipulated, or their religious devotion is spurious and a product only of indoctrination, coercion, opportunism or laziness. This is where an NSM approach may be useful. From the point of view of NSM theorists, social change is not the result of a conspiracy and those involved are not the unwitting dupes of conspirators. We are encouraged to take participants in NSMs seriously as competent and committed actors, even if their goals are antipathetic or alien to us.

An NSM approach also raises important challenges to standard interpretations of the power of Catholicism in contemporary Irish society. While we discussed the position of religion in Irish society in some detail in Chapter 14, here we wish to revisit some of the more influential interpretations of religion in Irish society that have been produced by sociologists, and ask how these might relate to our suggestion that Catholic fundamentalism should be treated as a social movement.

The first writer we examine, very briefly, is Tony Fahey, author of a broad range of sociological papers on Catholicism and Irish society. In his (1992a) paper, 'Catholicism in Ireland', Fahey's primary concern is with secularisation: how well has modernisation theory predicted the progress (or otherwise) towards secularism in Irish society? He suggests that although recent data on the falling numbers of Catholic clerical and religious personnel working in Ireland might indicate fairly strong secularisation tendencies, when placed in a broader historical perspective this conclusion could be quite misleading. Fahey suggests that the numbers of recruits to the church in the late nineteenth and early twentieth centuries was abnormally high. This was a remarkable period of Catholic resurgence and reconstruction in the years after the Famine. Since the 1960s there has been an inevitable return to more normal and 'sustainable' levels (1992a, p.308).

By so treating change in the church, Fahey creates the impression that we are witnessing a process of Irish society 'normalising or renormalising itself'. This obscures the fact that church influence in social affairs was the focus of sustained mobilisations and struggles throughout the 1970s and 1980s. For example, Fahey does not refer to the part played by the women's movement in challenging Catholic teaching, particularly in areas to do with family relationships and the control of fertility. To that extent, Connolly's complaint that 'the centrality of the women's movement to the rapid pace of *social change* in Ireland has not been adequately demonstrated by mainstream sociology' (1996, p.44) seems justified. But in ignoring the challenges to the church during this period, Fahey also ignores the possibility that movements to *defend* it against secularising pressures also developed. The only 'activists' he recognises in recent Irish Catholicism are those 'church groups taking a leading role in highlighting problems of poverty and social justice in Irish society . . . providing a dynamism of sorts in the shape of a new, poverty-centred oppositional role for the church' (1992a, p.311). This helps to buttress the assumption, which we question further below, that social movements are inherently oppositional and on the side of the weak, excluded or powerless.

We should also note that for Fahey — and he is by no means alone in this — 'Catholicism in Ireland' refers first and foremost to the institutional church and its members (priests, nuns, monks, brothers) and only in a quite limited way to the laity. He justifies this position by arguing that the resurgence and reconstruction of the nineteenth-century church was primarily focused on the institutional church and left little room for lay activity to develop. The new 'strongly devotional Catholic culture' that did emerge among the laity was, he says, strongly oriented to and dependent on church ritual, and he suggests that lay religious behaviour remains quite ritualised — 'for many adherents, their religion is not a very profound thing' (1992a, p.311). It is not surprising, then, that Fahey does not consider the possibility that a strong force in securing 'continuity' for Catholicism in Ireland in recent years might have been the emergence of a lay Catholic social movement.

This may encourage us to ask why lay Catholics, in contemporary Ireland, would continue to support their church. A possible answer is offered by two other analyses of the position of the contemporary church: Inglis (1998a) and Nic Ghiolla Phádraig (1995). Each answers in terms of *power*: the power of the church over its lay members. We suggest that an NSM perspective might have produced a rather different understanding of power to those offered.

Nic Ghiolla Phádraig, like Fahey, disputes the relevance for Ireland of the secularisation thesis. She suggests that 'the greatest puzzle facing sociologists examining religion in Ireland [is] its continuing strength' (1995, p.594) and offers as a solution an analysis of the church in terms of its power over Irish society. She suggests that Irish Catholics continue to practice their religion and to support their church's political positions because the church has some power to compel them to do so. Nic Ghiolla Phádraig argues that this power derives from two key sources: ideological control and control of significant material, organisational and human resources.

Nic Ghiolla Phádraig pays little attention to the Catholic laity. She notes the presence in Irish Catholicism of 'a very clear radical movement' (1995, p.613) which is critical of the institutional church, and talks about the contribution the church makes to the reproduction of inequality in Irish society. But in both cases her discussion focuses almost entirely on the actions of priests and members of religious orders. Only belatedly does she raise the possibility that the activities of lay Catholics may also be important for sociologists to examine, suggesting that the current decline in religious vocations may be opening a gap that could be filled by greater lay involvement. She notes, significantly, that this may have happened as lay Catholics have 'been . . . taking the lead on political matters such as the campaign against divorce and abortion' (1995, p.616). But she does not develop this point in relation to her overall thesis about the power of the Catholic Church.

In terms of power, how should we interpret this involvement by the laity? Is it evidence for a decline in the power of the religious institution or, on the contrary, evidence for a resurgence and regrowth in that power? This leads us to ask how we should define the Catholic Church itself: does it consist only of the hierarchy, priests and religious, or does it also incorporate the laity. If the laity are indeed part of the church, how does the church exercise power over this part of its own institution?

The issue of power is also central to Inglis's (1987; 1998a) work. Inglis argues that the Catholic Church should be recognised as a 'power bloc' in Irish society, and refers to similar 'power resources' (ideological authority, organisational strength) as those cited by Nic Ghiolla Phádraig. But Inglis pays far more attention to the position of the Catholic laity. He does not believe that Irish lay Catholics are coerced, compelled or manipulated into supporting their church, but insists that as rational, self-interested people they have something to gain from their membership. Since the church is a power bloc, participation allows ordinary Irish people access to some power for themselves, whether in the form of occupational advancement, material wealth, or social prestige and the respect of their fellow-citizens. Inglis (1987, p.64) is quite explicit about his view of human nature, saying that people's involvement in society:

> presupposes a more fundamental, calculated and selfish struggle to get their own way. Even when people appear to be acting on the basis of a non-rational commitment to a norm such as 'love thy neighbour as thyself', their actions can be understood as an attempt to gain a more immediate goal such as the moral respect of others.

This is a rather pessimistic view of human nature that ignores the possibility that people can act in support of values and ideals, not just their interests. Inglis seems to back away from this perspective as he develops his argument further; ultimately his analysis reflects two contradictory understandings of power and its exercise. One is the *zero-sum* theory of power, where power over another involves no more than coercion and control. The other is the *non-zero-sum* theory of power, where power is a relationship between two parties where each has something to gain: the 'powerless' party has co-operation to offer, and may gain some reward — and some power — from compliance. The latter approach to power may apply in particular to legitimate power, based on a level of agreement and used to some degree for the common good rather than for selfish sectional interests. Weber tells us that these are the most stable, successful and durable forms of power, because subordinates do not experience their obedience as bowing to compulsion; rather they feel that in obeying they increase their own capacities to live the way they want.

Inglis's analysis moves ambiguously between these two concepts of power. Sometimes he presents the church as supremely powerful, coercing a powerless laity; at other times he suggests that in complying with, supporting, or even trying to expand the power of the church lay Catholics can expand their own power and their capacity to realise their interests. In discussing the 1983 pro-life campaign he says that it was 'from the beginning a lay Catholic movement which attained the full support of the Church. The issue . . . was whether the Constitution should be changed to reflect the interests of this lay Catholic pressure group and the Church as a whole' (1998a, p.87). But he follows this almost immediately with an analysis of the referendum campaign that presents it as a matter of pressure, from the institutional church, on the state and individual lay Catholics, to accept that its teachings on abortion should enter Irish law.

A similar ambiguity can be seen in Inglis's discussion (1998a, pp.88–91) of the 1986 divorce campaign. We might conclude that he rejects the zero-sum approach to power, recognising that there are ways that membership in a powerful church and obedience to its rules can be empowering for the laity; but in the end he is unwilling to treat the church as in any sense a 'legitimate authority' in Irish society. To put this another way, Inglis is one of the few sociologists writing on Irish religion to recognise the importance of treating the laity as more than simply dupes of the church — and that must be regarded as a major advance. However, ultimately, his approach is not as effective as it could have been as he does not pay enough attention to differences among the laity — neither to those who experience membership in the church as empowering, nor to those who do not.

How does this relate to our attempt to connect religious fundamentalism to NSM theory? If we think of what happened in the 1980s and early 1990s as the emergence of a religious social movement, we can be alert to issues of power, and of lay membership of the church, in rather different ways. In particular, we can think of the laity, at least certain sections of it, as more actively involved with their religion and more committed to specific values and ideological world views than most commentators appear to recognise. We must stop thinking that it is only 'the church' that resists secularisation, for example, by trying to tighten its coercive and manipulative grip over a relatively passive lay membership. The laity may also resist secularisation and may even outflank the institutionalised church in how it does so.

This may lead us to reconsider the power of the Catholic Church in Irish society. It now appears not to be dependent on the passive obedience of the laity but perhaps more on the active work of lay members as they repair and redevelop the vulnerable power resources of the church as an institution. As both Inglis and Nic Ghiolla Phádraig point out, powerful groups or institutions in society stay in power because they possess both material and ideological resources. But ideological control is never static, it must constantly be re-created and reproduced in the face of threats and challenges. The fundamentalist campaigns of the last twenty-five years can be seen as mobilisations by certain sections of the Irish Catholic laity to defend and promote a world view and a set of values. The concept of social movement offers a useful way to understand the practices and strategies involved. Sociologists of religion in Ireland should perhaps refocus their attention away from the single social movement organisation — the institutional church — and broaden it to encompass the wider social movement, including significant groups of lay members. The resource mobilisation approach has been used, for example, by Aldridge (2000, pp.106–122) to explain the rise in power and influence of two modern religious groups: the Mormons and the Jehovah's Witnesses: interestingly, two religions that are lay-based.

Can we legitimately talk of a religious movement in terms of NSM theory? Perhaps not if religious beliefs and affiliations are no more than vestiges of the pre-modern stage of social development. But this only makes sense if we assume that modernisation implies secularisation and the triumph of reason and science over faith and theology. It may be time to re-examine this idea, particularly in the light of Giddens's suggestion that late modernity is accompanied by the emergence of life politics movements that attempt to give meaning and purpose to individual lives. If Giddens is right, should we expect a resurgence of religion in late modernity, rather than its disappearance? And is this more likely to generate 'new religions' (such as Scientology) that spring directly from the struggle to make sense of contemporary experience and the self, rather than to appear as a movement by an established religion to retain its ideological and material power base in society?

NSM theorising may lead us to make distinctions between 'new' and 'old' movements that are too rigid. The Catholic fundamentalist movement in Ireland suggests that 'traditional' ideas can be transformed as they are brought into play in new circumstances; they can indeed become part of a late modern politics of choice and lifestyle (we can perhaps see parallels here with the trajectory of the Irish language).

A more serious barrier to acceptance of Catholic fundamentalism as an NSM lies in the genealogy of the term itself. We have seen how in Europe the NSM concept has been directly linked to a progressive politics and philosophy through its treatment in the works of Habermas and Touraine. It is hard to see Catholic fundamentalism as progressive in this sense. If we term it an NSM, does this open up the category to *any* social movement — the French National Front, for example? For the RMT perspective, this is not an issue, as it does not involve any evaluation of the nature of a social movement. Should social movements be studied simply as organisations, or is it necessary to link them to specific theories about societal change? We will try to develop these issues further with our final case study.

The Irish Travellers' movement

Roman Catholics remain a majority group in Irish society and this colours any assessment of a social movement that pursues their interests. On the other hand, Travellers are one of the most significant minority groups in Irish society. With Ireland's increasing religious, political, cultural and sexual diversity, greater attention is now being paid to the experiences and human rights of minority groups. The pressure to adapt to diversity is exerted both from within elements of the majority — not least sections of the state — but also from minority groups. One of the most significant sources is the Traveller movement: does this make it a new social movement and, if so, what are the implications of NSM theory for an understanding of the changing position of Travellers in Irish life?

One view suggests that there has been an increased tolerance of diversity within Irish society, and that Travellers have benefited from this. This optimistic view would point to expanded educational provision, the role of the media, EU membership, foreign travel and a general improvement in living standards as positive factors. According to this view, greater tolerance of diversity is another mark of a successfully modernising society. A more pessimistic view of the position of Travellers in Irish society would draw attention to the increasing intolerance of diversity in Ireland, as indicated in the racist response to refugees, asylum seekers, New Age Travellers and any others who display 'visible difference' (Pollack, 1999; McVeigh, 1998; Kuhling, 1998). It would stress the continuing difficulties experienced by Travellers in gaining basic human rights and how legal and bureaucratic structures help to maintain an institutional structure of discrimination.

Generally missing from either the positive or negative accounts is any recognition of how Travellers themselves, as a social movement, have helped to shape their incorporation into modernity. By and large, recent sociological research on issues related to Travellers in Ireland has paid little direct attention to this aspect of their lives, tending to focus on the emergence of new understandings of Travellers as a social group within social science and policy discourses, rather than within the Travelling community itself (McCann et al., 1994; Hayes, 2006).

It is widely recognised that there has been a radical transformation of how the position of Travellers has been interpreted over the past twenty-five years: from a subgroup of the poor, or subculture (see Chapter 12), to a distinct ethnic group. Hayes has described in detail the complex and comprehensive range of discourses whereby Travellers have been constituted as 'others' in Irish society, in terms variously of their 'secrecy, dishonesty, licentiousness, violence and "a society within a society"' (2006, p 230). Hayes shows how these constructions of Traveller identity have persisted over an extended period of time (at least since the nineteenth century) and are also reflected in the discursive construction of nomadic peoples elsewhere in Europe. He also outlines how, in more recent times, Travellers' own actions have consciously sought to recreate common notions of Traveller identity and community and, in particular, to assert a distinct ethnic identity.

According to McCann et al. (1994, p.xi) 'the concept [of ethnicity] has radical implications for the study of Irish Travellers because it approaches Traveller culture as distinct and valuable in its own right with its own historical path of development, rather than as a short-term adaptation to poverty or marginality.' It has also, they claim, encouraged major changes in policy towards Travellers, identifying 'the need for policies which respect cultural differences, rather than ones which seek to erode them in the name of the settled community's image of "social improvement" or its administrative convenience' (1994, p.xii).

The claim that Irish Travellers constitute a distinct ethnic group is controversial within academic research and in Traveller/State relations (for example, the then Minister of Justice Michael McDowell referred to a previous edition of this book in support of his argument that Travellers are not an ethnic group (Joint Committee on Foreign Affairs, Sub-Committee on Human Rights, 11 March 2004). Where Ní Shúinéar (1994) argues strongly for recognising Travellers as a distinct ethnic group, McLoughlin (1994) responds just as strongly that this is not a useful or productive way to understand their experience. We pause briefly here to discuss how *ethnicity* has been conceptualised in these debates and suggest that an NSM approach could add important dimensions to our understanding of social change in this area.

For Ní Shúinéar ethnicity is a matter of possession of objective social and cultural characteristics that can be used as criteria to decide, in relation to any social group, whether it is an 'ethnic group' or not. The main characteristics are:

- biological self-perpetuation
- racial difference
- shared fundamental cultural values and cultural difference
- social separation from other groups
- the presence of language barriers
- hostility or antipathy between the group and members of other groups.

In her view, Irish Travellers can be shown to exhibit all of these and thus 'meet all the objective scientific criteria of an ethnic group' (1994, p.54).

There is an alternative way to understand ethnicity that has received attention from sociologists and anthropologists. It focuses on the *subjective* dimensions of ethnic group membership rather than on an objective possession of racial or cultural characteristics. Here, ethnicity resides:

- in the belief by members of a social group that they are culturally distinctive and different to outsiders
- in their willingness to find symbolic markers of that difference (for example, food habits, religion, forms of dress, language) and to emphasise their significance
- in their willingness to organise relationships with outsiders so that a kind of 'group boundary' is preserved and reproduced.

McLoughlin (1994) treats ethnicity not as a set of objective characteristics but as a *claim* that groups make about themselves or about others. Claiming to be an ethnic group is, in her view, part of a larger social and political agenda. Instead of asking: does this group really meet the objective criteria that constitute ethnicity? we should ask: does it help this group's situation to be pursuing this agenda — to 'play the ethnic card' — rather than some other one?

We may clarify the debate further if we briefly shift from thinking about ethnicity to a related phenomenon: national identity. The system of national identities that we know today emerged during the nineteenth century with the universal growth of nationalism (see Chapter 12). Nationalism is best understood as a social movement attached to a clear social and political agenda. We can also distinguish between nationalism and nationality: the latter refers to cultural or social differences that exist between groups (such as language), while the former refers to social movements that claim equality of status and self-determination for groups that feel themselves to be distinct.

By analogy it might be useful to use the term 'ethnicism' to talk about how groups make claims based on cultural difference and 'ethnicity' to refer to observable cultural differences. But we would have to recognise (where neither McLoughlin nor Ní Shúinéar do) that there is no necessary correlation between the two: a group can seek to establish its cultural worth even if it does not appear to possess anything that clearly distinguishes it culturally from others; and conversely groups that may be culturally very distinctive may not embark on an ethnicist movement at all.

This discussion suggests that the debate around Travellers' ethnicity is to a degree misplaced. It may be more useful to study how an ethnicist movement has arisen among Travellers in recent years and how this has profoundly affected both Travellers themselves and policy-makers and members of Irish society more generally. We can investigate whether this change in the Traveller discourse has been of benefit. For example, has the shift from a 'culture of poverty' discourse towards ethnicity helped to empower Travellers themselves?

Hayes's study does go some way to showing how Travellers have actively sought to develop expressions of distinctive cultural identity. One of these is through autobiography, and he outlines a number of books that have allowed individual Travellers (e.g. Nan Joyce and Pecker Dunne) to talk about their lives and Traveller culture. Hayes (2006, p.259) argues that these autobiographical accounts represent an expression of ethnicity that can be linked to broader patterns: they have, he suggests, 'coincided with a re-engagement on the part of Irish people with the questions of identity and cultural difference in an era where increasingly globalised societies are seeing transformations and new complexities in the cultural interactions between different peoples and cultures'. They form a marked contrast with some of the media perceptions of Travellers, which have tended to recycle the dominant negative 'myths' and 'stereotypes' of the past.

Pavee Point, formerly the Dublin Travellers' Education and Development Group, should be regarded as a very significant organisation in terms of the development of ethnicism within the Travellers' movement. It developed in the early 1980s as an organisation that involved equally both settled people (mainly social workers or researchers with a professional interest in Travellers) and Travellers. This signalled a major difference from previous bodies, such as the National Council for Travelling People, which had been set up by and included only settled people and which worked *for* rather than *with* Travellers. John O'Connell (1992, p.7), Director of the DTEDG, described this difference:

When we formally established the DTEDG in 1985 we acknowledged Travellers as an ethnic group. We decided that any work with Travellers should support their right to retain and develop their identity . . . We also wanted to offer our skills in support of Travellers in their struggle for justice and acceptance in Irish society.

Gmelch, an anthropologist who has written extensively on Traveller culture, has focused on the development of a Traveller ethnicity that can be traced back to the 1880s (Gmelch and Gmelch, 1976). She has documented (Gmelch, 1989) in particular the growing politicisation and mobilisation among Travellers during the 1980s. An important step was the establishment in 1984 of the organisation Mincéir Misli — significant because it was a Traveller-run organisation and also because it used for its title Gammon or Shelta words, signalling to the world at large for perhaps the first time that Irish Travellers saw themselves as a distinctive ethnic group that counted possession of a distinct language as a central symbol of this distinctiveness (see Binchy, 1994; Ó Baoill, 1994).

Gmelch's account of Mincéir Misli suggests that it closely resembles many NSM organisations in the multi-faceted nature of its analysis of Travellers' problems and of possible solutions to them. It has acted variously as a political lobby for Travellers' rights, a training ground for movement spokespeople, a contact point for group members and a cultural agency (publisher, film-maker) intervening in the perceptions of Travellers held both by Travellers themselves and by members of the settled society.

Although language has emerged as a significant marker of ethnicity for Travellers, a more significant symbol that summarises and captures for them their essential identity and difference from other groups in Irish society is *nomadism*. There is a certain irony in this, given Gmelch's suggestion that the emergence of ethnicism among Irish Travellers is linked to their transformation from a predominantly rural, mobile group in the 1960s to a substantially urban, 'immobile' group in the late 1980s.

Gmelch argues that the experience of urban migration (by 1981 over a quarter of all Traveller families were based in Dublin) has been a particularly important factor for the emergence of the Traveller movement. It contributed to a situation where settled people's anger and hostility towards Travellers greatly increased, which in turn helped to politicise Travellers themselves. It also helped to create the conditions under which collective mobilisation of Travellers was made easier. Urbanisation gave Travellers 'the logistical ability' to organise themselves (Gmelch, 1989, p.309) and, in the forging of an explicit group identity that followed, nomadism or at least the cultural transmission of 'a nomadic mindset' from one generation of Travellers to the next has become their most important distinctive attribute. Stimulating this development has been the growth of contacts between Irish Travellers and Traveller and Gypsy organisations elsewhere in Europe, also engaged in creating ethnic identity systems to symbolise their own distinctiveness.

We suggested earlier that an NSM perspective on the situation of Irish Travellers might be useful. In particular, it helps us to recognise that Travellers have been actively involved in a movement for recognition as an ethnic group and that this claim is not only a result of changes in thinking or practice among policy-makers, community workers or academic researchers. But considering the Irish Travellers' movement as an ethnicist social movement does lead us to the question: how has social research and theorising among professionals helped to produce this new phenomenon? And has sociology actively contributed to social change?

The 'culture of poverty' approach to interpreting their situation, first developed by McCarthy (1971), profoundly influenced how ordinary Irish people thought about Travellers and helped to shape the policies that were introduced to deal with 'the itinerant problem' during the 1970s. McCarthy has since rejected this approach and admitted that it 'has done them a great disservice in so far as the theory has been used by certain people to discredit Travellers and to negate their separate cultural identity' (1994, p.128). Although the development of a different theoretical approach to Travellers, based on the idea of a distinct ethnicity, has been in part a result of the fact that Travellers have become more vocal and that researchers have begun to listen, it is also clear that outside professionals and intellectuals have contributed in no small way to the elaboration of ethnic identity and ethnicist claims that Travellers have experienced.

O'Connell (1992) documents how researchers and community workers who operate with conceptions of Travellers as a culturally oppressed (not simply economically marginalised) group were involved in running workshops and consciousness-raising courses with Travellers in the early to mid-1980s. McCann *et al.* (1994) also indicate the extent of dialogue between researchers and Travellers around the concept of ethnicity. To a certain extent concepts of cultural oppression and ethnicity were already gaining currency among sociologists and social activists in Ireland as a way of understanding social exclusion and marginalisation in general, before they were specifically used to understand the situation of Travellers. The role of intellectuals both from within and outside social movements in developing movement ideas and practices is an issue that has generated much interesting sociological research in recent times. We mention it here to show that sociology itself, inasmuch as it helps to develop conceptual tools, has a potential role in bringing about social change.

SOCIOLOGY AND THE STUDY OF SOCIAL MOVEMENTS

We started this chapter by asking: why should sociologists be interested in NSMs? To end, we turn that question around and ask: what does the recent growth in sociological interest in NSMs tell us about the development of sociology itself? The development of a burgeoning NSM literature does suggest some profound changes in the discipline of sociology. In particular, it indicates a shift away from *structural* types of analysis towards an interest in *action* and *agency* — a desire to identify those social actors that actively bring about or resist change.

For some sociologists this is a victory for Weberianism over Marxism. Marx suggested that capitalist society produced two opposing classes with an *objective* reality: we can explain why people act in certain ways by drawing attention to their class membership. Weber agreed that we can deduce a certain class structure from an examination of the organisation of capitalist society, but this may reveal little of what happens in terms of struggles for power and social honour and about dominant ideas and values. For Weber, this requires an analysis of *subjective* reality: whether people recognise themselves as a class, or perhaps another sort of collectivity such as an ethnic, religious or occupational one. It is only then that we can identify the significant agents of modern society.

It would be wrong to overemphasise the differences between Weber and Marx on this point. Each sought to address the fact that, to paraphrase Marx, it is people who make history but they do not choose the circumstances in which they do so. Sociologists have always had to deal with the dilemma of structure and agency (see Chapter 7) — what weight to give to the external and unchosen social circumstances that shape our action, and to the voluntary meaning-creating and choice-making activities of individual or collective actors. The current focus on NSMs suggests that sociological theorising has moved towards the agency side of the equation, without wanting to entirely abandon structure.

What we have termed the European perspective on social movements has tended towards a more structural interpretation of NSMs whereas the dominant American perspective is more action- or agency-oriented. Hence the European insistence that NSMs are of structural importance to modern (late capitalist, post-industrial, post-materialist) society, and so should be studied by sociology; American research lacks such a rationale. As European researchers increasingly emphasise the symbolic creativity and cultural innovation of NSMs, they move towards a position that recognises the limited value of structural analysis. Increasingly, the movements have to be regarded as the *source* of (new) social structure, rather than simply the product of it. Social cleavages, including class cleavages, can be seen to emerge from the ideological and political struggles of the movements rather than just being part of a determinant social structure. In the second part of this chapter we looked at some cases that may benefit from a social movements analysis. We hope this may illustrate how this approach can open up issues to do with agency in Irish society and focus on the active participation of Irish people in creating their own distinctive social world.

18
Environmentalism

Environmentalists: a small group of supposedly posh Dublin-based intellectuals lobbying against needed 'national development', motivated by allegedly snobbish ideas about conservation (Flynn, 2006, p.87).

If the growth of consumerism is one of the most striking features of contemporary society, another is the rise of environmentalism as a critical response. In this chapter we look more closely at environmentalism: at the sorts of concerns and ways of thinking that have characterised the environmental movement internationally and in Ireland. We ask what environmental disputes and conflicts can tell us about the sort of society we are, or are becoming, and conclude with a brief discussion of the implications of these emergent concerns, not only for society but also for sociology.

While many would suggest the women's movement has perhaps been more influential, few sociologists would dispute the proposition that environmentalism is one of the key social forces of our time. Yet it has really only existed in its modern form for some forty years. Its origins are in the early 1960s, when a new environmental consciousness began to take hold, first among natural scientists and researchers, then in the public imagination. The emerging environmental movement was strongly influenced by a number of popular scientific books, the best known being Rachel Carson's *The silent spring* (1962). As these were taken up in the media, the significance of the natural world and of human intervention in it became a topic for widespread public debate.

During the late 1960s and early 1970s public awareness and concern began to manifest itself in new organisational forms. Long-established environmental organisations, such as (in the UK) the Royal Society for the Protection of Birds or (in Ireland) An Taisce were joined by many new organisations. These generally had a different sort of membership — younger, middle rather than upper class, urban rather than rural, possessing what Bourdieu calls symbolic capital as part of the new 'knowledge class' of late capitalist society. They also tended to differ in their organisational activities, usually being more activist and ready to take part in protest demonstrations and media campaigns rather than engaging in private lobbying of government and influential politicians, as the older organisations did. In some countries, such as West Germany and The Netherlands, the 'new left' mobilisations of the late 1960s came to incorporate environmental issues and the developing discourse of ecology was influenced by left-wing ideas, though in other countries this was much less the case. This was a particularly crucial period, it is often claimed, for the development of an ecological perspective and world view. Although it spanned less than a decade, it was a time when the new environmental protest groups were most creatively engaged in working out what would become the central themes in environmental knowledge, philosophy and concern.

During the 1970s the environmental movement grew rapidly — particularly in North America, some European countries and Australasia. Some of the struggles and protests in which environmental groups became involved, such as those against the building of nuclear power stations in a number of European countries, including Ireland, attracted worldwide attention and helped to generate more resources and recruits for environmental organisations. The period was also characterised by the 'greening' of government policy debates and discourses: 'by this time, environmental issues had become generally recognised political and social problems; they commanded the attention of governments and industry, as well as activists and the mass media' (Jamison *et al.*, 1990, p.10). At this time governments in the US and some European countries began to establish agencies and bodies with an environmental remit. As a result of their success, environmental organisations began to find themselves enlisted by governments in the search for practical solutions. What had previously been oppositional, protest organisations, against any participation in conventional politics, had to find ways to accommodate established institutions. In many countries the environmental movement became fragmented as a result, particularly over the issue of whether green activists should form themselves into a political party and look for an electoral mandate, or whether they should remain outside the political arena and work to change the personal awareness and behaviour of individuals instead.

In a sense, this simply means that environmentalism has become normalised. As environmental awareness and concern have come to play a more dominant role in state policies and public debate, differences of opinion about how problems should be tackled and about the ethical and scientific bases of various approaches will almost inevitably lead to new forms of organisational mobilisation and action. Indeed, just as societies that did not divide politically along a left-right axis in terms of economic policies have often been regarded as less modern, so today the presence of a strong environmental movement and of publicly expressed environmental concern is widely assumed to be a feature of the more developed societies. We are familiar with this in Ireland, where our level of environmental awareness is often taken to be an indicator of how much (or how little) we have 'become modern'.

In Europe environmental concern has now become institutionalised and taken for granted. Surveys reveal that most people support measures to conserve the environment, and environmental outcomes are increasingly taken into consideration in the formulation of economic policy. This policy and attitudinal shift has been termed 'ecological modernisation' or 'ecomodernisation' (Spaargaren and Mol, 1995; Flynn, 2006, p.20). Supporters of the ecomodernisation project argue that the state now adopts a preventive and precautionary approach to environmental problems by building advance strategies to combat environmental pollution into development planning. This also, it is claimed, helps to bring about more participative forms of environmental governance and ends the historical antagonism between the state and the environmental movement. Environmental concern has thus become normalised, expressed through a growing body of regulatory practices presided over by the state.

Critics of ecomodernisation argue that its discourse of achieving 'sustainable development' is merely a camouflage for continued support of economic growth. But it is popular as it suggests we can 'overcome the environmental crisis without leaving the path of modernisation' (Spaargaren and Mol, 1995, p.334). Thus, for example, pollution control is desirable not only for ecological reasons, but because it increases economic competitiveness. Taylor (2001) argues that this new way of thinking has helped to shift the Irish environmental policy approach from one of environmental protection to one of environmental *management* — particularly associated with the establishment in Ireland in 1993 of the Environmental Protection Agency (EPA), whose licensing regulations can be seen as an example of ecomodernisation practices. Taylor argues that: 'put simply, environmental policy debate in Ireland is concerned no longer with the extent of ecological degradation, the quality of the environment or encouraging environmental sensitivity, but with the complicated process of organising consent around new definitions of the *extent to which pollution can be justified*' (2001, p.5, original italics). Keohane's (1998) study of an EPA oral hearing on industrial development proposals for Clare and Limerick critically concluded that the body 'acts as the choreographer in a power play enacted to deceive those whom it is supposed to serve, and to corrupt one of the fundamental institutions of democracy'. Ecological modernisation has also penetrated Irish agriculture (Tovey, 2001, p.124) where it has become a management strategy that provides farmers and agricultural experts with a way to reconcile agriculture and environment in terms that support continued agricultural production.

The above short history suggests that the environmental movement embraces many different political positions and strands of thought. However, here we cover briefly just two ways to categorise green movements that are fairly widely used in the literature: the distinction between deep and shallow ecology, and the distinction between radical ecologists and conservationists.

Deep and shallow greens

The first point to note here is that 'deep' is a term that some green groups have claimed for themselves, in order to suggest that the approach of other groups is too shallow to bring about effective change. But some social theorists, especially Marxists, consider the ideas of the deep greens themselves to be quite superficial, at any rate in terms of their understanding of society and social structures. Deep ecologists are characterised by two features (Naess, 1997):

- a belief that there is no valid difference or separation between 'human beings' and 'the rest of nature'
- a commitment to a spiritual rather than a scientific orientation to nature.

Deep ecology is thus concerned about the fate of the earth as a total system, rather than of individual elements within it such as the human species. This total system — nature — is something to be revered by humans, who should try to understand its workings, through intuitive or mystical means, in order to adapt to and co-operate with it, instead of using an aggressive scientific perspective to dominate and manipulate parts of the system in the human interest. The Gaian philosophy (Lovelock, 2000) is probably one of the best-known examples of this way of thinking.

Shallow, or sometimes light, greens often accept elements of the deep ecology perspective, but combine a reverence for and desire to conserve nature with a belief that political intervention is essential if we are to address and control the root causes of environmental degradation, generally identified as human ignorance, greed and social wastefulness. This implies a rejection of the deep ecologists' subordination of humans to the wider system in which they live; instead, human action in the world remains the key to progress, and this includes both political intervention and the continued use of science to solve problems — even those that science earlier helped to create. This can be termed a human-centred rather than nature-centred form of environmentalism. One of its clearest expressions is the 'limits to growth' thesis, which conceptualises the natural world as a set of resources for meeting human needs and absorbing human waste, and argues that we cannot take for granted that these resources are unlimited. It is in the human interest to identify the limits (for example, the level of population that the planet can carry) and then to take steps to ensure we remain within them.

Radical ecologists and conservationists

Cutting across the deep/shallow division is another: radical ecologists and conservationists. The distinction refers to the extent of social and political change thought necessary to resolve and reverse the problems of the natural environment. Radical environmentalists believe that environmental degradation is the outcome not just of aspects of human behaviour like ignorance, greed or carelessness, but of the particular forms of social organisation and social relationships found in the developed capitalist world: the pressure exerted by multinational capital on natural and social resources over increasing areas of the globe; the technocratic rationality that dominates contemporary capitalist society; and the hierarchical and oppressive authority relationships that persist in work places, educational institutions and families — these are ultimately the causes of the destructive way we behave towards our natural environment. Radical ecologists are clearly influenced by Marxist analyses of capitalism, but differ crucially in rejecting the Marxist belief in continued economic growth as the key to progress.

By contrast, conservationists tend to believe in the capacity of the existing social system to manage environmental problems without having to change very much or alternatively do not hold any detailed social and political theories. In the former case, they characteristically adopt the positions referred to as green consumerists or green capitalists. They argue that either capitalist entrepreneurs, or consumers, or both, as rational individuals, will come to recognise that it is in their best interest to insist on organising production in ways that do the least damage to nature. Some who adopt this position claim that capitalist industrialists already recognise that avoidance of waste and pollution actually increases profits, so need no further incentive to move to cleaner forms of production. Others argue that a careful adjustment to tax and market systems, such as energy taxes or 'polluter pays' charges, can provide compelling incentives for cleaner industry, while remaining within the capitalist market system. Similarly, green consumerists argue that if consumers refuse to buy products that are not environmentally friendly, then capitalist businessmen will quickly stop producing them. A well-known and well-publicised example of both green capitalism and green consumerism is the Body Shop company, a chain of cosmetics outlets that has spread across much of the developed world and has made substantial profits from marketing products that are not tested on animals and are claimed to be less depleting of natural resources and less polluting than other cosmetics.

Both pro-capitalist and politically indifferent greens tend to share a belief that environmental change means starting with change at the level of *individual* knowledge, attitudes and behaviour. They see education and regulation as the main ways to achieve this, and look to the state as a central source of support in both cases. Education is seen as preferable, as it provides individuals with enlightened self-interest, but some regulation by the state is also required as some social groups are thought to be particularly resistant to persuasion and education. By contrast, radical ecologists see the state as a major part of the problem. It is the state's commitment to and support for capitalist enterprise that encourages the continuing development of environmentally destructive forms of technology, such as opencast mining or nuclear power. Radical ecological organisations thus tend to remain primarily protest and oppositional organisations outside the sphere of state policy formation. They seem to have diminished in importance in the past decade, whereas non-radical groups have been able to establish themselves as advisors, consultants and educators on behalf of the state.

WHY ENVIRONMENTALISM NOW?

Later in this chapter we examine the environmental movement in Ireland in the light of these distinctions and ask what sort of social movement it is and what impact it may be having on Irish society. But first we briefly discuss a question that is particularly central for sociologists, although probably not for most environmentalists: why has environmentalism developed on such an international scale now? What is it about the contemporary period that has given rise to such strongly felt concerns about environmental damage and danger, shared by apparently very diverse social groups and across a range of societies and cultures?

An obvious answer is that environmental concern has developed in response to increasing environmental destruction. As more people have become aware of how urban industrial society has polluted and degraded the natural environment, the air we breathe and the water we drink, and the habitats of numerous animal and plant species, more are starting to voice their anger and opposition. In other words, the dangerous condition that the physical environment is now in is sufficient reason for people to mobilise to protect and conserve it.

But there are some reasons to doubt this explanation. The countries where environmental movements are most strongly organised are not necessarily those that are experiencing the greatest environmental damage (compare, for example, environmental conditions in northern Europe with those in oil-rich regions of Nigeria); and those involved in environmental protests tend to be drawn from particular social classes and groups, not necessarily those who face the greatest environmental risks (usually the urban working class or rural poor). Many people are concerned about environmental problems of which they have no direct experience (for example, whaling) or that they cannot directly perceive for themselves but must rely on science to tell them about (the hole in the ozone layer). Thus, in taking up environmental issues people are not simply responding to 'facts' about the physical environment.

Durkheim stresses that social events and phenomena should always be explained in terms of *social* causes. Since the environmental movement is a social phenomenon, to explain its existence we should examine the social context in which it has developed, and its social consequences. We cannot simply point to physical changes: acid rain, high levels of nitrates in water, the disappearance of the corncrake or the last remnants of unspoilt countryside in Europe.

Environmental organisations as moral entrepreneurs

Yearley (1991) suggests that the contemporary significance of environmental organisations and pressure groups can be explained through a general study of societal response to 'social problems'. Why is it that, at a particular point in time, some issues figure prominently on society's list of 'things that have to be dealt with', and others are hardly visible? Quite often, the public prominence of a problem bears little relationship to its actual severity; for example, studies of public panics about crime and deviance suggest they are just as likely to occur when official crime statistics are declining as when they are increasing; or that the public may 'panic' about one type of activity (say, taking Ecstasy) that can be much less dangerous than another (say, drinking alcohol). An important factor in such cases is the activities of individuals or groups who, for whatever reason, have decided to organise a crusade in relation to a particular issue.

Sociologists have termed such people moral entrepreneurs. Although their concerns are moral rather than business ones, such people have much in common with business entrepreneurs: they take risks in launching their product on the market; they are good at identifying ways to sell the product; and they are prepared to invest their personal status, as well as their own and others' resources, in the promotional campaign. The global organisation Greenpeace fits well into this entrepreneurial model, though we might be less sure about organisations such as An Taisce or the Irish Wildbird Conservancy. But Yearley's general point is that a considerable part of the prominence now enjoyed by environmental issues is a result of the promotional, lobbying and organisational activities carried out by environmental protection organisations. This implies that the environmental concern we find in any society today is significantly shaped by the nature and characteristics of environmental organisations, that is, the sort of membership they appeal to; their relationships with government and the media; the sources of their funds; and what sort of paid or unpaid staff they recruit.

Yearley's has been called a *social constructionist* approach: instead of treating public concern about the environment as a reflection of physical processes, he draws our attention to the active part played by environmental agencies as they construct public perceptions of environmental problems. This helps us to understand some features about public concern, for example, its rather selective focus of attention. The threatened extinction of a species of beetle or spider generally draws much less public attention than that of a bird or a whale. We could explain this on the grounds that where environmental organisations are very dependent on the public for support and funds, they are most likely to take up the cause of the more appealing endangered natural species. Conversely, organisations that have easy access to private or public funds can afford to worry more about threats to the survival of organisms that are scientifically important but not visually attractive — but then these organisations probably play a smaller part in shaping public environmental awareness.

The social background of an organisation's membership may also help to explain why it tries to awaken interest in some issues but not others. The Irish Georgian Society, for example, is a good example of a moral entrepreneur organisation that was very active in promoting public concern about developments in the Irish urban environment in the 1970s, such as the destruction in south inner-city Dublin of Georgian houses to make way for modern office blocks. But the Society largely ignored other developments in relation to the built environment, such as the urban redevelopment that was undertaken to house those moved out of the north inner-city into new suburban estates. We could relate this selective interest in Dublin's architectural problems to the class position and, perhaps, the Anglo-Irish cultural identity of leading members in the Society.

Environmental organisations also differ in their relationships to and the use they make of the work of scientists, physical planners, economists and other professionals; in their readiness to work with party politicians; and in their interest in becoming a political organisation. They also vary in the extent they think it important to make connections between the emergence of significant problems in the natural environment and trends within contemporary society. Differences like these affect the world view within which they talk about the environment, environmental problems and environmental solutions. In turn these specific world views are conveyed to the wider public through the promotional and campaigning activities of the major organisations.

The social constructivist perspective is very useful for developing a sociological account of contemporary environmentalism. But it may also have the effect (as in Yearley, 1995) of encouraging us to over-focus on formally constituted environmental organisations such as Greenpeace, the World Wildlife Fund, and so on, and we may thus lose sight of an essential feature of modern environmentalism: that it is not just a series of formal organisations but a *social movement*. To develop this point further we now look in some detail at the Irish experience of environmentalism.

ENVIRONMENTALISM IN IRELAND

Environmentalism in Ireland exhibits a range of richly varied forms. It includes at one end of the spectrum variants of deep ecology such as the beliefs of Celtic religion revivalists, New Age Travellers and the growing Wicca movement, with, at the other end, scientists and other environmental professionals employed in the Environmental Protection Agency and the Department of the Environment. It encompasses eco-warriors and tree-lovers; local activists involved in one-off battles over forms of economic development proposed for their localities (from chemical factories to fishfarms); long-established residents' associations and leisure and sporting organisations that lobby the state to protect their local areas and amenities; political activists in the Green Party; and spokespersons for the leading environmental organisations who shade over, at times, into the official state policy-making community.

Yet this rich texturing of the Irish environmental movement is not at all evident from most public or academic discussion, and particularly not from how politicians, state policy-makers and policy advisors speak about it. Within Irish environmentalism, then, there are evidently conflicts about who is to be included as a legitimate environmental voice and who is not; who is on the 'lunatic fringe' and who is mainstream. As sociologists, whenever we write or speak about the environmental movement in Ireland we need to remind ourselves of the contested status of the object of our analysis.

The history of environmentalism in Ireland is similarly contested. Most discussions open with the claim that environmental awareness has come late to Irish society, compared with our more advanced European colleagues (Flynn, 2006, p.87). Thus, Coyle (1994, p.63) remarks that 'attitude surveys during the 1980s revealed Ireland to be consistently at or near the bottom of the league in terms of concern for the environment, especially when the issue was a trade-off between economic growth and environmental protection'. This late development is usually ascribed to one or both of two causes:

- the generally low level, until quite recently, of *cultural modernisation* in Irish society, a result of our native traditionalism and isolation from Britain and the European core
- our low level of *economic development*, which meant not only that job creation was seen as the over-riding priority until well into the 1980s, but also that the Irish environment thus fortuitously escaped the extensive degradation of rapid industrial growth, meaning that there was, until recently, little environmental damage for Irish people to be concerned about.

In opposition to the received wisdom, Baker (1990) has pointed out that ecological movements emerged on the Irish scene as early as the 1960s, at much the same time as in other European countries. She also argues that activism was significantly shaped and strengthened by the Irish experience of being an economically peripheral region of Europe, subject to specific patterns of economic relations with the developed world and particular cultural concerns as a result of colonial domination. The early environmentalism that emerged in Ireland reflected radical environmentalism. Even if it was confined to a small minority of the population, it contrasted markedly with the conservationist and state-oriented form of environmentalism that now dominates the Irish scene. This movement away from radicalism is fairly characteristic of the general trajectory of European environmentalism, so we may conclude that there is nothing particularly backward or different about the Irish experience.

Baker links the emergence of ecological politics in Ireland to the period of rapid economic change and industrialisation of the 1960s and early 1970s. This process helped to stimulate a range of new social movements in Ireland, most notably the feminist movement. For Baker (1990, p.53) the most significant of the early ecological movements was the anti-nuclear movement, which emerged in the 1970s in response to the state's decision to use nuclear power to generate electricity. This decision was supported by all main political groups at the time, including (with some internal conflict) Labour and Fine Gael. Moreover, the announcement that a nuclear power station was to be built at Carnsore Point in Wexford was also, initially, greeted with enthusiasm by local people. But by 1973, local resistance had started to crystallise as local activists formed themselves into a Nuclear Safety Association and started to make contact with Irish branches of Friends of the Earth (founded in Dublin in 1974) and a range of other groups in what was to become an expanding anti-nuclear national coalition. Baker reports (1990, p.55) 'the bulk of the anti-nuclear campaign . . . was conducted within the context of loosely woven, informal and locally based campaign groups. These numbered at one point approximately 102 separate groups and operated throughout Ireland.'

By the time of the first Carnsore protest festival in 1978, the campaign was attracting widespread support from young people across Ireland, especially from third-level students, and from groups in the United States, France and Italy. Of the protest Flynn (2006, p.89) remarks 'the sixties had arrived, but in 1979!' In that year Fianna Fáil set up an Interdepartmental Committee to re-examine the case for nuclear energy in Ireland and in the following year it was announced that the Carnsore plan had been 'postponed'. As it subsequently emerged, the nuclear energy option had been abandoned at this point by all the main political parties. The anti-nuclear campaign in Ireland thus turned out in the end to be more successful than a number of others, notably those in the European core countries of France and Britain. While the links with the military nuclear establishment were probably central to the outcome in these countries, it is also plausible that the success of the Irish movement was in many respects attributable to its ability to draw on and exploit aspects of that 'traditional culture' (in particular, the religiosity of Irish people and their commitment to international peace and neutrality) that many commentators later were to claim held back the development of a 'modern' attitude to the environment in Ireland.

Tovey (1992b; 1993) argues that commentators on Irish environmentalism, especially those within certain strands of the environmental movement, have not only forgotten about this early radical manifestation but tend also to ignore other historical dimensions. She argues that we should recognise two distinct environmentalisms in Ireland which have different histories and social locations, and which express different and even opposed interpretations of Irish development. She suggests we call one of these *official* environmentalism, as it is led primarily by environmental experts from a range of academic disciplines (planners, economists, agriculturists, chemists, botanists, zoologists) who usually work through the established environmental organisations. A significant number work in the public sector, directly or indirectly employed by the state.

The other strand Tovey labels *populist* environmentalism as it represents a relatively independent movement of dissent, by ordinary people working at the local level, from the dominant ideologies of modernisation, development and growth. Populist environmentalism reflects the activities of a different set of organisations, such as the community development movement in rural Ireland, and its activists may not necessarily see themselves as environmentalists (though they are increasingly likely to claim this label as it becomes more politically legitimate). Tovey links populist environmentalism to local communities' experiences of economic underdevelopment, rather than to cultural modernisation; thus it may be seen as a more direct descendant of Baker's 'early ecological politics' in Ireland than the official variant. An excellent example of the clash between such populist environmentalism on the one hand, and expert discourses of the state and business on the other, can be found in Garavan's (2006) analysis of the conflict in relation to the construction of the Shell gas pipeline in Co. Mayo.

As well as noting the varied history of Irish environmentalism, we can look at some of the main social or political factors that helped to shape it. Two can be picked out in particular — one external and one internal: the growing importance placed by the EU Commission on implementing environmental legislation; and the change in urban — rural relationships within Ireland.

Membership of the EU has obliged Irish governments to introduce a wide array of environmental initiatives. The evidence suggests that Ireland has had a mixed record in relation to the implementation of such moves. Certainly, in the early 1990s a series of EU directives in areas such as air and water pollution and wildlife protection were incorporated into Irish law or framed as government regulations. In 1990 the Environment Information Service (ENFO) was established, followed by the Environmental Policy Research Centre within the ESRI which was to examine economic aspects of environmental policy. In 1993 the Environmental Protection Agency was established, and the National Development Plan 1994–1999 contained an entire chapter on the 'environmental situation', a substantial increase on the previous Plan (Coyle, 1994, p.65).

In Coyle's view, these initiatives partly reflect the government's desire for us to show ourselves to be 'good Europeans', but are also an attempt to capitalise on the shift in European tastes towards green consumption, especially in the areas of food and tourism. A consequence of this activity has been to greatly expand the occupational opportunities available to environmental professionals in Ireland, beyond the traditional niches within third-level education and the public service. There are now many more public service jobs (including in local government) and independent environmental consultants increasingly find work in monitoring, advising and recommending strategies for environmental management under the new environmental regime. Those groups active in environmental organisations and campaigns, and most in favour of expanding state intervention in environmental regulation in Ireland, are members of the new 'knowledge class', arguably the class most likely to benefit from such expansion.

More recently, and certainly since the turn of the millennium, Ireland's compliance with EU legislation and initiatives has been far less thoroughgoing. As Flynn (2006, pp.138–145) convincingly demonstrates, Ireland has moved from being one of the more progressive European states in relation to the environment, to one of those most likely to be in breach of EU directives, along with major industrial countries such as France, Germany and Italy. Flynn maintains (2006, p.10) that the key issue is institutional inertia and resistance and a failure to implement policy at both local and national level: 'on paper Ireland has a modern environmental regulatory apparatus much like any advanced industrial democratic state. Yet the reality in practice can be very different.' Those who are employed in environmental regulatory roles, such as town planners or the staff of the EPA, confront a political system that is marked by lack of strategic direction, a tendency towards confrontation and adversarialism, and a dependence on threats of litigation from the EU Commission to bring about action. Such barriers to action, and the difficulties posed by political involvement in the planning process, have been graphically illustrated by McDonald and Nix (2005). Flynn, however, sees the solution to such barriers as located within the realm of institutional change at the national level, rather than in local mobilisation. He calls for a process of ecological modernisation, where 'environmental issues (can be) successfully repackaged as national technical, political and economic challenges' (2006, p.20). He sees this as a realistic strategy to reconcile the pressures of global competiveness and 'sustainable development'.

A second important factor that has shaped Irish environmentalism is the changing urban — rural relationship. Urbanisation has meant more than just an increase in the proportion of the population living in towns and cities rather than in small villages or the open countryside. It has included changes in the balance of political power between agrarian and industrial interests, and an increasing dominance of urban-based cultural practices and assumptions over rural ones (Tovey, 2002). Brody (1986) interpreted what was happening to the west of Ireland during the 1950s and 1960s as a process of rural *demoralisation* in that the skills, values and way of life of country people were increasingly perceived by rural dwellers themselves to be worthless, as they began to internalise dominant urban cultural positions. During the 1970s and 1980s, profound changes in Irish agriculture and agribusiness helped to weaken the political strength of farmers as the numbers engaged in commercial food production contracted steadily and as their interests began to take a back seat within the policy-making process to those of the food industry. These changes have contributed to a significant change in our perceptions of what the Irish countryside is for, and how it should be managed.

Until quite recently it was widely taken for granted that farmers had the prior right to determine the use of rural land, and this was reflected in, for example, the exemptions from planning permission allowed to certain kinds of agricultural development. While most Irish people also took for granted that they had a right of access to farm land for recreational purposes, this was subject to common-sense rules about not interfering with agricultural production, and it was the farmers, as the land-owners and food producers, who were seen as the natural managers of the countryside. But in the last decade these assumptions have been challenged. Urban-based conservationists, recreational groups and tourism interests have begun to make claims on the Irish countryside that undermine and attack the management role previously accorded to farmers.

Coinciding with the economic and political retreat of agriculture, the emergence of new sets of interests in relation to land has opened up a new debate about the future of rural Ireland, reflecting similar debates across Europe. Increasingly dominant in this debate is the claim that rural Ireland must be managed and regulated in the interests of the urban population. This tends to mean that the availability of rural space for leisure, recreation and education is increasingly given priority over the use of rural land to produce food. This is not true of all areas but is particularly evident in relation to large tracts of the west and north-west where any belief that small farms can be viable food-producing enterprises has been more or less abandoned. Similar arguments exist in relation to areas of the country where landscape and recreational values are high and where farming is still relatively small-scale and capital-extensive. The government/EU-sponsored Rural Environment Protection Scheme (REPS), for example, has been concentrated particularly on these sorts of areas. Tovey (1997) argues that the scheme encourages farmers to think of themselves increasingly not as food producers but as environmental conservationists working on behalf of an increasingly urbanised Irish society. Flynn (2006, p.102) is more sceptical, suggesting that REPS is first and foremost an income suport scheme for less well-off famers, with no 'coherent monitoring of its environmental effects'. Nevertheless it represents some evidence that, in line with changes to the EU's Common Agricultural Policy (CAP), parts of rural Ireland are moving towards what has been termed 'post-productivist agriculture' (see Chapter 3).

'Conservationist' environmentalism, as we previously suggested, tends to find itself in opposition to 'radical' ecological movements. It is generally 'deep' rather than 'social' ('shallow') in its prioritising of the needs of nature over those of human beings. It does not locate environmental problems within an analysis of societal development, but sees them as the outcome of individual human failings such as greed or carelessness. It looks for solutions, not in a transformation of society, but in keeping human intervention in nature to the barest possible minimum level. The dominant trend in current Irish environmentalism, at least of the 'official' variety, is now towards conservation and the identification and preservation of 'our natural heritage'. How do we explain this particular preoccupation?

Some writers see it as the profoundly conservative (in the political sense) response of a society that has experienced traumatic or demoralising changes in its sense of national identity. In relation to British experience, Hewison (1987) argues that the rise of a 'heritage industry' feeds on and encourages a nostalgia for the past when Britain was an imperial power and its culture was globally dominant. As a historian, he is very critical of the misleading version of the past that he claims is generated through the heritage industry's packaging of nostalgia. He is also concerned about the snobbishness, lack of faith or interest in contemporary popular culture, and the right-wing political stance that he detects within it. We might feel this to be a harsh judgment on the growth of a heritage movement in Ireland, while noticing how well that movement has successfully rehabilitated similar social icons for the Irish past, for example, in the focus on conserving the Irish 'great house'. Are there any grounds to suppose that Irish national identity has recently undergone similar traumatic changes to the British one? It could be argued that since the late 1960s all the conventional symbols of Irishness — Catholicism, rurality, communality, possession of a distinct language — have been systematically stripped of their value and legitimacy, necessitating a new version of our identity and a revaluation of our past. But the search for heritage in Ireland has also produced new populist versions of history, as people have come to value the traces — implements, buildings, clothing, emigrants' letters — left by ordinary Irish people in their passing through previous centuries.

It may also be that the rise of conservationist concerns and the preoccupation with heritage, natural and built, is a reflection of how consumption and consumerism have become drivers of contemporary Irish society. Within modern consumer society, we suggested in Chapter 16, people find a sense of personal identity less in their work roles or productive activities than in their consumption behaviour. Tourism, like shopping, has become a defining activity of late modern society. We visit and consume heritage sites, interpretive centres, recreational amenities, nature. The past and the physical world are turned into commodities that can be purchased and consumed by the tourist, who does not have to be a visitor from another country but can be anyone who spends time gazing at and enjoying in a detached way signs of the lives of others. Forms of tourism help us to signal to others and confirm to ourselves the sort of person we are, our tastes and interests and the social group we (would like to) belong to.

The rise of conservationist environmentalism in Ireland can thus be interpreted as a further indication of how 'developed' Irish society has become. We can understand environmental conflicts as struggles between those who want to use nature for productive purposes — to exploit natural resources — and those who wish to consume nature for personal satisfaction or as part of their social identity. To so link the rise of environmentalism in Ireland to the rise of consumerism is rather ironic, given that many environmental and ecological thinkers have identified consumerism as a major *cause* of environmental degradation. Given its embeddedness in late modern social life, a reduction in consumption as a solution to environmental destruction now seems unlikely. Whether a change in how we consume — such as consuming nature by appreciating it — may present a solution, remains to be seen.

A NEW SOCIOLOGY FOR AN ECOLOGICAL AGE?

Recent research interest in the area of consumption is part of a broader movement away from *structure* and towards a focus on *action* and *process*. We see this in how research and theorising on consumption has fed into sociological accounts of social class. In trying to explain variations in consumer behaviour across social groups, theorists like Bourdieu have recognised that purely structuralist accounts of class are no longer tenable. While important connections remain between class position and consumer practices, we must recognise that people are not automatically prompted by their class background to consume in specific ways. Rather people may use specific forms of consumption as a strategy to achieve, claim or maintain a particular class position (Devine *et al.*, 2005). The image of the individual as a self-conscious, strategic social actor who responds to images of self and identity is supported by much of the sociology of consumption.

The interest in consumption and consumerism is moving sociology in a direction that is different from, but connects with, earlier interests within the discipline. The implications of ecology and environmentalism are perhaps more challenging. Some writers go so far as to warn that once sociologists start to take on environmental issues in a serious way, they may find the enterprise of sociology itself cannot be continued — unless extraordinary changes occur in the fundamental assumptions of the discipline. The threat of environmental catastrophe is forcing profound changes, they argue, in our conventional political and economic rationality. Why should sociology expect to be immune?

The argument may be overstated but there are at least three ways that it can be developed further. The first concerns how and whether sociology can take into account *physical* as well as social causes and impacts on the social world. The second concerns the boundaries of *society*: as we become more aware of the rights of non-human animals, do we need to rethink our conception of society to include them, or some of them? And the third concerns the nature and status of *science*, as it is increasingly challenged by the growing environmental risks that result from its application.

The issue of physical impact reprises our earlier discussion about the social constructionist perspective, where environmental concerns are best understood as the product of moral entrepreneurs. This approach implies that public concern is not generated primarily from a recognition of potentially catastrophic changes in the natural world, and that it does not really matter — from a sociological point of view — whether such changes are 'real' or not. Some sociologists find themselves unable to accept such a conclusion: thus Martell (1994, p.124) finds problems with Yearley's social constructionist approach. Martell does not believe that environmental problems can simply be manufactured by organisations who want to manipulate public morality — they must have a physical or scientific base or they would be quickly discounted by the public or challenged by the many groups and organisations with a reason to oppose environmentalism. A study of how and why environmental problems become socially defined as problems is useful, certainly, but 'ought to complement rather than be counterposed to explanations based on the objective existence of environmental problems'. Yearley has now come closer to this position, noting that the 'marketing' role undertaken by environmental agencies is only one factor in a situation that must also include 'the state of the environment itself' (1995, p.657).

But sociology is not very well equipped to build 'the state of the physical environment' into its perspectives and theories. It is a discipline concerned with the study of the *social* world. In its early decades its practitioners worked hard to establish the difference between social and physical reality and to establish that quite different sciences are needed for the study of each. Durkheim, for example, insisted that social processes and events should always be explained by *social* causes, not psychological or physical ones. The development of sociology in the century or so since Durkheim elaborated this view has been predominantly in line with this approach: it explains the social by means of the social. Thus, while early theories of crime sought physical or psychological causes, a sociological approach has concentrated on analysing the social processes through which people become defined as criminal (see Chapter 11). Similarly, while early discussions of gender focused on physical difference, contemporary sociologists are generally very unwilling to concede that men's and women's biological or physical attributes determine or explain their social roles or position in society (see Chapter 9). Sociology has progressively defined its reality as a purely social reality, in that physical systems and environments play virtually no part other than to provide the context for social relations and actions. If sociologists now have to accept that changes in the physical world have major consequences for the organisation of social life, perhaps even for its survival, the nature of the discipline itself may have to be reconsidered.

The second way that environmentalism challenges sociology relates to the boundaries of society. Though not true for all environmentalists, there has been a strong drive by some, certainly within deep ecology, to rethink the position that human beings have traditionally accorded to other animals. Such philosophies reject the anthropocentric view that humans are separate from and superior to the rest of nature, and therefore entitled to use it, its physical resources and animal species, as mere objects for their own satisfaction. Even those who do not embrace deep ecology have been led by their interest in the operations of nature in general to reconsider their attitude to animals and to the suffering that humans cause to them. Considerable efforts have been made by environmental philosophers (Singer, 1997) to establish a theory of 'animals rights' that, while it recognises the inability of animals to claim such rights for themselves, finds ways to argue that they should still be accorded some level of rights.

Sociologists (for example, Franklin, 1999) have investigated how the different social settings in which we encounter animals lead us to define animals differently:

from 'almost human' in some settings (the family sitting-room) to 'almost a material object' in others (the scientific laboratory) — even when we are dealing with the same type of animal (a dog) in each setting. This has encouraged the idea that there is nothing intrinsic to animals that means they should be treated as if they merited no respect or consideration. To the extent that we agree to accord animals certain rights, or recognise human obligations towards them, we define them as part of the social community. This opens up the possibility that the boundaries of 'society', the fundamental entity studied by sociology, need to be redrawn so as to include at least some animal species. Even if we do not consider that interactions between animals are part of 'our' society, we might want to include aspects of human — animal interaction.

The third way that the encounter with environmentalism may prove profoundly unsettling for sociology is in relation to the connections between sociology and modernity. As a child of the Enlightenment, sociology's development was shaped by beliefs and assumptions that were at the core of modernity itself — in particular, the belief in progress, science and rationality. The rise of environmentalism has fundamentally challenged each of these tenets. The discovery that the advance of civilisation and prosperity in much of the world directly contributes to environmental damage that may threaten the viability of human life on earth, if not the earth itself, makes it very hard to maintain a belief that the history of humankind is a history of progress. Environmentalism has revealed to many the integral role in environmental damage that has been played by science itself and by the use of scientific knowledge to control the material world. Even if we still need science to identify the damage for us, and perhaps to offer remedies, the authority of science and the credibility of scientists have been among the most obvious victims of the rise of environmentalism. Finally, environmentalism poses questions about our capacity to act to solve environmental problems, or our capacity to identify and activate a rational strategy to deal with environmental risks. Within the movement worldwide, there is a strong if minority strand that no longer believes that normal methods of political intervention can solve the problems. For these environmentalists, the solution has to be found elsewhere, in terms of a personal conversion. The well-springs for this are not rationality, but emotions, values or religious mysticism.

Rejection of progress as a grand narrative of history; rejection of a blind faith in science; a preference for emotionally and value-based forms of action over rational strategic forms — these are all commonly said to be features of post-modern culture. The encounter with environmentalism might thus lead towards a post-modern sociology. What would such a sociology be like? We can hypothesise that it would be a sociology that is most concerned with the local and immediate, and then only in a provisional way, that distrusts the idea that we can produce any overarching explanation for social development. It would be a sociology that prefers qualitative methods of research, perhaps, and that sees itself as closer to history, anthropology or cultural studies, than to the economic or natural sciences. It would be a sociology of human beings as not just minds but also bodies, multidimensional creatures shaped as much by non-rational wants and desires as by their capacities for intentional, planned action. But in the end, would such a sociology help us to understand post-modernity, or would it merely reflect it?

References

Åberg, A.
(1999)

'Modern nature? Images of nature and rurality in Swedish cinema'.
Paper to European Rural Sociological Society conference, Lund.

Akenson, D.
(1991)

Small differences: Irish Catholics and Irish Protestants, 1815–1922.
Montreal and Kingston: McGill-Queen's University Press/
Dublin: Gill & Macmillan.

Aldridge, A.
(2000)

Religion in the contemporary world. Cambridge: Polity.

Alexander, J.
(1998)

'Civil Society I,II,III — Constructing an empirical concept from
normative controversies and historical transformations' in J.
Alexander (ed.) *Real civil societies: Dilemmas of institutionalisation.*
London: Sage.

Allen, K.
(1997)

Fianna Fáil and Irish Labour: 1926 to the present. London: Pluto.

Allen, K.
(1999)

'The Celtic Tiger, inequality and social partnership'.
Administration 47(2). pp.31–55.

Allen, K.
(2000)

The Celtic Tiger: The myth of social partnership in Ireland.
Manchester: Manchester University Press.

Allen, M.
(1998)

The bitter word: Ireland's job famine and its aftermath. Dublin:
Poolbeg.

Anderson, B.
(1983)

*Imagined communities: Reflections on the origin and spread of
nationalism.* London: Verso.

Ang, I.
(1985)

Watching Dallas: Soap opera and the melodramatic imagination.
London: Methuen.

Aniagolu, C.   'Being black in Ireland' in E. Crowley and J. Mac Laughlin (eds)
(1997)   *Under the belly of the tiger: Class, race, identity and culture in the
                    global Ireland*. Dublin: Irish Reporter.

Anthias, F.   'Theorising identity, difference and social divisions' in
(1999)   M. O'Brien, S. Penna and C. Hay (eds) *Theorising modernity*.
                    London: Longman.

Appadurai, A.   *Modernity at large: cultural dimensions of globalisation*.
(1996)   Minneapolis: University of Minnesota Press.

Arensberg, C.   *Family and community in Ireland*. 3e. Ennis: CLASP.
and S. Kimball
(2001) [1940]

Atkins, P.   *Food in society: Economy, culture, geography*. London: Arnold.
and I. Bowler
(2001)

Atkinson, A.   'Poverty in Ireland and anti-poverty strategy: A European
(1997)   perspective' in A. Gray (ed.) *International perspectives on the Irish
                    economy*. Dublin: Indecon.

Bacik, I.   'Women and the criminal justice system' in P. O'Mahony (ed.)
(2002)   *Criminal justice in Ireland*. Dublin: Institute of Public
                    Administration.

Bail, K. (ed.)   *DIY feminism*. Sydney: Allen and Unwin.
(1996)

Baker, J.,   *Equality: From theory to action*. Basingstoke: Palgrave.
K. Lynch,
S. Cantillon
and J. Walsh
(2004)

Baker, J.   'Studying equality'. *Imprints* 2(1). pp.57–71.
(1997)

Baker, S.   'The evolution of the Irish ecology movement' in W. Rudig (ed.)
(1990)   *Green politics I*. Rotterdam: Erasmus University Press.

Balanda, K. and   *Inequalities in mortality 1989–1998: A report on all-Ireland
J. Wilde   mortality data*. Dublin: Institute of Public Health in Ireland.
(2001)

Banks, M.
(1990)

'Irish television and society'. *Media, culture and society* 12. pp.403–407.

Barbrook, R.
(1992)

'Broadcasting and national identity in Ireland'. *Media Culture and Society* 14. pp.203–227.

Barrett, A.,
J. Fitz Gerald
and B. Nolan
(2000)

'Earnings inequality, returns to education and low pay' in B. Nolan, P. O'Connell and C. Whelan (eds) *Bust to boom? The Irish experience of growth and inequality.* Dublin: Institute of Public Administration.

Barry, A. and
B. Brunt
(2002)

'Female employment in the multinational electronics industry in Ireland's south-west planning region'. *Irish Geography* 35(1). pp.28–39.

Barth, F.
(1969)

Ethnic groups and boundaries: The social organisation of cultural difference. London: Allen and Unwin.

Barthes, R.
(1973)

Mythologies. St Alban's: Paladin.

Bartley, B.
(1999)

'Spatial planning and poverty in North Clondalkin' in D. Pringle, J. Walsh and M. Hennessy (eds) *Poor people, poor places: A geography of poverty and deprivation in Ireland.* Dublin: Oak Tree/Geographical Society of Ireland.

Barton, R.
(1997)

'From history to heritage: some recent developments in Irish cinema'. *The Irish Review* 21, pp.41–56.

Bauman, Z.
(1995)

Life in fragments: Essays in postmodern morality. Oxford: Blackwell.

Bauman, Z.
(2001)

Community: Seeking safety in an insecure world. Cambridge: Polity.

Bauman, Z.
(2002)

'Individually, together' in U. Beck and E. Beck-Gernsheim: *Individualization: Institutionalised individualism and its social and political consequences.* London: Sage.

Bayley, D.
(1991)

Forces of order: Policing modern Japan. Berkeley: University of California Press.

Beale, J.
(1986)

Women in Ireland: Voices of change. Basingstoke: Macmillan.

Beardsworth, A. and T. Keil (1997)   *Sociology on the menu: An invitation to the study of food and society*. London: Routledge.

Beck, U. (1992)   *Risk society: Towards a new modernity*. London: Sage.

Beck, U. and E. Beck-Gernsheim (2002)   *Individualization: Institutionalised individualism and its social and political consequences*. London: Sage

Belasco, W. (2006)   *Meals to come: A history of the future of food*. Berkeley: University of California Press.

Bell, D. (1982)   'Community studies: the new anthropological heritage and its popularity in Ireland'. *International Journal of Anthropology and Social Policy* 1. pp.22–36.

Bell, D. (1991)   'Cultural studies in Ireland and the postmodernist debate'. *Irish Journal of Sociology* 1. pp.83–95.

Bellah, R. (1967)   'Civil religion in America'. *Daedalus* Winter. pp.1–19.

Benington, J. (2001)   'Partnerships as networked governance?' in M. Geddes and J. Benington (eds) *Local partnerships and social exclusion in the European Union: New forms of local social governance?* London: Routledge.

Bennett, T. and D. Watson (2002)   'Understanding everyday life: introduction' in T. Bennett and D. Watson (eds) *Understanding everyday life*. Oxford: Blackwell/Open University.

Benson, M. (2007)   Changing cityscapes and the process of contemporary gentrification: an examination of the transformation of Ringsend within the context of post-industrial growth in Dublin. Unpublished PhD thesis, Department of Sociology, NUI Maynooth.

Berger, A. (1998)   *Media analysis techniques*. Thousand Oaks: Sage.

Bhreatnach, A. (2006)   *Becoming conspicuous: Irish Travellers, society and the state, 1922–70*. Dublin: University College Dublin Press.

Binchy, A.
(1994)

'Travellers' language: a sociolinguistic perspective' in
M. McCann, S. Ó Síocháin and J. Ruane (eds) *Irish Travellers: Culture and ethnicity*. Belfast: Institute of Irish Studies, Queen's University Belfast, for the Anthropological Association of Ireland.

Blaxter, M.
(1995)

'What is health?' in B. Davey, A. Gray and C. Seale (eds) *Health and disease: A reader*. Buckingham: Open University Press.

Blumler, J. and
M. Gurevitch,
(1981)

'Politicians and the press: an essay on role relationships' in D. Nimmo and K. Sanders (eds) *Handbook of political communication*. London: Sage. pp.467–93.

Bocock, R.
(1992)

'Consumption and lifestyles' in R. Bocock and K. Thompson (eds) *Social and cultural forms of modernity*. Cambridge: Polity Press/Open University.

Bocock, R. and
K. Thompson
(eds)
(1985)

Religion and ideology. Manchester: Manchester University Press/ Open University.

Bonner, K.
(1996)

Review of P. Clancy *et al.* (eds) *Irish society: Sociological perspectives* in *Irish Journal of Sociology* 6. pp.212–20.

Boston Women's
Health Book
Collective
(1973)

Our bodies, ourselves: A book by and for women. Boston: Boston Women's Health Book Collective.

Bourdieu, P.
(1984)

Distinction: A social critique of the judgement of taste. London: Routledge and Kegan Paul.

Box, S.
(1983)

Crime, power and mystification. London: Tavistock.

Boylan, T.
(1996)

'Rural industrialisation and rural poverty' in C. Curtin *et al.* (eds) *Poverty in rural Ireland*. Dublin: Oak Tree.

Boylan, T. and
T. Foley
(1992)

Political economy and colonial Ireland: The propagation and ideological function of economic discourse in the nineteenth century. London: Routledge and Kegan Paul.

Brady, J.
(2001)

'The heart of the city: commercial Dublin, c.1890–1915' in J. Brady and A. Simms (eds) *Dublin through space and time (c.900–1900)*. Dublin: Four Courts.

Breathnach, P.   'Rural industrialisation in the West of Ireland' in M. Healey and
(1985)   B. Ilbery (eds) *The industrialisation of the countryside*. Norwich: Geo.

Breathnach, P.   'Women's employment and peripheralisation: The case of
(1993)   Ireland's branch plant economy', *Geoforum* 24(1). pp.19–29.

Breathnach, P.   'Gender and employment in Irish tourism' in U. Kockel (ed.)
(1994)   *Culture, tourism and development: The case of Ireland*. Liverpool:
                    Liverpool University Press.

Breen, M.,   'Citizens, loopholes and maternity tourists: media frames in the
A. Haynes and   citizenship referendum' in M. Corcoran and M. Peillon (eds)
E. Devereux   *Uncertain Ireland: A sociological chronicle, 2003–2004*. Dublin:
(2006)   Institute of Public Administration.

Breen, R.,   *Understanding contemporary Ireland: State, class and
D. Hannan,   development in the Republic of Ireland*. London: Macmillan.
D. Rottman and
C. Whelan
(1990)

Breen, R. and   *Crime victimisation in the Republic of Ireland*. Dublin: Economic
D. Rottman   and Social Research Institute. [Paper no. 121].
(1985)

Breen, R. and   *Social mobility and social class in Ireland*. Dublin: Gill & Macmillan.
C. Whelan
(1996)

Breen, R. and   'Social mobility in Ireland: a comparative analysis' in A. Heath,
C. Whelan   R. Breen, and C. Whelan (eds) *Ireland North and South:
(1999)   Perspectives from social science*. Oxford: Oxford.

Brennan, E.   '*Fair City*: A case study in the proletarianisation of cultural
(2004)   production' in *Irish Journal of Sociology*, Special Issue on the
                    Media, Vol. 13(2). pp.66–83.

Brett, D.   *The construction of heritage*. Cork: Cork University Press.
(1996)

Brody, H.   *Inishkillane: Change and decline in the west of Ireland*. London:
(1986)   Faber and Faber.

Brown, S. and A. Patterson (2000)
'Knick-knack Paddy-whack, give a pub a theme'. *Journal of Marketing Management* 16. pp.647–62.

Buckingham, D. (2000)
After the death of childhood: Growing up in the age of the electronic media. Cambridge Polity.

Buckley, M. (1997)
'Sitting on your politics: the Irish among the British and the women among the Irish' in J. Mac Laughlin (ed.) *Location and dislocation in contemporary Irish society: Emigration and Irish identities.* Cork: Cork University Press.

Bunton, R. (1998)
'Inequalities in late-modern health care' in A. Petersen and C. Waddell (eds) *Health matters: A sociology of illness prevention and care.* Buckingham: Open University Press.

Burke, S., C. Keenaghan, D. O'Donovan and B. Quirke (2004)
Health in Ireland: An unequal state. Dublin: Public Health Alliance Ireland.

Burnett, J. (1999)
Liquid pleasures: A social history of drinks in modern Britain. London: Routledge.

Butler, M. (2002)
Evaluation in the Irish health sector. [CPMR Discussion paper 21] Dublin: Institute of Public Administration.

Butler, S. (2002)
Alcohol, drugs and health promotion in modern Ireland. Dublin: Institute of Public Administration.

Byrne, A. and Leonard M. (eds) (1997)
Women and Irish society: A sociological reader. Belfast: Beyond the Pale.

Byrne, A. and R. Lentin (eds) (2000)
(Re)searching women: Feminist research methodologies in the social sciences in Ireland. Dublin: Institute of Public Administration.

Byrne, A., R. Edmondson and T. Varley (2001)
'Introduction to the third edition' in C. Arensberg and S. Kimball, *Family and community in Ireland.* Ennis: CLASP.

Calhoun, C.   'Social theory and the public sphere' in B. Turner (ed.) *The*
(1996)   *Blackwell companion to social theory*. Oxford: Blackwell.

Callan, T. and   *Measuring trends in poverty over time*. Dublin: Economic and
B. Nolan   Social Research Institute [Working paper no. 7].
(1988)

Callan, T. and   'Poverty and policy' in S. Healy and B. Reynolds (eds) *Social policy*
B. Nolan   *in Ireland*. Dublin: Oak Tree.
(1998)

Callan, T. *et al*   *Poverty in the 1990s: Evidence from the Living in Ireland Survey*.
(1996)   Dublin: Oak Tree.

Campbell, C.   *The romantic ethic and the spirit of modern consumerism*. Oxford:
(1987)   Blackwell.

Campbell, H.   'Masculine hegemony and leisure sites' in P. Share (ed.)
and E. Phillips   *Communication and culture in rural areas*. Wagga Wagga (NSW):
(1995)   Centre for Rural Social Research, Charles Sturt University.

Carey, M.   'Women in non-traditional employment in Northern Ireland: a
(1997)   marginalised form of femininity' in A. Byrne and M. Leonard (eds)
                   Women in Irish society: A sociological reader. Belfast: Beyond the Pale.

Cassidy, E.   'Modernity and religion in Ireland, 1980–2000' in E. Cassidy
(2002)   (ed.) *Measuring Ireland: Discerning values and beliefs*. Dublin: Veritas.

Cassidy, T.   'Sober for the sake of the children: a discussion of alcohol use
(1997)   amongst Irish women' in M. Leonard and A. Byrne (eds)
                   Women in Ireland: A sociological profile. Belfast: Beyond the Pale.

Cassidy, T.   'Just two will do' in M. Peillon and E. Slater (eds) *Encounters*
(1998)   *with modern Ireland: A sociological chronicle 1995–1996*.
                   Dublin: Institute of Public Administration.

Castles, S. and   *The age of migration: International population movements in*
M. Miller   *the modern world*. Basingstoke: Palgrave.
(1998)

Chatterton, P.   *Urban nightscapes: Youth cultures, pleasure spaces and corporate*
and R. Hollands   *power*. London: Routledge.
(2003)

Clancy, P.
(1982)
Participation in higher education: A national survey. Dublin: Higher Education Authority.

Clancy, P.
(1988)
Who goes to college? A second survey of participation in higher education. Dublin: Higher Education Authority.

Clancy, P.
(1995)
'Education in the Republic of Ireland: the project of modernity?' in P. Clancy *et al.* (eds) *Irish society: Sociological perspectives.* Dublin: Institute of Public Administration in association with the Sociological Association of Ireland.

Clancy, P.
(2001)
College entry in focus: A fourth national survey of access to higher education. Dublin: Higher Education Authority.

Clark, J. and
M. Diani (eds)
(1996)
Alain Touraine. London: Falmer.

Clarkson, L. and
M. Crawford
(2001)
Feast and famine: A history of food and nutrition in Ireland 1500–1920. Oxford University Press.

Cleary, A.
(2005)
'Death rather than disclosure: struggling to be a real man' in *Irish Journal of Sociology,* Special issue on Masculinities, Vol. 14(2). pp.155–176.

Cleary, A.
(1997)
'Gender differences in mental health in Ireland' in A. Cleary and M. Treacy (eds) *The sociology of health and illness in Ireland.* Dublin: University College Dublin Press.

Cleary, A.,
M. Corbett,
M. Galvin and
J. Wall
(2004)
Young men on the margins. Dublin: Katherine Howard Foundation.

Clegg, M.
(2003)
'Trusteeship: A model in progress' in N. Prendergast and L. Monahan (eds) *Reimagining the Catholic school.* Dublin: Veritas.

Clinch, P., F.
Convery and
B. Walsh
(2002)
After the Celtic Tiger: Challenges ahead. Dublin: O'Brien.

Cloke, P. and N. Thrift (1990)	'Class and change in rural Britain' in T. Marsden, P. Lowe and S. Whatmore (eds) *Critical perspectives on rural change*. London: Fulton.

Coakley, J. (1998)   'Sports and religion: is it a promising combination?' in *Sport in society: Issues and controversies*. Boston: McGraw-Hill.

Coleman, D. (1992)   'The demographic transition in Ireland in international context' in J. Goldthorpe and C. Whelan (eds) *The development of industrial society in Ireland*. Oxford: Oxford University Press/ The British Academy.

Collins, C. and E. Shelley (1997)   'Social class differences in lifestyle and health characteristics in Ireland' in A. Cleary and M. Treacy (eds) *The sociology of health and illness in Ireland*. Dublin: University College Dublin Press.

Collins, G. (2006)   'Germs, globalisation and gender: the making of a food scare' in M. Corcoran & M. Peillon (eds) *Uncertain Ireland: A sociological chronicle, 2003–2004*. Dublin: Institute of Public Administration.

Commins, P. (1985)   'Rural community development — approaches and issues'. *Social Studies* 8. pp.165–78.

Commins, P. (1995)   'The European Community and the Irish rural economy' in P. Clancy *et al.* (eds) *Irish Society: Sociological perspectives*. Dublin: Institute of Public Administration in association with the Sociological Association of Ireland.

Commins, P. (1996)   'Agricultural production and the future of small-scale farming' in C. Curtin *et al.* (eds) *Poverty in rural Ireland*. Dublin: Oak Tree.

Commins, P. and M. Keane (1994)   *Developing the rural economy: Problems, programmes and prospects*. Report no. 97. Dublin: National Economic and Social Council.

Commission on the Points System (1999)   *Consultative process: Background document*. Dublin: Stationery Office.

Competition Authority (1998)   *Interim study on the liquor licensing laws and other barriers to entry and their impact on competition in the retail drinks market*. Dublin: Competition Authority.

Coniffe, D.   *Alcohol use in Ireland: Some economic and social implications.*
(1993)   Dublin: Economic and Social Research Institute [Report no. 160].

Connell, R.   *Gender and power: Society, the person and sexual politics.* Sydney:
(1987)   Allen and Unwin.

Connolly, B.   'Women in community education and development — liberation
(1997)   or domestication?' in A. Byrne and M. Leonard (eds) *Women and*
                   Irish society: A sociological reader. Belfast: Beyond the Pale.

Connolly, L.   'The women's movement in Ireland 1970–1995 — a social
(1996)   movements analysis'. *Irish Journal of Feminist Studies* 1 (1). pp.43–77.

Connolly, L.   *The Irish women's movement: From revolution to devolution.*
(2002)   Basingstoke: Palgrave.

Conway, B.   'Foreigners, faith and fatherland: the historical origins,
(2006)   development and present status of Irish sociology'. *Sociological*
                   Origins 5 (1) [special supplement] pp.5–35. [available at
                   www.sociological-origins.com].

Cook, F. *et al.*   'Media effects and agenda setting'. *Public Opinion Quarterly,*
(1983)   Vol. 47 (1) pp.16–35.

Corcoran, F.   *RTÉ and the globalisation of Irish television.* London: Intellect.
(2004)

Corcoran, M.   'Informalization of metropolitan labour forces: the case of Irish
(1991)   immigrant in the New York construction industry'. *Irish Journal*
                   of Sociology 1. pp.31–51.

Corcoran, M.   *Irish illegals: Transients between two societies.* Westport,
(1993)   CT/London: Greenwood.

Corcoran, M.   'Heroes of the diaspora?' in M. Peillon and E. Slater (eds)
(1998)   *Encounters with modern Ireland.* Dublin: Institute of Public
                   Administration.

Corcoran, M.   'Mall City' in E. Slater and M. Peillon (eds) *Memories of the*
(2000)   *present: A sociological chronicle of Ireland, 1997–1998.* Dublin:
                   Institute of Public Administration.

Corcoran, M.   'On the waterfront' in M. Corcoran and M. Peillon (eds)
(2002a)   *Ireland unbound: A turn of the century chronicle.* [Irish Sociological
                   Chronicles, vol. 3]. Dublin: Institute of Public Administration.

Corcoran, M.   'The process of migration and the reinvention of self: The
(2002b)   experiences of returning Irish emigrants.' *Éire-Ireland: Journal of
                   Irish inter-disciplinary studies*, 37 (1–2). pp.175–191.

Corcoran, M.   'Global cosmopolities: issues of self-identity and collective
(2003)   identity among the transnational Irish elite'. *Études Irlandaises*,
                   28(2) pp.135–150.

Corcoran, M.   'Portrait of the absent father: the impact of non-residency on
(2005)   developing and maintaining a fathering role'. *Irish Journal of
                   Sociology*, Special issue on Masculinities, Vol. 14(2) pp.134–154.

Corcoran, M.,   'Ties that bind? The social fabric of life in the new suburbs' in
J. Gray and   T. Fahey, H. Russell and C. Whelan (eds) *The best of times?
M. Peillon   The social impact of the Celtic Tiger*. Dublin: Institute of Public
(2007)   Administration.

Cormack, P.   'Angels, bells, television and Ireland: the place of the Angelus
(2005)   broadcast in the Republic in *Media Culture and Society*, 27(2)
                   pp.271–287.

Corrigan, Á.   Irish immigrant entrepreneurs in the United States: Ethnic
(2006)   strategies and transnational identities. Unpublished PhD thesis,
                   Department of Sociology, NUI Maynooth.

Corrigan, P.   'Backstage dressing: Clothing and the urban family.' Unpublished
(1988)   PhD thesis, Department of Sociology, Trinity College Dublin.

Corrigan, P.   *The sociology of consumption: An introduction*. London: Sage.
(1997)

Corsaro, W.   *The sociology of childhood*. Second edition. California: Pine
(2005)   Forge Press.

Coulter, C.   *Are religious cults dangerous?* Cork: Mercier.
(1984)

Coulter, C.   *Contemporary Northern Irish society: An introduction*. London:
(1999)   Pluto.

Coulter, C. and   *The end of Irish history? Critical reflections on the Celtic Tiger*.
S. Coleman   Manchester: Manchester University Press.
(eds)
(2003)

Council of
Europe (2001)
Recent demographic developments in Europe, 2001. Strasbourg:
Council of Europe.

Courtney, D.
(1995)
'Demographic structure and change in the Republic of Ireland
and Northern Ireland' in P. Clancy *et al.* (eds) *Irish society:
Sociological perspectives.* Dublin: Institute of Public Administration
in association with the Sociological Association of Ireland.

Courtney, D.
(1997)
'The quantification of Irish migration'. Paper to conference *The
scattering: Ireland and the Irish diaspora: A comparative perspective.*
Irish Centre for Migration Studies, University College Cork,
September.

Courtney, D.
(2000)
'A quantification of Irish migration with particular emphasis on
the 1980s and 1990s' in A. Bielenberg (ed.) *The Irish diaspora.*
Harlow: Pearson Education.

Coveney, J.
(2006)
Food, morals and meaning: The pleasures and anxieties of eating.
London: Routledge.

Coyle, C.
(1994)
'Administrative capacity and the implementation of EU
environmental policy in Ireland' in S. Baker *et al.* (eds)
Protecting the periphery. Ilford: Cass.

Crawford, E.
(1995)
'Food retailing, nutrition and health in Ireland, 1839–1989: one
hundred and fifty years of eating' in A. den Hartog (ed.) *Food,
technology, science and marketing: European diet in the
twentieth century.* East Lothian: Tuckwell.

Cresser, F.
(2001)
'Women's experiences of on-line e-zine publication' in *Media
Culture and Society,* Vol. 23: 457–473.

Cresswell, R.
(1969)
Une communaute rurale d'Irlande. Paris: Institut de Ethnographie.

Crompton, R.
(1998)
Class and stratification: An introduction to current debates.
Cambridge: Polity.

Cronin, M.
(2000)
Across the lines: Travel, language, translation. Cork: Cork
University Press.

Crotty, R.
(1974)
The cattle crisis and the small farmer. Mullingar: National Land
League.

Crotty, R.   'Modernisation and land reform: real or cosmetic, the Irish case'.
(1983)   *Journal of Peasant Studies* 11 (1) pp.101–16.

Crotty, R.   *Ireland in crisis: A study in capitalist colonial undevelopment.* Dingle:
(1986)   Brandon.

Crotty, P.   'Food and class' in J. Germov and L. Williams (eds) *A sociology*
(1999)   *of food and nutrition: The social appetite.* Melbourne: Oxford.

Crow, G. and   *Community life: An introduction to local social relations.* London:
G. Allen   Harvester Wheatsheaf.
(1994)

Crowley, E.   'Making a difference? Female employment and multinationals in
(1997)   the Republic of Ireland' in A. Byrne and M. Leonard (eds) *Women*
    and Irish society: A sociological reader. Belfast: Beyond the Pale.

CSO [Central   *That was then, this is now: Change in Ireland 1949–1999.*
Statistics Office]   Dublin: Central Statistics Office.
(2000)

CSO [Central   *Population and migration estimates, April 2002.* Dublin: Central
Statistics Office]   Statistics Office [Ref 183/2002].
(2002a)

CSO [Central   *Census 2002: Principal socio-economic results.* Dublin: Central
Statistics Office]   Statistics Office. [Ref. Pm 1037].
(2002b)

CSO [Central   *Ireland North and South: A statistical profile, 2003 edition.*
Statistics Office]   Dublin: Central Statistics Office.
(2006)

CSO [Central   *Irish life tables no. 14, 2001–2003.* Dublin: Central Statistics
Statistics Office]   Office. [Ref. 118/2004].
(2004a)

CSO [Central   *Quarterly national household survey: Crime and victimisation,*
Statistics Office]   *Quarter 4, 1998 and 2003.* Dublin: Central Statistics Office.
(2004b)   [Ref. 150/2004].

CSO [Central   *Census 2002. Volume 12: Religion.* Dublin: Central Statistics
Statistics Office]   Office. [available at www.cso.ie/census/documents/vol12_entire.pdf].
(2004c)

CSO [Central Statistics Office] (2006a)
Deaths from principal causes registered in the years 1998 to 2005. Dublin: Central Statistics Office. [available at www.cso.ie/statistics/principalcausesofdeath.htm].

CSO [Central Statistics Office] (2006b)
Women and men in Ireland 2006. Dublin: Central Statistics Office. [Ref. PM A6/2508].

CSO [Central Statistics Office] (2006c)
Statistical yearbook of Ireland 2006. Dublin: Stationery Office. [Ref. Prn A6/1071]. [available at www.cso.ie/releasespublications/statistical_yearbook_ireland_2006.htm.

Cuff, E., W. Sharrock and D. Francis (1998)
Perspectives in sociology. London: Routledge.

Cullen, L. (1987)
An economic history of Ireland since 1600. London: Batsford.

Curran, C. (1996)
'Fianna Fáil and the origins of the Irish Press'. *Irish Communications Review* 6: pp.7–17.

Curry, J. (2003)
Irish social services. Dublin: Institute of Public Administration.

Curtin, C. (1988)
'Social order, interpersonal relations and disputes in a West of Ireland community' in M. Tomlinson, T. Varley and C. McCullagh (eds) *Whose law and order? Aspects of crime and social control in Irish society.* Belfast: Sociological Association of Ireland.

Curtin, C. (1996)
'Back to the future? Communities and rural poverty' in C. Curtin *et al.* (eds) *Poverty in rural Ireland.* Dublin: Oak Tree.

Curtin, C., T. Haase and H. Tovey (eds) (1996)
Poverty in rural Ireland: A political economy perspective. Dublin: Oak Tree.

Curtin, C. and C. Ryan (1989)
'Clubs, pubs and private houses in a Clare town' in C. Curtin and T. Wilson (eds) *Ireland from below.* Galway: Galway University Press.

Curtin, C. and
T. Varley
(1986)
'Bringing industry to a small town in the West of Ireland'.
Sociologia Ruralis 26 (2). pp.170–85.

Curtin, C. and
T. Varley
(1995)
'Community action and the state' in P. Clancy *et al.* (eds)
Irish society: Sociological perspectives. Dublin: Institute
of Public Administration.

Curtin, C. and
T. Wilson
(1989)
Ireland from below: Social change and local communities.
Galway: Galway University Press.

CWC
[Community
Workers
Cooperative]
(1996)
*Partnership in action: The role of community development and
partnership in Ireland*. Galway: Community Workers Cooperative.

Daly, M.
(1997)
*The spirit of earnest inquiry: The Statistical and Social Inquiry
Society of Ireland 1847–1997*. Dublin: Institute of Public
Administration.

Daly, M.
(1998)
'The Statistical and Social Inquiry Society of Ireland' in
K. Kennedy (ed.) *From famine to feast: Economic and social change
in Ireland 1847–1997*. Dublin: Institute of Public Administration.

Daly, M. and
M. Leonard
(2002)
Against all odds: Family life on a low income in Ireland. Dublin:
Combat Poverty Agency.

Daniel, A.
(1998)
'Trust and medical authority' in A. Petersen and C. Waddell
(eds) *Health matters: A sociology of illness, prevention and care*.
Buckingham: Open University Press.

Davies, B.
(1990)
Frogs and snails and feminist tales: Preschool children and gender.
Sydney: Allen and Unwin.

Davis, A. and
J. George
(1993)
States of health: Health and illness in Australia. Sydney:
Harper Collins.

Day, G.
(1998)
'A community of communities? Similarity and difference in
Welsh rural community studies'. *Economic and Social Review*
29(3). pp.233–258.

De Botton, A.
(2004)

Status anxiety. London: Hamish Hamilton.

de Guistino, D.
(1995)

'Finding an archbishop: the Whigs and Richard Whately in 1831'. *Church History* 64(2). pp.218–236.

Delaney, E.
(1998)

'State, politics and demography: The case of Irish emigration, 1921–71'. *Irish Political Studies* 13, pp.25–49.

Delanty, G.
(1996)

'Beyond the nation-state: national identity and citizenship in a multicultural society. A response to Rex'. *Sociological Research Online* 1(3). [http://www.socresonline.org.uk/1/3/1.html]

Department of
An Taoiseach
(2006)

Report on active citizenship consultation process. Dublin: Task Force on Active Citizenship, Department of An Taoiseach.

Department of
Arts, Culture and
the Gaeltacht
(1995)

Active or passive? Broadcasting in the future tense. [Green paper on broadcasting]. Dublin: Stationery Office.

Department of
Education
(1965)

Investment in education. Report of the survey team appointed by the Minister for Education in October, 1962. Dublin: Stationery Office.

Department of
Education and
Science
(1998)

Adult education in an era of lifelong learning (Green paper on adult education). Dublin: Stationery Office.

Department of
Education and
Science
(2000)

Learning for life: White paper on adult education. Dublin: Stationery Office.

Department of
Education and
Science
(2007)

Key statistics about the Department's customers. [http://www.education.ie/home]

Department of
Foreign Affairs
(1995)

Facts about Ireland. Dublin: Department of Foreign Affairs.

Department of Health and Children (2002a)
Acute hospital bed capacity: A national review. Dublin: Department of Health and Children.

Department of Health and Children (2002b)
Quality and fairness: A health system for you. Dublin: Stationery Office.

Department of Health and Children (2002c)
Traveller health: A national strategy 2002–2005. Dublin: Department of Health and Children

Department of Health and Children (2002d)
Strategic taskforce on alcohol — Interim report. Dublin: [http://www.doh.ie/pdfdocs/stfa.pdf]

Department of Health and Children (2004)
Strategic task force on alcohol: Second report. Dublin: Health Promotion Unit, Department of Health and Children.

De Tona, C. (2004)
"I remember when years ago in Italy": Nine Italian women in Dublin tell the diaspora'. *Women's Studies International Forum*, 27(4). Special Issue: Representing Migrant Women in Ireland and in the EU. pp.315–334.

Devereux, E. (1988)
Muintir na Tire: The theory and practice of community development 1931–88. Unpublished MA thesis, National University of Ireland, Galway.

Devereux, E. (2003)
Understanding the Media. London: Sage Publications.

Devine, F. (1997)
Social class in America and Britain. Edinburgh: Edinburgh University Press.

Devine, F., M. Savage and R. Crompton (eds) (2005)
Rethinking class: Culture, identities and lifestyle. Basingstoke: Palgrave Macmillan.

Devlin, J.
(1997)

'The state of health in Ireland' in J. Robins (ed.) *Reflections on health: Commemorating fifty years of the Department of Health 1947–1997*. Dublin: Department of Health.

Dillon, L.
(2001)

Drug use among prisoners: An exploratory study. Dublin: Health Research Board.

Dixon, J.
(2002)

Changing chicken: Chooks, cooks and culinary culture. Sydney: University of New South Wales Press.

Doorley, P.
(1998)

'Health status' in E. McAuliffe and L. Joyce (eds) *A healthier future? Managing healthcare in Ireland*. Dublin: Institute of Public Administration.

Drudy, P.
(1995)

'From protectionism to enterprise: A review of Irish industrial policy' in A. Burke (ed.) *Enterprise and the Irish economy*. Dublin: Oak Tree.

Drudy, S.
(1991)

'Developments in the sociology of education in Ireland 1966–1991'. *Irish Journal of Sociology* 1 pp.107–127.

Drudy, S. and
K. Lynch
(1993)

Schools and society in Ireland. Dublin: Gill & Macmillan.

Dunlevy, M.
(1989)

Dress in Ireland. London: Batsford.

Durkheim, E.
(1964)

The rules of sociological method. New York: The Free Press.

Dwyer, M. and
P. Taaffe
(1998)

'Nursing in 21st century Ireland: Opportunities for transformation' in A. Leahy and M. Wiley (eds) *The Irish health system in the 21st century*. Dublin: Oak Tree.

Edley, N. and
M. Wetherell
(1995)

Men in perspective: Practice, power and identity. London: Prentice Hall.

Edmondson, R.
(1997)

'Older people and life-course construction' in A. Cleary and M. Treacy (eds) *The sociology of health and illness in Ireland*. Dublin: University College Dublin Press.

Eipper, C.
(1986)
The ruling trinity: A community study of church, state and business in Ireland. Aldershot: Gower.

Entwistle, J.
(2000a)
The fashioned body: Fashion, dress and modern social theory. Cambridge: Polity.

Entwistle, J.
(2000b)
'Fashion as culture industry'. *Consumers, commodities, and consumption newsletter* 1(2).
[http://socrates.berkeley.edu/~nalinik/newsletter.html]

Entwistle, J.
and E. Wilson
(eds)
(2001)
Body Dressing, Oxford: Berg.

ESRI [Economic
and Social
Research Institute]
(2007)
'Irish economy'. Available at http://www.ersi.ie/irish_economy/

Etzioni, A.
(1995)
The spirit of community. London: Fontana.

Etzioni, A.
(1997)
The new golden rule. London: Profile.

Euromosaic
(1996)
The production and reproduction of the minority language groups in the European Union. Luxembourg: Office for Official Publications of the European Communities.

Evans, P.
(1995)
Embedded autonomy. Princeton: Princeton University Press.

Fagan, H.
(1995)
Culture, politics and Irish school dropouts. Westport CT/London: Bergin and Garvey.

Fahey, T.
(1987)
'Nuns in the Catholic Church in Ireland in the nineteenth century' in M. Cullen (ed.) *Girls don't do honours: Irish women in education in the 19th and 20th centuries.* Dublin: Women's Education Bureau.

Fahey, T.
(1992a)
'Catholicism in Ireland' in P. Clancy, M. Kelly, J. Wiatr and R. Zoltaniecki (eds) *Ireland and Poland: Comparative perspectives.* Dublin: Department of Sociology, University College Dublin.

Fahey, T.
(1992b)
'State, family and compulsory schooling in Ireland'. *Economic and Social Review* 23(4). pp.369–95.

Fahey, T.
(1994)
'Catholicism and industrial society in Ireland' in J. Goldthorpe and C. Whelan (eds) *The development of industrial society in Ireland.* Oxford: Oxford University Press/The British Academy.

Fahey, T
(1998a)
'Progress or decline? Demographic change in the political context' in W. Crotty and D. Schmitt (eds) *Ireland and the politics of change.* London/New York: Longman.

Fahey, T.
(1998b)
'Housing and social exclusion' in S. Healy and B. Reynolds (eds) *Social policy in Ireland: Principles, practice and problems.* Dublin: Oak Tree.

Fahey, T.
(2002a)
'The family economy in the development of welfare regimes: A case study'. *European Sociological Review* 18(1). pp.51–64.

Fahey, T.
(2002b)
'Is atheism increasing? Ireland and Europe compared' in E. Cassidy (ed.) *Measuring Ireland: Discerning values and beliefs.* Dublin: Veritas.

Fahey, T. and
J. Fitz Gerald
(1997)
Welfare implications of demographic trends. Dublin: Oak Tree/ Combat Poverty Agency.

Fahey, T. and
R. Layte
(2007)
'Family and Sexuality' in T. Fahey, H. Russell and C.T. Whelan (eds) *The best of times? The social impact of the Celtic Tiger.* Dublin: Institute of Public Administration.

Fahey T. and
H. Russell
(2001)
Family formation in Ireland: Trends, data needs and implications. Dublin: ESRI.

Fahey, T.,
B. Hayes and
R. Sinnott
(2005)
Conflict and consensus: A study of values and attitudes in the Republic of Ireland and Northern Ireland. Dublin: Institute of Public Administration.

Fahy, P.
(1978)
Dependency in the Irish mass communications system (an exploratory study). Unpublished paper read at the Sociological Association of Ireland Conference, Cork.

Fairweather, J.   *Public drinking and social organisation in Methven and Mt Somers.*
and H. Campbell   Canterbury (NZ): Agribusiness and Economics Research Unit,
(1990)   Lincoln University.

Fallon, B.   *An age of innocence: Irish culture 1930–1960.* Dublin: Gill &
(1998)   Macmillan.

Fanning, B.   *Racism and social change in the Republic of Ireland.* Manchester:
(2002)   Manchester University Press.

Farrell, F. and   *Responding to racism in Ireland.* Dublin: Veritas.
P. Watt (eds)
(2001)

Fay, I.   *Beyond belief: A mind-blowing pilgrimage through religious Ireland.*
(1997)   Dublin: Hot Press.

Featherstone, M. 'Lifestyle and consumer culture'. *Theory, Culture and Society*
(1987)   4(1). pp.55–70.

Featherstone, M. Travel, migration and images of social life' in W. Gungwu (ed.)
(1997)   *Global history and migrations.* Boulder: Westview.

Ferguson, H.   *Strengthening families through fathers: developing policy and*
and F. Hogan   *practice in relation to vulnerable fathers and their families.*
(2004)   Waterford: The Centre for Social and Family Research,
                  Waterford Institute of Technology.

Ferriter, D.   *A nation of extremes: The Pioneers in twentieth-century Ireland.*
(1999)   Dublin: Irish Academic Press.

Findlater, A.   *Findlaters: the story of a Dublin merchant family, 1774–2001.*
(2001)   Dublin: Farmar.

Fine, R.   'Civil society and violence: a critique of John Keane'. *Soundings*
(2000)   16. pp.113–121.

Fiske, J.   'Cultural studies and the culture of everyday life' in L. Grossberg,
(1992)   C. Nelson and P. Treichler (eds) *Cultural studies.* London:
                  Routledge.

Fiske, J., B.   *Myths of Oz: Reading Australian popular culture.* Sydney: Allen
Hodge and   & Unwin.
G. Turner
(1987)

Fitz Gerald, J.
(2002)
'Ireland — a multicultural economy' in W. Crotty and D.
Schmitt (eds) *Ireland on the world stage*. Harlow: Longman.

Flanagan, S.
and C. Conlon
(eds)
(1999)
The business of tourism: Urban-led growth? Dublin: Blackhall.

Flynn, B.
(2006)
*The blame game: Rethinking Ireland's sustainable development
and environmental performance.* Dublin: Irish Academic Press.

Foucault, M.
(1973)
The birth of the clinic: An archaeology of medical perception. New
York: Vintage.

Foucault, M.
(1980)
The history of sexuality. Vol 1. A introduction. New York: Vintage.

Fox, N.
(1998)
'Postmodernism and "health"' in A. Petersen and C. Waddell
(eds) *Health matters: A sociology of illness, prevention and care.*
Buckingham: Open University Press.

Fox, R.
(1978)
The Tory Islanders: A people of the Celtic fringe. Cambridge:
Cambridge University Press.

Frank A.
(1967)
'The development of underdevelopment'. *Monthly Review,*
September. pp.17–30.

Franklin, A.
(1999)
Animals and modern cultures. London: Sage.

Friel, S. &
C. Conlon
(2004)
Food poverty and policy. Dublin: Combat Poverty
Agency/Crosscare/St Vincent de Paul. [available at
www.cpa.ie/health/foodpoverty/].

Friel, S.,
O. Walsh and
D. McCarthy
(2004)
The financial cost of healthy eating in Ireland. [Working paper
04/01]. Dublin: Combat Poverty Agency.

Fuller, L.
(2002)
Irish Catholicism since 1950: The undoing of a culture. Dublin:
Gill & Macmillan.

Fuller, L.
(2005)
'Religion, politics and socio-cultural change in twentieth-
century Ireland'. *The European Legacy,* 10(1). pp.41–54.

Furedi, F. (1997)	*Population and development: A critical introduction*. Cambridge: Polity.
Galligan, Y. (1998a)	*Women and politics in contemporary Ireland*. London: Pinter.
Galligan, Y. (1998b)	'The changing role of women' in W. Crotty and D. Schmitt (eds) *Ireland and the politics of change*. London/New York: Longman.
Gamson, W. and A. Modigliani (1989)	'Media discourse and public opinion on nuclear power: a constructivist approach' , *American Journal of Sociology*, 95(1). pp.1–37.
Garavan, M. (2006)	'Seeking a real argument' in M. Corcoran & M. Peillon (eds) *Uncertain Ireland: A sociological chronicle, 2003–2004*. Dublin: Institute of Public Administration.
Garvin, T. (1982)	'Theory, culture and Fianna Fáil — a review' in M. Kelly *et al.* (eds) *Power, conflict and inequality*. Dublin: Turoe.
Garvin, T. (1998)	'Patriots and republicans: an Irish evolution' in W. Crotty and D. Schmitt (eds) *Ireland and the politics of change*. London/New York: Longman.
Garvin, T. (2004)	*Preventing the future: Why was Ireland so poor for so long?* Dublin: Gill and Macmillan.
Garvin, T. and A. Hess (2006)	'Introduction: Tyranny in Ireland?' in G. de Beaumont *Ireland: Social, political and religious*. Cambridge [MA]: Harvard University Press.
Geary, R. (1951)	'Irish economic development since the Treaty'. *Studies* Vol. Xl. No. 160. pp.399–419.
Geddes, M. (1998)	*Local partnership: A successful strategy for social cohesion?* Dublin: European Foundation for the Improvement of Living and Working Conditions.
Gellner, E. (1983)	*Nations and nationalism*. Oxford: Blackwell.
Gibbon, P. (1973)	'Arensberg and Kimball revisited'. *Economy and Society* 4. pp.479–98.

Gibbons, L.
(1996)

Transformations in Irish culture. Cork: Cork University Press.

Giddens, A.
(1985)

The nation-state and violence. Cambridge: Polity.

Giddens, A.
(1991)

Modernity and self-identity: Self and society in the late modern age. Cambridge: Polity.

Giddens, A.
(2006)

Sociology. Cambridge: Polity.

Gillespie, M.
(1995)

Television, ethnicity and cultural change. London: Routledge.

Gmelch, G.
and S. Gmelch
(1976)

'The emergence of an ethnic group'. *Anthropological Quarterly* 49. pp.225–38.

Gmelch, S.
(1989)

'From poverty subculture to political lobby: the Traveller Rights movement in Ireland' in C. Curtin and T. Wilson (eds) *Ireland from below: Social change and local communities*. Galway: Galway University Press.

Goldblatt, D.
(1996)

Social theory and the environment. Cambridge: Polity.

Goldthorpe, J.
and others
(1968–9)

The affluent worker in the class structure. 3 vols. Cambridge: Cambridge University Press.

Goldthorpe, J.,
L. O'Dowd and
P. O'Connor
(2002)

'A sociology of Ireland: a review symposium'. *Irish Journal of Sociology* 11(1). pp 97–111.

Gould, S.
(1997)

The mismeasure of man. Harmondsworth: Penguin.

Granberg, L.,
I. Kovách and
H. Tovey (eds)
(2001)

Europe's green ring. Aldershot: Ashgate

Gray, B.
(1997)
'Unmasking Irishness: Irish women, the Irish nation and the Irish diaspora' in J. Mac Laughlin (ed.) *Location and dislocation in contemporary Irish society: Emigration and Irish identities*. Cork: Cork University Press.

Greeley, A.
(1999)
'The religions of Ireland' in A. Heath, R. Breen and C. Whelan (eds) *Ireland north and south: Perspectives from social science*. Oxford: Oxford University Press.

Gripsrud, J.
(1995)
The Dynasty years: Hollywood television and critical media studies. London: Routledge.

Guinnane, T.
(1997)
The vanishing Irish: Households, migration and the rural economy in Ireland, 1850–1914. Princeton: Princeton University Press.

Guiomard, C.
(1995)
The Irish disease — and how to cure it. Common sense economics for a competitive world. Dublin: Oak Tree.

Gunning, M.
(1997)
'Children and television pleasure' in M. Kelly and B. O'Connor (eds) *Media audiences in Ireland: Power and cultural identity*. Dublin: University College Dublin Press.

Habermas, J.
(1971)
Towards a rational society. London: Heinemann.

Habermas, J.
(1987)
'Life-forms, morality and the task of the philosopher' in P. Dews (ed.) *Autonomy and solidarity — Interviews with Jurgen Habermas*. London: Verso.

Habermas, J.
(1989)
The structural transformation of the public sphere. Cambridge: Polity.

Hanlon, G.
(1991)
'The emigration of Irish accountants: economic restructuring and producer services in the periphery'. *Irish Journal of Sociology* 1. pp.52–65.

Hannan, D. and P. Commins
(1992)
'The significance of small-scale landholders in Ireland's socio-economic transformation' in J. Goldthorpe and C. Whelan (eds): *The development of industrial society in Ireland*. Oxford: Oxford University Press/The British Academy.

Hannan, D. and L. Katsiaouni
(1977)
Traditional families? From culturally prescribed to negotiated roles in farm families. Dublin: Economic and Social Research Institute.

Hannan, D., B. McCabe and S. McCoy. (1998) — *Trading qualifications for jobs: Overeducation and the Irish labour market*. Dublin: Oak Tree/ Economic and Social Research Institute.

Hannan, D., E. Smyth, J. McCullagh, R. O'Leary, D. McMahon (1996) — *Coeducation and gender equality: Exam performance, stress and personal development*. Dublin: Oak Tree/ Economic and Social Research Institute.

Hannigan, J. (2004) — 'Boom towns and cool cities: the perils and prospects of developing a distinctive urban brand in a global economy.' Paper presented at the Resurgent City Symposium, London School of Economics. April 19–21.

Hardiman, N. (1998) — 'Inequality and the representation of interests' in W. Crotty and D. Schmitt (eds) *Ireland and the politics of change*. London/New York: Longman.

Harris, L. (1984) — 'Class, community and sexual divisions in North Mayo' in C. Curtin *et al.* (eds) *Culture and ideology in Ireland*. Galway: Galway University Press.

Harris, L. (1989) — 'Women's responses to multinationals in Co. Mayo' in D. Elson and R. Pearson (eds) *Women's employment and multinationals in Europe*. London: Macmillan.

Haughton, J. (1995) — 'The historical background' in J. O'Hagan (ed.) *The economy of Ireland*. Dublin: Gill & Macmillan.

Haughton, J. (1998) — 'The dynamics of economic change' in W. Crotty and D. Schmitt (eds) *Ireland and the politics of change*. London/New York: Longman.

Hayes, M. (2006) — *Irish Travellers: Representations and realities*. Dublin: Liffey.

Hayles, N. (1995) — 'The life cycle of cyborgs' in C. Hay (ed.) *The cyborg handbook*. London: Routledge.

Haynes, A. (2004) — 'Social capital and regional growth' in M. Peillon and M. Corcoran (eds) *Place and non-place: The reconfiguration of Ireland*. Dublin: Institute of Public Administration.

Hazelkorn, E. (1980)   'Capital and the Irish question'. *Science and Society* 44(3). pp.326–356.

Hazelkorn, E. (1991)   'British labour and Irish capital: evidence from the 1980s' in Galway Labour History Group (ed.) *The emigrant experience: Papers presented at the second annual Mary Murray Weekend seminar.* Galway: Galway Labour History Group.

Hazelkorn, E. (1996)   'New technologies and changing work practices in the media industry: the case of Ireland'. *Irish Communications Review* 6: pp.28–38.

Hazelkorn, E. (1997)   'New digital technologies, work practices and cultural production in Ireland'. *Economic and Social Review* 28(3). pp.

Healy, T. (2004)   'Social capital: old hat or new insight?' *Irish Journal of Sociology*, 13 (1). pp.5–28.

Heath, A. and M. Savage (1995)   'Political alignments within the middle classes, 1972–89' in T. Butler and M. Savage (eds) *Social change and the middle classes.* London: University College London Press.

Hederman O'Brien, M. (1998)   'Healthcare — the context' in E. McAuliffe and L. Joyce (eds) *A healthier future? Managing healthcare in Ireland.* Dublin: Institute of Public Administration.

Heidensohn, F. (1989)   *Crime and society.* London: Macmillan.

Heidensohn, F. and M. Farrell (eds) (1991)   *Crime in Europe.* London: Routledge.

Hems, L. and F. Tonkiss (2000)   'Introduction' in F. Tonkis and A. Passey (eds) *Trust and civil society.* Basingstoke: Macmillan.

Hess, A. (2000)   'Introduction: after success — the politics of civil society'. *Soundings* 16. pp.90–95.

Hettne, B. (1990)   *Development theory and the three worlds.* Harlow: Longman.

Hewison, R.
(1987)

The heritage industry: Britain in a climate of decline. London:
Methuen.

Higgins, M.
(2004)

'Culture, democracy and public service broadcasting'
in M. Corcoran and M. O'Brien (eds) *Censorship
and the democratic state.* Dublin: Four Courts.

Hill, M.
(2005)

Bibliography of Martineau's writings on Ireland. [available at
www.sociological-origins.com/HMSSIrishCD.html].

Hillery, G.
(1955)

'Definitions of community: areas of agreement'. *Rural Sociology*
20(2). pp.111–23.

Hindley, R.
(1990)

The death of the Irish Language: A qualified obituary. London:
Routledge.

Hobsbawm, E.
(1990)

Nations and nationalism since 1780. Cambridge: Cambridge
University Press.

Hodgins, M.
and C. Kelleher
(1997)

'Health and well-being in social care workers'. *Women's Studies
Review* 5. pp.37–48.

Hoggart, K.,
H. Buller and
R. Black
(1995)

Rural Europe: Identity and change. London: Arnold.

Horgan, J.
(2001)

Irish media: A critical history since 1922. London/New York:
Routledge.

Hornsby-Smith,
M. and
Whelan, C.
(1994)

'Religious and moral values' in C. Whelan (ed.) *Values and social
change in Ireland.* Dublin: Gill & Macmillan.

Hourigan, N.
(2001)

Comparison of the campaigns for Raidio na Gaeltachta and TnaG.
Irish Sociological Research Monographs vol. 1. Maynooth:
Department of Sociology, NUI Maynooth.

Hourihane, A.
(2000)

She moves through the boom. Dublin: Sitric.

Hourihane, J.   *Ireland and the European Union: The first thirty years, 1973–2003.*
(ed.)   Dublin: Lilliput.
(2003)

Hout, M. and   'Dimensions of occupational mobility in the Republic of
J. Jackson   Ireland'. *European Sociological Review* 2 pp.114–37.
(1986)

Howkins, J.   *The creative economy: How people make money from ideas.*
(2002)   London: Penguin.

Hug, C.   *The politics of sexual morality in Ireland.* London: Macmillan.
(1999)

Hummon, D.   'Community attachment: local sentiment and sense of place' in
(1992)   I. Altman and S. Low (eds). *Place Attachment.* NY: Plenum
                 Press, 1992.

Humphreys, A.   *The new Dubliners: Urbanisation and the Irish family.* London:
(1966)   Routledge and Kegan Paul.

Humphreys, E.   'Social capital in disadvantaged neighbourhoods: a diversion
(2007)   from needs or a real contribution to the debate on area-based
                 regeneration?' *Irish Journal of Sociology*, NYP.

Hyde, A.   'The medicalisation of childbearing norms: Encounters between
(1997)   unmarried pregnant women and medical personnel in an Irish
                 context' in A. Cleary and M. Treacy (eds) *The sociology of health
                 and illness in Ireland.* Dublin: University College Dublin Press.

Hyde, A. and   *Understanding teenage sexuality in Ireland.* [Report no. 9].
E. Howlett   Dublin: Crisis Pregnancy Agency.
(2004)

Hyde, A.,   *Sociology for health professionals in Ireland.* Dublin: Institute of
M. Lohan and   Public Administration.
O. McDonnell
(2004)

IDA [Industrial Business sectors — pharmaceuticals and medical technologies.
Development   [http://www. idaireland.com]
Authority]
(2007)

Illich, I.
(1976)
Limits to medicine. London: Marion Boyars.

Inglehart, R.
(1977)
The silent revolution: Changing values and political styles among western publics. Princeton: Princeton University Press.

Inglis, T.
(1987)
Moral monopoly: The Catholic church in modern Irish society. Dublin: Gill & Macmillan.

Inglis, T.
(1998a)
Moral monopoly: The Rise and Fall of the Catholic church in modern Ireland. Dublin: University College Dublin Press.

Inglis, T.
(1998b)
Lessons in Irish sexuality. Dublin: University College Dublin Press.

Inglis, T.
(1998c)
'A religious frenzy' in M. Peillon and E. Slater (eds) *Encounters with modern Ireland*. Dublin: Institute of Public Administration.

Inglis, T.
(1998d)
'Foucault, Bourdieu and the field of Irish sexuality'. *Irish Journal of Sociology* 7. pp.5–28.

Inglis, T.
(1998e)
'From sexual repression to liberation?' In M. Peillon and E. Slater (eds) *Encounters with modern Ireland*. Dublin: Institute of Public Administration.

Inglis, T.
(2002)
'Pleasure pursuits' in M. Corcoran & M. Peillon (eds) *Ireland unbound: A turn of the century chronicle*. Dublin: Institute of Public Administration.

Institute of Public Health in Ireland
(2007)
Consultations in relation to all-Ireland Traveller health study. [available at www.publichealth.ie].

Irish Universities Nutrition Alliance
(2001)
North/South Ireland food consumption survey: Summary report on food and nutrient intakes, anthropometry, attitudinal data physical activity patterns. Dublin: Food Safety Promotion Board.

Jackson, J.
(1998)
Social science in Ireland. Unpublished paper for the Sociology Department, Trinity College Dublin.

Jackson, J.
(2004)

'Research policy and practice in Ireland: a historical perspective' in M. MacLachlan & M. Caball (eds) *Social science in a knowledge society: Research policy in Ireland*. Dublin: Liffey.

Jackson, J. and
U. Barry
(1989)

'Women's employment and multinationals in the Republic of Ireland: the creation of a new female labour force' in D. Elson and R. Pearson (eds) *Women's employment and multinationals in Europe*. London: Macmillan.

Jacobson, D.
(1989)

'Theorising Irish industrialisation: the case of the motor industry.' *Science and Society* 53 (2). pp.165–91.

Jamison, A.
et al.
(1990)

The making of the new environmental consciousness. Edinburgh: Edinburgh University Press.

Jenkins, E.
(1999)

Tongue first: Adventures in physical culture. London: Virago.

Jessop. B.
(1997)

'The entrepreneurial city' in N. Jewson and S. McGregor (eds) *Transforming cities: Contested governance and new spatial divisions*. London: Routledge.

JNLR [Joint
National
Listenership
Research]
(2006)

'Research'. http://www.bci.ie/research_reports/jnlr.html.

Jorgensen, A.
(2006)

'Fields of knowledge' in M. Corcoran and M. Peillon (eds) *Uncertain Ireland: A sociological chronicle, 2003–2004*. Dublin: Institute of Public Administration.

Kane, E.
(1996)

'The power of paradigms: social science and intellectual contributions to public discourse in Ireland' in L. O'Dowd (ed.) *On intellectuals and intellectual life in Ireland*. Belfast: Institute of Irish Studies/Royal Irish Academy.

Keane, J.
(1988)

Civil society and the state. London: Verso.

Keane, J.
(1998)

Civil society: Old images, new visions. Cambridge: Polity.

Kearney, R. (ed.) (1990)
Migrations: The Irish at home and abroad. Dublin: Wolfhound.

Kearns, K. (1996)
Dublin pub life and lore: An oral history. Dublin: Gill & Macmillan.

Keating, P. and D. Desmond (1993)
Culture and capitalism in contemporary Ireland. Aldershot: Avebury.

Kelleher, C. (1997)
'Preface'. *Women's Studies Review* 5. pp.vii–viii.

Kelley, A. (2006)
'Ireland's "crack" habit: explaining the faux Irish pub revolution'. *Slate* 16 March. [Available at www.slate.com].

Kelley, P. *et al.* (1997)
'Children's accounts of risk' in *Childhood*, Vol.4 (3). pp.305–324.

Kelly, A. (2002)
Compulsory Irish: Language and education in Ireland, 1870s–1970s. Dublin: Irish Academic Press.

Kelly, F. (1998)
Early Irish farming: A study based mainly on the law-texts of the 7th and 8th centuries AD. Dublin: Dublin Institute of Advanced Studies.

Kelly, M. and B. O'Connor (eds) (1997)
Media audiences in Ireland: Power and cultural identity. Dublin: University College Dublin Press.

Kelly, M. and B. Rolston (1995)
'Broadcasting in Ireland — issues of national identity and censorship' in P. Clancy *et al.* (eds) *Irish society: Sociological perspectives.* Dublin: Institute of Public Administration.

Kennedy, F. (2001)
Cottage to crèche: Family change in Ireland. Dublin: Institute of Public Administration.

Kenny, M. (1997)
'Who are they, who are we? Education and Travellers' in E. Crowley and J. Mac Laughlin (eds) *Under the belly of the tiger: Class, race, identity and culture in the global Ireland.* Dublin: Irish Reporter.

Keogh, D.
(1998)
Jews in twentieth century Ireland: Refugees, anti-semitism and the Holocaust. Cork: Cork University Press.

Keohane, K.
(1997)
'Traditionalism and homelessness in contemporary Irish music' in J. Mac Laughlin (ed.) *Location and dislocation in contemporary Irish society: Emigration and Irish identities*. Cork University Press.

Keohane, K.
(1998)
'Reflexive modernisation and systematically distorted communications: an analysis of an Environmental Protection Agency hearing'. *Irish Journal of Sociology* 8. pp.71–92.

Keohane, K. and
D. Chambers
(2002)
'Understanding Irish suicides' pp.36–50 in M. Corcoran and M. Peillon (eds) *Ireland unbound: a turn of the century chronicle*. Dublin: Institute of Public Administration.

Keohane, K. and
C. Kuhling
(2004a)
Collision culture: Transformations in everyday life in Ireland. Dublin: Liffey.

Keohane, K. and
C. Kuhling
(2004b)
'The "gift" relationship and Irish consumerism' in M. Peillon and M. Corcoran (eds) *Place and non-place: The reconfiguration of Ireland*. Dublin: Institute of Public Administration.

Kerbo, H. and
M. Inoue
(1990)
Deviant behaviour. Washington: Taylor and Francis.

Kerr, A.
(2006)
The business and culture of digital games: Gamework/gameplay. London: Sage.

Kilkelly, U.
(2006)
Youth justice in Ireland: Tough lives, rough justice. Dublin: Irish Academic Press.

Kirby, P.
(1984)
Is Irish Catholicism dying? Cork: Mercier.

Kirby, P.
(1997)
Poverty amid plenty: World and Irish development reconsidered. Dublin: Gill & Macmillan/Trócaire.

Kirby, P.
(2002)
The Celtic Tiger in distress: Growth with inequality in Ireland. Basingstoke: Palgrave.

Kirkham, G. (1990)   'The origins of mass emigration from Ireland' in R. Kearney (ed.) *Migrations: The Irish at home and abroad*. Dublin: Wolfhound.

Kitchin, R. and B. Bartley (2007)   'Ireland in the twenty-first century' in B. Bartley and R. Kitchin (eds) *Understanding contemporary Ireland*. London: Pluto.

Klein, N. (2000)   *No logo: Taking aim at the brand bullies*. London: Flamingo.

Komito, L. (1984)   'Irish clientelism: a reappraisal'. *Economic and Social Review* 15(3). pp.173–94.

Kropiwiec, K. and R. Chiyoko King-O'Riain (2006)   *Polish migrant workers in Ireland*. Dublin: National Consultative Committee on Racism and Interculturalism. [Community Profiles Series]

Kuhling, C. (1998)   'New Age Travellers on Cool mountain' in M. Peillon and E. Slater (eds) *Encounters with modern Ireland*. Dublin: Institute of Public Administration.

Kumar, K. (1995)   *From post-industrial to post-modern society*. Oxford: Blackwell.

Lace, S. (2005)   *The glass consumer: Life in a surveillance society*. Bristol: Policy/National Consumer Council.

Lambe, M. (2001)   'At the Cross: a shop in rural Ireland 1880–1911' in D. Cronin, J. Gilligan and K. Holton (eds) *Irish fairs and markets: Studies in local history*. Dublin: Four Courts.

Langer, J. (1992)   *Emerging sociology: An international perspective*. Aldershot: Avebury.

Langman, L. (1992)   'Neon cages — shopping for subjectivity' in R. Shields (ed.) *Lifestyle shopping: The subject of consumption*. London: Routledge.

Language Planning Advisory Committee (1988)   *The Irish language in a changing society — Shaping the future*. Dublin: Bord na Gaeilge.

Larragy, J. (2006)	'Origins and significance of the community and voluntary pillar in Irish social partnership'. *Economic and Social Review* 37(3). pp.375–398.
Lash, S. and J. Urry (1994)	*Economies of signs and space*. London: Sage.
Leane, M. and E. Kiely (1997)	'Single lone motherhood — reality versus rhetoric' in A. Byrne and M. Leonard (eds) *Women and Irish society: A sociological reader*. Belfast: Beyond the Pale.
Lee, D. and H. Newby (1983)	*The problem of sociology*. London: Hutchinson.
Lee, D. and B. Turner (eds) (1996)	*Conflicts about class: Debating inequality in late industrialism*. London: Longman.
Lee, J. (1989)	*Ireland 1912–1985: Politics and society*. Cambridge: Cambridge University Press.
Leeuwis, C. (1989)	*Marginalisation misunderstood: Different patterns of farm development in the west of Ireland*. Wageningen: Wageningen Agricultural University.
Lennon, M., M. McAdam and J. O'Brien (1988)	*Across the water: Irish women's lives in Britain*. London: Virago.
Lentin, R. (1993)	'Feminist research methodologies'. *Irish Journal of Sociology* 3. pp.119–38.
Lentin, R. (1998)	'"Irishness", the 1937 Constitution, and citizenship: a gender and ethnicity view'. *Irish Journal of Sociology* 8. pp.5–24.
Lentin, R. (1999)	'Racializing our Dark Rosaleen: feminism, citizenship, racism, antisemitism'. *Women's Studies Review* 6. pp.1–17.
Lentin, R. (2002)	'Anti-racist responses to the racialisation of Irishness: disavowed multiculturalism and its discontents' in R. Lentin and R. McVeigh (eds) *Racism and anti-racism in Ireland*. Belfast: Beyond the Pale.

Lentin, R. and R. McVeigh (eds) (2002)   *Racism and anti-racism in Ireland.* Belfast: Beyond the Pale.

Leonard, M. (1997)   'Women caring and sharing in Belfast' in A. Byrne and M. Leonard (eds) *Women and Irish society: A sociological reader.* Belfast: Beyond the Pale.

Leonard, M. (2006)   'Sectarian childhoods in North Belfast' in M. Corcoran and M. Peillon (eds) *Uncertain Ireland.* Dublin: Institute of Public Administration.

Leyden, B. (2002)   *The home place.* Dublin: New Island.

Leyton, E. (1966)   'Conscious models and dispute regulation in an Ulster village'. *Man* [new series] 1. pp.534–42.

Leyton, E. (1975)   *The one blood: Kinship and class in an Irish village.* Newfoundland: Institute of Social and Economic Research.

Lincoln, C. (1993)   'City of culture — Dublin and the discovery of urban heritage' in B. O'Connor and M. Cronin (eds) *Tourism in Ireland: A critical analysis.* Cork: Cork University Press.

Liston, K. (2002)   'The gendered field of Irish sport' in M. Corcoran and M. Peillon (eds) *Ireland unbound: A turn of the century chronicle.* Dublin: Institute of Public Administration.

Lodge, A. (2005)   'Gender and children's social world: esteemed and marginalised masculinities in the primary school playground'. *Irish Journal of Sociology* 14(2). pp.177–192.

Lodge, A. and K. Lynch (2004)   *Diversity at school.* Dublin: Institute of Public Administration/ Equality Authority.

Loughran, H. and M. McCann (2006)   *A community drugs study: Developing community indicators for problem drug use.* Dublin: Stationery Office.

Lovelock, J. (2000)   *Gaia: A new look at life on earth.* Oxford: Oxford University Press.

Luibheid, E.
(2004)
'Childbearing against the state? Asylum seeker women in the Irish republic'. *Women's Studies International Forum*, 27(4). Special Issue: Representing Migrant Women in Ireland and in the EU. pp.335–349.

Lumby, C.
(1997)
Bad girls: The media, sex and feminism in the 90s. Sydney: Allen and Unwin.

Lynch, C.
(1997)
'Literacy is a human right: an adult underclass returns to education' in E. Crowley and J. Mac Laughlin (eds) *Under the belly of the tiger: Class, race, identity and culture in the global Ireland.* Dublin: Irish Reporter.

Lynch, K.
(1987)
'Dominant ideologies in Irish educational thought: consensualism, essentialism and meritocratic individualism'. *Economic and Social Review* 18(2). pp.101–22.

Lynch, K.
(1999a)
Equality in education. Dublin: Gill & Macmillan.

Lynch, K.
(1999b)
'Equality studies, the academy and the role of research in emancipatory social change'. *Economic and Social Review* 30(1). pp.41–69.

Lynch, K. and
A. Lodge
(2002)
Equality and power in schools: Redistribution, recognition and representation. London: Routledge.

Lynch, K. and
C. O'Riordan
(1999)
'Inequality in higher education: a study of social class barriers' in K. Lynch *Equality in education.* Dublin: Gill & Macmillan.

Lynch, K. and
E. McLaughlin
(1995)
'Caring labour and love labour' in P. Clancy *et al.* (eds) *Irish society: Sociological perspectives.* Dublin: Institute of Public Administration.

MacCurtain, M.
(1997)
'Godly burden: The Catholic sisterhoods in twentieth-century Ireland' in A. Bradley and M. Valiulis (eds) *Gender and sexuality in modern Ireland.* Amherst: University of Massachusetts Press.

Mac Éinrí, P.
(2001)
'Immigration policy in Ireland' in F. Farrell and P. Watt (eds) *Responding to racism in Ireland.* Dublin: Veritas.

Mac Éinrí, P.
(2007)
'Immigration, labour migrants, asylum seekers and refugees' in B. Bartley and R. Kitchin (eds) *Understanding contemporary Ireland*. London: Pluto.

MacFarlane, A.
(1997)
'The changing role of women as health workers in Ireland.' *Women's Studies Review* 5. pp.18–36.

Mac Gréil, M.
(1996)
Prejudice in Ireland revisited. Maynooth: Survey and Research Unit, Department of Social Studies, NUI Maynooth.

Mac Laughlin, J.
(1994)
Ireland: The emigrant nursery and the world economy. Cork: Cork University Press.

Mac Laughlin, J.
(1997)
Location and dislocation in contemporary Irish society: Emigration and Irish identities. Cork: Cork University Press.

Macionis, J.
and K. Plummer
(1998)
Sociology: A global introduction. London: Prentice Hall.

MacLachlann,
M. and M.
O'Connell (eds)
(2000)
Cultivating pluralism: Psychological, social and cultural perspectives on a changing Ireland. Dublin: Oak Tree.

MacVeigh, T.
(2006)
'Education, life chances and disadvantage' in B. Fanning and M. Rush (eds) *Care and social change in the Irish welfare economy.* Dublin: University College Dublin Press.

Maguire, M.
(2004)
Differently Irish: A cultural history exploring twenty-five years of Vietnamese Irish identity. Dublin: Woodfield.

Maheu, L. (ed.)
(1995)
Social movements and social classes: The future of collective action. London: Sage.

Mahon, E.
(1994)
'Feminist research: a reply to Lentin'. *Irish Journal of Sociology* 4. pp.165–9.

Mahon, E.
(1995)
'From democracy to femocracy: the women's movement in the Republic of Ireland' in P. Clancy *et al.* (eds) *Irish society: Sociological perspectives.* Dublin: Institute of Public Administration/Sociological Association of Ireland.

Mahon, E.   'The development of a health policy for women' in J. Robins
(1997)   (ed.) *Reflections on health: Commemorating fifty years of the*
                 Department of Health 1947–1997. Dublin: Department of Health.

Mair, P.   'Explaining the absence of class politics in Ireland' in J. Goldthorpe
(1994)   and C. Whelan (eds) *The development of industrial society in Ireland*
                 Oxford: Oxford University Press/The British Academy.

Marmot, M.   *The status syndrome: How social standing affects health and*
(2004)   *longevity.* London: Bloomsbury.

Marsden, T.   'Food matters and the matter of food: towards a new food
(2000)   governance?' *Sociologia Ruralis* 40(1), pp.20–29.

Marshall, T.   *Citizenship and social class, and other essays.* Cambridge:
(1950)   Cambridge University Press.

Martell, L.   *Ecology and society.* Cambridge: Polity.
(1994)

Mass   *The pub and the people: A Worktown Study.* London: Cresset.
Observation
Library.
(1987[1943])

Matthews, A.   *Farm incomes: Myths and reality.* Cork: Cork University Press.
(2000)   [*Undercurrents* 13]

May, T.   *Social research: Issues, methods and processes.* Buckingham:
(1997)   Open University Press.

Mayer, M.   'Urban governance in the post-Fordist city' in P. Healey et al.
(1995)   (eds) *Managing cities: The new urban context.* Chichester: Wiley.

Maynard, M.   *Dress and globalisation.* Manchester: Manchester University
(2004)   Press.

McAdam, M.   'A paradoxical dilemma in nurse education' in A. Ryan and
(2004)   T. Walsh (eds) *Unsettling the horses: Interrogating adult*
                 education perspectives. Maynooth: MACE.

McBrierty, V.   *Ireland and the knowledge economy: The new techno-academic*
and R. Kinsella *paradigm.* Dublin: Oak Tree.
(1998)

McCabe, C. and F. Keyes (2005) — *A review of Travellers' health using primary care as a model of good practice: Pavee Point primary healthcare for Travellers' project.* Dublin: Pavee Point.

McCafferty, D. (2007) — 'Urban systems' in B. Bartley and R. Kitchin (eds) *Understanding contemporary Ireland.* London: Pluto.

McCann, M., S. Ó Síocháin and J. Ruane (eds) (1994) — *Irish Travellers: Culture and ethnicity.* Belfast: Institute of Irish Studies, Queen's University Belfast, for the Anthropological Association of Ireland.

McCarthy, G. (1997) — 'Nursing and the health services' in J. Robins (ed.) *Reflections on health: Commemorating fifty years of the Department of Health 1947–1997.* Dublin: Department of Health.

McCarthy, J. and M. Zald (1977) — Resource mobilization and social movements: a partial theory'. *'American Journal of Sociology* 82(6). pp.1212–1241.

McCarthy, P. (1971) — *Itineracy and poverty: A study in the subculture of poverty.* MA thesis. University College, Dublin.

McCarthy, P. (1994) — 'The sub-culture of poverty reconsidered' in McCann, M., S. Ó Síocháin and J. Ruane (eds) *Irish Travellers: Culture and ethnicity.* Belfast: Institute of Irish Studies, Queen's University Belfast, for the Anthropological Association of Ireland.

McCombs M. and D. Shaw (1972) — 'The agenda-setting function of the press' in *Public Opinion Quarterly,* 36. pp.176–187.

McCrone, D. (1992) — *Understanding Scotland: The sociology of a stateless nation.* London: Routledge.

McCrum, E. (1996) — *Fabric and form: Irish fashion since 1950.* Stroud: Sutton/Ulster Museum.

McCullagh, C. (1995) — 'Getting the criminals we want — the social production of the criminal population' in P. Clancy *et al.* (eds) *Irish society: Sociological perspectives.* Dublin: Institute of Public Administration.

McCullagh, C. (1996) — *Crime in Ireland: A sociological introduction.* Cork: Cork University Press.

McCullagh, C.   'How dirty is the white collar? Analysing white-collar crime' in
(2002)   P. O'Mahony (ed.) *Criminal justice in Ireland*. Dublin: Institute
of Public Administration.

McCullagh, C.   'Random attacks?' in M. Peillon and M. Corcoran (eds) *Place*
(2004)   *and non-place: The reconfiguration of Ireland*. [Irish Sociological
Chronicles, vol. 4]. Dublin: Institute of Public Administration.

McDonald, F.   *The destruction of Dublin*. Dublin: Gill & Macmillan.
(1985)

McDonald, F.   *The construction of Dublin*. Kinsale: Gandon.
(2000)

McDonald, F.   *Chaos at the crossroads*. Kinsale: Gandon.
and J. Nix
(2005)

McDonnell, O.   'Ethical and social implications of technology in medicine: new
(1997)   possibilities and new dilemmas' in A. Cleary and M. Treacy
(eds) *The sociology of health and illness in Ireland*. Dublin:
University College Dublin Press.

McGinnity, F.   'Gender, work life balance and quality of life' in T. Fahey,
H. Russell and   H. Russell and C.T. Whelan (eds) *The best of times? The social
E. Smyth.   impact of the Celtic Tiger*. Dublin: Institute of Public
(2007)   Administration.

McGrath, B.   'Environmentalism and property rights: the Mullaghmore
(1996)   Interpretive Centre dispute'. *Irish Journal of Sociology* 6.
pp.25–47.

McGrew, A.   'A global society?' in S. Hall *et al* (eds) *Modernity and its
(1992)   futures*. Cambridge: Open University/Polity.

McHugh, S.   *A Sense of Ireland*. Dublin: A Sense of Ireland. [exhibition
(ed.)   catalogue]
(1980)

McKeown, K.,   *Changing fathers? Fatherhood and family life in modern Ireland*.
H. Ferguson   Cork: Cork University Press.
and D. Rooney
(1999)

McKevitt, D. (1998)   'Irish healthcare policy' in E. McAuliffe and L. Joyce (eds) *A healthier future? Managing healthcare in Ireland*. Dublin: Institute of Public Administration.

McKevitt, P. (1944)   *The plan of society*. Dublin: Catholic Truth Society of Ireland.

McLoone, M. (ed.) (1991)   *Cultural identity and broadcasting in Ireland: Local issues, global perspectives*. Belfast: Institute of Irish Studies, Queen's University.

McLoughlin, D. (1994)   'Ethnicity and Irish Travellers: reflections on Ní Shúinéar' in M. McCann, S. Ó Síocháin and J. Ruane (eds) *Irish Travellers: Culture and ethnicity*. Belfast: Institute of Irish Studies, Queen's University Belfast, for the Anthropological Association of Ireland.

McNabb (1964)   'Social structure' in J. Newman (ed.) *The Limerick rural survey, 1958–1964*. Tipperary: Muintir na Tíre.

McQuail, D. (2005)   *McQuail's mass communication theory*. London: Sage.

McSorley, C. (1997)   *School absenteeism in Clondalkin: Causes and responses*. Clondalkin: Clondalkin Partnership.

McVeigh, R. (1995)   'Cherishing the children of the nation unequally: sectarianism in Ireland' in P. Clancy *et al.* (eds) *Irish society: Sociological perspectives*. Dublin: Institute of Public Administration.

McVeigh, R. (1998)   'Irish Travellers and the logic of genocide' in M. Peillon and E. Slater (eds) *Encounters with modern Ireland*. Dublin: Institute of Public Administration.

McWilliams. D. (2005)   *The pope's children: Ireland's new elite*. Dublin: Gill & Macmillan.

Melucci, A. (1989)   *Nomads of the present*. London: Hutchinson Radius.

Melucci, A. (1995)   'The new social movements revisited: reflections on a sociological misunderstanding' in L. Maheu (ed.) *Social movements and social classes: The future of collective action*. London: Sage.

Mennell, S., A. Murcott and A. van Otterloo (1992) *The sociology of food: Eating, diet and culture.* London: Sage.

Merchant, C. (1980) *The death of nature: Women, ecology and the scientific revolution.* San Francisco: Harper Collins.

Messenger, J. (1969) *Inis Beag: Isle of Ireland.* New York: Holt, Rinehart and Winston.

Mikunda, C. (2004) *Brand lands, hot spots and cool spaces.* London: Kogan Page.

Millar, R. (1998) 'Worklife mobility typologies as background to current class position — a research note'. *Economic and Social Review* 29(3). pp.259–84.

Millen, D. (1997) 'Some methodological and epistemological issues raised by doing feminist research on non-feminist women'. *Sociological Research Online* 2(3). [http://www.socresonline.org.uk/socresonline/2/3/3.html]

Miller, D. and D. Slater (2000) *The Internet: An ethnographic approach.* Oxford and New York: Berg.

Mills C. Wright (1970) *The sociological imagination.* Harmondsworth: Penguin.

Moane, G. (1997) 'Lesbian politics and community' in A. Byrne and M. Leonard (eds) *Women and Irish society: A sociological reader.* Belfast: Beyond the Pale.

Molloy, C. (2002) *The story of the Irish pub.* Dublin: Liffey.

Morris, J. (1995) 'Inequalities in health: ten years and a little further on' in B. Davey, A. Gray and C. Seale (eds) *Health and disease: A reader.* Buckingham: Open University Press.

Morrison, A. (2004) 'Irish and white-ish mixed "race" identity and the scopic regime of whiteness'. *Women's Studies International Forum*, 27(4). Special Issue: Representing Migrant Women in Ireland and in the EU. pp.385–396.

Morrow, V.
(1999)

'Conceptualising social capital in relation to the well-being of children and young people: a critical review'. *The Sociological Review.*

Murcott, A.
(ed.)
(1998)

The nation's diet: The social science of food choice. Harlow: Longman.

Murphy-
Lawless, J.
(1992)

The adequacy of income and family expenditure. Dublin: Combat Poverty Agency.

Murphy-Lawless,
J., L. Oaks and
C. Brady
(2004)

Understanding how sexually active women think about fertility, sex and motherhood. Dublin: Crisis Pregnancy Agency Report No. 6.

Murray, M.
(2007)

'Cosmopolitans versus the locals: community-based protest in the age of globalisation'. *Irish Journal of Sociology*, NYP.

Murray. P.
(2004)

The transatlantic politics of productivity and the origins of public funding support for social science research in Ireland, 1950–1979. [Working Paper series 22]. Maynooth: National Institute for Regional and Spatial Analysis.

Mutwarasibo, F.
(2002)

'African in Ireland'. *Studies* vol. 91, no. 364. pp.348–358.

Naess, A.
(1997)

'Sustainable development and the deep ecology movement' in S. Baker, M. Kousis, D. Richardson and S. Young (eds) *The politics of sustainable development.* London/New York: Routledge.

Nash, C.
(1997)

'Embodied Irishness: gender, sexuality and Irish identities' in B. Graham (ed.) *In search of Ireland: A cultural geography.* London: Routledge.

National
Nutrition
Surveillance
Centre
(2003)

Dietary habits of the Irish population: Results from SLÁN Annual Report 2003. Dublin: National Nutritional Surveillance Centre, Department of Public Health Medicine, University College Dublin.

NCCRI
[National
Consultative
Committee on
Racism and
Interculturalism]
(2002)
Cultural diversity in the Irish health care sector: Towards the development of policy and practice guidelines. Dublin: National Consultative Committee on Racism and Interculturalism.

NCV [National
Committee on
Volunteering]
(2002)
Tipping the balance: Report and recommendations to government on supporting and developing volunteering in Ireland. Dublin: National Committee on Volunteering.

Negra, D. (ed.)
(2006)
The Irish in us: Irishness, performativity and popular culture. Durham [NC]: Duke University Press.

NESC [National
Economic and
Social Council]
(2005)
The developmental welfare state. Dublin: National Economic and Social Council.

Nettleton, S.
and J. Watson
(1998)
The body in everyday life. London: Routledge.

Nic Ghiolla
Phádraig, M.
(1995)
'The power of the Catholic Church in the Republic of Ireland' in P. Clancy *et al.* (eds) *Irish society: Sociological perspectives.* Dublin: Institute of Public Administration.

Ní Laoire, C.
(2001)
'A matter of life and death: Men, masculinities and staying "behind" in rural Ireland'. *Sociologia Ruralis* 41(2), pp.220–236.

Ní Shúinéar, S.
(1994)
'Irish Travellers, ethnicity and the origins question' in M. McCann, S. Ó Síocháin and J. Ruane (eds) *Irish Travellers: Culture and ethnicity.* Belfast: Institute of Irish Studies, Queen's University Belfast, for the Anthropological Association of Ireland.

Nolan, B. and
B. Maitre
(2007)
'Economic growth and income inequality: setting the context' in T. Fahey, H. Russell and C. Whelan (eds) *The best of times? The social impact of the Celtic Tiger.* Dublin: Institute of Public Administration.

Nolan, B. and C. Whelan (1997) 'Unemployment and health' in A. Cleary and M. Treacy (eds) *The sociology of health and illness in Ireland*. Dublin: University College Dublin Press.

Norberg-Hodge, H., T. Merrifield and S. Gorelick (2000) *Bringing the food economy home: The social, ecological and economic benefits of local food*. Dartington: International Society for Ecology and Culture [ISEC].

Ó Baoill, D. (1994) 'Travellers' Cant — language or register?' in M. McCann, S. Ó Síocháin and J. Ruane (eds) *Irish Travellers: Culture and ethnicity*. Belfast: Institute of Irish Studies, Queen's University Belfast, for the Anthropological Association of Ireland.

O'Brien, M. (2001) *De Valera, Fianna Fáil and the Irish Press; the truth in the news?* Dublin: Irish Academic Press.

Ó Buachalla, S. (1974) 'Permanent education in the Irish context'. *Studies* Winter. pp.355–65.

O'Byrne, R. (2000) *After a fashion: A history of the Irish fashion industry*. Dublin: Town House.

O'Carroll, J. (1985) 'Community programmes and the traditional view of community'. *Social Studies* 8(3/4). pp.137–48.

O'Carroll, J. (1998) 'Blood' in M. Peillon and E. Slater (eds) *Encounters with modern Ireland*. Dublin: Institute of Public Administration.

O'Connell, J. (1992) 'Working with Irish Travellers' in DTEDG File. *Irish Travellers: New analysis and new initiatives* (originally 1989). Dublin: Pavee Point.

O'Connell, M. (2001) *Changed utterly: Ireland and the new Irish psyche*. Dublin: Liffey.

O'Connell, M. (2002) 'Assessment of the crime rate in Ireland — issues and considerations' in P. O'Mahony (ed.) *Criminal justice in Ireland*. Dublin: Institute of Public Administration.

O'Connell, P., D. Clancy and S. McCoy (2006) *Who went to college in 2004? A national survey of new entrants to higher education*. Dublin: Higher Education Authority.

O'Connor, B.   'Gender, class and television viewing: audience response to the
(1997)   *Ballroom of Romance*' in M. Kelly and B. O'Connor (eds)
                  Media audiences in Ireland: Power and cultural identity. Dublin:
                  University College Dublin Press.

O'Connor, N.   *Bringing it all back home: The influence of Irish music*. London:
(1991)   BBC.

O'Connor, P.   *Emerging voices: Women in contemporary Irish society*. Dublin:
(1998)   Institute of Public Administration.

O'Donovan, O.   'The plan for women's health and the politics of knowledge: A
(1997a)   brief commentary'. *Women's Studies Review* 5. pp.159–62.

O'Donovan, O.   'Contesting concepts of care: The case of the home help service
(1997b)   in Ireland' in A. Cleary and M. Treacy (eds) *The sociology of health
                  and illness in Ireland*. Dublin: University College Dublin Press.

O'Donovan, O.   'Industrial development and rural women in Ireland' in
and C. Curtin   T. Varley, T. Boylan and M. Cuddy (eds) *Rural crisis: perspectives
(1991)   on Irish rural development*. Galway: Centre for Development
                  Studies, National University of Ireland, Galway.

O'Dowd, A.   *Common clothes and clothing 1860–1930*. Dublin: National
(1990)   Museum of Ireland.

O'Dowd, L.   *The state of social science research in Ireland*. Dublin: Royal Irish
(1988)   Academy.

O'Dowd, L.   'Church, state and women: The aftermath of partition' in
(1989)   C. Curtin, P. Jackson and B. O'Connor (eds) *Gender in Irish
                  society*. Galway: Galway University Press.

O'Dowd, L.   'The states of Ireland: some reflections on research'. *Irish Journal
(1991)   of Sociology* 1. pp.96–106.

O'Dowd, L.   'State legitimacy and nationalism in Ireland' in P. Clancy,
(1992)   M. Kelly, J. Wiatr and R. Zoltaniecki (eds) *Ireland and Poland:
                  Comparative perspectives*. Dublin: Department of Sociology,
                  University College Dublin.

O'Dowd, L. (ed.) *On intellectuals and intellectual life in Ireland*. Belfast: Institute of
(1996)   Irish Studies/Royal Irish Academy.

O'Dowd, M. and S. Wichert (eds) (1995)
Chattel, servant or citizen: Women's status in church, state and society. Belfast: Institute of Irish Studies, Queen's University Belfast.

O'Hara, P. (1998)
Partners in production: Women, farm and family in Ireland. New York and Oxford: Berghahn.

O'Hara, T. (1998)
'Current structure of the Irish health care system — setting the context' in A. Leahy and M. Wiley (eds) *The Irish health system in the 21st century.* Dublin: Oak Tree.

O'Hearn, D. (1992)
Putting Ireland in a global context. Occasional Papers Series 8. Cork: University College Cork, Department of Sociology.

O'Hearn, D. (1998)
Inside the Celtic Tiger: The Irish economy and the Asian model. London: Pluto.

O'Loingsigh, D. (2001)
'Intercultural education and the school ethos' in F. Farrell and P. Watt (eds) *Responding to racism in Ireland.* Dublin: Veritas.

O'Mahony, P. (1993)
Crime and punishment in Ireland. Dublin: Round Hall.

O'Mahony, P. (1997)
Mountjoy prisoners: A sociological and criminological profile. Dublin: Stationery office.

O'Mahony, P. (ed.) (2002)
Criminal justice in Ireland. Dublin: Institute of Public Administration.

O'Malley, E. (1992)
'Industrialisation in Ireland' in P. Clancy *et al.* (eds) *Ireland and Poland: Comparative perspectives.* Dublin: University College Dublin.

O'Reilly, C. (1996)
'The Irish language — litmus test for equality? Competing discourses of identity, parity of esteem and the Peace Process'. *Irish Journal of Sociology* 6. pp.154–78.

O'Reilly, E. (1992)
Masterminds of the right. Dublin: Attic.

Ó Riagáin, P. (1988)
'Bilingualism in Ireland 1973–1983: an overview of national sociolinguistic surveys'. *International Journal of the Sociology of Language* 70. pp.29–51.

Ó Riain, S. (2000)   'Soft solutions to hard times' in E. Slater and M. Peillon (eds) *Memories of the present: A sociological chronicle of Ireland, 1997–1998*. Dublin: Institute of Public Administration.

Ó Riain, S. (2004a)   Remaking the service class? Class relations among software developers in Ireland. [Working Paper series 23]. NUI Maynooth: National Institute for Regional and Spatial Analysis.

Ó Riain, S. (2004b)   *The politics of high tech growth: Developmental network states in the global economy*. Cambridge: Cambridge University Press.

Ó Riain, S. (2006)   'Social partnership as a mode of governance: introduction to the special issue'. *Economic and Social Review* 37(3). pp.311–318.

O'Shea, D. (1998)   'A particular problem in the East . . .' In A. Leahy and M. Wiley (eds) *The Irish health system in the 21st century*. Dublin: Oak Tree.

O'Sullivan, D. (1989)   'The ideational base of Irish educational policy' in D. Mulcahy and D. O'Sullivan (eds) *Irish educational policy: Process and substance*. Dublin: Institute of Public Administration.

O'Sullivan, D. (1992)   'Shaping educational debate: a case study and an interpretation'. *Economic and Social Review* 23(4). pp.423–38.

O'Sullivan, O. (1997)   *The silent schism: Renewal of Catholic Spirit and structures*. Dublin: Gill & Macmillan.

O'Sullivan, S. (1997)   '"The Ryanline is now open . . . " Talk radio and the public sphere' in M. Kelly and B. O'Connor (eds) *Media audiences in Ireland: Power and cultural identity*. Dublin: University College Dublin Press.

O'Toole, F. (1997)   'The ex-isle of Erin: emigration and Irish culture' in J. Mac Laughlin (ed.) *Location and dislocation in contemporary Irish society: Emigration and Irish identities*. Cork: Cork University Press.

O'Toole, F. (1998)   *The lie of the land. Dublin*: New Island.

O'Toole, F. (1995)   *Meanwhile back at the ranch: The politics of Irish beef*. London: Vintage.

Oakley, A. and J. Mitchell (eds) (1998)

Who's afraid of feminism: Seeing through the backlash. Harmondsworth: Penguin.

OECD (2004)

Review of higher education in Ireland. Paris: Organisation for Economic Co-operation and Development. [OECD ref. EDU/EC(2004)14].

OECD (2006)

Education at a glance 2006. Paris: Organisation for Economic Co-operation and Development.

OECD/Statistics Canada (2000)

Literacy in the information age: Final report of the International Literacy Survey. Paris: Organisation for Economic Co-operation and Development. [OECD ref 812000051P1].

Offer, A. (1981)

Property and politics. 1870–1914: Landownership, law, ideology and urban development in England. Cambridge: Cambridge University Press.

Oldenburg, R. (1999)

The great good place: Cafes, coffee shops, bookstores, bars, hair salons, and other hangouts at the heart of a community. New York: Marlowe.

Oram, H. (1993)

Paper tigers: Stories of Irish newspapers by the people who make them. Belfast: Appletree/RTÉ.

Owens, M. (1992)

'Women in rural development: a hit or miss affair'. *Womens Studies Centre Review* 1. pp.15–19.

Parker, A. (1999)

'Retail trends and the suburbanisation of Dublin's retailing: into the twenty-first century' in J. Killen & A. MacLaran (eds) *Dublin: Contemporary trends and issues for the twenty-first century.* Dublin: Geographical Society of Ireland. [Special Publication 11].

Parker, L. (1993)

'Rising crime rates and the role of police in the Czech Republic'. *Police Studies* 16 (2). pp.39–42.

Paterson, M. (2006)

Consumption and everyday life. London: Routledge.

Peace, A. (1986)

'"A different place altogether": diversity, unity and boundary in an Irish village' in A. Cohen (ed.) *Symbolising boundaries.* Manchester: Manchester University Press.

'Environmental protest, bureaucratic closure: the politics of discourse in rural Ireland' in K. Milton (ed.) *Environmentalism: The view from anthropology*. London: Routledge.

Peace, A.
(2001)
A world of fine difference: The social architecture of a modern Irish village. Dublin: University College Dublin Press.

Peillon, M.
(1982)
Contemporary Irish society: An introduction. Dublin: Gill & Macmillan.

Peillon, M.
(1992)
'State and society in the Republic of Ireland' in P. Clancy *et al.* (eds) *Ireland and Poland — Comparative perspectives*. Dublin: University College Dublin.

Peillon, M.
(1995)
'Interest groups and the state' in P. Clancy *et al.* (eds) *Irish Society: Sociological perspectives*. Dublin: Institute of Public Administration in association with the Sociological Association of Ireland.

Peillon, M.
(1998)
'Community of distrust' in M. Peillon and E. Slater (eds) *Encounters with modern Ireland*. Dublin: Institute of Public Administration.

Peillon, M.
(2000)
'Information overload' pp.165–181 in M. Peillon and E. Slater (eds) *Memories of the present*. Dublin: Institute of Public Administration.

Peillon, M.
(2001)
Welfare in Ireland: Actors, resources and strategies. Westport, CT: Praeger.

Peillon M.,
M. Corcoran
and J. Gray
(2006)
Civic engagement and the governance of Irish suburbs. Dublin: Policy Institute.

Pollack, A.
(1999)
'An invitation to racism? Irish daily newspaper coverage of the refugee issue' in D. Kiberd (ed.) *Media in Ireland: The search for ethical journalism*. Dublin: Open Air.

Poole, M.
(1997)
'In search of ethnicity in Ireland' in B. Graham (ed.) *In search of Ireland: A cultural geography*. London: Routledge.

Porter, S.
(1997)
'Why should nurses bother with sociology?' in A. Cleary and M. Treacy (eds) *The sociology of health and illness in Ireland*. Dublin: University College Dublin Press.

Powell, F. (2000)
'State, welfare and civil society' in F. Tonkiss and A. Passey (eds) *Trust and civil society*. Basingstoke: Macmillan.

Power, R. and M. Roche (1993)
The national farm survey 1992. Dublin: Rural Economy Research Centre, Teagasc.

Pringle, D., J. Walsh and M. Hennessey (eds) (1999)
Poor people, poor places: A geography of poverty and deprivation in Ireland. Dublin: Oak Tree/Geographical Society of Ireland.

Putnam, R. (2000)
Bowling alone: The collapse and revival of American community. New York: Simon and Schuster.

Rand, E. (1995)
Barbie's queer accessories. Durham NC: Duke University Press.

Rapple, C. (1997)
'Ownership, standards, diversity: a way forward' in D. Kiberd (ed.) *Media in Ireland: The search for diversity*. Dublin: Open Air.

Re:public (ed.) (1997)
Planet Diana: Cultural studies and global mourning. Sydney: Research Centre in Intercommunal Studies, University of Western Sydney, Nepean.

Reiger, K. (1985)
The disenchantment of the home: Modernizing the Australian family 1880–1940. Melbourne: Oxford.

Restivo, S. (1991)
The sociological worldview. Oxford: Blackwell.

Rex, J. (1996)
'National identity in the democratic multi-cultural state'. *Sociological Research Online* 1(2). [http://www.socresonline.org.uk/1/2/1.html]

Richardson, N (2004)
Getting inside men's health. Kilkenny: Health Promotion Department, South Eastern Health Board.

Ritzer, G. (1996)
The McDonaldization of society. [revised ed.] Thousand Oaks CA: Pine Forge.

Robertson, A. (1991)
Beyond the family: The social organization of human reproduction. Oxford: Polity.

Robertson, R.   'Globalisation and societal modernisation: a note on Japan and
(1987)   Japanese religion'. *Sociological Analysis* 46. pp.35–42.

Robins, J. (ed.)   *Reflections on health: Commemorating fifty years of the Department*
(1997)   *of Health 1947–1997*. Dublin: Department of Health.

Rogers, E. and   'Agenda-setting research: Where has it been? Where is it going?'
J. Dearing   in J. Anderson (ed.) *Communication yearbook*. London: Sage.
(1987)

Rolston, B. and   *Encounters: How racism came to Ireland*. Belfast: Beyond the Pale.
M. Shannon
(2002)

Roos, G. and   *Disparities in food habits: Review of research in 15 European*
R. Prättälä   *countries*. Helsinki: National Public Health Institute.
(1999)

Rose, M.   *The post-modern and the post-industrial*. Cambridge: Cambridge
(1991)   University Press.

Rostow W.   *The stages of economic growth*. Cambridge: Cambridge University
(1960)   Press.

Rottman, D.   *The criminal justice system: Policy and performance*. Dublin:
(1984)   National Economic and Social Council.

Rottman, D.,   *The Distribution of income in the Republic of Ireland: A study in*
D. Hannan,   *social class and family-cycle inequalities*. Dublin: Economic and
N. Hardiman   Social Research Institute.
and M. Wiley
(1982)

Ruane, J.   'Success and failure in a West of Ireland factory' in C. Curtin
(1989)   and T. Wilson (eds) *Ireland from below*. Galway: Galway
                    University Press.

Rundle, K.,   *Irish Contraception and Crisis Pregnancy* [ICCP] *study: a survey*
C. Leigh,   *of the general population*. Dublin: Crisis Pregnancy Agency.
H. McGee and
R. Layte
(2004)

Russell, H. *et al.*   *Work poor households. The welfare implications of changing*
(2004)   *household employment patterns.* Dublin: Economic and Social
                         Research Institute.

Ryan, A.   'Gender discourses in school social relations' in Byrne, A. and
(1997)   Leonard M. (eds) *Women and Irish society: A sociological reader.*
                         Belfast: Beyond the Pale.

Ryan, L.   'Irish emigration to Britain since World War 2' in R. Kearney
(1990)   (ed.) *Migrations: The Irish at home and abroad.* Dublin: Wolfhound.

Sabel, C.   *Ireland: Local partnerships and social innovation.* Paris: OECD.
(1996)

Sacks, P.   *Donegal mafia: An Irish political machine.* New Haven: Yale
(1976)   University Press.

Saris, A.   'The asylum in Ireland: A brief institutional history and some
(1997)   local effects.' In A. Cleary and M. Treacy (eds) *The sociology of
                         health and illness in Ireland.* Dublin: University College Dublin Press.

Sassen, S.   *The mobility of labour and capital.* Cambridge: Cambridge
(1988)   University Press.

Savage, M.   'Class analysis and social research' in T. Butler and M. Savage
(1995)   (eds) *Social change and the middle classes.* London: UCL.

Savage, R.   *Irish television: The political and social origins.* Cork: Cork
(1996)   University Press.

Schaffer, K.   *Women and the bush: Forces of desire in the Australian cultural
(1988)   tradition.* Melbourne: Cambridge University Press.

Scheper-Hughes,   *Saints, scholars and schizophrenics: Mental illness in rural Ireland.*
N.   California: University of California Press.
(1979)

Schiller, H.   'Transnational media and national development' in
(1979)   K. Nordenstreng and H. Schiller (eds) *National sovereignty and
                         international communication.* Norwood NJ: Ablex.

Schlosser, E.   *Fast food nation: What the all-American meal is doing to the world.*
(2001)   London: Allen Lane/Penguin.

Schubotz, D. and B. Rolston (2004)
'Playing the second fiddle? Young men and masculinity in Northern Ireland.' In M. Peillon and M.P. Corcoran (eds) *Place and non-place: The reconfiguration of Ireland*. Dublin: Institute of Public Administration.

Scott, A. (1992)
'Political culture and social movements' in J. Allen, P. Braham and P. Lewis (eds) *Political and economic forms of modernity*. Cambridge: Open University Press/Polity.

Seidler, V. (1988)
'Fathering, authority and masculinity' in R. Chapman and J. Rutherford (eds) *Male order: Unwrapping masculinities*. London: Lawrence and Wishart.

Seligman, A. (1992)
The idea of civil society. New Jersey: Princeton University Press.

Sennett, R. (1977)
The fall of public man. Cambridge: Cambridge University Press.

Share, P. (2002)
'Trust me: I'm organic' in M. Corcoran & M. Peillon (eds) *Ireland unbound: A turn of the century chronicle*. Dublin: Institute of Public Administration.

Shaughnessy, L. (1997)
'Female genital mutilation: beyond mutilating mothers and foreign feminists'. *Women's Studies Review* 5. pp.123–34.

Sheehan, H. (1987)
Irish television drama: A society and its stories. Dublin: Radio Telefís Éireann.

Sheehan, J. (1979)
'Education and society in Ireland, 1945–1970' in J. Lee (ed.) *Ireland: 1945–70*. Dublin: Gill & Macmillan.

Sheerin, E. (1998)
'Heritage centres' in M. Peillon and E. Slater (eds) *Encounters with modern Ireland*. Dublin: Institute of Public Administration.

Shortall, S. (1997)
'Women, farming and access to land'. *Irish Journal of Sociology* 7. pp.111–18.

Shutes, M. (1991)
'Kerry farmers and the European Community: capital transitions in a rural Irish parish'. *Irish Journal of Sociology* 1. pp. 1–17.

Silverman, M. (1993)
'An urban place in rural Ireland: an historical ethnography of domination, 1841–1989' in C. Curtin, H. Donnan and M. Wilson (eds) *Irish urban cultures*. Belfast: Institute of Irish Studies, Queen's University.

Simmel, G.
(1971)

Georg Simmel on individuality and social forms. [D. Levine, ed).
Chicago: University of Chicago Press.

Singer, P.
(1997)

Animal liberation. London: Pimlico.

Sinha, S.
(2002)

'Generating awareness for women of colour in Ireland' in R.
Lentin and R. McVeigh (eds) *Racism and anti-racism in Ireland.*
Belfast: Beyond the Pale.

SIRC [Social
Issues Research
Centre]
(1998)

*Social and cultural aspects of drinking: A report to the Amsterdam
Group.* Oxford: Social Issues Research Centre.

Skeldon, R.
(1997)

'Of migration, great cities and markets: Global systems of
development' in W. Gungwu (ed.) *Global history and migrations.*
Boulder: Westview.

Skilbeck, M
(2001)

*The university challenged: A review of international trends and
issues with particular reference to Ireland.* Dublin: Higher
Education Authority.

Sklair, L.
(1995)

Sociology of the global system. London/New York: Prentice
Hall/Harvester Wheatsheaf.

Slater, E.
(1993)

'Contested terrain: differing interpretations of Co. Wicklow's
landscape'. *Irish Journal of Sociology* 3. pp.23–55.

Slater, E.
(2000)

'When the *local* goes global' in E. Slater and M. Peillon (eds)
*Memories of the present: A sociological chronicle of Ireland,
1997–1998.* Dublin: Institute of Public Administration.

Slowey, M.
(1987)

'Education for domestication or liberation? Women's
involvement in adult education' in M. Cullen (ed.) *Girls don't
do honours: Irish women in education in the 19th and 20th centuries.*
Dublin: Women's Education Bureau.

Smelser, N.
(1998 [1962])

Theory of collective behaviour. London: Routledge.

Smith, A.
(1986)

The ethnic origins of nations. Oxford: Blackwell.

Smyth, E.
(1997)
'Labour market structures and women's employment in the Republic of Ireland' in A. Byrne and M. Leonard (eds) *Women and Irish society: A sociological reader*. Belfast: Beyond the Pale.

Smyth, E.
(1999)
Do schools differ? Academic and personal development among pupils in the second-level sector. Dublin: Oak Tree/ Economic and Social Research Institute.

Smyth, E. and
Hannan, D.
(1997)
'Girls and coeducation in the Republic of Ireland' in A. Byrne, and M. Leonard (eds) *Women and Irish society: A sociological reader*. Belfast: Beyond the Pale.

Sorlin, P.
(1994)
Mass media. London: Routledge. [Key ideas series].

Spaargaren, G.
and A. Mol
(1995)
'Sociology, environment and modernity: ecological modernisation as a theory of social change' in M. Redclift and G. Woodgate (eds) *The sociology of the environment* Vol. 3, part 4. Aldershot: Elgar.

Stein, M.
(1964)
The eclipse of community. New York: Harper and Row.

Stevenson, N.
(1999)
The transformation of the media. London: Longman.

Stiglitz, J.
(2003)
Globalisation and its discontents. New York: Norton.

Stiglitz, J.
(2006)
Making globalization work: The next steps to global justice. New York: Norton.

Stivers, R.
(2000)
Hair of the dog: Irish drinking and its American stereotype. New York: Continuum.

Storey, J.
(2001)
Cultural theory and popular culture: An introduction. Harlow: Prentice Hall.

Street, J.
(1997)
'"Across the universe" — the limits of global popular culture' in A. Scott (ed.) *The limits of globalization*. London/New York: Routledge.

Sullivan, M.
(1997)
The Visit, incarceration and film by women in Northern Ireland: an interview with Orla Walsh'. *The Irish Review* 21, pp.29–40.

Sutherland, E.
(1961[1949])
White collar crime. New York: Holt, Rinehart and Winston.

Sweeney, P.
(1998)
The Celtic tiger: Ireland's economic miracle explained. Dublin: Oak Tree.

Sweetman, P.
(2001)
'Shop window dummies? Fashion, the body and emergent socialities' in J. Entwistle and E. Wilson (eds) *Body dressing.* Oxford: Berg.

Swingewood, A.
(1984)
A short history of sociological thought. Basingstoke: Macmillan.

Symes, D.
(1972)
'Farm household and farm performance: a study of twentieth century changes in Ballyferriter, Southwest Ireland'. *Ethnology* 11. pp.25–38.

Symes, D. and T. Marsden
(1983)
'Complementary roles and asymmetrical lives: farmers' wives in a large farm environment'. *Sociologia Ruralis* 23(3/4).

Szasz, T.
(1961)
The myth of mental illness: Foundations of a theory of personal conduct. New York: Harper and Row.

Szuchewycz, B.
(1989)
'"The growth is in the silence": The meanings of silence in the Irish Catholic charismatic movement' in C. Curtin and T. Wilson (eds) *Ireland from below: Social change and local communities.* Galway: Galway University Press.

Tam, H.
(1998)
Communitarianism: A new agenda for politics and citizenship. London: Macmillan.

Tannam, M.
(1999)
'At home from abroad: the experiences of some migrant women in Ireland'. *Women's Studies Review* 6. pp.19–32.

Taylor, G.
(2001)
Conserving the Emerald Tiger: The politics of environmental regulation in Ireland. Galway: Arlen House.

Taylor, L.
(1989)
'The mission: An anthropological view of an Irish religious occasion' in C. Curtin and T. Wilson (eds) *Ireland from below: Social change and local communities.* Galway: Galway University Press.

Teagasc
(2007)

'Agriculture in Ireland'. http://www.teagasc.ie/agrifood/index.htm.

Thompson, E.
(1982)

'Time, work discipline and industrial capitalism' in A. Giddens and D. Held (eds) *Classes, power and conflict*. London: Macmillan.

Thompson, J.
(1984)

Studies in the theory of ideology. Cambridge: Polity.

Thompson, J.
(1990)

Ideology and modern culture. Cambridge: Polity.

Tobin, F.
(1996)

The best of decades: Ireland in the 1960s. Dublin: Gill & Macmillan.

Tonkiss, F. and
A. Passey
(eds)
(2000)

Trust and civil society. Basingstoke: Macmillan.

Tönnies, F.
(2001 [1887])

Community and civil society. [Gemeinschaft und Gesellschaft]. Cambridge: Cambridge University Press. [Cambridge Texts in the History of Political Thought.]

Touraine, A.
(1982)

The voice and the eye. Cambridge: Cambridge University Press.

Touraine, A.
(1983)

Anti-nuclear protest: The opposition to nuclear energy in France. Cambridge: Cambridge University Press.

Tovey, H.
(1982)

'Milking the farmer? Modernisation and marginalisation in Irish dairy farming' in M. Kelly *et al.* (eds) *Power, conflict and inequality*. Dublin: Turoe.

Tovey, H.
(1985)

'"Local community": in defence of a much-criticised concept'. *Social Studies* 8(3/4). pp.149–64.

Tovey, H.
(1992a)

'Rural sociology in Ireland: a review'. *Irish Journal of Sociology* 2. pp.96–121.

Tovey, H.
(1992b)

'Environmentalism in Ireland — modernity and identity' in P. Clancy, M. Kelly, J. Wiatr and R. Zoltaniecki (eds) *Ireland and Poland: Comparative perspectives*. Dublin: Department of Sociology, University College Dublin.

Tovey, H. (1993)	'Environmentalism in Ireland — two versions of development and modernity'. *International Sociology* 8 (4). pp.413–30.
Tovey, H. (1997)	'Food, environmentalism and rural sociology: on the organic farming movement in Ireland'. *Sociologia Ruralis* 37(1). pp.21–37.
Tovey, H. (1999a)	'Rural poverty — a political economy perspective', in D. Pringle, J. Walsh and M. Hennessey (eds) *Poor people, poor places: A geography of poverty and deprivation in Ireland*. Dublin: Oak Tree/Geographical Society of Ireland.
Tovey, H. (1999b)	'"Messers, visionaries and organobureaucrats": dilemmas of institutionalisation in the Irish organic farming movement'. *Irish Journal of Sociology* 9. pp.31–59.
Tovey, H. (2000)	'Milk and modernity: dairying in contemporary Ireland' in H. Schwarzweller and A. Davidson (eds) *Dairy industry restructuring*. [Research in Rural Sociology and Development vol. 8]. New York: Elsevier.
Tovey, H. (2001)	'Agricultural development and environmental regulation in Ireland' in H. Buller and K. Hoggart (eds) *Agricultural transformation, food and environment*. Aldershot: Ashgate.
Tovey, H. (2002)	'Rethinking urbanisation: struggles around rural autonomy and fragmentation' in M. Corcoran and M. Peillon (eds) *Ireland unbound: A turn of the century chronicle*. [Irish Sociological Chronicles, vol. 3]. Dublin: Institute of Public Administration.
Tovey, H., D. Hannan and H. Abramson (1989)	*Why Irish? A sociological interpretation of Irish national identity and the Irish language*. Dublin: Bord na Gaeilge.
Townsend, P. and N. Davidson (eds) (1982)	*Inequalities in health: The Black Report*. Harmondsworth: Penguin.
Tucker, V. (1987)	'State and community: a case study of Glencolumbcille' in C. Curtin and T. Wilson (eds) *Ireland from below: Social change and local communities*. Galway: Galway University Press.

Tucker, V.   'From biomedicine to holistic health' in A. Cleary and
(1997)   M. Treacy (eds) *The sociology of health and illness in Ireland.*
                Dublin: University College Dublin Press.

Turkle, S.   'Cyberspace and identity'. *Contemporary Sociology* 28 (6).
(1999)   pp.643–648.

Turner, B.   'Introduction' in B. Turner (ed.): *The Blackwell companion to*
(1996)   *social theory.* Oxford: Blackwell.

Tussing, A.   *How Ireland cares: The case for health care reform.*
and M. Wren   Dublin: NewIsland.
(2006)

Tuthill, D.   'Crime analysis and the use of alternative data'.
(2005)   *Communique (Garda management journal).* June. pp.25–30.

TWG [Technical *Interim report to the Steering Committee on the Future of Higher*
Working Group] *Education.* Dublin: Higher Education Authority.
(1995)

UNICEF   *A league table of educational disadvantage in rich nations.* Innocenti
(2002)   Report Card No.4. Florence: UNICEF Innocenti Research
                Centre.

Vandergeest, P. 'Real villages: national narratives of rural development' in
(1996)   E. DuPuis and P. Vandergeest (eds) *Creating the countryside.*
                Philadelphia: Temple University Press.

Varenne, H.   'Dublin 16: accounts of suburban lives' in C. Curtin, H. Donnan
(1993)   and T. Wilson (eds) *Irish urban cultures.* Belfast: Institute of Irish
                Studies, Queen's University.

Veblen, T.   *The theory of the leisure class: An economic study of institutions.*
(1925)   London: Allen and Unwin.

Volunteering   'Facts and figures'. http://www.volunteeringireland.com/facts &
Ireland   figures.
(2007)

Wagner, P.   *A sociology of modernity: Liberty and discipline.* London/New York:
(1994)   Routledge.

Walklate, S. (1995)   *Gender and crime: An introduction.* London: Prentice Hall/Harvester Wheatsheaf.

Wallerstein, I. (1983)   *Historical capitalism.* London: Verso.

Walls, P. (2006)   *The 2006 Irish in Brent health profile report: A report of research undertaken for Brent Irish Advisory Service and Brent Health Action Zone.* Brent: Brent Irish Advisory Service. [available at open.charityblog.org.uk/wp-content/uploads/2006/03/BIASreportjan06.pdf].

Walsh, J., S. Craig and D. McCafferty (1998)   *Local partnerships for social inclusion?* Dublin: Oak Tree/Combat Poverty Agency.

Walter, N. (1998)   *The new feminism.* London: Little, Brown.

Wang, Y. and R. Chiyoko King-O'Riain (2006)   *Chinese students in Ireland.* Dublin: National Consultative Committee on Racism and Interculturalism. [Community Profiles Series]

Wapner, P. (1996)   *Environmental activism and world civic politics.* Albany: State University of New York Press.

Ward, C. (2002)   'Intimations of immorality; An analysis of the international Social Survey Programme (ISSP) 1998' in E. Cassidy (ed.) *Measuring Ireland: Discerning values and beliefs.* Dublin: Veritas.

Warde, A. and M. Tomlinson (1995)   'Taste among the middle classes, 1968–88' in T. Butler and M. Savage (eds) *Social change and the middle classes.* London: UCL.

Watson, D. (2000)   *Victims of recorded crime in Ireland.* Dublin: Oak Tree/ESRI.

Watson, D. (2002)   ' "Home from home": the pub and everyday life' in T. Bennett & D. Watson (eds) *Understanding everyday life.* Oxford: Blackwell/Open University.

Watson, D., S. McCoy and S. Gorby (2006) *The post-leaving certificate sector in Ireland: A multivariate analysis of educational and employment outcomes.* Dublin: Economic and Social Research Institute/Department of Education and Science.

Watson, I. (1997) 'A history of Irish language broadcasting: national ideology, commercial interest and minority rights' in M. Kelly and B. O'Connor (eds) *Media audiences in Ireland.* Dublin: University College Dublin Press.

Weber, E. (1976) *Peasants into Frenchmen.* Stanford: Stanford University Press.

Weber, M. (1970) [1920] *The Protestant ethic and the spirit of capitalism.* [Trans. Talcott Parsons]. London: Unwin.

Weeks, J. (1989) *Sex, politics and society: The regulation of sexuality since 1800.* London: Longman.

Weeks, J. (2005) 'Fallen heroes? All about men' in *Irish Journal of Sociology,* Special issue on Masculinities, Vol. 14(2) pp.53–65.

Wellman, B. and K. Hampton (1999) 'Living networked on and off line'. *Contemporary Sociology* 28(6). pp.648–654.

WHC [Women's Health Council] (2003) *Women, disadvantage and health: A position paper of the Women's Health Council.* Dublin: Women's Health Council [available at www.whc.ie/publications/31657_WHC_Disadvantage.pdf].

WHC [Women's Health Council] (2006) *Women and cancer in Ireland 1994–2001.* Dublin: Women's Health Council [available at www.whc.ie/publications/WomenCancer.pdf].

Whelan, C. (1994) *Values and social change in Ireland.* Dublin: Gill & Macmillan.

Whelan, C. (1995) 'Class transformation and social mobility in the Republic of Ireland' in P. Clancy *et al.* (eds) *Irish society: Sociological perspectives.* Dublin: Institute of Public Administration in association with the Sociological Association of Ireland.

Whelan, C. and R. Layte (2007) 'Opportunities for all in the new Ireland?' in T. Fahey, H. Russell and C. Whelan (eds) *The best of times? The social impact of the Celtic Tiger.* Dublin: Institute of Public Administration.

Whelan, C. and   *Social mobility in the Republic of Ireland: A comparative perspective.*
B. Whelan   Dublin: Economic and Social Research Institute.
(1984)

Whitehead, A.   'Sexual antagonism in Herefordshire' in D. Barker and S.
(1976)   Allen (eds) *Dependence and exploitation in work and marriage.*
                     London: Longman.

Whyte, J.   *Church and state in modern Ireland 1923–1970.* Dublin: Gill &
(1971)   Macmillan.

Whyte, J.   'Church, state and society, 1950–70' in J. Lee (ed.) *Ireland:*
(1979)   *1945–70.* Dublin: Gill & Macmillan.

Whyte, J.   *Church and state in modern Ireland 1923–1979.* Dublin: Gill &
(1980)   Macmillan.

Wickham, J.   'Industrialisation, work and unemployment' in P. Clancy *et al.*
(1986)   (eds): *Ireland — A sociological profile.* Dublin: Institute of Public
                     Administration/Sociological Association of Ireland.

Wickham, J.   'Where is Ireland in the Global Information Society?' *Economic*
(1997)   *and Social Review* 28 (3)

Wickham, J.   'An intelligent island?' in M. Peillon and E. Slater (eds)
(1998)   *Encounters with modern Ireland.* Dublin: Institute of Public
                     Administration.

Wickham, J.   *Gridlock: Dublin's transport crisis and the future of the city.*
(2006)   Dublin: Tasc/New Island.

Wigham, M.   *The Irish Quakers: A short history of the Religious Society of Friends*
(1992)   *in Ireland.* Dublin: Historical Committee of the Religious
                     Society of Friends in Ireland.

Wilkinson, R.   *Unhealthy societies: The afflictions of inequality.* London:
(1996)   Routledge.

Wilkinson, R.   'Putting the picture together: prosperity, redistribution,
(1999)   health and welfare' in M. Marmot and R. Wilkinson (eds)
                     Social determinants of health. Oxford: Oxford University Press.

Wilkinson, R.   *The impact of inequality: How to make sick societies better.*
(2005)   London: Routledge.

Williams, R.
(1976)

Keywords: A vocabulary of culture and society. London:
Fontana.

Williams, R.
(1996)

'The health legacy of emigration: the Irish in Britain and
elsewhere'. *Irish Journal of Sociology* 6. pp.56–78.

Willis, P.
(1977)

Learning to labour: How working class kids get working class jobs.
Farnborough: Saxon House.

Wilson, T.
and H. Donnan
(2006)

The anthropology of Ireland. Oxford: Berg.

WODC
[Wetenschappelijk
Onderzoeken
Documentatie-
centrum]
(2006)

European sourcebook of crime and criminal justice statistics, 2006.
The Hague: Wetenschappelijk Onderzoeken Documentatie-
centrum. [available at www.europeansourcebook.org/esb3_
Full.pdf].

Woolgar, S.
(1988)

Science: The very idea. Chichester: Horwood/London and
New York: Tavistock.

Wren, M.
(2003)

Unhealthy state: Anatomy of a sick society.
Dublin: New Island.

Wright, E.
(1989)

The debate on classes. London: Verso.

Yearley, S.
(1991)

The Green case. London: Routledge.

Yearley, S.
(1995)

'The social shaping of the environmental movement in
Ireland' in P. Clancy, S. Drudy, K. Lynch and L. O'Dowd
(eds) *Irish society: Sociological perspectives*. Dublin: Institute of
Public Administration in association with the Sociological
Association of Ireland.

Young, I.
(1990)

'The ideal of community and the politics of difference' in
L. Nicholson (ed.) *Feminism/postmodernism*. London: Routledge.

Index